This book is a pioneering study of politics in the early middle ages, based on the middle Rhine valley.

Whereas it is believed widely that the source materials for early medieval Europe are too sparse to allow sustained study of the workings of social and political relationships on the ground, this book focuses on a uniquely well-documented area to investigate the basis of power. Topics covered include the foundation of monasteries, their relationship with the laity, and their role as social centres; the significance of urbanism; the control of land, the development of property rights and the organisation of estates; community, kinship and lordship; justice and dispute settlement; the uses of the written word; violence and the feud; and the development of political structures from the Roman Empire to the high middle ages.

Although a local study, the book offers persuasive and challenging generalisations about the nature of power in the early middle ages. It places its findings in an explicitly comparative perspective, identifying the peculiarities of the early medieval west and their implications for the broader sweep of European history.

MATTHEW INNES is Lecturer in History, Birkbeck College, University of London

Cambridge Studies in Medieval Life and Thought

STATE AND SOCIETY IN THE EARLY MIDDLE AGES

Cambridge Studies in Medieval Life and Thought
Fourth Series

General Editor:
D. E. LUSCOMBE
Leverhulme Personal Research Professor of Medieval History, University of Sheffield

Advisory Editors:
CHRISTINE CARPENTER
Reader in Medieval English History, University of Cambridge, and Fellow of New Hall

ROSAMOND McKITTERICK
Professor of Medieval History, University of Cambridge,
and Fellow of Newnham College

The series Cambridge Studies in Medieval Life and Thought was inaugurated by G. G. Coulton in 1921; Professor D. E. Luscombe now acts as General Editor of the Fourth Series, with Dr Christine Carpenter and Professor Rosamond McKitterick as Advisory Editors. The series brings together outstanding work by medieval scholars over a wide range of human endeavour extending from political economy to the history of ideas.

For a list of titles in the series, see end of book.

STATE AND SOCIETY IN THE EARLY MIDDLE AGES

The Middle Rhine Valley, 400–1000

MATTHEW INNES

CAMBRIDGE
UNIVERSITY PRESS

PUBLISHED BY THE PRESS SYNDICATE OF THE UNIVERSITY OF CAMBRIDGE
The Pitt Building, Trumpington Street, Cambridge CB2 1RP, United Kingdom

CAMBRIDGE UNIVERSITY PRESS
The Edinburgh Building, Cambridge CB2 2RU, United Kingdom
http://www.cup.cam.ac.uk
40 West 20th Street, New York, NY 10011-4211, USA
http://www.cup.org
10 Stamford Road, Oakleigh, Melbourne 3166, Australia

First published 2000

Printed in the United Kingdom at the University Press, Cambridge

Typeset in 11/12pt Monotype Bembo   [SE]

A catalogue record for this book is available from the British Library

Library of Congress Cataloguing in Publication data

Innes, Matthew.
State and society in the early Middles Ages: the middle Rhine
valley, 400–1000/Matthew Innes.
    p.   cm. – (Cambridge studies in medieval life and thought)
Includes bibliographical references and index.
ISBN 0 521 59455 3
    1. Political culture – Rhine River Valley – History – To 1500.
2. Cities and towns, Medieval – Rhine River Valley.   3. Elite (Social
sciences) – Rhine River Valley – History.   4. Rhine River Valley –
Social conditions.   5. Church and state – Rhine River Valley –
History – To 1500.   6. Local government – Rhine River Valley –
History – To 1500.   7. Monasticism and religious orders – Rhine River
Valley – History – Middle Ages, 600–1600.   8. Germany – History – To
843.   9. France – Social conditions – To 987.   10. Germany – Religious
life and customs – Middle Ages, 843–1517.   I. Title.   II. Series.
DD801.R76I56   2000
306.2′09434–dc21   99–33218   CIP

ISBN 0 521 59455 3 hardback

CONTENTS

vii

Contents

FIGURES

ABBREVIATIONS

AF	*Annales Fuldenses*, ed. F. Kurze, *MGH SRG* 7 (Hanover, 1891).
BM	*Regesta Imperii I. Die Regesten des Kaiserreiches unter den Karolingern 751–918*, ed. J. F. Böhmer, revised by E. Mühlbacher with J. Lechner, 2nd edn (Innsbruck, 1908).
CDF	*Codex diplomaticus Fuldensis*, ed. E. F. J. Dronke (Kassel, 1850).
CL	*Codex Laureshamensis*, ed. K. Glöckner, Arbeiten der historischen Kommission für den Volkstaat Hessen 3, 3 vols. (Darmstadt, 1929–36).
DA	*Deutsches Archiv für Erforschung des Mittelalters.*
Einhard, letters [cited by letter number]	
	Einhard, *Epistolae*, ed. K. Hampe, *MGH Epp.* V (Berlin, 1899), pp. 105–45. I have drawn on the translation of P. Dutton, both in *Carolingian Civilisation: A Reader* (Peterborough, Ontario, 1993) and *Charlemagne's Courtier: The Complete Einhard* (Peterborough, Ontario, 1997).
EME	*Early Medieval Europe.*
Klostergemeinschaft	*Die Klostergemeinschaft von Fulda im früheren Mittelalter*, ed. K. Schmid *et al.*, 3 vols. in 5, Münstersche Mittelalter-Schriften 8 (Munich, 1978).
MGH	*Monumenta Germaniae Historica*
	AA *Auctores Antiquissimi*, 15 vols. (Hanover, 1877–1919).
	Cap. *Capitularia Regum Francorum*, 2 vols., eds. A. Boretius and V. Krause, *MGH Leges sectio* III (Hanover, 1883–97).

Const.	*Constitutiones et acta publica imperatorum et regum*, vol. I, ed. L. Weigand (Berlin, 1893).
	D plus ruler's name: *Diplomata* [for full details see bibliography section I(b)].
Epp.	*Epistolae*, 8 vols. (Hanover, 1887–1939).
Form.	*Formulae*, ed. K. Zeumer, *MGH Leges sectio* V (Hanover, 1887).
PLAC	*Poetae Latini aevi Karolini*, 4 vols. (Hanover, 1881–99).
SRG	*Scriptores rerum Germanicarum* (Hanover, 1871–1995).
SRM	*Scriptores rerum Merovingicarum*, 7 vols. (Hanover, 1884–1920).
SS	*Scriptores*, 32 vols. (Hanover, 1826–1934).
MIÖG	*Mitteilungen des Instituts für Österreichische Geschichtsforschung.*
N	*Regesta des ehemaligen Benediktinerklosters Hornbach*, ed. A. Neubauer, Mitteilungen des Historischen Vereins der Pfalz 27 (Speyer, 1904).
NCMH	*New Cambridge Medieval History II: 700–900*, ed. R. McKitterick (Cambridge, 1995).
P&P	*Past and Present.*
PL	*Patrologia cursus completus, series Latina*, ed. J.-P. Migne, 221 vols. (Paris, 1841–66).
Settimane	*Settimane di Studio del Centro italiano di studi sull'alto medioevo* (Spoleto, 1953–).
TAF	*Traditiones et antiquitates Fuldenses*, ed. E. F. J. Dronke (Fulda, 1844).
TW	*Traditiones Wizenburgenses: Die Urkunden des Klosters Weissenburg, 661–864*, eds. K. Glöckner and A. Doll (Darmstadt, 1979).
UBF	*Urkundenbuch der Kloster Fulda*, ed. E. E. Stengel, Veröffentlichungen der historischen Kommission für Hessen und Waldeck 10, 2 vols. (Marburg, 1913–58).
UBH	*Urkundenbuch der Reichsabtei Hersfeld*, ed. H. Weirich, Veröffentlichungen der historischen Kommission für Hessen und Waldeck 19 (Marburg, 1936).
UBMR	*Urkundenbuch zur Geschichte der, jetzt die Preußischen regierungsbezirke Coblenz und Trier bildenden*

	mittelrheinischen Territorien, eds. H. Beyer, L. Eltester
	and A. Goerz, vol. 1 (Koblenz, 1860).
VF	Vörträge und Forschungen.
VMPIG	Veröffentlichungen des Max-Planck-Instituts für
	Geschichte.
ZGO	*Zeitschrift für die Geschichte des Oberrheins.*
ZSRG	*Zeitschrift der Savigny-Stiftung für Rechtsgeschichte.*
	GA Germanische Abteilung.
	KA Kanonische Abteilung.

A NOTE ON NOMENCLATURE
AND CITATIONS

In matters of nomenclature, I have been guided by purely pragmatic considerations. I have silently standardised personal names, where possible using modern forms: thus Hruadpertus, Rodbertus, Hrutbertus and so on, all become Rupert. Where a particular form has become normal in the historiography, I have adopted this. On occasion this can lead to inconsistency: thus the eighth-century landowner Otakar and the ninth-century archbishop of Mainz, Otgar, in fact shared a name. In particular, the Germanic name-forms corresponding to Rupert and Robert were identical, as in the case of the man known to posterity as Robert the Strong. I have endeavoured throughout to ensure that the identity of individuals is easily traced, and have been guided by this in my use of name-forms.

Unidentified medieval place-names are given in italics; otherwise I have modernised silently. Place-names are given in the form of the modern country in which they lie, where no standard English form exists: thus Cologne not Köln, but Wissembourg not Weissenburg.

When citing editions of acta and charters, I have indicated the charter number, not a page reference.

Throughout, I have given readers only the relevant prosopographical information for the current argument, in an effort not to leave them snowed under with names. The tables in particular are designed as aids in negotiating the text, not as statements of the findings of research.

In citing four of the key narrative sources, I have silently rested on excellent modern translations: namely P. Dutton, *Charlemagne's Courtier: The Complete Einhard* (Peterborough, Ontario, 1998) for Einhard's *Translatio* and his letters; J. L. Nelson, *The Annals of Saint-Bertin* (Manchester, 1991); and T. Reuter, *The Annals of Fulda* (Manchester, 1992). This is the appropriate point to acknowledge my debt to them.

ACKNOWLEDGEMENTS

The debts built up in the completion of a work of this kind are inevitably legion, and in what follows I can only acknowledge a few specific and particularly important gratitudes. I must begin by acknowledging the constant encouragement and guidance of Rosamond McKitterick, who first stimulated my interest in Carolingian history and supervised the thesis out of which this book grew. Jinty Nelson and Chris Wickham, who examined that thesis, have been generous with advice and support, as has Mayke De Jong. In addition to their comments, drafts of various sections of this book have also been improved immeasurably thanks to Marios Costambeys, Paul Fouracre and Guy Halsall. The trustees of the Seeley Prize and Prince Consort Medal stimulated the speedy completion of this work by adjudging an earlier draft worthy of an equal share in their award for 1997. William Davies and the staff at Cambridge University Press have been a model of efficiency. Thanks for financial support are due to the British Academy, a postgraduate award from whom supported the first two years of my research; and to the Master and Fellows of Peterhouse, Cambridge, for electing me to a Research Fellowship which allowed me to continue my work over the next three years. Subsequently I have been lucky enough to work in the Department of Medieval History at the University of Birmingham and the Department of History at the University of York. Much that is in this book has been presented and discussed both formally and informally with very many friends and colleagues: I am happy to be working in an environment in which early medieval history is flourishing. Particular thanks are due to colleagues in the Cambridge History Faculty, the School of Historical Studies at the University of Birmingham, and the Centre for Medieval Studies at the University of York. Karin and Werner Grüber and family hosted a memorable stay in the Odenwald. Finally, I must thank my family for their support and encouragement, and particularly my wife, Jayne, for helping me see this project to completion.

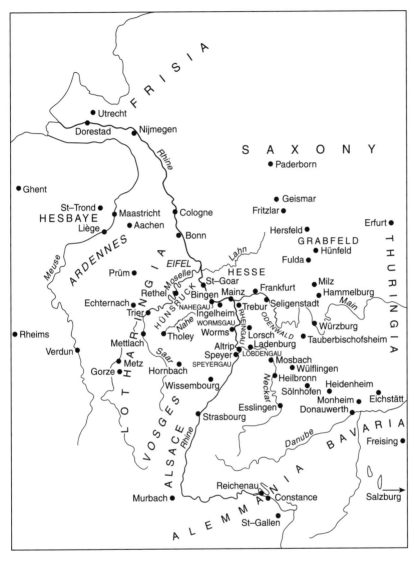

1 The Carolingian Rhineland

2 The Carolingian middle Rhine valley

INTRODUCTION

REGION, SOURCES AND SCOPE

On the morning of 18 January 838 an earthquake hit the middle Rhine valley. One local observer recorded this prodigy for posterity in his account of his time. Disruption occurred 'at St Nazarius and in the regions of Worms, Speyer and Ladenburg'.[1] The geographical focus of this study coincides neatly with the epicentre of the 838 earthquake, and, just as tremors must have been felt well beyond this immediate area in 838, so on occasion in what follows we will also move beyond the Rhine valley. Our observer, probably writing at Mainz, identified the region in terms of four important centres. Worms and Speyer were both seats of bishops, under the jurisdiction of the archbishop of nearby Mainz: all three bishoprics stood on the site of Roman cities on the Rhine's west bank; Mainz and Worms were vibrant urban centres already in the ninth century, although Speyer remained a backwater until royal patronage in the eleventh century effected a transformation. East of the river, Ladenburg likewise stood on a Roman fortified site, but lacked a bishop. It was, nonetheless, an important local centre which was described by some Carolingian observers as a city: hence in the description of the 838 earthquake it was acknowledged as a central place which supplied an identifying label for its rural hinterland.[2] The final place mentioned as being affected by the earthquake was the resting-place of St Nazarius, the royal abbey of Lorsch, which was situated around 10 kilometres east of the Rhine, opposite Worms. Its inclusion here reminds us of the living power of dead saints, and the significance of monasteries as social centres, in the Carolingian world.

This region – the Rhine valley between Bingen and Speyer – is

---

[1] *AF*, s.a. 838, p. 28.
[2] The choice of labels in the 838 annal coincides with the basic geographical units into which the region was divided, each styled a *pagus*. See below, pp. 118–24.

referred to by German historians as the middle Rhine. Its current division between three *Länder* mirrors its fate through much of its history, but in spite of the recurrent utility of the Rhine as a geographical and on occasion political boundary, in social terms the region can be seen as a historical unity. Topographically, it was dominated by the Rhine itself. The fertile lands of the valley were the social, political and economic heartland of the surrounding areas. To both west and east, the valley is bounded by escarpments which rise dramatically. On the eastern bank, a strip of between 10 and 30 km in width – much of which is still heavily wooded today – leads abruptly to the forested hills of the Odenwald. From the Rhine, the natural routes east lie along the Main and the Neckar: in the early middle ages the valleys of both rivers were tendrils of population and communication reaching eastwards. To the west of the Rhine valley lies, similarly, a fertile band bounded by sharply rising wooded uplands, which form a natural barrier between our area and the Moselle valley. The Nahe, which meets the Rhine at Bingen, cuts into this block, which was also traversed in the early middle ages by the old Roman road from Metz to Worms. Despite this, westwards contacts in the early middle ages were limited, perhaps even more so than those with the regions to the east: the main thoroughfare was the Rhine itself, the journey downriver leading northwards to the political and economic centres of the Frankish world. The cities of the river's banks, the villages in its valley, and even those settlements perched in the woods and hills, all looked towards the Rhine.

The middle Rhine is a viable region for study thanks to the monks of the abbeys of Lorsch and Fulda. Lorsch, which we have already visited, was both wealthy and politically significant, the mausoleum of the east Frankish kings in the ninth century. Fulda, although situated around fifty kilometres east and a little north of our region, likewise enjoyed rich holdings in the middle Rhine and an intimate and important relationship with Mainz: it was, after all, the resting-place of Mainz's first archbishop, Boniface. Extensive compilations of legal deeds detailing the acquisition of rights over land in the middle Rhine in the eighth and ninth centuries survive from both Lorsch and Fulda. These monastic riches – over 4,000 Carolingian charters are transmitted in total – make the region uniquely well documented.[3] To them can be added material from other abbeys with interests – albeit less extensive – in the region. The monks who preserved these legal deeds also recorded the payments and services extracted from the peasants who worked monastic land, in documents known in historian's jargon as polyptychs. The most precious of all these registers

---

[3] For full references to the sources discussed in this section, see the bibliography of primary sources.

outlines the burdens imposed on the inhabitants of royal estates in the area; compiled in the middle decades of the ninth century, it was blithely copied amongst a series of surveys of monastic property by a twelfth-century scribe.[4] This vast documentary database is complemented by the survival of a portion of what was clearly once a much larger epistolary tradition. The selection of the correspondence of Boniface, collected at Mainz after his death, is the best-known letter collection from the region. More valuable for the social historian are the surviving letters of Charlemagne's biographer, Einhard, most concerning the affairs of his monastery at Seligenstadt on the Main; they give a priceless glimpse of the social and political life of the region in the 820s and 830s. There is relatively little from the middle Rhine in the way of narrative sources, either historiographical or hagiographical. The account of ninth-century politics known as the 'Annals of Fulda', from which the description of the 838 earthquake with which we began was taken, gives a regional perspective on the great political events of the ninth century, and the occasional local insight. There is also a series of saints' lives associated with the circle of Boniface. The most useful and vivid narrative undoubtedly comes, again, from the pen of Einhard. Like his letters, his account of the coming of the relics of Marcellinus and Peter from Rome to the Main valley and eventually to Seligenstadt puts flesh on the bare bones of social structure evident from the charters. Archaeology, both the traditional fare of cemeteries with grave-goods, and more recent excavations of settlements, likewise adds to our understanding of early medieval society.

For the historian of the early medieval middle Rhine, scarcity of sources is hardly a problem. It is vital, though, to realise that the surviving evidence has an essentially Carolingian horizon, and preserves the interests and perspectives of a small but closely knit elite. We must remain acutely aware of the influence that these sources – and those who wrote them – have over our image of the society which they both record and represent. A society which has left primarily documentary sources, like the Carolingian middle Rhine, will look dramatically different from one which has left literary narratives, but the difference may be more apparent that real.[5] In that received views of early medieval society still largely

[4] CL3671–5, whose true nature was first demonstrated by K. Glöckner, 'Ein Urbar des rhein-fränkischen Reichsgutes aus Lorsch', *MIÖG* 38 (1920), 381–98. For its date towards the middle of the ninth century, see M. Gockel, *Karolingische Königshöfe am Mittelrhein*, VMPIG 31 (Göttingen, 1970), pp. 27–40. I have not been able to obtain a copy of E. Menzer, 'Das Lorscher Reichsurbar', in W. Wackerfuß (ed.), *Beiträge zur Erforschung des Odenwaldes* 5 (Neustadt, 1992), which argues on philological grounds that the polyptych dates from the middle of the eighth century. Even if the name-forms used are early, there are real historical problems in assigning the document as a whole to such an early date.
[5] Cf. T. Reuter, 'The "Feudal" Revolution', *P&P* 155 (1997), 177–95 at 192–5.

rest upon royal legislation and literary narrative, the reconstruction of politics and society from documentary material is historiographically important: it allows the development of a new perspective. This book takes the opportunity the richness of the middle Rhine offers to study social power in the early middle ages. The results are of global significance because they demonstrate that the familiar sources to which scholars habitually turn, the well-thumbed products of the royal court, are in need of radical reinterpretation.

EARLY MEDIEVAL POLITICS:
PROBLEMS OF APPROACH

If we are to interrogate our sources successfully, it is vital to pose the right questions. There is a range of issues about politics and power in the early middle ages on which extant scholarship, addressing the canon of standard sources, has been unable to elicit a meaningful response. How was royal power articulated and exercised in the localities? What was the relationship between kings and local power? In a world where kings were dependent on local elites to carry out their will, what can we identify as constituting royal power? How can we differentiate royal power from aristocratic power?[6]

The very act of posing these questions underlines the peculiarity of early medieval polities. Nonetheless, a long tradition of scholarship has sought to describe early medieval politics in familiar terms, delineating the roles of officials whose power rested on wholesale delegation from the centre. Thus nineteenth- and early twentieth-century pioneers attempted to reconstruct the 'Germanic' constitution.[7] In reaction to this, German scholarship of the inter-war period and later argued that aristocratic power was autogenous, originating in neither delegated royal powers nor popular institutions, but in relationships of personal dependence between lord and man. Lordly rights over dependants – so they argued – were the basis of the Frankish polity, and kings enjoyed jurisdiction over royal land and royal dependants alone.[8] This approach has exerted a deep influence, and offers a fascinating perspective on the

---

[6] Cf. P. Fouracre, 'Cultural Conformity and Social Conservatism in Early Medieval Europe', *History Workshop Journal* 33 (1992), 152–60.

[7] Classically G. Waitz, *Deutsche Verfassungsgeschichte*, 8 vols. (Berlin, 1876–96).

[8] The best statement is T. Mayer, 'Die Ausbildung der Grundlagen des modernen deutsches Staat im hohen Mittelalter', *Historische Zeitschrift* 159 (1938–9), 457–87; the ground-breaking local studies were O. Brunner, *Land und Herrschaft*, which was first published in 1939 (a later edition is now available in translation as *Land and Lordship: Structures of Governance in Medieval Austria*, trans. H. Kaminsky and J. Melton (Philadelphia, 1992)) and W. Schlesinger, *Die Entstehung der Landesherrschaft*, first published in 1941; second edn Darmstadt, 1964.

development of the medieval state from an entity held together by personal relationships within the elite to a territorially defined administrative unit. It has not, however, dealt a fatal blow to legal-constitutional approaches to political structures, because it involved a championing of the Germanic heritage of early medieval institutions which cannot find support in the surviving evidence; the counts and counties of the Carolingian world cannot be derived from allegedly archaic forms of personal lordship whose very existence is shadowy and open to question. As a result most research has turned towards something not unlike nineteenth-century constitutionalism, often without being fully aware of the fact.[9]

When scholars have gone hunting Carolingian government, they have had a clear idea of the kind of beast they were tracking: a hazy silhouette. glimpsed from afar, but recognisably of the same species as the modern state. F. L. Ganshof, the doyen of twentieth-century Carolingian history, used royal decrees (capitularies) to fill in the details of tangible and centralised governmental institutions. Despite the enduring value of his work as a guide to Carolingian legislation, his picture of Frankish institutions can be challenged. This is not only because of the inevitable messiness of actual practice when compared with royal wishes. Ganshof's Frankish state was built up of local institutions (counts, counties and so on) which were defined by the delegation of regalian prerogative. His reading was based on an interpretation of the term *bannus*, found in the capitularies, as a right of command which was invested in royal officials. The actual uses of the term are relatively rare, and tend to concern obedience to specific royal orders, making it difficult to see the *bannus* as a fundamental constitutional principle.[10] We cannot assume that the basic structures of politics were either brought into being, or legitimated, by kings, even in theory. Ganshof's picture of an institutionalised governmental hierarchy nonetheless remains more or less unchallenged as a representation of what Carolingian rulers wanted to do. Those historians who have bravely stalked the thickets of local documentary evidence seeking Carolingian government have used it as a guide. Tracking a beast resembling the modern state, they have returned empty handed, unable

---

[9] A good recent example of modern criticism of the Germanist thesis, and the return to constitutionalism which has tended to follow, is A. C. Murray, 'The Position of the *Grafio* in the Constitutional History of Merovingian Gaul', *Speculum* 64 (1986), 787–805.

[10] F. L. Ganshof, *Frankish Institutions under Charlemagne* (Providence, 1968), esp. pp. 11–12, where the *bannus* as a legal principle is extrapolated from far more specific uses in the sources. For more recent views of political theory as far more concerned with the moral and personal, see J. Fried, 'Der karolingische Herrschaftsverband im 9. Jahrhundert zwischen "Kirche" und "Königshaus"', *Historische Zeitschrift* 235 (1982), 1–43; H.-W. Goetz, '*Regnum*. Zum politische Denken der Karolingerzeit', *ZSRG GA* 104 (1987), 110–90.

even to point to a strong scent or a footprint. Rather than halting to reconsider their assumptions about their quarry, they have tended to see Carolingian government as a rare, short-lived and soon extinct import prematurely introduced into a harsh and hostile landscape.[11]

In other words, the basic assumptions which inform the Ganshofian view from the capitularies remain unquestioned. Indeed, they thrive in certain historiographical traditions, particularly those which have eschewed the study of the localities in their own right. In one strand of recent Francophone scholarship, for example, the evident power and effectiveness of Carolingian kings has been taken as a tell-tale sign of the existence of a highly institutionalised state infrastructure, inherited from the Roman Empire (using similar logic, historians of tenth- and eleventh-century England have argued from the evident organisational strength of royal government for a 'maximum view' of structured state power).[12] Both optimists and pessimists share the assumption that the Carolingians were attempting to forge a unitary polity run via the routine delegation of royal power through administrative institutions. They reach differing conclusions largely because they study different sources, but they share a similar view of the Carolingian state, while disagreeing over whether it was hale and hearty or pale and pathetic. Both often share an almost Prelapsarian image of a Carolingian Eden, where peaceful peasants frolic freely under the protection of strong justice-loving kings and deep-rooted public institutions. In such a scheme of things, the Carolingian period ultimately becomes little more than an interesting blip in the long run of European history, a short-lived predecessor to, and antithesis of, the 'feudal' age of private, normatively brutal, aristocratic power.[13]

This is not to deny that there have been important developments in our understanding of Carolingian politics in the past half-century. Broadly speaking, the most innovative work on early medieval politics has proceeded on two fronts. First, prosopography – the identification of networks of kinship – has allowed a much deeper understanding of the

---

[11] A position exemplified by J.-P. Poly and E. Bournazel, *The Feudal Mutation* (New York, 1990).

[12] For French scholarship on the Carolingians, see J. Durliat, *Les finances publiques de Dioclétian aux Carolingiens (284–888)*, Beihefte der Francia 21 (Sigmaringen, 1990). For England, see J. Campbell, 'The Late Anglo-Saxon State: The Maximum View', *Proceedings of the British Academy* 87 (1994), 39–65.

[13] As is evident in such high-quality work as H. Keller, 'Zum Charakter der "Staatlichkeit" zwischen karolingischer Reichsreform und hochmittelalterliche Herrschaftsausbau', *Frühmittelalterliche Studien* 32 (1989), 248–64; or T. N. Bisson, 'The "Feudal" Revolution', *P&P* 142 (1994), 6–42. The classic statement of the ultimate insignificance of the Carolingian period was that of Bisson's teacher, J. R. Strayer, *On the Medieval Origins of the Modern State* (Princeton, 1970), pp. 10–12.

interests and motivations of the aristocracy.[14] Second, and more recently, political ritual has been shown to have played a central role in the transmission of political rules and the mobilisation of political support: kings used ritual to manipulate early medieval 'consensus politics'. In the most challenging recent work, these two strands of research have come together to put our reading of high politics on a new level of fluency: the rich and complex lexicon of early medieval public life is beginning to be decoded.[15] We are now far more aware of the importance of the interaction between the royal court and local politics, and the processes of group formation which created the basic units of early medieval society.[16] Nonetheless, we are no closer to explaining how armies were equipped and put in the field, and tribute and services extracted from rural society.

In fact, even in the best current scholarship, something not unlike the Ganshofian institutionalist approach holds the field by default.[17] This is shown most clearly in the flourishing series of local studies, whether written in the German tradition of *Landesgeschichte*, or the French regional *thèse* inspired by the *Annales* school's championing of history 'from the bottom up'. In that such work provides a local perspective it has the potential to qualify the view from the royal court. Indeed, regional studies have played an important role in further underlining the centrality of local elites to the political system, thus merging with the work of the prosopographers.[18] But the empirical data local studies

---

[14] Where I have used the term 'aristocracy', it is in recognition of the social fact of a dominant group which was born powerful and was conscious of the fact; I do not mean to suggest in my use of the term that the early medieval elite was closed, static or defined legally, merely that it was based on the inheritance of extensive landholdings. For more on the problems of definition, see pp. 82–5.

[15] Compare two recent biographies of early medieval rulers, J. L. Nelson, *Charles the Bald* (London, 1992) and G. Althoff, *Otto III* (Darmstadt, 1996); see also the work collected in Nelson, *Politics and Ritual in Early Medieval Europe* (Woodbridge, 1986) and *The Frankish World, 750–900* (Woodbridge, 1994) and in Althoff, *Spielregeln der Politik im Mittelalter. Kommunikation im Friede und Fehde* (Darmstadt, 1997).

[16] G. Althoff, *Verwandte, Freunde und Getreue. Zum politische Stellenwert der Gruppenbindungen im früheren Mittelalter* (Darmstadt, 1990); S. Reynolds, *Kingdoms and Communities in Western Europe, 900–1300* (Oxford, 1984); J. M. H. Smith, *Province and Empire: Brittany and the Carolingians* (Cambridge, 1992).

[17] Thus, for all their merits, the best two treatments of Carolingian government: J. L. Nelson, 'Kingship and Royal Government', in *NCMH*, pp. 383–430; K.-F. Werner, '*Missus–marchio–comes*. Entre l'administration centrale et l'administration locale de l'empire carolingien', in W. Paravicini and K.-F. Werner (eds.), *Histoire comparée de l'administration (IVe–XVIIIe siècles)*, Beihefte der Francia 9 (Munich, 1980), pp. 191–239.

[18] Studies of the middle Rhine, in either a prosopographical or a *Landesgeschichte* tradition, are F. Staab, *Untersuchungen zur Gesellschaft am Mittelrhein in der Karolingerzeit*, Geschichtliche Landeskunde 11 (Wiesbaden, 1975); Gockel, *Königshöfe*; K. Bosl, *Franken um 800. Strukturanalyse einer fränkischer Königsprovinz* (2nd edn, Munich,1969). French scholarship has concentrated on France and the Mediterranean and, following Duby, on the post-Carolingian period (partly because of the relative lack of Carolingian documentary evidence in France at least): the classics

have uncovered have continued to be processed within an institutional-ist understanding of royal power. This is clearly evident in a series of recent works which investigate the key figures in the Frankish polity, the counts. In 1973 H. K. Schulze, working from the charter evidence from the provinces east of the Rhine, pointed to the ubiquity of counts, and of territorial divisions into geographical units styled *pagus* and roughly equivalent to the later English county; here were the royal institutions and officials which constituted the Frankish state. Ulrich Nonn's 1983 study of the upper reaches of the Rhine similarly investigated *pagus*-labels and the appearance of counts in the charter evidence, arguing that the Carolingians divided up regional political units led by *duces*, and imple-mented a system of *pagi* and counts. Both works were based upon con-stitutionalist assumptions about the nature of local power: both Schulze and Nonn saw understanding Frankish government as a matter of iden-tifying administrative institutions through which royal agents exercised delegated royal power. Once they found counts and *pagi*, they made no attempt to investigate what royal officials actually did.[19]

Michael Borgolte's controversial work on Carolingian Alemannia (roughly modern Switzerland and that area of southern Germany imme-diately to the north) marked an important attempt to get closer to the realities of early medieval society. The system of regular *pagi* run by counts which can be identified in parts of Alemannia was not, he argued, a reflection of an unchanging Frankish polity, but a state of affairs consciously created by Carolingian rulers in the course of eighth-century reconquest. In some outlying areas, complexes of aristocratic power which looked very much like autogenous lordship rights could be identified as late as the ninth century, whilst elsewhere efforts to reshape society in terms of counts and counties could be detected. In spite of heavy criticism, the broad outline of Borgolte's work is convinc-ing. Yet even Borgolte ultimately fails to explain how political power was exercised on a local level. Despite accentuating the importance of aris-tocratic kinship networks – something which his predecessors had also

Footnote 18 (*cont.*)

are P. Bonnassie, *La Catalogne du milieu du Xe à la fin du XIe siècle* (Toulouse, 1975) and P. Toubert, *Les structures du Latium médiéval* (Paris, 1973); the best Carolingian local study is C. Lauranson-Rosaz, *L'Auvergne et ses marges (Velay, Gévaudan) du VIIIe au XIe siècle: la fin du monde antique?* (Le Puy-en-Velay, 1987).

[19] H. K. Schulze, *Die Grafschaftsverfassung der Karolingerzeit in den Gebieten östlich des Rheins* (Berlin, 1973); U. Nonn, *Pagus und comitatus in Niederlothringen. Untersuchungen zur politischen Raumgliederung im früheren Mittelalter*, Bonner Historische Forschungen 49 (Bonn, 1983); Nonn, 'Probleme der frühmittelalterlichen Grafschaftsverfassung am Beispiel des Rhein-Mosel Raum', *Jahrbuch für westdeutsche Landesgeschichte* 17 (1991), 29–50.

acknowledged – he took the actual power of counts as a given, resting on varying combinations of delegated royal rights and family power. Although his work has placed our understanding of counts on a new footing, we still have little idea about what being a count actually involved; here we once again turn back to Ganshof's reading of the capitularies.[20]

In other words, in spite of much important new work on early medieval politics, the basic framework within which findings are assimilated and interpreted has remained remarkably stable.[21] Yet this framework is based on assumptions about the delegation of power from the top down, and the ruler as the sovereign source of legitimate power, which are looking increasingly dated. What is needed is a shift of paradigm, the creation of a new interpretative framework to replace the often unspoken institutionalism which underpins our thinking about early medieval politics.[22] Rather than searching for insitutions, we need to study the generation and transmission of power: that is, to examine the structures of social action, and the political strategies which it was possible to pursue within these structures (remembering, of course, that even the most basic structures were not static but were reproduced and so subtly altered over time).[23] A series of recent studies which have exploited the potential of the documentary evidence to analyse the exercise of power in the localities point the way forward. So far, this kind of local documentary work

---

[20] See M. Borgolte, *Geschichte der Grafschaften Alemanniens in fränkischer Zeit*, VF Sonderband 31 (Sigmaringen, 1984), and the companion prosopography, *Die Grafen Alemanniens im merowingischer und karolingischer Zeit. Eine Prosopographie* (Sigmaringen, 1986). Also Borgolte's 'Die Geschichte der Grafengewalt im Elsaß von Dagobert I bis Otto dem Großen', ZGO 131 (1983), 3–54. For criticism, H. K. Schulze, 'Grundprobleme der Grafschaftsverfassung', *Zeitschrift für Württembergische Landesgeschichte* 44 (1985), 265–82; and Schulze, 'Die Grafschaftsorganisation als Element der frühmittelalterlichen Staatlichkeit', *Jahrbuch für Geschichte des Feudalismus* 14 (1990), 29–46; the most constructive discussion is T. Zotz, 'Grafschaftsverfassung und Personengeschichte. Zu einen neuen Werk über das karolingerzeitliche Alemannien', ZGO 97 (1988), 1–14. Of Borgolte's work on counts, the essay which comes closest to describing the mechanics of local power is 'Die Alaholfingerurkunden. Zeugnisse vom Selbstverständnis einer adligen Verwandtengemeinschaft des frühen Mittelalters', in Borgolte and D. Geuenich (eds.), *Subsidia Sangallensia I. Materialen und Untersuchungen zu den Verbrüderungsbüchern und zu den älteren Urkunden des Stiftsarchivs St. Gallen* (St Gallen, 1986), pp. 297–354.

[21] Cf. R. E. Sullivan, 'The Carolingian Age: Reflections on its Place in the History of the Middle Ages', *Speculum* 64 (1989), 267–306.

[22] For paradigm-shifts, how they occur and their relationship to empirical research, see T. Kuhn, *The Structure of Scientific Revolutions* (Chicago, 1962).

[23] For power as the object of historical enquiry, see M. Mann, *The Sources of Social Power I: A History of Power from the Beginning to A.D.1760* (Cambridge, 1986). Power as strategy, and the structuring of social action, is a recurrent subject in recent social theory: see e.g. P. Bourdieu, *Outline of a Theory of Practice*, trans. R. Nice (Cambridge, 1977). But for all the recent stress on agency and the renegotiation of the social process over time, we should not underestimate the extent to which action is historically delimited.

has concentrated on illuminating the workings of early medieval society, although the obvious implications for our understanding of political structures have been highlighted.[24] By examining the ways in which societies handle conflict, we can observe the surge of currents of power; the documentary evidence allows us to plot the connections through which power flowed, and the objectives for which that power was harnessed. This study investigates the circuits of power in the 'small worlds' which made up the Carolingian Empire as a means of reformulating our views of political power in the early middle ages.

Local power was problematical, something that needed constant maintenance, and if we ignore this basic fact we inevitably misunderstand the Frankish polity. The more we look at local leaders, the more it becomes clear that legalistic constitutional ideas about delegated rights of command simply do not explain the realities of power. In the localities, we meet forms of political leadership which were inherently personal, resting on one-to-one obligation and the recognition of transcendent moral qualities. Power, deeply unequal in its distribution within a profoundly hierarchical society, rested in reciprocity. It depended on informal channels of moral obligation and social pressure, not constitutional positions.[25] In such a world, power could only be negotiated and shared; only when power is institutionalised can it be delegated and controlled. One central concern of this study is the process by which power came to be presented in formal, legal terms, separated from the web of personal relationships involved in its exercise. In analysing the transformation of power there is a series of diagnostic questions which must be borne constantly in mind. Were political leaders more than particularly influential social actors, their power immersed in normal patterns of social action? Could they exercise

---

[24] Cf. W. Davies, *Small Worlds: The Village Community in Early Medieval Brittany* (London, 1989), esp. pp. 201–10; also W. Davies and P. Fouracre (eds.), *The Settlement of Disputes in Early Medieval Europe* (Cambridge, 1986).

[25] The pathbreaking study of reciprocity was, of course, M. Mauss, *The Gift: Forms and Functions of Exchange in Archaic Societies*, trans. I. Cunnison (New York, 1967); most recently, see A. Weiner, *Inalienable Possessions: The Paradox of Keeping-while-Giving* (Berkeley, Los Angeles and New York, 1992). For reciprocity and political leadership see M. Sahlins, 'Poor Man, Rich Man, Big-Man, Chief', *Comparative Studies in Society and History* 5 (1962–3), 285–303; useful additional material in M. Godelier and M. Strathern (eds.), *Big Men and Great Men* (Cambridge, 1991); and see W. G. Runciman, *A Treatise on Social Theory II: Substantive Social Theory* (Cambridge, 1989), esp. pp. 78–9, 185–6, 323–6. On reciprocity as the foundation of emergent political systems see H. J. M. Claessen and P. Skalník (eds.), *The Early State* (The Hague, 1977). On reciprocity in early medieval political and social structures, C. J. Wickham, 'Problems of Comparing Rural Societies in Early Medieval Europe', *Transactions of the Royal Historical Society* 6 (1992), 221–46; J. Hannig, '*Ars donandi*. Zur Ökonomie des Schenkungs im früheren Mittelalter', *Geschichte in Wissenschaft und Unterricht* 3 (1986), 149–62; B. H. Rosenwein, 'The Family Politics of Berengar I, King of Italy (888–924)', *Speculum* 71 (1996), 247–81.

their power as of right, or did they rely on their personal standing to carry out their official role? Was the act of ruling seen as something separate and distinct from the everyday functioning of society?[26]

The political structures of the early middle ages need to be analysed in their own right and on their own terms. We cannot go on seeing early medieval polities as simply inchoate or less developed forms of the 'perfected feudalism' of the high middle ages, or degenerate and messy continuations of ancient society. On the most general of levels, European society throughout the first millennium AD was traditional and agrarian, and so political power was closely tied to control of the land and those who worked it. Generalisations of this scale, however, do not make for penetrating analysis, and the moment we try to be more specific about the construction of political power, we are faced with manifest and important changes. In the Roman world, political power was mediated through the infrastructure of the state, and in particular through the city and the nexus of administrative and fiscal law. By the twelfth century, political power was rooted in jurisdictional rights which were understood as a form of property, the legal and proprietorial combining to define control of land and people.[27] The intervening period cannot satisfactorily be reduced to either a hangover from antiquity or a melting-pot out of which high medieval society emerged. In both schemes there is more than a hint of the Dark Ages paradigm which has not quite been exorcised yet – for is not the characterisation of five centuries of gradual synthesis an effective writing off of any independent value to those centuries? Historical development cannot be seen as a simple progression from chaos to order, irrational to rational. Unless we recognise that the early middle ages have their own legitimacy as a historical period we fall victim to a self-fulfilling teleology, describing it in terms of what came before and after and thus positing a natural and seamless transition from one to the other. In other words, we must take care before we characterise the early middle ages in terms of a simple polarity between the heritage of the ancient world and the birth of a new, medieval society – a polarity prolonged by the tendency of specialists to discuss the period in

[26] Cf. K. Polanyi, 'The Economy as Instituted Process', in Polanyi, C. M. Arensberg and H. W. Pearson (eds.), *Trade and Market in Early Empires: Economics in Theory and Practice* (New York, 1957), pp. 243–69; and S. N. Eisenstadt, 'The Study of the Process of Institutionalisation', in Eisenstadt, *Essays on Comparative Institutions* (New York, Sydney and London, 1965), pp. 1–68.

[27] If one defines 'feudalism' as a system of social organisation, in which power is articulated in terms of a hierarchy of proprietorial and jurisdictional rights, here we have it – and it has no necessary or causal connection with the prevalence or otherwise of specific forms of tenure, personal lordship or military organisation. On account of the confusion caused by the different senses of the word 'feudalism', I have not used it in this study.

terms of unreflective and one-dimensional categories of 'continuity' and 'change'.[28] The early middle ages were both dynamic and distinct, characterised by a particular relationship between 'state' and 'society' which was radically different from what went both before and after. The peculiarity of this relationship, indeed, was such that our modern categories of 'state' and 'society' tend to collapse into each other when encountering with early medieval evidence.[29]

What follows is divided into two parts. In the first, consisting of chapters 2–5, I adopt a broadly 'horizontal' approach, focusing on the 'source-rich' Carolingian period and analysing the fundamentals of social and political organisation. I begin by attempting to explain precisely why the Carolingian period is so well documented, examining the relationship between monasteries and lay society. I go on to examine the nature of landownership and the relationships between kinship, social status and the land; the texture of power, the places at which collective action took place, and the activities of those who ruled this society; and, finally, the ability of the political centre to impinge on the locality, to raise armies and tap the agrarian surplus. None of these discussions, however, stays wholly rooted in the Carolingian period, or presents a picture of stasis; they glance forward and back, and attempt to locate the vivid Carolingian evidence in longer patterns of development. I then present a diachronic analysis of the process of political change. Within this analysis, I offer a history of middle Rhenish politics from the late Roman period to the eleventh century – not a conventional political narrative so much as an analysis of changing political structures and the key points in their evolution. In conclusion, I identify the key characteristics of the political structures of the early medieval west, and trace the implications of those structures and their peculiarities.

---

[28] See G. Halsall, *Settlement and Social Organisation: The Merovingian Region of Metz, 500–800* (Cambridge, 1995).

[29] Hence it is only in my concluding analysis that I reintroduce the term 'state': to do otherwise would be to court confusion. I should underline that I am not claiming to discover 'the state' in my period, but analysing the peculiarities of the organisation of political power in the early middle ages, as the conclusion makes clear.

2

MONASTICISM, SPIRITUAL PATRONAGE AND SOCIAL STRUCTURE

GIFTS TO THE CHURCH: PATTERNS AND POTENTIAL

'Total history' is an impossibility, because in studying any historical society we are totally reliant on the highly selective and carefully selected views transmitted to us by that society and its successors. Any serious attempt at reconstructing a past society must therefore begin by confronting the problem of the representativeness or otherwise of the surviving sources. The evidence which survives from the early medieval period is only a tiny subset of what once existed, but its survival is not necessarily random. Those documents which were transmitted were not just lucky enough to avoid the random variables of destruction and loss; most were copied because of conscious decisions made to preserve them by later generations.[1]

In the Carolingian middle Rhine, documents were copied in large numbers because they recorded an important process of social change, which saw monasteries acquiring rights over land on an unprecedented scale. If we consider what is lost, it is clear that more or less random destruction through decay, war or natural disaster played a part: hence the absence of Carolingian material from the archives of the cathedrals of Mainz, Worms and Speyer. Similarly, the abbey of Hersfeld preserved the originals of its royal grants, but not documents recording its dealings with non-royal individuals. The odd non-royal documents that do survive from Hersfeld are, essentially, lucky: three ninth-century charters were used as bookbindings in the tenth century and thus preserved and later rediscovered.[2] But the majority of the documents which made this study possible did not owe their transmission to such happy chances. In

---

[1] These issues have recently begun to attract the attention they deserve: the classic medieval study is P. J. Geary, *Phantoms of Remembrance: Memory and Oblivion at the End of the First Millennium* (Princeton, 1994), esp. pp. 81–113; see also A. Esch, 'Überlieferungs-Chance und Überlieferungs-Zufall als methodisches Problem des Historikers', *Historische Zeitschrift* 240 (1985), 529–70.
[2] *UBH* 21, 26, 35.

13

particular, what survived from Fulda and Lorsch did so because of the comprehensive attempts made to maintain an institutional memory and record of the abbey's patrimony in the Carolingian period. Whilst only a handful of original charters survive, none earlier than the ninth century, large collections of copies of documents – cartularies – were made in the Carolingian and post-Carolingian periods.[3] This makes the middle Rhine, in terms of the charter evidence, the best-documented part of Carolingian Europe north of the Alps.

A full-length cartulary from Lorsch, copied in the twelfth century, records over 3,000 transactions, the vast majority dated between 764 (the abbey's foundation) and the end of the ninth century.[4] The credentials of the material as overwhelmingly genuine are unchallenged and unchallengeable. The inclusions and omissions within the Lorsch material show that we are reliant on the active choices made by monastic archivists: a record of dispute settlement (*placita*) only made it into the cartulary where no written act of donation for the property concerned survived, and written records of lettings of monastic land were consciously excluded. Two sides of Lorsch's relations with its neighbours were thus almost totally obscured.[5] The compilers of the Lorsch cartulary, moreover, did not copy out surviving documents willy-nilly: rather, they were consciously organised by geographical units, first of all by the *pagus*, then by individual settlement units, each called a *villa*, within the *pagus*; for each *villa* the documents were ordered chronologically. This suggests that much of the twelfth-century cartulary which survives is actually a copy of an earlier Carolingian compilation: *pagus* units were redundant by the twelfth century, but we know that Carolingian archives and cartularies elsewhere organised documents *pagus* by *pagus*. One might suggest a compilation date of *c.* 870, given the more or less total absence of material after that date, other than in the introductory cartulary-chronicle.[6]

---

[3] On the rarity of non-royal originals from east of the Rhine in this period see H. Breßlau, *Handbuch der Urkundenlehre für Deutschland und Italien*, 2 vols. (2nd edn, Leipzig, 1912–31), II, p. 117. See A. Bruckner and R. Marichal (eds.), *Chartae Latinae Antiquiores: Facsimile Edition of Latin Charters prior to the Ninth Century*, 12 nos. 540, 542 for the only two non-royal originals from the area from before 800. [4] *Codex Laureshamensis*, ed. K. Glöckner, 3 vols. (Darmstadt, 1929–36).

[5] On precarial grants, see the explicit statement in CL167. That *placita* were similarly excluded is my explanation for the often-noted lack of such documents in CL. Certainly *placita* were only transmitted where no 'better' document with no hint of dispute about the estate in question was available: CL228, CL532 are both fine examples. (Other *placita* are not strictly speaking court proceedings but record boundaries, and are thus more likely to be preserved and on occasion interpolated: CL6a is the classic example.)

[6] On its compilation and transmission more work is needed, but see Glöckner's comments in CL I, pp. 1–62. See also F. Staab's important discussion of the organisation of the Lorsch archive before the compilation of CL, 'Aspekte der Grundherrschaftsentwicklung von Lorsch vornehmlich aufgrund der Urbare des Codex Laureshamensis', in W. Rösener (ed.), *Strukturen der Grundherrschaft im frühen Mittelalter*, VMPIG 92 (Göttingen, 1989), pp. 285–333.

Cartulary-compilers did not, however, blindly copy what lay before them. Most of the non-royal charters were severely abbreviated, precisely because vital details for the social historian such as the names of witnesses and scribes, and the places at which documents had been enacted, were of little interest to later generations of monks, whose interests centred on the specific pieces of property being given and the identity of the donors. At the abbey of Fulda fragments of Carolingian cartularies, organised *pagus* by *pagus*, survive, most usefully for us one dealing with the Mainz area.[7] This Carolingian material is complemented by a series of twelfth-century registers of donations. On one hand, random decay and destruction played a role in determining what survives, in that we have only parts of a once larger Carolingian compilation; on the other, the active institutional agency of the monastery was crucial, for it was a matter of choice that these compilations were made, preserving records of monastic land dealings over preceding generations, and that further efforts at archival preservation were made in the twelfth century. The other diplomatic sources – above all the evidence from Wissembourg, from which two sections of a Carolingian cartulary survive, preserving documents from two particular *pagi* – confirm this picture.[8]

Whilst it cannot be denied that the evidence is 'pretty laconic in its present form', the real challenge is to understand the mind-numbingly formulaic tradition of the documents and thus open up a vast database.[9] The surviving charters are, in a sense, wholly unrepresentative. The interests of the cartulary-compilers, and of the compilers and keepers of monastic archives, edited the material. The surviving documents tell us about pious gifts to the church, and a little about later challenges to these transactions, but stand in an uncertain relationship to the wider field of social intercourse. Little is known about transactions not involving the new rural monasteries of the eighth and ninth centuries. We can rest

---

[7] On the transmission of the Fulda material see E. E. Stengel, *Abhandlungen und Untersuchungen zur Hessischen Geschichte*, Veröffentlichungen der Historischen Kommission für Hessen und Waldeck 26 (Marburg, 1960), pp. 27–265. The corpus was edited by E. F. J. Dronke in *Codex diplomaticus Fuldensis* (Aalen, 1850) and *Traditiones et antiquitates Fuldenses* (Fulda, 1844); a systematic re-edition was planned by Stengel, but he was only able to publish a modern edition for the period up to 802: *Urkundenbuch der Kloster Fulda*, ed. E. E. Stengel, Veröffentlichungen der historischen Kommission für Hessen und Waldeck 10, 2 vols. (Marburg, 1913–58). The completion of Stengel's project is a desideratum. K. Schmid *et al.* (eds.), *Die Klostergemeinschaft von Fulda im früheren Mittelalter*, 3 vols. in 5, Münstersche Mittelalter-Schriften 8 (Munich, 1978) is an invaluable companion in working with the Fulda material, diplomatic and necrological.
[8] *Traditiones Wizenburgenses: Die Urkunden des Klosters Weissenburg, 661–864*, ed. K. Glöckner and A. Doll (Darmstadt, 1979). For the compilation of the Wissembourg cartulary see Doll's introduction.
[9] C. J. Wickham, 'European Forests in the Early Middle Ages: Landscape and Land Clearance', in Wickham, *Land and Power: Studies in Italian and European Social History 400–1200* (Rome, 1994), pp. 155–200 at p. 182.

assured from the references in surviving charters and the occasional surviving document that written documents were used before the foundation of these monasteries.[10] Patterns of documentary survival were determined by initiatives of archival preservation, not patterns of original production.[11] The surviving documents present a snapshot of specific types of social relationships at a particular date: a spectacular snapshot, but one from a very particular and carefully chosen viewpoint, carefully posed and taken close up, and without comparable shots of 'before' and 'after'. In recent years some historians have acknowledged the problems of the evidence, attempting to place it in a fuller context by posing questions about the uses of writing, the factors encouraging gifts of land to the church, and the nature of landownership.[12] By asking why some documents survive we can avoid being misled by the provenance of the surviving evidence into accepting a partial view of social interaction at face value. Whilst we obviously cannot work outside the transmitted evidence, we can avoid the main pitfall facing the historian of early medieval Europe, that of being 'source-driven'. Once we have understood the contemporary function of the documentation, and the factors determining its survival, we are in a stronger position to pose questions about social change.[13]

The surviving documentary evidence is concerned first and foremost with the interaction between church and society. From the middle Rhine, we have several thousand charters transferring rights over land to the church – or rather, to a small number of particularly popular monastic communities. Each pious gift can be understood as an individual transaction in terms of the family exercising and transferring property rights, and in the context of the relationship between the donors and the recipient monastery. But when we look at pious gifts in aggregate, clear patterns of distribution across time and space also emerge. We have one hundred times more documents from the 780s than from the 850s, and virtually no documents after the 870s. As well as this long chronological

---

[10] See p. 112.

[11] Cf. the discussion of changing forms of documentation by P. Johanek, 'Zur rechtlichen Funktion von Traditionsnotiz, Traditionsbuch und früher Siegelkunde', in P. Classen (ed.), *Recht und Schrift im Mittelalter*, VF 23 (Sigmaringen, 1977), pp. 131–62.

[12] E.g. R. McKitterick, *The Carolingians and the Written Word* (Cambridge, 1989), pp. 77–134; C. J. Wickham, *The Mountains and the City: The Tuscan Apennines in the Early Middle Ages* (Oxford, 1989); and B. H. Rosenwein, *To Be the Neighbor of Saint Peter: The Social Meaning of Cluny's Property, 909–1049* (Ithaca and London, 1989).

[13] Cf. D. Barthélemy's criticisms of French historians of the tenth and eleventh centuries, who, he claims, have been misled by changing patterns of documentation into exaggerating the scale of the social changes taking place at the time: 'La mutation féodale a-t-elle eu lieu?', *Annales ESC* 47 (1992), 767–77; also P. Stafford, 'La mutation familiale: A Suitable Case for Caution', in J. Hill and M. Swan (eds.), *The Community, the Family and the Saint* (Turnhout, 1998), pp. 103–25.

tide, shorter and more local eddies and currents can be detected: gifts ebb and flow in particular localities, or from particular kin groups, at particular dates. Of course, we must allow for the random loss of some documents, but this cannot explain the patterns in the surviving evidence. The cartularies which preserve the evidence were composed in precisely that period in which the tide of gift-giving had very visibly gone out – the middle decades of the ninth century. The chronological patterning of gifts cannot thus be explained by the existence of a cut-off date after which documents were not preserved, because the gradual going out of the tide of giving is apparent over the decades pre-dating cartulary compilation. Moreover, if we concentrate on areas for which there is a good transmission from one or more institution, there is no reason why documents from a particular decade or a particular locality should be more susceptible to random loss on a sufficient scale to explain the patterns of pious gifts. The broad chronological profile is consistent across different institutions whose different archives had very different histories, and at Fulda the picture of the cartularies can be checked against, and confirmed by, the evidence preserved in twelfth-century registers.

These waves of pious giving are thus challenging phenomena which were at once both universal and highly local. They were universal as, at broadly similar dates, a similar dynamic can be detected across a vast area of Europe, down the Rhine and in the provinces to its east, in the Moselle and Saar valleys, even into Italy. The tide gathered momentum in the middle of the eighth century, but was in retreat by the first decades of the ninth.[14] They were local as ultimately each donation can only be understood in its specific social, chronological and geographical context. They are challenging as each donation was simultaneously a legal act transferring rights over property, a social act involving kin, lords and neighbours, and a spiritual act patronising the church. Above all, they are invaluable, as each donation concerns land and rights over the exploitation of land, the basic resource in this society, and thus relates to the most significant social relationships, providing insight into the fundamentals of power.

Gifts of land to the church were 'total occasions': social, legal and spiritual factors were simultaneously operative. There is thus no need to debate the relative merits of 'religious' versus 'materialist' explanations. To draw attention to the social logic of giving to the church is not to

---

[14] In the region between the Loire and Seine a different pattern is apparent, with a very gradual and more or less continuous increase in the number of surviving gifts from the seventh century through to the high middle ages. See R. Le Jan, *Famille et Pouvoir dans le Monde Franc* (Paris, 1995), p. 26, for figures. Whether this pattern is to be explained in terms of genuine social difference or differences in the process of transmission is clearly an important issue. In Italy, we have a similar distribution, with a gradual and continuous increase in the number of surviving documents, but one also marked by a shift from gifts to leases in the course of the ninth century.

argue that those who gave land were calculating self-interest in the absence of any spiritual motivation; similarly, to insist that the religious motives stated by the charters must be taken seriously is not to assert that those who gave land were simply particularly pious individuals.[15] To argue that the best way to explain the startlingly concentrated chronological and geographical distribution of pious gifts is to look for local social, economic and political factors avoids the obvious danger of ignoring the fact that gifts of land were transfers of power: it should not involve reducing religious motivation to a superstructural epiphenomenon. But we cannot afford to forget that pious gifts of land were acts with legal, social and political significance, and that they take on a very particular pattern in their distribution in space and time.

The best starting-point for any study of gifts of land to the church in the middle Rhine is the foundation of the abbey of Lorsch by the powerful landowner Cancor and his widowed mother Williswind in 764, on their portions of an important family centre.[16] Cancor and Williswind gave their abbey to their kinsman Chrodegang, bishop of Metz, monastic reformer, papal legate in Francia and the driving force behind the reform of the Frankish church.[17] Lorsch was staffed with monks from Chrodegang's foundation at Gorze, led by Guntland, Chrodegang's brother, who became abbot. A stress on contemporary Roman usage lay at the heart of Chrodegang's reform agenda; Chrodegang was responsible for one of the earliest translations of Roman martyrs to Francia in 761 when he acquired the relics of Gorgonius, Naborius and Nazarius from

[15] C. B. Bouchard, *Sword, Miter, and Cloister: Nobility and the Church in Burgundy, 980–1198* (Ithaca and London, 1987) seems to me to stress religious motivation *at the expense of* practical implications. Both Wickham's 'patronage' model and Rosenwein's 'association' model acknowledge the many layers of pious giving: see, respectively, *The Mountains and the City*, pp. 54–5, 191–7, 256–68, and *To Be the Neighbor, passim*. See also M. McLaughlin, *Consorting with Saints: The Ideology of Prayer for the Dead in Early Medieval France* (Ithaca, 1993).

[16] On the Lorsch estate see below, pp. 53–9. The following discussion of Lorsch's early years expands upon material in M. Innes, 'Kings, Monks and Patrons: Political Identity at the Abbey of Lorsch', in R. Le Jan (ed.), *La royauté et les élites dans l'Europe carolingienne* (Lille, 1998), pp. 301–24. On Lorsch's holdings, and their history, see F. Hülsen, *Die Besitzungen des Klosters Lorsch in der Karolingerzeit. Ein Beitrag zur Topographie Deutschlands im Mittelalter*, Historische Studien 104 (Berlin, 1913), and F. Knöpp (ed.), *Die Reichsabtei Lorsch. Festschrift zum Gedenken an ihre Stiftung 764*, 2 vols. (Darmstadt, 1974–7), esp. J. Semmler, 'Die Geschichte der Abtei Lorsch von der Gründung bis zum Ende der Salierzeit, 764 bis 1125', I, pp. 75–173.

[17] See J. Semmler, 'Chrodegang, Bischof von Metz, 747–766', in F. Knöpp (ed.), *Die Reichsabtei Lorsch. Festschrift zum Gedenken an ihre Stiftung 764* (Darmstadt, 1974–7), I, pp. 229–45; J. Semmler, 'Pippin III und die fränkische Klöster', *Francia* 3 (1975), 88–146 and the conference *Saint Chrodegang* (Metz, 1967). For the ties between Chrodegang and Cancor's family, see below, p. 55.

18

the pope. Gorgonius and Naborius found their way to Gorze and Chrodegang's other foundation near Metz, St Avold, respectively, whilst Lorsch was dedicated to Nazarius.[18] The twelfth-century cartulary chronicle preserves what may be a Carolingian description of the crowds, Cancor at their head, who welcomed the Roman saint to his new home.[19] The charter evidence confirms that locals really did welcome Nazarius; Lorsch received over a hundred donations of land each year in the first five years of its existence. In giving land to the new Roman saint brought to the middle Rhine by Chrodegang and Cancor, donors were buying into a network of spiritual patronage: in one donation charter a benefactor refers to 'my peculiar patron, St Nazarius'.[20] Concerns about prestige and local position informed the early waves of donations. Things really took off in March 766. From 8 to 14 March we have ten donations, all bar one of land at Mannheim and neighbouring settlements, most made at Weinheim. These gifts were made before the local elite, the great and good of the area just south of Lorsch on the lower Neckar. They were very public acts. Being seen to patronise the new saint expressed social status. After this wave of gifts, the urge to buy into Nazarius' charisma was felt by another elite grouping which dominated a different locality, across the Rhine from Lorsch: on 21 March we have three donations from Oppenheim and two from nearby villages, on 23 and 31 March further donations from Oppenheim. The men who gave were not just buying into saintly patronage and expressing their local position by doing so: they were also associating themselves with Cancor and Chrodegang, the two political patrons *par excellence* in the area. After all, Lorsch was staffed with monks from Chrodegang's Gorze, run by Chrodegang's brother, funded by Cancor and his kin. Giving to the new foundation not only expressed and confirmed social status, it also claimed a link with the wider political world via Cancor and Chrodegang. (See fig. 3, overleaf)

Nazarius made a huge and immediate impact on middle Rhenish

---

[18] See *Annales Laureshamenses*, ed. G. H. Pertz, *MGH SS* I, pp. 22–39, s.a. 761, 764, 765 respectively. For the significance of the translation of Roman martyrs, see F. Prinz, 'Stadtrömisch-Italienische Märtyrreliquien und fränkischer Reichsadel im Maas-Moselraum', *Historisches Jahrbuch* 87 (1967), 1–25, and, in general, M. Heinzelmann, *Translationsberichte und andere Quellen des Reliquienkultes*, Typologie des sources du Moyen Age occidental 33 (Turnhout, 1979).

[19] *CL* c. 3. Glöckner argues that this rests on the lost ninth-century collection of miracles associated with Nazarius. Two charters refer to *miracula* wrought by the relics: CL178, 221 (both, significantly, gifts by the close kin of the abbey's founders).

[20] CL281. On saints as patrons, in addition to the works on the charter evidence cited from n. 8 above, see T. Head, *Hagiography and the Cult of the Saints: The Diocese of Orléans 800–1200* (Cambridge, 1990), using literary evidence in a scholarly tradition which goes back to P. R. L. Brown, 'The Rise of the Holy Man in Late Antiquity', *Journal of Roman Studies* 61 (1971), 80–111, on living saints, and extended to the relics of dead saints by Brown in *The Cult of the Saints: Its Rise and Function in Latin Christianity* (Chicago, 1981).

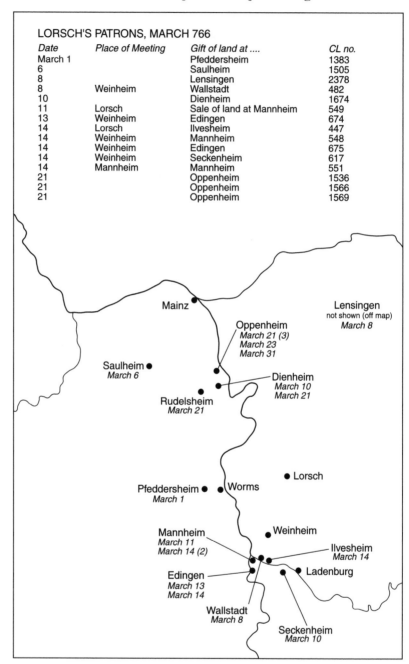

LORSCH'S PATRONS, MARCH 766

Date	Place of Meeting	Gift of land at	CL no.
March 1		Pfeddersheim	1383
6		Saulheim	1505
8		Lensingen	2378
8	Weinheim	Wallstadt	482
10		Dienheim	1674
11	Lorsch	Sale of land at Mannheim	549
13	Weinheim	Edingen	674
14	Lorsch	Ilvesheim	447
14	Weinheim	Mannheim	548
14	Weinheim	Edingen	675
14	Weinheim	Seckenheim	617
14	Mannheim	Mannheim	551
21		Oppenheim	1536
21		Oppenheim	1566
21		Oppenheim	1569

Mainz

Lensingen
not shown (off map)
March 8

Oppenheim
March 21 (3)
March 23
March 31

Saulheim
March 6

Dienheim
March 10
March 21

Rudelsheim
March 21

Lorsch

Pfeddersheim
March 1

Worms

Mannheim
March 11
March 14 (2)

Weinheim

Ilvesheim
March 14

Edingen
March 13
March 14

Ladenburg

Wallstadt
March 8

Seckenheim
March 10

3 Lorsch's patrons, March 766

society: from 765 to 770 we have a vast swell of donations, over 500 in total. It would be possible to examine the material in very great detail, outlining a pattern of waves such as that we have already seen in March 766, with local eddies and ripples. Substantial donations continued for three-quarters of a century, but their volume fell off, in a gradual but perceptible process. Both the scale and immediacy of Lorsch's impact were unparalleled. Of course, there were other monasteries which had a wide appeal and generated similar waves of pious gifts. The closest comparison with Lorsch is Fulda, founded in 744 under the aegis of Boniface, the Anglo-Saxon missionary active under Frankish protection in the provinces east of the Rhine. The written accounts of Fulda's foundation depicted an isolated spot in a remote wilderness, but archaeology shows that the monastic complex actually overlay an important site, probably a centre of Frankish lordship over the Grabfeld.[21] Fulda made a slow start in terms of attracting benefactions: non-royal gifts only really began after 750 and slowly reached a high-tide mark in the decades around 800. Although Fulda stood over 50 km to the east of the middle Rhine valley, its early benefactors were from the Mainz and Worms areas; indeed, gifts made by 'easterners' of more local estates only really began in the 780s, and this regional catchment area only eclipsed the middle Rhine as the focus of the abbey's interests in the first decades of the ninth century. By 810 the tide of giving was going out in the middle Rhine, although the abbey never lost its connections with the area. The tide of giving to Fulda turned slightly later in Fulda's other catchment areas, the upper Main and the Grabfeld, but it was retreating even there by the middle of the ninth century.[22]

Given sufficient contextual knowledge, it is possible to be very specific about the social mechanics of patronage. In the Fulda donations a number of discrete and definable groups of benefactors are immediately apparent. Many of the earliest patrons of Fulda were involved in one way or another with Lull, Boniface's disciple and successor as bishop of Mainz. Most of them must have known Boniface: one donation, by Otakar, was made as the body of Boniface, killed in Frisia in 751 and

---

[21] See H. Hahn, 'Eihloha – Sturm und das Kloster Fulda', and K. Heinemeyer, 'Die Gründung des Klosters Fulda im Rahmen der bonifatianischen Kirchenorganisation', *Fuldaer Geschichtsblätter* 56 (1980), 56–82, 83–132, respectively. For the background, W. Levison, *England and the Continent in the Eighth Century* (Oxford, 1946) and T. Schieffer, *Winfrid-Bonifatius und die christliche Grundlegung Europas* (Freiburg, 1954), remain fundamental. On Fulda see most recently G. Schrimpf (ed.), *Kloster Fulda in der Welt der Karolinger und Ottonen*, Fuldaer Studien 7 (Frankfurt, 1996).

[22] E. Friese, 'Studien zur Einzugsbereich der Kloster von Fulda', in *Klostergemeinschaft*, II:iii, pp. 1003–1269 is fundamental. See also F. Staab, 'Der Grundbesitz der Abtei Fulda bis zur Mitte des 9. Jahrhundert und seine Stifter', in W. Böhne (ed.), *Hrabanus Maurus und seine Schule: Festschrift der Rabanus-Maurus-Schule* (Fulda, 1980), pp. 48–63, with useful maps.

proclaimed a martyr, was moved from Mainz, where it had lain for some time, to its final resting-place at Fulda. Here is a documentary counterpart to the written accounts which depict pious well-wishers rushing to glimpse the martyr's body as it went east.[23] Boniface's contacts and patrons and their descendants continued to provide the backbone of Fulda's middle Rhenish benefactions into the ninth century. The children of Otakar and his brother, and some of their descendants, maintained the links made in the time of Boniface by keeping up a steady flow of gifts, some large, some small, and thus reaffirming their relationship to Boniface's foundation at Fulda.[24] If initial gifts to Fulda were from Otakar and his kin and contacts, by the 770s more gifts were coming, many on a less elevated social level. There may have been an element of emulation at work here: if the powerful Otakar and his kin were Fulda's patrons *par excellence*, imitating them and giving to Fulda was a way of expressing status, and aligning oneself with this potent patron, on a more local level. Certainly by the 790s members of very local elites were active patrons of Fulda, including some men whose social horizons may have barely extended beyond the immediate neighbourhood and who were well-to-do peasants. Lorsch had enjoyed a similar profile in the middle Rhine since its foundation. For a case study, the *villa* of Dienheim on the Rhine is probably the most richly documented rural settlement in Carolingian Europe. Here one faction of local landowners identified itself, from the late 780s, by its patronage of Fulda. This settlement was politically split. The series of gifts to Fulda from one group of landowners can be compared with a parallel series of gifts to Lorsch, made by a different group of landowners which showed very little overlap with the Fulda benefactors. The pious donations recorded by the charters were part of a very local political game of patronage and conspicuous display, two local factions expressing their opposition by making benefactions to different saints, and aligning themselves with different patrons beyond the village by doing so.[25]

A fascinating series of donations to Fulda made in January 813 illustrate precisely how gifts of land were central to local networks of patron-

---

[23] Willibald, *Vita Bonifatii*, ed. W. Levison, *MGH SRG* (Hanover, 1905), c. 8, pp. 53–4. Eigil, *Vita Sturmi*, ed. P. Engelbert, *Die Vita Sturmi des Eigil von Fulda*, Veröffentlichungen der Historische Kommission für Hessen und Waldeck 29 (Marburg, 1968), c. 15b, pp. 149–50.

[24] *UBF*23 and see A. Gerlich, '"Fidelis noster Otakarus". Aus den Anfängen der Bonifatius-verehrung am Mittelrhein', *Mainzer Zeitschrift* 48/49 (1953–4), 1–3. On Otakar see also below, pp. 61–5.

[25] On Dienheim see Friese, 'Einzugsbereich', pp. 1187–99, who assembles and analyses the basic data, plus analysis by Wickham, 'Rural Society in Carolingian Europe', in *NCMH*, pp. 510–37 at pp. 519–23, Staab, *Gesellschaft*, pp. 262–78, and Gockel, *Königshöfe*, pp. 184–203. See also below, pp. 101, 106–9, 126–8.

age which had their roots in rural settlements like Dienheim and tied together local elites as clients of saint and abbot. Gifts of Dienheim land to Fulda were made, at Dienheim, on 25 and 26 January; the bulk of the witnesses to these two donations were the well-to-do landowners who dominate charter witnessing at Dienheim. But in a remarkable piece of detective work, Eckhard Friese has also identified a handful of witnesses from outside Dienheim in each donation, who are part of a larger group of thirty-three men who witnessed Fulda charters across the region, from the middle Rhine to the Saale, right through the period 811–16. The two Dienheim donations from January 813 can be related to a series of others from the middle Rhine in the same month, tied together by the activity of these outside witnesses: at the monastery of Fischbach, north of Mainz, on 11 January; at the doors of the monastery of St Alban's, Mainz, on the 16th; then, after the Dienheim gifts of the 25th and 26th, at Wackernheim, just south of Mainz, on the 27th; at the unidentified *Marahabergen* on the 30th; and at Altheim near Worms on 8 February. This was precisely the period at which a great reform council was held at Mainz, and the revivalist tenor of the church's leaders obviously percolated down to local elites. The charter witness-lists show laymen in the service of Abbot Ratgar – a powerful and controversial figure – actively priming the abbey's patronage network, applying social pressure to solicit further gifts.[26] (See fig. 4).

Lorsch and Fulda were by no means the only churches in the eighth-century middle Rhine: we need to ask why it was these particular monastic foundations at this particular date which attracted such enthusiastic patronage. Christianity had a continuous history in the middle Rhine, in spite of the dislocation of the fifth and sixth centuries and the transition from Roman to Frankish rule. Judging by episcopal lists, bishops may have briefly disappeared in this period, but the archaeological record demonstrates that Christian communities and churches continued to exist in the cities of Mainz and Worms, and in Roman forts such as Alzey, Bad Kreuznach and Bingen. But this Christian continuity remained very much tied up with former Roman sites: in the middle Rhine in the sixth

---

[26] Friese, 'Einzugsbereich', pp. 1199–1204. The Dienheim charters are *CDF*281, 282; the others are *CDF*279, 280, 282, 283, 284, 285. Friese is surely correct to link the peculiar visibility of this group in the charters to Abbot Ratgar's controversial managerial style, and particularly his use of trusted laymen in key offices (see the complaints voiced in *Supplex Libellus*, ed. J. Semmler, in K. Hallinger (ed.), *Corpus Consuetudinum Monasticarum I* (Siegburg, 1963), pp. 319–27, at cc. 5, 16, pp. 323, 325); but the existence of such a group would be more normal (e.g. Abbot Hraban's legates in *CDF*456). On the controversy over Ratgar's regime see *Supplex Libellus*; Candidus, *Vita Eigil*, c. 3, ed. G. Waitz, *MGH SS* 15:1, pp. 221–33 at p. 223; Candidus, *De Vita Eigil*, ed. E. Dümmler, *MGH PLAC* 2, V:6, pp. 94–117 at p. 99; J. Semmler, 'Studien zum Supplex Libellus und zur anianischen Reform in Fulda', *Zeitschrift für Kirchengeschichte* 69 (1958), 268–98.

FULDA'S PATRONS, JANUARY TO FEBRUARY 813

Date	Place of meeting	Gift of	CDF no.
11 January	'in the monastery called Fischbach,under the jurisdiction of Count Liutfrid'	Four slaves (*mancipia*)	279
13 January	'at the basilica of St Alban in the city of Mainz'	Three slaves (*mancipia*)	280
25 January	Dienheim	Vineyard	281
26 January	Dienheim	Paternal inheritance in Dienheim, excluding one field, one dwelling and one slave, plus land in Uelversheim and Gimbsheim	282
27 January	Wackernheim	Fourteen slaves, plus paternal inheritance in Rüdesheim and vineyard in Dromersheim	283
30 January	*Marahbergun* (Wormsgau)	All property in Dienheim and Harxheim in Wormsgau and *Eggistat* in Niddagau, with four slaves	284
8 February	Altheim	Vineyard, five ploughlands (*jurnales*) and two slaves, all at Dienheim	285

NIDDAGAU

'in the monastery called Fischbach' ●
January 11

Frankfurt ●

●
Mainz
Wackernheim   'at the basilica of St.Alban'
Rüdesheim ●   January 27   January 16

●Dromersheim
Harxheim ●

Dienheim
January 25
January 26

Uelversheim ●

Gimbsheim ●

Marahbergen
(unidentified)
January 30

Altheim ●
February 8

4 Fulda's patrons, January–February 813

Monasticism, spiritual patronage and social structure

and seventh centuries – like much of the rest of the Frankish realm – churches were predominantly found in urban and suburban contexts. In the seventh century the first rural monasteries were founded. By the eighth century, monastic foundations were increasingly favoured by the elite. By the time of Lorsch's foundation the surrounding countryside was dotted with small family monasteries, nunneries and proprietary churches (to the extent that the three can be clearly distinguished). The charters also witness a growing number of small basilicas in the rural communities, often built of wood but sometimes of stone, in the eighth and ninth centuries, the earliest dating back to the seventh century.[27] These processes supply an important context in which the charters of pious gifts can be placed. A society in which rural elites were increasingly prepared to invest in a local church or a family monastery was one in which they might also be prepared to make donations to large-scale monastic foundations to build up their local prestige.

Most aristocratic church foundations were foci of family identity, the points around which kin groups crystallised; many were little more than 'house' monasteries, little bigger than the average elite household, with perhaps a dozen inmates, led by a family member.[28] Daughters and widows often found themselves at the head of such communities, under the protection of a lay relative, a father, brother or son; in the charters such women are frequently styled *deo sacrata*, implying that they had sworn to live by a set of precepts including celibacy. This made sense in view of the importance of women as conduits of family memory. In the early Lorsch and Fulda charters we see a series of tiny foundations,

[27] K. Heinemeyer, *Das Erzbistum Mainz in römischer und fränkischer Zeit I. Die Anfänge der Diözese Mainz*, Veröffentlichungen der Historischen Kommission für Hessen und Waldeck 39 (Marburg, 1979) is the best discussion of the Merovingian church in the area; see also H. Büttner, 'Frühes fränkisches Christentum am Mittelrhein', *Archiv für mittelrheinische Kirchengeschichte* 3 (1951), 9–55. The inscription evidence is vital: *Die frühchristliche Inschriften des Mittelrheingebietes,* ed. W. Boppert (Mainz, 1971). On the spread of monasticism see F. Prinz, *Frühes Mönchtum im Frankenreich: Kultur und Gesellschaft in Gallien, den Rheinlanden und Bayern am Beispiel der monastischen Entwicklung (4 bis 8 Jahrhundert)* (Munich and Vienna, 1965); on the elite and church foundation, K.-F. Werner, 'Le rôle de l'aristocratie dans la christianisation du nord-est de la Gaule', *Revue de l'Histoire de l'Eglise de France* 62 (1976), 45–73; on Merovingian religious culture in general see Y. Hen, *Culture and Religion in Merovingian Gaul* (New York, Leiden and Cologne, 1995), and the regional study of F. Staab, 'Heidentum und Christentum in der Germania Prima zwischen Antike und Mittelalter', in Staab (ed.), *Zur Kontinuität zwischen Antike und Mittelalter am Oberrhein*, Oberrheinische Studien 11 (Sigmaringen, 1994), pp. 117–52.
[28] See Bosl, *Franken um 800*, pp. 30–42, 73–83. Friese, 'Einzugsbereich', p. 1006 notes the contrast between foundations like Lorsch and Fulda, which attract wide-scale patronage, and more family-oriented abbeys such as Schäftlarn in Bavaria. Certainly the landholdings of Amorbach in the eleventh century, or even Seligenstadt in the tenth century, suggest that they were attracting patronage on a very different scale to Lorsch. See W. Störmer, 'Die Reichskirche im Spessart-Odenwald-Gebiet von der Karolinger bis zur Salierzeit', *Jahrbuch für fränkische Landesforschung* 48 (1988), 1–16.

notably convents at Baumerlenbach and Roden, each headed by a daughter and given to Lorsch in the 780s; Fulda received similar communities such as the nunnery at Milz, headed by the redoubtable Emhild.[29] That is, these early monastic structures were shaped by familial relationships, as they in turn offered elite families new strategies for the reproduction of power. In the eighth century, they contributed to a distinctive religious culture which has left traces in the record of manuscript production, and in texts such as the nun Huneburc of Heidenheim's *Lives* of her relatives, Willibald of Eichstätt and Wynnebald of Heidenheim.[30] By the ninth century, the kind of small, familial establishment in which women could play an important role was no longer so prominent. Already at Chrodegang's Gorze, Carolingian reform emphasised large-scale, ordered, male monasticism focused on the liturgy of the mass, an emphasis which was to be redoubled by the triumph, with royal backing, of Benedict of Aniane's brand of monasticism in the first quarter of the ninth century.[31] The gifts of family houses to the monks of Lorsch and Fulda, visible in the charters, mark the start of the process by which an edifice of discipline and jurisdiction was constructed, with resultant changes in religious culture as a whole, and in the role of women in particular. By the 820s the Fulda monk Rudolf, in his *Life* of Leoba (a relative of Boniface's who had headed a small nunnery at Tauberbischofsheim on the Main), presented a sanitised version of earlier tradition designed not to conflict with the decrees of Carolingian reformers.[32]

Even eighth-century foundations were not wholly female, but they represented monasticism on a different scale, and with a different rationale, from that offered by the great all-male houses of the Carolingian

---

[29] *CL* 12, 13, also 18; *UBF*265 (799). On the latter see M. Gockel, 'Zur Verwandtschaft der Äbtissin Emhilt von Milz', in H. Beumann (ed.), *Festschrift für Walter Schlesinger*, 2 vols. (Cologne and Vienna, 1974), II, pp. 1–70.

[30] *Vita Willibaldi episcopi Eichstetensis*, ed. O. Holder-Egger, *MGH SS* 15:1 (Hanover, 1887), pp. 86–106; *Vita Wynebaldi abbatis Heidenheimensis*, ed. O. Holder-Egger, ibid, pp. 106–17. See P. Dronke, *Women Writers of the Middle Ages* (Cambridge, 1984), pp. 33–5; R. McKitterick, 'Frauen und Schriftlichkeit im Frühmittelalter', in H.-W. Goetz (ed.), *Weibliche Lebensgestaltung im frühen Mittelalter* (Cologne, Weimar and Vienna, 1991), pp. 65–118; English trans. 'Women and Literacy in the Early Middle Ages', in McKitterick, *Books, Scribes and Learning in the Frankish Kingdoms, 6th to 9th centuries* (Aldershot, 1994), XIII, esp. pp. 22–3, 30–1.

[31] The best introduction to Carolingian monasticism is M. De Jong, 'Carolingian Monasticism: The Power of Prayer', in *NCMH*, pp. 622–53.

[32] See Rudolf of Fulda, *Vita Leobae abbatissae Biscofesheimensis*, ed. G. Waitz, *MGH SS* 15:1 (Hanover, 1887), pp. 118–31. On female piety in the ninth century see J. M. H. Smith, 'The Problem of Female Sanctity in Carolingian Europe', *P&P* 146 (1995), 3–37; J. Martindale, 'The Nun Immena and the Foundation of the Abbey of Beaulieu: A Woman's Prospects in the Carolingian Church', *Studies in Church History* 27 (1990), 27–42, emphasises the importance of the new forms of intercessory and commemorative liturgy centred on the mass, necessarily performed by men.

renaissance. The type of structure that the charters describe can be envis-
aged in more detail thanks to the excavation of the monastic *cella* built by
one Hafti and his family in the middle of the eighth century at Esslingen
on the upper Neckar. The complex was based around a stone nave
approximately 10.5 by 9.5 m, under which eighteen burials, sixteen adults
and two children, were found. Just as Lorsch had initially been given to
Chrodegang, so Esslingen was given by Hafti to Abbot Fulrad of Saint-
Denis.[33] Given the intense pressure on family resources that even such a
modest foundation created, the giving of such a community to the likes
of Fulrad or Chrodegang, or to a great abbey such as Lorsch or Fulda,
made sense. After all, these local churches continued to exist, and maintained their links with the families of their founders, but now they were
part of a wider and more potent network of prayer centred upon a great
abbey. Only the grandest foundations were able to continue as self-
sufficient entities for more than a couple of generations. Hornbach, for
example, was founded at a strategic site on the Blies by a powerful local
family in co-operation with St Pirmin in the early eighth century, but
throughout its existence housed tens rather than hundreds of monks; its
inmates and patrons were predominantly associates of the founder's
family.[34]

Because they were larger, Lorsch and Fulda took in far more child
recruits, thus relating to more communities and kindreds.[35] They offered
spiritual patronage to wide, and relatively well-defined, catchment areas.
It is remarkable that Lorsch received donations primarily in the middle
Rhine and the region immediately east of the Rhine from Hesse to
Alemannia, but only limited gifts in the Moselle and Liège areas, where
its founders also had kin, interests and contacts. This neatly complemented the interests of Chrodegang's Gorze: whereas Gorze received
land which lay mainly in the Moselle and the area to the west, Lorsch's
holdings began on the other side of the Hunsrück, in the Rhine valley,
and spread east and south-east from there.[36] The scope of Lorsch's eastern
holdings was defined by the interests of its founders and their contacts.
Cancor was active as a Frankish agent in Alemannia in the middle of the

---

[33] See G. P. Fehring and F. Stein, 'Frühmittelalterliche Kirchenbauten unter St. Dionysius zu
Esslingen am Neckar', *Germania* 44 (1966), 354–85. On Fulrad's patrons and land-acquisitions, see
now A. Stoclet, *Autour de Fulrad de Saint-Denis (v.710–784)* (Geneva, 1993).

[34] On Hornbach see A. Neubauer's *Regesta des ehemaligen Benediktinerklosters Hornbach*, Mitteilungen
des Historischen Vereins der Pfalz 27 (Speyer, 1904) and A. Doll, 'Das Pirminskloster Hornbach.
Gründung und Verfassungsentwicklung bis Anfang des 12 Jahrhunderts', *Archiv für mittelrheinische
Kirchengeschichte* 5 (1953), 108–42.

[35] On monastic recruitment, see M. De Jong, *In Samuel's Image: Child Oblation in the Early Medieval
West* (Leiden, New York and Cologne, 1996).

[36] For Gorze's patrimony see *Cartulaire de l'abbaye de Gorze. MS 826 de la Bibliothèque de Metz*, ed. A.
d'Herbomez (Paris, 1898).

eighth century, and in the Briesgau, the area where Lorsch later acquired significant holdings. He was active alongside Ruthard, the Frankish agent in the newly conquered duchy. Ruthard was, like Cancor, close to Chrodegang. He granted estates in the Moselle valley to Gorze and founded monasteries at Amorbach, close by Lorsch on the Main, and at Gengenbach on the east bank of the upper Rhine, the latter like Lorsch given to Chrodegang and staffed by Gorze monks.[37] Lorsch's acquisition of holdings along the upper Rhine and the lower Neckar underlines the importance of Cancor's contacts, particularly those with Ruthard, for the new foundation.[38] The abbey's extensive holdings further to the north, but still east of the Rhine, above all in Hesse, owed more to Cancor's own family interests. Here the key figures may have been Cancor's mother, and another relation, Swicgar, active as a Frankish agent in Hesse – perhaps the same Swicgar who had extensive interests on the Bavarian frontier and who worked hand in hand with Boniface's follower, Willibald, in establishing the landed base for the diocese of Eichstätt.[39]

The mechanisms by which these landholdings east of the Rhine were acquired are suggested by the activities of another of Cancor's contacts, Abbot Fulrad of Saint-Denis. Fulrad was one of the key figures in Frankish politics in the east in the mid-eighth century, and was close to Cancor's father and to Ruthard. His will, drawn up in 777, indicates that he had inherited substantial estates in the Alsace–Alemannia borderlands, estates which he had supplemented by attracting gifts both in the vicinity of his inherited estates and east of the Rhine from local men eager to receive his patronage, including, indeed, Hafti, who handed the church at Esslingen over to Fulrad. Esslingen was one of a series of monastic cells which were the focal points of Fulrad's property, and which Fulrad, in turn, in his will, handed on to the monastery of Saint-Denis in Paris. These property links facilitated the political and ecclesiastical integration of Alsace and Alemannia into the Frankish realm.[40] Whether those who gave him land and monastic cells expected them to end up in the hands of Saint-Denis is unclear: they were essentially

---

[37] Borgolte, *Die Grafen Alemanniens*, pp. 229–36, with references. For Amorbach see F. Oswald and W. Störmer (eds.), *Die Abtei Amorbach im Odenwald* (Sigmaringen, 1984).
[38] Note also the contacts with St Gallen: H. Büttner and J. Duft, *Lorsch und St-Gallen*, VF Sonderband 1 (Sigmaringen, 1963).
[39] On Swicgar, see Staab, *Gesellschaft*, pp. 422–7, for his kin and his activity in Hesse, and *Vita Willibaldi*, c. 5, ed. Holder-Egger, pp. 104–5, for Eichstätt.
[40] J. Fleckenstein, 'Fulrad von St-Denis und der fränkische Ausgriff in den süddeutschen Raum', in G. Tellenbach (ed.), *Studien und Vorarbeiten zur Geschichte des großfränkisches und frühdeutschen Adels* (Freiburg, 1957), pp. 9–39, and see now Stoclet, *Fulrad*. For an edition and discussion of Fulrad's will, the key document, see M. Tangl, 'Das Testament Fulrads von Saint-Denis', in Tangl, *Das Mittelalter in Quellenkunde und Diplomatik: Ausgewählte Schriften*, Forschungen zur mittelalterliche Geschichte 12, 2 vols. (Graz, 1966), I, pp. 540–81, or *Chartae Latinae Antiquiores* 12, nos. 622–4.

patronising a Holy man who also allowed direct access to the Frankish court. Fulrad worked in concert with laymen like Ruthard to create networks of support and patronage amongst the elites of the regions in which they were active – and these networks were primed by gifts of land. We can certainly see Willibrord acting precisely so a generation earlier, and presumably Chrodegang's appeal was similar.[41] The wave of gifts to Lorsch and Fulda in this area in the second half of the eighth century effected the final integration of the eastern provinces into the Frankish realm, as members of local elites who were already Frankish clients expressed their allegiance by giving gifts of land to the churches of the Frankish elite. Fulda won support from the elite of the Mainz area, where Boniface himself had been based. Hence gifts to Fulda begin around Mainz and point east along the Main, before taking off in the physical vicinity of the abbey, further to the east. Fulda was also heavily involved in the conversion of Saxony from its very inception, and was thus able to build up links with the Saxon elite which became increasingly important in the ninth century.[42] Lorsch won the backing of the elite of the middle Rhine valley from Mainz southwards, winning patronage east of the Rhine and south-east down the upper Rhine and the lower Neckar as far as the Alemannian borderlands, thanks to their influence in the region.

These monasteries were founded at strategic points, which also functioned as important social centres: Fulda a meeting place for the 'men of the Grabfeld', Lorsch a 'public place' (*locus publicus*).[43] The *Life* of Sturm, the first abbot of Fulda, includes a remarkable account of the foundation of the new monastery: after a royal charter giving the site of his new monastery to Boniface had been drawn up, it was carried to Fulda by royal messengers who assembled 'all the noble men of the Grabfeld', read the charter aloud and delivered, on the king's behalf, sermonising exhortations to give land to Boniface's church. These sermonising exhortations, judging from the charter evidence, had little immediate effect, and it was the translation of the relics of Boniface after his death that led to significant lay patronage.[44] Similarly, gifts of land to Lorsch immediately followed the translation of a new Roman saint to the church, and its subsequent rebuilding beginning in 767. Relics were potent repositories of supernatural power, focal points from which charisma radiated into the

---

[41] For this pattern see M. J. Costambeys, 'An Aristocratic Community on the Northern Frankish Frontier, 690–726', *EME* 3 (1994), 39–62; Stoclet, *Fulrad*. I must thank Marios Costambeys for helping me clarify my thoughts here.

[42] Friese, 'Einzugsbereich', is fundamental on the changing pattern of gifts to Fulda.

[43] Fulda: n. 21 above. Lorsch: pp. 101–3 below.

[44] Eigil, *Vita Sturmi*, c. 12, ed. Engelbert, p. 143.

secular world. The shift from devotion to living Holy men to devotion to dead relics is part and parcel of the institutionalisation of religious charisma through the ordering of large-scale communities of intercessory prayer at places like Gorze, Lorsch and Fulda. It also had the effect of locking up gifts to the Holy in an undying institution, rather than leaving them in the hands of a living patron.[45]

If we wish to understand the workings of spiritual patronage, we must move forward half a century to Einhard's vivid account of his translation of the relics of Marcellinus and Peter to the Odenwald, and, eventually, to the monastery at Seligenstadt, in 827. Here locals and a vagabond army of pilgrims, cripples and paupers flock to the relics to seek intercession, to end injustice, infirmity or illness. Einhard, like Boniface, Chrodegang or Fulrad a generation earlier, was a powerful patron who also offered access to the sacred, and so combined secular and spiritual patronage – although unlike his predecessors half a century earlier, Einhard's contact with the sacred came unambiguously through relics.[46] Even in the middle of the eighth century, it was relic-cults in particular that were central to the acquisition of land: relics were the crucial agents in the solidifying of the fluid networks which emerged around Holy men into an institutional patrimony. At Lorsch, an account of the *Miracula* performed by Nazarius existed by the first years of the ninth century, although unfortunately all that survives are dry, factual fragments in the twelfth-century cartulary chronicle. Similarly, ninth-century Fulda writers were anxious to chronicle the quantity and potency of the relics housed in their monastery's churches.[47] When we encounter the marked geographical shifts in patterns of giving which were so visible in the micro-studies pursued above – the giving to Lorsch in March 766 or to Fulda in January and February 813 – we have to think in terms of monks publicly parading their relics and advertising their powers, just as Einhard did with his newly acquired Roman relics in 827–8.

Indeed, Einhard's account indirectly pays testimony to Fulda's and Lorsch's success in penetrating middle Rhenish society. Of the four

[45] For dispute over Boniface's relics, n. 23 above. On various aspects of the Carolingian hostility to living sanctity, and the centrality of relic-cults, see Smith, 'Female Piety', and P. J. Geary, *Furta Sacra: Thefts of Relics in the Central Middle Ages* (2nd edn, Princeton, 1990).

[46] Einhard, *Translatio et miracula sanctorum Marcellini et Petri*, ed. O. Holder-Egger, MGH SS 15:1 (Hanover, 1887), pp. 238–64, and see J. Fleckenstein, 'Einhard, seine Gründung und sein Vermächtnis im Seligenstadt', in K. Hauck (ed.), *Das Einhardskreuz. Vorträge und Studien der Münsteraner Diskussion zur arcus Einhardi*, Abhandlungen der Gesellschaft der Wissenschaften in Göttingen, phil.-hist. Klasse 87 (Göttingen, 1974), pp. 96–121, and H. Schefers, 'Einhards römische Reliquien. Zur Bedeutung der Reliquientranslations Einhards von 827/828', *Archiv für Hessische Geschichte und Altertumskunde* 48 (1990), 272–92.

[47] Semmler, 'Lorsch', p. 146, n. 79; Rudolf of Fulda, *Miracula sanctorum in Fuldensium ecclesias translatorum*, MGH SS 15:1 (Hanover, 1887), pp. 328–41.

books of Einhard's *Translatio* only one concerns the miracles wrought by
Marcellinus and Peter in our area, the rest recounting their origins, their
success in miracle working at court and their sojourns at Einhard's other
abbeys. The documentary evidence which survives shows that
Seligenstadt's estates were small both in size and in scope. Evidently even
Einhard's best efforts could only summon up a minor eddy of pious
giving. In part, this may be due to site: Marcellinus and Peter found their
home in the wooded uplands of the lower Main, not the rich and densely
settled Rhine valley. But Einhard was clearly too late entering the game;
the tide of donations had well and truly turned by the time of the translation, and the coming of a new source of spiritual patronage could not
end the underlying dynamic. Quite simply, by the 820s there were few
groups in the area in need of spiritual patronage precisely because Lorsch
and Fulda between them had been so efficient at mopping up potential
benefactors and fulfilling their needs. Einhard himself acknowledged this
when he gave his church at Michelstadt to Lorsch.[48]

Despite his limited success, Einhard's account offers valuable insight
into the rituals and practices which created bonds of association between
monasteries and their benefactors: the importance of relics and a shrine,
prayer and the liturgy, and the intercession offered. The charters can add
to our knowledge of the religious atmosphere in which donations took
place. Some have long introductory statements of pious intent. One
popular statement is a citation from Psalm 123 of a verse prominent in
the liturgy.[49] The fact that donors placed their charters on the altar of the
church, that is onto the relics of the saint who was receiving the gifts,
suggests that the liturgical quotation may have been performed as they
made their gift.[50] The most common opening likened pious gifts to
water, extinguishing the fire of sin, and then made a citation from Luke

[48] Seligenstadt's holdings can be reconstructed from tenth-century lists of dues discovered by A.
Schmidt, 'Mitteilungen aus Darmstädter Handschriften', *Neues Archiv* 13 (1888), 603–22. *CL*20
for the gift of Michelstadt.
[49] In this paragraph I rely heavily on the Wissembourg material as its formulae have been subjected
to detailed scrutiny by Doll in his introduction. See *TW*, pp. 82–3, with table 53, p. 595, for the
opening of 15 charters: *Adiutorium nostrum in nomine domini qui fecit celum et terram*. On the importance of the Psalter in lay religiosity, McKitterick, *The Carolingians and the Written Word*, pp. 218–19.
[50] For gifts on the altar see (e.g.) *CL*12, 13, gifts of nunneries in which this element of the ritual is
explicitly spelt out. *Lex Alamannorum*, I:i, and *Lex Baiuvariorum* I:i (ed. K. Eckhardt, *Die Gesetze
des Karolingerreiches 2. Alemannien und Bayern*, Germanenrechte 2:ii (Weimar, 1934), pp. 2, 78,
respectively) see placing the charter on the altar as standard practice. On the correlation between
liturgy and diplomatics see W. John, 'Formale Beziehungen der privaten Schenkungsurkunden
Italiens und des Frankenreiches und die Wirksamkeit der Formulare', *Archiv für Urkundenforschung*
14 (1936), 1–104 at 11 (tenth-century Gorze), and K. Leyser, *Rule and Conflict in an Early Medieval
Society* (Oxford, 1979), p. 103 (tenth-century Germany); also L. K. Little, *Benedictine Maledictions:
Liturgical Cursing in Romanesque France* (Ithaca and London, 1993), esp. pp. 52–9. Again, I must
thank Marios Costambeys for alerting me to the possibilities of this evidence.

11.41: 'Give alms and all the world shall be yours.' This pair of statements
was copied by a variety of scribes writing for different individuals and
institutions.[51] On occasion more unusual openings, nonetheless clearly
influenced by standard formulae, were used to explain the motives for
giving. One donation to Wissembourg, from 757, began: 'And I have
done as admonished, as is said: *gift-giving pleases God*; and, *as water extinguishes fire, so alms extinguish sin*.'[52] The charters thus show the dissemination of a set of standard justifications for pious gifts, and suggest a ritual
context in which pious hopes were voiced. The constant barrage of biblical glosses upon the act of giving affected the conceptualisation of transfers of land to the church. In the late eighth century middle Rhinelanders
begin to describe the giving of land to the church as 'giving in alms'. This
was a regional phenomenon: whilst by the ninth century almost half the
surviving Fulda documents style themselves as 'gifts in alms', the phrase
is almost wholly absent beyond the middle Rhine.[53] Since late antiquity,
giving gifts to saints and the church had been presented as a noble and
pious act which was also a form of charity. A sixth-century grave inscription from Bingen records the alms-giving of the noblewoman Berthild:
presumably her alms were moveable goods. In the seventh century,
Frankish charters began to depict gifts of *land* to the church as a species
of alms-giving which did good for the donor's soul.[54] In the eighth-
century middle Rhine this was taken one stage further, with the charitable ideal invading the legal heart of the charter, the dispositive clause.
In donations to Wissembourg gifts 'in alms' first appeared in 783, and sub-

---

[51] *Marculfi Formularum Libri Duo*, ed. A. Uddholm (Uppsala, 1962), II:1, p. 164 is the source for the gift:water analogy. See John, 'Formale Beziehungen', 58–60 and H. Zatschek, 'Die Benutzung der Formulae Marculfi und anderer Formelsammlungen in den Privaturkunden des 8. bis 10. Jahrhunderts', *MIÖG* 42 (1927), 165–267 at 179.

[52] *TW*144. For other non-standard openings which nonetheless rest on Biblical formulae see *CL*552, Wampach, *Grundherrschaft Echternachs* 21, d'Herbomez, *Cartulaire de Gorze* 14, 15, *TW*52, 204.

[53] And yet some St Gallen charters use the Biblical citations which, on the middle Rhine, inform the idea of gifts in alms: for example *Urkundenbuch der Abtei St.Gallen*, ed. H. Wartmann, 2 vols. (Zurich, 1863–6), I, nos. 116, 117. Cf. *Die älten Mönchslisten und die Traditionen von Corvey*, ed. K. Honselmann, Veröffentlichungen der Historischen Kommission für Westfalen 10, Abhandlungen zur Corveyer Geschichtsschreibung 6 (Paderborn, 1982), and *The Cartulary of Flavigny*, ed. C. B. Bouchard (Cambridge, MA, 1991).

[54] In general see P. Jobert, *La notion de donation: Convergances 630–750*, Publications de l'Université de Dijon (Paris, 1977); also B. Beaujard, 'Dons et piété à l'égard des saints dans la Gaule des Ve et VIe siècles', in M. Sot (ed.), *Haut Moyen Age: Festschrift P. Riché* (Paris, 1990), pp. 59–68, and H. Fichtenau, *Arenga: Spätantike und Mittelalter im Spiegel der Urkundenformeln*, *MIÖG* Ergänzungsband 18 (Graz, 1957), pp. 141–4. Berthild: *Die frühchristliche Inschriften*, ed. Boppert, pp. 108–18. On the centrality of notions of gift-exchange and salvation to early medieval Christianity, see P. R. L. Brown, 'Vers la naissance de purgatoire', *Annales: ESC* 52 (1997), 1247–62, and S. MacCormack, 'Sin, Citizenship and the Salvation of Souls: The Impact of Christian Priorities on Late Roman and Post-Roman Society', *Comparative Studies in Society and History* 39 (1997), 644–73.

sequently on thirteen successive occasions; the earliest use of all is in a Fulda charter written by a Mainz scribe in 765. The Echternach material points to the regional nature of the phraseology: there are just four 'gifts in alms', the first in 789, all by middle Rhinelanders, none by Echternach's patrons elsewhere.[55]

These phrases may be formulaic stereotypes, but they are formulaic stereotypes which influenced action and have to be taken seriously. Concerns about redemption were pervasive. How did pious gifts ensure the health of the giver's soul? Do the charters document a form of gift-exchange, laymen giving gifts of land to the church and receiving spiritual countergifts in return? The charters presented a world of spiritual patronage in which gifts to a particular saint and a particular church created an associative bond between donor and church, building a relationship between benefactor and saint and thus aiding the redemption of the donor's soul. Commemoration of the dead was a constant preoccupation. A gift 'in alms' for a parent or friend was a way to ensure their *memoria* and do good for their soul. Indeed, a gift could place the responsibility for commemoration in the hands of a particular church. Lorsch and Fulda built up a vast network of patrons along the Rhine and to its east, establishing themselves as the spiritual patrons for local elites by offering prayers which consolidated political and personal ties. Lorsch and Fulda attracted donations of land because they were particularly potent centres of spiritual patronage. They differed even from other episcopal and aristocratic foundations, in that they offered spiritual patronage on a larger scale, and, because of this, acquired more extensive landholdings.

The history of the early medieval cemetery and church at Flonheim, near Alzey, is indicative of the social and religious changes we have been tracing. The cemetery was founded *c.* 500 with a spectacularly rich male burial. Nine other burials of the sixth and seventh centuries, each complete with lavish grave-goods, surrounded this 'founder grave'; this group was probably the nucleus of a larger cemetery. At some point, probably in the seventh century, a church was built over this exclusive set of burials; here, past met present at a place of prayer and commemoration. In eighth-century charters, we meet the owners of the church, a family with widespread property interests for whom Flonheim, with its dynastic mausoleum, was a special place. At some point between 764 and 767, the basilica was given to the monks of Lorsch, who offered more effective prayer still. The gift of the Flonheim church also reflected

---

[55] Wissembourg: *TW*20, 23, 31, 33, 81, 117, 127, 134, 165, 175, 180, 182, 236. Fulda: *UBF*39 and *passim* thereafter. Echternach: C. Wampach, *Geschichte der Grundherrschaft Echternach* I (Luxembourg, 1930), pp. 101, 112, 137, 141.

political alliance between the Flonheim family and Lorsch's founders.[56] This use of prayer as the adhesive of political and familial alliance can be seen more clearly still at the church of St Lambert in Mainz. St Lambert's was founded in the first decades of the eighth century, its dedication to a recent and controversial political saint reflecting the political stance of its founders. By 800, no fewer than eighteen men and women had property rights to shares of the church. In the first decades of the ninth century, one by one they gave their shares to Lorsch, as they did so transferring responsibility for commemoration of their kin to the monks. This decision seems to have been informed by the links of kinship and patronage binding them to the founders of Lorsch. One way to look at the rapid growth of Lorsch's importance in middle Rhenish society is to think of the many similar gifts of churches, and the many more gifts of land, each transferring responsibility for intercession and commemoration on behalf of a social group to the huge monastery with its powerful relics and potent liturgy, resting on the prayers of hundreds of specialists. Therein lies the key to the triumph of Lorsch and Fulda, and the type of monasticism they represented.[57]

FUNERARY RITUAL, INHERITANCE AND GIFT EXCHANGE

Giving land to the church was a way of gaining the spiritual patronage of saints, expressing political allegiance and ensuring commemoration after death. The surge of pious gifts of land in the eighth century thus points to an increased concern on the part of the laity with spiritual patronage, and above all with intercessory prayer and commemoration beyond the grave.[58] To understand why these concerns emerged so strongly at this moment in time, it is necessary to place the pious giving of land in the context of relationships between the living and the dead suggested by the long-term development of funerary ritual.

In the sixth and seventh centuries the inhabitants of the middle Rhine

---

[56] See H. Ament, *Fränkische Adelsgräber aus Flonheim in Rheinhessen*, Germanische Denkmäler der Völkerwanderungszeit B5 (Berlin, 1970) for the archaeology and *CL*933–943 for the charters, plus comments by P. J. Geary, 'Problems of Using Archaeological Evidence for Religious and Cultural History', in Geary, *Living with the Dead in the Middle Ages* (Ithaca and London, 1994), pp. 30–45 esp. pp. 37–8, and M. Borgolte, review of Heinemeyer's 'Das Erzbistum Mainz', *ZGO* 131 (1983), 467–8.

[57] On St Lambert, Gockel, *Königshöfe*, pp. 238–58, and *CL*1966–7, 1969–72, 1974. Cf. also M. Borgolte's comments on gifts of churches to St Gallen, 'Gedenkstiftungen im St.Galler Urkunden', in K. Schmid and J. Wollasch (eds.), *Memoria. Die geschichtliche Zeugniswert des liturgischen Gedenkens im Mittelalter*, Münstersche Mittelalter Schriften 48 (Munich, 1984), pp. 578–602.

[58] On the significance of the dead in these terms, see P. Geary, 'Exchange and Interaction between the Living and Dead in Early Medieval Society', in Geary, *Living with the Dead in the Middle Ages* (Ithaca and London, 1994), pp. 77–94, and Le Jan, *Famille et Pouvoir*, pp. 35–57.

practised a rite of furnished inhumation in communal cemeteries which involved the deposition of grave-goods with the dead. Grave-goods cannot be seen as inherently pagan, a hangover whose elimination by the end of the seventh century demonstrated the final victory of Christianity.[59] The most lavish early Merovingian burial from the middle Rhine, that of an adult male buried at Planig in the first third of the sixth century, included a golden helm decorated with Christian symbols; other sixth-century grave-goods were decorated with crosses. Although we cannot say that those buried with such artefacts were Christians, Christianity was in the air.[60] The Merovingian church made no attempt to stamp out the practice of burial with grave-goods; indeed, it used grave-goods to help define the power of saints and churchmen. The spectacular finds recently unearthed at Frankfurt demonstrate how the church had no reservations about turning the use of grave-goods to its own advantage. Underneath the Carolingian palace complex, a series of inhumation burials beneath a stone church of the late seventh century have been found. These burials include that of a girl of four or five with fabulously rich grave-goods, interred in a tunic embroidered, in gold, with a cross, but also with amulets near her head and pots containing burned animal flesh. Here, the spectacular display of wealth and power through the deposition of lavish grave-goods helped establish the standing of the new church in a local idiom with strong syncretic elements. Other finds, such as the burials at Esslingen, demonstrate the use of grave-goods in a religious culture whose Christianity was less idiosyncratic.[61]

In the Merovingian period, churchmen may have inherited the ambitions of the late antique episcopal establishment regarding the regulation of mortuary ritual, but in a world where churches and priests were few and far between outside the cities, they could not hope to control or define mortuary practice. Although there is no reason why priests should not have been present at the occasions on which furnished burials were made, such occasions were not organised by the church; they were secular rituals run by kin and heirs. In the sixth century, the heyday of grave-goods, the lavish and expensive ritual of deposition was central to the

---

[59] B. Young, 'Paganisme, christianisme et rites funéraires', *Archéologie Médiévale* 7 (1977), 5–81; B. Effros, 'Symbolic Expressions of Sanctity: Gertrude of Nivelles in the Context of Merovingian Mortuary Custom', *Viator* 27 (1996), 1–10.

[60] Planig: P. T. Kessler, 'Merowingisches Fürstengrab von Planig in Rheinhessen', *Mainzer Zeitschrift* 35 (1940), 1–12. On this and other grave-goods with Christian symbols, see Heinemeyer, *Erzbistum Mainz*, pp. 62–4.

[61] Frankfurt: A. Hampel, *Der Kaiserdom zu Frankfurt am Main:Ausgrabungen 1991–3* (Nußloch, 1994); Esslingen: Fehring and Stein, 'Frühmittelalterliche Kirchenbauten'. See also the useful catalogue of grave-goods with Christian references, and burials beneath churches, assembled by H. W. Böhme, 'Adel und Kirche bei den Alemannen der Merowingerzeit', *Germania* 74 (1996), 477–507.

community's commemoration of the deceased. By the middle of the seventh century the church's role was growing rapidly. In the seventh and eighth centuries, most old cemeteries were abandoned and many new cemeteries founded, some around a church from the beginning, others having a church built over them later in their history. Esslingen is another case in point, a cemetery of eighteen furnished burials beneath the eighth-century church. Although 'founder-graves', like that at Frankfurt, needed spectacular assemblages of grave-goods to legitimate the new site, in general seventh-century burials contain fewer and less varied artefacts than their predecessors, as at Esslingen, which has yielded only pottery shards and a few, unspectacular, artefacts. The actual grave-goods were becoming less central to the rite, with the commemoration of the deceased less dependent on grave-goods leaving a vivid impression of the memory of its contemporary audience, and increasingly coming under the auspices of the church. By the eighth century, furnished burials were rare and anomalous; and as a rule burial took place in churchyard cemeteries. Burial in the churchyard placed one in the community of believers. It marked the triumph of a new ideal of community, as an inclusive grouping united by faith. One was inaugurated into this community through baptism as a child; churchyard burial gave one a permanent place – and thus continued remembrance – within it in death. There was no opting out.[62]

The deposition of grave-goods was an assertion of the rank of the deceased and, by implication, the family of the deceased.[63] Connections between burial, kin and inheritance are suggested by a rare written account of burial with grave-goods: in sixth-century Metz, a childless woman received a lavish burial, but one of her relatives (who, given the woman's childlessness, would have had claims of inheritance over her property) had his followers rob the grave to bring the wealth back into

[62] G. Halsall argues convincingly that the abandonment of burial with grave-goods can be explained by an increased concern with long-term commemoration of the dead: 'Burial Ritual and Merovingian Society', in J. Hill and M. Swan (eds.), *The Community, the Family and the Saint,* (Turnhout, 1998), pp. 325–38. On the shift from secular to ecclesiastical mortuary ritual, and the importance of churchyard burial, see Young, 'Paganisme'; D. Bullough, 'Burial, Community and Belief in the Early Medieval West', in P. Wormald *et al.* (eds.), *Ideal and Reality in Frankish and Anglo-Saxon Society* (Oxford, 1983), pp. 177–201; J. M. H. Smith, 'Religion and Lay Society', in *NCMH*, pp. 654–78 at pp. 672–8

[63] See Halsall, *Settlement and Social Organisation,* pp. 76–163; Halsall, 'Female Status and Power in Early Medieval Central Austrasia: The Burial Evidence', *EME* 5 (1996), 1–24; building on E. James, 'Cemeteries and the Problem of Frankish Settlement in Gaul', in P. H. Sawyer (ed.), *Names, Words and Graves: Early Medieval Settlement,* pp. 55–89; E. James, 'Burial and Status in the Early Medieval West', *Transactions of the Royal Historical Society* 39 (1989), 23–40; also R. Samson, 'Social Structures from the *Reihengräber:* Mirror or Mirage?', *Scottish Archaeological Review* 4 (1987), 116–26. See also Young's discussion of social emulation in changing burial rites: 'Exemple aristocratique et mode funéraire dans la Gaule mérovingienne', *Annales: ESC* 41 (1986), 379–407.

circulation.[64] The giving of grave-goods may have been connected to the division of the legacy of the deceased, constituting a symbolic redistribution of wealth effecting an exchange of gifts between living and dead, in which the deposition of goods with the deceased reciprocated for the inheritance of their wealth. The disappearance of grave-goods does not mean that such ritual giving ceased, but it took on new forms. Charlemagne himself expected his heirs to pass some of his vast moveable wealth on to the church, and to carry out charitable acts on his behalf: his will is typical of the Carolingian evidence in seeing the distribution of a part of a legacy for the health of the deceased's soul as a responsibility of the heirs.[65] The church mediated in gift-exchange between the living and the dead. Liturgical ritual fulfilled the needs once met by lavish displays of grave-goods, and in doing so changed the cosmological justification for such funerary giving. Long-established teachings about the beneficial effects of charity became a potent justification for the church's new mediatory function: the message preached again and again from the seventh century onwards was that alms-giving from a legacy cleansed the soul of the deceased. This set of cultural changes cannot be seen in terms of progress from a less to a more perfect Christianity: they are indices of the church's changing social function, not of the quality of spiritual life.[66]

Not that even the Carolingian church established total control. From the ninth century there are hints at the continuation of presumably much older secular rituals involving feasting at the graveside. Such banquets were defined by the presence of kin, and also by local associations based on formal mutual obligation, part of whose *raison d'être* was to ensure

---

[64] Gregory of Tours, *Historiae*, ed. B. Krusch and W. Levison, *MGH SRM* I, VIII:21, pp. 387–8, discussed in Halsall, 'Female Status', 1–2.

[65] See M. Innes, 'Charlemagne's Will: Ideology, Inheritance and the Imperial Succession in the Early Ninth Century', *English Historical Review* 112 (1997), 833–55, with bibliography.

[66] Most accounts stress continuity *à la longue durée*, looking at ecclesiastical teaching from late antiquity to the high middle ages: see O. G. Oexle, 'Mahl und Spende im mittelalterlichen Totenkult', *Frühmittelalterliche Studien* 18 (1984), 401–14; J. Wollasch, 'Gemeinschaftsbewußtsein und soziale Leistung im Mittelalter', *Frühmittelalterliche Studien* 9 (1975), 268–86; B. Effros, 'Beyond Cemetery Walls: Early Medieval Funerary Topography and Christian Salvation', *EME* 6 (1997), 1–25. Also A. Angenendt, 'Theologie und Liturgie der frühmittelalterliche Toten-Memoria', in K. Schmid and J. Wollasch (eds.), *Memoria. Die geschichtliche Zeugniswert des liturgischen Gedenkens im Mittelalter*, Münstersche Mittelalter Schriften 48 (Munich, 1984), pp. 79–199, and F. S. Paxton, *Christianising Death: The Creation of a Ritual Process in Early Medieval Europe* (Ithaca, 1990), are important studies of the evolution of Christian ideas and practices. See also G. Duby, *The Early Growth of the European Economy: Warriors and Peasants from the Seventh to the Twelfth Century*, trans. H. B. Clarke (Cornell, 1974), pp. 47–59, esp. pp. 55–9; and most recently C. La Rocca, 'Segni di distinzione. Dai corredi funerari alle donazioni "post obitum" nel regno langobardo', in L. Paroli (ed.), *L'Italia centro-settentrionale in età langobarda* (Florence, 1997), pp. 31–54. We should not allow the clear similarity of social function between grave-goods and alms to obscure changes in the intention and destination of giving, nor see continuity on a formal or legal level (as earlier scholars did).

secular commemoration by friends and peers. Such associations also, by the ninth century, ensured some charitable giving on behalf of the deceased. But Carolingian reformers were uneasy about the essentially secular bonds of group solidarity involved, the amount of alcohol imbibed to cement them, and the dancing and mask-wearing which were performed in celebration of the dead; they drew on late antique teaching and attempted to redefine such occasions in terms of their potential for charitable action alone. Thus associations, inevitably made up of notables and the well-to-do, were urged to become more inclusive; priests were to have the poor invited to funerary feasts, and to try to prevent drunkenness and ribaldry.[67]

Two vivid examples from the ninth-century middle Rhine open the door to a fuller understanding of Carolingian mortuary custom. Einhard tells the following story:

a man by the name of Willibert, who had a house not far from [Seligenstadt] approached the bier [which held the relics of Marcellinus and Peter] among others who gathered to pay reverence to the saints, and offered up a gift of forty silver coins. When he was asked by us who he was and what he wished to achieve with the offering of this gift, he answered that a few days before he had sunk to such an extreme point that, despaired of by all who had seen him, he had been urged, for the good of his soul, to give away all his possessions (*facultates*) immediately, and so he had done. With all the bequests arranged now and to holy places to which they should be given, one of his servants lamented loudly that they had managed matters wrongly and negligently because none of his property had been given to the saints who had recently arrived from Rome. Then he had asked those standing nearby if they knew of any possession left to him that could be sent to the martyrs . . . Then someone answered him, saying that from all his goods only one pig remained and that it had not been decided to whom it should be given. He rejoiced and gave orders that it should be sold and that after his death the value of it should supply candles for the martyrs. As soon

---

[67] For hints at such practices, all in the context of episcopal condemnation, see Hincmar of Rheims, *Collectio de Ecclesiis et Capellis*, ed. M. Stratmann, *MGH Fontes iuris Germanici antiqui, n. 5.* (Hanover, 1990), p. 100; Hincmar of Rheims, First Capitulary, *MGH Capitula episcoporum* II, ed. R. Pokorny and M. Stratmann (Berlin, 1993), cc. 14, 16, pp. 41–2; anonymous Capitulary from Trier, c. 11, *ibid.* p. 56. On sworn associations ('gilds') see O. G. Oexle, 'Conjuratio und Gilde im frühen Mittelalter. Ein Beitrag zum Problem der sozialgeschichtlichen Kontinuität zwischen Antike und Mittelalter', in B. Schwineköper (ed.), *Gilden und Zünfte: kaufmännische und gewerbliche Genossenschaften im frühen und hohen Mittelalter*, VF 28 (Sigmaringen, 1985), pp. 151–214; 'Gilden als soziale Gruppen in der Karolingerzeit', in H. Jankuhn *et al.* (eds.), *Das Handwerk in vor- und frühgeschichtlicher Zeit I*, Abhandlungen der Akademie der Wissenschaften in Göttingen, philologisch-historische Klasse 122 (Göttingen, 1981), pp. 284–354. For the implications of such secular ritual for attitudes towards death and the dead, see O. G. Oexle, 'Die Gegenwart der Toten', in W. Verbeke and D. Verhelst (eds.), *Death in the Middle Ages* (Louvain, 1983), pp. 15–77; N. Caciola, 'Wraiths, Revenants and Ritual in Medieval Culture', *P&P* 152 (1996), 3–45.

as he had uttered these words, he claims, he felt so sudden a relief from his malady that straightaway, all his pain vanished and he wanted to eat. After eating, he recovered his strength so quickly that the next day he was able with great ease to go about all the business and work which the nature of his business demanded. After this the pig was sold and he gave the money, according to his vow, to the blessed martyrs.[68]

This story centres around the fate of Willibert's moveable possessions. They were divided between as many holy places as possible, to maximise the intercession for Willibert's soul. Willibert's gifts were votive, part of an explicit system of gift-exchange: Willibert was asked, directly, what he wished to achieve by making a gift. Willibert knew that once Marcellinus and Peter had restored his health, he must keep his promise of making a gift or their aid would be withdrawn, underlining the almost contractual nature of the transaction. Willibert's goods were sold to raise money for gifts whose function was specific, and in which Willibert's identity inhered: candles were symbols of the commemoration of their giver.

In 851 Ercanfrida, widow of the former count of Trier, left an elaborate set of instructions for her heirs. As a condition of receiving their various inheritances of land and moveables, they were each to pay a *census* of a specified value on her behalf; these payments, totalling 200 pounds of silver, were to be divided between twenty-one churches in the Moselle and middle Rhine (including Lorsch), given as alms for Ercanfrida's soul. These churches defined the world of Ercanfrida and the elite set within which she moved: by her conspicuous patronage of them in death she was reaffirming the allegiances that had shaped her life. In addition, one particular estate, which Ercanfrida had received from her husband as a morning-gift on the occasion of their marriage, was to be held by the monks of St Maximian at Trier, to whom it had previously been given by charter: as a condition of their ownership they were to hold each year on this estate a *convivium*, a banquet, in memory of Ercanfrida and her husband. Ercanfrida's will demonstrates the workings of a moral economy of alms-giving and inheritance, a moral economy driven by the binding personal obligation on those who inherited wealth to give alms on behalf of the individual from whom they had inherited. Like Willibert and, indeed, Charlemagne in his will, Ercanfrida gave alms to as many churches as possible. This was an economy of gift in which inheritance and alms-giving were two sides of a gift-exchange between living and dead. Funerary feasting remained a central practice,

---

[68] Einhard, *Translatio* III:iii, ed. Waitz, p. 249.

ecclesiastified by Ercanfrida. It was also combined with a typically ninth-century concern with liturgical intercession: Ercanfrida's death day was assiduously celebrated by the monks of St Maximian. Ercanfrida, that is, met traditional concerns in the best possible contemporary taste.[69]

GIFTS OF LAND AND SOCIAL POWER

Nothing would be known of Ercanfrida's posthumous patronage of Lorsch were it not for the preservation of her will by the monks at St Maximian. This underlines the partial nature of the surviving evidence: gifts of moveable wealth like Ercanfrida's and Willibert's, although important social practices, are invisible to us except in the most exceptional circumstances. The development of funerary ritual sheds light on important changes in the relationship between church and laity in the seventh and eighth century. How does this context relate to the giving of land as recorded in the charters? Were pious gifts of land, too, part of the system of gift-exchange between living and dead which the Carolingian church mediated?

Ercanfrida's will demonstrates that the currency of post mortem alms-giving was moveable wealth, not land; in this, it is at one with other Carolingian wills. The donation of Ercanfrida's morning-gift to St Maximian was not an integral part of her funerary alms-giving; it was not related to the responsibility of her heirs to distribute moveable wealth on her behalf. In fact, this pious gift of land was not effected by her will; it had already been made in an earlier document, a standard charter of donation which recorded the transfer of the land as a pious gift made for the salvation of Ercanfrida's, and her husband's, souls. Ercanfrida was allowed to keep the land until her death. This gift continued a special association between Ercanfrida and St Maximian, an association she inherited from her husband, and above all from his secular lord, Adalard, who was lay-abbot there. It was thus no accident that St Maximian was the special church where she and her husband were commemorated: by making the initial gift and building on her existing associations with the monastery, Ercanfrida was demonstrating that St. Maximian was *the* special spiritual patron of herself and her husband. It is only in the will

---

[69] *Urkunden- und Quellenbuch zur Geschichte der altluxembourgischen Territorien*, ed. C. Wampach (Luxembourg, 1935), I, no.87. See J. L. Nelson, 'The Wary Widow', in W. Davies and P. Fouracre (eds.), *Property and Power in the Early Middle Ages* (Cambridge, 1995), pp. 82–113; Le Jan, *Famille et Pouvoir*, pp. 69–70; and B. Kasten, 'Erbrechtliche Verfügungen des 8. und 9. Jahrhunderts. Zugleich ein Beitrag zur Organisation und zur Schriftlichkeit bei der Verwaltung adeliger Grundherrschaft am Beispiel des Grafen Heccard aus Burgund', *ZSRGGA* 107 (1990), 236–338 at 240–84. On wills in general see Innes, 'Charlemagne's Will', with full bibliography.

that an explicit link was made between the spiritual and liturgical services performed by the monks and Ercanfrida's gift of land – here Ercanfrida was reminding the monks of her previous generosity, and her special association with their community, before instructing them as to how she wished to be commemorated. That is, in the long run it was the gift of land which built up associations between donors and the church they patronised.

Land was not the only thing which could be given to the church. To give land was to alienate a permanent source of power and wealth – a momentous choice for an individual and family. It was a choice which was made because gifts of land could do things which gifts of mere moveables could not. Land was exceptional because it was immoveable. The immoveability of land meant that even after ownership was formally transferred, the memory of previous owners lived on. This kind of emotional attachment between gift and giver is admirably illustrated by Ercanfrida's dealings with St Maximian: Ercanfrida gave the land which had been given to her by her husband as she entered into marriage, and so into a new family, land which thus had special significance for Ercanfrida and her kin. This special significance was what made it a particularly suitable place to celebrate the memory of Ercanfrida and her husband by holding an annual banquet on her death day. Ercanfrida's case may be particularly vivid, but when the compilers of necrologies remembered important benefactors they characteristically listed the estates that the church had received: the specific land given remained closely tied to the memory of the giver. In fact, the vast majority of gifts of land – like Ercanfrida's – did not involve any immediate change in the actual use or possession of the estate in question. Donors characteristically maintained a life-interest in their gifts, and many explicitly reserved usufruct for their heirs. Nominal gifts of moveable wealth on the day of the patron saint to whom the land had been given might be included in such arrangements, but they only served to underline the fact that what the gift had effected was a relationship of spiritual patronage between donor and saint. The ties between land and erstwhile owners were thus durable, and gifts of land were ways of expressing patronage relationships with a particular saint. Although in the long term the land given would pass beyond the control of heirs, and hence was likely to be contested, in the short term giving to the saints could be painless, on occasion even profitable. By placing an estate under the spiritual patronage of a saint a donor might put it beyond the reach of political opponents or acquisitive kinsmen. Certainly there was now no question of its partition between heirs, or expropriation by enemies. Legislation also suggests that giving the ultimate rights over land to the church was a way of avoiding demands for royal service, which would now have to be met by the church.[70]

Why did the tide of gifts of land begin to turn in the second and third decades of the ninth century? Gifts, in whatever medium, were presented as spiritually beneficial throughout the early middle ages, but the concerns which made giving land attractive to the laity were evidently only active in a short period. Giving land cannot be seen as a static or normative structure, a standard form of piety. If it is seen as an active phenomenon which created bonds between church and society, the chronological patterning becomes easier to explain because it relates to a significant shift in the social impact of the church, through the building up of concrete links between church and laity offered by monasticism of a Carolingian model. One intelligent guesstimate has suggested that the wave of donations recorded by the charters led to the transfer of between one-half and one-third of land in the typical eastern Frankish rural settlement to various churches in the course of a hundred years.[71] Even given that much of the land may have remained in the usufruct of kin, or have been let out to villagers integrated into monastic patronage networks, this kind of transfer over a few generations constituted a social earthquake. Once a monastery had built up holdings on this scale, those living within the community were scarcely likely to want to increase the church's muscle still further. Indeed, by the middle of the ninth century there was no need to create bonds with the church by giving it land: one was born into a world where spiritual patronage was very immediate and real precisely because the church was a landowner on such a huge scale. In a very concrete way, what made the church much more involved in rural communities than it had been hitherto was precisely the fact that it was now 'lord and neighbour'.[72] The patronage of the church was now part of the fabric

[70] See, in addition to the important discussions by Rosenwein and Wickham, J. Jahn, '*Tradere ad sanctum*. Politische und gesellschaftliche Aspekte der Traditionspraxis im agilolfingischen Bayern', and W. Hartung, 'Adel, Erbrecht, Schenkung. Die strukturellen Ursachen der frühmittelalterlichen Besitzübertragungen an die Kirche', both in F. Seibt (ed.), *Gesellschaftsgeschichte: Festschrift für K. Bosl zum 80. Geburtstag,* 2 vols. (Munich, 1988), II, pp. 400–16, 417–38, respectively. On legislation and royal service see E. Müller-Mertens, *Karl der Große, Ludwig der Fromme und die Freien. Wer waren die liberi homines der karolingischen Kapitularien (742/3–832)? Ein Beitrag zur Sozialgeschichte und Sozialpolitik des Frankenreiches,* Forschungen zur mittelalterlichen Geschichte 10 (Berlin, 1963).
[71] Based on F. Schwind, 'Beobachtungen zur inneren Struktur des Dorfes in karolingischer Zeit', in H. Jankuhn *et al.* (eds.), *Das Dorf der Eisenzeit und des frühen Mittelalters,* Abhandlungen der Akademie der Wissenschaften in Göttingen, phil.-hist. Klasse 101 (Göttingen, 1977), pp. 444–93, looking at specific settlements. For a macro-study, D. Herlihy, 'Church Property on the European Continent, 701–1200', *Speculum* 36 (1961), 81–102.
[72] To follow McKitterick, *The Carolingians and the Written Word,* p. 79, in adopting R. Sprandel's phrase (*Das Kloster St. Gallen in der Verfassung des karolingischen Reiches,* Forschungen zur oberrheinischen Landesgeschichte 7 (Freiburg, 1958), p. 57).

of everyday life. The land owned by the church was bordered by familial plots, and some was let out to villagers. Why give land to the saints when they were already the largest landowners in the community, and when one was already wholly implicated in their patronage networks, both spiritual and material? Of course, giving land to the church was still sometimes useful as a way of cementing previous bonds and restating relationships, signalling that one wished to take up the relationship with a particular church begun by an ancestor. Giving land thus never totally stopped; but by a certain point gifts of land ceased to be necessary to set in motion associative relationships, because the relationships were already there and could be pursued in different ways, using different media.

This shift in the social role of the church is the backdrop against which the rhetoric of Carolingian church reform must be placed: 'reform' was not an attempt to apply timeless standards to a previously moribund or corrupt church, but a response to the dramatic increase in the church's local profile. Indeed Carolingian reform led to the institutionalisation of some of the church's new roles. The rapid increase in the number of rural churches which begins in the seventh century meant that, by the ninth century, many large rural settlements had a priest and a church. Hence a concern with the lives of rural priests, and the quality of the pastoral care they provided, is a recurrent interest of Carolingian legislation. In the Carolingian period a network of rural parishes began to crystallise: to be sure, a network of relatively large parishes which was later to be added to, but a basic grid centred on the most important rural settlements nonetheless. The church came home with a vengeance as an actor in rural society. And the Carolingians imposed tithe: a pious gift which was now legally enforceable and legally enforced, and involved parcelling the countryside up into geographical units each dependent on a particular church.[73]

These developments, and particularly the enforcement of tithe, obviously had profound effects on a local level. For the elite, the foundations and gifts of the eighth and early ninth centuries created relationships which future generations inherited and could maintain without further gifts of land. Hence the golden age of liturgical commemoration of lay aristocrats post-dated the wave of gifts of land: the descendants of those

[73] On parishes and tithe see J. Semmler, 'Mission und Pfarrorganisation in den rheinischen, mosel- und maasländischen Bistümern 5–10 Jahrhundert', *Settimane* 28 (1982), 813–88; J. Semmler, 'Zehntgebot und Pfarrtermination in karolingischer Zeit', in H. Mordek (ed.), *Aus Reich und Kirche: Festschrift F. Kempf* (Sigmaringen, 1983), pp. 33–44. G. Constable, *Monastic Tithes from their Origins to the Twelfth Century* (Cambridge, 1964) remains the best discussion of Carolingian tithe; more work is needed. On rural priests see Nelson, 'Making Ends Meet: Poverty and Wealth in the Carolingian Church', *Studies in Church History* 24 (1987), 25–35; on church reform, R. McKitterick, *The Frankish Church and the Carolingian Reforms* (London, 1977).

who had made initial endowments and ensured the church's success could keep up the bonds of patronage between monks and elites through exhibiting the fashionable pieties of the age. Nor should we forget that the interface between church and society was always a personal one, centring on the familial and social identities of monks themselves. At Dienheim, for example, it was the presence of monks administering a local estate complex, monks who were personally related to the local elite, which allowed Fulda to act as an effective patron and attract donations in the 790s and 800s; but monks continued to be present at Dienheim thereafter, responsible for the administration of the monastery's estates in the area and thus potent patrons in purely secular terms. In the 820s Einhard offers a glimpse of the interaction between elite and church. The basilica of the *villa* of Suntilingen in the Wetterau was held by a priest Waltbert, who, suffering from a mental disorder, was brought to Einhard at Seligenstadt by three of his brothers – one of whom was also a priest – and a close relative who was a monk of the monastery of Hornbach, where Waltbert himself had been educated and which owned the Suntilingen living.[74]

The ways in which these new relationships worked can be vividly traced in the career of Folcnand, who built up a formidable position in the woodlands of the Wingarteiba, a settlement area remote in the uplands of the Odenwald. Land given to St Cyriacus' in Worms in 858 was located 'in the *pagus* of the Wingarteiba' and the charter 'enacted in the county of Count Megingoz, in the *ministerium* of Folcnand the tribune'.[75] Folcnand's power within his *ministerium* owed much to his relationship with the churches of the region. A mid-ninth-century notice commemorates the gift of land made by a Sigehard to Seligenstadt: Sigehard's land was located in the Maingau, in the county of Ruochar, and in addition to six witnesses Sigehard's lord (*senior*) Eberhard and Seligenstadt's advocate Folcnand were present; the charter was written by Seligenstadt's *praepositus*.[76] Folcnand was also Fulda's advocate; his dominance of this small woodland backwater may have been so complete that all the great churches of the region, and local counts, relied on Folcnand to guard their interests and keep order within his *ministerium*. But acting as advocate helped develop this power base, as it involved taking respon-

---

[74] Dienheim: above, p. 107. Hornbach monk: Einhard, *Translatio*, III:20, ed. Waitz, pp. 255–6. Cf. also, from the tenth century, *CL*273, 278, and the scandal at Aschaffenburg discussed by H. Fichtenau, *Living in the Tenth Century: Mentalities and Social Order*, trans. P. Geary (Philadelphia, 1991), pp. 224–6.

[75] Ed. A. Lamey, *Acta Academiae Theodoro-Palatinae* 7 (Mannheim, 1789), pp. 64–5.

[76] Schmidt, 'Mitteilungen aus Darmstädter Handschriften', 612–13.

sibility for all a church's possessions in a given area; allied to this right of protection may have been a role in overseeing the collection of tithe, judging from the Fulda evidence in which Folcnand allegedly testified as to the extent of the monastery's claims to tithe.[77] Such power complexes were perhaps easiest to build up in a social, economic and political backwater like the Wingarteiba. There are hints that as early as *c.* 800 one Manold may have used his relationship with the church to build up a similar position in more or less the same area.[78] If whole blocks of property and rights were more likely to be granted out to laymen in remote forest areas, the kind of practical patronage enjoyed by Folcnand, and its importance in creating power in the localities, was not unusual. Unfortunately, evidence for the letting out of church lands, and the role of advocates, is rare because later cartulary-compilers had little use for the documents recording such arrangements.

That the falling off of gifts of land in the ninth century can be related to the heightened political and social profile of church property is confirmed by the changing ways in which the church acquired, and used, land. At Lorsch the majority of surviving documents from the second half of the ninth century did not record pious gifts at all, but exchanges between laity and the monastery. This pattern was typical. The monks were conscious of the change this involved. In 847 Abbot Samuel obtained a written licence from the king allowing him to make exchanges as and when he chose, without needing to obtain royal permission for each one (kings were the protectors of monastic property, and were supposed to approve even the most humble exchange).[79] To some extent, then, there was a change of policy. Exchanges were pre-eminently sociable transactions: they underlined the importance of Lorsch's bonds with the laymen with whom swaps were made. But exchanges drew on an existing social network rather than creating new associations. They were one of a variety of new ways – alongside lettings and advocacy – in which

---

[77] *CDF*610 is a forged royal charter, purporting to date from 871, connected with Fulda's claims to tithes; it does list Folcnand as an advocate and the witness-list looks like it was written by an informed observer. Folcnand's status makes him a regular witness: see also *CDF*631 (again alongside Count Rouchar, in 889, and concerning the Maingau), 633, 638, 647, 679. Charters recording exchanges between church and laity increasingly come to include grants of tithe in the tenth century: e.g. *CL*70, 83.

[78] *CL*3337, from *c.* 800, lists many of Lorsch's possessions in the Maingau as lying in the *ministerium* of Manold. *CL*6a, from 795, has the *viculus* of Manold marking the eastern boundary of the woodland appended to the *villa* of Heppenheim. *CL*21, from 821, has *Manegoldescella* marking the boundary of the woodland rights enjoyed by the *villa* of Michelstadt.

[79] *CL*29. Whereas exchanges are typical of the end of the cycle of pious giving, buying land, interestingly, is most typical of the period after a monastery has been founded but before gift-giving has really taken off.

church land was used, as the relationship between church and laity altered.[80]

A second change in the evidence underlined the shift towards the priming of extant networks. Cartulary-compilation – the copying out of charters of donation, settlement by settlement, into handbooks recording the extent of church landownership and the means by which land had been acquired – was a phenomenon of the middle years of the ninth century. Fulda's archives were worked through, and donations recorded in a series of dossiers, under the order of Abbot Hraban in 828. Wissembourg's title-deeds were similarly copied *c.* 855 under the orders of Abbot Grimald. Like Abbot Samuel's licence to transact exchanges, these initiatives were admissions that the golden age of pious gifts of land was over, and represented shifts of policy which centred on making full use of extant possessions. They also cemented links between monks and patrons, for cartularies were ways of registering and commemorating the identities of those who had given land: their commemorative function was on occasion made explicit. And the second half of the ninth century was the period in which the commemoration of benefactors was put on a new footing, as the monastic liturgy increasingly came to include laymen, and important benefactors were given special treatment.[81] By the tenth century, those pious gifts which were made were recorded in a new way. The classic Carolingian pious gift was recorded in a formal, first-person charter of donation. By the tenth century gifts that were recorded were recorded as terse, third-person notices, often giving simply the name of the donor, the location of the property and a witness list. This is not evidence for declining literacy. Notices were still useful written documents, both as records of title and as ways of remembering the identity of benefactors, as embodiments of *memoria*: their prevalence articulated a different set of priorities by the monks, in a world where the

---

[80] The best discussion of changing relationships between church and aristocracy are those of W. Störmer, *Früher Adel. Studien zur politischen Führungsschicht im fränkisch-deutschen Reich von 8. bis 11. Jahrhundert*, 2 vols., Monographien zur Geschichte des Mittelalters 6 (Stuttgart, 1973), II, pp. 374–81, focusing on Bavaria, and of Wickham, *The Mountains and the City*, on Lucca, to whom my discussion is deeply indebted. Also E. Boshof, 'Untersuchungen zur Kirchenvogtei in Lothringen im 10 und 11 Jht.', *ZSRGKA* 65 (1979), 55–119, and see below pp. 238, 247.

[81] Geary, *Phantoms of Remembrance*, pp. 81–113, is the best discussion of cartulary compilation; see also R. Kottje, 'Schriftlichkeit im Dienst der Klosterverwaltung und des klösterlichen Lebens unter Hrabanus Maurus', in G. Schrimpf (ed.), *Kloster Fulda in der Welt der Karolinger und Ottonen* (Frankfurt, 1996), pp. 177–92 The classic statement of the commemorative function is *Die Traditionen des Hochstifts Freising*, ed. T. Bitterauf, Quellen und Erörterungen zur bayerischen und deutschen Geschichte 4 (Munich, 1905), vol. I, p. 1. For the dates of cartulary compilation see above, pp. 14–15; for benefactor commemoration at Lorsch and Fulda see, respectively, Staab, 'Grundherrschaftsentwicklung', pp. 287, 290–3; and F. Jacobi, 'Die weltlichen und geistlichen Magnaten im Fuldaer Totenannalen', in *Klostergemeinschaft* II:ii, pp. 792–887.

economy of giving land to the church, an economy centred around the formal charter of donation, was a thing of the past.[82]

THE IMPLICATIONS OF MONASTIC LANDHOLDING

There are few other historical societies in which between a quarter and a half of the basic socio-economic resource changed hands in so short a period as a hundred years. The quantity of land they were given made monasteries the 'multinationals' of the ninth century. This was a transfer of control, which was relocated beyond the reach of those immediately implicated in the exploitation of land. It was thus ultimately a redistribution of political as well as economic and social power, particularly as it was the secular elite who gained control, thanks to their thorough integration into relationships of reciprocal patronage with the church. Members of the elite, whether laymen acting as advocates or tenants, or monks acting as abbots or provosts, controlled, and profited from, the vastly extended scope of monastic landholding.

This was not a revolution which occurred silently or invisibly. From the last decades of the eighth century the duty of rulers to protect the powerless but free, the *pauperes*, was again and again emphasised in moral instruction and royal edict. Of particular concern were the social pressures which might lead to the decline of the small freeholder, and encroachment on peasant landholding. The normative sources supply lurid stories of impoverished peasant smallholders losing their property, through trickery, threat, and desperation brought on by famine or hardship.[83] Such stories reflected real worries: loss of property is a perennial concern of any peasant society, and expropriation through trick or threat a similarly widespread phenomenon which we must expect to meet in the Carolingian period. But normative sources need careful handling: moral panics focus on cases which are rich in contemporary resonance,

---

[82] See Johanek, 'Zur rechtlichen Funktion'; the best discussion of changing diplomatic form in a defined area is H. Fichtenau, *Das Urkundenwesen im Österreich*, *MIÖG* Ergänzungsband 23 (Vienna, 1971), which is fundamental on the distinction between charter and notice.

[83] For the practices condemned in capitulary and synodal legislation, see Müller-Mertens, *Karl der Große*; R. [Le Jan] Hennebicque, '"Pauperes" et "Paupertas" dans l'occident carolingien aux IXe et Xe siècles', *Revue du Nord* 50 (1968), 169–87; and W. Ullmann, 'Public Welfare and Social Legislation in the Early Medieval Councils', *Studies in Church History* 7 (1971), 1–39. See also K. Bosl, '*Potens* und *pauper*. Begriffsgeschichtliche Studien zur gesellschaftlichen Differenzierung im frühen Mittelalter und zur "Pauperismus" des Hochmittelalters', in Bosl, *Frühformen der Gesellschaft in mittelalterlichen Europa. Ausgewählte Beiträge zu einer Strukturanalyse der mittelalterlichen Welt* (Munich–Vienna, 1964), pp. 106–34, and J. Schmitt, *Untersuchungen zu den Liberi Homines der Karolingerzeit* (Frankfurt, 1977). For 'moral panics' see S. Hall et al., *Policing the Crisis* (London, 1973).

encapsulating the stresses engendered by social change, without necessarily being an objective representation of the actual process of change. It is no accident that the normative sources focus upon particular outrages which hit at the self-image of this society as consisting of property-owning free peasants, a community in which social relations were conducted according to Christian norms. This self-image was at once stressed by the increasingly coherent ideological statements of the church, and put under stress by the shift in power in the localities. Peasants tricked out of their patrimonies may have been the exception, rather than the rule, but this was a period of mounting social differentiation and increasing pressure on the bottom strata of the peasantry. The shrill voices of the articulate were thus responses to the reality of change, albeit responses which did not identify the underlying pressure for change. The moral panic they created was not ignored: royal edicts from the 810s and 820s stressed the dangers of the erosion of the landed basis of the free peasantry, permitting gifts of land to the church but showing concern for the fate of heirs. The extent to which such edicts were enforced as law is a complex and separate issue; the current point is that they were reactions to real worries.[84] These worries, indeed, lay behind the ebbing of the tide of gifts of land to the church as members of rural communities increasingly chose to relate to the church in ways which did not involve handing over land.

It would probably be a mistake to believe that famine or coercion lay behind more than a handful of the thousands of charters recording pious gifts to the church in this region. The patterning of gift-giving cannot be related to documented instances of famine or disorder. Less than a dozen surviving documents involve loss of personal freedom on the part of the donor. Donations of entire patrimonies were uncommon. Many gifts may have led to the establishment of formal relationships of dependence between donor and church, particularly when, as often happened, the donor received a life-interest in the land he had given; such formal relationships did not, however, abstract the donor from the local community or give the church exclusive jurisdiction over him or control of his labour. In that there was a dramatic increase in the quantity of land ultimately owned by the church, the proportion of land owned by the

---

[84] Capitulary legislation is rehearsed in detail in the works of Schmitt and Müller-Mertens, with differing views as to its application in practice. It reaches a culmination in a series of capitularies in the early years of the reign of Louis the Pious. Particularly important is the insistence that, whilst pious gifts are to be allowed, they must meet with the consent of potential heirs: see *MGH Cap.* I, no. 138, c. 7, p. 277. Note also that legislation from this period begins to distinguish between free proprietors and free men without land: K. Nehlsen-von Stryck, *Die boni homines des frühen Mittelalters unter besonderer Berücksichtigung der fränkischen Quellen*, Freiburger Rechtsgeschichtlichen Abhandlungen 2 (Berlin, 1981), pp. 253–4.

peasantry must have declined, a substantial, if not overwhelming, number of peasants ending their days as free tenants rather than owner-cultivators.[85] The evidence from Dienheim confirms that those who did decline were, in all probability, those whose holdings had been limited: here the top strata of the peasantry, who dominated witness-lists, were more reluctant to give land to the church, and, in any case, could probably afford to give the odd parcel of land without jeopardising the lot of future generations. We should not, therefore, exaggerate the scale of the change: the peasantry as a group did not disappear, but internal divisions within the peasantry between the landless and those who owned land became increasingly important. In the immediate post-Carolingian period this remained a society in which between a half and a third of the human population were legally free, and a critical mass of this group enjoyed full rights of ownership. Although more free peasants were dependent on landlords as tenants, and those who hung on to their property were likely to be more fully integrated in networks of patronage centred on churches and aristocrats, the peasantry was not subject to lordly jurisdiction or restrictive control or command. In the tenth century, local business continued to take place in neighbourhood meetings attended by substantial numbers of medium-sized proprietors; disputes were settled by the collective testimony of a community of free owner-cultivators.[86] The creation of rights of territorial control and jurisdiction over free men was a separate process from the acquisition of land by the church, a process which is not apparent in the evidence until the eleventh century.

Nonetheless, the flow of land to the church had significantly altered the balance of power in the localities. In the eighth and ninth centuries, gifts of land to the church had built up bonds between churches and lay groupings, allowing the church to become an important patron and social actor from the level of the elite to that of the village. Land given to the church was not wholly or immediately abstracted from the world of kin, but the rules governing its redistribution were different from those pertaining to land owned by kin. Ultimate rights over church land remained in the hands of the saints; they could not be redistributed as kinship groups fissured and coalesced. The church was thus integrated into kinship structures and inheritance strategies. This changed the practical

<hr/>

[85] Cf. Davies, *Small Worlds*, pp. 185–7, expanded in 'On Servile Status in the Early Middle Ages', in M. L. Bush (ed.), *Serfdom and Slavery: Studies in Legal Bondage* (London, 1996), pp. 225–46; also P. Freedman, *The Origins of Peasant Servitude in Medieval Catalonia* (Cambridge, 1991). For our area see D. Neundörfer, *Studien zur ältesten Geschichte des Kloster Lorsch*, Arbeiten zur deutschen Rechts- und Verfassungsgeschichte 3 (Berlin, 1920), pp. 27–69.

[86] Local meetings: CL278, 382, 428, 660, CDF679, 708. Dispute settlement: CL532, and, from an area further to the east, CDF690, 692.

workings of kinship, inheritance and thus social reproduction: as families shared property rights with, and defined themselves with reference to, local churches which they did not wholly control, so kinship ties became necessarily extensive, outward looking and in need of constant renegotiation. That is, the landholdings of the Carolingian church ensured the prevalence of a kinship system which was comparatively fluid and malleable.[87]

---

[87] I thus follow J. Goody's diagnosis of the peculiarity of western kinship structures and their early medieval origins, but not his interpretation in terms of a 'conspiracy theory' on the part of the church: *The Development of the Family and Marriage in Europe* (Cambridge, 1983); for the extrinsic nature of western kinship, see also his 'Inheritance, Property and Women: Some Comparative Considerations', in Goody, J. Thirsk and E. P. Thompson (eds.), *Family and Inheritance: Rural Society in Western Europe, 1200–1800* (Cambridge, 1976), pp. 10–36.

3

LAND, KINSHIP AND STATUS

THE ELITE: KINSHIP, LAND AND INHERITANCE

To explore the articulation of the interests of the elite through strategies of kinship, land and inheritance, I turn to the three families which we can examine in greatest detail. Their relationships with Fulda and Lorsch were so close that a series of well-focused images survive. The resulting family albums consist of carefully posed group portraits taken on a handful of important occasions. They need comparing and contrasting with the snapshots – often shaky and poorly focused – which can be snatched from a wide range of other sources. Then we may be in some position to generalise about the world of the elite. It should be underlined at the outset that what follows is not an exhaustive survey of important or influential families in the area, but an attempt to analyse the relationship between land, kinship and social status in the Carolingian middle Rhine.

LORSCH'S FOUNDERS

The first individuals on whom we can zoom in are the founders of Lorsch. The monastery founded at Lorsch in 764 was the successor of a nearby church which was likewise dedicated to St Peter and under the lordship of Chrodegang of Metz.[1] In addition to supplying the site on which Chrodegang founded the new monastery, Cancor and Willeswind gave further estates to support the monks; when it was decided, in 767, that the monastery's popularity necessitated the building of a new church

---

[1] *CL*429 for St Peter's at Heppenheim. A full bibliography of works dealing with Lorsch's foundation is given above; I draw here on my earlier discussion, 'Kings, Monks and Patrons'. On the family of Lorsch's founders, K. Glöckner, 'Lorsch und Lothringen, Rupertiner und Capetinger', *ZGO* 50 (1936), 301–54, remains fundamental.

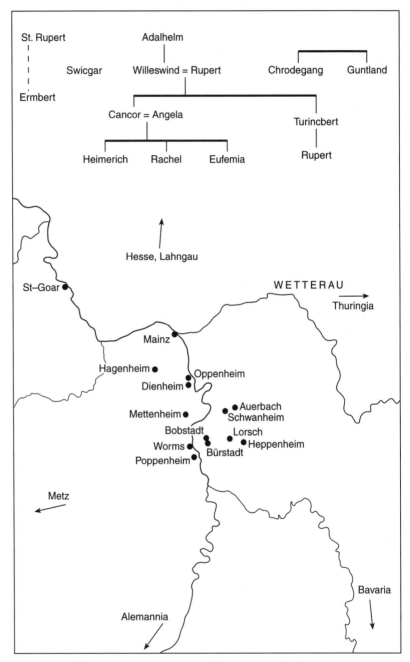

5 Lorsch's founders: kinship and property

on a larger site, once again it was Cancor and his kin who supplied the land needed, giving important estates and woodland by the Weschnitz in a series of donations.[2] These family bonds defined Lorsch's status until Cancor's death late in 771.

Historians have labelled Cancor's kin the 'Rupertines', but this is a term of art, not a contemporary label. We must be careful not to use such terms in an uncritical manner which might import misleading assumptions about early medieval kinship. Family labels of this type were coined in the pioneering days of prosopographical research, when scholars aimed to reconstruct vast kin groups which placed a high premium on bilateral and collateral relationships, in which maternal kin were as important as paternal, and cousins were close relations. In the past quarter century, this image of huge and cohesive early medieval clans has been successfully qualified. First, the fact that kinship was bilateral and marriage exogenous meant that kinship groups were fluid and subject to constant reformation. Second, the ties which bound together distant kin were not operative automatically or all of the time.[3] Among Lorsch's early patrons a large number of relatives of Cancor and Chrodegang can be identified, but few make substantial donations: most may have felt it necessary to acknowledge their ties to the foundation without entering into a close bond. The label 'Rupertine' is in danger of imposing a misleading homogeneity of interest and unity of political will. Within wide groups of 'official' kin, like those relatives of Cancor and Chrodegang who acknowledged the new abbey, were a smaller group of 'practical' kin with whom a political and social strategy was shared. The kernel of a group of 'practical' kin was a relatively restricted immediate family, who made gifts for each other's souls, and through whose hands the vast bulk of family land was inherited.

At Lorsch we can see the intensity of bonds between kinship, land and identity. Before it was given to Chrodegang's monks, Lorsch was an important centre for Willeswind's close kin. Land at Lorsch was owned exclusively by Willeswind's children and grandchildren. The property of one family, the Lorsch estate lay on the boundary between two neighbouring

---

[2] Initial endowment: *CL* c. 1, *CL*1, 598. Support for later rebuilding: *CL*167/3788 (767, gift to build *claustrum*); also 168/3789 (?767), 3780 (770), 10 (770), 3783 (771).

[3] Modern work on the Carolingian aristocracy goes back to G. Tellenbach (ed.), *Studien und Vorarbeiten zur Geschichte des großfränkischen und frühdeutschen Adels*, Forschungen zur oberrheinische Landesgeschichte 4 (Freiburg, 1957); the crucial studies are accessible in K. Schmid's collected essays, *Gebetsgedenken und adliges Selbstverständnis im Mittelalter* (Sigmaringen, 1983). The most important recent work is Le Jan, *Famille et Pouvoir*, and her earlier essay, 'Structures familiales et structures politiques au IXe siècle: un group familiale de l'aristocratie franque', *Revue Historique* 265 (1981), 289–333. See now S. Airlie, 'The Aristocracy', in *NCMH*, pp. 431–50.

settlements, the *villae* of Bürstadt and Heppenheim.[4] Within a decade of the foundation of a monastery at Lorsch, the totality of the estate was in the hands of the monks. The series of charters transferring rights between 764 and 772 provide a detailed picture of the estate there. Cancor held the large tract of woodland between Bürstadt and Lorsch, and gave it to the monks in 770: this gift attracted the consent of Cancor, his wife, son and brother.[5] Cancor had given another part of the estate, which bordered on this woodland, to his wife, Angela, as her morning-gift. The precise structure of the land and rights involved was obscure, but when Angela gave it to Lorsch for the health of her soul in 771, less than a month before her husband's death, it included cultivated land, meadows, woodland and water.[6] Cancor's brother, Turincbert, also had interests at Lorsch: in 767 he gave, with his nephew Heimerich acting as his witness, one *mansus*, on the natural mound where the abbey's remains still stand, to be the site of the new cloister, as well as another nearby *mansus* with a meadow and six iugates of ploughland; this was quickly followed by a half-*mansus* which was particularly linked to Turincbert's son Rupert.[7] Finally, in 770 the monks acquired the remainder of Turincbert's interests at Lorsch, in exchange for twenty-two ploughlands elsewhere, and three ounces of silver.[8] Possession of land at Lorsch had defined a tightknit group of practical kin to such an extent that Cancor's wife, Angela, was given a portion of the Lorsch complex as her morning-gift: on the day that her marriage had effected her entry into that kin group, she had been given land at its focal point, Lorsch. Gifts of portions of the Lorsch estate – notably the gift of Angela's morning-gift – were linked to the commemoration of dead ancestors of those who held land there.[9]

From Lorsch and those who held land there spread out a web of threads linking this group of 'practical kin' to a series of 'official kin'. The web could spread wide, and in more than one direction. Hence when Willeswind made important gifts to support the thirteen monks whom

---

[4] On the Lorsch estate, H.-P. Wehlt, *Reichsabtei und König. Dargestellt am Beispiel der Abtei Lorsch mit Ausblicken auf Hersfeld, Stablo und Fulda*, VMPIG 28 (Göttingen, 1968), pp. 16–25; for archaeology, I have not seen P. Rhein, *Altmünster und Kloster Lorsch* (Mainz, 1986); for older excavations see F. Behn, 'Ausgrabungen in Lorsch', in *Laurissa Jubilans: Festschrift zur 1200-Jahrfeier* (Lorsch, 1964), pp. 115–20. In spite of the presence of a Roman *villa* no link has yet been established between Roman and Carolingian inhabitation. On patterns of aristocratic landholding, see W. Rösener, 'Strukturformen der adeligen Grundherrschaft in der Karolingerzeit', in Rösener (ed.), *Strukturen der Grundherrschaft im frühen Mittelalter* (Göttingen, 1989), pp. 126–80, and A. Bergengruen, *Adel und Grundherrschaft im Frankenreich*, Vierteljahrsschrift für Sozial- und Wirtschaftsgeschichte 41 (Berlin, 1958).   [5] *CL*10.   [6] *CL*3783.   [7] *CL*167/3788, 168/3789.   [8] *CL*3780.
[9] Gifts and ancestors: *CL*10, 168. Cf. the parallel case of Ercanfrida, above, pp. 39–40. On the transfer of land to effect marriage, and its significance, see Le Jan, *Famille et Pouvoir*, pp. 263–87, 333–81; R. Le Jan-Hennebicque, 'Aux origines du douaire medieval (VIe–Xe siècles)', in M. Parisse (ed.), *Veuves et Veuvage dans le Haut Moyen Age* (Paris, 1993), pp. 107–21; Nelson, 'The Wary Widow', pp. 82–94.

Chrodegang brought to Lorsch in 764, the bishops of Utrecht, Trier and Constance all travelled to the new monastery to witness the transaction.[10] Cancor and Willeswind were not particularly close to Chrodegang in biological terms – he was at best a cousin – but common political interests, resulting from and reinforced by co-operation at Lorsch, meant that this distant kin tie was vitally important to both parties in the 760s. Through his kinship with Chrodegang, Cancor gained links with the elite of the Carolingian heartland around Liège and down the Moselle – hence the presence of the bishops of Utrecht and Trier at Lorsch's dedication in 764. Cancor's interests in Alemannia were also acknowledged in 764 by the presence of the bishop of Constance. The interests in Alemannia and the Moselle had been pursued by Cancor in alliance with the Carolingians, but they may have pre-dated this alliance. Cancor was a scion of the indigenous elite of the middle Rhine, descended from Rupert, who had been bishop of Worms in the decades around 700. Cancor's father had been named after Rupert, as was his nephew; Rupert, indeed, is the most common name among Lorsch's early benefactors, pointing to a web of cousins in the locality ready to support Cancor's new foundation. The historical Rupert had been an opponent of the ancestors of the Carolingians, and he forged important links with Bavaria, where he engaged in missionary activity, refounding Salzburg: he was venerated as a saint. Cancor's children were to draw on the links they inherited from their saintly ancestor, working alongside Ermbert, another descendant of Rupert's and bishop of one of his erstwhile sees, Worms.[11] Through his mother, Cancor also inherited kin and property in the middle Rhine's eastern hinterland: Willeswind's father, Count Adalhelm, had been involved with the foundation of the church of St Bilihildis (the Altmünster or Hagenmünster) in Mainz, and was involved with the politics of the early eighth-century *duces* of Würzburg, east along the Main. The name Willeswind gave to Cancor's brother, Turincbert, is best explained by these links: the *duces* of Würzburg styled themselves rulers of the Thuringians, and the first two syllables of Turincbert's name advertised Thuringian credentials.[12]

---

[10] *CL*1. Lorsch tradition made the first thirteen monks all inmates of Chrodegang's Gorze.

[11] E. Zöllner, 'Woher stammte der heilige Rupert?', *MIÖG* 57 (1949), 1–22, established the kinship between St Rupert and Cancor. For Worms as Rupert's initial resting-place see H. Beumann, 'Zur Textgeschichte der Vita Ruperti', in *Festschrift für Hermann Heimpel*, 3 vols., VMPIG 36 (Göttingen, 1972), III, pp. 166–96 at 192–3, and E. Gierlich, *Die Grabstätten der Rheinische Bischöfe vor 1200*, Quellen und Abhandlungen zur mittelrheinische Kirchengeschichte 65 (Mainz, 1990) pp. 204–8. For Bishop Ermbert see *CL*15.

[12] See Innes, 'Kings, Monks and Patrons', pp. 307–8; also below, pp. 185–6. On Adalhelm and St Bilihildis, see M. Weidemann, 'Urkunden und Viten der Heiligen Bilihildis aus Mainz', *Francia* 21:1 (1994), 17–84 at 32–9, and E. Ewig, 'Zur Bilihildisurkunde für das Mainzer Kloster Altmünster', in K.-U. Jäschke and R. Wenskus (eds.), *Festschrift für H. Beumann* (Sigmaringen,

These familial and political structures were fluid. The ties of kinship which an individual played on at a particular moment were elective, and might be played down at a different moment in a different political context. In the earliest Lorsch charters, the alliance between Cancor and Chrodegang determined the shape of their kin group. However, after the two men's deaths, in 767 and 771 respectively, things inevitably changed. By 772 Chrodegang's brother, Abbot Guntland, apparently preferred royal lordship to the interference of Cancor's descendants, and gave the abbey to Charlemagne, after establishing his rights against those of Cancor's son, Heimerich, in an important judgement made at the royal court. Their dispute eloquently makes another important point. Thus far, ties of kinship have been presented in terms of the potential for alliance – but kinship inevitably also generated conflict precisely because it transmitted claims to property, claims which were always likely to be contested. It is no accident that the dispute over ultimate control of Lorsch took place immediately after Cancor's death. And when control of Lorsch was contested in 772, it was a royal lord, Charlemagne, who intervened. Kin groups were not closed worlds: they overlapped and interacted with other kin groups, of allies, clients and lords, and so disputes within them affected the fabric of politics and society – a fabric which had to be rewoven each generation through the processes of inheritance and marriage, and the reallocation of roles and relationships which inheritance effected.[13] The dispute over Lorsch in 772 turned on precisely such a reallocation through inheritance, for the central issue was Heimerich's precise relationship to the abbey founded by his father. The charter evidence demonstrates that other parts of Heimerich's inheritance from his father were also disputed: in 792 Heimerich's sister, Rachel, remembered that her brother had inherited one estate '*contra* Count Warin'.[14] In a world of partible inheritance, where a variety of kin had different claims for a part of an individual's estate, the process of inheritance was inevitably a matter for negotiation within the restricted family group of spouses, children, siblings, grandchildren and parents; and also between these 'practical' kin and the web of 'official' kin. Inheritance thus reaffirmed, but also reshaped, kin groups. Partition meant that the basic units which made up a kin group, and the distribution of landed resources between these units, was altered with each act of inheritance.

Footnote 12 (*cont.*)

1977), pp. 137–48. Turincbert's name: Le Jan, *Famille et Pouvoir*, p. 54, noting also the property at *Hagenheim* which Willeswind gave to Lorsch (*CL*1).

[13] *MGH DCharlemagne* 65, for more on the political context see below, pp. 180–2.

[14] *CL*15. Gockel, *Königshöfe*, p. 302, argues for kinship between Warin and Heimerich on the basis of this statement – but, in the absence of any supporting evidence for this, it may be more realistic to see Warin intervening in his office as count.

After Cancor's death, Heimerich and his two sisters, Rachel and Eufemia, worked in concert to secure the bulk of their father's estate. This co-operation was made easier by the status of Rachel and Eufemia. Neither appears to have married, the rich charter evidence mentioning neither husbands nor offspring. Both were styled *deo sacrata*, a term usually used of widows, signifying that they had taken a religious vow and were placed under special episcopal protection, in the person of a kinsman, Ermbert, bishop of Worms. In middle Rhenish charters, *deo sacrata* was also a title used to refer to women who contributed to their family by heading a family religious foundation, becoming 'house-nuns' or abbesses of small family convents.[15] Eufemia evidently performed just such a role as abbess of St Peter's at Metz, a position pointing to continuing contacts with Metz after Chrodegang's death, perhaps through his brother, Abbot Guntland of Lorsch. She certainly remained close to one of her father's erstwhile contacts at court, Abbot Fulrad of Saint-Denis, with whom she conducted property deals.[16] Their parents thus ensured that the interests of their daughters furthered those of their son. This was a strategy which integrated the church within the family. It enabled Heimerich to succeed to his father's position, with his sisters as allies and preservers of family tradition and family property. It certainly gives the lie to those who would see partible inheritance as inevitably leading to the fragmentation of holdings, and to those who would see gifts to the church as harmful of family fortunes. In 782, for example, Heimerich gave Lorsch an estate which he had received from his parents, and accepted from his sisters in inheritance.[17] In 776 Eufemia gave Lorsch a neighbouring estate which had been left by her parents and inherited by her and her brother and sister 'by law' (*legaliter*); the donation was witnessed by her brother.[18] Land was presented as a shared inheritance between the three direct heirs, Heimerich, Rachel and Eufemia, and was then assigned to one or the other of them. Hence both of Cancor's daughters received land and rights, and indeed Rachel inherited land from her brother Heimerich, whom she outlived.[19] The memory of those who had exercised rights over inherited land lived on with the title to that land: when Rachel gave an estate to Lorsch in 792 she did so not only for the health of her soul, but also for her parents'

---

[15] For kinship between Ermbert and the founders of Lorsch, Le Jan, *Famille et Pouvoir*, p. 54. For *deo sacrata* in general see M. Parisse (ed.), *Veuves et Veuvage dans le Haut Moyen Age* (Paris, 1993); Le Jan, *Famille et Pouvoir*, pp. 365–78; Nelson, 'The Wary Widow', pp. 82–94; for *deo sacrata* of the latter kind, see CL12, 13, 18 and cf. J. L. Nelson, 'Parents, Children and the Church in the Early Middle Ages', *Studies in Church History* 31 (1994), 81–114 at 110.
[16] *MGH DCharlemagne* 136 (781).   [17] *CL*178.   [18] *CL*182.
[19] *CL*15, 182, 1679, 2918/3747a, 2919/3747b, 3170/3686dd.

and her brother Heimerich's, via whom the land had been passed on to her and eventually the abbey.[20] This is the world of the ninth-century mother who advised her son to pray for 'those who have left their property in legal inheritance': 'To the same extent that they have bequeathed, pray for the possessor'.[21] Here we once again see the special status of land as a gift, and its association with prayer for the cleansing of the soul. These concerns could shape relations between lay people as well as the relationship between laity and church – these exchanges of land and prayer between close kin underlined their family identity and co-operation.

The foundation of a monastery at Lorsch may, initially, have sacralised this place of identity and thus reinforced its significance. It may be that the church of St Germain at *Scarra*, which, along with the extensive estate complex which supported it, was the first gift made by Willeswind to Lorsch, had fulfilled this commemorative function for Willeswind's family before the advent of the monks at Lorsch.[22] Many monastic foundations – Hornbach, for example – continued for generations as focal points for family identity. Whilst Lorsch was surrounded by, and interleaved with, land and residences belonging to Cancor's kin, the monks were physically and socially a part of Cancor's *familia*, and their role can be understood as acting within the family structure. The translation of Roman relics in 765 and the beginning of new, large-scale building in 767 may have already indicated that this was to be a foundation of a different kind, on a different scale. Certainly by 772 the entire Lorsch complex was in the hands of the monks, the imposition of royal lordship in that year confirming that the monks were no longer legally or socially a part of an elite *familia*. Nonetheless, links between Lorsch and the kin of its founders were not severed. All three of Cancor's children gave estates to the monastery: Rachel a huge gift in Hesse in 772 within a year of her father's death, Heimerich and Eufemia neighbouring estates at Bobstadt near Bürstadt, Eufemia and Rachel a pair of donations in the Wetterau for the health of their souls in 775.[23] None of the three, however, was commemorated in the necrology there, unlike their ancestors, Willeswind and her husband Rupert, Cancor and his wife Angela.[24] Eufemia's activities as an abbess in Metz and a benefactor of St Goar point to her involvement with family interests in the Moselle area,

---

[20] *CL*15.
[21] Dhuoda, *Liber Manualis*, ed. P. Riché, Sources chrétiennes 225 (Paris, 1975), 10:5 and 8:14, pp. 354–5 and 318–23 respectively. See Geary, 'Exchange and Interaction', pp. 79–81. [22] *CL*598.
[23] *CL*178, 182, 2918/3747a, 2919/3747b, 3170/3686dd. See also *CL*15, 1539.
[24] For commemoration see the thirteenth-century necrology, 'Kalendarium necrologium Laureshamense', ed. J. F. Böhmer, *Fontes rerum Germanicarum* III (Stuttgart, 1853), pp. 144–52.

west of Lorsch.[25] Heimerich and Rachel, however, increasingly pursued more easterly interests. In this they worked with a kinsman from a different part of their kinship web to Chrodegang and Guntland: Ermbert, bishop of Worms and abbot of Wissembourg, who gave land to Lorsch for the health of Heimerich's soul and in turn was commemorated by Rachel in the same breath as her parents and her brother.[26] The estates in question here were not at Lorsch, but at Dienheim and a neighbouring settlement east of the Rhine; Rachel and Eufemia made gifts for the health of their souls of land that was situated to the north and east of Lorsch, beyond the Main in the Wetterau. An exchange transacted between Rachel and Lorsch around 790 perhaps gives a hint of the new centre of family activity, with Dienheim, as Rachel's transactions with Ermbert and Heimerich suggested, the residence in the middle Rhine, but the overall focus more easterly, on property in Hesse and along the Main.[27] Shifts in interest not only led to new residences and family centres, but also were expressed by gifts to the church. Thus although relationships with Lorsch were kept up, from 776 there were also donations to Fulda by Rachel.[28] It is certainly no surprise that the descendant of Willeswind who rose to local prominence after Heimerich's death, a man imaginatively named Rupert, based his earliest activities on Dienheim.[29] The loss of the estate at Lorsch had not ruined Cancor's kin: these were wealthy landowners with far-flung interests from the Moselle to the Main, notably holdings in the wine-rich middle Rhine and vast estates in Hesse.[30] But, whilst they still enjoyed a useful proximity to the abbey and its monks, their world no longer revolved around Lorsch – it was Eufemia, Ermbert, and their foundations, not the monks of Lorsch, who prayed for their souls. The kin group re-formed around other centres.

---

[25] For Eufemia's career, in addition to *MGH DCharlemagne* 136, see Wandalbert of Prüm, *Miracula S.Goaris*, c. 10, ed. O. Holder-Egger, *MGH SS* 15:1 (Hanover, 1887), pp. 361–73 at p. 366.

[26] *CL*15.   [27] *CL*1679, and cf. *CL*15.

[28] *UBF*76 for Rachel's gift to Fulda in 776 (with Abbot Guntland of Lorsch witnessing). Note also Cancor, son of Rupert, who is an important benefactor of Fulda: *UBF*140b, *CDF*275, *TAF* c. 42, nos. 209, 282; on him see Staab, *Gesellschaft*, p. 413. A Thuringian woman named Willeswind, whose *domus* lay beyond the Tauber, was amongst the inmates of Leoba's convent at Tauberbischofsheim, closely related to Fulda: Rudolf, *Vita Leobae*, c. 15, ed. Holder-Egger, p. 128.

[29] For Count Rupert at Dienheim from 796, see *UBF*236, 246, 277. His precise relationship to Willeswind, Cancor and Heimerich is unclear: Cancor's brother, Turincbert, had a son named Rupert, and this count Rupert may be this man (as Glöckner, 'Lorsch und Lothringen', argued) or his son. Certainly his property interests, and those of his son, make it clear that he was a descendent of Willeswind.

[30] Middle Rhine: *CL*178, 182 (both Bobstadt), 15 (Dienheim and *Sunnincstete*), 1539 (Oppenheim and Auerbach). Hesse: *CL*2918/3747a, 2919/3747b (*Duraheim* in Wetterau and 2 places in the Lahngau with 10 *mancipia*), 3170/3686dd (a dozen places in the Lahngau with 44 *mancipia*).

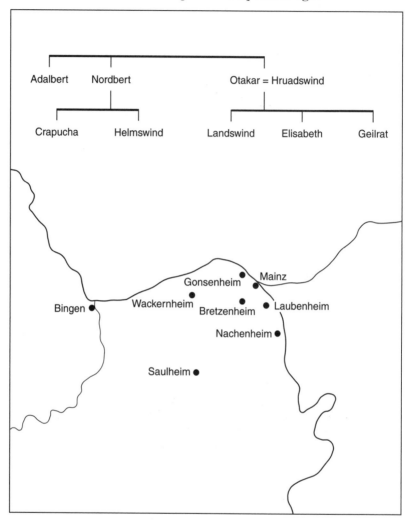

6 Otakar: kinship and property

Land, kinship and status

The second figure who can be viewed in close-up was a near contemporary of Cancor. Otakar dominated the area around Mainz from the middle of the eighth century until the end of the 770s – scarcely a charter was redacted in the area without his subscription as a witness. As Otakar's kin and contacts were the key patrons and supporters of Fulda in these decades, their interests can be reconstructed in comparable detail to those of Cancor. As with Cancor, we can see both the workings of the small group of 'practical' kin and the web of ties to a wider group of 'official' kin radiating outwards. Like Cancor, this wider web gave Otakar contacts beyond the middle Rhine, in particular to Bavaria and the founders of the monastery of Tegernsee, and also possibly with Burgundy.[31] Unlike Cancor, however, none of these wider links can be seen as operative factors affecting Otakar's actions, perhaps because, unlike Cancor, Otakar did not have property in the distant areas where he had official kin – the charters show that Otakar held land exclusively in the middle Rhine valley and remained a regional figure, not a member of a supra-regional elite. Otakar and his family had rich estates in a 20 km arc south and west of Mainz, but little property beyond this arc.

Like Cancor, Otakar's world circulated around a family residence where property rights were held by a small group of practical kin, and whose importance was underlined by its role as a centre for family commemoration. Wackernheim was a rich centre of viniculture just south of Mainz. Otakar, his brother Nordbert, and Adalbert, a relative and in all probability a third brother, all gave Fulda vineyards here. A small group of men in Wackernheim owned land which bordered on to each other's holdings, and acted as witnesses for one another: Otakar's vineyard was bordered by land of Nordbert's and Adalbert's, Nordbert's by Otakar's, and other neighbours such as Ragambert held land jointly with Adalbert and acted as witnesses with Otakar and his kin.[32] If there were odd outsiders with interests in the rich vineyards around Wackernheim, the core of the *villa* was very much the affair of Otakar and his close kin. In 772

---

[31] These relationships have been postulated by historians mainly on the admittedly difficult basis of naming-patterns, but the evidence is strong enough to make Otakar's relationship to the founders of Tegernsee probable: see M. Mitterauer, *Karolingische Markgrafen im Südosten. Fränkische Reichsaristokratie und bayerischer Stammesadel im österreichischen Raum*, Archiv für österreichische Geschichte 123 (Vienna, Graz and Cologne, 1963), pp. 50–3. On Otakar and his kin see Gerlich, 'Otakarius'; Gockel, *Königshöfe*, pp. 247–56, 305–6; Staab, *Gesellschaft*, pp. 380–403; Le Jan-Hennebicque, 'Structures familiales', 309–12; Le Jan, *Famille et Pouvoir*, pp. 198–9.

[32] *UBF* 23, 26, 27. Cf. Le Jan, *Famille et Pouvoir*, pp. 72, 80–3, on the witnessing patterns, and note her important comments on the significance of subdivided property at p. 409. On the Wackernheim estate see also Rösener, 'Strukturformen', pp. 167–8.

Otakar gave the bulk of the Wackernheim estate to Fulda, for the health of his soul, and that of his wife Hruodswind and one of his daughters, Lantswind: this gift consisted of an estate centre with demesne land, which was Otakar's residence, plus a half of what he had inherited from his mother and father in Wackernheim and Saulheim, and a half of his acquisitions in the surrounding *marca* (presumably mainly vineyards, in which there was a lively exchange) and a third of the unfree dependants – forty-one named individuals – who worked these two estates.[33] The heart of the Wackernheim and Saulheim estates, as opposed to the acquired vineyards away from the main settlement, were the core of Otakar's inheritance, and from this he had supplied Hruodswind with a morning-gift, which was, in turn, given to Fulda in 774.[34] The remainder of the Wackernheim and Saulheim estate passed on to Otakar's daughters, and a further portion was given to Fulda by two of them, Elisabeth and Geilrat, in 779.[35] It was a donation from 802, however, which underlined the centrality of Wackernheim and Saulheim to Otakar's kin: Helmswind and Crapucha gave to Fulda, for the soul of their father Nordbert, Otakar's brother, their share of the church of St Martin's, Wackernheim, and land at Wackernheim and Saulheim. The transaction was important enough to be witnessed by two counts and an Imperial *missus*.[36] Note again the agency of women in the commemoration of family and thus the cultivation of identity. Just as the widow Willeswind and her granddaughters Rachel and Eufemia had played a central role in defining the identity of Cancor's kin, so Otakar's women, particularly his nieces and daughters, gave for the souls of their menfolk and thus commemorated the dead and transmitted a family identity. Just as Cancor's wife was given a morning-gift at Lorsch to underline the new identity and role she took on when she married into her husband's family, so Otakar's wife, Hruodswind, was given a morning-gift at Wackernheim and Saulheim. The pieces of land given as morning-gifts were obviously specially chosen and specially treated, as was particularly evident in the case of Ercanfrida, who gave her morning-gift to a monastery on condition that an annual feast be held there in commemoration of herself and her husband. These women were not an alternative vector of memory to that supplied by the church; rather their interests clustered around Wackernheim and the church there, and were reinforced by gifts to the

---

[33] *UBF59*: gift of the residence *curte dominicato* with the *casa ubi ego manere videor*. *UBF60* for the associated list of 41 *mancipia*. The date may be no accident: the aftermath of the death of Carloman, Charlemagne's brother, in 772 led to a reworking of royal patronage which affected the middle Rhine dramatically (see pp. 180–2 below).   [34] *UBF66*.   [35] *UBF82*.

[36] *UBF267*. Bosl, *Franken um 800*, pp. 94–5, argued from the presence of royal representatives and the dedication to St Martin that the church had originally been royal property: this is one possibility.

monks of Fulda.[37] The residence of Otakar's close kin at Wackernheim, at the centre of a complex of rights over land and men, stood beside a proprietary church owned by the family, and dedicated to St Martin, the Franks' patron saint. At this church the family were remembered, and Nordbert's daughters wished to leave their father's soul in the hands of the monks of Fulda, the monastery of which the family had been patrons for over half a century. Patronage of Fulda defined this family and thus the church which stood at the centre of the family identity was eventually given to the care of the monks: the church attracted gifts precisely because it was, in a sense, a part of family structures.

The sizable estate at Wackernheim was supported economically by a scattering of holdings in other nearby settlements: Gonsenheim, where Otakar's daughters owned, *inter alia*, eighty ploughlands; and Laubenheim, Nachenheim and Bretzenheim, where Adalbert had considerable interests.[38] And above all, Otakar and his kin had large holdings in Mainz: in 779 Lantswind gave Fulda two plots, twenty ploughlands, one vineyard, thirty unfree dependants and the lettings held by a client, Berahtolah, whilst Elisabeth and Geilrat gave three plots, two vineyards, sixty ploughlands and a dozen unfree dependants; in 788 the latter pair added another two plots, three vineyards, forty ploughlands and eight unfree dependants.[39] These interests probably sustained dwellings in Mainz – in the 788 charter the scribe glossed the plots (*areales*) 'id est hofasteta', making it clear that these were estate centres.

Otakar ranked as a royal *fidelis* – not quite a count, a man who wielded political power in the localities, but an influential local whose position and importance the king acknowledged, and who was significant enough to enter into a personal relationship of obligation to the king. In acknowledging Otakar's local dominance, the king helped entrench it, for Otakar held a sizable benefice from Charlemagne which, like so much else associated with Otakar, ended up being given to the monks of Fulda, albeit in this case by Charlemagne rather than directly by Otakar. The scale and type of resources thus acquired raised Otakar well above his kin in terms of wealth and power – Otakar's benefice consisted of twenty-five *mansi*, sixty-six unfree dependants, sixteen half-free tenants and vineyards in Mainz, plus additional property near his holdings in Laubenheim

---

[37] Ercanfrida: pp. 39–40 above. On women, family memory and identity see K. Leyser, *Rule and Conflict*, pp. 73–83; Geary, *Phantoms of Remembrance*, pp. 48–80; Le Jan, *Famille et Pouvoir*, pp. 35–57; B. Pohl-Resl, 'Vorsorge, Memoria und soziales Ereignis: Frauen als Schenkerinnen in den bayerischen und alemannischen Urkunden des 8. und 9. Jahrhunderts', *MIÖG* 103 (1995), 265–87; M. Innes, 'Memory, Orality and Literacy in an Early Medieval Society', *P&P* 146 (1998), 3–36 at 23–8; and Innes, 'Keeping it in the Family: Women and Aristocratic Memory, 700–1200', in E. van Houts (ed.), *Medieval Memories: Men, Women and the Past* (London, forthcoming).
[38] *UBF*52, 72, 179.   [39] *UBF*87, 88, 174.

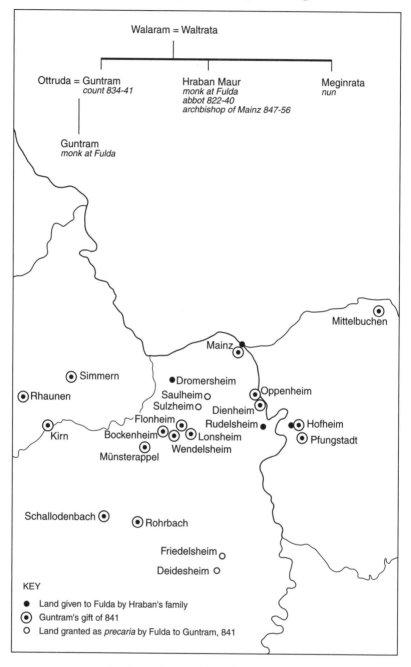

7 The family of Hraban Maur: kinship and property

and Gonsenheim, and underdeveloped land on an islet in the Rhine and at the confluence of the Rhine and the Nahe.[40] Royal patronage effectively cemented his hegemony in the Mainz area.

THE FAMILY OF HRABAN MAUR

Otakar's appearances in the charters ended in 779; thereafter a younger man, Walaram, monopolised the witness-lists for transactions involving property in the Mainz area. Walaram was a contact of Otakar's, whose niece he may have married.[41] Walaram witnessed an extraordinary corpus of forty-one charters, concerning property transactions in the Mainz area in the period 754–802. That this reflected some formal rank on Walaram's part is suggested by the rapid transformation in his activity in 772: before this date he was active as a witness but only inconsistently, and lowly placed in the witness-lists, but after 773 he acquired a new and consistent pre-eminence in the eyes of charter scribes. Walaram was certainly in contact with the count in the region, Hatto, but Walaram was far more frequent a witness, far closer to the locality. When groups of locals made the pilgrimage to Fulda to remember the dead, to witness the oblation of a local boy, or merely to celebrate holy days in holy company, Walaram went with them frequently, Count Hatto less often.[42] Walaram's activity as a local dispenser of patronage and figure of influence was confined to Mainz and its vicinity. When he wished to deal with his property interests east of the Rhine, in the lower Neckar area, he rode to Ladenburg, and had his charter witnessed by the resident count, Warin, and drawn up by a local notary.[43]

Walaram is visible not only thanks to his witnessing activity, but also because he too was an important patron of Fulda. His gifts to the monastery did not only consist of land: he also gave up one of his sons to the monks, as a child oblate. That the gift of a son was the ultimate associative gift, the boy remaining a member of his earthly kindred as well as of his monastic community, is well demonstrated by the intimate links which continued between Walaram's family and Fulda after the oblation.[44] Indeed, Walaram's son enjoyed such a successful career as a monk that the fortunes of the family and the continuing associations between family and monastery can be followed through the next generation and

[40] *MGH DCharlemagne* 127 (779).
[41] *UBF*22 for contacts. For the marriage see K.-F. Werner, 'Bedeutende Adelsfamilien im Reich Karls des Großen', in H. Beumann, (ed.), *Karl der Große I: Persönlichkeit und Geschichte* (Düsseldorf, 1965), pp. 83–142 at p. 135, and Gockel, *Königshöfe*, p. 256, n. 303 (for), and Staab, *Gesellschaft*, p. 390 (against).   [42] *UBF*158, 190, 219, 220, 237, 277, 279.   [43] *UBF*38.
[44] On child oblation see De Jong, *In Samuel's Image*.

beyond. For Walaram's son was none other than Hraban, given the nick-
name Maur, after St Benedict's favourite pupil, during time spent at
Charlemagne's court, on account of his academic promise. Hraban
became a prolific author and the leading intellectual of the first half of
the ninth century, abbot of Fulda from 822 to 841 and archbishop of
Mainz from 847 to his death in 856.[45]

Hraban was born shortly before 784, perhaps in 780.[46] On 25 May 788
Walaram and his wife Waltrata made two donations to Fulda: the first of
the family's residence in Mainz, with the usufruct reserved for the couple
and Hraban; the second of Waltrata's estate at Dromersheim. These gifts,
which the infant Hraban subscribed as a witness, were clearly connected
to the family's decision to place Hraban in the monastery, and in all probability linked to the physical act of oblation. Hraban's relations made
further gifts which were witnessed by the young oblate in 791 and 801.
The child oblate was a bridge between monastery and family: both later
gifts were made on the occasion of trips to Fulda by Hraban's kin and their
contacts. The charter of 791 gives a vivid insight into the type of sociability such visits involved, for the standard formulae are given a new life by
the subtle change which addresses Abbot Baugolf as 'most jocund' rather
than the conventional 'most venerable'.[47] As with Cancor, so with
Walaram, choices concerning the career of offspring were made in such a
way as to ensure the continuation of the family into the future: Hraban's
sister, Meginrata, was also dedicated to God as a nun. Walaram thus cleared
the way for his son Guntram to inherit his secular position, with a well-
placed brother at Fulda to assist him in his career. And the patronage which
Hraban, as a monk, could offer was not only spiritual: the early charters
demonstrate the attraction of having a monk in the kindred, and thanks to
the success of his career Hraban was later able to assist his brother,
Guntram, in his secular career at key political points in 834 and 841, and
have his nephew, another Guntram, professed a monk at Fulda, placed as

[45] On Hraban's family and career see R. Kottje and H. Zimmermann (eds.), *Hrabanus Maurus. Lehrer, Abt und Bischof*, Mainzer Akademie der Wissenschaften und der Literatur, Abhandlungen der Geistes- und Sozialwissenschaften 4 (Wiesbaden, 1982); W. Böhne (ed.), *Hrabanus Maurus und seine Schule. Festschrift der Rabanus-Maurus-Schule* (Fulda, 1980); D. Schaller, 'Der Junge "Rabe" am Hof Karls des Grossen (Theodulf Carm. 27)', in J. Autenrieth and F. Brunhölzl (eds.), *Festschrift B. Bischoff* (Stuttgart, 1971), pp. 123–41. There is a vast bibliography on Hraban's schol-arship, but for the links between intellectual output and politics see M. De Jong, 'The Empire as *Ecclesia*: Hrabanus Maurus and Biblical Commentary for Rulers', in Y. Hen and M. Innes (eds.), *Using the Past in the Early Middle Ages*, (Cambridge, 2000), pp. 191–226.
[46] On Hraban I follow F. Staab, 'Wann wurde Hrabanus Maurus Mönch in Fulda? Beobachtungen zur Anteilnahme seiner Familie an den Anfängen seiner Laufbahn', in R. Kottje and H. Zimmermann (eds.), *Hrabanus Maurus. Lehrer, Abt und Bischof* (Wiesbaden, 1982), pp. 75–101 noting the criticisms of De Jong, *In Samuel's Image*, pp. 73–7. See also E. Friese, 'Zum Geburtsjahr des Hrabanus Maurus', in Kottje and Zimmermann (eds.), *Hrabanus Maurus*, pp. 18–74.
[47] *UBF*177, 178, 219.

a royal chaplain at the court of Lothar II and then as provost of Sölnhofen.[48] Complex though these family structures were, men like Walaram made them work. They were not impoverishing their heirs by giving to the church, nor was inheritance custom allowed to fragment family holdings.

Like the other families we have been investigating, Walaram's crystallised around a rural estate complex and an associated proprietary church. Hofheim, east of the Rhine more or less opposite Worms, was not an ancient settlement site; indeed, rather like Lorsch, it was not presented by charter scribes as a self-standing settlement in its own right but rather as isolated. As with Cancor and his kin at Lorsch, Walaram and his offspring are the only documented Carolingian landowners at Hofheim. Perhaps setting up such a seat was one way of marking oneself off as a member of the local elite. Certainly Walaram, like Otakar and Cancor, used church foundation as a way of advertising his status: a church dedicated to St Boniface stood at the heart of the Hofheim estate, its dedication indicating that the complex was relatively recently developed and thus perhaps a reflection of prospering family fortunes. The church at Hofheim was linked to the commemoration of Walaram and Waltrata – a donation to Fulda of 807 acknowledged the link – and, given that it must have been dedicated after 754, Walaram and Waltrata had probably founded the church.[49] Guntram and his wife Ottruda were buried there, and the church was remembered by Hraban, who composed verses for his brother's epitaph.[50] Other than Hofheim, Walaram and his kin demonstrated a close attachment to Mainz; indeed, it is to Mainz that he went when he had business to transact. Again the parallel with Otakar is clear. Hraban, in the verse epitaph he wrote for himself, played on the centrality of the *urbs* – Mainz needed no further introduction – to his social world. Here he was born, here he was baptised, here he was buried (with a little matter of eight years as archbishop in the meantime).[51] Walaram and Waltrata's initial gift to Fulda, possibly made as they handed their son over to the monks, had been of a town house in the city, of which the usufruct was reserved to Walaram, Waltrata and then Hraban: evidently a city residence was not only necessary for important laymen, but also desirable for a well-connected monk.[52] In addition, Walaram and Guntram also enjoyed a scattering of holdings of various size and origin

---

[48] Hraban and his brother, see below, pp. 200–2, 208–9. For his nephew Guntram see *Klostergemeinschaft*, pp. 439–40; Staab, 'Wann wurde Hrabanus Maurus?', pp. 85–6, and Ermanic of Ellwangen, *Sermo de Vita Sualonis*, ed. O. Holder-Egger *MGH SS* 15:1 (Hanover, 1887) pp. 153–63 at p. 155, 161, and *MGH Epp.* V, no. 27, p. 529.   [49] CDF487.

[50] Hraban Maur, *Carmina*, ed. E. Dümmler, *MGH PLAC* 2, pp. 154–258, no. 86, p. 238 and see Gockel, *Königshöfe*, pp. 41–2, n. 42.   [51] Hraban, *Carmina*, no. 97, p. 244.

[52] UBF177: *aream unam cum casa et cum omni aedificio, in qua nos commanere videamur*, bounded on three sides by the *strata publica* and on the fourth by the holding of Zotan.

over the middle Rhine valley as a whole, concentrated in the triangle with Bingen, Mainz and Worms at its corners. Interestingly, none of these other interests was given to Fulda, which received only the Hofheim core of the family's estate, and gifts linked to Hraban's career, most of which were from Waltrata's inheritance from her parents. Indeed, an overview of family holdings is only possible as Guntram, facing ruin in the political crisis of 841, granted his lands to his brother's abbey as a safeguard, receiving back the usufruct – no wonder, after this act of desperation, that Guntram's son ended up a Fulda monk rather than launched on a secular career![53]

LAND AS PROPERTY

These detailed reconstructions illuminate the fundamentals of kinship structure: the fluidity of families as groups of practical kin operated in a web of potential patrons and allies; the periodic re-formation of familial relationships through death, inheritance and marriage; and the importance of women and the church in maintaining a cultural veneer of continuity. All these relationships were defined with reference to land. Kinship ties were renegotiated through the inheritance of land: women, when they married into the family, received special pieces of land, as did favoured monasteries like Lorsch and Fulda. That is, land was not only the basic economic resource, from which most wealth was derived. It was also the primary social resource, something around which and with which relationships were created. And, if we remember that the families which we have been tracing were part of an elite, land also defined social status. The ability to exercise rights over land marked out the fundamental division in society, and the possibility of pursuing a familial strategy was dependent on the extent of those rights.[54]

In legal documents, rights over land were presented unproblematically, in a Latin terminology inherited from late Roman law. When an individual handed over a named piece of land to the church, the rights being transferred were self-evident to contemporaries because they were living, practised rights, part of the fabric of experience. Whilst the formulaic opacity of the majority of the charters of donation prevents them revealing much about the practice of landownership[55], written records of dis-

---

[53] *CDF*534, 535. On the context, above, pp. 208–9.
[54] For an ethnographic survey of the significance of land in a peasant society, J. Davis, *Land and Family in Pisticci* (London, 1973).
[55] Cf. the classic discussion of the Anglo-Saxon material, E. John, *Land Tenure in Early England* (Leicester, 1960). In general on custom, law and power I have been strongly influenced by E. P. Thompson, *Customs in Common* (London, 1991), and see E. P. Thompson, 'The Grid of

putes over land (*placita*) are more helpful. For *placita* record the contestation of rights over land, and are thus more revealing about the types of rights which were being disputed, and the basis by which these rights were established – not least as the ability to dispute rights suggests the presence of some legal or moral case that attracted some local support and demanded an answer.

The type of claim that might be at stake is suggested by a case from 806, when Binin and Rudwig claimed that one Waltolf, whilst he had lived, had begged Willibert and themselves to give land at Eimsheim in alms for his soul to Fulda. The property in question seems originally to have been given by Waltolf to Binin, Rudwig and Willibert, with the expectation that it would be given, posthumously, for his soul. Such transactions were common, and should be linked to the associations for alms-giving mentioned in capitulary legislation.[56] However, Willibert had not given the land at Eimsheim to Fulda – hence the case against him. In the transmitted document, Binin and Rudwig alone granted the Eimsheim land to Fulda; Willibert, however, was eventually forced to make a *traditio*, a ritual transferring rights over the land to Fulda, in the presence of two Imperial agents. The case evidently turned on the plausibility of Binin and Rudwig's assertions about the now dead Waltolf's wishes as to the fate of the Eimsheim land. This proof was oral: no deed documenting Waltolf's wishes was mentioned. No one disputed that Waltolf had given the Eimsheim land to Willibert; Binin and Rudwig argued that Willibert had been given the land on the understanding that when Waltolf died it would be given to Fulda for the good of Waltolf's soul. So, although the proof was oral testimony and not a document, a legal norm informed the case: that land given for alms-giving should be used for alms-giving as the original owner had wished. Binin and Rudwig's testimony as to Waltolf's original wishes may have been upheld as those at the meeting remembered the initial transaction. Willibert was obliged to use the land as the man who had given it to him, Waltolf, had wished. This was not simply a case of Binin and Rudwig establishing fact where Willibert failed: Binin and Rudwig invoked norms about the obligations created by gifts of land, norms which were enforceable at law. In that these norms about gifts for the soul were not laid down in any law-code, but were shaped by collective experience, this case turned on

---

Inheritance: A Comment', in J. Goody, J. Thirsk and E. P. Thompson (eds.), *Family and Inheritance: Rural Society in Western Europe, 1200–1800* (Cambridge, 1976), pp. 328–60; and W. C. Neale, 'Land is to Rule', in R. E. Frykenberg (ed.), *Land Tenure and Social Structure in Indian History* (Madison, Milkwaukee and London, 1965), pp. 3–16.

[56] Cf. *MGH Cap.* I, no. 20, c. 16, p. 51, on *gildonia* for the purpose of alms-giving. and see above, pp. 37–8, for the basis in death-ritual.

custom. It may have helped the application of this custom that it favoured the most powerful party in this case, the abbey of Fulda: custom is notoriously malleable and open to social pressure. That the document did not explicitly state a normative rule to the effect that Willibert, having acquired the property as he did, had to give it as Waltolf had wished, need not mean that these obligations were not expressed as general rules – the document is too opaque to permit insight into the precise way that legal arguments were marshalled in the hearing in 806.[57]

A comparable case, concerning the same area, was resolved in a legal assembly held at Eimsheim in 825. Hatto had ordered that land at Dalheim should be given to Fulda on his death, for the health of his soul. Theotamar, Hatto's son, held on to the land and resisted pressure to carry out his father's wishes. Like Willibert in 806, Theotamar lost, and ended up respecting the wishes of the dead former owner of the disputed land. Unlike Willibert, Theotamar could have pointed to inheritance custom to buttress his claims, but the wishes of his father were upheld in a local assembly. That is, Theotamar lost out because of the invocation of a similar norm to that which had sealed Willibert's fate. The assembly in 825 must have had to adjudicate between one norm, rooted in mortuary custom, about the inviolability of expressed wishes to give land to the church; and another norm, rooted in inheritance custom, about the rights of sons to take over family land. What sealed Theotamar's fate in 825 was the feeling that heirs receiving property were obliged to make some gift for the soul of the person from whom they inherited.

The resolution of Theotamar's case was, however, more complex than Willibert's. Theotamar received the contested land back to be held as a life-grant from Fulda. That is, Theotamar's claim to some rights over his father's land was stronger than Willibert's claim to a legacy given by a friend and on the condition that it be given to the church. Despite the language of absolute judgement in the document recording the transaction, Theotamar was able to force the monks of Fulda to offer a compromise, and succeeded in gaining tenure of the disputed land for the rest of his life. This compromise did not only concern the Dalheim estate, for the history of the Dalheim estate was preserved within a charter recording a pious donation of land and rights at Dienheim made by Theotamar to Fulda. Although Theotamar obtained a life-interest in the Dalheim estate, he did not keep any rights at Dienheim. The gift of land at

---

[57] CDF228. On the opacity of archival records as to actual debate, cf. S. Roberts, 'The Study of Disputes: Anthropological Perspectives', in J. Bossy (ed.), *Disputes and Settlements: Law and Social Relations in the West* (Cambridge, 1983), pp. 1–24 at p. 20. My treatment of disputes owes much to S. D. White, 'Inheritances and Legal Arguments in Western France, 1050–1150', *Traditio* 43 (1987), 55–103.

Dienheim was made 'in alms', that is with an eye on the spiritual benefits which would accrue to his soul and – importantly – also his father's. Moreover, through his tenure of the Dalheim estate Theotamar was placing himself under Fulda's patronage in a formal, secular sense. Theotamar was anxious to keep up a relationship of spiritual and secular patronage with Fulda, and to perform his filial duty towards his father. Theotamar had been forced at law to respect his father's wishes about Dalheim, and in order to maintain the patronage of Fulda, he had to make a further gift, that of the Dienheim land. This 'gift' evidently was part of the compromise hammered out in 825; its presentation as a gift 'in alms' confirms that it served to rebuild the relationship between Theotamar's family and the monks. Theotamar's is a familiar story: gifts of land to the church being contested by the heirs of those who had made them. By contesting rights over family land which had been used to create a relationship between his family and the church, Theotamar was renegotiating that relationship, and attempting to reassert control over a lucrative resource. The judgement made in 825 was only enacted through the brokering of a settlement which did not ruin Theotamar, whilst acknowledging Fulda's title to the disputed land. Whilst the documents are again too opaque to allow a full view of the arguments advanced at Dienheim in 825, it is clear that Fulda's legal victory could only be enacted and enforced by acknowledging the social pressures which had brought Theotamar to court in the first place.[58]

Both cases show that the language of the charters, presenting gifts of land as absolute alienations, did not tell the whole story. In both cases, customary restraints, and above all the wishes of the previous owner of the land, had continuing moral and legal force. Such a state of affairs was far from irrational: it guarded the interests of kin, anxious not to see their inheritance granted away, but also ensured the performance of good deeds for the souls of dead ancestors. Although none of the transmitted cases shows grants to the church revoked and returned to disinherited kin, such cases were hardly likely to have been transmitted through monastic archives. Nonetheless, heirs were able to occupy estates which

[58] *CDF*459. For norms, pp. 37–40 above. On compromise, the best study is S. D. White, '*Pactum ... legem vincit et amor judicium*: The Settlement of Disputes by Compromise in Eleventh-Century Western France', *American Journal of Legal History* 22 (1978), 281–308; for the use of 'hidden' compromises within a framework of courts and judgements, see C. J. Wickham, 'Land Disputes and their Social Framework in Lombard-Carolingian Italy, 700–900', in W. Davies and P. Fouracre (eds.), *The Settlement of Disputes in Early Medieval Europe* (Cambridge, 1986), pp. 105–24 at pp. 118–23. On the tension between giving to the church and continuing familial rights over land, see Rosenwein, *To Be the Neighbor*; S. D. White, *Custom, Kinship and Gifts to Saints: The Laudatio Parentum in Western France, 1050–1200* (Chapel Hill, 1988); B. H. Rosenwein, T. Head and S. Farmer, 'Monks and their Enemies: A Comparative Approach', *Speculum* 66 (1991), 764–96.

had been given to the church by their ancestors, and their cases had sufficient strength to force the church into compromise, as with Theotamar. Both phenomena imply local sympathy, perhaps even active support, for disinherited heirs. In a sense, then, rights of ownership over land clearly were not absolute: what could be done with a particular piece of land was limited by obligations towards past and potential future owners of that land.

Such constraints were primarily a matter of responsibilities towards an inheritance group limiting freedom of action. Willibert's case, however, provides priceless evidence that similar obligations were transmitted with land that passed beyond the inheritance group. It may be that the real distinction in terms of freedom of action was not so much between inherited and acquired land, as between land which was given, and land which was bought or exchanged. Because a sale or exchange was a complete transaction, in which one received an agreed return for a piece of land, no residual personal obligations were created between the parties involved – whereas because a gift was essentially asymmetrical, it created a moral and social relationship between recipient and donor, and was, in a sense, incomplete. That is, whilst land which was given would have remained, in some sense, subject to the wishes of its donor, sales and exchanges may have effected more absolute transfers of rights.[59]

Land was not a commodity, an object which could be absolutely passed from one party to another: rights persisted after changes in possession.[60] The vocabulary, Latin or vernacular, which was used to refer to land was undifferentiated: plots were *portiones*, the *possessio* or *eigen* of an individual. There was no real interest in classifying property in terms of dues incumbent on it, or the rules governing its use. When rights were contested, local witnesses recounted the history of a particular estate, cataloguing the social relationships tied up with a piece of land and the obligations that they created, rather than attempting to place an estate in a particular legal category. Despite these constraints on the exercise of rights over land, individuals were in a real sense owners of land. Although ownership was relative and conditional, land was normally under the effective control of one individual, not subject to shared rights of control: kin had moral checks but did not, as a rule, administer their property jointly. Hence the charters talk of land being transferred into the *ius* or

[59] On sales and exchanges as transactions, Rosenwein, *To Be the Neighbor*, pp. 70–108; C. I. Hammer, 'Land Sales in Eighth- and Ninth-century Bavaria: Legal and Social Implications', *EME* 6 (1997), 47–75; and cf. J. Campbell, 'The Sale of Land and the Economics of Power in Early England', *Haskins Society Journal* 1 (1989), 23–37.

[60] See Rosenwein, *To Be the Neighbor*, and A. Gurevich, 'Représentations et attitudes à l'égard de la propriété pendant le haut moyen âge', *Annales: ESC* 27 (1972), 523–47.

dominium of an individual, and of *proprietas*. The term 'allod', so well-loved by historians, was actually astonishingly rarely applied to specific pieces of land. It is only in the eleventh century that *allodium* starts to be used in a manner more familiar to modern historians, as a blanket term for all land free of obligations towards a lord. Before the eleventh century, full ownership, subject to moral and customary checks, was the standard form of rights over land, and needed no special label. Indeed, where possession and ownership did not coincide, problems arose. Although tenancies became more common in the Carolingian period, thanks to the letting out of church land, the moral tie between land and possessor always made them problematical. Very few tenancies were economic arrangements, with significant rents being collected, rather than social arrangements. Tenure of land *in beneficium* or *in precarium* (the two terms were interchangeable) was essentially the gift of uninhibited possession, in return for the demonstration of ultimate ownership by the payment of an annual sum.[61]

Can we project back this pattern, revealed by eighth- and ninth-century charters, into the Merovingian period? The chronology of gifts of land to the church suggests that the ways in which land was used changed in the seventh century: before that date, gifts of land were not used to create obligations and define relationships between the church and laity. Written documents conveying rights over land were rare before the late seventh century; the reintroduction of the charter may have met an urgent social need for a means of recording new ways of using land.[62] It may even be possible to find traces of earlier tenurial patterns in the transmitted charter evidence. Some eighth- and ninth-century documents contain opaque references to complex tenurial arrangements which cannot be explained in conventional terms of landownership, and already seem to have been archaic. In this handful of documents we meet groups of free men securely holding and inheriting land which was

---

[61] See H. Dubled's work, primarily on the Wissembourg charters: 'La notion de propriété en Alsace du VIIIe au IXe siècles', *Le Moyen Age* 65 (1959), 429–52; '*Allodium* dans les textes latins du moyen âge', *ibid.* 67 (1961), 241–6; also G. Köbler, 'Eigen und Eigentum', *ZSRGGA* 95 (1978), 1–33. Note that distinctions between ownership and possession were blurring in late Roman law: E. Levy, *West Roman Vulgar Law: The Law of Property* (Philadelphia, 1951).

[62] See below, p. 112, and cf. McKitterick, *The Carolingians and the Written Word*, pp. 66–75; Halsall, *Settlement and Social Organisation*, pp. 46–8; and Costambeys, 'An Aristocratic Community', 47–55. F. Theuws, 'Landed Property and Manorial Organisation in Northern Austrasia: Some Considerations and a Case Study', in Theuws and N. Roymans (eds.), *Images of the Past: Studies on Ancient Societies in Northwestern Europe* (Amsterdam, 1991), pp. 299–407, is an important study drawing on both archaeological and documentary evidence. The classic discussions concern changing notions of property and their relationship to the church and the charter in Anglo-Saxon England: see P. Wormald, *Bede and the Conversion of England: The Charter Evidence* (Jarrow, 1985).

ultimately owned by the king, or a favoured church which had acquired its rights from the king. Their tenurial position cannot be adequately described in the language of Roman property law: they were something more than tenants, but rather less than full owners. That is, they inherited a form of property right, but not one that was absolute ownership.[63] These customary tenures usually appeared because they were under threat, as kings or ecclesiastical lords reorganised their holdings. Thus in 771 Dagaleich, who held land at Umstadt, had his case heard before Charlemagne. The entire *villa* of Umstadt had been given by Pippin to Fulda, and Fulda now attempted to turn the rather abstract *possessio* it had thus acquired into something more tangible. Dagaleich objected to his holding being exploited *ab utilitatibus ecclesie*, and, unsurprisingly, lost. But Fulda needed a royal judgement to ensure its victory: Dagaleich's case was that he was more than a tenant and therefore he, not Fulda, was the ultimate owner of his land.[64] Similarly, in the 820s, Fulda, having obtained a judgement confirming its ownership of the settlement of Hünfeld, forced the residents to acknowledge the monastery's claim, performing rituals in which they were invested by the monastic landlord with the land which they already held. Little was said about the previous status of the inhabitants of Hünfeld, but Fulda was clearly imposing a new interpretation of their position: the care with which the granting back of land was recorded, individual by individual, and the insistence that they were now mere tenants with a life-interest, suggests that it recorded a *de facto* change. The inhabitants of Hünfeld were being forced to renounce their customary rights over land which they had previously inherited; Fulda, whose rights at Hünfeld may previously have amounted to little more than the collection of customary dues, was restyling two sets of complementary customary right as more absolute ownership.[65]

At Hünfeld and Umstadt, the monks were transforming the rights they exercised over land, turning the collection of dues from a community of free men into full-blooded landownership. This point is underlined by events at Schwanheim in 782. Here a group of free men lost out in a similar way, when a royal court decided that Charlemagne had given the entire *villa* of Schwanheim to Lorsch. Yet in the decades before 782, free men at Schwanheim had treated their rights over land there as rights of full ownership: their charters gave land as full property, with no reference to any other individual's interests. At Schwanheim, then, it was not the imposition of a written legal tradition that transformed property rights.

---

[63] See Wickham, 'European Forests', pp. 162–8 on such tenures.   [64] *MGH DCharlemagne* 63.
[65] *CDF*456.

The minutiae of the case are revealing: the monks argued that Charlemagne had given Lorsch the *villa* of Hurfeld and its appurtenances, and that Schwanheim was included in this grant, buttressing their case with local testimony which, presumably, confirmed that Schwanheim was an outlier of Hurfeld. Schwanheim was probably a relatively young settlement, the product of clearances – hence its dependence on an older core settlement, and the insistence by the residents that they held their land as full property. Whatever the case, here free peasants lost out as the monks, with a monopoly of royal and supernatural patronage, argued that they were the real holders of full property rights at Schwanheim, in succession to the king.[66]

Prior to 700, then, the middle Rhenish peasantry enjoyed *de facto* control of the land they worked, but their substantial property rights did not quite add up to full ownership. They owed relatively light dues, presumably mainly renders in kind, which were collected on a community level from the *villa* as a whole, or even from a group of connected *villae*; this kind of structure, based on personal rather than proprietorial right, was widespread in Roman and pre-Roman northern Gaul.[67] Who collected these dues and how are matters for speculation: kings presumably attempted to establish a theoretical control, but much must have ended up sticking to local fingers. Perhaps the substantial royal estates in the region, which we can first see in the eighth-century evidence, were originally this type of loose lordship, and were reorganised into a more intensive exploitation when kings began to visit the middle Rhine more, and thus needed a firmer economic base in the region. The large tenurial units, made up of several settlements and known as 'marks', which are visible in some eighth-century documents, may be survivals of these archaic tenurial units, undergoing a swansong as they were granted out to loyal followers of the Carolingians to facilitate full Frankish control east of the Rhine. Swicgar, a relative of Lorsch's founders, exercised quasi-proprietorial rights over an area around Wetzlar which was referred to as

---

[66] CL228 for the hearings and judgement, and CL225–7 for earlier transactions using charters to transfer ownership of land within the settlement.
[67] See C. R. Whittaker, 'Rural Labour in Three Roman Provinces', in P. Garnsey (ed.), *Non-Slave Labour in the Greco-Roman World* (Cambridge, 1980), pp. 73–99; also J. Percival, 'Seigneurial Aspects of Late Roman Estate Management', *English Historical Review* 82 (1969), 449–73 and E. Wightman, 'Peasants and Potentates: An Investigation of Social Structure and Land Tenure in Roman Gaul', *American Journal of Ancient History* 3 (1978), 97–128, although both with unfortunate tendencies to seek the origins of high medieval manorial structures. For the absence of demesnes and the importance of rent in Merovingian estates, M. Tits-Dieuaide, 'Grands domaines, grandes et petits exploitations en Gaule mérovingienne', in A. Verhulst (ed.), *La grande domaine aux époches mérovingienne et carolingienne* (Ghent, 1985), pp. 23–50; and S. Sato, 'L'*agrarium*: la charge paysanne avant la régime domanial, VIe–VIIIe siècles', *Journal of Medieval History* 24 (1998), 103–25.

his *ministerium*, or in the vernacular *ambath*.[68] Older forms of lordship and land tenure survived predominantly in woodlands and uplands: the topographical context shared by Hünfeld, Schwanheim and Umstadt is striking. Here we can see monasteries transforming older forms of lordship into full ownership of large blocks of territory. But such a pattern was the exception rather than the rule. By the Carolingian period, across most of the area, and above all in the Rhine valley itself, full ownership of land by the possessors of land was the rule. Presumably what had happened here was what we saw the first stages of at Schwanheim, before Lorsch's acquisition of the settlement: possessors establishing rights which came to amount to full ownership. Where no outside force intruded (unlike at Schwanheim), the customary rights of kings or aristocrats over a community became fossilised dues – the payments for the use of woodland and so on, or the head-taxes, which were recorded in Carolingian surveys. That is, these payments ceased to have any organic connection to the ownership of land, and became dues levied from the local community as a whole.[69] A charter of 897 perhaps even gives a glimpse of the kind of rights that these dues could evolve into. Count Erenfrid had inherited rights in the area around Alzey – the *villae* of Alzey, Schafhusen, Ilbesheim, Rockesheim and their appurtenances, to be precise – which the Emperor Arnulf had seized from him. As well as landholdings, styled *salicae terrae*, in the area, Erenfrid's inheritance included a series of levies (*decimationes*) on pigs, hens and woodland in the area. But Erenfrid did not own the area as a whole: these were customary dues, not property rights.[70]

In the seventh century, then, we have the transformation of rights over land, with the development of a new model of full ownership. Part and parcel of this change was the emergence of land as a medium of social exchange, and the adoption of the charter as a means of transferring rights over land. Whilst there were areas – above all the hills and woodlands – where kings and churches were able to transform their traditional

[68] On the mark system, F. Schwind, 'Die Franken in Althessen', in W. Schlesinger (ed.), *Althessen im Frankenreich*, Nationes 2 (Sigmaringen 1975) pp. 211–80, is the fullest discussion, including Swicgar at Wetzlar, on which see *CL*3684b/3066, and *MGH DCharlemagne* 142; see also H. Büttner, 'Die politische Kräfte zwischen Rhein und Odenwald bis zum 11. Jht.', in Büttner, *Zur frühmittelalterliche Reichsgeschichte am Rhein, Main und Neckar*, ed. A. Gerlich (Darmstadt, 1975), pp. 253–66. Note when describing these tenurial units 'mark' has a sense which is distinct from, but related to, its more familiar usage as the wood and waste pertaining to a settlement nucleus, on which see pp. 105–6 below.
[69] For example, some of the dues levied by Carolingian kings as recorded in *CL*3671–4 would fit this pattern well.
[70] *MGH DArnulf* 154. Erenfrid's rights around Alzey look very close to those exercised in the eighth century in the 'marks' east of the Rhine, except that they are here firmly not proprietorial in nature, whereas in the eighth-century cases this is more ambivalent.

rights into outright ownership of vast tracts, as a rule free peasants were able to consolidate their rights over land into full ownership. Older dues, which had been associated with the control of large units made up of several settlements, survived, but only as customary dues which did not impede the property rights of the peasantry.

THE EXPLOITATION OF LAND AND THE ORGANISATION OF ESTATES

The fundamental fact about the property rights which emerged at the end of this process, in the eighth and ninth centuries, was their fragmentation. Holdings were scattered over a wide area: a couple of holdings in this settlement, a vineyard in the next, an estate in the next still. Even within rural settlements large, compact blocks of land or sizable estates comprising an entire settlement were extremely rare. Of course, the degree of fragmentation varied, and in part depended on local factors – a settlement's history, its topography and economy.[71] But this society was based upon a complex mosaic of parcels of land of various sizes, held by a variety of individuals. This was true even of the most influential families, as we have seen in the cases of Cancor, Otakar and Walaram.

There were occasional settlements where property rights were less fragmented, most often monopolised by the king or a great church. By the eighth and ninth centuries some such settlements were organised as manors – bipartite estates, where dependants were housed on their own plots but also made to work on demesne land, whose produce went directly to the lord.[72] These structures were new. Resting on the

---

[71] For fuller discussion of the sociology of rural settlement in Carolingian Europe, and the importance of tenurial fragmentation, see esp. Wickham; 'Rural Society'; for case-studies see Davies, *Small Worlds*; Schwind, 'Beobachtungen zur inneren Struktur des Dorfes'; H. Dannenbauer, 'Fränkische und schwäbische Dörfer am Ende des 8. Jahrhunderts', in Dannenbauer, *Grundlagen der mittelalterlichen Welt* (Stuttgart, 1958), pp. 271–83. See also R. Sprandel, 'Die frühmittelalterliche Grundbesitzverteilung und Gerichtsordnung im fränkischen und alemannischen Raum', in F. Quarthal (ed.), *Alemannien und Ostfranken im Frühmittelalter*, Veröffentlichung des Alemannisches Instituts Freiburg-im-Br. 48 (Bühl and Baden, 1984), pp. 47–59, developing the thesis advanced in 'Gerichtsorganisation und Sozialstruktur Mainfrankens im früheren Mittelalter', *Jahrbuch für fränkische Landesforschung* 38 (1978), 7–38. I draw on all these studies freely in what follows.

[72] There is a vast bibliography on Carolingian estate structures. A. Verhulst's seminal articles are collected in *Rural and Urban Aspects of Early Medieval Northwest Europe* (Aldershot, 1992); for an overview of the current state of play, see Y. Morimoto, 'Autour du grand domaine carolingien', in Morimoto and A. Verhulst (eds.), *Economie rurale et économie urbaine au moyen âge* (Kyushu, 1993), pp. 25–79. For our area as a whole Staab, *Gesellschaft*, pp. 250–86, 313–71 is the best discussion. On royal estates the starting-points are W. Metz, *Das Karolingische Reichsgut. Eine verfassungs- und verwaltungsgeschichtliche Untersuchung* (Berlin, 1960) and for our area Gockel, *Königshöfe*; on ecclesiastical estates J.-P. Devroey, '*Ad utilitatem monasterii*: mobiles et préoccupations de gestion dans l'économie monastique du monde franc', *Revue bénédictine* 103 (1993), 224–40; D. Hägermann,

imposition of labour services upon the peasantry, they had first arisen in the Frankish heartland north of the Loire and west of the Rhine in the seventh century and spread outwards from there.[73] Their inhabitants could be free, unfree, or a mixture of both: their legal status was relatively unimportant compared to their economic function as tied tenants bound to work the lord's land. Charter scribes recognised that, despite the legal heterogeneity of the groups who worked on manorial estates, they formed a distinct social and economic group; they were consistently termed *servi* and distinguished from other tenants and dependants.[74] The very earliest manors in the area were situated on royal land, and by the second half of the eighth century the church was also acquiring estates of this kind, often through royal gifts.[75] But it would be a mistake to read the estate surveys of the first decades of the ninth century as indicating that royal and ecclesiastical land was, as a rule, organised into manors. A Carolingian estate survey from Fulda points to a variety of estate structures: some large estates, more often than not those which originated in royal gifts, are organised as manors, but other land is let out to free tenants or for exploitation by unfree dependants.[76] That is, manorial organisation was never an exclusive or total strategy; bipartite estates always coexisted with other structures. This may seem a self-evident point, but it is worth spelling out as students of estate structures tend to work from Carolingian surveys which, in effect, biases them in favour of the manor. In the middle Rhine, on the other hand, surveys can be read in the context of the

Footnote 72 (*cont.*)

'Die Abt als Grundherr: Kloster und Wirtschaft im frühen Mittelalter', in F. Prinz (ed.), *Herrschaft und Kirche. Beiträge zur Entstehung und Wirkungsweise episkopaler und monastischer Organisationsformen*, Monographien zur Geschichte des Mittelalters 33 (Stuttgart, 1988), pp. 345–85; W. Metz, 'Zu Wesen und Strukturen der geistlichen Grundherrschaft', *Settimane* 27 (1981), 147–69; and, on individual institutions, L. Kuchenbuch, *Bäuerliche Gesellschaft und Klosterherrschaft im 9. Jahrhundert: Studien zur Sozialstruktur der Familia der Abtei Prüm*, Vierteljahrschrift für Sozial- und Wirtschaftsgeschichte 66 (Wiesbaden, 1978); U. Weidinger, 'Untersuchungen zur Grundherrschaft des Klosters Fulda in der Karolingerzeit', in W. Rösener (ed.) *Strukturen der Grundherrschaft in frühen Mittelalter* (Göttingen, 1989), pp. 247–65; W. Rösener, 'Die Grundherrschaft des Kloster Fulda in karolingische und ottonische Zeit', in G. Schrimpf (ed.), *Kloster Fulda in der Welt der Karolinger und Ottonen* (Frankfurt, 1996), pp. 202–24; and (on Wissembourg) W. Rösener, *Grundherrschaft im Wandel*, VMPIG 102 (Göttingen, 1991), pp. 83–146.

[73] The seminal study remains A. Verhulst, 'La génèse du régime domanial classique en France au haut moyen âge', *Settimane* 13 (1966), 135–60; for our region see Verhulst, 'Die Grundherrschaftsentwicklung im ostfränkischen Raum vom 8. bis 10. Jahrhundert. Grundzüge und Fragen aus westfränkischer Sicht', in W. Rösener (ed.), *Strukturen der Grundherrschaft im frühen Mittelalter* (Göttingen, 1989), pp. 29–46. For other recent work, adding detail but not altering the basic picture, see previous note.   [74] Staab, *Gesellschaft*, pp. 342–52.

[75] See Weidinger, 'Grundherrschaft des Kloster Fulda', pp. 251–4, on the estate at Hammelburg given by Charlemagne to Fulda in 777.

[76] Weidinger, 'Grundherrschaft des Kloster Fulda', esp. p. 258, in the course of a useful discussion of the problems of creating a manorial system, pp. 258–65.

charter evidence. Manors need to be understood as a particular form of economic organisation with a specific function, rather than as a universal model.

The charter evidence strongly suggests that in the Carolingian period lay estate structures were more conservative than those of church or king: most aristocratic land was cultivated by unfree dependants, who were consistently labelled *mancipia*.[77] The vocabulary was inherited, ultimately, from Roman law. These unfree dependants were treated in legal transactions as objects, given, received, bought and sold. In some charters *mancipia* were even thrown in along with buildings and tools in pertinence clauses; in others, they were listed by name (presumably to make it clear precisely which *mancipia* residing on a given estate were being given). To all intents and purposes they were a part of a given estate, making it economically viable; hence gifts of land were accompanied by gifts of the relevant *mancipia*. Female *mancipia* performed slightly different duties from male, characteristically including textile production. A sizable estate may have been worked by a hundred or more unfree dependants: when Otakar gave Fulda a third of his estates at Wackernheim and Saulheim, he also gave a third of the *mancipia*, and an appended document recorded forty-one names. The system of unfree labour practised by Otakar and his peers was not, however, one of classical slavery: the *mancipia* were not treated, simply, as sources of labour. They lived in family units focused on the conjugal couple, presumably to ensure the production of a new generation of dependant labourers. Otakar's *mancipia* at Wackernheim and Saulheim, the centres of his holdings where he held large quantities of land and could exercise direct control, would have been subject to far more direct and intense control than most *mancipia* – those who tended a small, isolated plot, residing there with their family and passing what surplus there was on to their lord, were coming close to being tied tenants. *Mancipia* were treated as humans rather than cattle: there are few hints in Carolingian law of slave-branding and the other dehumanising practices which are such a marked feature of the treatment of the classical slave. They might be subject to total economic and legal subjection, but they were also seen as moral actors in their own right. Their names indicate that they were

---

[77] For *mancipia* in these sources see Staab, *Gesellschaft*, pp. 331–42. For shifting systems of the exploitation of dependant labour in the early middle ages see Davies, 'On Servile Status'; H.-W. Goetz, 'Serfdom and the Beginnings of a 'Seigneurial System' in the Carolingian Period: A Survey of the Evidence', *EME* 2 (1993), 29–51 and P. Bonnassie, 'On the Survival and Extinction of the Slave Regime in Early Medieval Europe', in Bonnassie, *From Slavery to Feudalism in Southwestern Europe*, trans. J. Birrell (Cambridge, 1991), pp. 1–59; on the late Roman background, C. R. Whittaker, 'Circe's Pigs: From Slavery to Serfdom in the Roman World', *Slavery and Abolition* 8 (1987), 88–122.

considered a part of the *familia* of their lord.[78] Einhard's letters give vivid insight into the concerns of lords in their dealings with their unfree dependants: most centre around the contracting of marriages, and in particular marriages which involved free partners, mirroring the recurrent concern in contemporary legislation about such marriages. That the legal consequences of such marriages were a matter of recurrent concern must indicate that they were common, suggesting that there was no real social gulf between free and unfree. Even if we adopt a social, rather than a purely economic, definition of slavery, this cannot be described as a slave society.[79]

Manors were rare, as the type of intensive control upon which they rested was difficult to achieve. Creating a manor necessitated territorial control of a sizable and more or less discrete block of land, land of a type appropriate for large-scale cultivation – hence the concern of churches like Fulda to establish proprietorial rights over large blocks of land at Umstadt and Hünfeld. For most lay property, manorial organisation was simply out of the question precisely because of the phenomena of fragmentation and scattering: how could one create a manor out of a motley collection of land parcels? A trawl through the thousands of surviving charters produces just a handful of manors or parts of manors being given by the laity to Lorsch and Fulda: a tiny figure, even allowing for the problems of the evidence.[80] Clearances may have been important for both aristocracy and church in allowing a more intensive exploitation: here was one way to acquire a large block of cultivable land. This may be the kind of structure that was being created when Heimerich, son of Count Cancor, gave his father's foundation at Lorsch eight *mancipia* with 'all the *laboratum* of Herman' in Auerbach, an outlier of the *villa* of Bensheim.[81] It is the need for political control of a sizable block of land that helps explain the close link between gifts of fiscal land, the assertion of pro-

<hr/>

[78] On the humanisation of slaves see, in addition to works cited above, H. Hoffmann, 'Kirche und Sklaverei im frühen Mittelalter', *DA* 42 (1988), 1–47. For names as indicative of inclusion in the *familia*, see Le Jan-Hennebicque, 'Structures familiales', 317–20; C. I. Hammer, 'Servile Names and Seigneurial Organisation in Early Medieval Bavaria', *Studi Medievali* 36 (1995), 917–28; and in general Hammer, 'Family and *Familia* in Early Medieval Bavaria', in R. Wall *et al.* (eds.), *Family Forms in Historic Europe* (Cambridge, 1983), pp. 217–48.

[79] Einhard, letter 46 and cf. letter 60. G. Bois, *The Transformation of the Year 1000: The Village of Lournand from Antiquity to Feudalism*, trans. J. Birrell (Cambridge, 1992), suggests that the slave:free gulf remained real and therefore talks of a 'slave society' in the ninth and tenth centuries.

[80] See *CL*659, 697, 799, 936 and *UBF*237, 249, and Staab, *Gesellschaft*, pp. 342–52. Even if, as is likely, I have missed some instances among the 3,000 plus charters, we are dealing with less than 1% of the gifts: manors can scarcely have been common among the laity.

[81] *CL*1539. On the role of clearances cf. Weidinger, 'Grundherrschaft des Kloster Fulda', pp. 258–9; Verhulst, 'La génèse', 147, 149; and Theuws, 'Landed Property and Manorial Organisation'.

prietorial rights by king and church, and the establishment of manorial structures. Most lay landholding was organised along traditional lines precisely because of the organisational limitations inherent in its size and distribution – the tenure of fiscal and ecclesiastical land, as benefices, precarial grants or outright gift, was the main way by which laymen could gain control over manors.

Manors played an important role in provisioning the royal court and monastic houses. The greatest secular households were also of such a scale that it was worth establishing this style of estate. But most land was not organised in these complex structures, and remained a mass of tiny fragments, some worked by unfree labourers with family plots, some by tenants, some formed directly by its owners, at the lowest level of free society. The fragmentation of landholdings, which is so typical of the Carolingian period, has often been seen by previous historians as the end point of a process of subdivision due to generations of partible inheritance. Property holdings, on this model, were originally large, discrete blocks, which were either granted by the king or areas settled by pioneer forefathers; division between heirs created the fragmentation of the Carolingian evidence. To extrapolate back from a messy eighth-century reality to a hypothetical model of earlier simplicity is dangerous. Moreover, if we trace back documented dispersed holdings to original compact royal grants, subsequently subdivided, we are postulating a sixth-century kingship which owned vast, uninterrupted tracts of land, which is difficult to credit. It may make more sense to see the fragmentation of landholding in the Carolingian period as the result of the consolidation of property rights over individual holdings in the seventh and eighth centuries. No society is a helpless prisoner of inheritance custom, and the three families we began by investigating manipulated custom to safeguard familial interests. Investigation of the interplay between inheritance custom and social pressures towards the maintenance and reintegration of family holdings is difficult because we do not have sufficient detail about the estates of any one family over three or four generations. But the charters show that in the eighth and ninth centuries, fragmented and scattered landholdings were a constant structural phenomenon. Inheritance involved both carving up the totality of holdings, old and new, and the subdivision of particular pieces of long-standing family land. These patterns, of scattered land-parcels being constantly dispersed and agglomerated, meant that the exchange of land was one of the basic social actions. Hence the importance of transfers of rights over land in creating relationships and alliances, and not only in a constantly revolving cycle of inheritance – the charters make it clear that the sale, exchange and straightforward giving of land were regular occurrences. This society, and the family groups of which it consisted, were defined and maintained by a pattern of constant exchange.

VERTICAL INTEGRATION: SOCIAL STATUS

So far we have looked at familial structures, and the economic resources which were transmitted through these familial structures, as a means of understanding the elite's position within society. What we have not investigated are the ways in which the elite transformed its control of these resources into social power: that is, the ways in which this raw economic strength was translated into influence over the options open to, and the choices made by, those who controlled fewer resources. Nor have we looked at the ways in which the elite were able to construct a group identity that underwrote their claims to represent the locality. Therefore, we need to investigate the processes through which the ascription and consolidation of social status both transformed economic muscle into social influence, and dressed that economic muscle in clothes that demonstrated legitimacy, making an unequal social order appear natural. When we look at social status, whilst we will remain rooted in the middle Rhine, we must also look beyond, for the elite participated in a political culture which spread across most of western Europe, and expressed their power in the idiom provided by this culture.[82]

It is indubitable that the highest echelon of the elite can be described as an aristocracy: their economic power was based on inherited rights over land and people, thanks to which they enjoyed a virtual monopoly on the exercise of formal political power.[83] But beyond these raw social facts, the processes through which the aristocracy defined itself are more difficult to discern: there is no evidence in the charters, or in early medieval law-codes, of 'noble' or 'magnate' as an objective legal status, or of the aristocracy attempting to set itself up as a caste with different rights and duties from the remainder of society. The lack of a legal definition did not make this aristocracy weak or insecure – law is not a naive reflection of social reality, and legal barriers are most likely to be erected

---

[82] See Fouracre, 'Cultural Conformity and Social Conservatism'.

[83] On the problem of definition, see H.-W. Goetz, 'Nobilis'. Der Adel im Selbstverständnis der Karolingerzeit', *Vierteljahrsschrift für Sozial- und Wirtschaftsgeschichte* 70 (1983), 153–91; J. Martindale, 'The French Aristocracy in the Early Middle Ages: A Reappraisal', *P&P* 75 (1977), 5–45; and T. Zotz, 'Adel, Oberschicht, Freie', *ZGO* 125 (1977), 3–20. Usefully, recent scholarship has begun to stress the existence of different layers within the aristocracy: see e.g. H. K. Schulze, 'Reichsaristokratie, Stammesadel und fränkischer Freiheit', *Historische Zeitschrift* 227 (1978), 353–73; Airlie, 'The Aristocracy', esp. pp. 448–50; Le Jan-Hennebicque, 'Structures familiales'; Lauranson-Rosaz, *L'Auvergne et ses marges*.

at precisely that point in time when *de facto* dominance begins to be contested. Yet the lack of an objective guarantee of noble status had profound implications for the process by which the aristocracy defined and transmitted its power. In terms of legal definition or social identity, there were no fundamental divisions within the ranks of the property-owning free. In ideological terms the fundamental divide was that between the free and the unfree: it was this image which suffused legislation and defined the bounds of society. The image of the free Frank conflated the ownership of property, the ability to act at law, to bear weapons, hunt, and fight, and, through all of this, to perform royal service.[84] Hence when one courtier wished to denigrate his opponents and suggest that their behaviour was unbecoming, he had to compare them with slaves; as there was no identity resting on the opposition between aristocrat and non-aristocrat which he could mobilise, the courtier and historian Nithard had to draw on the traditional polarity of free:unfree. Similarly, the churchman Thegan condemned his *bête noire*, Archbishop Ebbo of Rheims, by drawing upon the distinction between free and unfree, which could be overcome by the legal act of manumission, and contrasting this legal barrier with the socially constructed one between noble and non-noble, for true nobility of behaviour could not be created by legal act, but only ingrained through descent and upbringing.[85]

As Thegan pointed out, in social fact if not in legal theory there were huge and growing differences between aristocrats and freeholders: these were differences in wealth and power, which were to a very great extent determined by birth. But both aristocrat and freeholder participated in a single culture. The identity of the free Frank encompassed a very broad section of society, and 'noble' was a largely subjective label given to some members of this group. It was not wholly subjective in that all observers would agree that the richest, most powerful free Franks were noble; but subjective to the extent that different observers would draw the cut-off point between aristocrat and freeholder at different points, informed by their different positions in the social continuum.[86] 'Nobility' was a moral distinction, a moral distinction which (as moral distinctions usually do) tended to reflect social status. To be 'noble' in this sense was to exercise social power in the proper manner. Thus groups like the well-to-do locals

---

[84] Cf. the comments *à propos* royal legislation in Lombard Italy of Wickham, *Early Medieval Italy: Central Power and Local Society, 400–1100* (London, 1981), p. 115.

[85] Nithard, *Historiae*, ed. P. Lauer, *Histoire des fils de Louis le Pieux* (Paris, 1926), II:3, p. 44, and see J. L. Nelson, 'Public Histories and Private History in the Work of Nithard', *Speculum* 60 (1985), 251–93 at 271–2. Thegan, *Gesta Hludovici*, c. 20, ed. E. Tremp, *MGH SRG* 64 (Hanover, 1995), p. 232.

[86] Cf. the earlier comments of D. Bullough, '*Europae Pater:* Charlemagne and his Achievement in the Light of Recent Scholarship', *English Historical Review* 85 (1970), 59–105 at 73–84.

who judged the boundaries of Fulda's estate at Hammelburg in 777 were called 'noble men', underlining their legal competence and the validity of their testimony; *viri nobiles* was here the equivalent of a label like *boni homines*, pointing to truthfulness and good character.[87] Meaning was dependent on context: the men who were 'noble' to a Fulda scribe in 777 would have been *minores* to a courtier or ecclesiastic writing narrative history. The titles used in charters and letters rested on a similar set of templates which again essentially reflect personal and ultimately moral qualities. Charters use the term *illustris*, whilst Einhard's letters use a complex hierarchy of compliments encompassing *illustris*, *clarissimus* and *excellentissimus*: all these terms are inherited from the Roman past but have lost their objective anchoring in a defined hierarchy and become subjective ascriptions.[88] We might wonder whether this literary etiquette had physical and material correlates in norms of greeting, precedence on public occasions, dress and deportment – but in the current state of research we simply do not know. Although terms like *nobilis* were most often used about the aristocracy, they were not exclusive to them precisely because they referred to personal qualities. They were thus rarely used in the plural to denote a class. Rather, when commentators talked about the collective action of the aristocracy as a political force, they normally used a more neutral vocabulary of relative social observation: of *proceres*, *potentes*, *maiores* and *primores*. The modern historian's sense of the aristocracy rests on similar concerns of political influence, political influence allowed by wealth but reflected by collective involvement in political action.[89]

The pre-eminence of the highest echelon of the elite was defined by their supra-regional influence. A man like Cancor doubtless got his way in the middle Rhine when he wanted it, but his political strategy was pursued not in the locality but on a more distant stage through alliance with other aristocrats – many of them kin – from other regions. In the absence of any routine method of maintaining direct local control other than by physical presence, the day-to-day running of the localities was thus left to a lower tier of the elite. These were the men who were the backbone of the charter evidence, whom we might want to term a gentry.[90] Their status was advertised in a code suffused by the social iden-

---

[87] Hammelburg: see *UBF*86. On the meaning of *boni homines* and similar terms, see Nehlsen-von Stryck, *Die boni homines*, convincingly showing the lack of a fixed legal definition, but the common concerns leading to the frequent adoption of the vocabulary of status and goodness.

[88] See K. Brunner, 'Das fränkische Fürstentitel im neunten und zehnten Jahrhundert', in H. Wolfram (ed.), *Intitulatio II: Lateinische Herrscher- und Fürstentitel im neunten und zehnten Jahrhundert*, *MIÖG* Ergänzungsband 23 (Vienna, 1973), pp. 179–340, esp. pp. 179–92.

[89] As was first pointed out by Martindale, 'The French Aristocracy'.

[90] The term is floated by Bullough, '*Europae Pater*', pp. 73–84.

tity of the free Frank and the example of their social betters; it is visible both in use of titles like *nobilis* in charters and epitaphs, and in the foundation of residences like that of Hraban's family at Hofheim. This was a broad group, with its own internal gradations which are difficult to recover from the charter evidence: frequent charter-witnessing, and a geographical range which suggests activity on a regional level rather than in one or two settlements, are useful indices. Below them, we have a peasantry, free owner-cultivators, who are just visible in the charters, occasionally witnessing or giving land. These men had a very local social horizon, restricted to a handful of settlements.[91] As we descend through the peasantry to those who can barely scrape together a living from a tiny plot, the division between free and unfree which was so clear to legislators begins to break down. Indeed, in economic terms the better off unfree may have been more prosperous than the poorest free. At this level legal and ideological distinctions naturally blurred: there were free tenants, and many must have combined the cultivation of parcels of inherited land with wage labour and small-scale tenancy.

VERTICAL INTEGRATION: KINSHIP AND LORDSHIP

We must also factor in the possibility of social mobility – not just across generations but also across an individual's life cycle. This is above all the case within the elite, where good fortune and patronage might enable a member of the regional elite to cut a figure on a supra-regional stage.[92] The image of a relatively open elite, whose members moved upwards or downwards under their own steam, is essentially accurate, but there were also vertical bonds linking people at different levels, bonds which could aid upward mobility by supplying patrons, or stabilise one's position by creating a support system of clients and allies. First and foremost was kinship. Practical kinship, determined by the immediate family group and

---

[91] The charter evidence makes clear the existence of a critical mass of owner-cultivators who can safely be labelled a peasantry. However, theories about legal identity have proved so pervasive that even the derivation of this class has been much debated, some scholars claiming that, as the nobility was the only truly free class in ancient Germanic society, so the free property-owners of the charters must all be impoverished nobles. The circularity of the claim, thus stated, is clear. For historiography and discussion see F. Staab, 'A Reconsideration of the Ancestry of Modern Political Liberty: The Problem of the so-called "King's Freedmen" (Königsfreie)', *Viator* 11 (1980), 52–69; H. K. Schulze, 'Rodungsfreiheit und Königsfreiheit. Zu Genesis und Kritik neuer verfassungsgeschichtlicher Theorien', *Historische Zeitschrift* 219 (1974), 529–550; R. Sprandel, 'Grundherrliche Adel, rechtsständige Freiheit und Königszins. Untersuchungen über die alemannischen Verhältnis in der Karolingerzeit', *DA* 19 (1963), 1–29.
[92] On men raised from the dust, see S. Airlie, 'Bonds of Power and Bonds of Association in the Court Circle of Louis the Pious', in P. Godman and R. Collins (eds.), *Charlemagne's Heir: New Perspectives on the Reign of Louis the Pious (814–40)* (Oxford, 1990), pp. 191–204.

bound together by inheritance, was largely a 'horizontal' factor, binding together a group whose members stood mostly on the same social stratum as one another. Official kin, however, could include powerful uncles and impoverished cousins, and thus this wider kin group could aid vertical integration and mobility. This was not only a question of local figures needing powerful patrons at court; Imperial aristocrats needed local power bases to fall back on in times of crisis, and to supply them with the followers they needed. The significance of kinship in mobilising support is most vividly illustrated in a pair of Einhard's letters, in which, late in 833, he takes up the case of one Frumold. Einhard asks that two of his contacts at court intervene on Frumold's behalf:

To a certain U.
Frumold, son of Count N., whose sister is the wife of N., has a rather small benefice in Burgundy, in the Geneva region, where his father was count, but he is suffering from infirmity rather than old age, being troubled with a chronic case of severe gout, and is afraid that he will lose the benefices unless you kindly come to his aid, because in consequence of the infirmity that weighs upon him he cannot appear at court . . .

To a Count.
Frumold, the lord's vassal and brother of Count N.'s wife, wanted to come to the lord emperor but was troubled by gout and old age and was not able [to travel] because of his illness. As soon as he can, he will come to his duty. In the meantime, he requests that he be permitted to hold his benefice, the one in Burgundy that the lord emperor Charles gave him, until he [can] appear before him and commend himself into his hands. It also seems right and useful to me that this be done just as he wished, because he is a good and prudent man and of good reputation among his neighbours. You would be doing the right thing, if you could consider helping him in this business.[93]

Frumold was a pathetic figure, who must have dreamed of a countship and a glittering political career in his youth, but ended up a backwoodsman. Einhard was evidently wary of playing too much on Frumold's age, and instead stressed his usefulness as a royal vassal – his praise of his good character and reputation takes us to the very heart of Carolingian society. Nonetheless, look at how his kinship network, so assiduously rehearsed by Einhard, was mobilised in his defence, at a time when the deposition of Louis the Pious and his replacement by Lothar threatened disruption and the redistribution of benefices. Frumold, in spite of his old age and gout, still had a political position because of his kin, and this prevented further social descent. Frumold's kinsmen, and those patrons who helped him now, could, in their turn, expect a warm welcome in Burgundy

---

[93] Letter 27, 28.

when they needed it, and useful support from Frumold and those neighbours who held him in such high esteem.

These vertical bonds of patronage encompassed relationships involving personal lordship as well as kinship. Lordship is a concept which is difficult to discuss as the charters rarely mention it: it was an unacknowledged fact. In this period, lordship was a relationship defined by mutual ties between two people, most likely expressed through a legal ritual which invoked a set of norms, certainly not a contractual relationship involving written declarations of rights and dues. At the outset, we must be clear about the fact that there was nothing dishonourable in a free man entering into a relationship of personal lordship; it did not diminish his personal freedom, or weaken his hold on inherited land. When ninth-century kings enjoined that every free man should have a lord – and should be free to chose that lord – they were acknowledging the reality of a society which had been shaped by personal patronage for centuries, not resigning themselves to the decline of the class of free landowners.[94] Throughout the Carolingian period lordship remained a purely personal relationship, not one in which the possession or tenancy of land played a *defining* role. Lords did sometimes grant out or give land to their followers, but there is no evidence in the local charter or letter evidence that such grants or gifts were constitutive: they did not create relationships of lordship between the two parties. Throughout the period this was a society in which there were very, very few free tenants, and in which landownership was necessary for social or political significance; there is certainly no sign of feudal tenure replacing landholding as the basic tenurial form even in the tenth century.[95] The charter evidence does not show large numbers of vassals whose status was dependent on the tenure of benefices. Laymen did, on occasion, grant out estates *in beneficium* in the eighth and ninth centuries, but the instances are rare, and show benefices being used as ways to build up the local muscle of existing clients, rather than to endow followers as they entered an individual's lordship. The best-documented case is that of a Count Baugolf, active from the 750s to the early 770s, who had granted an estate *in beneficium* to one Waning. Waning – who is never called a vassal – was a local landowner, active in concert with his master, and the grant simply cements this relationship.[96] Although the charters are overwhelmingly concerned with gifts of land

---

[94] See *MGH Cap.* II, no. 204, iii:2, p. 71 (Meersen, 847) and cf. F. L. Ganshof, *Feudalism* (London, 1953), pp. 30–1.

[95] Cf. S. Reynolds, *Fiefs and Vassals: The Medieval Evidence Reconsidered* (London, 1993).

[96] For Waning's *beneficium*, *UBF* 53; for his career, Staab, *Gesellschaft*, pp. 408–9. Ganshof, *Feudalism*, p. 12, gives parallel cases from the early eighth century, judiciously refusing to see in them early instances of feudal lordship.

to the church, the fact that they give no hint at widespread grants of land *in beneficium* must suggest that it was not a common practice – charters tend to give additional information about the history of a piece of land (which is how we know of Waning's *beneficium*) and supply plentiful circumstantial information, but the grants of benefices that are documented in the thousands of charters can be counted on the fingers of one hand. Indeed, in the charters the phrase *in beneficium* was used primarily about the tenure of ecclesiastical land, but without much technical precision: it is virtually a synonym for *in precarium*, both phrases pointing to the granting out of land in relatively light tenures which did not specify labour services on the lord's land, with *beneficium* perhaps also carrying overtones of reward for support.[97] The titles used to refer to those who held benefices were similarly untechnical, suggesting that we are dealing with relationships of patronage and mutual obligation which were not defined by any general, legal template. *Vassus*, for example, was simply not used in the local charters before the tenth century (although it was used in Einhard's letters), whilst even holders of royal benefices were more often called *fideles* than *vassi*.[98]

By the second half of the eighth century, tenure of royal or ecclesiastical land in benefice was widespread, and an important feature of the relationship between king and the powerful.[99] Otakar is once again the best example from the middle Rhenish evidence, although he is far from alone. And benefices like Otakar's were not *post hoc* rewards for particular actions. Einhard's letters are again the best entry point into the world of benefice-holding. Einhard presented loyalty and good service as reasons for the granting of benefices. There are hints that the granting of a benefice could be constitutive of service and took place as one entered a particular king's service: hence Einhard's appeal to Louis the German 'on behalf of an intimate friend of mine . . . that you may deign to receive him, and when he has commended himself to your protection give him

---

[97] See already Dubled, 'La notion de propriété', and cf. more recently Reynolds, *Fiefs and Vassals*, drawing on E. Lesne, 'Les diverses acceptions du terme 'beneficium' du VIIIe au IXe siècle', *Revue historique du droit français et étranger* 3 (1924), 5–56. Lesne's finding, that *beneficium* simply denotes a life-tenure, is good for the tenth century, too, in the middle Rhine.

[98] *Vassus* in local charters: CDF651, 683, 695, 710.3, 724. In Einhard's letters *vassus* is used more often of *vassi dominici* than of aristocratic retainers, but for the latter sense see letters no. 62, 63 (but cf. *fidelis* in 55, 60, 62 and *homo* in 7, 23, 42, 51, 55). Royal benefice-holders as *fideles*, rather than *vassi*: MGH DCharlemagne 127, MGH DLouis the German 94, and see above all C. E. Odegaard, *Vassi and Fideles in the Carolingian Empire* (Cambridge, MA, 1945). Cf. Ganshof, *Feudalism*, pp. 21–2.

[99] On the origins of this style of grant, see H. Wolfram, 'Karl Martell und das fränkische Lehenswesen. Aufnahme eines Nichtbestandes', in J. Jarnut et al. (eds.), *Karl Martell in seiner Zeit*, Beihefte der Francia 37 (Sigmaringen, 1994), pp. 61–77; I. Wood, 'Teutsind, Witlaic and the History of Merovingian *Precaria*', in W. Davies and P. Fouracre (eds.), *Property and Power in the Early Middle Ages* (Cambridge, 1995), pp. 31–52.

some consolation from the benefices which are known to be free and open here in our neighbourhood. For he is noble and faithful, and well trained for good service in any kind of duty which may be entrusted to him. For he served your grandfather and your father faithfully and energetically, and is ready to do the same by you if God wills . . .'[100] That is, the granting of benefices was a central part of entry into royal lordship amongst the political elite – hence Einhard's fears about the loss of his own benefices in 833, when Louis the German was effective ruler of his area but Einhard was unable to meet Louis and perform commendation. The letters make it clear that benefices were sought after, and one had to be careful not to give rulers any reason to seize them and give them to new favourites.[101]

The point made again and again by Einhard's letters was that it was not just the Imperial aristocracy who received benefices: efficient lords were able to intercede and get benefices for their clients, men who could work usefully for kings in the localities. These were the *vassi dominici* of the narrative and normative sources: locally based but bound into royal lordship and royal service thanks to a lucrative grant. The capitularies make it clear that *vassi dominici* were expected to perform a varied and extensive range of services for the king, most of them locally – the kind of local usefulness that Einhard played on in the case of Frumold.[102] But we should remember that in these very narrative and normative sources the term *vassus* is used to denote a particular class of royal servant, somewhat similar in its organisation and function to lay property, and that royal patronage was a factor of the utmost importance in the constitution of social hierarchies in the localities. Land that could be given by the king, whether technically fiscal or ecclesiastical, was a strategic resource whose distribution created political power.

These were practices of royal service. Aristocratic lordship is painfully under-researched, but it need not have taken the same forms as royal lordship, not least as aristocrats simply did not have the resources to grant out large amounts of land to followers. The successful aristocrat could tap into these royal and ecclesiastical resources through his access to the

---

[100] Letter 34. Cf. also letter 39. But in letters 1 and 28, men have already performed commendation and entered a king's lordship and still seek benefices.

[101] Letter 25. Cf. letter 39: 'I know of the wicked desires and boundless greed of certain people who have no regard for the injury done to their neighbours in cases where they have the power to satisfy their own most grasping greed.'

[102] F. L. Ganshof, 'Benefice and Vassalage in the Age of Charlemagne', *Cambridge Historical Journal* 6 (1939), 147–75, and more recently W. Kienast, *Die fränkische Vasallität von den Hausmeiern bis zu Ludwig dem Kind und Karl dem Einfältigen* (Frankfurt, 1990) collect the references, but their attempts to seek a single legal template to explain the variety of contexts in which we find benefices, and the heterogeneity of terms used to describe benefice-holders, are unconvincing.

court. Again, Einhard's letters are the best source as they allow insight into the relationships between Einhard and his local followers. Relationships here varied in form and function. Einhard wrote letters for a wide circle of clients, some of whom were not under his formal lordship. At the heart of Einhard's lordship stood his *familia*, those who were attendant upon him for at least part of the year. Within this group, unfree dependants might acquire an important function. Carolingian legislation is much concerned with the unfree priests, who would fall into this category; a secular equivalent comes in the case of Hraban's brother, Guntram, whose household is headed by an unfree dependant named Camareri, literally chamberlain.[103] Other household officials were, of course, free men. But the *familia* was a social unit which transcended the legal boundaries between free and unfree: another letter concerns the case of a free vassal who wishes to marry an unfree female member of his lord's *familia*.[104] Other household members, whilst not dedicated to a particular function such as chamberlain, had a more or less full-time job active in their lord's service: two letters concern the activities of some of his men, led by Willebald whom Einhard styles 'my faithful priest', who travelled 'to receive our dues . . . both fully and in good money', and also to procure a donkey load of wax, on the feast of St Bavo, the patron of an abbey held by Einhard in Ghent.[105] But not all of Einhard's clients were household retainers. Some may have held benefices of land belonging to Einhard's abbeys (Carolingian legislation laid down that such benefices were held on payment of a nominal money rent) and others may have been patrons of the abbeys who had made donations and received back their land as a precarial grant (which likewise attracted nominal rents payable on patronal feast days); others still may have been free men who simply had entered into the personal lordship of Einhard, without any tenancy or property being involved (by the tenth century Einhard's foundation at Seligenstadt had seventy such dependants).[106] Given the charter evidence for widespread, if often small-scale, landownership, there is no reason to presume that there were large numbers of landless retainers dependent upon royal benefices or lordly favour for their upkeep. Perhaps the bulk of a lord's household were young men receiving an education in matters political and martial; the commendation of adolescent males into the household of a lord and patron (the king

---

[103] *CDF*534 and see Staab, *Gesellschaft*, pp. 333–6 on dependants and *familia*, particularly p. 335 on Guntram's following.   [104] Letter 46 and see Staab, *Gesellschaft*, pp. 333–6.   [105] Letters 55, 56.

[106] See G. Constable, '*Nona et decima*: An Aspect of the Carolingian Economy', *Speculum* 35 (1960), 224–50, for the legal background. On Seligenstadt, see Schulze, 'Mitteilungen aus Darmstädter Handschriften'.

for the most well-born) is well documented.[107] One letter of Einhard's sheds tantalising light on the generational structure of his following:

> To my *fidelis* . . .
> I do not doubt that you remember how you committed yourself and yours to me . . . Be it known, therefore, that that *vassus* of ours and your daughter desire . . . with your consent to obtain each other as man and wife . . . It seems suitable to the mother and brother and all the relatives [of the vassal], if it is your pleasure, that the marriage be contracted. I not only wish that it be confirmed, but if you give me authority to carry it through, I desire in honourable fashion as quickly as may be, to provide worthily both in the matter of benefices and of other things. Moreover this same vassal will give the dowry and is increasing the gifts . . .[108]

Here we meet a client who had evidently entered Einhard's service in the relatively distant past and did not reside in his lord's household – Einhard styles him a *fidelis*. A second man, a vassal who was a part of the household, on contracting a marriage, was to receive benefices, and presumably then leave the household. That is, youths spent their adolescence in a lord's household in his direct service but upon marriage left it, although remaining under his personal lordship. The young vassal in the letter evidently came from a landowning family – hence he could provide a dowry. Einhard, as lord, brokered the marriage, obtaining consent from both kin groups, and then procured the young man a benefice, placing him in royal service in the process. The marriage within Einhard's following helps cement the ties of horizontal solidarity. Tenancy of (normally royal) land was important not to feed Einhard's vassal, who evidently had inherited property, but to give him the additional resources which allowed him to embark on a political career.

The charters do show aristocrats giving land to their followers. The fact that, in the surviving charters, outright gifts of land by lords to their men are far more common than grants of benefices cannot be explained away as a distortion – there is no inherent reason why we are more likely to hear about gifts between lord and man than tenancies in the surviving evidence. (We may also suppose that gifts of moveables – weapons or horses, say – were the normal currency of lordship, but they are difficult

---

[107] On this practice see C. Dette, 'Kinder und Jugendliche in der Adelsgesellschaft des frühen Mittelalters', *Archiv für Kulturgeschichte* 76 (1994), 1–34; D. Bullough, '*Alboinus deliciosus Karoli regis*: Alcuin of York and the Shaping of the Early Carolingian Court', in L. Fenske *et al.* (eds.), *Institutionen, Kultur und Gesellschaft im Mittelalter. Festschrift J. Fleckenstein* (Sigmaringen, 1984), pp. 73–92; M. Innes, '*A Place of Discipline*: Aristocratic Youth and Carolingian Courts', in C. Cubitt (ed.), *Court Culture in the Early Middle Ages*, (forthcoming). Cf. also T. Charles-Edwards, 'The Distinction between Land and Moveable Wealth in Anglo-Saxon England', in P. H. Sawyer (ed.), *Early Medieval Settlement* (London, 1979), pp. 97–104.   [108] Letter 62.

to trace in the surviving evidence). Lordship was a personal, social relationship which varied in its form and implications: we simply cannot see
a legal blueprint which subsumes all lordship. That it was predominantly
informed by social, rather than legal, norms is underlined by the charters
which give some insight into the practice of lordship. Thus Heimerich
gave one Herman rights over land which the latter was active in clearing
and which was eventually given to Lorsch for both men's souls; in the
early ninth century Engilhelm made gifts for the souls of two successive
lords, Counts Rupert and Werner; in 834 Hraban's brother Guntram
made a gift for the soul of his kinsman and erstwhile lord Count Rupert;
in 837 Guntram himself had a retainer, Batdagis, make a gift for his soul;
c. 940 Gerold and his wife made a gift for the souls of their *parentes* and
their lord, Count Conrad. Lordship and kinship, moreover, overlapped
and reinforced one another: these really were relationships of sociable
patronage, not legal obligation. Guntram and Engilhelm, for example,
were both kinsmen of their lord, Count Rupert. Einhard's letters supply
further examples, such as the vassal Agantheo, 'my relative who has been
for some time in my service'.[109] In that kinship was an important vertical bond which one could manipulate to find a powerful patron, and in
that local lordship seems to have rested on the *familiaritas* engendered by
the upbringing of adolescent males in a patron's household, this overlap
between kinship and lordship is scarcely unexpected. Nonetheless, it is
important. It is, after all, the language of kinship which is dominant in
the Carolingian period: fictive or spiritual kinship and bonds of *familiaritas* cement relationships of dependence or alliance where there is no
biological kinship. Lordship and patronage actualised bonds, but they
were often presented in familial terms. Indeed, it is only in the tenth
century that lordship becomes more visible in the local evidence, particularly the charters. Whilst in Carolingian charters, it is clear that patterns
of witnessing reflect lordship and patronage relationships, it is only in the
late ninth and tenth centuries that such relationships are explicitly
acknowledged, and words like *domnus* and *senior* become more common
in the charters. By the middle of the tenth century *vassus* was a familiar
term, a catch-all for those in the service of the greatest aristocrats; by the
first half of the eleventh century, Fulda scribes at least were beginning to
specify in formal, written terms precisely what military service was owed
by the abbey's vassals in respect of their tenures.[110] Even then, it may be
that the structures of lordship were relatively constant, resting on kinship

---

[109] See *CL*1539, 219, 271, 534, 222, 532, Einhard, letter 63 (and cf. nos. 31–2, 43).
[110] See e.g. *CL*532, *CDF*651, 683, 695, 710.3, 724, 740, 749. Cf. R. LeJan-Hennebicque, 'Domnus,
illuster, nobilissimus: les mutations de pouvoir au Xe siècle', in M. Sot (ed.), *Haut Moyen Age:
Festschrift P. Riché* (Paris, 1991), pp. 439–48.

and *familiaritas*; there is still no sign of territorially or tenurially based lordship in the charter evidence. But lordship has an increasingly high social profile: there is a shift from the presentation of relationship in terms of kinship towards its presentation in terms of lordship.

THE RELATIONSHIP BETWEEN LAND AND POWER

Inevitably, as the overwhelming proportion of wealth came from the control of land, the ownership of land was central to the creation of power in this society. But land did not lead, simply and automatically, to power: control of land was necessary to fund a lifestyle and to enter the social spheres in which one could create the personal contacts which allowed one to exercise power. By the eighth century, the exchange of land – normally by outright gift – was a central tactic in the creation of power networks. One gave land to favoured churches, key clients and followers; marriage, likewise, involved gifts of land. Land was a medium with which politically important relationships were created, as well as the basic economic resource. Carolingian society was based on the creation and manipulation of these types of relationships: this was not yet a world of *territorial* power, of rights of command over land that one did not own. It was a world of tenurial fragmentation, where power over land was a direct consequence of the possession of that land. As such, it contrasts with the society which emerges so clearly from the twelfth-century documentation. By 1200 power rested on lordship rather than property, on the ability to extract rent and services from territories, and on the control of spatially-defined blocks over which one was lord. 'Justice was the ordinary name of power.'[111] In early medieval society, territorial power of this type was rare; lordship over men was not combined with lordship over space. One implication of the centrality of possession of land, together with tenurial fragmentation and profound continuities in social status, was that power was created and expressed through personal relationship: it was defined socially, in terms of one's ability to mobilise allies and followers, rather than legally, in terms of justice.

---

[111] P. Anderson, *Passages from Antiquity to Feudalism* (London, 1974), p. 153.

4

LOCAL POWER: COLLECTIVE ACTION, CONFLICT AND CONSENSUS

PATTERNS OF PUBLIC ACTION

The charter evidence allows us to investigate the relationships between those who exercised political power and the localities they ruled.[1] The transactions recorded in the charters involved not only the transfer of rights over land, but also the definition of relationships between people. In that charters also list a supporting cast of those who witnessed and guaranteed the legitimacy of the transactions they record, they illuminate power relations between the principal actors and the supporting cast. They also supply information about stages and performances: they tell us where and when the public meetings were held, and supply identities for those who presided over, and recorded, these performances.[2] That is, in the charters we can clearly see structured patterns of collective action. In what follows, we will first investigate the stages on which transactions took place, and the relationship between public meetings and the physical and social structure of rural and urban settlement. We will then move on to look at the legal traditions which informed the conduct of these meetings, in particular focusing on the scribes to whom we owe our surviving written records. Next, we will plot the activities of those who sought to rule the localities, uncovering the basis of their power. Finally, we will analyse the relationship between local structures of public action and the initiatives of kings and aristocrats, particularly in the crucial areas of law and violence.

Charter scribes chose to present the transactions they recorded as public actions. Deeds were 'enacted publicly'; cases were heard in 'public' meetings; places at which such meetings were held were styled 'public *villa*', 'public *vicus*', 'public city' or simply 'public place'. Local collective

---

[1] I examine the relationship between personal presence, place and power in 'Space, Place and Power in Carolingian Society: A Microcosm', in M. De Jong and F. Theuws (eds.), *Topographies of Power in the Early Middle Ages* (Leiden, Boston and Cologne, forthcoming).

[2] Cf. S. Humphreys, 'Social Relations on Stage: Witnesses in Classical Athens', *History and Anthropology* 1 (1985), 313–69.

action was represented as 'public' because it took place on agreed stages which ensured its visibility to a watching public. This sense of the 'public' was not fixed, or definable in narrowly legal terms. The notion of public action had deep roots in early medieval political culture. The formulae used by middle Rhenish charter scribes ultimately derived from formularies – manuals of models – put together to the west, in Gaul, during the Merovingian period. These models linked the 'public' to city institutions and formal legal procedures which had survived from the late Roman period.[3] By the eighth and ninth centuries, when such formal continuity was problematical, invocation of the public came to signal local knowledge of, and consent to, potentially controversial transactions: sales, marriages, changes in the ownership of slaves.[4] That is, despite its roots in late Roman legal practice, the Carolingian sense of the public which we are investigating was not defined by formal institutions or procedures. Rather, it rested on a sense of visibility and access informed by local collective action. Public action was what was not secret, hidden, or fraudulent; transparency and accessibility granted legitimacy.[5] Patterns of collective social action and public meetings filled the void left by the atrophy of late Roman institutional and procedural regulation of legal action which had ensured the legitimacy of transactions.[6] In that by the Carolingian period, public action was open, manifest and consensual, this was 'representative publicness', a sphere of action distinct from – and mediating between – the household and the royal court.[7]

CITIES, MONASTERIES AND COLLECTIVE ACTION

'Representative publicness' was not defined by formal rules, but rested on social patterns. In the charters from the eighth- and ninth-century middle Rhine, there was a clear hierarchy of places for such public action. Some

---

[3] For example: *Formulae Andecavenses* nos. 1, 32, 48 (pp. 4, 15, 21); *Turonenses* 2, 3, 20, 27, 28 (pp. 136, 137, 146, 147–8, 151); *Bituricenses* nos.3, 7, 15c (pp. 169, 171, 176); *Cartae Senonenses* Appendix 1b, 1c (p. 209); *Marculfi* II.17, II.38 (pp. 86, 98). (Here and hereafter all formularies cited from *MGH Formulae Merowingici et Karolini aevi*, ed. K. Zeumer (Hanover, 1886)).

[4] For the legal frameworks see H. Siems, *Handel und Wücher im Spiegel frühmittelalterlicher Rechtsquellen*, Schriften der MGH 35 (Hanover, 1992), pp. 60–108, and P. L. Reynolds, *Marriage in the Western Church: The Christianisation of Marriage during the Patristic and Early Medieval Periods* (Leiden, New York and Cologne, 1994), pp. 386–412. For specific cases from the formularies see (e.g.) *Augienses Collectio A* nos. 14, 15, 18 (pp. 345, 345, 346); *B* nos. 1, 2, 6 (pp. 347–8, 347–8, 351–2); *Collectio Sangallensi* nos. 8, 9, 17, 21 (pp. 401–2, 402–3, 406, 407–8); *Bituricenses* no. 15 (pp. 174–5).

[5] Cf. (e.g.) *Formulae Arvernenses* no. 3 (p. 30); *Turonenses Addimenta* no. 1 (p. 159); *Cartae Senonenses* no. 9 (p. 189), *Extravagentes* no. 23 (p. 547). See also Bisson, 'The "Feudal" Revolution', 12.

[6] Cf. P. Classen, 'Fortleben und Wandel spätrömischen Urkundenwesen im frühen Mittelalter', in Classen (ed.), *Recht und Schrift im Mittelalter*, VF 23 (Sigmaringen, 1977), pp. 13–54, esp. pp. 50–4.

[7] In the sense of J. Habermas, *The Structural Transformation of the Public Sphere: An Inquiry into a Category of Bourgeois Society*, trans. T. Berger (London, 1989), esp. pp. 1–13.

of these stages were seen as 'public places' in their own right, places which were by definition visible in the eyes of the community. In the eighth century, it was the cities of the middle Rhine which were the favoured places at which important property transactions were made. Worms and Mainz were each consistently styled a 'public city'. There is, however, a long-established interpretation, deeply embedded in the scholarship, which holds that the label 'public', particularly when used in royal charters, indicated royal ownership of the place in question.[8] Yet neither Worms nor Mainz were wholly owned by the king, and identical phrases were used about a range of other places where royal interests were far from dominant.[9] In fact, the practice of labelling certain places as 'public' had its origins in local scribal traditions and cannot be reduced to an index of royal interest. No transmitted Merovingian royal charter described its place of redaction as 'public', but from the seventh century, non-royal documents did refer to some places (most unconnected with the king) as public, and this usage was adopted by the royal chancery immediately upon Pippin's accession to the throne.[10] Thus scribes of royal charters, when they called Worms a 'public city', were drawing on an older, local sense of representative publicness which legitimated the status of particular places as important stages for legal action. Doubtless royal residence and interests in Worms heightened this sense of the city as a public place, but it did not call it into being. Rather, Mainz and Worms were places where public actions habitually took place, as the interchangeability of the formulae 'enacted in the public city' and 'enacted publicly in the city' shows.[11]

Patterns of legal action evident in the charters show that here formu-

---

[8] See the often-cited classic statement, F. Prinz, 'Herzog und Adel in Agilulfingischen Bayern. Herzogsgut und Konsensschenkungen vor 788', *Zeitschrift für bayerische Landesgeschichte* 25 (1962), pp. 283–301, esp. p. 299, n. 20. For Worms see P. Classen, 'Bemerkungen zur Pfalzenforschung am Mittelrhein', in *Deutsche Königspfalzen. Beiträge zu ihrer historischen und archaeologische Erforschung* I, VMPIG 11 (Göttingen, 1963), pp. 75–96. R. Kraft, *Das Reichsgut im Wormsgau*, Quellen und Forschungen zur Hessischen Geschichte 16 (Darmstadt, 1934) already linked the phrase 'public city' to the alleged royal ownership, e.g. at p. 118.

[9] By the end of the ninth century Murbach was the principal landowner in Worms, whilst the charters show significant non-royal lay holdings: see n. 21 below for further bibliography. For Mainz, see n. 11 below. For parallels see the cases of Lorsch and Dienheim below, n. 29, 30.

[10] See e.g. Wampach, *Echternach*, 8, 14, 15, 17, 22, 25, 26; *MGH DPippin* 2, 4 and so on. Similarly, whilst Gregory of Tours did not describe places as being 'public', both Jonas of Bobbio's *Life of Columbanus* and (following Jonas) 'Fredegar' did: see J. M. Wallace-Hadrill, *The Fourth Book of the Chronicle of Fredegar with its Continuations* (Oxford, 1960), IV:36, p. 24, Conts. 36, p. 104 with n. 1 (with a 'fiscalist' interpretation).

[11] Mainz: the evidence is conveniently assembled in *Mainzer Urkundenbuch*, ed. M. Stimming, Arbeiten der historischen Kommission für den Volkstaat Hessen 4 (Darmstadt, 1932). Classen 'Pfalzenforschung', pp. 80–2 suggests that the Mainz evidence is grammatically confused and exceptional. *Pace* Kraft, *Das Reichsgut im Wormsgau*, pp. 118, 200–14, the Fulda charters seem to me to make it inconceivable that property in Carolingian Mainz was overwhelmingly owned by the king, or originated from recent royal grants.

lae reflected social practice. The evidence is richest for Mainz, thanks to the close links between the city and the circle of Boniface. In the eighth century, Mainz was the place where locals went to give, buy or exchange land, and to have the charters confirming these transactions written up and witnessed by the great and good. Members of the local elite – the families of Hraban Maur and Otakar, for example – owned town houses in Mainz.[12] The vast number of urban churches underline the city's role as a regional centre. The numerous churches within the city were the foundations of the local elite, and their dedication to political saints from other regions like St Lambert, St Emmeram or St Bilihildis reflected the extensive contacts that radiated from the city.[13] Mainz was thus the focus for the local elite, and the gateway between the region and the rest of the Frankish world.

Given this regional significance, and its location on the Rhine, it was only natural that Mainz likewise served as the centre of long-distance exchange, when regularised long-distance exchange took off in the seventh century. Trade down the Rhine to Dorestad, the valve linking Mainz's regional hinterland into an exchange network encompassing the North Sea littoral, was largely conducted by Frisian middlemen: in the late ninth century the trading area within Mainz, which lay along the bank of the Rhine, was known as the 'Frisian quarter'. Here, at some point in the half-century centred on 700, the old Roman wall of the city was dismantled and the land divided into a series of long strips, stretching around 25 m down to the Rhine. These strips were served by a road which ran parallel to the river, the *via communis*, and their owners each paid a *cens*: here were warehouses and workshops, like the *fabrica* owned by one of the young Hraban's kin.[14] The archaeology makes it clear that at the heart of this economic activity was the manufacture and exchange of high-status metalwork used in conspicuous display.[15] However, long-distance

---

[12] See above, pp. 63, 67. Note also *UBF2* for an influential local buying a townhouse from Bishop Lull, paying with gold and horses. On aristocratic interests in Mainz see L. Falck, *Mainz im frühen und hohen Mittelalter (Mitte 5. Jht. bis 1244)* (Düsseldorf, 1972) [vol. II of A. P. Brück and L. Falck (eds.), *Geschichte der Stadt Mainz*], pp. 13–17, 21–2, in particular noting the documentary and archaeological evidence for fortified aristocratic residences; also Staab, *Gesellschaft*, pp. 122–32.

[13] Churches in Mainz: H. Büttner, 'Mainz im Mittelalter: Gestalten und Probleme', in Büttner, *Mittelrhein und Hessen. Nachgelassene Studien*, ed. A. Gerlich, Geschichtliche Landeskunde 33 (Stuttgart, 1989), pp. 1–50 at pp. 12–13.

[14] See E. Wamers, *Die frühmittelalterlichen Lesefunde aus der Löhrstraße (Baustelle Hilton II) in Mainz* (Mainz, 1994), for exciting new finds which supplement the documentary material already assembled by K. Weidemann, 'Die Topographie von Mainz in der Römerzeit und dem frühen Mittelalter', *Jahrbuch des Römisch-Germanisches Zentralmuseums Mainz* 15 (1968), 146–99. For the *fabrica* owned by Lantfrid see *UBF219* (791).

[15] See the fine study of E. Wamers, 'Frühmittelalterliche Funde aus Mainz. Zur karolingische-ottonischen Metalschmuck und seinen Verhältnissen zum angel-sächsischen Kunsthandwerk', in Wamers (ed.), *Frankfurter Beiträge zur Mittelalter-Archäologie* I (Bonn, 1986), pp. 1–55.

exchange operated in tandem with more local networks, and in the later ninth and tenth centuries it was the increasing vitality of local markets and exchange which allowed continued economic growth.[16] Still, we must remember that Mainz's importance within local society did not rest on these economic developments. Mainz was a regional centre before its economic 'take-off' in the seventh century.[17] The key to understanding early medieval Mainz lies in its role as a multi-functional central place, fulfilling a whole array of specialist functions – religious and political as well as economic – for its hinterland. No wonder that when seventh- and eighth-century rulers visited the region, they resided at Mainz![18]

Mainz's population must have numbered thousands rather than hundreds, and the city was clearly differentiated from the rural settlements around it. Within the city, however, population, may not have been particularly dense, and certainly was not uniformly distributed. Both archaeology and the charter evidence suggest that a significant proportion of the area within the Roman walls was used for agriculture or viniculture; we should probably imagine a series of clusters of habitation and activity, around important residences and churches (some, like the burial place of the archbishops, the monastery of St Alban's, beyond the Roman walls). Early medieval Mainz's urban morphology was thus very different from that of a Roman city.[19] Yet it was precisely this early medieval style of urbanism which led a seventh-century author to describe the aristocracy of the middle Rhine as the *Macanenses*. These 'men of Mainz' were not necessarily the permanent residents of Mainz, but the elite who dominated the city and its hinterland.[20]

---

[16] I hope to discuss the relationship between 'international' and local economic networks elsewhere: cf. R. Hodges, *Dark Age Economics: The Origins of Towns and Trade AD 600–1000* (London, 1982); R. Balzaretti, 'Cities, Emporia and Monasteries: Local Economies in the Po Valley, c. 700–875', in N. Christie and S. T. Loseby (eds.), *Towns in Transition* (Woodbridge, 1997), pp. 213–34; R. Balzaretti, 'Cities and Markets in Early Medieval Europe', in G. Ausenda (ed.), *After Empire: Towards an Ethnology of Europe's Barbarians*, pp. 113–34; W. Van Es, 'Dorestad Centred', in J. C. Bestemann *et al.* (eds.), *Medieval Archaeology in the Netherlands* (Assen, 1990), pp. 151–82. New local markets are evident in documentary sources: see F. Hardt-Friederichs, 'Markt, Münze und Zoll im Ostfränkischen Reich bis zum Ende der Ottonen', *Blätter für deutsche Landesgeschichte* 116 (1980), 1–32; W. Bleiber, 'Grundherrschaft und Markt zwischen Loire und Rhein während des 9. Jahrhunderts. Untersuchungen zu ihrem wechselseitigen Verhältnis', *Jahrbuch für Wirtschaftsgeschichte* III (1982), 105–35; W. Heß, 'Geldwirtschaft am Mittelrhein in karolingischer Zeit', *Blätter für deutsche Landesgeschichte* 98 (1962), 26–63.

[17] See Jonas of Bobbio, *Vita Columbani*, Quellen zur Geschichte des 7. und 8. Jahrhunderts, ed. A. Kusterning and H. Wolfram (Darmstadt, 1982), c. 27, p. 483.

[18] C.-R. Brühl, 'Königspfalz und Bischofstadt in fränkischer Zeit', *Rheinische Vierteljahrsblätter* 23 (1958), 161–274 at 229–36.

[19] K. Böhner, 'Urban and Rural Settlement in the Frankish Kingdom', in M. W. Barley (ed.), *European Towns: Their Archaeology and Early History* (London, 1977), pp. 185–207 talks of 'the disintegration of the late Roman town into private domestic units' (p. 193).

[20] *Fredegar*, ed. Wallace-Hadrill, IV:87, pp. 73–4. Gregory of Tours used *civitas* labels in a similar

98

Local power: collective action, conflict and consensus

Up the Rhine the charter evidence shows that Worms and Strasbourg, both similarly Roman cities and the seats of bishops, played a multi-functional role for their hinterlands which makes them comparable to Mainz.[21] The evidence is not so vivid as that supplied by the early Fulda charters for Mainz, because the archives of the monastic foundations of Wissembourg and Murbach which had large-scale interests in these two cities are transmitted only fragmentarily, and there is little archaeology. Nonetheless, there are important similarities to Mainz. Both Worms and Strasbourg were centres for the writing of charters and for the transfer of property rights; both were political centres, Worms the site of a royal palace and seventh- and early eighth-century Strasbourg the home of the *duces* of Alsace; at both we find a sizable number of urban and suburban churches whose dedications point to supra-regional contacts, plus hints of the existence of aristocratic urban residences; at both the physical fabric of the Roman city, above all the walls, survived.[22]

The one exception to this pattern of *civitates* acting as central places in early medieval society is Speyer.[23] Like Mainz, Worms and Strasbourg, Speyer probably lost continuous contact with its episcopal tradition: there is a fifth- and sixth-century gap which can be filled with no known bishops. But unlike its neighbours Speyer also lost direct contact with its Roman past. The actual site of the city shifted to the north-west, and the Roman *civitas*-name was replaced by the name of the tributary of the Rhine on which the new settlement stood. The archaeological evidence suggests that the new 'city' was all but indistinguishable from a rural *villa*, despite its status as the seat of a bishopric. Bishops were present at Speyer from the beginning of the seventh century but, unlike their counterparts in Worms, Mainz or Strasbourg, they were not important or high-profile figures until the eleventh century, when the bishopric was strategically developed by powerful patrons. Speyer is interesting precisely because it

manner. On *civitates* and spatial perception see F. Cardot, *L'espace et le pouvoir. Etude sur l'Austrasie Mérovingienne* (Paris, 1987), pp. 90–6, 139–63.

[21] The best discussion of early medieval Worms is H. Büttner, 'Zur Stadtentwicklung von Worms im Früh- und Hochmittelalter', in *Aus Geschichte und Landeskunde. [Festschrift F. Steinbach]* (Bonn, 1960), pp. 389–407; for the archaeology, M. Grünewald, 'Worms zwischen Burgunden und Salier', in K. van Welck (ed.), *Die Franken. Wegbereiter Europas*, 2 vols. (Mainz, 1996), I, pp. 160–2. The material for Strasbourg can be approached through *Urkundenbuch der Stadt Strasburg I. Urkunden und Stadtrecht bis zur Jahr 1288* (Strasbourg, 1879), ed. W. Wiegand. See Staab, *Gesellschaft*, pp. 118–36 on the significance of physical heritage of Roman urbanism in the middle Rhine.

[22] Charter redaction: below, pp. 114–6, and note the importance of Strasbourg as a place at which sales of land took place, on which see Doll's comments, *TW*, pp. 46–8. Walls and residences at Worms: see Staab, *Gesellschaft*, pp. 120–3, Büttner, 'Stadtentwicklung', p. 393. Worms as a political centre: Brühl, 'Königspfalz und Bischofstadt', 259–67, and Classen, 'Pfalzenforschung'. For Strasbourg see esp. *UBF*187, 281, and TW *passim*.

[23] On Speyer see F. Staab, 'Speyer im Frankenreich', in W. Eger (ed.), *Geschichte der Stadt Speyer* I (Stuttgart, Cologne, Mainz, 1982), pp. 163–247.

State and society in the early middle ages

provides a case of the non-development of a distinctive set of social and political functions: episcopal seats and ex-Roman cities did not automatically become the central points of early medieval society.

Failure at Speyer can be usefully counterpointed with a success story across the Rhine, at Ladenburg on the Neckar. The area east of the Rhine, of course, inherited no Roman urban network. Ladenburg had, however, been the site of an important Roman fort: recent excavations have confirmed the evidence of charters and place-names in demonstrating the physical continuity of the Roman settlement into the Carolingian period. The charter evidence shows that, by the eighth century at the latest, it was an important local centre – something like a surrogate 'city' for the lower Neckar, even styled *civitas* by charter scribes, its hinterland forming a *pagus* named after it.[24] Here, then, we see that the early medieval settlement hierarchy was not merely a simplified version of that of the late Roman period, fossilised by the church and passively maintained in the early middle ages for the want of anything better. Rather, Roman and ecclesiastical inheritances were actively reshaped to serve new functions in a new society, with the rise of Ladenburg, east of the Rhine and controlling the socially and strategically important lower Neckar, reflecting new realities.[25]

Early medieval urban settlements were central in the definition of regional economic, political and social networks. They thus played a mediating role in the creation and distribution of power. The early medieval aristocracy did not sit on their rural estates and run things from home: they had to work through local traditions of collective action which continued to centre on cities.[26] Between cities, at the apex of the

---

[24] On Ladenburg see H. Büttner, 'Ladenburg am Neckar und das Bistum Worms bis zum Ende des 12. Jahrhunderts', *Archiv für Hessische Geschichte und Altertumskunde* 28 (1963), 83–98, with H. Keller et al. 'Mittelalterliche Städte auf römischer Grundlage im einstigen Dekumatenland', *ZGO* 96 (1987), 1–64, for the archaeological evidence. F. Trautz, *Das untere Neckarland im Mittelalter*, Heidelberger Veröffentlichungen zur Landesgeschichte und Landeskunde 1 (Heidelberg, 1953) is fundamental on the locality.

[25] Places such as Würzburg may have developed in the region east of the Rhine, where there was no Roman heritage, precisely because of the need for this kind of regional centre.

[26] This has been emphasised by some historians of early medieval Italy for some time: e.g. C. Wickham, 'Italy and the Early Middle Ages', in Wickham, *Land and Power: Studies in Italian and European Social History, 400–1200* (London, 1994), pp. 99–118, esp. pp. 107–13; R. Harrison, *The Early State and Cities in Lombard Italy* (Lund, 1993). For cities as mediating institutions in tenth- and eleventh-century England see R. Fleming, 'Rural Elites and Urban Life in Late-Saxon England', *P&P* 141 (1993), 3–37. For recent work suggesting that Roman cities in northern Gaul continued to exercise important functions as central places in the early middle ages see Halsall, *Settlement and Social Organisation*, pp. 214–42; Halsall, 'Towns, Societies and Ideas: The Not-So-Strange Case of Late Roman and Early Merovingian Metz', in N. Christie and S. T. Loseby (eds.), *Towns in Transition* (Woodbridge, 1997), pp. 235–61; S. Schütte, 'Continuity Problems and Authority Structures in Cologne', in G. Ausenda (ed.) *After Empire:Towards an Ethnology of Europe's Barbarians* (San Marino, 1993), pp. 163–76.

settlement hierarchy, and villages, the basic units of rural society, there were some intermediate centres, important rural settlements which acted as local focal points for action that did not merit a trip to the city. Charter scribes, indeed, sometimes used the label 'public' to refer to some of these places, although more intermittently than they did for cities.

The settlement hierarchy on the lower Neckar is clearly visible in the first waves of gifts to Lorsch. The half-dozen gifts of lands Lorsch received in the summer and autumn of 765 were mainly transacted at Ladenburg, which stood at the apex of the settlement hierarchy. Gifts of land from the lower Neckar region to the monks at Lorsch began again in March 766, when a series of gifts were made, in public, at Lorsch itself and at the nearby settlements of Weinheim and Mannheim. On 14 March five gifts were made, all recorded by the same scribe: one at Lorsch, one at Mannheim and three at Weinheim, the three within a day's ride of one another. The witness-lists show that these actions took place before the well-to-do of the lower Neckar region as whole. Interestingly, Weinheim and Mannheim lay on the boundary between the two *pagi* into which the area was divided, the Rheingau and the Lobdengau, which indicates that *pagi* were not closed or cohesive social units. Both Mannheim and, in particular, Weinheim, were important places in the locality, and acted as centres for charter redaction at other dates, too. Weinheim, indeed, was located on the most important north–south route; counts held land here and by the tenth century it was the site of a local market.[27]

The village of Dienheim was a local centre of a similar kind for its hinterland, a rich wine-growing region on the Rhine's west bank. Dienheim was the site of a *portus* on the Rhine, and a place at which local counts had interests and from which Fulda monks ran their local estates. Numerous land transactions were made, and recorded in charters, at Dienheim, and public meetings at which disputes were resolved were also held there.[28] In the first years of the ninth century it was even styled 'public *vicus*', which must relate to this contemporary importance – which may have owed much to the interests there of powerful landowners, notably one Count Rupert to whom we will be introduced properly anon – rather than a past period of royal ownership.[29]

Lorsch, too, was evidently already an important place for the surrounding locality before the new monastery was founded in 764. In the immediate aftermath of the foundation of the monastery, charter scribes called Lorsch a 'public place', a coinage which they saw reflecting the frequency of public meetings held at Lorsch, for they used the clauses

<hr/>

[27] See Trautz, *Das untere Neckarland*, pp. 46–8.   [28] Cf. pp. 116–7, 126–8.
[29] Cf. Gockel, *Königshöfe*, p. 187, for a fiscalist interpretation.

'enacted publicly at Lorsch' and 'enacted at Lorsch, the public place' interchangeably. Lorsch was not owned by the king, nor is there any evidence that it ever had been royal property, so the label 'public place' must be an index of this aristocratic residence's role as a local centre.[30] By the end of the 760s, thanks to the completion of the monastic complex and the presence of Holy relics, Lorsch became still more prominent, but as a different kind of centre from the aristocratic residence which it had been previously. In the final third of the eighth century, Lorsch became increasingly dominant as the place at which the overwhelming majority of transmitted charters from the lower Neckar region were enacted: in the area within a 30 km radius of the abbey, for which we are best informed, only a handful of transmitted charters were not redacted at the abbey.[31] A similar pattern is visible in the Fulda material. Fulda's distance from the middle Rhine means there are far more charters involving Fulda that record transactions which did not take place within the abbey's walls. Nonetheless, in the 790s some benefactors began to make pious journeys to Fulda, and they took friends, neighbours and on occasion lords with them; from Dienheim we have records of half a dozen such journeys in the 790s. This trend continued into the ninth century.[32] It is noteworthy that at a similar date inhabitants of the Worms area wishing to make gifts to the abbey of Gorze, near Metz, began to make the journey to Gorze, in the company of friends and neighbours, in order to have their benefactions recorded, rather than having them written up in local meetings.[33] This was collective action which transcended mere neighbourliness.

In the last third of the eighth century scribes became increasingly reluctant to present meetings held at Lorsch or Fulda as 'public'. In the Lorsch charters this change in scribal presentation can be closely related to a change in the monastic complex itself. As a rule, meetings at Lorsch stopped being seen as 'public' *c.* 767, the time at which the monks had acquired a critical mass of land at Lorsch and began to build a new monastic complex. Lorsch became a place dedicated to the monks, rather than an aristocratic centre at which secular lords and their monks lived

[30] Cf. Wehlt, *Reichsabtei und König*, p. 25, with older literature. The fiscalist hypothesis that the label 'public place' indicated sometime royal ownership of Lorsch is largely circular, resting on Prinz's argument that such labels were indices of fiscal property. The only other supporting prop is the view that the family of Lorsch's founders were interlopers implanted by the Carolingians, whose holdings must therefore have originated in royal grants – but cf. pp. 51–61, 175–9, for qualifications to this reconstruction.
[31] Unfortunately we cannot compare Lorsch's total domination of the immediate neighbourhood with what was surely a more complex picture in more distant areas, because the place of redaction is only transmitted for charters copied near the beginning of the Lorsch cartulary, i.e. those concerning land very close to Lorsch.
[32] Travel to Fulda from Dienheim: *CDF*216, 237, 261, 228a, 264, 305.
[33] d'Herbomez, *Cartulaire de Gorze* 70, 71. Cf. Costambeys, 'An Aristocratic Community', 46.

cheek by jowl. As Lorsch and Fulda were by definition dedicated sacred spaces, they gave a particular aura to transactions which took place there, in the eyes of scribes at least: in early medieval law there was a recurrent and strong opposition between the sacred and the public, which was by definition secular.[34] There were occasionally charters after 767 which saw meetings at the monastery as 'public'. For example, a document of May 782 was 'enacted publicly', perhaps because royal *missi* were active in the area at this date.[35] Other occasions were 'public' on account of their over-riding local significance. Thus in the charter recording Abbess Hiltisnot's grant of her nunnery at Baumerlenbach to the monks of Lorsch, an important transaction which took place in the presence of her brothers (one a count), Lorsch was referred to as a 'public place'.[36] Similarly, when counts travelled to Lorsch to make pious donations, charters were seen as recording action 'in public'.[37] On these occasions the whiff of secular-ity was so strong that even monastic scribes acknowledged it. But as a rule, actions which took place in monasteries, even though they took place in the presence of groups of laymen, were presented as manifesta-tions of a different kind of collective action. In seeing the community united before the Holy as something distinct from the secular and the public, charter scribes were following the usage of the Bible.[38]

It is hardly surprising that locals travelled to Lorsch or Fulda to make pious donations. It was not just a formulaic nicety, however, which marked the distinction between these occasions and secular public meet-ings. It is significant that when the monks acquired land by sale or exchange, transactions rarely took place at Lorsch or Fulda. The division between pious gift and secular business was entrenched in the conven-tions of charter-writing, which presented gifts as actions involving a donor and a saint, from which spiritual benefits accrued, in contrast to sales and exchanges, in which the abbot, not a saint, was the legal actor representing the monastery. But the habit of transacting sales and exchanges beyond the monastic complex itself suggests that these con-ventions corresponded to wider perceptions of a contrast between sacred gifts and secular business. Indeed, sales and exchanges give rare glimpses

[34] See G. Köbler, *Das Recht im frühen Mittelalter: Untersuchungen zu Herkunft und Inhalt frühmittelalter-licher Rechtsbegriffe im deutschen Sprachgebiet*, Forschungen zur deutschen Rechtsgeschichte 7 (Cologne and Vienna, 1971) pp. 68–70, 93, 141.
[35] CL957, and for royal *missi*, CL228. The only other charter fully transmitted from these months, CL468, was not seen as 'public'. [36] CL16 and cf. CL12.
[37] This is not, of course, a hard-and-fast rule, but a tendency: see e.g. CL27, 33. Cf. L. Genicot, '*Publicus*. Sur la survivance de la notion de l'Etat', in L. Fenske *et al.* (eds.), *Institutionen, Gesellschaft und Kultur im Mittelalter: Festschrift J. Fleckenstein* (Sigmaringen, 1984), pp. 147–64 at pp. 152–3.
[38] Cf. A. Borst, 'The Invention and Fissure of the Public Persona', in Borst, *Medieval Worlds: Barbarians, Heretics and Artists in the Middle Ages* (Cambridge, 1991), pp. 37–60 at pp. 39–40.

of the continuation of a world of public action which extended beyond the monastery walls. Local meetings, such as that at Bermersheim in 782, during which an exchange of land was confirmed 'in public', or that at which another exchange was made at Oppenheim in 784, evidently continued much as before, but pious gifts were no longer, as a rule, made in them, but in direct contact with the saintly recipient at the monastery itself.[39]

These changing patterns show the profound impact of the new large-scale rural monasticism represented by Lorsch and Fulda upon middle Rhenish society. The build-up of vast holdings of land by both abbeys made them centres of social and political power in their own right. Complex and wide-reaching webs of patronage extended outwards from the monastery walls. The scale and density of these networks was unprecedented. Their continued existence over time was guaranteed, because saints were undying patrons whose holdings could only be redistributed temporarily, not given away, and were not subject to the vagaries of inheritance. Monasteries thus became the stable points in the ever-changing web of familial relationships and property rights. Monastic networks were therefore imprinted onto society and reproduced over time where those of even the most powerful secular figures were not. And although monasteries were defined with reference to the sacred, the networks which were woven around them inevitably had secular implications. Monasteries were multi-functional centres. There is good evidence that they served as centres of redistribution, for benefactors of Lorsch and Fulda received gifts of weapons, status symbols and livestock from the monks; they would have been centres of production. They were also centres of sociability: Hraban's family, for example, made repeated trips to Fulda, and the charters show laymen from more humble backgrounds likewise journeying to the homes of the saintly patrons. We may, indeed, be witnessing a new type of sociability involving feasting with the abbot, praying in the abbey church and hunting in the monastic woods.[40]

---

[39] *CL*1048, 1047 respectively, and see the register to *CL* for more examples. At Gorze, too, exchanges and precarial grants were more 'public' than pious gifts: d'Herbomez, *Cartulaire de Gorze* 19, 51, 53, 55, 57, 58, 61.

[40] Monasteries as multi-functional centres: Innes, 'Space, Place and Power'. Monasteries as centres of production: F. Schwind, 'Zu karolingerzeitlichen Klöstern als Wirtschaftsorganismen und Stätten handwerklicher Tätigkeit', in L. Fenske *et al.* (eds.), *Institutionen, Gesellschaft und Kultur im Mittelalter. Festschrift J. Fleckenstein* (Sigmaringen, 1984), pp. 101–23. Sustained research on the sociability of the interaction between laymen and monasteries is a *desideratum*: for some suggestive comments see D. Bullough, *Friends, Neighbours and Fellow-Drinkers: Aspects of Community and Conflict in the Early Medieval West*, H. M. Chadwick Memorial Lecture 1 (Cambridge, 1993); J. Campbell, 'England in 991', in J. P. Cooper (ed.), *The Battle of Maldon: Fiction and Fact* (London, 1993), pp. 1–17.

Local power: collective action, conflict and consensus

This is not to argue that the new monasteries swept previous patterns of collective action aside and took on a role which had earlier been the preserve of the cities. The continuation, beyond the monastery walls, of public meetings at which sales and exchanges were made, should serve as a reminder that the dominance of Lorsch and Fulda as stages for legal action is inevitably exaggerated by the surviving evidence, which is overwhelmingly concerned with gifts to these two abbeys. There are enough glimpses of the world beyond the monasteries to suggest that extra-monastic traditions of collective action continued, with a similar hierarchy of stages, centring on the cities, to that which can be reconstructed so clearly in the eighth century. The emergence of rural monasteries as social centres did mark a substantive change to patterns of local collective action, but it did not sweep earlier traditions aside. Monasteries, after all, did not directly rival the cities: they were a new kind of central place, dedicated to the sacred. Indeed, the arrival of rural monasteries was important and led to an increase in functional differentiation between types of social action. Whereas in the middle of the eighth century there had been relatively little functional specialisation within this society – economic, social, political and legal matters all tending to concentrate in the cities – by the ninth century there was a series of overlapping networks which were more specialised, some leading back to the cities, some to the monasteries. In 750 one went to the city to buy or sell, to encounter the sacred, to meet a patron – in short, for virtually any activity which could not be undertaken in the countryside. By 850 one could go to either the city or the monastery to engage in important business, the choice depending on what kind of business it was, and with whom one wanted to interact. This was an increase in social complexity, which led to a corresponding increase in the complexity of the settlement hierarchy.

RURAL SETTLEMENTS

Cities and monasteries were dominated by kings and aristocrats, nodal points in the topography of power. Were they part of the world of the mass of the population? Can we see the actions of peasant smallholders as confined to rural settlements, essentially self-governing, closed and only intermittently impinged upon by outsiders? The countryside was divided up into settlement units: a relatively densely exploited core, the *villa*, and woodlands and surrounding areas, the *marca*. Thus one narrative tells the story of an unfortunate villager who, according to her neighbours, became possessed by demons, and was persecuted and forced to live outside the *villa*, in the surrounding fields: the *villa* was a core area, where people resided.[41] The boundaries between these units were real: a flood in 869 was so serious that it took flotsam and jetsam from the *villa* of Bingen over the boundary of the next *villa*.[42] Occasionally charters give an idea of what defined these boundaries, normally when delineating the scope of rights over large blocks of woodland: the stream as far as such-and-such a stone, which marked the end of so-and-so's land, then to the tumulus named after so-and-so . . . Even in the Odenwald such boundaries, and the constant naming of landmarks after landowners, do not give the impression of an alien or unlived in landscape.[43] That is, these were living units deeply embedded in the microtopography. They were defined by the practice of everyday life. Whilst it is possible that the origins of these units are to be found in Roman tenurial and fiscal arrangements, it would be ludicrous to see these arrangements, which gave the *villa* its initial definition, continuing through the radical changes in political and social structure which took place between the fourth and seventh centuries. The continuation of the *villa* unit may have owed something to the fact that it continued to be the unit in which kings thought about legal action or fiscal exaction. But by the ninth century, although dues and services were levied *villa* by *villa*, the *villa* was not a unit that could be defined in fiscal terms; it was a physical reality, a unit grounded in social experience, through which kings worked. Indeed, it may well be the case that the impingement of kings or lords on such a pre-existing social unit was a crucial factor in the formation of a deeper sense of community: collective action *vis-à-vis* an outsider is the crucible of community consciousness. It is thus in the twelfth century and after, when the legal and political organisation of rural settlements crystallised, normally under the formal jurisdiction of outsiders, that the local sense of community really came to the fore.[44]

To understand how these settlements were defined in the Carolingian period, it is necessary to look at them as functioning social units. The charter evidence permits a very detailed understanding of their social structure. For settlements such as Bürstadt or Dienheim in the Rhine valley there are almost a hundred documents revealing the names and

[41] *AF*, s.a. 858, pp. 51–3.   [42] *AF*, s.a. 869, pp. 71–2.   [43] See, for example, *CL6a*.
[44] My reading of *villa* is thus similar to that of Halsall, *Settlement and Social Organisation*, pp. 189–98. See also R. Schmidt-Weigand, 'Das Dorf nach den Stammesrechten des Kontinents', in H. Jankuhn *et al.* (eds.), *Das Dorf der Eisenzeit und des frühen Mittelalters*, Abhandlungen der Akademie der Wissenschaften in Göttingen, philologisch-historische Klasse 101 (Göttingen, 1977), pp. 408–43, M. Heinzelmann, '*Villa* d'après les œuvres de Grégoire de Tours', in E. Magnou-Nortier (ed.), *Aux sources de la gestion publique I: Enquête lexicographique sur 'fundus', 'villa', 'domus', 'mansus'* (Lille, 1993), pp. 45–70, and, against a 'fiscalist' reading of *villa*, Wickham, 'La chute de Rome n'aura pas lieu. A propos d'un livre récent', *Le Moyen Age* 49 (1993), 107–26. Schwind, 'Beobachtungen' is the best discussion of rural reality. There is still no adequate study of high medieval formalisation.

connections of dozens of landowners. Bürstadt stood a kilometre or so west of Lorsch along the Worms road. At the heart of the settlement stood a two-storey wooden hall where kings occasionally stayed. These buildings had a symbolic importance: kings issued charters and gave judgements there on occasion. There was, of course, royal land at Bürstadt too, but most of the land there was owned by laymen. Much belonged to the very richest local families: the descendants of Cancor, for example, held land at Bürstadt more or less to a man. But there were also less exalted men with more local horizons who appeared in Bürstadt charters as witnesses, or gave holdings at Bürstadt to Lorsch.[45] Dienheim, on the Rhine's west bank halfway between Mainz and Worms, we have already visited. The focus of the settlement may again have been a large estate complex and hall, in this case owned before 792 by the king, and after that date by Fulda. Monks resided there as administrators, and the economic life of the settlement may have revolved around the abbey's estate. But Fulda's holdings were not the only focus of social and economic life at Dienheim: other churches owned land there also, notably Lorsch, but also the distant cathedral of Liège. Within the *villa* there was evidently a defined sense of social hierarchy, as demonstrated above all by charter witness-lists; a hierarchy cut through by, but not defined by, the patronage networks radiating from the abbeys of Lorsch and Fulda. The social spectrum ran from powerful lords, whose scattered holdings included plots at Dienheim, to free peasants, who scratched together a living and appeared in the charter evidence only on exceptional occasions, to the unfree, presented simply as human objects in the charter evidence.[46]

These social and tenurial patterns make it difficult to equate settlement and community: it is not possible to see a *villa* as an organic social unit, exclusive, inward-looking and homogeneous.[47] Wealthy landowners would only have visited many of the settlements where they had holdings rarely or in passing; indeed, where their holdings amounted to a vineyard or a few smallholdings, they had no reason to visit at all, so long as rent or renders were forthcoming. Moreover, tenurial patterns conspicuously crisscrossed from *villa* to *villa*, with illustrious landlords owning parcels in dozens of settlements scattered over a wide area, and even relatively humble men owning land in two, three or four *villae*. It was really only the very lowest strata of free society – peasant owner-cultivators basically practising subsistence agriculture – whose holdings were confined to a single settlement. This was, therefore, a society

---

[45] On Bürstadt see Gockel, *Königshöfe*, pp. 258–310.   [46] Cf. pp. 22–3, 101, 126–8.
[47] Cf. Wickham, 'Problems of Comparing', pp. 213–14, 'Rural Society', pp. 520–21.

characterised by a high degree of structural, geographical mobility. Even well-to-do peasants with perhaps half a dozen scattered plots needed to travel substantial distances, especially as their half-dozen plots were not necessarily situated in half a dozen neighbouring settlements. Thus Ripwin and Giselhelm, two brothers whose holdings were concentrated on Bensheim near Lorsch (where they made substantial clearances), also held land at Cloppenheim and Dossenheim on the lower Neckar, and at Dienheim across the Rhine. Their more distant interests can be explained by involvement in the wider world of politics and lordship: scattered holdings and mobility made for a complex system of patronage and kinship which bound the regional elite together but also cut across settlements.[48]

To deny any sense of community would, however, be to risk throwing the baby out with the bathwater. In that the property-owners of a *villa* were neighbours who enjoyed some common rights (for example in the surrounding mark), a rough and ready sense of collectivity was indubitable and indeed, inevitable. This was as true of the Merovingian, or the Ottonian, as the Carolingian period.[49] This sense of a *villa* collectivity is much in evidence in the charters; the property-owners of a *villa* played an important role in establishing proof of ownership of land within the *villa*. Dienheim supplies a vivid example of the role of the *villa* as a legal collectivity: in 796 a dispute about tolls payable at the *portus* was resolved by the testimony of 'those who have inheritances in Dienheim'.[50] The men who witnessed were that same loose elite who dominated charter witness-lists at Dienheim; here was a group of village elders who were the backbone of the *villa* collectivity. These men had no title, no objective position and the charters give no hint at a rigid or legal definition. But there was the ascription of a certain local standing, a status within the settlement. When the toll case stressed the possession of inherited interests, it was underlining the stake that these witnesses had in Dienheim. These were not newcomers with perhaps a parcel or two, but men whose interests centred on Dienheim. They presumably also resided locally. Absentee landlords with local interests might interact with these more humble groups when their affairs necessitated it, but they were not

[48] On the pair see below, pp. 147–52. Cf. Wickham's example from Dienheim, 'Rural Society', pp. 522–3. Davies, *Small Worlds*, is fundamental on structural mobility.

[49] For suggestions about rituals (such as bound-walking) as defining 'community', see Wickham, 'Rural Society', pp. 529–31. Also, in general, Reynolds, *Kingdoms and Communities*, pp. 101–54. For an attempt to see early medieval community in legal terms, see Staab, *Gesellschaft*, pp. 250–86. A. C. Murray, *Germanic Kinship Structure: Studies in Law and Society in Antiquity and the Early Middle Ages* (Toronto, 1983), pp. 67–87, shows that the legal competence of rural communities has its roots in the administrative practice of the late Roman state. On the notion of community and its application to medieval society, see M. Rubin, 'Small Groups: Identity and Solidarity in the Late Middle Ages', in J. Kermode (ed.), *Enterprise and Individuals in Fifteenth-Century England* (Stroud, 1991), pp. 132–50.   [50] *UBF*246.

a part of the *villa* community. Nor was the community exclusive: charter witnesses were not all *villa* 'elders', and some Dienheimers witnessed at other, nearby, settlements. But it was there, doubtless reinforced by participation in other spheres of common ritual action today untraceable: for example, annual perambulations of the settlement's bounds. *Villa* churches also played an important role in the definition of community and collective action, with the church *atrium* the typical focus of rural communities right across Carolingian Europe. The church door was thus the locus for public marriage, whilst many a charter tells us that it was redacted at the *villa* church.[51] The church, with the cemetery around it, was the ritual focus of the community by the Carolingian period.[52]

Archaeology suggests that these settlements underwent important changes in the seventh and eighth centuries.[53] Merovingian cemeteries, typically distant from actual settlements, were abandoned as the dead came to be relocated around newly founded churches at the physical heart of the community. Excavated Merovingian rural settlements typically shifted their focus over time, within a relatively large, but also a defined, area; settlement may have been relatively dispersed.[54] Thus in the southern suburbs of modern Speyer a small Merovingian settlement – distinct from the surviving shell of the Roman city and medieval bishopric – shifted its location along a terrace by the Rhine. The eventual,

---

[51] Although most charters simply give the name of the settlement unit in which they are redacted, a few add further localisation. See *CDF*382, 417, d'Herbomez, *Cartulaire de Gorze* nos. 19, 33, 42, 47, 51, 55. See P. J. Geary, 'Living with Conflicts in Stateless France: A Typology of Conflict Management Mechanisms, 1050–1200', in Geary, *Living with the Dead in the Middle Ages* (Ithaca and London, 1994), pp. 125–62 at pp. 153–4 for illuminating discussion (centring on a case from eleventh-century southern France). On public marriage and the church door see Reynolds, *Marriage in the Western Church*, pp. 386–412. Note also the frequent royal injunctions against holding local assemblies in church, which were places of peace and were therefore not to be disturbed by legal conflict: their frequency demonstrates that churches were the foci of rural society.

[52] See *CL*428 for a local meeting in the cemetery; cemeteries continued to be important foci for the local community into the high middle ages.

[53] For reviews of settlement archaeology, each reflecting the interests of the author and the state of research at the date of publication, see W. Janssen, 'Dorf und Dorfformen des 7. bis 12. Jhts. im Lichte neuer Ausgrabungen in Mittel- und Nordeuropa', in H. Jankuhn *et al.* (eds.), *Das Dorf der Eisenzeit und des frühen Mittelalters*, Abhandlungen der Akademie der Wissenschaften in Göttingen, philologisch-historische Klasse 101 (Göttingen, 1977), pp. 285–356; H. Steuer, 'Standortverscheibunger früher Siedlungen – von der vorrömischen Eisenzeit bis zum frühen Mittelalter', in G. Althoff *et al.* (eds.), *Person und Gemeinschaft im Mittelalter. Festschrift K. Schmid* (Sigmaringen, 1988), pp. 25–59; and H. Hamerow, 'The Archaeology of Rural Settlement in Early Medieval Europe', *EME* 3 (1994), 167–79. See also H. Steuer, 'Zur Berechnung von Bevölkerungsgröße und Bevölkerungsentwicklung in einer Siedlungslandschaft der Merowingerzeit', *Saeculum* 39 (1988), 119–28; H. Hamerow, 'Shaping Settlements: Early Medieval Communities in Northwest Europe', in Hamerow and J. Bintliff (eds.), *Europe between Late Antiquity and the Middle Ages*, British Archaeological Reports International Series 617 (Oxford, 1995), pp. 8–37.

[54] See Halsall, *Settlement and Social Organisation*, pp. 276–8; Theuws, 'Landed Property and Manorial Organisation'.

permanent, site of Carolingian and Ottonian settlement emerged 500 m south-west of the original Merovingian centre. This eighth-century settlement was larger and more complex than its predecessors; it included one building which was evidently a centre of textile manufacture.[55] At Wülflingen on the Kocher, a tiny Merovingian settlement of a few poor buildings was reorganised, *c.* 700, when a large hall served by a metalled track was constructed, surrounded by smaller dependent dwellings: presumably this hall was the property of the ancestors of the Count Cunicpert who granted the Wülflingen estate to the monks of Fulda in 779.[56] To some extent, mobility may simply be a correlate of the need to rebuild wooden buildings each generation or so, although less mobile Carolingian settlements consisted of wooden buildings, too. Nonetheless, there is very clear evidence for a twofold shift in the decades around 700, with the creation of more permanent settlement centres, and a decrease in dispersal within the larger settlement unit. By the Carolingian period 'village' is a viable translation for the *villa* of the charters. At Wülflingen we can detect the smack of firm lordship in the archaeological record, and in some cases settlement reorganisation may have proceeded hand in hand with manorialisation.[57] It is necessary, however, to remember that large numbers of owner-cultivators survived into the eighth and ninth centuries: most of the *villa* settlements of the Carolingian period were not manors. Of course, royal, ecclesiastical and secular estates could determine basic economic and social patterns without swallowing up entire settlements. That is, smallholders may have existed in many areas in a symbiotic relationship with larger, more complex estates, perhaps supplying some lordly estates, renting odds and sods of aristocratic land to add to their inheritances, or making ends meet by working as part-time or seasonal hired labour in addition to cultivating their own holdings. These concerns explain the concentration of settlement. And these settlements acquired new, fixed, focal points, above all rural churches whose locus was sacred and unmovable, which ended settlement mobility.

In spite of this new stability, even Carolingian villages were not closed or inward-looking: the settlement hierarchy corresponded with a series

---

[55] H. Bernhard, 'Die frühmittelalterliche Siedlung Speyer "Vogelgesang"', *Offa* 39 (1982), 217–33.

[56] M. Schulze, 'Die Wüstung Wülflingen in Nordwürttemberg', *Offa* 39 (1982), 235–43, and see UBF86.

[57] Thus Halsall, *Settlement and Social Organisation*, pp. 276–8 and Theuws, 'Landed Property and Manorial Organisation'. This is, in effect, precisely the process which R. Fossier claims to be the central feature of social development in the *post-Carolingian* period – but whether Fossier takes full account of the rich Carolingian evidence is another matter. See e.g. 'Les tendences de l'économie: stagnation ou croissance?', *Settimane* 27 (1981), 261–74, esp. the exchange with E. Ewig in the discussion at 281–4.

of overlapping and superimposed spheres of social action, with no strong, formal barriers between them. The base unit, however, was the settlement and the locality around it. We are ill-informed about legal action on this level in charters of any type. Nonetheless, we can piece together scraps. Thus one charter, precisely because it was relatively unformulaic, explained how one Egiher entrusted his legacy to Lorsch to the priest Liebant, and the free men Liutolf, Eberhard, Rudit and Eberwine; they in turn elected Eberhard to act as their *missus* and perform the ritual transferring the legacy to Lorsch before 'all the free men of Weiblingen, Bergheim, Eppelheim, Plankstadt and Schwetzingen'.[58] A concern with local knowledge and consent underlined the whole transaction, and it was a drama which was acted out on the most local of stages. For the peasantry, cities and rural monasteries were places that were visited occasionally. They were not the stage for normal action. Indeed, the hierarchy of stages for public action reflected and reinforced the gradations of status and deference which characterised middle Rhenish society. By underlining the legitimacy of stages that they dominated, the elite were claiming to underwrite legal action and to represent those whose horizons were more local.

SCRIBES AS GUARDIANS OF LEGAL TRADITION

The legal rituals which we glimpse in the record of Egiher's legacy were rarely recorded in the written documents, although there can be no doubt that they were pervasive in practice. It has been claimed that precisely because this type of action underlay most charters, the written documents we work from are the superficial creation of a clerical minority supplying a misleading view of Carolingian society.[59] Charters did not, however, somehow stand outside the contemporary legal world, but were a central element within it. After all, in Egiher's case, the face-to-face arrangements made with his trustees, and the local ritual performed to transfer ownership, needed confirmation in a written document. Written documents were useful precisely because they could be read aloud and brandished aloft before the inhabitants of a locality. For example, in 821 Hugh, Count of Tours and the most powerful landowner along the Rhine south of Worms, completed a series of property transactions with the abbot of Wissembourg; the charter recording them was drawn up at the palace at Quierzy and witnessed by the flower of the Frankish

---

[58] CL730.
[59] As argued by Cheyette, 'The Invention of the State', pp. 149–56; M. Richter, '*Quisquis scit scribere, nullam potat abere labore*. Zur Laienschriftlichkeit im 8. Jahrhundert', in J. Jarnut *et al.* (eds.), *Karl Martell in seiner Zeit*, Beihefte der Francia 37 (Sigmaringen, 1994), pp. 393–404.

aristocracy. But the deals were also broadcast to the inhabitants of the settlements in which property was changing hands, and Hugh's scribe took
care to record their knowledge and consent.[60] Royal judgements and
orders were likewise enacted and publicised in local meetings, as in 777
when a charter transferring the royal estate at Hammelburg to Fulda was
carried to Hammelburg by two royal vassals who then carried out the
ritual of transfer, the *vestitura*.[61]

Written documents were used in the middle Rhine before the monastic foundations of the eighth century. The earliest monastic documents
were drawn up not by monks from the new monastic foundations, but
by local scribes steeped in a common regional tradition.[62] The earliest
transmitted document dealing with property rights in the middle Rhine,
the will of Adalgisel-Grimo, perhaps suggests the path by which standard
templates reached the middle Rhine. Adalgisel's will was drawn up in
Verdun, where he was a deacon, in 634, its jargon informed by late
Roman legal culture.[63] The formulae which dominated middle Rhenish
documents were derived from models from the more Romanised areas
of central and southern Gaul, probably disseminated through the personal interests of the likes of Adalgisel.[64] This suggests that in our region
charters were being adopted as a means of transferring property in the
early seventh century, perhaps because in this period rights over land were
being redefined in more absolute terms, which made the transfer of land
through processes other than inheritance a more frequent occurrence.[65]
Whereas in central and southern Gaul the beginnings of charter transmission in the seventh century might reflect a shift from papyrus to parch-
ment, and from municipal institutions to the church as the agent of
preservation, the middle Rhine does genuinely seem to have been an area
where the charter was reintroduced.[66]

The charter was not, then, introduced to the middle Rhine with the
wave of monastic foundations which reached its height in the middle of
the eighth century, but emerged as a result of social and legal changes in
the seventh century. Law-codes and royal decrees from the seventh to the

---

[60] *TW*69.   [61] *UBF*83. Cf. below, p. 138.

[62] For scribal traditions, see John, 'Formale Beziehungen'; for non-monastic scribes, Bresslau,
'Urkundenbeweis'.

[63] W. Levison, 'Das Testament des Diakons Adalgisel-Grimo von Jahre 634', in Levison, *Aus rheinischer und fränkischer Frühzeit* (Düsseldorf, 1948), pp. 118–138.

[64] For formulaic models for middle Rhenish scribes see John, 'Formale Beziehungen' and Zatschek,
'Die Benutzung der Formulae Marculfi'.

[65] For the argument that the reintroduction of charters was linked to changes in property rights over
land, see below, pp. 73–7.

[66] Cf. I. N. Wood, 'Disputes in Fifth- and Sixth-Century Gaul', and P. Fouracre, '"Placita" and the
Settlement of Disputes in Later Merovingian Gaul', in W. Davies and P. Fouracre (eds.), *The
Settlement of Disputes in Early Medieval Europe* (Cambridge, 1986), pp. 7–22, 23–44 respectively.

ninth century suggest that there were officially recognised local scribes, called *cancellarii*, who were charged with recording legal business in written form. Attempts to see here evidence for a state-sponsored infra-structure of notaries are probably misleading: we should avoid picturing *cancellarii* in institutional terms, and think instead of official recognition of local scribes as the record-takers at local meetings.[67] Those scribes who can be traced in the charters were mainly churchmen, which has been seen as militating against the existence of public scribes. But the fact that a scribe was a monk or a priest did not make him solely an agent of the church. Indeed, the provision of writing may have been one important function of priests in their neighbourhoods.[68] Any assessment of the status of scribes should rest on their observed actions, not on a priori classifications opposing public notaries and private ecclesiastical scribes.

The charters provide clear evidence for the existence of personal scribes in the service of the powerful, who acted as recorders of official business. Ratleig, Einhard's scribe, was one such figure and his career serves as an illustration of the avenues opened up by such service. His role as Einhard's notary involved acting as a general purpose agent. From a relatively humble background in Cologne, Ratleig's work in Einhard's service allowed him to create a power base in the middle Rhine and emerge as an influential local figure.[69] Ratleig was not alone. One royal official active in the middle Rhine in the late eighth century, Count Warin, was similarly served by a personal scribe: the charter in which Herirac gave property at Dolgesheim in the Wormsgau to Gorze in 793 was written by Libfarius, 'the *cancellarius* of Count Warin'.[70] He was nearly contemporary to a *cancellarius*, Herirad, who was active as a royal agent in dispute settlement in 782.[71] Herirad was a local man, not an official from the royal chancery. The charters show him to have been a layman with scattered property interests, extensive contacts, and enough

[67] The fundamental study, seeing a state notariate, was Breßlau, 'Urkundenbeweis'. Subsequent critics have convincingly demonstrated that there was no such institutional system, but perhaps thrown out the baby with the bathwater in denying any system of officially-recognised scribes whatsoever: D. P. Blok, 'La notariat franc: a-t-il existé?', *Revue du Nord* 42 (1960), 320–2; Classen, 'Fortleben und Wandel', p. 45; I. Heidrich, 'Titulatur und Urkunden der arnulfingischen Hausmeier', *Archiv für Diplomatik, Schriftsgeschichte und Wappenkunde* 11/12 (1965–6), 71–279 at 207–12. The charter evidence certainly suggests that there were officially-recognised scribes: Staab, *Gesellschaft*, pp. 137–53, and McKitterick, *The Carolingians and the Written Word*, pp. 118–20. For a good discussion avoiding most of the pitfalls of thinking too institutionally about early medieval arrangements, see Johanek, 'Zur rechtlichen Funktion', esp. p. 141.
[68] Cf. Johanek, 'Zur rechtlichen Funktion', for a good discussion of the legislation; also Fichtenau, *Urkundenwesen*, p. 79, for ecclesiastical scribes on official business. For priests in local communities, W. Davies, 'Priests and Rural Communities in East Brittany in the Ninth Century', *Etudes Celtiques* 20 (1983), 177–97.
[69] See *Translatio*, esp. I:4, ed. Waitz p. 241, and on Ratleig see above, p. 207, and *MGH PLAC* II, p. 241.   [70] d'Herbomez, *Gorze*, no. 32, accepting Staab, *Gesellschaft*, p. 142, n. 586.   [71] CL228.

standing to act as a regular witness across a wide area.[72] Herirad was one of the 'illustrious men' who testified to the boundaries of the Heppenheim mark in 795.[73] Herirad was also close to the royal agent Guntram, whom he aided in 782.[74] Herirad's position also brought him into contact with other royal officials: the charter evidence points to links with Counts Raffold, Cancor and Warin.[75] Yet Herirad wrote just two other transmitted charters. As an influential local landowner his living was not made as a scribe, despite his role as *cancellarius*; his charter-writing was confined to a handful of particular occasions.[76]

In the eighth and ninth centuries, there was also organised charter redaction at Mainz. When a local wished to make a gift to Fulda, or indeed a property transfer of another kind, they travelled to Mainz, where they found a scribe. Thirteen transmitted charters from the third quarter of the eighth century were written in 'the public city of Mainz', whilst other charters which give no place of enactment shared formulaic traits with this corpus. One particular scribe, Wolfram, drew up most of the charters in question; on occasion he styled himself 'Wolfram, notary of Mainz'.[77] Wolfram's activities, when they were localised, were always in Mainz; in five of his charters a count led the witnesses. He styled himself *emmanuensis* or *notarius*, titles inherited from late antiquity. Scribes similar to Wolfram were active at Worms and Strasbourg. The priest Hiaebo (Jacob) wrote charters at Worms, and styled himself *ammanensis* (sic).[78] As at Mainz, the city acted as a focus for the local population: hence in 754 Aggiold, wishing to give land to Fulda, travelled to Worms and had Hiaebo draw up a charter.[79]

These city notaries had a defined role: all were succeeded by scribes using similar jargon and writing for similar clients. After 775 there is a

---

[72] Witnessing: CL170, 215, 456; UBF49. Donations: CL281, 422; CDF28; d'Herbomez, *Cartulaire de Gorze* 32. As a neighbour: CL187, 188, 190. For a prosopographical investigation of Herirad, see Gockel, *Königshöfe*, pp. 262–5.   [73] CL6a.
[74] CL228. The pair also witness together in a transaction involving property at Bensheim in 789, CL256.
[75] Herirad and Raffold: CL14, land at Weinheim in 790, where Herirad is 'leading-witness'. In CL429 (755x6) a titleless Raffold and Herirad witness a donation of land at Ladenburg; the charter is written by a public notary, Hiaebo. If Herirad is the same man as the donor in d'Herbomez, *Cartulaire de Gorze* 32 he had his charter drawn up by Count Warin's *cancellarius*. CL281 (765) shows links between Herirad, giving land at Ladenburg to Lorsch, and Count Warin, the leading-witness. In CL482 Herirad, Count Warin and Count Cancor all witnessed. The Gorze donation is intriguing. If Herirad really were a *cancellarius* like those of the normative sources, his actions would have a geographical limit: hence when he made a donation west of the Rhine, he would have it drawn up by another official.
[76] CL520 (770); CL976 (774). It is possible that Herirad wrote other charters which are transmitted with no scribal subscription.
[77] On Wolfram, Breßlau, 'Urkundenbeweis', pp. 34–5; Stengel's introduction to UBF, pp. lv–lvii; Staab, *Gesellschaft*, pp. 145–50.   [78] Staab, *Gesellschaft*, pp. 140–3.
[79] UBF42, see also UBF50, CL429.

thirty-four-year caesura in explicit evidence for charter redaction in Mainz, because Wolfram's successors Weliman and Hiltibald did not localise the enactment of the documents they wrote, although they used the same formulae and orthography as Wolfram had.[80] Hiltibald's successor was one Theotrich, whose charters concerned property scattered across a wide area. On occasion Theotrich travelled as far as Ingelheim, Bruheim near Frankfurt, and even Erfurt and Hersfeld.[81] Does this geographical spread mean that city scribes were actually episcopal officials?[82] Theotrich's successor, the priest Starcharius, was active as a charter scribe in Mainz in 819 and 827, but in the latter year also travelled to Haßloch, west of Worms and well beyond Mainz's diocesan boundary, to write a charter; what is more, his charters recorded transactions involving both Fulda and Hornbach.[83] In Theotrich's last charter, recording an exchange between the archbishop and the abbot of Fulda (and written at Fulda), he may have been working for the archbishop, but most of his charters recorded gifts to Fulda.[84] As his predecessors were, like him, priests, they may have had similar connections to the church of Mainz. But this does not necessarily make them archiepiscopal functionaries. Theotrich, for example, travelled to 'the public palace' at Erfurt in 802 and attended the assembly at which the *Lex Thuringiorum* was drawn up by royal agents: his activities as a charter scribe at this assembly, writing up a donation to the abbey of Hersfeld with which he had no personal links, must suggest some degree of official recognition.[85] These scribes all wrote charters for the local population as a whole, not for any particular institution alone.

The Mainz evidence is more detailed than that for Worms, but a similar pattern can be detected there. Hiaebo, a contemporary of Wolfram's, wrote charters transacted at Worms and travelled to nearby rural settlements to record transactions made there, too.[86] After Hiaebo, the scribe active in Worms was one Geroin, who wrote charters recording transactions involving Wissembourg and land around Speyer and on the Saar, as well as transactions involving Fulda and Wissembourg in the Worms area. Geroin was no monastic scribe but neither was he a city-based notary, in that he wrote charters in a variety of rural contexts as

---

[80] Zatschek, 'Die Benutzung der Formulae Marculfi und anderer Formelsammlungen in den Privaturkunden des 8. bis 10. Jahrhunderts', *MIÖG* 42 (1927), 165–267, and H. Kletschke, *Die Sprache der Mainzer Kanzlei nach der Namen der Fuldaer Urkunden* (Halle, 1933).

[81] *CDF* 283, 224, 222. *UBH*26 is probably to be redated to 842, and written by a Lorsch monk Theotrich.

[82] See Stengel's comments in *UBF* I, p. lvi, and Staab, *Gesellschaft*, p. 147. But cf. Fichtenau, *Urkundenwesen*, p. 79: such scribes could be secular as well as ecclesiastical officials.

[83] *CDF*382, 416; N13, ed. C. Crollius, *Acta Academiae Theodoro-Palatinae* I (Mannheim, 1766), pp. 295–6.   [84] *CDF*270.

[85] *UBH*21, and see Schlesinger, *Die Entstehung der Landesherrschaft*, pp. 50–1.

[86] *UBF*50, 53, *TW*60.

well as in Worms.[87] There were also scribes linked to the 'public city' of Ladenburg. Notbald, Alapsi and Hessi all only wrote charters at Ladenburg; Notbald at least was a local landowner and (apparently) a layman. The three produce the charters surviving from a meeting held at Ladenburg in March 766, at which two counts were present.[88]

There were other scribes active who served locals over a wide area without apparent attachment to any institution or forum. The best documented is the notary Wiglar, who wrote charters in the area around Lorsch and Ladenburg in the middle of the eighth century.[89] By 770 Wiglar had retired from charter-writing; after this date Lorsch monks wrote the vast bulk of charters concerning property on the middle Rhine's east bank. Around Mainz and Worms, most of the transmitted documents were likewise written by Lorsch and Fulda monks.[90] It is hardly surprising that monasteries were increasingly providing would-be donors with monastic scribes to record gifts. It would, however, be rash to see a shift from an earlier system of notaries serving the community as a whole to a new system of recipients taking responsibility for recording donations. The bias of the documentation makes it difficult to assess whether monks really were monopolising charter-writing, or just writing donations to the church. We also have little way of knowing whether they worked solely for their own institution or supplied notarial skills for the locality as a whole.[91] That scribal skills continued to be enjoyed by a variety of individuals serving a plurality of interests throughout the period is demonstrated by charter production at Dienheim. Before the late 780s, property rights at Dienheim were discussed and conveyed in the public forum supplied by Mainz. In the late 780s and early 790s, charters concerning Dienheim were written by Fulda monks, and enacted at Fulda, several days' travel away. On other occasions in the late eighth century scribes, from Mainz wrote charters witnessed by locals and concerning land at Dienheim. From the late 790s, Dienheim grew in impor-

---

[87] *TW*60 and *UBF*53 are Geroin's charters from Worms. *TW*193 is written at Ungstein in the southern part of the Wormsgau. On Geroin, Doll's comments, *TW*, pp. 133–5.

[88] *CL*226, 274, 673, from 766. Notbald also wrote *UBF*38 (763 at Ladenburg); and acted as a witness in *CL*283.   [89] On Wiglar, Staab, *Gesellschaft*, p. 144, and Breßlau, 'Urkundenbeweis', p. 33.

[90] On monks as charter scribes see Stengel, *UBF* I, pp. lix–lxix; Doll, *TW*, pp. 115–51; M. Sandmann, 'Wirkungsbereiche Fuldaer Mönche', in *Klostergemeinschaft* II:ii, pp. 692–791 at pp. 704–14.

[91] Previous discussion, following Breßlau, have tended to assume that the increasing dominance of monastic scribes in the ninth-century documents points to the decline of 'public scribes', and a shift from a system of official recognition of scribes to one in which recipients were responsible for having documents drawn up. But see Johanek, 'Zur rechtlichen Funktion', esp. pp. 141–2 for cases which he describes as 'fictive continuity', with monastic scribes continuing to describe themselves as *cancellarii*: the continuity may, however, not be so fictive, and monastic scribes may simply have taken over the 'public' role earlier filled by non-monastic scribes.

tance as a forum in its own right. In the early ninth century it was a place where charters were regularly enacted, not only concerning property in Dienheim but also in the surrounding neighbourhood. A variety of scribes wrote these charters: Fulda monks, often based at Dienheim where the abbey had an important centre; local priests; and some anonymous scribes, whose documents are most politely described as monuments to the depth of pragmatic literacy.[92] Clearly, at Dienheim we are not witnessing a shift from public notaries to monastic recipient-redaction, but the impact of a new source of scribal skills, the monastery, onto an already complex picture.

Scribes, whether monks or not, worked with a common set of stereotyped templates which they used to describe legal actions right through the seventh, eighth and ninth centuries. This phenomenon is of the utmost importance. Standardisation guaranteed legitimacy.[93] Scribes – whether monks, clerics or laymen – were the guardians of a legitimating tradition. The regional tradition within which these scribes worked was one recorded in formularies: these collections of actual documents were used as models for future generations of scribes. Working with a formulary or a collection of actual documents did far more than teach one how to write a charter; it also educated one in how law ought to be practised, transmitting a set of legal norms. And scribal education may have involved more than extensive work with actual documents and formularies. A handful of documents demonstrated acquaintance with royal law-codes: scribes in Alsace and the Moselle, for example, were clearly aware of some clauses at least of *Lex Ribuaria*.[94] Monastic scribes at least knew written law from monastic libraries, and translations of written law into the Germanic vernacular were made both in the Moselle and at Fulda.[95] The translations remind us of the existence of a linguistic gulf

<hr>

[92] In discussion of Dienheim scribes I draw on the prosopographical information collected in volume V of the Münster *Klostergemeinschaft*. Charters redacted at Fulda are written by Asger (p. 105) and Inguis (in 812: p. 258). Hiltibald (*UBF*257) is evidently the Mainz scribe of that name. Otfridus (*CDF*217) writes at Dienheim but is also a Fulda monk (p. 126). Reccheo, *cancellarius* (*CDF*213 from 803) writes charters elsewhere and is thus to be identified with one of the two monks named Reccheo in the 820s (p. 311). Reginbert writes two charters at Dienheim (*CDF*281, 282), makes a gift himself (*CDF*222), serves as a witness (*CDF*244) and writes three charters elsewhere; he never claims any sacerdotal status, but two men named Reginbert were Fulda monks in the 820s (p. 307). The majority of Dienheim charters are local redactions which give no scribe, although important differences between Lorsch and Fulda charters can be observed.

[93] See W. Davies and P. Fouracre (eds.), *The Settlement of Disputes in Early Medieval Europe* (Cambridge, 1986), pp. 212–13; Costambeys, 'An Aristocratic Community', 47–55.

[94] See Doll, introduction to *TW*, pp. 46–8, and note also the Gorze charters discussed above, n. 39.

[95] For a general overview see R. Schmidt-Weigand, 'Stammesrecht und Volkssprache in karolingischer Zeit', in H. Beumann and W. Schröder (eds.), *Aspekte der Nationenbildung im Mittelalter*, Nationes 2 (Sigmaringen, 1978), pp. 171–204, with full discussion of the translation of capitulary

between the spoken language of the population of the area and the Latin of the charters, albeit a gulf of differing depth in different contexts – on the most local, village level it may well have been above the vernacular, oral, ritual aspect of legal action which mattered to participants, whilst the Latin literacy of the charter became more important as one moved to the city or the monastery. But this gulf was never unbridgeable. Charters were worth having, and their contents were communicated in the vernacular and through ritual. The ability to read, still less to write, a charter did not need to be widespread for the written word to play a central part in law in practice.

In that legal training and the ability to write charters went hand in hand, scribes were, in effect, the legal experts in the community, and thanks to this role they could act as conduits of legal knowledge. The role of scribes as guardians of legal tradition explains the evident high status that went with being a scribe. Lay scribes like Herirad were evidently in a very real sense local elders. Monks who worked as scribes were not workaday brethren, but among the elite of their communities, often ending up as abbot or in other high-profile positions. It is a remarkable fact that all of Lorsch's first five abbots spent time in their youth as charter scribes, whilst amongst Fulda and Wissembourg scribes one looks at the young Einhard, Rudolf and Otfrid. Such men were educated in legal tradition, even if they never engaged in abstract legal formulation to a sufficient extent for us to characterise them as lawyers.[96] They stood at the heart of the operation of a binding local tradition, a binding tradition in which written documents played a central role.

COUNTS AND PUBLIC MEETINGS

The traditions of collective action which we have been studying were crucial to the exercise of local power. Rulers needed to acknowledge, and work through, them. Traditionally, however, counts have been seen as officials to whom the king delegated plenipotentiary power within a

---

Footnote 95 (*cont.*)

legislation made in the Moselle, and that of *Lex Salica* made at Fulda. For law in monastic libraries, and lay knowledge of law, see McKitterick, *The Carolingians and the Written Word*; see also C. I. Hammer, '*Lex Scripta* in Early Medieval Bavaria: Use and Abuse of *Lex Baiuvariorum*', in E. B. King and S. Ridyard (eds.), *Law in Medieval Life and Thought* (Sewanee, 1990), pp. 185–95.

[96] Cf. R. McKitterick, 'Perceptions of Justice in Europe in the Ninth and Tenth Centuries', *Settimane* 44 (1997), pp. 1075–1102 at 1096–1100, criticising the specific conclusions of C. Radding, *The Origins of Medieval Jurisprudence: Pavia and Bologna 850–1150* (London and New Haven, 1988) about early medieval law. Cf. also J. L. Nelson, 'Dispute Settlement in Carolingian West Francia', in W. Davies and P. Fouracre (eds.), *The Settlement of Disputes in Early Medieval Europe* (Cambridge, 1986), pp. 45–64, esp. p. 63.

recognised territorial competence, the *pagus*.[97] In the middle Rhine, documents from the late seventh century onwards divide the region into geographical areas each called a *pagus*; their vernacular names often end with the suffix -*Gouwe*, modernised as -*Gau*.[98] Legal documents used *pagus* labels to locate places and property, as did normative and literary sources.[99] Given the ubiquity and relative clarity of the *pagus* as a spatial construct, it is hardly surprising that generations of historians have claimed it as the basic administrative unit.[100] However, *pagus* was primarily a geographical term. An alternative vocabulary existed to describe politically defined space: the term *comitatus* developed in the royal chancery in the late eighth century, and from the 830s became the standard term for administrative units in treaties and royal charters.[101] Middle Rhenish scribes received the vocabulary of *comitatus* early, and on occasion used it as a means to provide extra detail about the location of property.[102] Significantly, when they use the term *comitatus*, scribes link it to the person of an individual count rather than giving it an independent territorial designation: property was located 'in *pagus* X, in the *comitatus*

---

[97] See above, pp. 8–9.

[98] Earlier discussions of counts and counties in the middle Rhine are those of Staab, *Gesellschaft*, pp. 416–27, and Schulze, *Grafschaftsverfassung*, pp. 173–214. On *pagi*, see the monumental W. Niemeyer, *Der Pagus des frühen Mittelalters in Hessen*, Schriften des Hessischen Landesamtes für geschichtliche Landeskunde 30 (Marburg, 1968). Also influential have been the geographical studies of G. Wagner, which mapped *pagus* labels as used in the charters, as in 'Comitate zwischen Rhein, Main und Neckar', *ZGO* 64 (1955), 1–34.

[99] P. von Polenz, 'Gaunamen oder Landschaftsnamen? Die *pagus*-Frage sprachlich betrachtet', *Rheinische Vierteljahrsblätter* 21 (1956), 77–96, shows that *pagus* names seem to be organic west of the Rhine, but east of the Rhine the language of charter scribes implies that they are more artificial. Nonn, *Pagus und Comitatus*, pp. 37–40, in the context of an important discussion of the term *pagus*, pp. 35–51, criticises von Polenz from the capitulary evidence. Literary texts like Einhard's *Translatio* also use *pagus* labels, implying that they had a currency in society at large.

[100] Staab, *Gesellschaft*, p. 416, claiming that as late ninth-century charters locate property 'in the county of Count N. and in the *pagus* X.[-Gouwe]', a clear-cut *pagus* system supplied administrative units throughout the Carolingian period. Schulze, *Grafschaftsverfassung*, pp. 180–8, makes a similar assumption. The best modern discussion of the complex relation between count and *pagus* is Nonn, *Pagus und Comitatus*, esp. pp. 199–258.

[101] Nonn, *Pagus und Comitatus*, pp. 40–51. See T. Reuter, *Germany in the Early Middle Ages* (London, 1992), pp. 92–4 for an overview, and pp. 237–8 below.

[102] See CL3637 (in *Waltgouwe in comitatu Geroldi*, 777x84); 3139/3687c (in *comitatu Cunradi in pago Logengouwe*, 773); and compare CL1132 (no date). I.[Dienemann-]Dietrich, 'Die Traditionsnotiz des CL Nr.3139 und ihr vermeintliches Datum von 772/73', *Hessisches Jahrbuch für Landesgeschichte* 3 (1953), 283–91 argues on prosopographical grounds that the second of these charters may be misdated by the cartulary's compiler. In part she is attacking the idea that the royal chancery, when it adopted similar phrases in the second half of the ninth century, was borrowing them from local practice; she would rather see local scribes following the court. Given the rarity of such phrases, it would be a mistake to see formulae and it is surely unnecessary to suggest that the idea of locating property in terms of a count needed borrowing from anywhere. Staab, *Gesellschaft*, pp. 421–2 extends the argument to the other Lorsch charter and CL3066/3684b. But the *in comitatu* phrase was used in charters from Gorze and Bonn as well as Lorsch in the late eighth century: see d'Herbomez, *Cartulaire de Gorze* 18; Wisplinghoff, *Rheinische Urkundenbuch* 55.

held by N'.[103] Other documents used terms such as *ministerium* and its vernacular equivalent, *ambath*, in a similar way.[104] Contemporaries evidently did not see *pagus* and *comitatus* as wholly equivalent terms: a *pagus* was a named geographical area, whereas a *comitatus* was simply the area ruled over by a count, and thus a personal competence, not a geographical entity. The extent to which *pagus* and *comitatus* tended, in fact, to overlap is another issue; comital power was not firmly identified with *pagus* units.

According to the local charter tradition, absolutely everywhere lay within a *pagus*. Both *pagus* and *comitatus* were all-encompassing: immunities were located within their *pagus* time and time again, and on occasion they were also seen as lying within a *comitatus*.[105] In many areas, particularly east of the Rhine, *pagi* were settlement areas in the broadest sense of the term.[106] They had clear boundaries: the Wormsgau, for example, was defined by the course of the Rhine in the north and the east, and the Nahe in the north-west, so that when the Rhine changed course in the 880s, the two *villae* of Oppau and Edingen, which had previously been on the east bank but now lay to the west of the river, became a part of the Wormsgau.[107] The presence of agreed boundaries is underlined by the case of Bingen, a settlement whose own boundaries straddled the Nahe. Property within Bingen could thus lie in either the Wormsgau or the Nahegau, depending which side of the river it was on.[108] But the existence of boundaries of this type does not make the *pagus* a unit defined by a political act. Locals – and local rulers – could work with a unit like the *pagus* without it being administratively defined.

The origins of the *pagus* system are unclear: it simply emerges, ready-formed, at the end of the seventh century in the earliest transmitted charters. There is no hint that *pagi* were political or administrative units at this date, and Merovingian law-codes hardly ever used the term *pagus*.[109] Nor

---

[103] The one exception d'Herbomez, *Cartulaire de Gorze* 18 (*in pago Wabrinse in comitatu Virdunensi*). Verdun's hinterland appears in Adalgisel's will in the first half of the seventh century as the '*territorium* of Verdun' (Levison, 'Das Testament des Diakons Adalgisel-Grimo'); this provides an important reminder that although *pagi* are fully-fledged by the time the charter evidence sheds light on the area they are not necessarily units which go back to the initial Frankish settlement.

[104] CL3684b (edited alongside CL3066). MGH DCharlemagne 142 confirms the equivalence with *ministerium* (and demonstrates that Staab, *Gesellschaft*, p. 422 is wrong to equate *ambath* with a *pagus*); in general on *ambath-ministerium*, F. Staab, 'Zur Organisation des früh- und hoch mittelalterlichen Reichsgutes an der unteren Nahe', in A. Gerlich (ed.), *Beiträge zur Geschichtliche Landeskunde*, Geschichtliche Landeskunde 21 (Wiesbaden, 1980), pp. 1–29.

[105] *Pagus*: countless charters locate Lorsch within the *pagus* of the Rheingau. For *comitatus* see the Prüm evidence cited by Zotz, 'Personengeschichte und Grafschaftsverfassung', 12–13, n. 87, or CL53 for Lorsch.

[106] Niemeyer, *Der Pagus des frühen Mittelalters in Hessen*, especially pp. 185–222.

[107] See Trautz, *Das untere Neckarland*, p. 15 (later followed by Niemeyer and Schulze).

[108] See in general Niemeyer, *Der Pagus*, pp. 83–8. These boundaries were probably marked by cairns and so on: see CL6a, 21.   [109] Nonn, *Pagus und Comitatus*, p. 38.

can the *pagus* be seen as a Frankish form of social organisation: *pagi* rested, albeit in a messy and indirect way, on the Roman settlement hierarchy, in that they were broadly defined by the Roman *civitas* system. There was, however, no correlation between diocesan boundaries and the *pagus* system, even though both ultimately grew out of the Roman *civitas* network. *Pagus* boundaries must have arisen from a similar piecemeal process, resting on the influence of powerful individuals, to that by which diocesan boundaries were formed.[110] If *pagus* units ever reflected the exercise of political power, it was during the period in which they crystallised, *c.* 600 or slightly earlier.[111]

The charter evidence from the Carolingian period suggests a rough and ready correlation between the activities of counts and the *pagus* system. This does not necessarily make the *pagus* system an administrative grid, and there is no sense in the transmitted evidence of the *pagus* as a jurisdictional territory rather than a social unit. To the extent that the *pagus* corresponded with local patterns of collective action, it was inevitably the framework within which counts worked. But collective action was not delimited by *pagus* boundaries, and so the *pagus* supplied only the haziest of frameworks for local rulers. A series of donations made to Lorsch in March 766 shows this clearly. Three of the men who witnessed these charters were counts: Cancor, his son Heimerich, and Warin, a figure well known from the charter evidence whose activities were centred in Ladenburg and the city's hinterland.[112] The main interests of the men involved, and the locations at which they had charters redacted, spanned two *pagi*, the Lobdengau and the Rheingau. This was certainly not a *pagus* meeting, precisely because the *pagus* system cut across patterns of social intercourse and was thus of limited value as a social or political unit. Indeed, it was held on the boundary between the *pagi*. It was not a case of Warin and Cancor each identifying certain transactions as pertaining to his competence, but of the pair working through existing patterns of social intercourse.

If we wish to understand these patterns, we should begin in the area around Fulda where the charter evidence for counts ruling through public meetings is particularly good. Two cases are transmitted from the Grabfeld. On 20 February 825, in the *villa* of Geismar, a 'public meeting' was held by 'Count Poppo and all of his county': an assembly which we

---

[110] For the formation of diocesan boundaries see Heinemeyer, *Das Erzbistum Mainz*; F. Staab, 'Episkopat und Kloster. Kirchliche Raumerschließung in den Diözesen Trier, Mainz, Worms, Speyer, Metz, Straßburg und Konstanz im 7. Jht. durch die Abtei Wissembourg', *Archiv für mittelrheinische Kirchengeschichte* 42 (1990), 13–56; E. Ewig, 'Zu Wimpfen und Worms, St-Dié und Trier im 7. Jht.', *Jahrbuch für westdeutsche Landesgeschichte* 1 (1975), 1–9.
[111] For this date, see below, p. 172. [112] See below, pp. 19–20 with fig. 3.

know of thanks to the 'great investigation' into the property of the monastery at Hünfeld which arose in its course. This record was written by the Fulda scribe Theotamar. The 'county' consisted of the most influential local landowners, listed as witnesses. Interestingly, whilst a judgement was made at the comital assembly, a further, local meeting is set up to be supervised by Poppo's agents to effect the judgement. Comital assemblies are perhaps best seen as political and social occasions at which local worthies met to discuss local affairs, rather than as purely judicial institutions. The charter does not make the hearing of the Hünfeld case a principal object of the meeting, rather leaving the impression of a dispute which arose in the course of the assembly.[113] This impression is confirmed by the record of another case from 827, when Poppo and the 'better born of his county' met at a place known as *Swarzesmuore* in another 'public meeting'. Thirteen individuals are listed as present in addition to Poppo and Abbot Hraban – the 'better born' here, like the 'county' in the earlier case, being the local landowning elite, a county community.[114] The comital *mallus* of the Saalegau, which heard another dispute involving Fulda in 837, was a similar grouping, a regular meeting of the great and good of the locality at which business affecting the locality was discussed. Again a further, local, assembly is set up to resolve the dispute recorded in our charter.[115] These meetings seem to be held at special venues which were acknowledged as central places by the inhabitants of the locality. Geismar, where the 'county' assembled in 825, was an important *villa* which had been a social and religious centre before the coming of Frankish Christianity.[116] The *Swarzesmuore*, where the 'better born of the county' met in 827, was an acknowledged public space: at some point in 827 before the county meeting recorded in the charter, Abbot Hraban of Fulda had met there with a number of local men and a series of property dealings had been concluded, mainly Fulda purchasing clearances in return for valuable moveable goods.[117] Given the overlapping patterns of landowning and witnessing in the charters, we cannot see these groupings as strictly defined or exclusive. We are not dealing with the inhabitants of territorial units, but with broadly based local elites; it was their collective action which determined matters in their locality and allowed them to represent the 'county'. Carolingian initiatives to formalise the places and times of local meetings, to use these

[113] CDF456. There are penetrating discussions of the Fulda material in Schlesinger, *Die Entstehung der Landesherrschaft*, pp. 68–73; and R. Sprandel, 'Gerichtsorganisation und Sozialstruktur'.
[114] CDF471. For the elite 'communities' in medieval England, see C. Carpenter, 'Gentry and Community in Medieval England', *Journal of British Studies* 33 (1994), 340–80; P. R. Coss, *Lordship, Knighthood and Locality: A Study of English Society, c. 1180 to c. 1280* (Cambridge, 1991).
[115] CDF659. [116] Willibald, *Vita Bonifatii*, c. 6, ed. Levison, p. 31. [117] CDF471.

meetings as the interface between locality and royal representatives, and to force all to swear loyalty to the king before the local count at such meetings, may have strengthened these bonds, and helped crystallise the identities to which they gave rise: again, collective encounters with external forces were the crucible of community.[118]

Let us look at one case in more detail to underline the primary significance of the broadly based collective action of local elites as the interface between locality and royal officials. In 795 Count Warin held a meeting to determine the boundaries of the Heppenheim mark, which had been given to Lorsch almost a quarter of a century earlier. The meeting point was a *tumulus* known as the *Walineshouw*. Men from the *pagus* within which Lorsch and Heppenheim lay, the Rheingau, gathered there, as did men from neighbouring *pagi*, the Maingau, the Wingarteiba and the Lobdengau.[119] Although the royal *praeceptum* which Warin carried to the *Walineshouw* set up the meeting, it looks like a traditional site for local public meetings, not least given the presence of a *tumulus* with a special name. Twelve 'illustrious men' served as joint representatives of the Rheingau and the Maingau, led by Count Rupert; from the Lobdengau and the Wingarteiba came separate contingents. Although the meeting took place in the Rheingau and concerned the boundaries of property within that *pagus*, its president was Count Warin, whose activities as a charter witness focus on Ladenburg and the Lobdengau, whilst Count Rupert, who seems to have dominated the Rheingau, was simply an interested participant. If we try to see the *pagus* as a unit of jurisdiction, it is extremely difficult to make sense of this case. In an important recent study of dispute settlement in the Carolingian middle Rhine, Jürgen Hannig has pointed out that this state of apparent confusion in matters jurisdictional is common in the charter evidence. He attempts to rescue the inherited model of the 'integrated *pagus*'[120] as a unit of jurisdiction by arguing that these cases are exceptional, resting on the exercise of special *ad hoc* powers in specific cases. Certainly Count Warin may have acted as president of the 795 meeting because of his local knowledge, for he had previously held the land in question. But the whole procedure adopted, not least the presence of contingents of men from beyond the *pagus* within which Heppenheim lay, makes it difficult

---

[118] For Carolingian legislation on local meetings see F. N. Estey, 'The Meaning of "Placitum" and "Mallum" in the Capitularies', *Speculum* 22 (1947), 435–439; P. Fouracre, 'Carolingian Justice: The Rhetoric of Improvement and the Contexts of Abuse', *Settimane* 42 (1995), 771–803. We await a full study of its social logic.   [119] CL6a.

[120] To coin a phrase: cf. J.-F. Lemarignier, 'La dislocation du "pagus" et le problème des "consuetudines" (Xe–XIe siècles)', in *Mélanges d'histoire du moyen âge dédiés à la mémoire de Louis Halphen* (Paris, 1951), pp. 401–10, and see the comments of Nelson, 'Dispute Settlement', pp. 61–2.

to rescue any sense of the *pagus* as a judicial unit. Special pleading in this particular case might be convincing, if most disputes fitted the model of the *pagus* as a neat unit on which counts based their power. But *none* of the transmitted cases from the middle Rhine fit the 'integrated *pagus*' model unproblematically.[121]

It is time to abandon the model and admit that comital power was personal, as it was exercised through groups of people, overlapping collectivities. Royal legislation, when it referred to local units and courts, was attempting to order this local diversity, not presupposing centrally-defined institutions. We are dealing with the collective judgements of social units, not the exercise of jurisdictional right. Judgements took place in meetings of local worthies, groups like the 'better born of the county' of 827, or the twelve 'illustrious men' of 795. Ultimate settlement often rested on the setting up of a further, local assembly, to which representatives would as like as not be sent. Some sense of a wider audience watching was necessary for legitimacy. Einhard, concerned about Seligenstadt's human possessions, wrote to a local count informing him that he was about to enter into a legal defence of his Saints' *mancipia*: the advocate of Saints Marcellinus and Peter would come into the comital presence and make an enquiry. Presumably an inquest on a more local level would then be ordered.[122] Comital power rested on illustrious presence and public performance, not instituted jurisdiction.[123]

LOCAL POLITICAL LEADERSHIP

We can investigate the basis of comital power further by looking at the activities of specific counts. The one about whom we know most is Hatto, who was active in the second half of the eighth century. He was a large-scale landowner, his interests lying along the Main, and has been convincingly identified with the founder of the monastery of Neustadt-am-Main in the Spessart, and thus a close contact (and possibly relative) of Megingoz, bishop of Würzburg, one of Boniface's followers.[124] Hatto

---

[121] Cf. J. Hannig, 'Zentrale Kontrolle und regionale Machtbalance. Beobachtungen zum System der karolingischen Königsboten am Beispiel des Mittelrheingebietes', *Archiv für Kulturgeschichte* 66 (1984), 1–46 at 27–40.   [122] Einhard, letter 50.

[123] To borrow Bisson's phrase: 'The "Feudal" Revolution', 12. Cf. Sprandel, 'Gerichtsorganisation und Sozialstruktur', who sees early medieval systems of judgement within social groups (counties for the elite, villages for peasants) evolving into high medieval systems of formal jurisdiction.

[124] Friese, *Herrschaftsgeschichte*, pp. 73–6, 139–62, and Staab, *Gesellschaft*, pp. 411–13, 416. Hatto's land and origins seem to lie on the middle Main, around Hünfeld, rather than in the middle Rhine proper, despite Gockel, 'Zur Verwandtschaft der Äbtissen Emhilt von Milz', pp. 37–41, arguing that there is no evidence that the Wormsgau Count Hatto should be equated with the Count Hatto who owned land in the east (the compelling point being that Count Hatto is active only as a witness, never a donor, around Mainz, but always a donor, never a witness, in the east).

also acted as a witness more than any other count in the transmitted charters; the twenty-two documents from 767 to 802 which have his subscription are thus a priceless database for the workings of comital power. The charters deal with donations of land and property concentrated within one *pagus*, the Wormsgau, plus its smaller neighbour, the Nahegau.[125] This witnessing was not concentrated in the region where Hatto's inherited interests lay, on the Main; it must therefore have related to his position as a count. These witnessing activities were not confined to meetings held within the Wormsgau and Nahegau: Hatto also witnessed transactions concerning property in these *pagi* at sites beyond their bounds, for example at both Fulda and Lorsch.[126] His presence at the monasteries when locals chose to make pious donations is better explained in terms of the bonds between Hatto and the groups he ruled than in terms of jurisdiction. Hatto was not sedentary: not all these charters gave a place of redaction, and just one explicitly mentioned 'the public city of Mainz'.[127] Yet the scribes who wrote these charters were Mainz notaries; Hatto's activities were not dissociated from the city or reliant on any alternative centre, but based on itineracy through the city's hinterland.

Hatto could also intervene in actions far beyond Mainz's immediate hinterland. In 788 when Abbess Emhild of Milz and her brothers staged a meeting with Fulda's representatives over the nunnery at Milz, at Milz itself, a *vicus publicus* far to the east of Mainz, Count Hatto was present. This was a high-profile case, part and parcel of regional politics, and Emhild was in all probability kin.[128] Similar concerns might explain his actions *vis-à-vis* the abbey of Hornbach: in the reign of Louis the Pious, the monks complained about depredations which had taken place in the ⸱ime of Charlemagne, when one member of the family of the monastery's founders, Werner, had seized control of some monastic estates. Here we have conflict within a kingroup, for Werner and his brother, Count Wido, were joint owners of the monastery. Wido, though, had found his fortune in royal service on the Breton march, and Werner seems to have been trying to seize control of the family's inherited power base in his absence. What is striking is that to do this, Werner allied with two local counts: Hatto, who connived at the seizure of Göllheim in the Wormsgau, and Wicbert, who had helped Werner seize property in the Bliesgau. Göllheim was not in an area where Hatto was usually active, but his status as a count allowed him to intervene, with the support of a powerful local.[129]

---

[125] *UBF*59, 61, 160–2, 165, 178, 180, 182, 185, 195, 248–50, 252, 255, 267, 283; *CL*198, 859, 917.
[126] *CL*198, 859, 917. Cf. also *UBF*180.   [127] 'Public city of Mainz': *UBF*59.
[128] *UBF*180. Hatto was probably a relative of Emhild: see *UBF*145a for their common interests at Roisdorf (although compare Gockel, 'Zur Verwandtschaft der Äbtissen Emhilt von Milz').
[129] BM699 = N11 (edition: *Monumenta Boica* 31.1 (Munich, 1836), no. 17).

State and society in the early middle ages

These interventions were based on bonds of kinship and alliance within the regional elite. The basis of Hatto's activity needs to be understood in terms of his relationship to the city of Mainz and the social groups around it. That the logic was social rather than jurisdictional is shown by the presence of another count simultaneously with Hatto in the same *pagus*. A notice about tolls from 796 demonstrates the power of Count Rupert at Dienheim, which lay within the Wormsgau.[130] Count Rupert was a descendant of the founders of Lorsch, with interests throughout the middle Rhine, who witnessed charters as count from 795. Rupert's action in the Wormsgau in 796 was not isolated: he travelled to Fulda to act as a leading witness to donations of property in Dienheim, Dolgesheim and Mainz in charters from 796 and 801.[131] Rupert was also active on the Rhine's east bank, in the Rheingau. His power crossed the Rhine and spanned *pagus* boundaries because he exercised power within groups of people, not over a defined territory.

Dienheim was the focal point of Rupert's power, and in all probability his residence. Although it lay on the Rhine's west bank, it was the centre of a locality which included settlements on both sides of the Rhine: settlements around Dienheim on the Rhine's west bank paid the same forest dues as the settlements opposite them, across the river, surely implying that Dienheimers and their neighbours exercised customary rights in woods and waste on both sides of the Rhine.[132] Interestingly, a similar group of settlements around Dienheim are also treated as a collectivity in a late Carolingian document detailing *corvées* due at Worms.[133] This group of settlements formed a legal collectivity: hence in 806 a case concerning property at Dalheim and Dienheim was settled in a 'public meeting' (*conventus publicus*) attended by local property-owners, whilst in 825 a case concerning Dienheim land was heard in a 'public court' (*mallus publicus*) held at nearby Eimsheim.[134] This particular collectivity is not named or referred to in any transmitted documents, although terms such as *centena*, 'hundred', were used in legislation. It is equivalent to the grouping of five *villae* on the lower Neckar which one charter shows holding a common meeting, its constituency all the free men of the locality.[135] By the high middle ages, units of this size constituted the territorial jurisdictions, *Zenten*, within which most petty disputes were settled. Whilst there is undoubtedly continuity of a kind here, the early medieval

[130] *UBF246*, and for discussion pp. 108–9. [131] *UBF213, 236, 277*. [132] *CL3671*.
[133] See below, p. 162–4. [134] *CDF228, 459*.
[135] *CL730*. In the more Romanised west *centena* is often used, like *pagus* and *villa*, as a geographical label in charters. In the middle Rhine it is used just once, to refer to the Wingarteiba, an area deep in the Odenwald: see above, p. 44, n. 75. On *centenae* in Frankish legislation see A. C. Murray, 'From Roman to Frankish Gaul: *Centenarii* and *Centenae* in the Administration of the Frankish Kingdom', *Traditio* 44 (1988), 59–100.

evidence contains nothing to suggest that such units enjoyed a formal, judicial identity in the Carolingian period. Social units within which disputes were settled, and through which the king's demands were met, gradually hardened into jurisdictional territories.[136]

The nature of the Dienheim collectivity in the eighth and ninth centuries is further illuminated by the patterns of charter witnessing within it. In the toll inquest of 796, one Zeizo appeared immediately after Rupert, in second place in the witness-list. Zeizo appeared frequently at Rupert's side as a 'witness-leader', particularly in transactions from the area around Dienheim in the Wormsgau, but also in transactions involving property across the Rhine in the Rheingau.[137] Zeizo, who had married a niece of Otakar's, was well-to-do, his property interests concentrated around Dienheim and, immediately across the Rhine, around Pfungstadt. His witnessing was centred in these areas, too. However, Zeizo's witnessing was indicative of something more concrete than local influence: he consistently headed witness-lists when he subscribed charters. Whilst witness-lists were extremely sensitive to matters of precedence, the mechanics of social standing in these communities as a rule prevented any one individual from monopolising the first position in witness-lists. The 'witness-leader' phenomenon thus cannot be explained by social status alone. This is underlined by the precedence given to Zeizo on official occasions, such as the Dienheim toll inquest and also two other important inquests when royal *missi* were present, and by his proximity to Count Rupert. His activities were typical of a class of untitled 'witness-leaders' in the charter evidence. The official nature of their position was suggested by charter evidence from St Gallen in Alemannia, and from Wissembourg concerning the upper Saar, in which similar figures were consistently styled *centenarius*, 'hundred-man'.[138]

Thanks to the unparalleled richness of the charter evidence, Zeizo's

136 Cf. M. Schaab, 'Die Zent im Franken von der Karolingerzeit bis ins 19. Jahrhundert. Kontinuität und Wandel einer aus dem Frühmittelalter stammenden Organisationsform', in W. Paravicini and K.-F. Werner (eds.), *Histoire comparée de l'adminstration (IVe–XVIIIe siècles)*, Beihefte der Francia 9 (Munich, 1980), pp. 345–62, seeing wholesale continuity, with Sprandel, 'Gerichtsorganisation und Sozialstruktur'.

137 *UBF*213, 277, 236, 246; *CL*6a, 186, 192, 221, 228, 268 and see Staab, *Gesellschaft*, pp. 430–1 wanting Zeizo to be 'hundredman of the Rheingau', and hence worried about his overlap with the career of the *vassus dominicus* Guntram, and having to explain away his activities around Dienheim in terms of his following his master, Rupert, who was acting as *missus* (despite the silence of the charters themselves on any such situation). On Zeizo's family and property see Staab, *Gesellschaft*, p. 263. Zeizo's second wife was a niece of Otakar's and, as Staab emphasises, his leading-witnessing in particular links to the group of families which dominated Dienheim.

138 See Staab, *Gesellschaft*, pp. 427–31. Gockel, reviewing Staab's book in *Naßauische Annalen* 87 (1976), at 315 criticised Staab's borrowing of the title *Zentenar*. Wissembourg: *TW* nos. 192, 194–6, 201–2, 218/239, 224, 227, 243–4, 256, 263, 265, 267, which await study. St Gallen: Sprandel, *Das Kloster St-Gallen*.

career does not stand isolated; he is one of a series of similar figures active as a witness-leader in the locality of Dienheim. Between 803 and 818 a Hadurih acted as 'witness-leader' in transactions from the Dienheim area, once travelling to Fulda and once to Mainz. Like Zeizo, his activities were not confined to the Rhine's west bank alone: he also acted as a 'witness-leader' for transactions east of the river, in the Rheingau. And as with Zeizo, his family hailed from Dienheim, and his holdings were concentrated there. As with Zeizo, he was something more than a local who rose organically to pre-eminence; his position was official enough to entail him presiding at a hearing into a property dispute concerning Dienheim land in 806.[139] The kind of title which men like Zeizo and Hadurih were given is hinted at by a further charter, again involving the Dienheim area, dating from shortly after Hadurih's demise. In it the witness-list was headed by a Wigrich, who was given the special title *'iudex'*. The evidence for Wigrich's local position is sparse: he was a local landowner who frequently witnessed from 792 onwards, but only achieved prominence in a handful of charters.[140] Guntram, Hraban Maur's brother, may have been a similar figure early in the 800s, 810s and 820s. He was a frequent witness, more often than not at the side of Count Rupert, and it was he who presided at the Eimsheim *mallus publicus* of 825. But Wigrich's and Guntram's careers also warn against equating the position of all these local court presidents and witness-leaders and seeing them as successors in a strictly-defined office: they acted side by side as leading witnesses in an important and politically sensitive transaction of 842. Guntram was a client and kinsman of Count Rupert, and also, through both his lord and his well-placed brother, a figure with access to elite circles; hence he reached the dizzying heights of a brief spell as a count in the 830s. Even earlier in his career these links are evident. He behaves, in the charters, rather more like Rupert's trusted agent and deputy than a truly local leader on the model of Hadurih or Zeizo.[141]

---

[139] *CDF*212, 228 (overseeing the resolution of a dispute), 229 (at Fulda), 252 (at Mainz), 253, 318 (not leading the witness-list), 320, 362; also 229 as a leading-witness in the Rheingau in 818. See Staab, *Gesellschaft*, p. 429, seeing him as 'hundredman of the Wormsgau', p. 264, for his property and family.

[140] *CDF*361. Staab, *Gesellschaft*, p. 429, sees him as a successor of Hadurih as 'hundredman of the Wormsgau'. For Wigrich's witnessing, *CDF*406 and *UBH*26 (probably from 842) are the only charters in addition to *CDF*361 where he heads the witness-list; it may be significant that *UBH*26 is a high-profile transaction. Wigrich subscribes a huge number of charters from 792 onwards: *UBF*195, 237, 245, 249, 250, 253, 255,256, 266; *CDF*199, 229, 283, 305, 417. Staab, *Gesellschaft*, pp. 429–30 for kin and property.

[141] 825: *CDF*459; 842: *UBH*26. His earlier witnessing is difficult to unpick from that of the *vassallus dominicus* and *comes* of the same name who flourished in the 770s and 780s, who was surely a relation (on him, p. 183 with n. 57 below). But from 788 a steady flow of witnessing, until 802 as a rule at his father's side, begins: see *UBF*177, 178, 179, 190, 196, 245, 249, 253, 255, 256 (note the two Guntrams here), 258, 280, 283.

Local power: collective action, conflict and consensus

The precise balance struck by each of these figures between local social pre-eminence and a more official position varied. Their style of local political leadership rested on social networks of mutual obligation. Despite their more or less regular position, stabilised through their links with the aristocracy, they never quite escaped the reciprocity inherent in such a position. They did not totally dominate charter witnessing in the Dienheim area. They needed to deliver to both their comital superiors and their local clients to maintain a delicate position, based on mediation between rulers and locality. The charters, however, are a graphic reminder that the influence of such men was far more pervasive and, on a local level, far more effective than that of counts. Zeizo and his ilk were the dominant actors in the day-to-day life of the localities, whilst counts had to fight, travel, attend court, and supervise family estates. Hence Zeizo, in a pattern which is absolutely typical, was far more frequent a charter witness than Count Rupert, and it was men like Wigrich and Hadurih who acted as court presidents in all but the most explosive cases. These local figures made government work: they ensured that counts were able to meet the king's demands, but also that the process of meeting these demands did not disrupt the social fabric of the locality.

VIOLENCE, RITUAL AND DISPUTE SETTLEMENT

To understand the exercise of political power in this world, we need to look at the balance between official demands and local pressures as it was felt by those men who were simultaneously local actors and royal agents. It is in records of disputes and their settlement that the raw bones of power are visible, naked and unencumbered by their everyday clothing, and so it is through the study of local conflict and its resolution that we can best understand the peculiar interpenetration of local social processes and supra-local contacts that constituted early medieval politics. The historian of the Carolingian middle Rhine is lucky to be able to draw on a rich vein of letters which supplement the courtroom dramas of the charters.

Violence, both threatened and actual, played a recognised and legitimate part in the conduct of dispute.[142] Hence Einhard wrote to Abbot Hraban of Fulda, on behalf of Hraban's *homo* Gundhart. Gundhart had

---

[142] The historical study of violence is still in its youth. For its role in early medieval society, see now G. Halsall (ed.), *Violence and Society in the Early Medieval West* (London, 1997); B. H. Rosenwein, (ed.), *Anger's Past: The Social Uses of an Emotion in the Middle Ages* (Ithaca, 1998). On the legitimacy and function of violence see Wickham, 'Rural Society', pp. 333–5; White, 'The "Feudal" Revolution'; for problems of defining and studying violence in medieval society cf. P. Maddern, *Violence and the Social Order: East Anglia, 1422–1442* (Oxford, 1992).

sought out Einhard's intercession as he was terrified of the anger (*ira*) and enmity (*inimicia*) of an unnamed count: these were technical legal terms, signifying a state of formally declared hostilities, for Einhard described Gundhart's disagreement with the count as constituting a feud (*faidosus*). Gundhart needed Einhard's intervention as he was scared of going on a military expedition which was to be led by the count with whom he was feuding. The letter is difficult, but it suggests that feud was a state of formal enmity which made certain types of physical violence legitimate, but which did not give an absolute *carte blanche* to burn and pillage. Certainly Gundhart's feud with the count was not a spontaneous outburst of bloodshed. It is the danger of contact with the count and his men through involvement in public affairs, and above all through going on campaign, that puts Gundhart in physical danger.[143] Violence, that is, was only legitimate when practised within certain social norms. Being 'in a feud' was to enter into a special legal state, through a formal declaration which was also a threat of possible violence. Einhard elsewhere described the peace-making wrought by the relics of his saints as ending such a state: the presence of the relics inspired two men who were in state of feud to end their enmity, and they swore friendship on the relics, the saints acting as their guarantors.[144]

The motivating force in conflict, and the concern which demanded the threat of inter-personal violence, was the sense of honour.[145] The close relationship between the denial of honour and the outbreak of open violence is clearest in the fragments of an epic poem known as the *Hildebrandslied*, copied, in the vernacular, at Fulda in the 830s. The action centres on the encounter between two warriors and their followers. Their exchange is replete with legal terminology and modelled on the conduct of a formal dispute. They began by declaring their ancestry before rehearsing the issue between them. One makes an offer of golden arm-rings – treasure demonstrating status and allowing the maintenance of honour intact. When this offer is refused, armed conflict between the pair commences. Although made in a work of imaginative literature, the

---

[143] Letter 42, for more on Gundhart, and bibliography, above, pp. 146–7. On feud, see S. D. White, 'Feuding and Peacemaking in the Touraine around the Year 1100', *Traditio* 42 (1986), 195–263; Le Jan, *Famille et Pouvoir*, pp. 85–98; J. M. Wallace-Hadrill, 'The Bloodfeud of the Franks', in Wallace-Hadrill, *The Long-haired Kings* (London, 1962), pp. 121–47.

[144] *Translatio*, II:8, ed. Waitz, p. 247. Cf. letter 65, where Einhard brokers a compromise concerning 'the matter of that composition for which [one of his clients] is in debt to [the recipient] by law'. Note that *amicitia* likewise denoted a formal, legal, state, into which one entered by ritual actions (oath-swearing, as here): cf. Le Jan, *Famille et Pouvoir*, pp. 83–6.

[145] On honour and its centrality to early medieval law see Fouracre, 'Carolingian Justice', and R. Le Jan, 'Justice royale et pratiques sociales dans le royaume franc au IXe siècle', *Settimane* 44 (1997), 47–86.

link between honour and legitimate and ritualised recourse to violence needed no elaboration.[146]

Individuals felt it necessary to enter into public enmity with opponents to right perceived wrongs; not to do so was to fail to do one's duty by family and allies, and worse still to jeopardise one's honour, to lose face and standing in the eyes of the community. Because formal enmity was necessary to maintain honour, the conduct of conflict was determined by the need to defend one's social standing – indeed, it helped define that standing. The threat of violence, and the potential for legitimate violence within certain limits, was thus woven into legal and social intercourse. Concerns about honour may have also played a role in property disputes, although it is an element which charters pass over in silence. We do know, from law-codes, literature and letters, that those engaged in disputes over land often exchanged gifts with other parties. Gifts of high-status objects were an integral part of any dispute, demonstrating mutual respect for the honour of others involved in the process and defining the social relationship between the involved parties. Hence the archbishop of Rheims, defending his church's rights in the woodlands on the upper Nahe, wrote to Erluin, a royal agent in the area who had been involved in the case, thanking him for his aid. Erluin was bound to Rheims in a relationship of *amicitia*, and the archbishop assured him of the gratitude of Rheims' patron saint, Remigius. But this gratitude also took the tangible form of gifts: a silver vase as a *munus,* a customary gift made to the resolver of a dispute, and gold and silver objects, which defined the *amicitia* between Rheims and Erluin.[147] Such practices may look like bribery to modern eyes, but they were central to the functioning of law in Carolingian society; legislators worried that the practice might disadvantage the poor, and attempted to draw a dividing line between necessary gift-giving and improper influence.[148]

Honour not only defined the conduct of conflict between individuals of similar status; it also helped define 'vertical' relationships. Legitimate controlled violence was an essential aspect of the exercise of lordship. Two of Einhard's letters concern the cases of runaway peasants, who fled

---

[146] *Hildebrandslied*: trans. J. K. Bostock, *A Handbook on Old High German Literature* (Oxford, 1976), 2nd edn rev. by K. C. King and D. R. McLintock, pp. 76–7. On the significance of feud in the social imagination, see the important study of the Icelandic sagas by W. I. Miller, *Bloodtaking and Peacemaking: Feud, Law and Society in Saga Iceland* (Chicago, 1990).

[147] Flodoard, *Historiae Remensis ecclesiae* III:26, eds. J. Heller and G. Waitz, *MGH SS*13, pp. 405–599, at p. 545, and see below, p. 226, for Erloin.

[148] See J. Hannig, '*Pauperiores vassi de infra palatio*? Zur Entstehung der karolingischen Königsbotenorganisation', *MIÖG* 91 (1983), 309–74; Fouracre, 'Carolingian Justice'; Le Jan, 'Justice royale'; Nelson, 'Dispute Settlement', p. 43.

to Seligenstadt to seek sanctuary, and won Einhard's intercession. In the first case, a dependent peasant of the archbishop of Mainz's had admitted to homicide, in a context of general disorder (*homicidia propter scandalum*) – perhaps the killing had happened in a brawl, for Einhard stressed that it was not cold-blooded. He faced 'punishment in limb and by scourging', but Einhard begged the archbishop to accept composition instead, arguing that the whole affair was unfortunate and should be dealt with leniently. In a similar case, two peasants from Hedabach, a Mainz estate, fled to Seligenstadt because their brother had killed another peasant on the estate, and pleaded for Einhard to ask that their brother be spared 'punishment of his life and limb', offering instead that 'the proper weregild' be paid.[149] Although both cases involved relationships between lords and their dependants, the logic was still one of vengeance as a means of preserving honour. In both cases the interests of the archbishop had been harmed by a killing, and he had a right to take revenge, not only on the perpetrator of the injustice, but also on their kin. The demonstration of punishment through physical violence was necessary to maintain face, and to warn potential future malefactors.

'Vertical' violence was considered a legitimate means of disciplining the unfree, but the letters suggest that there were social norms limiting its use.[150] In a series of enactments from Worms and Lorsch at the beginning of the eleventh century, lordly rights of vengeance were expressed as legal norms, to be exercised according to certain rules in specific circumstances – above all as a means of disciplining and controlling his following.[151] If we have no formal statements of such rules in the ninth century, Einhard, in pleading with the archbishop, echoed contemporary moral tracts which reminded lords to show justice and Christian charity towards their dependants. These moral checks came very close to legal norms. The phrases describing 'punishment in limb' and so on have a formulaic ring which suggests that they referred to established practice, whilst when Einhard petitioned for commutation from physical punishment to payment of 'the proper weregild' he was drawing on legal ideas about composition (ideas which, indeed, were recorded in written lawcodes). Law worked within, and reinforced, a hierarchical social order.[152] Although these disputes arose within judicial immunities, where rights of

---

[149] Letters 48, 49.

[150] Cf. J. L. Nelson, 'Violence in the Carolingian World and the Ritualisation of Ninth-Century Warfare', in G. Halsall (ed.), *Violence and Society in the Early Medieval West* (London, 1997), pp. 90–107 at pp. 92–3.

[151] *MGH Const.* I, ed. L. Weiland (Berlin, 1893) nos. 35, 438, pp. 78–81, 639–45, and below, p. 246, for their context.

[152] See Nelson, 'Dispute Settlement', pp. 51–2, and R. Balzaretti, 'The Monastery of San'Ambrogio and Dispute Settlement in Early Medieval Milan', *EME* 3 (1994), 1–18.

justice had been granted to their ecclesiastical lords, they were dealt with according to the same norms and procedures which informed legal action outside the immunity.[153] 'Private justice' is therefore a misnomer: although lords must have usually expected to get their way, they were not insulated from social pressures or legal norms. Indeed, they may not have been primarily concerned with the administration of petty justice on their estates, for which there was no real pay-off. Einhard's letters, and contemporary estate surveys, suggest that lordly *iustitia* centred largely on discipline and the control of marriage, and petty disputes may have been left to collective judgement.[154] Even vengeance was not instant. Rather, the physical punishment was decreed, just as Gundhart and his enemy had decreed that they were in a feud, and then a complex drama of intercession and appeal began.

The logic of making amends informed all legal action. In another Einhard letter, two *pauperes* fled to Seligenstadt to plead for intercession. Count Poppo had accused them of poaching, and they had admitted their guilt. They had been ordered to pay a fine to Poppo: 'a part of the fine they have paid and part they still have to pay, but, as they declare, they have not the means of paying on account of their poverty.' Einhard asked Poppo that 'so far as possible . . . they may not be utterly ruined for a transgression of this sort, but may feel that it has profited them in your eyes to have sought refuge at the tombs of the holy martyrs'.[155] Here the law legitimated aristocratic and royal property rights. Although the poachers might have resented the restrictive forest rights, they understood the form of the law and the need to stick to it to have their punishment ameliorated. For here, the law worked through a logic of personal conflict and making amends: the levying of fines, and Einhard's fear of 'utter ruin' (the possibility of judicial slavery and the loss of liberty), were practices of the official law, as recorded in written lawcodes. And Poppo was not acting as an aristocratic lord, but as a royal official guarding royal rights; the poachers had been caught in a *forestis dominicus*, a royal forest.[156]

In any society conflict is a recurrent action.[157] In early medieval society,

---

[153] See Nelson, 'Dispute Settlement', esp. p. 62; Balzaretti, 'The Monastery of Sant' Ambrogio', stressing the utility of the forms of public justice as a means of legitimising lordly power; J. Weitzel, *Dinggenossenschaft und Recht*, 2 vols. (Cologne and Vienna, 1985), I, pp. 717–47.

[154] Letters 37, 38, 48, 49, 50, 60 and *Liber Possessionum Wizenburgensis*, ed. C. Dette, Quellen und Abhandlungen zur mittelrheinische Kirchengeschichte 59 (Mainz, 1987), p. 104.

[155] Einhard letter 47, translated Dutton, pp. 303–4.

[156] Friese, *Herrschaftsgeschichte*, p. 108, identifies it as the Spessart. For the context of stricter definitions of forest rights in the Carolingian period, see Jarnut, 'Die frühmittelalterliche Jagd unter rechts- und sozialgeschictlichen Aspekten', *Settimane* 31 (1985), 765–808, and Wickham, 'European Forests'. [157] Geary, 'Living with Conflicts'.

recourse to violence was, in certain circumstances, acknowledged as proper; legitimate force was certainly not monopolised by the holders of official power. Indeed, no agency of enforcement external to society itself existed to implement legal decisions. Conflict was thus pursued and processed within parameters defined by local social pressures. But this did not make it merely a matter of private initiative: there were agreed norms, patterns of what was recognised as legitimate action, and local opinion was manifested in local collective action, which supplied a veneer of consensus.[158] This was a potent force which rulers could tap and canalise.

This legal world differs greatly from that presupposed in modern notions of law as an abstract set of rules imposed in an impersonal manner by an external agency. The local practices which emerge have much in common with systems of customary law studied in legal anthropology and historical sociology.[159] We need to qualify and refine our notion of custom, however, to enable it to fit fully the early medieval evidence. In this context, custom was not a seamless and unchanging tradition, but malleable, open to change and the subject of heated debate. Early medieval customary law, moreover, proved quite compatible with the pragmatic use of the written word in legal record: it was not a manifestation of an oral or archaic mindset.[160] Comparative work on customary law suggests that this type of legal system works through local consensus and collective action, rather than external agencies of definition and enforcement.[161] Both the epistolary and literary evidence for feud, and the charter evidence for disputes over land, suggest a conception of legal action which emphasised the inter-personal, conflict between individuals about the specific rights of those individuals. Was this compatible with

[158] On the very local logic informing most dispute settlement, see W. Davies, 'Disputes and their Settlement in the Village Communities of Eastern Brittany in the Ninth Century', *History and Anthropology* 1 (1985), 289–312; and W. Davies, 'People and Places in Dispute in Ninth-Century Brittany', in Davies and P. Fouracre (eds.), *The Settlement of Disputes in Early Medieval Europe* (Cambridge, 1986), pp. 65–84.

[159] I have found S. Roberts, *Dispute and Settlement: An Introduction to Legal Anthropology* (London, 1977) particularly useful; many of the works cited below also include good discussions of the comparative material.

[160] On customary law, recent work has stressed malleability and flexibility: for debate see M. T. Clanchy, 'Remembering the Past and the Good Old Law', *History* 55 (1970), 165–79; Reynolds, *Kingdoms and Communities*, pp. 12–66; H. Vollrath, 'Herrschaft und Genossenschaft im Kontext frühmittelalterlicher Rechtsbeziehungen', *Historisches Jahrbuch* 102 (1982), 33–71, and H.-W. Goetz's reply, 'Herrschaft und Recht in der frühmittelalterlicher Grundherrschaft', *Historisches Jahrbuch* 104 (1984), 392–410.

[161] Understanding the social logic of law in practice has been the major project of the new interest in early medieval law in the past two decades, exemplified in the processual microhistories pioneered in the UK by the Bucknell group, notably in Davies and Fouracre (eds.), *The Settlement of Disputes*, and by a series of American scholars. For the current state of play, two recent conferences on 'La giustizia nell'alto medioevo': *Settimane* 42 (1995), 44 (1997).

any sense of 'official' law as the creation of a ruling agency? Is it indicative of 'statelessness'?[162] Was there any concept of offence against society as a whole, any category of the criminal?[163] Given the legitimacy of resort to physical force by wronged parties, and the absence of any regular coercive agency of law enforcement, how were settlements made to stick? Were they essentially compromises informed by the relative strengths of the involved parties, or were they judgements resting upon the application of recognised legal rules?[164]

Legal action in the Carolingian middle Rhine valley was certainly not entirely a matter of private initiative. Although disputes were articulated in terms of personal claim and counter-claim, royal officials did, when necessary, step in.[165] But kings and their officials made no attempt to define the patterns of legal interaction, or the conduct of disputes: they did not have a distinct coercive agency with which they could impose their will. Rather, they worked through local forces to reinforce existing social norms. Indeed, ideas about making amends were useful precisely because they mobilised these forces, which tended to reproduction of the *status quo* and peaceful resolution. Hence Carolingian legislation on the bloodfeud did not strike at the logic of reciprocal action *per se*, but gave official backing to the inevitable local forces for pacification and compromise. If obtaining amends took the form of violent vengeance, the superior, official violence of the king was unleashed; but so long as making amends was a peaceful process, the patterns of inter-personal action and reaction were encouraged.[166]

---

[162] As argued for the post-Carolingian period by F. L. Cheyette, '"Suum cuique tribuere"', *French Historical Studies* 6 (1970), 287–99; Cheyette, 'The Invention of the State'; and Geary, 'Living with Conflicts'. And see now Geary's important discussion of the earlier period, 'Extra-Judicial Means of Conflict Resolution', *Settimane* 42 (1995), 569–605.

[163] Cf. Davies, *Small Worlds*, pp. 149–50, where such a conclusion is drawn from the charters.

[164] Much recent work has tended to blur the distinction between judgement and compromise, consensus and coercion: see M. T. Clanchy, 'Law and Love in the Middle Ages', in J. Bossy (ed.), *Disputes and Settlements: Law and Human Relations in the West* (Cambridge, 1983), pp. 47–67; J. Martindale, '"His Special Friend"? The Settlement of Disputes and Political Power in the Kingdom of the French, Tenth to Twelfth Centuries', *Transactions of the Royal Historical Society* 5 (1995), 22–42; S. D. White, 'Inheritances and Legal Arguments'; Wickham, 'Legal Disputes and their Social Context'.

[165] For example *MGH DCharlemagne* 63, CDF228, TW196a, CDF456, CDF471, CDF560, CL532, Einhard letters 7, 50.

[166] The crucial pieces of feud legislation are *MGH Cap.* I, no. 20, c. 22, p. 51 (779: exile for those in a feud who refuse to pay or accept amends); no. 44, c. 5, p. 123 (805: counts to pacify those involved in feuds; those who continue to feud to lose their hands and pay a fine); and no.136, c. 13, p. 284 (818/19: counts to pacify those in feuds; this legislation repeated in 829, *MGH Cap.* II, c. 8, p. 201). For the logic of these interventions cf. J. Wormald. 'The Blood Feud in Early Modern Scotland', in J. Bossy (ed.), *Disputes and Settlements: Law and Human Relations in the West* (Cambridge, 1983), pp. 101–44; on the 'peace in the feud', Wallace-Hadrill, 'The Bloodfeud of the Franks'.

Isolated but decisive official interventions sent chilling messages about the intermittent possibility of coercive force: conspicuous but occasional official violence is characteristic of a legal order in which rulers have to rely on intermittent threat rather than constant policing.[167] The strategic points at which rulers did intervene were precisely those at which the norms that defined society were broken, or social order threatened. Hence the worried letters of the archbishop of Mainz concerning the *scandalum* caused by a feud which had ended with a bloodbath in a local church. Here a Christian, moral order had been broken: the forces of order had the wrongdoers rounded up, and imposed public penance, which involved the laying aside of arms and thus exclusion from the society of the secular elite. It was where a moral order was threatened that we have the beginnings of a sense of the criminal.[168] One local account of an uprising against the archbishop of Mainz in 866 makes this graphically clear. Savage reprisals were taken against the ringleaders of the uprising – 'some were hanged, others had their fingers and toes cut off, or were even blinded; many left all their property to escape death and became exiles.'[169] These actions were presented as acts of rightful vengeance for two of the archbishop's men who had been killed in the unrest. Here the logic of revenge was entwined with the imposition of legal punishments reserved for offences against the proper order.

The charters, moreover, suggest that even property law was not simply a matter of the establishment of fact and the brokering of compromises to recreate local consensus. Written with hindsight from the winner's viewpoint, they used a vivid vocabulary of wrongdoing when discussing disputes. The 'unjust' seizure of property was a refrain, whilst losers were castigated for behaving with 'evil intent'.[170] Law was based on universal notions of right and wrong, just and unjust. Documents recording the outcome of disputes are often frustratingly opaque, and we should not expect them to tell us exactly what was debated, or how the parties involved put their cases. But it does seem clear that cases were settled with respect to argument, rather than the simple assertion of fact. In the previous chapter we studied in detail two disputes over land, one concerning the rights of an heir of a man who had given land to the church, one the rights of a 'trustee' who had been given land on condition that he in turn give it to the church. A close examination of the issues at stake and

---

[167] The classic, though controversial, statement is D. Hay *et al.*, *Albion's Fatal Tree* (London, 1973).

[168] *MGH Epp.* V, no.20, pp. 525–6, and see M. De Jong, 'What was "Public" about Public Penance? *Paenitentia Publica* and Justice in the Carolingian World', *Settimane* 44 (1996), 863–902, for the significance of *scandalum*, moral order, and public penance. Synodal legislation has much to offer on this subject.   [169] *AF*, s.a. 866, trans. Reuter, p. 65.

[170] *MGH DCharlemagne* 63, *CDF*228, 456, 459, 560.

the eventual outcome made it clear that legal norms must have been invoked: norms which held that the wishes of the dead to have gifts made for the health of their souls be respected, but which also militated against the wholesale impoverishment of heirs.[171] That is, reliance on local testimony did not make law simply a matter of establishing what had been past practice in a particular case. Arguments could be put forward, arguments both moral and legal. Hence, in the case of the poachers, discussed above, there were legal norms, which related to the injunctions of written law-codes, determining the punishment meted out for poaching, and the effects of the non-payment of fines. There were also, however, moral norms, a Christian framework of mercy, to which Einhard appealed. It was not a case of identifying the specific procedure and proofs applicable in a certain type of case, as in modern law. Rather, facts were established and then a multiplicity of arguments from a variety of sources were advanced. There was no external body of formal law which informed what had to be demonstrated. In this sense, it was a world of substantive moral legalism, not formal law.[172]

Putting a case seems to have followed set patterns: these were genuine legal procedures, however hard they may be to recover. We have already seen that feuds had a ritual grammar which regulated individual conduct. For land law, the surviving evidence is tantalisingly sparse, but full of hints. Charters point to the significance of topographical features, often named after landowners and some man-made, which functioned as boundary-markers and visible 'title-deeds'; one literary source describes a peasant striking a large stone which acted as a boundary-marker when he entered a plot and staked his claim to it.[173] There was a set of rituals used to conclude disputes, too. The *festuca*, a staff passed around a public meeting, would be grasped and wrongdoing admitted. This formal admission was seen as ending any challenge or accusation. Losers then usually had to make some kind of solemn promise or oath, probably involving a pledge or fine, to respect the outcome of the hearing. Most importantly of all, cases about land almost as a rule ended with a ritual re-giving of the disputed land – with a *revestitura*. On those occasions where disputes were settled in arenas distant from the land in question, symbolic objects – staffs or other insignia – represented the property. The enactment of the ritual of *revestitura* was emphasised in the charters,

---

[171] See above, pp. 68–73.
[172] For 'substantive legalism' in these terms see White, 'Inheritance and Legal Arguments'; White, *Custom, Kinship and Gifts*, esp. pp. 76–80, and cf. Fouracre, 'Carolingian Justice', and McKitterick, 'Perceptions of Justice'.
[173] *CL6a*, 21, and see Hincmar, *Vita Remigii*, ed. B. Krusch, *MGH SRM* 3, pp. 239–341, c. 27, p. 323.

presumably as it often confirmed a *de facto* change of possession.[174] Even royal judgements were acted out thus on local stages: on 6 July 782, following a hearing at the royal court about property rights in the *villa* of Schwanheim, two royal *missi* arrived at Schwanheim with those who had given sworn testimony at the royal court, brandishing the royal *praeceptum* which recorded the result of the case.[175] The *praeceptum* so conspicuous at Schwanheim, if it had survived, would have mentioned nothing of this second, local manifestation of royal justice; we only know of the acting out of the judgement on the local level because of the transmission of a local record. The record of the *vestitura* of Charlemagne's gift of the *fiscus* of Hammelburg to Fulda is a similar text, produced in the locality and recording the local rituals through which a distant decision was effected.[176] Such rituals were not, however, only used in the enactment of royal judgements: they were absolutely typical.[177]

The ritualisation of the conclusion of disputes was important because making a settlement stick was always likely to be difficult in a world where there was no ever present coercive agency of enforcement. Oath-swearing, the most recurrent ritual practice, took place on relics and thus invoked saints and God as witnesses to the truth, guaranteeing social visibility and publicity. Oaths were thus means of both legitimating and communicating decisions. Ritual practices which may appear odd and irrational to our eyes had a social logic which made them common sense.[178] Thus the Fulda monk Rudolf (in his youth a charter scribe and so a man well-versed in legal practice) recounted how, at some point in the late eighth century, a dead baby was found near the nunnery of Tauberbischofsheim on the Main. Locals, outraged, accused the nuns of living a loose life and breaking their vow of celibacy. The abbess, Leoba, led the nuns in parade around the nunnery walls, their arms outstretched in the shape of the cross, chanting the Psalms. In doing so, they were practising the ordeal of the cross, a ritual of proof attested in law-codes, although it had been banned by Louis the Pious by the time that Rudolf wrote (although not at the time he was writing about). The ritual worked. The invocation of the divine caused the dead baby's mother, actually a local laywoman, not a nun, to confess that she had left the baby before the nunnery. Here, ritual worked by mobilising local social

---

[174] These rituals emerged most clearly in royal charters thanks to the formulae used by the royal chancery: e.g. *MGH DCharlemagne* 63,65. For *revestitura* see e.g. *CDF*456.   [175] *CL*228.
[176] *UBF*83.   [177] E.g. *CL*428, *CDF*456, *TW*69: examples could be multiplied.
[178] More work has focused on ordeals than on oath-swearing or the more widespread phenomenon of the invocation of the supernatural. See P. Brown, 'Society and the Supernatural: A Medieval Change', *Daedalus* 104 (1975), 133–51; R. Colman, 'Reason and Unreason in Early Medieval Law', *Journal of Interdisciplinary History* 4 (1974), 571–91; and R. Bartlett, *Trial by Fire and Water* (Oxford, 1986).

pressure. By invoking the sacred through the ordeal of the cross, Leoba increased the stakes, forcing the mother, who must already have been the object of gossip, to confess. The ritual also helped to re-establish order: the perambulation of the nunnery walls by nuns singing Psalms and practising the ordeal of the cross, as well as shaming the dead baby's mother, re-established the sacred aura of the nunnery, an aura threatened by the gossip caused by the dead baby. It was a ritual of purification, emphasising that the nunnery walls enclosed a sacred space. Finally, we must remember that this highly ritualistic form of justice was used precisely because this was an unusual and intractable case. The type of common-sense proof provided by local testimony and production of documents could hardly have established the facts here, and so an ordeal was necessary.[179]

Ritual invocation of the divine may have been used in exceptional cases, such as the scandal of the dead baby at Tauberbischofsheim, but it was effective precisely because it was a rare event imbued with the solemnity of the sacred. As disputes were characteristically settled in local meetings attended by local men listening to local testimony, there was likely to be strong local pressure towards enforcing a settlement, and towards making sure that the settlement would stick. The rituals used to enact a settlement similarly may have acted to crystallise local consensus around a mutually acceptable resolution. That is, disputes were resolved with reference to the consensual view of the locality, stated in ritual form. These local pressures were the agency enforcing settlement, and when royal agents intervened, it was normally precisely because royal interests were threatened or these more local processes had broken down.

THE TEXTURE OF LOCAL POWER

In the absence of formal rights of territorial control, local power in the Carolingian world was ultimately dependent on the ability to carry a public meeting, to exert influence, pull in favours, cajole support. Coercion might be possible intermittently, but not as a lasting strategy: the exercise of power was rooted in the everyday, in the give and take of face-to-face relationships of co-operation, patronage and mutual back-scratching. Informality and interpersonality made local power almost impossible to delegate. Personal presence was necessary for the direct exercise of power, which was therefore bound up with patterns of movement and meeting. To a very large extent, then, the terminology of

---

[179] See Rudolf, *Vita Leobae*, ed. Waitz, c. 12, pp. 126–7, and see Bartlett, *Trial by Fire and Water*, pp. 4–13, esp. 9–10.

'government' and 'administration' is misleading. Politics was woven into the texture of local social relationships. Political leadership was exercised in local public meetings. Political power was claimed and negotiated through the collective action of a series of overlapping and interleaving groups on a hierarchy of public stages. These local patterns of the public, manifest and collective must replace administrative delegation in our minds as the foundation stones of the Carolingian polity.

5

LOCALITY AND CENTRE: MECHANISMS
OF EXTRACTION

APPROACHING EARLY MEDIEVAL GOVERNMENT

Carolingian kings wielded a formidable degree of structural power. They were able to maintain an efficient military machine and successfully extract the labour which enabled the building of palaces, fortifications, roads, bridges and other public works. For us, it is second nature to assume that structural power of this type must be based on a system of political organisation resembling the modern state: so begins a long search for administrative institutions.[1] Yet, as we have seen, political power in Carolingian society did not rest on a dedicated state infrastructure of delegated official roles. If it is difficult for us to reconcile such a state of affairs with real structural power on the part of kings, that is an indication of our ingrained 'statism'. To understand the foundations of the structural power enjoyed by Carolingian rulers, we need to start from the localities, and investigate the extent to which royal demands impinged on them, and the mechanisms through which these demands were met.

Uncovering these mechanisms is difficult: the primary interest of most of the surviving Carolingian documentation was not the day-to-day supply of palaces, messengers or soldiers. The problem facing any attempt to reconstruct rule from the bottom up is that whilst royal edicts can be made as general or specific as the reader wishes, the detailed local evidence – above all that of the polyptychs – inevitably concerns only ecclesiastical and fiscal property.[2] It is often claimed that the practices that can be seen on ecclesiastical and royal land demonstrate the workings of 'private' lordship, the king as landowner exploiting his own estates and ecclesiastical land under his protection. This hypothesis has become deeply embedded to the stage that it is more or less unconsciously a prop

---

[1] Thus Werner, *'Missus-marchio-comes'*, and cf. Campbell, 'The Late Anglo-Saxon State'.
[2] On the inventorying of fiscal and ecclesiastical land as a response to royal initiatives, see Metz, *Das karolingische Reichsgut*.

141

for 'empirical' research techniques. Where royal dues are documented it is assumed that they are a hangover resulting from an original, often long-past, period of royal ownership. Yet, for all the valuable results that such research has provided, its foundation remains simply a hypothesis; to assume, a priori, that royal dues must relate to royal ownership is to close down debate about the basis of royal power before it has begun.[3]

More recently, a group of French historians have reached contrasting conclusions, similarly based on a priori hypotheses about the nature of royal power in the early middle ages. They have championed the 'public' nature of the practices recorded in the polyptychs, seeing in them the legacy of the Roman state.[4] Yet to demonstrate the origins of early medieval practices in late Roman public law is one thing; to allege a continued sphere of state action quite another. It is equally possible that late Roman practices remained, fossilised and localised, to be picked up by later landowners, particularly kings and bishops.[5] We certainly cannot base our interpretation of early medieval documents on the assumption that their terminology retains the precise meanings it had in late Roman public law.[6] In fact, the 'maximum' view of Carolingian government ultimately rests on the assumption with which we began, that significant structural power must by definition be the product of a dedicated state infrastructure.

Let us eschew both the 'private' and 'public' hypotheses and observe Carolingian rule in action. The type of obligations which were central to the Carolingian political system are neatly defined in a diploma of Louis the Pious, granting royal foresters in the Vosges immunity from the 'public functions'. The document spelt out precisely what was meant by

---

[3] The 'regressive' method developed at the Max-Planck Institut für Geschichte, and exemplified for our area by Gockel, *Königshöfe*, is thus at once indispensable, but puzzling on account of the tendency to lead to a picture of a hypothetical Merovingian fisc of vast, compact blocks covering most of the kingdom. This is only really possible if we accept that fiscal 'ownership' in the early Merovingian period was a loose concept, as argued above, pp. 73–7.

[4] See above all Durliat, *Les finances publiques*, which supplies a full bibliography of recent work in a 'fiscalist' vein.

[5] Whilst one tenth-century commentator could gloss polyptych as *publica lex* (W. Goffart, 'Merovingian Polyptychs: Reflections on Two Recent Publications', in Goffart, *Rome's Fall and After* (London, 1989), pp. 233–53 at pp. 234–5) the continuation of a public element to such revenue raising needs demonstrating. F. Lot, *L'impôt foncier et la capitation personelle sous le bas-Empire et à l'époque franque*, Bibliothèque de l'Ecole des Hautes Etudes 253 (Paris, 1928), pp. 77–82, 107, discusses the continuity in form but rightly points out that Carolingian fiscality as seen in the capitularies is something quite different to that of the late Roman state. Cf. Goffart, 'From Roman Taxation to Medieval Seigneurie: Three Notes', in Goffart, *Rome's Fall and After* (London, 1989), pp. 255–73, and R. Kaiser, 'Steuer und Zoll in der Merowingerzeit', *Francia* 7 (1979), 1–17.

[6] Cf. Wickham, 'La chute de Rome n'aura pas lieu' on Durliat's tendency to read medieval texts in the light of Roman usage rather than contemporary social and economic relationships. I find the comeback by E. Magnou-Nortier, 'La chute de Rome a-t-elle eu lieu?', *Bibliothèque de l'Ecole des Chartes* 152 (1994), 521–41, unconvincing.

'public functions', exempting the foresters from payment of the army tax (the *haribannus*), performance of transport services (*paraveredi*), and obedience to other *ad hoc* orders (the *bannus*); they were, however, still to pay an impost (the *stoffa*).[7] 'Public functions' thus subsumed military service, royal imposts, and a variety of petty dues.[8] The problem is one of generalisation from the specific. After all, the Vosges foresters were men under a special form of royal lordship, who resided in a royal forest. It could be argued, quite correctly, that their case is direct evidence for services levied on royal land and its tenants alone. We must investigate the rubrics suggested by the diploma one by one, with a view to understanding how they related to other men in different communities.

MILITARY SERVICE

Military service is the place to begin any analysis of early medieval political organisation, precisely because questions about military service lie at the heart of debate about the nature of the early medieval state.[9] The nineteenth-century view was that fighting was an ancient duty of all free men, making the army the 'nation in arms', a levy of a mass of free property-holders all in a direct relationship to the king. This theory has proved difficult to part with, despite quite legitimate scepticism as to the possibility of such peasant militias being either useful or possible.[10] In

---

[7] *Formulae Imperiales* 43, ed. Zeumer, *MGH Form.*, pp. 319–20. The Vosges here includes the forests between the Moselle, the Saar and the middle Rhine: see Schneider, 'Reims und das Remigiusland im frühen Mittelalter (6 bis 9 Jht.)', *ZGO* 119 (1971), 47–80 at 79–80.

[8] Compare *MGH Cap.* I, no. 143, pp. 294–5: *Capitulare de functionibus publicis*, which discusses payments at the palaces, bridge work and service in royal hunting-ranges (*brogilii*); see esp. c. 4 limiting the imposition of 'public functions' to those legitimated by 'ancient custom'. Also *Cap.* I, no. 165, c. 2, p. 330 (banning gifts from the church motivated by desire to avoid military service or 'other public functions'). Most interesting of all *MGH Cap.* II, no. 241, p. 150. The term is already used in the late sixth century by Gregory of Tours, *Historiae* V:26, eds. Krusch and Levison, pp. 232–3. For 'public *servitium*' see *MGH Cap.* I, no. 93, c. 5, p. 196: gifts to the church do not end transport dues (*angraria*) '*seu servitio publico vel privato*'; and J. W. Bernhardt, *Itinerant Kingship and Royal Monasteries in Germany, 919–1056* (Cambridge, 1994), p. 77, n. 148 for some examples of its use in charters.

[9] For illuminating discussions of these interpretative problems elsewhere in early medieval Europe, see R. Abels, *Lordship and Military Obligation in Anglo-Saxon England* (Berkeley, 1988) (but see n. 31 below); N. Lund, 'The Armies of Swein Forkbeard and Cnut: *Leding* or *Lið*?', *Anglo-Saxon England* 15 (1984), 105–18.

[10] For a survey of the Merovingian background, see B. S. Bachrach, *Merovingian Military Organisation 481–751* (Minneapolis, 1972), pp. 65–9 who shows the lack of evidence for any Merovingian universal military service, and Reuter's discussion, 'The End of Carolingian Military Expansion', in P. Godman and R. Collins (eds.), *Charlemagne's Heir: New Perspectives on the Reign of Louis the Pious (814–40)* (Cambridge, 1990), pp. 391–405 at p. 396 and n. 25. Such ideas can permeate even the most empirical of discussions: for example C. Dette, 'Einige Bemerkungen zum ältesten Weißenburger Urbar', in A. Verhulst (ed.), *La grande domaine aux époques mérovingienne et carolingienne* (Ghent, 1985), pp. 112–24 at p. 114, sees the personal military service performed by some of Wissembourg's ninth-century tenants as a relic of this old peasant-based order.

reaction, since the beginnings of the twentieth century many have sought the origins of political society in lordship, and presented military service as originating in personal subordination.[11]

The normative sources for military service are problematic in that they only discuss obligations to fight in any detail during the first decades of the ninth century, at precisely the time when the orientation of the Frankish military was undergoing significant change. In the eighth century campaigns had been annual and offensive, and the plunder and prestige that they generated had added to the momentum of the military machine. Attempts to set up a responsive defensive system after the end of regular expansion led to a flood of rulings on military service after 800.[12] Indeed, injunctions claiming that military service was a universal obligation on all free men were first made in a defensive context in the ninth century. They were concerned, moreover, with the exceptional case of defence of the homeland (*patria*) against invaders.[13] These injunctions cannot be read as statements of fundamental principles of military organisation dating back to the forests of Germany, the Merovingian foundation of the Frankish kingdom, or even the annual offensive campaigns of the eighth century. The very fact that ninth-century rulers needed to legislate on the universality of the obligation to defend against invaders underlines how exceptional universal military service must have been.

The capitularies on military service, if handled with care and recognised as attempts to redefine practice to support a new defensive stance, can help us to identify some of the groups who did fight. They are frequently concerned with the service performed by the *pauperes*: those with little property were to club together to provide one soldier from a group.[14] Most historians have argued that this marked a move away from a supposed archaic levy of all free peasants, with military service becoming too onerous for the *pauperes* to perform. This thesis founders on the lack of evidence for a universal peasant levy in the Merovingian period. Indeed, as early as the sixth century it was reported as being customary that 'public functions' were not levied on *pauperes*; in the eighth century some *pauperes* received formal, written exemptions from military service.

[11] This is the central point of much German scholarship between the 1920s and 1950s: on the army, see H. Dannenbauer, 'Die Freien im karolingischen Heer', in Dannenbauer, *Grundlagen der mittelalterlichen Welt* (Stuttgart, 1958), pp. 240–56. Free men in the Carolingian army were actually those over whom the king enjoyed proprietorial rights.

[12] Reuter, 'Plunder and Tribute in the Carolingian Empire', *Transactions of the Royal Historical Society* 35 (1985), 75–94; Reuter, 'End', esp. pp. 391–5.

[13] See *MGH Cap.* II, no. 71, n. *, and the comments of Reuter, 'End', pp. 399–400; J. L. Nelson, 'Kingship and Empire in the Carolingian World', in R. McKitterick (ed.), *Carolingian Culture: Emulation and Innovation* (Cambridge, 1994), pp. 52–87 at p. 65; and K.-U. Jäschke, *Burgenbau und Landesverteidigung um 900*, VF Sonderband 16 (Sigmaringen, 1975), p. 22.

[14] Reuter, 'End', p. 395, with a full list of references at n. 22.

Carolingian capitularies were actually regularising a long-standing tradition of granting *ad hoc* exemptions, and clarifying precisely what services were owed by the *pauperes*, whose lack of military utility can scarcely have been a new development of the ninth century.[15]

Long before the ninth century there were mechanisms on a local level which made some men liable for military service, but not others. *Circa* 600 a legal document from Angers shows one man paying his son to fight in his stead, a case which is surely incompatible with the idea that all free men were expected to fight.[16] The existence of some criteria which identified certain individuals as liable for military service, and the close relationship between these criteria and local patronage systems, is vividly shown by a case from late Merovingian Paris: in 695 a free man named Ibbo was forced by the abbot of Saint-Denis to sell a piece of land to escape military service.[17] Carolingian legislation attempted to introduce a new degree of transparency to the whole issue of military service, in that grounds for exemption and performance were laid down in an explicit, universal manner. This was reinforced by the compilation of lists of those owing service.[18] In the reign of Louis the Pious, transmitted mobilisation orders aimed at the quick informing of known individuals, based on lists drawn up by royal officials, not at the mobilisation of all the free.[19]

Criteria of ability must have been the bottom line in determining the make-up of the Carolingian army: a free peasant was no use in the field unless equipped and trained. Abbot Hraban of Fulda, adapting a Roman commentator on military organisation for a Carolingian king, commented that 'in our days, youths are nourished in the houses of princes'. The sons of the highest aristocracy learned the arts of hunting, riding and fighting in a period at court in their adolescence; those of a less exalted status spent a similar training period in the households of aristocratic patrons.[20] Here was the supply of trained soldiers which fuelled the Carolingian military machine. To receive such a placement, one needed

---

[15] Reuter, 'End', pp. 398–400. From the Merovingian period see Gregory of Tours, *Historiae* V:26, eds. Krusch and Levison, pp. 232–3. From the eighth century see n. 49 below; *Formulae Salicae Merkmaliae* 41, ed. Zeumer, *MGH Form.*, pp. 256–7.

[16] *Formulae Andecavenses* 37, ed. Zeumer, *MGH Form.*, p. 16. See also Reuter, 'End', pp. 396–400.

[17] *MGH DMer* 68.

[18] *MGH Cap.* II, no. 185, p. 5. See also Flodoard, *Historia Remensis Ecclesiae* III:26, eds. Heller and Waitz, p. 545. For transparency cf. *MGH Cap.* I, no. 73, c. 3, pp. 164–5.

[19] See Frothar of Toul, letter 2, *MGH Epp.* V, p. 277, from Archbishop Hetti of Trier to Bishop Frothar of Toul (817) and also *MGH Cap.* II, no. 185, p. 5 (828). For comments see Ganshof, *Frankish Institutions*, pp. 63–4, Werner, '*Missus-marchio-comes*', p. 115, n. 25, and Reuter 'End', p. 394, n. 17.

[20] See Dette, 'Kinder und Jugendliche'; Innes, '*A Place of Discipline*'; K. Leyser, 'Early Medieval Canon Law and the Beginnings of Knighthood', in L. Fenske *et al.* (eds.), *Institutionen, Kultur und Gesellschaft im Mittelalter. Festschrift J. Fleckenstein* (Sigmaringen, 1984), pp. 549–66; J. L. Nelson, 'Ninth-Century Knighthood: The Evidence of Nithard', in C. Harper-Bill *et al.* (eds.), *Studies in Medieval History Presented to R. Allen Brown* (Woodbridge, 1989), pp. 255–66.

wealth and connections. The mechanisms through which the martial engine was kept turning over were thus essentially locally generated within the elite.

The primary role of those without the connections that allowed military training may have been the provision of logistical support. Charlemagne had demanded carts full of provisions as well as military contingents from his abbots.[21] The Wissembourg polyptych allows a view of how such demands were met from the abbey's estates. Military dues from tenants and dependants were organised over the abbey's estates as a composite unit. Free tenants were expected to provide horses, oxen and carts, and on occasion to serve themselves. Services were levied in an uneven manner; the abbatial estate at Altstadt, for example, was exempt altogether. Other estates were expected to co-operate with each other in producing supplies. The polyptych records a system which could annually place eight cavalry horses, thirty-six oxen, eight carts and twenty men in the field. Wissembourg's estates, that is, were organised so as to provide a neatly rounded military contingent.[22] Royal estates in the middle Rhine were organised similarly. The polyptych evidence gives no hint of a universal obligation on all free men to perform military service even here, on royal land at the heart of the Empire. All free tenants at Nierstein and *Wilauwilare* were to perform personal military service, but at these two settlements alone; the description of *Wilauwilare* explicitly contrasted the military dues of free tenants here with their absence in other neighbouring settlements.[23] On both royal land and Wissembourg's estates, it was the immediate landowner who was responsible for the organisation and provisioning of his contingent.[24] Such arrangements made the creation of a viable army from a mass of free and half-free peasants possible.

Flesh can be put on these dry bones thanks to Einhard's letters. Gundhart, a client of Fulda whom we have already met in a feud with the local count, asked Einhard to intercede for him with Abbot Hraban. Einhard asked that Gundhart:

---

[21] See *MGH Cap.* I, no. 75 (804xii), p. 168 and the comments of F. Prinz, *Klerus und Krieg im früheren Mittelalter. Untersuchungen zur Rolle der Kirche beim Aufbau der Königsherrschaft*, Monographien zur Geschichte des Mittelalters 2 (Stuttgart, 1971), pp. 73–9.

[22] *Liber . . . Wizenburgensis*, ed. Dette, cc. 1–25. Dette argues that this document dates to *c.* 818, suggesting a link between the making of the polyptych and the ordering of services from royal monasteries recorded in the 819 *Notitia de servitio monasteriorum* (ed. P. Becker, in K. Hallinger (ed.), *Corpus Consuetudinum Monasticarum I* (Siegburg, 1963), pp. 483–99). On the polyptych see Dette's introduction, *Liber . . . Wizenburgensis*; Dette, 'Einige Bemerkungen'; Dette, 'Die Grundherrschaft Weißenburg im 9. und 10. Jahrhundert im Spiegel ihrer Herrenhöfe', in W. Rösener (ed.), *Strukturen der Grundherrschaft im frühen Mittelalter* (Göttingen, 1989), pp. 181–96. The importance of such logistic support for successful campaigning is stressed by B. S. Bachrach, 'Animals and Warfare in Early Medieval Europe', *Settimane* 31 (1985), 707–751.   [23] CL3672–3.

[24] Ganshof, *Frankish Institutions*, p. 63; Verbruggen, 'L'armée', pp. 432–3.

may be allowed to absent himself from the muster which is to take place at this time, and may stay at home without offence to you, nay, with your approval. He asserts that he is driven to this staying at home by strong necessity in as much as he is in a feud and dare not attend this muster with his enemies and men who are plotting against his life especially with that count under whose commands the muster is to be held and whom, he says, is a most bitter enemy to him. Therefore he asks that he may not be pushed into such danger by an authoritative order of yours. He will attend to making provision to pacify the collector of the *haribannus* if he comes and summons him, and will do it without putting you to any trouble.[25]

The charter evidence shows that Gundhart was a free man who owned the land he cultivated, at Nordheim in the Grabfeld.[26] Rather than a full-time retainer of Hraban's, he was a well-to-do proprietor in a loose patron–client relationship with Fulda. Nonetheless, Gundhart's military service was performed as a part of the abbey's contingent, under the supervision of a local count.[27] The stress on the need for such a specific exemption parallels important passages in the capitularies, where specific legal summonses played a central role in defining military responsibilities.[28] Gundhart, having heard that an army was being summoned, was identified as a man who owed military service and so was expected to participate; if he failed to do so the *haribannus* would be levied. In this sense, he was a 'professional' soldier, and was recognised as such by royal officials.

The world of men like Gundhart can be further investigated from the charters. A brief notice, made 'in the twenty-fifth year of our lord King Charles the first' and transmitted in the Lorsch cartulary, concerned the estate of one Ripwin who was 'travelling to Lombardy with my lord, the aforesaid king' – that is, campaigning with the royal army in Italy.[29]

---

[25] Einhard, letter 42. For the social networks revealed by this letter, see Wickham, 'Rural Society', pp. 531–2.

[26] See CDF423–6, 435. Wickham suggests that Gundhart may be a benefactor of Seligenstadt who was also a client in a more formal sense of Fulda.

[27] It is not clear here whether the count acquires jurisdiction over Gundhart as Abbot Hraban will not be able to lead Fulda's military contingent in person (compare Lupus, *Epistolae*, no. 15, ed. L. Levillain, *Loup de Ferrières. Correspondance*, 2 vols. (Paris, 1964), I, pp. 92–5) or as the count in question is commander of the army as a whole.

[28] Reuter, 'End', pp. 396–8. Cf. Lupus, letter 72, ed. Levillain, ii:10–12.

[29] CL257: 'in Longobardiam cum domino meo iam dicto rege iturus'. The reference to Charlemagne as Charles the first is due to the status of Charlemagne's son Charles as king and chosen heir. There are problems with the dating: the 25th year of Charlemagne would be 792–3, the date given by Glöckner in his edition, but in this year the focus of campaigning was in the east, against the Avars (BM317b). However late in 792 a force was despatched to Italy under Charlemagne's son Charles, and Ripwin could just about be a member of this host (BM320c). Another possibility is that the date is confused (hardly surprising as the notice is idiosyncratic in form and thus probably not the work of a regular scribe).

Ripwin – worried about the possibility of death on campaign, and his inability to defend his property whilst absent in Italy – left his land to his brother Giselhelm, with instructions to give it to Lorsch if he (Ripwin) did not return from Italy. If Ripwin did return, Giselhelm was to return the estates to him. Ripwin made it back. He witnessed charters until 806. The charter evidence supplies important information about the social connections of this Carolingian soldier.[30] His brother, Giselhelm, appeared in many other charters, usually at his side. The pattern of Ripwin's activity as a donor and witness is not incompatible with the hypothesis that he customarily and regularly performed military service: he witnessed mainly in autumn, winter and spring, and never whilst a campaign was going on. That Ripwin's brother did not serve in the army is left beyond doubt by his appearances as a charter witness in the campaigning season; Ripwin's military service was not hereditary. His case, therefore, cannot be made to conform to the 'private' model of the royal services being due only from 'king's free men', individuals over whom the king enjoyed proprietorial rights. It is clear that Ripwin's family dealt with their property as theirs, and theirs absolutely; it was in no sense royal land. That is, although Ripwin's career suggests the existence of dedicated soldiers, their status was not hereditary, nor determined by a special tenurial position.[31]

Thanks to the charter evidence, we can investigate the effects of military service on Ripwin's family. Ripwin's close kin were well-to-do peasants, who owned a handful of parcels of land which they worked themselves (no tenants or dependants appear in the charters). The family's activities and holdings were overwhelmingly centred on one village, Bensheim. There they made a clearance, which, significantly, they then gave to Lorsch.[32] Of especial interest for understanding the evident relationship between this family and Lorsch is the first appearance made by Ripwin and Giselhelm in the charters: in 768 or 769 they sold land held in common to Lorsch, in return for a horse (the charter scribe used the term *caballus*, immediately reminding one of the *caballa-*

---

[30] On the family see Gockel, *Königshöfe*, pp. 260–2. His reconstruction differs slightly in emphasis from mine: he believes that Ripwin's military service makes him a royal vassal, and that his family are therefore aristocrats. This is at odds with the very full charter evidence.

[31] On the 'private' model, and the theory that in the early middle ages freedom meant royal ownership, see above, pp. 4–5, 85 n. 91. This theory, which is losing its ground in work on the Frankish Empire even in German historiography, underpins some of the work of Abels, *Lordship and Military Obligation*, on Anglo-Saxon England. An additional argument against the *Königsfreie* theory is the tying of state obligations to particular individuals and their descendants, or to specific pieces of land, in late Roman and Byzantine fiscal law (cf. below, n. 56): such practices, if we do detect them, need have nothing to do with royal ownership of land or Germanic forms of lordship. [32] CL245.

rii, cavalrymen mentioned in Carolingian capitularies as making up a monastery's military contingent). Horses – particularly quality cavalry horses – were a scarce commodity in this society and possession of one immediately marked out a certain status on Ripwin's part.[33] Significantly, Ripwin and Giselhelm's activity as charter witnesses began in the late 760s, suggesting that the sale to Lorsch and the acquisition of a horse may have been accompanied by changes in his social position.[34] The acquisition of a horse may represent a conscious strategic decision to enter the clientele of the monastery, one of the brothers serving as a soldier and winning the support of the monks, and the family thus avoiding the sub-division and resulting fragmentation of family land. It is no accident that Ripwin's will, should he fail to return from Italy, was preserved at Lorsch, and recorded his wish that Lorsch be given land in such an eventuality. The family's later gift of cleared land to the monks was likewise significant: this transaction would have cut both ways, with the family cementing their relationship with the monks without alienating inher-ited land, whilst the monks gained a newly cultivated plot, which had been cleared by one of their clients and his kin. There are tantalising hints at similar relationships being formed in a handful of other charters, in which Lorsch and Fulda gave swords to donors. These transactions remind us that the foundation and consolidation of rural monasteries in the eighth century created new centres of wealth, centres from which high-status goods were redistributed, creating bonds of mutual obligation between the monastery and its patrons. They also explain why kings insisted that lords were to ensure their followers were fully equipped when they went on campaign.[35]

Ripwin's soldiering and relationship with the monks allowed him to acquire a certain social standing. He began to witness charters more

---

[33] CL247. Note that this charter is eccentric in language and form, as are others associated with the brothers, notably CL245 and CL257. In CL245 a monk Folcrad, otherwise unattested as a charter scribe, writes up a donation for the family. On *caballarii* see *MGH Cap.* I, no. 49, c. 3, p. 136; no. 75, p. 168, and so on; for other transactions involving *caballi* see CL1895, 2522.

[34] Ripwin's father last witnesses in CL245. The buying of the horse is the first appearance for the two brothers. Ripwin's gift to Lorsch in 806, his last appearance, looks like that of an old man making a gift for his soul.

[35] See Schwind, 'Klöstern als Wirtschaftsorganismen', p. 115. From Lorsch, the prime example is CL508, the gift of a sword in return for land; from Fulda, CDF336, a gift of a complete set of wargear, and the classic case, CDF471 (for discussion of the latter see M. Gockel, 'Die Träger von Rodung und Siedlung in Hünfelder Raum in der Karolingerzeit', *Hessisches Jahrbuch für Landesgeschichte* 26 (1976), 1–26 and Innes, 'Space, Place and Power'). Elsewhere – at Carolingian St Gallen or post-Carolingian Cluny, for example – such gifts are more often mentioned in the charters. Further in-depth study of this material would shed important light on the relationship between the bearing of arms, royal service, social status and landholding: cf. N. P. Brooks, 'Arms, Status and Warfare in Late Saxon England', in D. Hill (ed.), *Ethelred the Unready*, British Archaeological Reports British Series 59 (Oxford, 1978), pp. 81–103.

frequently than either his father, grandfather or uncle had, and stood shoulder to shoulder with the local landowners who probably did not have to dirty their hands in agricultural work. By 806 Ripwin personally was able to leave Lorsch a scattering of half a dozen parcels of land, including holdings at Dienheim, over the Rhine from his home village.[36] Ripwin's activity as a soldier and client of the monks also created bonds of association. In the key disputes cutting through the locality in the 770s and 780s, Ripwin followed his 'lord king' in the person of a local royal agent, Guntram, and brought family and neighbours with him.[37] But there were limits to mobility. Ripwin never became one of the select band with real local influence. The record of one dispute from 782 makes this clear, as Ripwin and his kin are numbered amongst a group of interested witnesses (styled *testes* by the charter scribe), but not among the group of *scabini* who ran the show. On other occasions, when the 'illustrious men' of the locality were summoned to deliberate and decide, Ripwin and his family had no part to play.

Ripwin is not the only soldier who can be identified from the charter evidence. At the assembly held at the royal palace of Paderborn in Saxony in June 785, Fulda received a series of gifts of land. The Paderborn meeting was also the embarkation point for a campaign against the Saxons, and these men were cementing links with the abbey which was playing a salient role in the conquest and conversion of Saxony.[38] One of the gifts concerns land in the middle Rhine, at Roxheim. Its witness-list reads like a veritable who's who of the area south of Mainz. Ratbod, who made the donation, was the owner of the church at Flonheim, a well-to-do local with contacts at the highest political level through his kin, who included Count Gerold, brother of the recently deceased Hildegard, who had been Charlemagne's wife. Among his witnesses were Count Hatto, whom we have already met as the royal agent in the Mainz area, and another familiar face, Walaram, Hraban Maur's father. Ratbod's charter graphically demonstrates the importance of local elites as the backbone of the Carolingian army, and the importance of the bonds of kinship and common action which bound them together and supplied links to the political centre. (Presumably more humble locals who were clients of monasteries like Fulda and Lorsch, or of brokers like Count Hatto and Count Gerold, were also present, but

[36] CL259.   [37] CL228.
[38] UBF163–5 (Ratbod's charter is UBF165), and see BM268c for the context. UBF160–2, which give no place of redaction, may also date to the Paderborn assembly (see D. Bullough, 'Aula Renovata: The Carolingian Court before the Aachen Palace', in Bullough, *Carolingian Renewal: Sources and Heritage* (Manchester, 1991), pp. 123–60, n. 32 at p. 154). Gockel, *Königshöfe*, p. 267, assembles useful information on the witnesses but assumes that those present must be royal vassals; similarly Bullough, 'Aula Renovata', n. 32 at p. 154.

not required to witness the legal deeds of the great and good.) Going on campaign, for all its manifest dangers, was attractive for these men precisely because it brought them to the political centre, into contact with powerful kin and patrons. One ninth-century source from Alemannia gives insight into the hopes which led men to go on campaign: it tells tales of two clients of Ratbod's relative, Gerold, who acquired public office after catching Charlemagne's eye through their valour in battle. The army was a potent engine of social mobility and political integration; in another story from the same source, two bastards from Colmar were rewarded for their vigilance in guarding Charlemagne's tent by being promoted into his personal bodyguard.[39]

The Carolingian army worked through social networks, but this did not make it simply an agglomeration of personal followings any more than the presence of free smallholders like Ripwin made it a peasant militia. The real problem is one of generalisation from fragmentary evidence: how do we ascertain the direction and processes of change? Here, the received view of a move from a peasant-based army based on public obligations to one based on private obligations between lord and man is so deeply embedded as to be difficult to budge.[40] But its evidential basis is almost non-existent. Capitularies insisting that all benefice-holders, *fideles* and *vassi* must fight when summoned, cluster in the first decade of the ninth century, and are normally taken as an index of the increasing importance of benefices and of a new form of private lordship defined by military obligation. Like so many other regulations about the Carolingian military, however, they date from precisely the point in time when the practices which had supported annual offensive campaigns were being redefined to meet new needs. Kings no longer wanted companions in profitable offensive plundering, but demanded onerous defensive duties, often removed from one's immediate locality, in the name of the public good. The capitularies were simply ensuring that all those who could fight, did fight, and do not necessarily reflect any substantive social change other than the end of the annual offensive campaign.[41] The local evidence confirms that in the ninth century, tenurial obligation was far from becoming the basis of military service. At Wissembourg, ten

---

[39] Notker, *Gesta Karoli* II:2–4, ed. Haefele, pp. 51–2. On the interpretation of these stories in Notker, see Innes, 'Memory, Orality and Literacy'.

[40] See e.g. J. Fleckenstein's otherwise admirable 'Adel und Kreigertum und ihre Wandlung im Karolingerreich', *Settimane* 27 (1981), 67–94. The old technologically determinist argument, that the need to develop heavy cavalry led to new military demands which were met by a new tenurial definition of military service, is now thoroughly discredited on grounds of military technology, let alone social history.

[41] See *MGH Cap.* I, no. 48 (807), cc. 1, 2, pp. 134–5; no.49, c. 3, p. 136; no. 50 (808) cc. 1, 9, pp. 137, 138; no.141 (819), c. 27, p. 291.

estates were granted out to laymen who performed a variety of services – political and administrative as well as military – for the abbey. Similarly, at Prüm a handful of local figures who were active in the abbey's service and sometimes referred to as vassals received land *in beneficium*, whilst a few powerful aristocratic patrons received estates *in precaria*. The relationships cemented by these grants did not centre on the performance of military service, and the handful of men involved only constituted a small portion of the lord's contingents, although they were doubtless the elite.[42]

This reading of the Carolingian material is confirmed by evidence from the tenth century. In 980 or 981 Otto II demanded military levies to reinforce his army in Italy. Their make-up is recorded in the *Indiculus loricatorum*. Round numbers of horse-borne soldiers, fully equipped, were to be supplied by bishoprics, royal monasteries, and counts: the archbishop of Mainz 100 men, the bishop of Worms 40, the bishop of Speyer 20, the abbot of Lorsch 50, Count Megingoz 30, Count Heribert 30, and his brother 30, or 40 if he did not come himself in person. The charter evidence, which shows that full ownership of property remained the dominant tenurial form, makes it unlikely that these armed retinues were significantly different in composition to their Carolingian predecessors: there simply were not enough benefices in the charter evidence for the large contingents recorded in the *Indiculus* to have been made up of soldiers supported by 'feudal' tenure. As in the Carolingian period, there clearly were a hard-core of benefice holders (most of them holding grants of ecclesiastical land) and a significant body of retainers who resided in the household of their lord, but the size of levies demanded by Otto II makes it inconceivable that men like Ripwin and Gundhart, local landowners who were clients of churches or aristocrats, did not also owe and provide military service when it was demanded of them.[43]

Even in the mid-eleventh century, benefice-holders constituted an elite military force, but many who owed military service were not tied into a 'feudal' nexus: Lorsch's twelfth-century chronicler tells us that in 1066 the abbey's military following was led by twelve *fideles* who held benefices on account of their military service, each of whom was responsible for

---

[42] Wissembourg: *Liber . . . Wizenburgensis* caps. 216–26. Prüm: Kuchenbuch, *Bauerliche Gesellschaft und Klosterherrschaft*, pp. 330–55. On the military service of benefice-holders in the Carolingian period see now Reynolds, *Fiefs and Vassals*, pp. 84–105.
[43] *MGH Const.* I, no. 436, p. 633, on the *Indiculus* and tenth-century military organisation see K.-F. Werner, 'Heeresorganisation und Kriegführung im deutschen Königsreich des 10 und 11 Jahrhunderts', *Settimane* 15 (1968), 799–845 and Reynolds, *Fiefs and Vassals*, pp. 423–8. Note that this is a list of reinforcements: the lay contingents at least are demanded from those who were not already participating, whilst the ecclesiastical ones may have been supplementary levies. On the charter evidence for tenth-century society, see pp. 49, 92–3, 240–1.

leading a large number of *milites*, who presumably were clients of a type not wholly unlike Ripwin or Gundhart.[44] A similar system is suggested by the charter evidence from Fulda, where in the late tenth and early eleventh century explicit contracts about the performance of military service, particularly military service on Imperial expeditions in Italy, began to be included in documents recording grants of ecclesiastical land to laymen *in beneficium*. The fact that precise legal stipulations about the military incidents of land tenure had to be made, in a written record of the transaction, implies some novelty. Yet it was hardly new that holders of ecclesiastical land were expected to fight for their landlord. The insistence on formal, defined, obligations in these documents suggests that in the eleventh century tenure of monastic land, which had previously created multifaceted patronage relationships, was beginning to be defined in terms of specific legal duties, in particular the duty to perform specified military services, especially those relating to distant and onerous royal service.[45] These grants presumably supported an elite fighting force like the twelve Lorsch *fideles* which in the normal run of things met royal and abbatial demands, but which, when necessary, could be supplemented by the monastery's clients. Eventually in the course of the eleventh century even the service of these clients came to be defined in terms of property law: as early as 1020 Burchard, bishop of Worms, had legislated for his *familia*, the clients of the church of Worms whose position was increasingly coming to be expressed in terms of the church's legal ownership of them. With the emergence of a society increasingly based upon legal obligations defined with reference to property rights over land and people, what had been systems of clientage run to supply royal demands became the incidents of lordship.[46]

THE ARMY TAX

Once we accept that the Frankish army was never a universal peasant militia, and that military service was not an incident of land tenure before the eleventh century, the inevitable question arises: how was military service defined before the emergence of proprietorial lordship in the eleventh century? Examination of the dues exacted from those who did not fight to support those who did supplies an answer. In the Carolingian period, there is clear evidence for an army tax, the *haribannus*. This is a facet of the Carolingian military system which has been

---

[44] *CL* i.415, discussed by Reynolds, *Fiefs and Vassals*, p. 427, which drew the significance of this episode to my attention.   [45] The Fulda charters are *CDF*724, 740, 749.
[46] Burchard of Worms, *Lex familia Wormatiensis ecclesiae, MGH Const.* I, ed. Weigand, no. 438, pp. 639–45, and see p. 246 below.

hitherto neglected, but it sheds important light upon the nature of the obligation to fight. The received view is that the *haribannus* was an ancient fine for non-performance of the military service.[47] Certainly Gundhart, Abbot Hraban's client, wished to pay it as an alternative to fighting, and much Carolingian legislation concerns comparable cases.[48] However, it is equally clear that by the Carolingian period the *haribannus* was levied as a matter of course from some individuals: it was not simply a fine for non-performance, but a payment in support of the army.[49] The polyptych evidence makes it crystal clear that for many men payment of the *haribannus* was a levy to support the army, not a fine for not fighting. For example, free tenants of the king at *Askemundesheim* in the Dreiech, and probably in other royal *villae* in the forest, gave one measure 'for the host'. At Morgenstadt, west of Worms, holders of free tenures similarly paid 'thirty smaller, or twenty-four larger, measures, in payment to the host'. These dues levied on the tenants of great land-owners tended to be taken from free tenants from whom personal military service was not expected.[50] In other words, the Carolingian *haribannus* was an incident on free men from whom military service was not expected, and used as a means of maintaining the army. A capitulary of 808 is suggestive of the kind of social contract involved: the *missi* were to check that the *pauperes* had been bonded together into soldier-providing groups, as ordered the previous year. Those 'who failed to support their peers (*pares*) in the host, in accordance with our decree' were to pay the *haribannus*. Exactly how these local groupings were constituted is unknown, but the *haribannus* was clearly a payment, enforced

---

[47] For example Verbruggen, 'L'armée', p. 424.

[48] *MGH Cap.* I, no. 64 (810), c. 12, p. 153 (those who should have served but did not fined); no. 74 (811), c. 1, p. 166 (to pay *haribannus* if ordered to fight but fail to appear); c. 9, p. 167 (to pay if fail to follow lord in host to pay *haribannus*, but lord to pay for those he orders to stay at home on guard); no. 141 (819), c. 27, p. 291 (bishops, abbots, counts and royal vassals who fail to fight and cannot demonstrate 'necessary cause' to pay *haribannus*). Analogous are *MGH Cap.* I, no. 50 c. 1, p. 137 (a *pauper* who fails to help *parem suum* to pay *haribannus*); c. 9, p. 138 (*fideles* who stay at home on royal orders not to pay *haribannus*). From Italy see *MGH Cap.* I, no. 98, p. 205 (free man who returns home from campaign in contempt of royal order to pay *haribannus*). Again, note the recurrent link to specific royal orders not general legal obligations.

[49] *Formulae Salicae Merkmaliae* 41, ed. Zeumer, *MGH Form.*, pp. 256–7, implies that payment of the *haribannus* is a different matter to service *in hostibus*. Compare also *Cartae Senonicae* 19, p. 193, and *Collectio Patavensis* 3, pp. 457–8. All three formulae date from the late eighth century. From the ninth century, see *MGH Cap.* I, no. 99, c. 13, p. 207: Italian capitulary talking of 'the *haribannus* or any other tax levied on account of the army'. Compare *MGH Cap.* I, no. 40, c. 5, p. 115. Annals of St Bertin, s.a. 866, ed. Grat *et al.*, p. 126; Verbruggen, 'L'armée', p. 428.

[50] *CL*3672–4. Local custom was inevitably messy in practice: thus freemen at Nierstein perform military service and pay the *haribannus*, whilst elsewhere there are unfree who pay the *haribannus*. Confusion resulting from the mismatch between tenure and legal status is only to be expected in this context. Cf., for the Prüm evidence, Kuchenbuch, *Bauerliche Gesellschaft und Klosterherrschaft*, pp. 139–41.

by landlords and royal officials, levied on the mass of free landowners to support local men who went on campaign.[51]

The origins of the *haribannus* are shadowy. The earliest references to its levying come from the seventh century: *c.* 665 the bishop of Speyer was granted immunity from the payment of judicial fines (*freta*), taxes (*sthupha*) or the *haribannus*, whilst the abbot of Wissembourg received a similar immunity towards 700.[52] Long before these references to the *haribannus*, individuals were fined for the non-performance of military service: in the early seventh-century law-code *Lex Ribuaria*, those who did not fight when summoned were liable for the standard fine for ignoring an official summons of any type.[53] Whilst those who were expected to perform military service but failed to meet their obligation were fined right through the Frankish period, the development of a dedicated army payment known as the *haribannus* took place in the course of the seventh century. Any explanation must relate it to the political and social changes of this period. At the beginning of the seventh century, the drafters of *Lex Ribuaria* saw the population as heterogeneous in legal identity, including Franks, Romans, 'royal men' and 'ecclesiastical men'. Being a Frank was closely linked to the performance of military and other services for the king, in return for exemption from those imposts inherited or adapted from the Roman past. But in the course of the seventh century, Frankish identity came to be universal and the Merovingians' ability to tax atrophied. The direct correlation between royal service and Frankish identity thus became untenable. In response, payments began to be levied on those who did not fight on the grounds that, as free Franks, they owed military service. These payments, perhaps originally local and *ad hoc*, quickly became known by the Franco-Latin term *haribannus*.[54] Some of these payments, particularly those levied on free tenants on great

---

[51] *MGH Cap.* I, no. 50, c. 1, p. 137. On *pares*, compare *MGH Cap.* I, no. 74, cc. 5, 6, p. 167, and *Formulae Imperiales* 47, ed. Zeumer, *MGH Form.*, pp. 319–20. The description of customary military service in Berkshire in Domesday Book, discussed most recently by Abels, *Lordship and Military Obligation*, pp. 85–196, is essentially a late version of precisely this type of early medieval military system.   [52] *MGH DMer* 28; *TW*12.

[53] See *Lex Ribuaria*, c. 65.1, ed. Eckhardt, p. 65: the fine is for disobedience when a Frank is '*in legibus in utilitatem regis sive in hoste seu in reliquam utilitatem bannitus fuerit*'. But a '*Romanus*' or a '*regius seu ecclesiasticus homo*' who is disobedient pays a different fine (65.2). Reuter, 'End', p. 397, n. 28, says that this is 'clearly the ... *haribannus* of Carolingian times': in substance it is, but it is not yet differentiated from the more general powers included under the *bannus* in the Carolingian evidence. Similarly, see Gregory of Tours, *Historiae*, V:26, eds. Krusch and Levison, pp. 232–3 (discussed above) and VII:42, p. 360, where a local judge fines those who do not go on campaign.

[54] For seventh-century changes see E. Ewig, 'Volkstum und Volksbewußtsein im Frankenreich des 7. Jhts.', in Ewig, *Spätantikes und fränkisches Gallien. Gesammelte Schriften 1952–73*, ed. H. Atsma, Beihefte der Francia 3, 2 vols. (Munich, 1976), I, pp. 231–73 and esp. W. Goffart, 'Old and New in Merovingian Taxation', in Goffart, *Rome's Fall and After* (London, 1989), pp. 213–31. For heterogeneity of legal identity in *Lex Ribuaria*, see e.g. c. 65.1, ed. Eckhardt, p. 65.

estates, may in essence have been continuations of imposts inherited from the Roman state, maintained by landlords and subsumed under a new label; certainly there are marked similarities between the military dues incumbent on the tied tenants of the later Roman period and those recorded in Carolingian polyptychs.[55] But such practices were subsumed under a larger rubric: the obligation of all free men to support the army either by serving in person or paying the *haribannus*. A comparison with the evolution of late Roman practices in Byzantium highlights the peculiar social logic of Frankish practice. In Byzantium, named free landowners and specific estates were identified by the state as liable for military service, and non-fighters were legally responsible for their financial support; the whole system was justified with reference to the fiscal law of the late antique state.[56] In Francia, the universalisation of Frankish identity and the atrophy of the legal and fiscal infrastructure of late antiquity left military obligations defined in terms of the personal obligation of Frankish free men to the king of the Franks. The social and political changes of the seventh century led to the emergence of a new, characteristically early medieval, military system.

ROYAL LEVIES

Although the ninth-century *haribannus* was to all intents and purposes an army tax, it is significant that it was never presented as a tax, but as the result of personal obligations owed by free men to their king. This in itself must shed doubt on Jean Durliat's controversial arguments for a taxing-and-spending Carolingian state based on the inheritance of the late Roman tax system. Durliat's case is based on the contention that Carolingian polyptychs were records not of estate management, but of state imposts.[57] Yet even a cursory inspection of the polyptychs makes it clear they were not tax-lists. They did not exist, Domesday Book fashion,

---

[55] The observation of similarities goes back to Lot, *L'impôt foncier*, pp. 126–7. Durliat 'L'impôt pour l'hoste' and *Les finances publiques*, pp. 196–7, would generalise from such payments to a centrally-defined fiscal system; Devroey, 'Problèmes de critique autour du polyptyche de l'abbaye de Saint-Germain-des-Près', in H. Atsma (ed.), *La Neustrie. Les Pays du Nord de la Loire de 650 à 850*, Beihefte der Francia 16, 2 vols. (Sigmaringen, 1989), I, pp. 441–65 here 441–2, draws attention to their uneven impact.

[56] For Byzantium, see J. F. Haldon, 'Military Service, Military Lands and the Status of Soldiers: Current Problems and Interpretations', *Dumbarton Oaks Papers* 47 (1993), 1–67.

[57] See J. Durliat, 'Le polyptyche d'Irminon et l'impôt pour l'armée', *Bibliothèque de l'Ecole des Chartes* 141 (1983), pp. 183–208, and 'Qu'est-ce qu'un polyptyche? A propos des documents de Tours (ChLA 659)', in *Media in Francia . . . Recueil des Mélanges offerts à K.-F. Werner* (Paris, 1989), pp. 129–38. J.-P. Devroey, 'Polyptyques et fiscalité à l'époque Carolingienne: une nouvelle approche', *Revue Belge de philologie et d'histoire* 63 (1985), 783–793, offers criticism. Lot, *L'impôt foncier*, p. 82, had already signalled the possibility of using polyptychs to discern the contours of taxation.

for all sectors of society, but rather for royal and ecclesiastical land alone, and most of the practices they describe were nitty-gritty concerns of agrarian tenure.[58] Nonetheless, they do include payments and practices made in response to the demands of kings, including, as we have seen, levies to support the army. The polyptych evidence thus provides a way into an investigation of the whole range of royal exemptions with which we began: namely the payment of a levy known as the *stoffa*, and the performance of corvées at the king's command.

Let us begin with the payment of royal levies. In 889 the bishop of Würzburg received a grant of one-tenth of all royal levies (*tributi*) from the eastern Franks and the Slavs 'whether in honey or in fur pelts or in any other form of payment'. This payment was known by the vernacular term *osterstufa* and was taken from the population of the area west of Würzburg along the Main and into the middle Rhine valley.[59] Similar payments were made by those further west still: royal foresters in the Vosges were exempt from the *stuofa*, whilst in 850 an inhabitant of the Moselle valley named Winebert gave his estate and his person to St Arnulf's at Metz and received royal exemption 'from all exactions, that is from payment of the *stofa* and expeditions in the host'.[60] There is further information about these levies in the polyptychs. For example, holders of free tenures at Nierstein paid four *denarios ad osterstuapha* each year, whilst free tenants at Königstedt in the Dreiech paid two *denarios ad osterstufa*, and the *osterstufa* was also paid at Florstadt in the Wetterau. These payments were not rent-based, even if they were levied alongside rent.[61] The surviving evidence makes most sense if the term *osterstufa* is read as a generic label which could cover a whole range of broadly similar levies – that is, nomenclature was a matter of local interpretation, not central edict. At Königstedt, the only *villa* in the Dreiech where *osterstufa* was

---

[58] In *Les finances publiques*, pp. 192–3, Durliat jumps from registers of 'la totalité de l'Etat'(church lands, *honores*, benefices) to 'l'universalité de la manse' as a unit of assessment. As Metz pointed out in 1960, the only inventories that we know of which made any kind of claim towards universality were those of 829: *Das Karolingische Reichsgut*, p. 18. The key document for the scope of such lists is an account of royal lands and dues in Rhaetia, probably dating from 843, and edited in an appendix to *Bündner Urkundenbuch I: 300–1199*, ed. E. Meyer-Marthaler and F. Perret (Chur, 1955).

[59] *MGH DArnulf 69*. This was a renewal of an earlier precept, confirming a grant allegedly first made by Pippin.

[60] *MGH DLothar* II 6. It is unclear what lay behind this remarkable transaction: it could be that Winebert was under some kind of royal lordship (like the foresters), but there is no indication that this is the case, as Winebert initiates the transaction and needs no royal licence for his donation. The unique total immunity which Metz had received from Charlemagne is relevant: *MGH DCharlemagne* 66.

[61] Nierstein: *CL3672*. Königstedt: *CL3673*. Florstadt: *CL3675*. Gockel, *Königshöfe*, pp. 96–100, is the best overview of the *osterstufa*, but cf. W. Metz, 'Zum Lorscher Reichsurbar', *Historisches Jahrbuch* 106 (1986), 407–17 at 410; also, *Das karolingische Reichsgut*, p. 74.

paid, there is no record of an *annona* of one measure of wheat which was levied elsewhere in the Dreiech: the two payments were equivalent, if not identical. The difference between Königstedt and the neighbouring settlements is explained by the fact that Königstedt had been the property of the monks of Fulda, who gave it to the king in an exchange in 823, whereas the rest of the Dreiech was royal property throughout the Carolingian period.[62] The implication, that these levies were not made on royal tenants alone, and that their nomenclature and content varied depending on local conditions, is supported by evidence from Worms. Here a charter in the name of Arnulf, heavily interpolated in the second half of the tenth century, granted the bishop of Worms market and toll rights within the city along with the 'king's measure which is also known as the *stuofchorn*'. Whether this particular clause is genuinely Carolingian or a later interpolation, the document does show that in the tenth century such a due existed and was worth claiming.[63]

This evidence for cash and kind levies from the middle Rhine and its eastern hinterland hardly points to a Durliat-style fiscal state operating on late Roman lines. Nonetheless, the ability to take a direct levy is important, not least as the *osterstufa* bears no resemblance to late Roman practice, and would be difficult to see as a fossilised survival.[64] Here an originally personal due had developed into a more regular royal exaction.[65] The name *osterstufa* is the only clue we have as to origins. It has normally been interpreted as denoting a payment made at Easter. However, some early Carolingian sources use a similar vernacular label, *ostarliudi*, to refer to the 'eastern folk', those east of the Rhine. There is thus a good philological case for seeing the *osterstufa* as a tribute levied on the 'easterners', originating before the eighth century.[66] The exaction of a tribute in kind, as outlined in the grant of the *osterstufa* to Würzburg,

---

[62] *CL*3673. The *annona* (the title from the sums at the end of the register) is doubled at Nivenheim. It looks similar to the army payment at *Askmundesheim*, although Nierstein makes both army payments and *osterstufa*. For Fulda and Königstedt, *CDF*325b.

[63] *MGH DArnulf* 166 and see J. Lechner, 'Die älteren Königsurkunden für das Bistum Worms und die Begrundung der bishoflichen Fürstenmacht', *MIÖG* 22 (1901), 361–419, 529–74 for the series of late tenth-century forgeries of which this is a prime example.

[64] There is little dispute that in southern Gaul there were some fossilised late Roman practices; for the argument that they were large-scale and significant see Magnou-Nortier, 'La gestion publique en Neustrie: les moyens et les hommes (VIIe–IXe siècles)', in H. Atsma (ed.), *La Neustrie. Les Pays du Nord de la Loire de 650 à 850*, Beihefte der Francia 16, 2 vols. (Sigmaringen, 1989), I, pp. 271–320.

[65] Lot, *L'impôt foncier*, p. 111, pointed to parallels in other regions, notably Alemannia, where further research might shed more light on the pattern of development I suggest.

[66] J. Schütz, 'Die Deutung alter fränkischer Beziehungen: Ortsname "Vougastisburc"-"ostarstuo-pha"- "Trusnasteti"', *Jahrbuch für fränkische Landesforschung* 56 (1996), 111–22, esp. 117–20. For the 'orientalium Francorum quos illi propria lingua osterliudos vocant' see *Annales Mettenses Priores*, s.a. 688, ed. B. von Simson, *MGH SRG* (Hanover, 1909), p. 4. Cf. also *Hildebrandslied*, l.58 for the *osterliudi*.

was typical of Merovingian hegemony.[67] This was presumably originally a tributary exaction imposed on the region in the sixth or seventh century, which by the Carolingian period had become a customary due paid by all free men.

This regularisation of tributary gifts was paralleled in Carolingian dealings with their elite generally. Although Merovingian kings received gifts from their more powerful subjects, the Carolingians demanded 'annual gifts' as obligatory.[68] By the ninth century, the request and receipt of such gifts was ordered and regulated by palace officials: thus Einhard advised Count Poppo on the *dispensa* required from him, whilst under Louis the German two horses, each with a shield and lance, were expected each year from royal abbeys.[69] This formalisation affected the peasant population of great estates. Einhard ordered that his estates provide *eulogiae* 'according to custom' for the emperor, whilst free and unfree tenants of Wissembourg were to take 'customary gifts', either produce (hens and eggs) or cash, to the palace at Worms when 'royal service' was demanded.[70]

By the ninth century, kings were also commandeering corvée labour to upkeep royal palaces. Again the tenants of bishoprics and royal abbeys had a particularly visible and important role.[71] In the middle Rhine, estate

[67] See I. N. Wood, *The Merovingian North Sea* (Alsingas, 1983); and, on Merovingian hegemony in the east; Wood, *The Merovingian Kingdoms, 481–751* (London, 1993), pp. 160–4; and Wood, 'The Frontiers of Western Europe: Developments East of the Rhine in the Sixth Century', in W. Bowman and R. Hodges (eds.), *The Sixth Century: Production and Demand* (Leiden, Boston and Cologne, 1998), pp. 231–57.

[68] Reuter, 'Plunder and Tribute, 85–6; Nelson, 'The Lord's Anointed and the People's Choice: Carolingian Royal Ritual', in D. Cannadine and S. Price (eds.), *Rituals of Royalty: Power and Ceremonial in Traditional Societies* (Cambridge, 1987), pp. 137–80 at p. 166.

[69] See Einhard, letter 8 (on *dispensa* see also *MGH Cap.* 1, no. 143, p. 294, and compare Lupus letters 45 and 47, ed. Levillain, i:192, 196). *MGH DLouis the German* 70 (cf. also *MGH DZwentibald* 18, where Trier's due is reduced to six horses each year). For discussion see Waitz, *Deutsche Verfassungsgeschichte* IV, pp. 106–10; Bernhardt, *Itinerant Kingship and Royal Monasteries*, esp. pp. 75–81.

[70] Einhard, letter 26; see Dette's introduction to *Liber . . . Wizenburgensis*, pp. 63–4. Also 'Einige Bemerkungen', pp. 114–15 for discussion of 'royal service': prominent as payments in pitch paralleled from royal forests and, like the *eulogiae*, useful but small scale. For a fuller discussion of royal service and *eulogiae*, A. Schäfer, 'Die Abtei Wissembourg und das karolingische Königtum', *ZGO* 114 (1966), 1–53 at 7–13, with plenty of parallels for small gifts and cash payments in west Frankish polyptychs (Schäfer's argument that such payments can be explained by the rights of the king over his 'proprietary church' is unconvincing). T. Zotz, 'Beobachtungen zur königlichen Grundherrschaft entlang und ostlich des Rheins vornehmlich im 9. Jahrhundert', in W. Rösener (ed.), *Strukturen der Grundherrschaft im frühen Mittelalter* (Göttingen, 1989), pp. 74–124 at pp. 113–21.

[71] For example: St Gallen [Notker II:21, ed. Haefele, p. 92 (St Gallen craftsmen help build Aachen)]; Rheims [Flodoard II:19, eds. Waitz and Heller, p. 469 (Louis the Pious frees Rheims from work at Aachen); also Einhard, *Translatio* IV:2, ed. Waitz, p. 256 (Rheims man involved in building at Aachen)]; Toul [Frothar, letter 9, ed. Dümmler, pp. 282–3 (Toul exempted from the *servitium onerosum* at Aachen but is to build and repair a wall and portico at nearby Gondreville instead)].

surveys show that free tenants of Wissembourg and the Nonnenmünster at Worms were to travel to palaces, carrying stone and sand, to perform building work.[72] Einhard, who was granted a dwelling at Aachen on account of his role as a courtier, had the abbey of St Servatius at Maastricht (close by Aachen) provide food to the palace; the abbey also supplied men 'to repair and restore'.[73] Corvées and royal orders were also used in the building and maintenance of churches.[74] Probably the most onerous royal demands came from the network of royal forest rights, which were closely related to the palace system and defined by the demands of the royal hunt, a social, political and ceremonial occasion of the utmost importance.[75] Inhabitants of settlements along both banks of the Rhine made customary payments to royal agents in acknowledgement of royal forest rights in their locality.[76] They also performed labour services preparing the way for the royal hunt, presumably keeping up fences and maintaining the forest so as to maximise royal and aristocratic enjoyment: work in royal *brogilii* was counted as one of the 'public functions', whilst in the Vosges royal foresters were freed from all other services to oversee and maintain royal hunting rights.[77]

It was the network of royal roads, and the bridges which were the nodal points of the transport system, that accounted for perhaps the most impressive of the 'public functions'. In the first decades of the ninth century, royal legislation shows a concerted attempt to make the upkeep of this infrastructure a universal duty.[78] The charter evidence from the

---

[72] Zotz, 'Beobachtungen', pp. 119–21; A. Schäfer, 'Mauerbaupflicht fränkischer Königsleute zu Ladenburg und an der karolingerzeitlichen Ringwallanlage "Heidenlöcher" bei Deidesheim. Eine Quelle der Karolingerzeit aus dem Kloster Nonnenmünster bei Worms', *ZGO* 74 (1965), 429–435.   [73] Einhard, letter 5.

[74] See G. Weise, 'Staatliche Baufronden in fränkischer Zeit', *Vierteljahrsschrift für Sozial- und Wirtschaftsgeschichte* 15 (1921), 341–80. For specific cases from our area, all involving churches, see Einhard, letter 33; *Rheinisches Urkundenbuch*, ed. Wisplinghoff, nos. 64, 65, 74.

[75] On the close relationship between palaces and forests, K. Bosl, 'Pfalz und Forst', in *Deutsche Königspfalzen. Beiträge zu ihrer historischen und archäologischen Erforschung* I (Göttingen, 1963), pp. 30–74. On the hunt's significance, J. Jarnut, 'Die frühmittelalterliche Jagd'; R. Le Jan-Hennebicque, 'Espaces sauvages et chasses royales dans le Nord de la France, VIIe–IXe siècles', *Revue du Nord* 244 (1980), 35–57 and K. Hauck, 'Tiergärten im Pfalzbereich', in *Deutsche Königspfalzen* I (Göttingen, 1963), pp. 1–29. Also H. Rubner, 'Vom römischen Saltus zum fränkischen Forst', *Historisches Jahrbuch* 83 (1964), 271–7, and Wickham, 'European Forests', on forest rights.

[76] CL3671, and see Metz, 'Zum Lorscher Reichsurbar', 414–15, arguing that it is a payment for use-rights (those who unequivocally live within the forests do not pay it). For the social and economic significance of woodland in the early middle ages, Wickham, 'European Forests'.

[77] *MGH Cap.* I, no. 143, pp. 294–5; *Formulae Imperiales* 43, ed. Zeumer, *MGH Form.*, pp. 319–20.

[78] On roads, bridges and their maintenance see M. Rouche, 'L'héritage de la voierie antique dans la Gaule du haut Moyen Age (Ve–XIe siècles)', in *L'homme et la route en Europe Occidentale*, Flaran 3 (Auch, 1982), pp. 13–32; T. Szàbo, 'Antikes Erbe und karolingisch-ottonische Verkehrspolitik', in L. Fenske et al. (eds.), *Institutionen, Gesellschaft und Kultur im Mittelalter. Festschrift J. Fleckenstein* (Sigmaringen, 1984), pp. 125–45; Siems, *Handel und Wücher*, pp. 461–8; and for a wider context

middle Rhine hints at how these initiatives might have been implemented locally. Lorsch was involved in the upkeep of roads and bridges from 777, when it received a large tract of royal land between the abbey and the Weschnitz, along with the right to maintain a road and bridge in the area, presumably with the labour of the inhabitants of the area granted.[79] In 815 Louis the Pious gave further property to Lorsch, in a gift explicitly linked to the upkeep of roads and which included within its immunity a bridge over the Weschnitz. This transaction is the earliest example of the upkeep of a bridge being presented as pious work: the monks were to build the bridge 'in alms' for Louis' soul, monastic resources being mobilised for the public good.[80] The complex relationship between kings, royal abbeys and the infrastructure of roads and bridges revealed by this charter is paralleled in an edict of 820, which encouraged the repair of bridges by powerful individuals or institutions *ex propriis facultatibus*, but forbade the levy of new or exploitative tolls in repayment.[81] A not dissimilar arrangement provided sustenance and support for eleven men from Worms who were born into a role as royal messengers, and who collectively constituted a *societas parafridorum*. These men, and the group of royal estates which were earmarked for their supply, were granted to the bishop of Worms by Arnulf at the end of the ninth century, but this did not end their role as royal servants, it merely passed responsibility to a more local agency. Messengers, now organised for the king by the bishop of Worms, continued to be active in royal service through the tenth century into the first years of the eleventh, when they were referred to as *ministeriales*, unfree servants.[82] At the heart of this messenger system lay a group of royal servants supported by ear-

N. P. Brooks, 'Medieval Bridges: A Window onto Changing Concepts of State Power', *Haskins Society Journal* 7 (1997), 11–29. Cf. the remarkable evidence from Rochester, N. P. Brooks, 'Church, Crown and Community: Public Work and Seigneurial Responsibility at Rochester Bridge', in T. Reuter (ed.), *Warriors and Churchmen in the High Middle Ages: Essays Presented to K. Leyser* (London, 1992), pp. 1–20.   [79] *MGH DCharlemagne* 114.

[80] BM577 = CL18. (And note Lorsch's rights to levy *paraveredi* at Weinheim in the eleventh century: CL3669 and Wehlt, *Reichsabtei und König*, p. 120). On bridges as pious works see Szàbo, 'Antikes Erbe', p. 145, missing the Lorsch case. See also Durliat, *Les finances publiques*, p. 236, on this document as an example of the delegation of governmental activity within ecclesiastical immunities. Cf. Rouche, 'L'héritage', esp. pp. 28–9, where he discusses a very similar case from Rheims: he is surely over-pessimistic in his characterisation of this type of interplay between royal and ecclesiastical resources as 'privatisation' resulting from the state's inability to maintain the infrastructure.

[81] *MGH Cap.* I, no. 143, c. 3, p. 295.

[82] *MGH DArnulf* 158 for the men and estates given to Worms. See Zotz, 'Beobachtungen', p. 118 and Dette, *Liber . . . Wizenburgensis*, pp. 63–6, for tenth- and eleventh-century evidence for their continued service. The royal huntsman and messenger Dagulf whom we meet in Einhard, letter 41, may have been one of the ancestors of these men: if so, his relationship to the bishopric of Worms suggested in BM834 (a property exchange, with imperial approval, between Dagolf and the bishop of Worms in 826) is surely significant. Possibly a similar *societas* was based in Paris: see Brühl, *Fodrum, Gistum, Servitium Regis*, pp. 65–6.

marked royal estates, but its efficiency was ensured by a complex infrastructure of stopping-points along the road system, supported by a series of corvées and payments levied from ecclesiastical and royal estates up and down the Rhine, painstakingly pieced together by Franz Staab.[83] This infrastructure did not only allow the speedy travel of royal messengers; it also facilitated the movement of those on royal business. A flavour of its functioning is given by Einhard's account of his journeys up and down the Rhine from Seligenstadt, moving along royal roads with conveniently sited *mansiones* where he could expect shelter and sustenance.[84] The complexity and sophistication of this system places it amongst the most impressive achievements of Carolingian kingship.

One late Carolingian document gives a priceless insight into the organisation of 'public functions'. A notice drawn up *c.* 900 records the work performed by the population of Worms and its rural hinterland on the city walls.[85] Worms' walls, of course, were ultimately Roman, but as elsewhere in Francia, refortification was a pressing need in the decades around 900, and at Worms, as elsewhere, responsibility was taken by the bishop.[86] The walls were divided into a series of sections, their boundaries the various towers and gateways on the circuit. Responsibility for the upkeep of each section was assigned to a different body: groups of villages from the rural hinterland, plus the *urbani*, the Frisian merchants, and the *familia* of the abbey of Murbach. Corvées of this type are paralleled in some Carolingian estate surveys: the tenants of the Nonnenmünster in Worms, for example, took sand and stone to repair the walls of Ladenburg and of an originally stone age fort near Deidesheim.[87] In the Worms document, corvées are levied from groupings of neighbouring rural settlements. These may correspond to the loose neighbourhood units which we detected in the charter evidence. There is a striking similarity, for example, between the group of villages around Dienheim which were responsible for one section of Worms' walls, and the settle-

---

[83] Staab, *Gesellschaft*, pp. 32–106.

[84] See *Translatio* III:11, ed. Waitz, p. 251, III:19, p. 255 (and see Staab, *Gesellschaft*, pp. 37–9), IV:7, p. 258. See also his letters 13–15, on travel from Maastricht to Valenciennes. In general, F. L. Ganshof, 'La *tractoria*. Contribution à l'étude des origines du droit de gîte', *Tijdschrift voor Rechtsgeschiednis* 8 (1927), 69–91; Brühl, *Fodrum, Gistum, Servitium Regis*, pp. 61–9; Siems, *Handel und Wücher*, pp. 468–76.

[85] 'Wormser Burgenbauordnung', ed. H. Boos, *Monumenta Wormatiensia*, Quellen zur Geschichte der Stadt Worms III (Berlin, 1893), pp. 223–5. For the date, Büttner, 'Zur Stadtentwicklung', pp. 395–7. For discussion, Jäschke, *Burgenbau*, esp. pp. 30–81, and F. Beyerle, 'Zur Wehrverfassung des Hochmittelalters', in *Festschrift Ernst Mayer (Würzburg)* (Weimar, 1932), esp. pp. 46–9.

[86] Prinz, *Klerus und Krieg*, pp. 136–7 (not mentioning Worms).

[87] The source is the 1146 confirmation and survey of the Nonnenmünster's lands, ed. Kraft, *Das Reichsgut im Wormsgau*, pp. 256–61, with a fine piece of detective work by Schäfer, 'Mauerbaupflicht fränkischer Königsleute'. Schäfer is unfortunately determined to interpret these fortifications as fiscal, that is 'private' and maintained only by land owned by the king.

MAINTAINING WORMS' WALLS c.900

Specific responsibilities for given sections of the city walls were allocated to groups of settlements in the city's hinterland, and to groups of the city's inhabitants, as follows:

- the Frisians
- Rudelsheim, Gimbsheim, Eich, Hamm, Ibersheim, Dürkheim, Alsheim and Mettenheim
- the *familia* of the abbey of Murbach
- the *urbani,* who were called in the vernacular the *Heimgereiden*
- Poppenheim, *Ligrisheim,* Roxheim, Oggersheim, and all those who dwelt by the Rhine, as far as the river known as the Karlbach (now the Eckbach)
- from the Karlbach as far as Kircheim
- all those dwelling along the Eisbach as far as Mertesheim
- all those dwelling along the Pfrimm as far as its confluence with the Mühlbach
- from Monzenheim to Dienheim

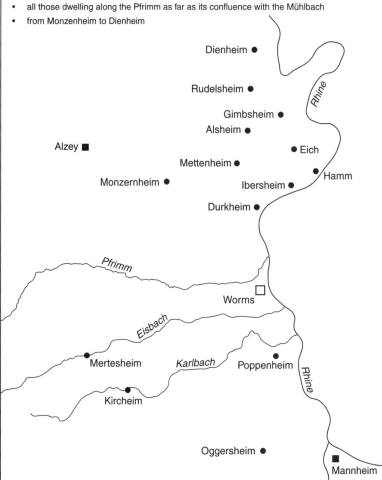

8 Maintaining Worms' walls, *c.* 900

ments that were listed in an earlier fiscal record as sharing a common liability for the payment to the royal *villa* of Gernsheim. This was essentially a social unit, whose existence has already been suggested from the rich charter evidence from the neighbourhood.[88] It was evidently through such collectivities that demands for the performance of 'public functions' were met: it might even be that their origins lie in the tenurial organisation of the Merovingian period, although by the Carolingian period they were social units from which customary exactions were made.[89]

It is at this most local of levels that we can trace the Carolingian system, based on communities, being transformed into a system of jurisdiction over territories. By the second half of the tenth century, localities were increasingly seen as units of proprietorial right. At Worms, for example, in the last decades of the tenth century, Bishop Hildebold was able to use his close links to the royal chancery to concoct a series of forged diplomas and extract confirmation and grants of royal rights. These grants – of market and toll rights, and royal levies in and around the city of Worms – became the basis of a formal, territorial power over Worms and its hinterland, and a number of similar units, for example around Ladenburg.[90] Before the eleventh century, these dues and the units from which they were levied were essentially defined by social bonds. By the eleventh century, their performance within a specified territory came to be the legal possession of specific individuals or institutions. With the emergence of jurisdictional powers and proprietorial rights, we move into a new era of law and lordship.

---

[88] *CL*3671 for the Gernsheim payments and see above, pp. 162–4.   [89] Cf. below, pp. 73–7.
[90] Lechner, 'Die älteren Königsurkunden', for the forgeries; below, pp. 247–50, for their interpretation.

6

POLITICAL POWER FROM THE FIFTH TO THE ELEVENTH CENTURY

INTRODUCTION

The Frankish polity was polycentric, a series of interleaved and interacting segments bound together by the personal interests of local elites at its core.[1] It is thus only possible to do justice to its complexity by adopting a local perspective. Unless we look at politics from the bottom upwards, we are in constant danger of forgetting the multiplicity of sources of legitimate power, and seeing a constant opposition between king and aristocracy, centre and locality. In fact, regional elites were what held the polity together, their interests straddling both centre and locality. Political conflict, therefore, was not articulated as centre against locality, but was generated as part of the constant process of negotiation between different actors at the centre. This makes political development a complex process. This complexity was compounded by the fact that power, if it was to be exercised over a larger area than a locality, was of necessity itinerant, and that in the absence of an institutionalised administrative infrastructure, delegation inevitably led to power sharing. Political power thus became more intermittent, and more dependent on association with local figures, the larger the unit within which it was exercised. It is only by examining the long-term development of the interactions between the various constituent parts of this polity that we can offer a convincing account of structural change in the distribution and derivation of political power.

ROMAN TO MEROVINGIAN

The middle Rhine valley lay on the very fringes of direct Roman power. Before the third century, the occupation of fortifications in the Taunus

---

[1] 'Polycentric' is used of the Ottonian polity (but implicitly denied of the Carolingian) by H. Keller, 'Zum Charakter der "Staatlichkeit"'; for comparative and theoretical material that I have found helpful in thinking about early medieval polities, see below, p. 261, n. 17, p. 262, n. 18.

and the Odenwald had marked an attempt to establish direct control over the east bank; by the fourth century, the Rhine itself was the limit of regular Roman rule. The Rhine, like the Empire's other frontiers, was not a sharp line of political demarcation. It was, rather, a zone of particularly intensive interaction – social, economic and political – between the Empire and those beyond Rome's direct sway. The transition from 'civilisation' to 'barbarism' was a gradual gradient, not a sudden precipice. We can even detect creeping Romanisation east of the Rhine, notably in the area between the Rhine and Neckar known as the *agri decumates*, a once Roman province where the barbarian elite continued to enjoy a thoroughly 'civilised' lifestyle.[2]

The frontier zone was characterised by a certain ethnic heterogeneity and ambivalence. As the frontier was the geographical locus of interaction between 'Roman' and 'barbarian', so the army was the social forum through which barbarian elites encountered *Romanitas*. By the fourth century largely 'barbarian' in origin, the army was a powerful organ of geographical and social mobility, and a melting-pot in which ideas and identities were combined and reformed, from which barbarian leaders could gain position within the Empire.[3] The presence of the Roman army, indeed, was central to the political and social structures of the region. Frontier forces were organised as a military command or *ducatus* whose headquarters lay at Mainz: the Roman army was deployed at a host of fortified sites along the Rhine from Andernach to Selz.[4]

Roman rule, then, was anything but marginal to this frontier society. The local economy was tied into an Empire-wide system of redistribution defined by the demands of the Roman government, which allowed the provisioning of the army. Local elites gained the possibility of consolidating their power through attaining an official role within the Roman administration. In the crisis of the third century, the Romanisation of local patterns of leadership became clear when, faced with a political vacuum, the local elite acted in alliance with military commanders to proclaim Laelianus emperor at Mainz. The ties between local elites and the Empire became stronger still when, in the fourth

[2] There is a large and quickly growing bibliography on Roman frontiers: see particularly C. R. Whittaker, *Frontiers of the Roman Empire* (Baltimore and London, 1994) and H. Elton, *Frontiers of the Roman Empire* (London, 1996). For the developments on the east bank of the Rhine, see E. Schallmeyer, 'Die Lande rechts des Rheins zwischen 260 und 500 nach Christ', in F. Staab (ed.), *Zur Kontinuität zwischen Antike und Mittelalter am Oberrhein* (Sigmaringen, 1994), pp. 53–68.
[3] See, in addition to Whittaker, J. W. H. G. Liebeschuetz, *Barbarians and Bishops: Army, Church and State in the Age of Arcadius and Chrysostom* (Oxford, 1990), pp. 7–85.
[4] See E. Ewig, 'Der Raum zwischen Selz und Andernach von 5 bis zur 7 Jahrhundert', in Ewig and J. Werner (eds.), *Von der Spätantike zum frühen Mittelalter. Aktuelle Probleme in historischer und archäologischer Sicht*, VF 25 (Sigmaringen, 1979), pp. 271–96.

century, the Imperial court was frequently based in northern Gaul, and proximity to the emperor brought favours and the possibilities of high office in the Imperial administration. The integration of the region into the Empire transformed the presentation and possibilities of local power.[5]

The political history of the Rhine frontier was a story of intermittent incursion. This should not obscure the continuation of less visible forms of interaction across the frontier, and the intensifying interplay of 'Roman' and 'barbarian' within the Roman army, which set the scene for the drama of the shift from Roman to barbarian rule. The first act began with the breach of the Rhine frontier and the defeat of garrisons at Strasbourg, Mainz and Worms in the winter of 406–7. The irruption of Vandals, Sueves and Alans did not break the western Empire. Indeed, between 425 and 454 the Roman general Aetius was remarkably successful at maintaining Roman control in the west. But Aetius' control was exercised in a different manner from that of the fourth-century emperors. Frontier provinces like the Rhine were increasingly expected to defend themselves under a loose Roman overlordship, and barbarian leaders within the Empire were recognised *qua* barbarian leaders, rather than previously, as Roman generals. The fifth-century western Empire, as it was reconstituted after the crisis which followed the 407 invasion, was a political system which bound together, rather than regulated, the activities of local men of influence, Roman generals and allied barbarian warlords. We should not write off this system: for much of the fifth century, the Roman state remained the ultimate political point of reference which legitimated more local forms of power, even if it no longer defined them. When the usurper Jovinus was proclaimed emperor at Mainz in 412, he was, like Laelianus 150 years earlier, asserting his local power in a thoroughly Roman Imperial idiom; moreover, his supporters were responding to crisis by creating an Imperial presence of a kind which they had come to expect in the course of the fourth century. The real change was, however, clear from the basis of Jovinus', and his opponents', military backing. He was supported not by Roman legions, but by Burgundian and Alan federates, and his regime was crushed not by Imperial troops but by Visigoths in 'Roman' service. Although local power continued to be seen as part of a Roman system, it was a Roman system in which barbarian federates rather than Roman armies were the

[5] On the interaction between local men of influence and the imperial government, R. van Dam, *Leadership and Community in Late Antique Gaul* (Berkeley and London, 1985), pp. 7–55 (pp. 28–9 on Laelianus), also Elton, *Frontiers*, pp. 41–58, on the earlier period. For the opportunities for power at the centre enjoyed by western elites, see J. F. Matthews, *Western Aristocracies and the Imperial Court, AD 364–425* (Oxford, 1975); for the history of Roman Gaul, E. Wightman, *Gallia Belgica* (London, 1985).

basis of military power: as Aetius' panegyrist put it, 'The Rhine has bestowed pacts, making the wintry world Rome's servant.'[6]

As we enter the finale of the drama in the second half of the fifth century, the distinctions between local influence, barbarian kingship and Roman military command have become blurred. Even before 407 there were signs of an increasing reliance on locally-based forces, and a new interest in the possibilities of barbarian allies.[7] The archaeological record from fortified sites on the Rhine frontier, such as Altrip and Alzey, points to the maintenance of an official military infrastructure into the middle decades of the fifth century. At Worms, held by Burgundian *foederati* in the second quarter of the fifth century, the presence of Mediterranean ceramics until mid-century suggests that something of the Imperial infrastructure of military provisioning continued to function under Aetius, even if a barbarian material culture from across the Rhine predominates in the archaeological record and speaks volumes as to the changes taking place.[8] After the middle of the century, the atrophy of the centrally administered system of taxation and redistribution which had provisioned the army meant that military rulers related to the inhabitants of the countryside and tapped their surplus directly, without the mediation of the infrastructure of the imperial government. We know little of the mechanisms through which civilian society related to its military protectors, but the very basis of power was changing radically.[9]

This process will inevitably remain shadowy owing to the paucity of pliable evidence of any kind for the crucial decades of the middle of the fifth century. It is clear that many former Roman military centres like Worms maintained their importance through the fifth and early sixth

---

[6] For the political history of the fifth-century middle Rhine see Whittaker, *Frontiers*, pp. 243–57, on changing fifth-century strategy; pp. 250–1, for the panegyric on Aetius.

[7] See Wightman, *Gallia Belgica*, pp. 206–11, for the increasingly localised basis of the military. Fourth-century cemeteries with weapon-burials have been seen as evidence for the settlement of barbarian soldier-farmers within the Empire. The interpretation of the evidence is difficult, and these sites are situated in the interior of northern Gaul rather than the Rhine frontier: see Wightman, *Gallia Belgica*, pp. 252–6; H.-W. Böhme, *Germanische Grabfunde des 4. und 5. Jahrhunderts zwischen Elbe und Loire*, 2 vols. (Munich, 1974); G. Halsall, 'Archaeology and the Late Roman Frontier in Northern Gaul: The so-called *Federatengräber* Reconsidered', in W. Pohl and H. Reimitz (eds.), *Grenze und Differenz im früheren Mittelalter* (Vienna, forthcoming).

[8] J. Oldenstein, 'Die letzten Jahrzehnte des römischen Limes zwischen Andernach und Selz unter besonderer Berücksichtigung des Kastells Alzey und der *Notitia Dignitatum*', and G. Stein, 'Kontinuität im spätrömischen Kastell Altrip (*Alta ripa*) bei Ludwigshafen am Rhein', both in F. Staab (ed.), *Zur Kontinuität zwischen Antike und Mittelalter*, pp. 69–112, 113–17, respectively; M. Grünewald, 'Worms zwischen Burgunden und Salier', in K. van Welck (ed.), *Die Franken. Wegbereiter Europas* (Mainz, 1996), I, pp. 160–2 at 161.

[9] Cf. Whittaker, *Frontiers*, pp. 257–78; Whittaker, 'Landlords and Warlords in the Later Roman Empire', in J. Rich and G. Shipley (eds.), *War and Society in the Roman World* (London, 1993), pp. 277–302; Halsall, 'Towns, Societies and Ideas', pp. 243–5; and van Dam, *Leadership and Community*, pp. 7–55.

centuries. There is evidence, mainly in the form of funerary inscriptions, for continued occupation by high-status individuals at least, in cities such as Mainz and also in forts like Alzey, Bingen and Kreuznach. In that the evidence also suggests some continuity of Christianity, even here, right on the former Roman frontier, so we are dealing with a process more complex than the simple takeover of fortified sites by incoming hordes.[10] The elaboration of funerary rites in the last quarter of the fifth century sheds some light on the emergence of new political and social structures. The last decades of the century saw the emergence of burials marked by the deposition of lavish grave-goods, particularly wargear, right across northern Gaul. Amongst the earliest of these burials are a series of male graves marked out by the presence of magnificent and ornately-decorated swords; those at Rommersheim and Flonheim are similar to that buried with the Frankish leader Childeric at Tournai *c.* 481. The distribution of these burials in the middle Rhine clearly relates to the Roman infrastructure of roads and fortifications.[11] Their material culture is characterised by a kaleidoscope of influences. The grave-goods typically include 'Roman' artefacts, notably Imperial military insignia and Byzantine coins; but much in the wargear had powerful central European parallels. The diffusion of this material culture points to the existence of a wide-ranging military elite, which had evolved in contact with the Empire but was receptive to 'barbarian' styles. The burial rite itself, inhumation with lavish grave-goods and particularly wargear, was an eclectic new synthesis: its closest precedents came from fourth-century graves in northern Gaul within the imperial frontier. Its sudden adoption across much of northern Gaul relates to a situation in which local leaders and military commanders could no longer legitimate their power with reference to 'Roman' authority, although they remained based in Roman fortifications linked by Roman roads. Here was the final militarisation and localisation of political power.[12]

[10] For continuity of occupation at Roman fortified sites, and the significance of the distribution of high-status burials, see H. Ament, 'Die Franken in der Römerstädten der Rheinzone', in K. van Welck (ed.), *Die Franken. Wegbereiter Europas* (Mainz, 1996), I, pp. 129–37; Heinemeyer, *Das Erzbistum Mainz*, pp. 51–7, and n. 8 above. Staab, *Gesellschaft*, pp. 13–32, shows that there was no wholesale change of population, and that on a local level there was much Roman continuity, although we need more work on settlement patterns.

[11] See Ament, *Fränkische Adelsgräber aus Flonheim*; A. Wieczoreck, 'Die Ausbreitung der fränkische Herrschaft in den Rheinland vor und seit Chlodowig I', in K. van Welck (ed.), *Die Franken. Wegbereiter Europas* (Mainz, 1996), I, pp. 241–60.

[12] Roman precedents and eclecticism: James, 'Cemeteries'; Halsall, 'The Origins of the *Reihengräberzivilisation* – Forty Years on', in J. F. Drinkwater and H. Elton (eds.), *Fifth-Century Gaul: A Crisis of Identity?* (Cambridge, 1992), pp. 196–207. For their adoption as a response to a legitimation crisis see Halsall, 'Towns, Societies and Ideas', pp. 251–2. For their ideology of martial power cf. H. Härke, 'Warrior Graves? The Background of the Anglo-Saxon Weapon Burial Rite', *P&P* 126 (1990), 22–43. These burials seem to me to fit D. H. Miller's model of the

Whether the changes in burial rite can be linked to Frankish conquest or colonisation is another issue. There are no grounds for seeing a Frankish identity as defining this shared material culture: there are no straightforward precedents in the Frankish homelands, and the material culture is eclectic, not narrowly Frankish. The argument that the spread of the new rite reflects Frankish colonisation is ultimately circular, because it rests on the assertion that the earliest burials of this style post-date Frankish conquest of the areas in which they are found, something which has not yet been demonstrated from the archaeological record (and is difficult to sustain for Rommersheim and Flonheim).[13] In any case, the Franks of the fifth century were scarcely a united or homogeneous group, either politically or ethnically: Clovis eliminated a series of rival Frankish dynasties with separate kingships.[14] One written source tells us that *c.* 500 the middle Rhine was divided in terms of its ultimate political loyalty, with Worms ruled by the Alemans, and Mainz and Bingen by the Franks.[15] It is striking that the earliest lavish assemblages of grave-goods cluster in the area between Worms, Mainz and Bingen; they should be seen as responses to political competition in this highly unstable zone, not as blanket indicators of Frankish ethnicity. It probably makes most sense to think of a series of essentially local leaders of diverse origins establishing themselves on the ground, beneath an umbrella of political alliances which were often expressed in terms of ethnic allegiance. In a largely invisible process in which conquest doubtless played an important role, the Merovingian dynasty under Clovis and his successors transformed its relationship with these local rulers, who were thus integrated into the Frankish realm. Our reliance on the linear narrative of Gregory of Tours,

---

Footnote 12 (*cont.*)

    new centrality of a frontier culture: 'Frontier Societies and the Transition between Late Antiquity and the Early Middle Ages', in H. Elton and H. Sivan (eds.), *Shifting Frontiers in Late Antiquity* (Aldershot, 1996), pp. 158–71. Their newness is made clear if one looks at rites practised in the fourth- and fifth-century cemetery at Lampertheim, on the east bank of the Rhine near Worms: F. Behn, 'Ein vorfränkisches Gräberfeld bei Lampertheim im Rheinhessen', *Mainzer Zeitschrift* 30 (1935), 56–65.

[13] The received 'Frankish colonisation' interpretation is given its most detailed exposition in Ament, *Fränkische Adelsgräber* and is followed most recently by Wieczoreck, 'Die Ausbreitung der fränkische Herrschaft'. For the general problem of circularity see James, 'Cemeteries', and also *The Franks* (Oxford, 1988), pp. 76–7. Ament has to resort to special pleading to make the archaeological horizon represented by Flonheim grave 5 fit the accepted chronology of Frankish conquest in the middle Rhine beginning in the final years of the fifth century; and Rommersheim is earlier still than Flonheim grave 5.

[14] Gregory of Tours, *Historiae*, II:40–2, eds. Levison and Krusch, pp. 89–93.

[15] See E. Ewig, 'Probleme der fränkischen Frühgeschichte in den Rheinlanden', in H. Beumann (ed.), *Historische Forschungen W. Schlesinger* (Cologne and Vienna, 1974), pp. 47–74, and H. Beumann, 'Die Franken am Rhein', in H. Beumann and W. Schröder (eds.), *Aspekte der Nationenbildung im Mittelalter* (Sigmaringen, 1978), pp. 109–26, for the political history of the fifth-century Rhineland.

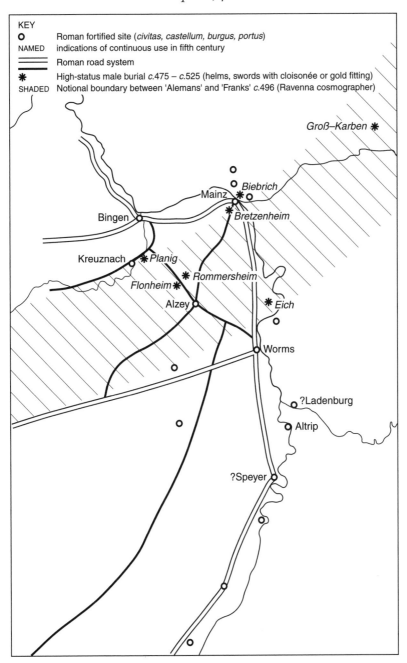

KEY
○   Roman fortified site (*civitas, castellum, burgus, portus*)
NAMED   indications of continuous use in fifth century
═══   Roman road system
✳   High-status male burial *c.*475 – *c.*525 (helms, swords with cloisonée or gold fitting)
SHADED   Notional boundary between 'Alemans' and 'Franks' *c.*496 (Ravenna cosmographer)

Groß–Karben ✳

○
○ *Biebrich*
Mainz ✳○
○
Bingen ✳ *Bretzenheim*

Kreuznach ✳*Planig*
✳ *Rommersheim*
Flonheim✳
Alzey ✳ *Eich*
○

Worms
○
○?Ladenburg
○ Altrip
○

?Speyer ○
○
○
○

9 The middle Rhine valley, *c.* 500

writing with hindsight in a generation to which political legitimacy had come to be defined by Merovingian blood, may make this process appear far simpler and quicker than was the actual case.

THE MEROVINGIAN MIDDLE RHINE

The internal organisation of the Merovingian middle Rhine must remain shadowy, given the lack of evidence. To talk of administration, though, is likely to be misleading: later documentary evidence suggests essentially self-regulating rural settlements passing on 'customary' dues, often under threat of coercion, to a militarised elite.[16] We know little about the actual mechanics of power. The archaeology strongly suggests that the cities and some other fortified Roman sites typically maintained their significance, whilst the minting of Merovingian coins at Mainz, Worms and Bingen underlines their continuing centrality.[17] It was probably in this earliest period of Frankish domination that *pagus* units, which were fully-fledged by the time of the earliest transmitted documents in the seventh century, were formed. That, on the west bank of the Rhine, a large *pagus* in the most prosperous and populous area was named after Worms, even though it also included Mainz, suggests that *pagi* initially crystallised around those fortified Roman sites from which secular rulers exerted their influence. By the time of our first written sources in the early seventh century, Mainz was the pre-eminent social and political centre of the region, so the *pagus* labels must originate somewhat earlier.[18] Possibly the pre-eminence of first Worms, then Mainz, can be explained in terms of the continuation of a regional military command, the ghost of the late Roman *ducatus*; the existence of such a large, loose, regional command is paralleled elsewhere in north-eastern Gaul.[19] Certainly the first written

---

[16] Cf. above, pp. 73–7.

[17] Archaeology: n. 10 above. Coins: W. Diepenbach, 'Die Münzpragungen am Mittelrhein im Zeitalter der Merowinger', *Mainzer Zeitschrift* 44–5 (1949–50), 141–52.

[18] A hypothesis supported by the fact that Ladenburg, which was linked to the bishopric of Worms from the early seventh century at least, supplied the name and the centre of the strategically most important *pagus* east of the Rhine. Cf. E. Ewig, 'Die Stellung Ribuariens in der Verfassungsgeschichte des Merowingerreiches', 'Die Civitas Ubiorum, die Francia Rinensis und das Land Ribuarien', and 'Civitas, Gau und Territorium in den Trierischen Mosellanden', all in Ewig, *Spätantikes und fränkisches Gallien. Gesammelte Schriften 1952–73*, Beihefte der Francia 3, 2 vols. (Munich, 1976–9), I, pp. 450–71, 472–503, 504–22 respectively, for *pagus*-formation elsewhere.

[19] E. Ewig, 'Der Mittelrhein im Merowingerreich. Eine historische Skizze', in Ewig, *Spätantikes und fränkisches Gallien* I (Munich, 1976), pp. 435–49 at pp. 438–40; Ewig, 'Der Raum', esp. p. 289. See now R. Butzen, *Die Merowinger östlich des mittleren Rheins. Studien zur militärischen, politischen, recht-lichen, religiösen, kirchlichen, kulturellen Erfassung durch Königtum und Adel im 6. sowie 7. Jahrhundert*, Mainfränkische Studien 36 (Würzburg, 1987) pp. 122–70. There is some support for this propo-sition in a putative partition of 839, which used old Merovingian political-geographical labels, and talks of duchies in Ripuaria and Alsace (north and south of our area), and on the Moselle

evidence suggests such a structure. In 639 King Sigebert embarked on a campaign against the Thuringians: 'Radolf [the Thuringian *dux*] was in touch with certain *duces* in Sigebert's army and knew that they would not attack him with their men. Radulf advanced on Sigebert's camp and, as battle was joined, the *Macanenses*, ['the men of Mainz'], 'turned traitor'.[20] Sigebert's army, then, was made up of regional contingents led by local leaders styled *dux*; one such unit was focused upon Mainz, a former Roman city and military centre.[21] To the extent that local power was structured, those who held local power were following in the footsteps of the *comes civitatus* of the late Empire, and may have styled themselves *comes* or with the vernacular equivalent, *grafio*.[22]

Again, we are reliant on the cemetery evidence to supply real insight into the basis of local power. Sixth-century burials suggest transient competitive display in a shared forum: grave-goods were lavish and varied, but apparently aimed at a present audience, whilst cemeteries seem to have served several settlements. Power could not be transmitted from one generation to the next without a spectacular demonstration of wealth before the entire community, a demonstration whose necessity and expense effected a certain degree of redistribution. Debate about the origins of the aristocracy may miss the point. The ruling elite were exercising new forms of power in a new situation: whilst it will doubtless have been recruited from both influential local landowners and incoming barbarian leaders, the dramatic shifts in the nature of power made it to all effects and purposes a new elite in a new society, regardless of personnel. This explains why those with power had to expend considerable time and energy legitimating its reproduction. The intense local competition evident in the burial evidence may have allowed kings to exert considerable local patronage. Certainly, in the southern Gaul described by

and the Main (to the west and east), lumping the *pagi* of Worms and Speyer rather anomalously in between: *Les Annales de St-Bertin*, eds. Grat *et al.*, s.a. 839, p. 32. This might support Butzen, *Die Merowinger*, p. 164 in his argument that the middle Rhine was anomalous as it had no *dux*.

[20] Fredegar IV:87, ed. Wallace-Hadrill, pp. 73–4.

[21] Ewig, 'Mittelrhein', pp. 439–40; Ewig, 'Raum zwischen Selz und Andernach', p. 288, Falck, *Mainz*, pp. 11–12. On the Würzburg *duces* and their links with the Rhenish aristocracy, Friese, *Herrschaftsgeschichte*, pp. 17–51; W. Störmer, 'Zu Herkunft und Wirkungkreis der merowingerzeitlichen "mainfränkischen" Herzöge', in K. R. Schnith and R. Pauler (eds.), *Festschrift für E. Hlawitschka* (Munich, 1993), pp. 11–21

[22] On the development of the office of count, the starting-point remains the controversy between R. Sprandel, 'Dux und comes in der Merowingerzeit', *ZSRG GA* 70 (1957), 41–84, and D. Claude, 'Untersuchungen zum frühfränkischen Comitat', *ZSRG GA* 83 (1966), 273–80, with a second round, Sprandel, 'Bemerkungen zum frühfränkischen Comitat', *ZSRG GA* 82 (1965), 288–91 and Claude, 'Zu Fragen frühfränkischer Verfassungsgeschichte', *ZSRG GA* 83 (1966), 273–80. On the equivalence between *comes* and *grafio*, A. C. Murray, 'The Constitutional Position of the *Grafio*'. On counts as royal officials, P. S. Barnwell, *Emperor, Prefects and Kings: The Roman West, 395–565* (London, 1992), pp. 108–13.

Gregory of Tours this was the case: here competition for royal patronage was not incompatible with a firmly embedded aristocracy because of the survival of an infrastructure of local office. If we accept the parallel with Gregory, it may be that the slow decline of this infrastructure can be detected in the changing social structures suggested by the archaeological record from our region. By the seventh century, grave-goods became, as a rule, more standardised and less lavish, suggesting an increased security in matters of status even at the most traumatic of moments, the point of inheritance. Burials increasingly advertised the continuity of power over time: sometimes with the erection of a church as a demonstration of status and a repository of family memory, as at Flonheim; sometimes with other forms of burial, such as the reuse of an imposing prehistoric barrow at Wallerstädt, just southeast of Mainz.[23]

By the seventh century, the dominance of the church was central to the political and social strategy of the aristocracy. In spite of the strong evidence for the continuity of Christianity, it is difficult to trace bishops before the seventh century: bishops from Worms and Speyer made their first appearances at Merovingian church councils as late as 614, and diocesan boundaries in the middle Rhine were not inherited from the Roman period but based on the new realities of the seventh and eighth centuries.[24] The evidence for the political power which bishops managed to amass is late but vivid. In the eighth century the Anglo-Saxon missionary Boniface complained about the Rhenish episcopate with the passion of a true zealot. For the social and political historian of the region, Boniface's letters are in many ways a disappointing source:

---

[23] For changing patterns of burial and their interpretation see Halsall, *Settlement and Social Organisation*, pp. 76–163, elaborating the interpretation of 'Social Change around 600: An Austrasian Perspective', in M. Carver (ed.), *The Age of Sutton Hoo* (Woodbridge, 1992), pp. 265–78; similar conclusions are reached, through different interpretative processes, by Steuer, 'Archaeology and History', and Young, 'Exemple aristocratique'. However, I would not see the aristocratic power as wholly secure or stable even by 700, and it does seem to me that the elite throughout the Merovingian period can be accurately described as an aristocracy: what the burials show is their power articulating itself in different ways in different contexts, and here the changing administrative infrastructure must be central (building here on the suggestion of Halsall, 'Social Identities and Social Relationships in Early Merovingian Gaul', in I. N. Wood (ed.), *Franks and Alamanni in the Merovingian Period: An Ethnographic Perspective* (Woodbridge, 1998), pp. 141–65, but seeing competition for royal favour and office as perfectly compatible with the existence of an aristocracy. For a catalogue of burials under churches, barrows and in separate cemeteries, likewise showing an increasing assertion of exclusiveness by the elite, see H.-W. Böhme, 'Adelsgräber im Frankenreich. Archäologische Zeugnisse zur Herausbildung einer Herrenschicht unter den merowingischer Königen', *Jahrbuch der Römisch-Germanischen Zentralmuseums Mainz* 40 (1995), 397–534; for Wallerstädt see W. Schnellenkamp, 'Ein Grabhügel bei Wallerstädten in Hessen-Starkenburg mit Bestattungen der Hallstatt-, Latène- und Merowingerzeit', *Mainzer Zeitschrift* 27 (1932), 59–74.

[24] Heinemeyer, *Erzbistum Mainz*; Büttner, 'Frühes fränkisches Christentum'.

their collector aimed to depict Boniface as an Old Testament-style prophet on a European stage, not to supply minutiae of local conflicts and disputes. Quarrels over jurisdiction beyond the Rhine may underlie much of Boniface's rhetoric; local bishops had long been active east of the Rhine, in an area where Boniface was attempting to carve out an episcopal and monastic power base.[25] But Boniface's essential complaint was about the wholesale adoption of the values of the secular elite by Rhenish churchmen, and in particular their passion for hunting and feasting. Boniface's opponents – men like Milo of Trier and Gewilib of Mainz – undertook such activities with gusto precisely because they were what was expected of the good patron. It was through such practices that their ancestors had succeeded in monopolising episcopal office as a basis of familial power.[26]

The importance of episcopal office for local and supra-local politics is best shown by the career of the most powerful man in the middle Rhine in the generation before Milo and Gewilib. St Rupert, whose career lay in the decades around 700, was an ancestor of Lorsch's founders. His familial pre-eminence was reinforced by his role as bishop of Worms, and led to wider political contacts, for Rupert was close to the Merovingian court in the late seventh century. When the political tide turned against him, with the rising power in Francia of the ancestor of the Carolingians, Pippin II, Rupert left Worms for Bavaria, where he found a political ally in the Agilolfing ruler. In Bavaria, Rupert refounded the see of Salzburg and engaged in missionary work, before returning to Worms at the end of his life. Rupert's *Life*, written in Salzburg at the end of the eighth century, celebrated his resolutely aristocratic sanctity. His career underlines the success of the late Merovingian church and was, in fact, a sign of its agility in adapting to the realities of late Merovingian society.[27]

---

[25] See Büttner, 'Mainz im Mittelalter', p. 10; Butzen, *Merowinger*, pp. 68–111, esp. 69–72; and H. Büttner, 'Mission und Kirchenorganisation des Frankenreiches bis zum Tode Karls des Großen', in H. Beumann (ed.), *Karl der Große. Persönlichkeit und Geschichte* (Düsseldorf, 1965), pp. 454–86.

[26] For Boniface's criticisms of 'Milo et eiusmodi similes', see letters 50, 60 and 87, ed. M. Tangl, *MGH Epistolae selectae* I (Berlin, 1955), pp 82–3, 122 and 199. The fundamental study remains Ewig, 'Milo et eiusmodi similes', in Ewig, *Spätantikes und fränkisches Gallien* II (Munich, 1979), pp. 189–219; see also T. Reuter, 'Saint Boniface and Europe', in Reuter (ed.), *The Greatest Englishman* (Exeter, 1980), pp. 69–93, and J. M. Wallace-Hadrill, 'A Background to St Boniface's Mission', in K. Hughes and P. Clemoes (eds.), *England Before the Conquest* (Cambridge, 1971), pp. 35–48. On Gewilib, F. Staab, '*Rudi populo rudis adhuc presul*. Zu den wehrhäften Bischöfe der Zeit Karl Martells', in J. Jarnut et al. (eds.), *Karl Martell in seiner Zeit* (Sigmaringen, 1994), pp. 249–75, suggests a positive reassessment. For the significance of hunting and feasting see Jarnut, 'Die frühmittelalterliche Jagd'; Althoff, *Verwandte, Freunde und Getreue*, pp. 203–11.

[27] On Rupert, the fundamental studies are H. Wolfram, 'Der heilige Rupert und die antikarolingische Adelsopposition', *MIÖG* 80 (1972), 4–34; and H. Wolfram, 'Vier Fragen zur Geschichte des heiligen Rupert. Eine Nachlese', *Studien und Mitteilungen zur Geschichte des Benediktiner-Ordens*

The career of Rupert also makes clear the increasing importance of the region east of the Rhine.[28] In the seventh century political control east of the Rhine, an area subject to Frankish overlordship since the sixth century, became formalised as the Frankish elite established themselves there. At some point before 639, the Frankish king implanted a ducal dynasty at Würzburg, to dominate the provinces east of the Rhine. The exact relation of these rulers to the Thuringian dynasty which had been defeated in 531 is obscure: they may have been Frankish appointees, but they were seen as rulers of the Thuringians. The divided loyalties of the men of Mainz reflected the close ties between the middle Rhine and the region to the east, solidarity with their neighbours and cousins winning out over obedience to the Frankish king in 639. The power of the Würzburg dynasty probably reached as far as the Rhine's east bank: an inscription dated 711 records the foundation of a church at Nilkheim, near Aschaffenburg on the lower Main, in the Odenwald, and its consecration by Bishop Rimibert of Mainz, under *dux* Theotbald.[29] In the middle decades of the eighth century, the Carolingians were to bring these rulers under direct Frankish control in a largely invisible (and apparently mostly peaceful) process.

These interests in the east were part and parcel of a widening of the scope of aristocratic interests which likewise becomes visible in the

---

Footnote 27 (*cont.*)

und seiner Zweige 93 (1982), 2–25. The main source is *Gesta sancti Hrodberti confessoris*, ed. W. Levison, *MGH SRM* 6, pp. 140–62, in essence a Salzburg work from the end of the eighth century; on its ideal of sanctity, see K. Bosl, 'Der Adelsheilige. Idealtypus und Wirklichkeit, Gesellschaft und Kultur im merowingerzeitlichen Bayern des 7. und 8. Jhts', in C. Bauer *et al.* (eds.), *Speculum Historiale. Festschrift für J. Spörl* (Freiburg and Munich, 1965), pp. 167–87. For the significance of episcopal power see M. Heinzelmann, 'L'aristocratie et les évêchés entre Loire et Rhin jusqu'à la fin du VIIe siècle', *Revue d'Histoire de l'Eglise de France* 62 (1976), 75–90; M. Heinzelmann, 'Bischof und Herrschaft vom spätantiken Gallien bis zur karolingischen Hausmeiern: die institutionellen Grundlagen', in F. Prinz (ed.), *Herrschaft und Kirche. Beiträge zur Entstehung und Wirkungsweise episkopaler und monastischer Organisationsformen* (Stuttgart, 1988), pp. 23–82; P. Fouracre, 'Merovingian History and Merovingian Hagiography', *P&P* 127 (1990), pp. 3–38; F. Prinz, 'Heiligenkult und Adelsherrschaft im Speigel merowingischer Hagiographie', *Historische Zeitschrift* 204 (1969), 529–44.

[28] The bibliography is vast: see most recently Butzen, *Merowinger*, with references. Note particularly W. Metz, 'Austrasische Adelsherrschaft des 8. Jhts. Mittelrheinische Grundherren in Ostfranken, Thüringen und Hessen', *Historisches Jahrbuch* 87 (1967), 257–304; R. Sprandel, *Die merovingische Adel und die Gebiete östlich des Rheins* (Freiburg, 1958); H. K. Schulze, 'Ostfranken und Alemannien in der Politik des fränkischen Reiches', in F. Quarthal (ed.), *Alemannien und Ostfranken im Frühmittelalter* (Baden-Bühl, 1984), pp. 13–37; W. Schlesinger, 'Zur politischen Geschichte der fränkischen Ostbewegung vor Karl dem Großen', in Schlesinger (ed.), *Althessen im Frankenreich* (Sigmaringen, 1975), pp. 9–62; Störmer, 'Herkunft und Wirkungkreis'; Wood, 'The Frontiers of Western Europe'.

[29] *MGH SRM* VII, p. 711, Cf. *CL*6a, from 795, where the history of the estate of Heppenheim, east of the Rhine, 'under kings and *duces*' is recorded; and Fredegar, IV:87, ed. Wallace-Hadrill, pp. 73–4, when Sigebert gets a safe conduct as far as the Rhine.

seventh century. Local men of influence had, even in the fifth century, been tied into a wider network of alliance and political contact. In the seventh century we begin to see these contacts take the form of extensive landholding and political influence in more than one region. Already in 634 Adalgisel-Grimo, a deacon from Verdun, had property interests which were scattered from a monastery at Tholey, in the Vosges, and then westwards through the heartland of the 'eastern kingdom', Austrasia.[30] Indeed Adalgisel's relations, the forefathers of the Carolingian dynasty, were able to establish themselves at the head of the Austrasian aristocracy by the end of the seventh century, thanks to their acquisition of interests in both the Meuse and Moselle areas. But the Carolingians were far from alone, as families like St Rupert's built up interests not only in the middle Rhine, but also in the eastern provinces. It was, presumably, precisely this tying into wider horizons, and the stabilising effect which the church had on local power structures, which lay behind the increasing solidity of social stratification suggested by the cemetery evidence.

In the first half of the eighth century, the power of families like that of Rupert was so assured that it was only their interest in a wider, court, political stage that held the polity together. This was not necessarily a matter of royal 'decline'. It was not that aristocrats ruled the localities as of right: the charters make it quite clear that local power continued to rest on winning the support of free landowners through complex systems of patronage rooted in reciprocity.[31] What happened in the seventh century was the emergence of the aristocracy as the integrative force in the polity, in the place of the administrative infrastructure of late antiquity. The aristocracy came to enjoy an effective monopoly on mediation between political centre and the regions. It was, however, through the court that political designs continued to be pursued. Indeed, the most important – and most easily missed – development in late Merovingian politics was the gradual expansion of the geographical scope of political conflict and contact. By the last decades of the seventh century, traditional political patterns which had compartmentalised the Merovingian polity into three discrete kingdoms, within which political manoeuvring was more or less self-contained, were on the wane. Although labels like 'Neustrian' or 'Austrasian' were political rallying points, those who used

---

[30] See Levison, 'Das Testament des Diakons Adalgisel-Grimo'; Heinemeyer, *Erzbistum Mainz*, pp. 120–35; M. Werner, *Der Lütticher Raum im frühkarolingischen Zeit. Untersuchungen zur Geschichte eine karolingische Stammeslandschaft*, VMPIG 62 (Gottingen, 1980), pp. 34–59.

[31] The best source for the nature of local power in the late Merovingian period is the Wissembourg cartulary: see R. Sprandel, 'Struktur und Geschichte des merowingische Adels', *Historische Zeitschrift* 193 (1961), 33–71 for an important discussion.

them in the decades around 700 used them to rally support in a struggle for political power across Francia as a whole.[32]

The breadth of the political stage on which late Merovingian politics was played is shown admirably by the careers of St Rupert's heirs. St Rupert's power base in the middle Rhine was inherited by a Count Rupert who died shortly before 764. Count Rupert was the father of Cancor, the founder of Lorsch, and a kinsman of Chrodegang, bishop of Metz, who was a member of a powerful family in the Liège area, and began his career at the court of Charles Martel. Precisely how these kinship links between the elites of the Liège and Worms areas arose we cannot know, but they clearly pulled St Rupert's successors into contact and eventually alliance with Charles Martel and his Carolingian dynasty, and may indeed have been designed to cement this alliance.[33] One of the key figures in these contacts was yet another Rupert, *dux* of the Hesbaye and an important benefactor of the abbey of St Trond, where his kinsman Chrodegang had been educated. Such alliances, and activity in the service of the Carolingians, allowed the extension of family interests, and ensured the effective delivery of patronage to local clients and the preservation of local influence.

Once Martel was clearly winning, even a family like that of St Rupert, which had opposed Martel's predecessors, had to change tack. And changing tack was profitable, given the opportunities for alliance with men like Chrodegang and *dux* Rupert, and for aggrandisement through expansion and favour. Indeed, the real story of the first half of the eighth century was the Carolingian family's struggle to establish itself as the political centre, despite the continued presence and symbolic significance of Merovingian kings. Increasingly, political factions within the Frankish aristocracy came to work by allying with different members of the Carolingian dynasty, rather than by bypassing the Carolingians as St Rupert had a generation earlier. This process was slow: in the crisis within the Carolingian family which followed the death of Pippin II, Martel's father, there were still those who seized the opportunity to

---

[32] P. Fouracre and R. Gerberding, *Late Merovingian France* (Manchester, 1996), pp. 11–26, bring out the increasing scope of political conflict; F.-R. Erkens, 'Divisio legitima und unitas imperii. Teilungspraxis und Einheitsstreben bei der Thronfolge im Frankenreich', *DA* 52 (1996), 423–85, points out that the late Merovingian polity, unlike the Carolingian, was never partitioned.

[33] Werner, *Die Lütticher Raum*, pp. 202–12, is a searching re-examination of the links between the founders of Lorsch and the elite of the Liège area. Werner argues that the normal reading of the Lorsch cartulary-chronicle as referring to kinship between Chrodegang and Cancor is a misunderstanding. Whilst close kinship seems unlikely, the evidence of shared political activity, property interests and naming-patterns, assembled by the authors Werner criticises, does point to some form of more distant kinship between the two men: Innes, 'Kings, monks and patrons'.

attempt to set up a system which excluded the Carolingians, but by Martel's death in 741 the aristocracy of the Frankish heartlands had been cajoled and forced into a political system in which Carolingian power – when necessary justified by Merovingian regality – was a given, and only on the periphery was it possible to follow an independent strategy.[34] Martel did not simply hammer out this system through brute force; his opponents were increasingly imprisoned rather than killed in true Merovingian fashion. Even a bitter opponent like Bishop Eucherius of Orléans was removed from the Loire by Rupert of Hesbaye, and delivered to the safekeeping of the monks of St Trond.[35]

The relationships which Martel built with both our Ruperts were essentially horizontal alliances which were mutually beneficial.[36] In the middle decades of the eighth century, Cancor was allowed a more or less free hand, his interests east of the Rhine proceeding hand in hand with those of the Carolingians. Cancor's contact, Fulrad, acted as a mediator between court and the region: bound to the Carolingians, thanks to the office of chaplain and the abbacy of Saint-Denis, he acquired vast amounts of land from clients in his homeland down the Moselle and Saar and east of the Rhine.[37] From the middle of the century, the Carolingian acquisition of rights over land in the region allowed them to prime these networks still more effectively: under Pippin and Charlemagne there is good evidence for alliance with local leaders being cemented through the tenure of royal land.[38] Although local rulers might seek to present their positions in terms of office – Cancor styled himself *comes*, as did aristocrats at the former Roman centres of Worms, Mainz, Bingen and

---

[34] For Martel's elimination of potential rivals within the Frankish heartlands, see Wood, *Merovingian Kingdoms*, pp. 273–87; Fouracre, 'Frankish Gaul to 814', in *NCMH*, pp. 85–109 at pp. 87–94; also J. Jarnut *et al.* (eds.), *Karl Martell in seiner Zeit* (Sigmaringen, 1994).

[35] *Vita Eucherii*, ed. W. Levison, *MGH SRM* 7, pp. 46–53 at pp. 50–1. For changing patterns of punishment see J. Busch, 'Vom Attentat zur Haft. Die Behandlung von Konkurrenten und Opponenten der frühen Karolinger', *Historische Zeitschrift* 263 (1996), 561–88; G. Althoff, '*Ira Regis*: Prolegomena to a History of Royal Anger', in B. H. Rosenwein (ed.), *Anger's Past: The Social Uses of an Emotion in the Middle Ages* (Ithaca and London, 1998), pp. 59–74.

[36] This is the important conclusion of two detailed regional studies by M. Werner, *Der Lütticher Raum* and *Adelsfamilien im Umkreis der frühen Karolinger. Die Verwandtschaft Irminas von Oeren und Adelas von Pfalzel*, VF Sonderband 28 (Sigmaringen, 1982). (Werner's account of the geographical origins of what was to become the Carolingian family has not won universal support: see E. Hlawitschka, 'Zu den Grundlagen des Aufstiegs der Karolinger', *Rheinische Vierteljahrsblätter* 49 (1985), 1–61.) Cf. P. Geary's important study of aristocratic power in southern Gaul: *Aristocracy in Provence: The Rhône Basin at the Dawn of the Carolingian Age* (Stuttgart and Philadelphia, 1985).

[37] See Stoclet, *Fulrad*, and above, pp. 27–9. See also *MGH Epp.* III, no. 17, p. 514, for a Rupert travelling to Rome with Fulrad of Saint-Denis in 758.

[38] E.g. at Heppenheim (*CL6a* and p. 149 above); and Mainz (*MGH DCharlemagne* 127 and p. 63 above). The acquisition of the royal title in 751 may have been significant precisely because of the landed resources it brought with it, and the resulting expansion of opportunities for patronage.

Ladenburg in the middle of the eighth century[39] there is very little evidence for royal interest in the creation and manipulation of local
command before the reign of Charlemagne. Until then, we have a series
of powerful patrons like Rupert, Cancor and Fulrad, at the apex of
regional elites and binding them to the centre. It was Charlemagne and
Louis the Pious who were to transform this pyramidal political system
into one based on an articulated hierarchy which the centre claimed to
control.[40]

FORGING THE *PAX KAROLINA*

Thanks to the charters, we can trace the imposition, challenge and final
acceptance of a new relationship between central and local power under
Charlemagne and Louis the Pious. The drama begins in 771, when
Charlemagne saw, and ruthlessly took, the chance of intervention in the
formidable political network built up by Cancor's family. Charlemagne's
chance came following Cancor's death, which more or less coincided
with that of Charlemagne's brother, Carloman. Carloman and
Charlemagne had each ruled one-half of the Frankish realm since their
father's death in 768, an arrangement full of tension.[41] The newly
founded abbey of Lorsch, the epicentre of Cancor's political system,
stood in Charlemagne's portion, but just to the south, in Alsace and
Alemannia, Carloman held sway. Cancor, whose interests straddled the
political division, maintained a policy of equidistance between the brothers, and Cancor's ally, Fulrad, was one of Carloman's key backers.[42] On
Cancor's death, his son, Heimerich, evidently expected to step into his
father's shoes: in March 772, Heimerich was styled count as he witnessed
a publicly made gift at Lorsch, whose abbot, Guntland, was a kinsman.[43]
Within weeks, however, Heimerich was at Herstal, at Charlemagne's
court, involved in a dispute with Abbot Guntland. The brief record of
the royal diploma recording the verdict of Charlemagne's court tribunal,

[39] Cancor: *CL1*, 482 (in *CL* c. 6 he was styled 'rhenensis pagus comes', but the cartulary-chronicle
is twelfth-century). Worms: *UBF*50, and probably also *UBF*53. Mainz: *UBF*24, 25, 40, 41, 59.
Ladenburg: *UBF*38. Bingen: *UBF*39, 40.
[40] For the distinction between 'pyramidal' and 'hierarchical' political systems, see A. Southall, 'A
Critique of the Typology of States and Political Systems', in M. Banton (ed.), *Political Systems and
the Distribution of Power* (London, 1965), pp. 113–40 at pp. 126–9.
[41] J. Jarnut, 'Ein Bruderkampf und seine Folgen. Die Krise des Frankenreiches (768–771)', in G.
Jenal *et al.* (eds.), *Herrschaft, Kirche, Kultur. Festschrift F. Prinz*, Monographien zur Geschichte des
Mittelalters 32 (Sigmaringen, 1992), pp. 165–77.
[42] *CL*1290, dated, uniquely amongst the Lorsch and Fulda material, by both brothers' regnal years.
[43] *CL*248 (17 March 772). Schulze, *Grafschaftsverfassung*, p. 197, argues that Heimerich was active as
a count before his father's death, his activity based in Hesse, and that on his father's death he
became a count in the middle Rhine. The idea that Heimerich was a count in Hesse before his

made up of Heimerich's peers, is frustratingly opaque.[44] Guntland complained that Heimerich had made 'challenges' to the abbey, which had been given in full property to Chrodegang by Cancor and then by Chrodegang to Guntland. Guntland won the case. Yet it would be unwise to assume that Heimerich was simply challenging Guntland's position, given his presence at Lorsch just weeks earlier.

The case is difficult precisely because Lorsch's legal status before 772 was unclear.[45] The initial gift to Chrodegang had made Lorsch a constituent of the constellation of Chrodegang's 'reform monasteries' centred on Gorze – a constellation which had held together his political network, linking Hesbaye, the Moselle and the Rhine. Lorsch was thus neither a royal monastery nor an episcopal house in the usual understanding of the term: Chrodegang was not the diocesan bishop, and Lorsch was not seen as a house of the bishops of Metz or a daughter house of Gorze. The trigger for the 772 dispute was Cancor's death; Heimerich's 'challenges' thus link to the issue of family relations to Lorsch. Whatever the precise issues in March 772, the key to understanding the case is Guntland's action on winning: he immediately gave the abbey, now legally his possession, to Charlemagne.[46] The king was the only real winner from the whole affair, at a politically vital juncture; he may have even engineered the entire case to impose royal lordship. The language used in the royal diploma recording Heimerich's defeat provides a further clue as to the issues at stake. Heimerich was described as simply *homo*, a normal free Frank, not as *fidelis* (which would have denoted personal bonds of fidelity to Charlemagne), or a count (as he had been called by a Lorsch scribe just weeks before).[47] Although the status of Lorsch may have been the issue which was fought over at the royal court, Heimerich suffered other challenges to his position after his father's death: land which he inherited

father's death rests on the identification of Heimerich with a Count Heimo in Hesse, which goes back to Glöckner. Glöckner's argument rested on the similarity between the names, and the fact that some of a group of charters redacted on 12 March 766 were witnessed by Heimerich whilst others were subscribed by a Heimo (*CL*548, 549, 551): this does not make the two men identical, and indeed a close look at the charter evidence suggests that they were quite separate. Heimerich was once styled 'count' in local charters before 772 (*CL*551).

[44] *MGH DCharlemagne* 65. For stimulating comments on the case and the issues around it, see Hannig, 'Zentralle Kontrolle', 28–33, Le Jan, 'Justice royale', 80–3, and cf. also Innes, 'Kings, Monks and Patrons', pp. 309–11.

[45] Semmler, 'Lorsch', pp. 79–80. Also A. Angenendt, 'Pirmin und Bonifatius. Ihr Verhältnis zu Mönchtum, Bischofsamt und Adel', in A. Borst (ed.), *Mönchtum, Episkopat und Adel zur Gründungszeit des Klosters Reichenau*, VF 20 (Sigmaringen, 1974), pp. 251–303, esp. pp. 267–9.

[46] *MGH DCharlemagne* 67, see also nos. 72, 73 for further patronage. Charlemagne was notoriously parsimonious in the giving away of land, and very selective as to which churches he patronised: the scale of his gifts to Lorsch underline the abbey's significance.

[47] *CL*248. See the comments of Kienast, *Die fränkische Vasallität*, p. 178, for the *homo*: *fidelis* division, made explicit in *MGH DCharlemagne* 210.

from his father came 'against Count Warin'.[48] In spite of these challenges, the family of Cancor and Heimerich did not disappear without trace; what Charlemagne was doing was changing the parameters within which their power worked in the locality. Rather than exercising unmediated power, embedded through their control of Lorsch, they had to learn to play a new game.

The rewriting of the political rule book was not an experience which men like Heimerich enjoyed. After his very public humiliation in 772, Heimerich was less conspicuous locally. He witnessed just one charter (recording a pious gift by one of his sisters) between the Herstal débâcle and 779, and in that he was given no special title.[49] In the meantime, he may have been politically active beyond Charlemagne's effective reach. In 774 the relics of St Rupert were translated from Worms to Salzburg, where they were housed in a massive new cathedral, whose construction was a demonstration of the political and cultural assertiveness of Bavaria.[50] Rupert's relics did not single-handedly decide on a change of scenery: in early medieval society, relic-translations expressed shifting balances of political power. Heimerich's precise role in the translation of St Rupert (like his precise relationship to St Rupert) is unknown, but the chronology is eloquent. The relics of Heimerich's saintly ancestor and family patron were moved beyond Charlemagne's reach in the same year that Charlemagne himself watched the consecration of a new church at Lorsch, now under royal lordship.[51]

Heimerich's effective exile from the middle Rhine lasted until 779. From then until 784 Heimerich was, once again, very much in evidence in the area, witnessing charters, entitled count and occupying first place in witness-lists.[52] Thanks to the preservation of a local document recording the legal conflict over the status of the *villa* of Schwanheim in 782, Heimerich's political position in this second period can be minutely reconstructed.[53] Legal conflict over Schwanheim was initiated by Heimerich and a group of local landowners, who contested Lorsch's claim that the monks had been given Schwanheim by Charlemagne and thus owned the *villa* in its entirety. Heimerich had family interests at

---

[48] *CL*15. Whilst it is possible that Warin was a kinsman of Cancor's and thus had a basis in inheritance custom for the contest, he can scarcely have been more than a distant relation and thus his contestation of Heimerich's inheritance from his father is best understood in terms of political ulterior motives. Cf. Gockel, *Königshöfe*, p. 302.

[49] *CL*182: Heimerich subscribed as 'germani eius'.

[50] *Annales Iuvavenses*, ed. H. Breßlau, *MGH SS* 30:2 (Hanover, 1926) pp. 727–44, s.a. 774, p. 734. For Rupert's initial burial at Worms, Gierlich, *Die Grabstätte*, pp. 204–8.

[51] Innes, 'Kings, Monks and Patrons', pp. 312–13.

[52] He last appears in 784x6, *CL*1539. Other charters from the period featuring Count Heimerich are *CL*178 (782); *CL*221 (779); *CL*248; *CL*268 (782).   [53] *CL*228.

Schwanheim.[54] Indeed, several of Heimerich's followers were long-term associates of his family: Heimerich's local power depended on his ability to maintain the bonds of patronage which his family had built up with influential local landowners over generations.[55] In January 782 – just months before the Schwanheim dispute was settled at Charlemagne's court – Heimerich visited Lorsch and made a pious donation to the monks. Informal discussions were clearly under way long before the formal court hearing was staged.[56] When the Schwanheim case was finally heard, Heimerich's faction were opposed by another local grouping, led by a local man named Guntram. His frequent activity as a charter witness allows us to trace his long-standing links with the local men he was able to mobilise in 782. The Schwanheim *placitum*, and subsequent documents, styled him 'count', whilst one earlier document had called him a royal vassal. Guntram was clearly very directly bound to the king, and acted as a royal agent, carrying out royal orders in 777, and again in the aftermath of the Schwanheim dispute. By recruiting this influential local as a royal vassal, Charlemagne gained a powerful and loyal local agent who could counter Heimerich's family and their long-standing dominance.[57]

There are striking parallels between the Schwanheim case and another high-profile dispute from the area, likewise heard before Charlemagne in 782. This concerned the status of the abbey of Mettlach in the Hünsruck, which had been founded by the ancestors of Milo, Martel's ally, and was dedicated to one of Milo's forefathers and predecessors in the family bishopric of Trier, St Liutwine. In 782 'reformed' Trier, no longer ruled by a descendent of Liutwine's, claimed ownership of the monastery, which

---

[54] *CL*226 for the earlier interests of Count Rupert, Heimerich's grandfather.

[55] See e.g. the close ties between Bernoin and Heimerich's family: *CL*228, 559, 221, 268.

[56] *CL*178. Note also *CL*268 from June 782 where Heimerich is active as a witness at Lorsch.

[57] Guntram's land-holding: *CL*1561, 1650, 1732, 2803. As a witness: *CL*860 (771); 249 (775); also in *CL*221, 178, 268; as count in *CL*228 and thereafter *CL*256 (782), 249. For Guntram as *vassus dominicus* see *UBF*83. *CL*544 (probably 782) is also probably this Guntram, here witnessing third. Guntram's witnessing at Heimerich's side in *CL*221, 178, 268 has led historians since Glöckner (most notably Gockel, *Königshöfe* at (for example) pp. 124, 257–8) to see Guntram as a 'Rupertine'. Staab, *Gesellschaft*, p. 430 sees Guntram as *centenarius* of the Rheingau on the evidence of his witnessing, and dismisses comital titles as a reflection of his vicecomital standing: the account of 782 in *CL*228 offers a far sharper and more defined picture than this interpretation would allow (see Hannig, 'Zentralle Kontrolle', 29–30, for an interpretation closer to mine). At pp. 387–93 Staab suggests links with the Mainz area and the family of Hraban Maur: it seems likely to me that the Guntram active in these circles at the very end of the eighth century is a different man from the one active around Lorsch in the 770s and 780s. Most recently M. Werner, *Der Lütticher Raum*, pp. 208–9, n. 54, has reminded us that there is no direct evidence for relationship between Guntram and the Rupertines, and that links between Hraban's family and the Rupertines arise a generation later in the wake of a marriage alliance. Note that other men involved in royal service followed Guntram in 782, notably the scribe Herirad (on whom, above, pp. 113–4) and the soldier Ripwin and his family (on whom, above, pp. 147–52).

was controlled by three grandsons of its founder. The case turned on the legal basis, and legitimacy, of this control. Trier won. The net effect of the judgement was to remove a monastery which was the epicentre of an aristocratic political system from the control of the family of its founders. It thus effectively replayed Charlemagne's seizure of Lorsch a decade earlier.[58]

The legal mechanism used to obtain the verdict demonstrates the success of royal efforts to build up direct influence in the localities, using royal patronage to challenge the local hegemony of powerful families. The royal charter recording the verdict presents it as settled by the testimony of the three bishops of the province of Trier, and the counts and *scabini* of the Moselle region. The records of the Mettlach and Schwanheim cases, both resolved in 782, are the two earliest surviving documents in which local judgement-finders were referred to as *scabini*.[59] Before 782, judgement-finders in the middle Rhine had been styled *boni homines* or *nobiliores homines*.[60] *Scabinus* was a newfangled title adopted by the court in royal edicts. Earlier historians, working from royal legislation alone, have seen in the adoption of the new term *scabinus* an attempted institutional reform; the *scabini* were close to being professional jurors, appointed for life on the grounds of legal knowledge.[61] Yet the *scabini* of 782 were exactly the same kind of men who had been described as *boni homines* previously: local men of property and influence.[62] There was no change of personnel, but the diffusion of a new title was clearly

---

[58] *MGH DCharlemagne* 148. See T .Raach, *Kloster Mettlach / Saar und sein Grundbesitz. Untersuchungen zur Frühgeschichte und zur Grundherrschaft der ehemaligen Benediktiner Abtei im Mittelalter*, Quellen und Abhandlungen zur mittelrheinische Kirchengeschichte 19 (Mainz, 1974), pp. 12–19. For events at Mettlach as typical of eighth-century Carolingian policy, see J. Semmler, 'Episcopi potestas und karolingische Klosterpolitik', in A. Borst (ed.), *Mönchtum, Episkopat und Adel zur Gründungszeit des Klosters Reichenau*, VF 20 (Sigmaringen, 1974), pp. 305–95. For the prosopography of this family, christened 'Widonid' by historians, up to the end of the ninth century see E. Hlawitschka, 'Waren die Kaiser Wido und Lambert Nachkommen Karls des Grossen?', *Quellen und Forschungen aus Italienischen Archiven und Bibliotheken* 49 (1969), 366–86; W. Metz, 'Miszellen zur Geschichte der Widonen und Salier, vornehmlich in Deutschland', *Historisches Jahrbuch* 85 (1965), 1–27; Metz, 'Austrasische Adelsherrschaft'; H. Schreibmuller, 'Die Ahnen Kaiser Konrads II und Bischof Brunos von Würzburg', in *Herbipolis Jubilans*, Würzburger Diozesangeschichtsblätter 14/15 (1952), pp. 173–233; Stoclet, *Fulrad*.

[59] Ganshof, *Frankish Institutions*, p. 77.

[60] *TW*196, 257, 267, *UBF*83. Cf. also *CL*6a (*viri illustres*) although slightly later (795). The title *rachimbourgi*, encountered in normative sources, is not attested in the local evidence from the middle Rhine, and only very, very occasionally elsewhere.

[61] See Ganshof, 'La preuve dans le droit franc', in *La Preuve*, 2 vols., Recueil de la Societé Jean Bodin 17 (Paris, 1965) II, pp. 71–98. For an exhaustive revisionist discussion see Weitzel, *Dinggenossenschaft und Recht*, pp. 776–913.

[62] Cf. Fouracre, 'Frankish Gaul', pp. 106–8. For the social background of *scabini* see F. N. Estey, 'The *Scabini* and the Local Courts', *Speculum* 26 (1951), 119–129.

significant, in that it occurred at such a politically explosive juncture. In the Schwanheim *placitum* this was explicit – its local scribe called some of those who backed the royal agent Guntram '*scabini*'. The new title was one of functional specialisation which replaced generalised labels of social standing: local influence was being presented in terms of official roles defined by the political centre.[63]

Charlemagne was not trying to force the aristocracy to its knees, but to make local power-holders more answerable to the centre by redefining their position in terms of office. Thanks to the successful prosecution of expansive warfare, and the possibility of high office through royal patronage, the aristocracy had a vested interest in the Carolingian system which eased the enactment of structural changes. The men who lost control of Mettlach, for example, stayed loyal; they and their kin had grown wealthy and powerful in Carolingian service beyond their home area, in western Francia and Italy. Indeed, Charlemagne went out of his way to court potentially disaffected groups in the region, notably in his marriage policy. Hildegard, his wife from 771 to 783, came from a family which had property interests in the middle Rhine, and the provinces east of the Rhine as far south as Alemannia; in 788, after Hildegard's death, one of her sons, Louis the Pious, was married to a daughter of Chrodegang's brother. The type of interaction between king and locality which was the result of these marriages is clear from the ninth-century *Life of Leoba*, which tells of Hildegard's devotion to the Anglo-Saxon Holy woman and Leoba's eventual move to an estate close by the royal residences of Mainz and Worms. Here, the local links cultivated by these local women were helping kingship to put down local roots in a region where the king was increasingly resident.[64]

Even these efforts, however, could not prevent an aristocratic reaction which reached a head in 785, when a sworn conspiracy of disaffected easterners was formed. Royal marriage again lay at the heart of politics: after Hildegard's death, Charlemagne had married another easterner, Fastrada, who hailed from the Main valley. The *Königsnähe* enjoyed by Fastrada and her kin seems to have dragged Charlemagne into very local factional infighting: certainly one informed local claimed that

---

[63] See e.g. *MGH Cap.* I, no. 40, c. 4, no. 44, c. 12; *MGH Cap.* II, no. 192, cc. 2–4, for the advancement of an ideology of office. As *scabini* were to swear oaths on taking up office, and lists of them were to be made, this ideology would have reached a local level: oath-swearing and list-making were amongst the elements of the capitulary programme which can be shown to have been carried out in the localities.

[64] See Rudolf, *Vita Leobae*, cc. 18–20, pp. 129–30; and Thegan, *Gesta Hludovici*, cc. 2, 4, ed. Tremp, pp. 176–8, 178–80. Hildegard's kin included the owners of the church at Flonheim, discussed above, pp. 33–4.

disaffection was caused by Fastrada's *crudelitas*.[65] Although Charlemagne's marriage to Fastrada may have been the final straw for the disaffected, a near contemporary local source suggests that the real bone of contention was structural political change. This account – known as the *Annales Nazariani* – gives a priceless insight into the world-view of the rebels, and the aims and form of their conspiracy. Their complaints were about royal encroachment on a regional world where the aristocracy had previously been left to their own devices. Charlemagne was accused of having ridden roughshod over regional custom, attempting to broker a marriage between one local aristocrat's daughter and a Carolingian lackey – again, marriage politics proving contentious and central. One conspirator even admitted to having sworn that he would kill Charlemagne if he ever again crossed the Rhine. The rebels couched their opposition to Charlemagne in terms of opposition to Frankish intervention: whereas sources close to the Carolingian court saw the conspirators as 'eastern Franks', the *Annales Nazariani* talked of 'Thuringians'. The revolt failed. When the conspiracy was discovered, the malcontents fled, significantly, to Fulda, where they begged for clemency in the name of St Boniface, and had Abbot Baugolf – a kinsman and neighbour, but as abbot also a royal official – intercede for them. The rebels met Charlemagne at Worms, and were then sent off to swear loyalty on various relics dispersed through Francia, whereupon they were promptly seized, some of them blinded and others forfeiting their property.[66] The complaints about royal intervention, in what had previously been a closed world of regional politics, were a striking indication of the direction of political change: these were not diehard anti-Carolingian rebels, but members of groupings which had previously prospered in a loose alliance with the Carolingians and now railed at royal intrusiveness.

Even the forms of organisation used by the rebels in 785 looked to the past. Sworn associations (*coniurationes*) had been forbidden in 779; political factions were no longer to be cemented by mutual oath-swear-

---

[65] Einhard, *Vita Karoli*, c. 20, ed. Holder-Egger, pp. 25–6. On Fastrada see F. Staab, 'Die Königin Fastrada', in R. Berndt (ed.), *Das Frankfurter Konzil von 794: Kristallisationspunkte karolingischer Kultur*, Quellen und Abhandlungen zur mittelrheinische Kirchengeschichte 80 (Mainz, 1997), pp. 183–217.

[66] On the rebellion see Schlesinger, *Die Entstehung der Landesherrschaft*, pp. 50–51; K. Brunner, *Oppositionelle Gruppen im Karolingerreich* (Vienna, 1979), pp. 48–53; U. Hussong, 'Studien zur Geschichte der Reichsabtei Fulda bis zur Jahrtausendwende, II', *Archiv für Diplomatik* 32 (1986), 129–303 at 141–6; Friese, *Herrschaftsgeschichte*, pp. 51–84; and, on the traditions around it recorded in the *Annales Nazariani*, K. Brunner, 'Auf den Spuren verlorener Traditionen', *Peritia* 2 (1983), 1–22; Innes, 'Kings, Monks and Patrons', pp. 313–15. For blinding as a new punishment, and its regal significance, see G. Bührer-Thierry, '"Just Anger" or "Vengeful Anger"? The Punishment of Blinding in the Early Medieval West', in B. H. Rosenwein (ed.), *Anger's Past: The Social Uses of an Emotion in the Middle Ages* (Ithaca and London, 1998), pp. 75–91.

ing. At the same time, the Carolingians had attempted to undermine the foundations of horizontal solidity which underpinned and embedded inherited forms of aristocratic leadership in the regions, banning the pursuit of bloodfeud through armed force and outlawing sworn military bands (*trustes*).[67] The significance of these measures is clear from the evidence for their application: when the relatives of a murdered man named Hroutmond took out their vengeance on his killer, Hortlaic, in Fastrada's presence at Frankfurt in 794, those involved on both sides were punished with the confiscation of land.[68] Oaths, and horizontal groupings cemented by oaths, were only permitted when articulated through a hierarchical structure of royal power. As a direct result of the conspiracy of 785, an oath of fidelity to Charlemagne was extracted from each free man in the kingdom, and the oath of fidelity was to be insisted upon by Charlemagne through the rest of his reign, and by his successors. Whereas previously a handful of influential aristocrats had sworn *fidelitas* on account of their personal position, now *fidelitas* was expected by all. Each man was placed in a direct relationship to the king, which was not to be complicated by mutual oaths sworn with neighbours and friends.[69]

These moves had a practical basis, too, in Charlemagne's concerted efforts to acquire aristocratic monasteries right across Austrasia, down the Rhine and in its eastern hinterland, and also in central and southern Gaul – efforts which we have already seen bearing fruit at Lorsch and Mettlach.[70] The foundation of rural monasteries was a real challenge for kings. By placing houses like Lorsch or Mettlach under his personal protection, granting privileges of immunity in return, Charlemagne was both limiting the exercise of effectively independent local power, and gaining a practical foothold in the localities. Royal lordship did not, however, end the relationship between the local elite and the new rural monasteries: Lorsch and Fulda continued to attract donations of land from the local elite long after they had become royal monasteries. Indeed, as the actions of the rebels in fleeing to Fulda in 786 show, they continued to be the hubs of regional aristocratic worlds. But they were hubs

---

[67] See *MGH Cap.* I, no. 20, cc. 1, 4, 22, pp. 50–1. On the political implications of these injunctions, and their centrality to the Carolingian political programme, see Althoff, *Verwandte, Freunde und Getreue*, pp. 119–33, 149–67; Geary, 'Extra-Judicial Means of Conflict Resolution', esp. pp. 584–5, 600–1; Le Jan, *Famille et Pouvoir,* pp. 122–30.

[68] *MGH Formulae*, no. 49, p. 523 – the restitution of Hortlaic's forfeited land to his grandson.

[69] On the oath of loyalty, and its relation to the conspiracy of 785, see M. Becher, *Eid und Herrschaft. Untersuchungen zum Herrscherethos Karls des Großen*, VF Sonderband 39 (Sigmaringen, 1993), and F. L. Ganshof, 'Charlemagne's Use of the Oath', in Ganshof, *The Carolingians and the Frankish Monarchy* (London, 1971), pp. 111–124. On the shift from personal *fidelitas* by the great to universal *fidelitas*, Le Jan, 'Structures familiales', 315–17.

[70] Semmler, 'Die Geschichte der Abtei Lorsch' pp. 80–2; Le Jan, 'Justice royale', pp. 80–3.

which were formally connected to the wider Frankish polity, as events of 786 likewise demonstrated: the rebels could not fortify themselves at Fulda, impregnable in the locality, because Fulda was a royal monastery. Abbots like Baugolf thus faced two ways, not only towards their royal lord but also towards the regional networks on whose support they relied. Indeed, the meaning of royal lordship was increasingly strictly defined, a process which reached its culmination under Louis the Pious in the years 814 to 819. Ultimately, of course, royal lordship meant much in practical terms: kings could tap on the resources and organisational power of monasteries, or at least attempt to regulate the ways in which the church's swollen holdings were used. By the ninth century the land and opportunities of patronage they offered were integral to royal strategies of local control, both through the grant of abbacies to trusted clerics and laymen, and through the sheer weight of monastic landholdings.[71] Rural monasteries were both the hubs of local worlds and points of contact between locality and centre; royal lordship over them thus articulated a new, king-centred, political system.

MAINTAINING THE *PAX KAROLINA*

Under Charlemagne, the channels which linked locality and court were formalised. It was on account of its role in this process that literacy was central to Carolingian government, recording the exhortations of kings and linking local agents to the royal court.[72] In that there was brisk local use of written documents, the Carolingian programme mobilised local traditions of public action, and placed them in a direct relationship with the centre. Central to the structured chain of command thus created was the role of the count. Counts were directly answerable to the king as local rulers, charged with carrying out a moral programme recorded in the capitularies and kept in contact with the king's wishes through written documents. Charlemagne's counts were not new men, outsiders implanted as royal snoopers. They were members of families which had long enjoyed local dominance, and had often long enjoyed the title

[71] On the development of royal lordship, see M. De Jong, 'Carolingian Monasticism', with reference to the path-breaking studies of J. Semmler. On royal lordship in action see F. J. Felten, *Äbte und Laienäbte im Frankenreich*, Monographien zur Geschichte des Mittelalters 27 (Sigmaringen, 1982); F. J. Felten, 'Herrschaft des Abtes', in F. Prinz (ed.), *Herrschaft und Kirche. Beiträge zur Entstehung und Wirkungsweise episkopaler und monastischer Organisationsformen* (Stuttgart, 1988), pp. 147–296; Wehlt, *Reichsabtei und König*; Innes, 'Kings, Monks and Patrons'.

[72] See McKitterick, *Carolingians and the Written Word*, esp. pp. 23–75; J. L. Nelson, 'Literacy in Carolingian Government', in R. McKitterick (ed.), *The Uses of Literacy in Early Medieval Europe* (Cambridge, 1990), pp. 258–96; R. Schieffer (ed.), *Schriftkultur und Reichsverwaltung unter den Karolingern*, Abhandlungen der Nordrhein-Westfälischen Akademie der Wissenschaften 97 (Opladen, 1997).

count, but whereas previously their power had rested on an inherited place in a social pyramid, now it was defined in terms of a political hierarchy. Although outsiders could be appointed, it was rare, and it would be misleading to see the appointment of an outsider as an index of royal power. Ricbod, abbot of Lorsch and archbishop of Trier, saw the use of 'poorer vassals' as royal officials as likely to encourage corruption and oppression, and the appointment of local aristocrats as preferable, indeed a measure of 'reform'.[73] Given the importance of local opinion and patronage networks, keeping things in the family made political sense for all involved: although coercion was an intermittent possibility for kings, in the long term they could only rule through informal structures of deference and patronage. Royal success should not, therefore, be measured by the appointment of outsiders, but by the degree of control that they maintained over local families.

Royal strategy and its success is most clearly visible in the fate of the family of Count Warin, whose power base lay on the lower Neckar around Ladenburg in the second half of the eighth century. Warin had held the royal *villa* of Heppenheim, and the associated land and rights, as an endowment to facilitate his performance of his *ministerium*. Warin had come into the endowment at Heppenheim after his father, Wegelenzo, who had held the *villa* as a *beneficium*.[74] Wegelenzo had been allied to the Carolingians and active down the middle and upper Rhine in the first half of the eighth century. The nature of his endowment at Heppenheim added to his local muscle and thus served both his interests and those of his Carolingian allies. Wegelenzo's local power remained informal, resting on patronage: this was typical of the late Merovingian political system which Pippin and Charlemagne inherited and transformed. Wegelenzo was occasionally styled count, but in necrological sources and royal charters rather than local documents – this was local dominance, not office.[75] Warin first appeared in Pippin's entourage in the 760s, his importance in maintaining Carolingian power in the middle Rhine apparent. Unlike his father, he was consistently titled count, even by local scribes.[76]

[73] *Annales Laureshamenses*, s.a. 802, ed. Pertz, p. 38, and see Hannig, 'Pauperiores vassi de infra palatio?'
[74] *CL6a*.
[75] On the family see Gockel, *Königshöfe*, pp. 302–5. See CL1091, 1200, 2024, 2117, 2151, MGH DPippin 16 UBF523, *Das Verbrüderungsbuch der Abtei Reichenau*, eds. Autenrieth et al. f.115, sector B3 (closely associated with Count Baugolf in all the last three, as in CL6a: the men were probably brothers). In identifying the Wielant of many of these charters with our Wegelenzo I am following Staab, *Gesellschaft*, p. 409, n. 717 (with bibliography) on the philology.
[76] On Warin, Gockel, *Königshöfe*, pp. 302–5; for his lands UBF173, CL3335, 1742. DPippin 16 (762) for his first appearance in a royal charter. Note that there are two men named Warin amongst the witnesses, confirming that our Warin is not the man who was the main Carolingian 'agent' in Alemannia.

The Carolingians needed Wegelenzo's family and its embedded power; Wegelenzo's family, in turn, needed Carolingian patronage. The reciprocity of the relationship is well illustrated in a complex transaction of 762. Wegelenzo, Count Baugolf and Erlebald gave the monastic *cella* on the island of Altrip, in the Rhine opposite Speyer, which they jointly owned, to Pippin, who in turn gave it to his favoured abbey of Prüm.[77] This two-way relationship could be renegotiated, and family power prevented from becoming too independent of royal backing. At some point before 773, Warin lost the Heppenheim endowment, which was granted to Count Baugolf, again *in ministerium ad opus regis*. Warin knew Baugolf well: the two had served Pippin together, and were kinsmen.[78] So in a way, the transfer of the Heppenheim endowment barely interrupted the steady maintenance of family power. What it did show was that families were not closed groups with static structures: kings could manipulate them, and ideas about the inheritance of claims to high office, for their own ends. The context of Baugolf's career confirms the picture. Baugolf witnessed charters as count at Worms in 770 and 771, a trustworthy backer of Charlemagne's installed at an important point in the period in which the Frankish kingdoms were divided between Carloman and Charlemagne.[79] In 773 the *villa* of Heppenheim was given to the now royal abbey at Lorsch, and Baugolf no longer witnessed local charters, so his presence at Worms was presumably no longer necessary after the death of Carloman.[80] Baugolf's links were still important in maintaining Carolingian power down the middle Rhine: they were probably the key factor in his promotion to the abbacy of Fulda from 779 to 802. As abbot, Baugolf was remembered at Fulda as a political figure, eventually forced into exile. His role as intermediary between the regional aristocracy which patronised the abbey and the Carolingian court was most visible in his role in the revolt of 785–6.[81]

---

[77] *MGH DPippin* 16.

[78] Baugolf was probably Warin's uncle; on him, see Gockel, *Königshöfe*, pp. 302–5. He is active in Carolingian service, as a *fidelis*, as early as 753 (*DPippin* 6); see also *DPippin* 16, *UBF*50, 53 (where he has endowed a follower, Waning, on whom see Staab, *Gesellschaft*, pp. 408–9), 523. *CL*909 (782) and 965 (788) may be a different Baugolf. Note that another Warin was one of Carloman's key backers in 768–71.

[79] *UBF*50 at Worms, and compare *UBF*53 with no place of redaction from 771. Previously Baugolf has invariably been seen as count in the Speyergau in *UBF*50, although a transaction which took place at Worms, concerns property in the Speyergau, as does *UBF*53 (although this latter transaction concerns Baugolf's personal property, granted out as a benefice to one Waning, and gives no *pagus* localisation): see (for example) Schulze, *Grafschaftsverfassung*, p. 192. Surely the Worms connection is the most significant point about these charters.

[80] *MGH DCharlemagne* 73.

[81] For Baugolf's probable identity as the man who was abbot of Fulda see Friese, 'Einzugsbereich', p. 1009 with older literature. On Baugolf as abbot, see M. Sandmann, 'Die Folge der Äbte', in *Klostergemeinschaft* I, pp. 178–204 at 182, with bibliography, and above, p. 185, for 785–6.

Warin was not ruined by the irruption of Baugolf. He continued to be active in the area, and presumably had little choice but to rally to his kinsman's side.[82] Warin last appeared as a charter witness in 795.[83] The kind of informal bonds on which he had relied are evident in a remarkable charter of 814, in which a group of locals gave Lorsch land at Ilvesheim for the souls of Warin (by now dead) and his wife Friderun.[84] Warin's children, and particularly his son Witagowo, on occasion acted as 'witness-leader' in their father's old stamping ground after his death.[85] Even more than Warin's, Witagowo's career demonstrates clearly the embedded but informal nature of family power, and the ability of kings to control its parameters. Throughout the first two decades of the ninth century, Witagowo appears active in the lower Neckar region, attempting to make the most out of his father's reputation. He was able to inherit land held by his father from the king, and even maintained family interest in the Heppenheim estate.[86] In 817, after almost two decades waiting, he suddenly and dramatically began to be styled 'count', and to make gifts of land to Lorsch.[87] Scholars who have seen father–son succession to office here miss the context which a close reading of the charters supplies: Witagowo was made to sweat, and was ultimately dependent on royal goodwill.[88] Moreover, it is not clear that Witagowo's office lay in the middle Rhine, since his appearances as count were limited to transactions in which he makes pious donations. By 820 Witagowo and his son, Adalbert, were actively building up power in Bavaria, making property dealings with Freising, a church close to Louis, the young king of Bavaria; here, not in the ancestral haunts on the middle Rhine, was where the political future of Witagowo's descendants lay.[89] It must be likely, therefore, that Witagowo's promotion came as he entered the service of

---

[82] *CL*15 is the only real evidence for his status in these years.

[83] *CL*6a is his last definite living appearance. If he was the *prefectus* of *CDF*228 he would still have been living in 806.   [84] *CL*477.

[85] *CL*193 (Witagowo, 'the son of Count Warin' in 799), 216 (Gerhoh, 'the cleric, son of Count Warin' in 806).

[86] Witagowo as leading-witness: *CL*193 (799), 427 (812), 512 (817). *CL*22 shows his inheritance of land which his father had held from the fisc; *CL*893 property rights at Heppenheim.

[87] Gifts entitled as count: *CL*774 (817); 893 (*c.* 818). Witagowo's only earlier gift had been made in 806/7, when he and his sister made a joint gift of extensive property and twenty *mancipia* at Frankenthal near Heilbronn, in the Gartachgau (*CL*2751). (But see the gift of a vineyard by a Witagowo near Alzey (near property of Warin's, *CL*1742) in 778: *CL*1841.)

[88] Cf. Metz, 'Miszellen', 5; Schulze, *Grafschaftsverfassung*, p. 195.

[89] *Die Traditionen des Hochstifts Freising*, ed. Bitterauf, no. 433. See Mitterauer, *Karolingische Markgrafen*, pp. 144–53. Witagowo's links to Louis 'the German' possibly also explain his patronage of Wissembourg, to which he gave, at an unknown date, property at *Witagowoshusun* (his Rhenish residence?): Wissembourg was close to Louis 'the German' from the 830s on. See Metz, 'Das Kloster Weißenburg', p. 460, for the gift and Gockel, *Königshöfe*, pp. 302–3 with n. 763 for discussion of *Witagowoshusun*.

the young Louis, dispatched as king to Bavaria. The donations of family land in the middle Rhine with which Witagowo marked his new status may owe much to the improved fortune which office, and the endowments which went with it, brought. Playing the patron was a far more affordable option for Witagowo after he became a count, and middle Rhenish property far less important when his political base lay in Bavaria. The multiplicity of potential sources of patronage, and the inability of the aristocracy to move beyond the Carolingian framework, were the foundation stones of the *pax Karolina*. By Witagowo's time, disaffected aristocrats sought patronage from alternative members of the Carolingian dynasty, most often from king's restless sons.

Sons might inherit their father's clout and hope to gain their father's offices, but inherited clout did not lead, automatically and inevitably, to inherited office: office remained something which one needed royal favour to take up, it could not be subsumed to the familial or proprietorial. Kings could work through family power but, by using patronage with care, they could also keep family power in the localities under ultimate royal control.[90] Carolingian control was the order of the day in the church, too, not only through royal lordship of monasteries, but also through creation of a hierarchical structure of church government. Whereas the Merovingian church had been a series of distinct episcopal islands, each with its own charisma, the Carolingian church – whilst still run by an episcopate which was overwhelmingly aristocratic in origin – was one in which sacred power flowed from the centre down. A regular chain of command led from court to metropolitan to bishop. Since the days of Boniface political control and church organisation had gone hand in hand. Boniface's successors at Mainz were, after Lull, well-connected locals who were also royal servants of impeccable pedigree: Riculf, who was closely connected to Charlemagne's wife Fastrada, played a huge role in furthering royal interests in the middle Rhine at the end of the eighth century, whilst his kinsmen and successors Otgar and Hraban dictated the political fate of the region in the ninth century.[91] The local roots, and kinship, of these high-profile royal servants reminds us that there was no absolute dichotomy between 'court' and 'local' appointments: royal control over episcopal appointment was

[90] Cf. D. C. Jackman, *Criticism and Critique: Sidelights on the Konradiner* (Oxford, 1997), who shows the power of inheritance-based claims to succeed to public office, but fails to demonstrate that such claims were more than powerful moral and social arguments which kings often heeded.

[91] On Riculf, Staab, 'Fastrada' is full of useful information. On Otgar see A. Gerlich, 'Zur Reichspolitik des Erzbischofes Otgar von Mainz', *Rheinische Vierteljahrsblätter* 19 (1954), 286–316; on Hraban, M. Sandmann, 'Hraban als Mönch, Abt und Erzbischof', *Fuldaer Geschichtsblätter* 56 (1980), 133–80.

a means of identifying and cultivating key local figures. The letter which Einhard received from Bernarius, bishop of Worms, as he lay on his deathbed, demonstrates the interaction between local concerns and royal appointment nicely:

I plead with you . . . that for the love of God and [your] friendship with me . . . you might devote your great attention to the churches which were entrusted to my small talents. In this way, after my death, hungry wolves will not be able to invade that holy place and scatter that very vulnerable flock, but instead a ruler will be given to them, one who will know that he should love, or, rather, fear God and mercifully help those placed under him.

Indeed, our most faithful brothers, who are also yours, at the monastery of [Wissembourg, which Bernarius held alongside Worms] have selected Fulco to preside over them. Of them, he is the one closest to me. He may, in fact, be young in age, but I believe him to be mature in character and conduct. You know his family well: he is the son of N., the brother of N., and the relative of many nobles. They sent him to Worms and, since I was still alive, they commended him in person, while N. deigned to visit me. With Count N. standing at his side, [Fulco] with many tears made promises to me and my relatives, Lord N., who was moved by the request, also agreed that, if God brought it about, [the brothers] might select Fulco in my place. Therefore, remember, my dearest, that this is not to be put off, but try as hard as you can to bring it about.[92]

Einhard, efficient as always, succeeded in arranging Fulco's succession at Worms and Wissembourg.

Hand in hand with the creation of an episcopal hierarchy went the creation of a secular hierarchy. The new church hierarchy defined the system of *missi dominici*. It is well known that the system of *missi* was no attempt to parachute in outsiders as royal agents: the role of this tier of government was to link centre and locality, and this necessitated trustworthy locals. Jürgen Hannig has shown that in the middle Rhine the archbishop of Mainz took on, *ex officio*, the role of *missus*, and was accompanied by a leading member of the secular elite. Through careful choices in the appointment of *missi*, kings were able to maintain a regional balance of power between local factions and families.[93] We can follow the career of one such figure in detail, and thus understand the workings of the system. Count Rupert was a descendant of the founders of Lorsch and his influence was pervasive in the middle Rhine between 795 and his

193

death in 834.[94] But the pattern of his activity was wholly different from
that of his ancestors. Whereas Cancor and Heimerich were essentially
local patrons, Rupert was first and foremost an agent of the political
centre. In a capitulary of 825, he was named as *missus dominicus* alongside
the archbishop of Mainz.[95] Charters and letters flesh out his regional role.
Rupert exercised a general oversight over the fisc in the region: he was
responsible for the running of fiscal estates deep in the Vosges, around
Kaiserslautern, which supported stopping places on the strategically
important road from Metz to Worms.[96] In the 830s Count Rupert acted
alongside an anonymous *missus*, organising the services of Imperial vassals
and assembling political support for the Emperor, and using the standard
procedure for the mobilisation of the host to do so.[97] Count Rupert was
also the royal official entrusted with effecting the return of illegally seized
lands to the archbishop of Rheims and with chairing the inquest into a
complex and politically sensitive dispute over property between the fisc
and the abbey of Hornbach. He was chided by Einhard for the tardiness
of his investigation of the case of one Alahfrid, which he had been asked
to investigate by the emperor and two counts of the palace.[98] Evidently
his role involved the handling of particularly tricky disputes involving the
delicate political balance of the region. Rupert's ancestry made him the
natural leader of regional society, but this position was redefined within
an administrative hierarchy; subscribing to this hierarchy confirmed
Rupert's dominance. The difference between regional power as exercised
by Rupert, and that enjoyed two generations previously by his ancestor
Cancor, points to the impact of Carolingian reform in the localities. Both
based their power on inherited land in the locality, and the influence
which this brought; both exercised political power which was essentially
based on patronage; both were allied to Carolingian rulers. But Rupert's

[94] Glöckner identified three Ruperts active as counts in the period 795–837. Most subsequent historians have inevitably followed Glöckner in the identification of individuals, given the influence
of his notes and index to the edition of the Lorsch cartulary. However, his separation of three
Ruperts remains a hypothesis. There is no clear break in the appearances of men named Rupert
in the charters from the period until 834, when a donation for the soul of a Count Rupert was
made (CL271). Any attempt to see a succession of Ruperts in the period between must be based
on subjective judgement: I have taken the equally unprovable position of assuming that one
Rupert was active between 795 and 834, as it seems the most straightforward reading of the evidence, and if I am wrong it has no effect on the substance of my argument about political structure. Compare Gockel, 'Zur Verwandtschaft der Äbtissen Emhilt von Milz', pp. 27–33. For
Rupert's activity at Dienheim in the 790s and 800s, below, pp. 126–8.
[95] *MGH Cap.* I, no. 151, p. 308.
[96] Kaiserslautern: CL3674a, and see Kraft, *Das Reichsgut im Wormsgau*, pp. 54–90.
[97] Einhard, letter 22.
[98] Flodoard, *Historia Remensis Ecclesiae* I:19, ed. Heller and Waitz, p. 467; BM 770 = N12 (edition:
Monumenta Boica 31:1 (Münich, 1836), no. 18); Einhard, letter 7.

power was exercised within the parameters which the Carolingians themselves had created.

The story as usually told is simple: in the ninth century the aristocracy were able to establish themselves as undisputed masters of the localities and thus undermine the *pax Karolina*. Once, however, we understand that the Carolingian system rested on a symbiotic relationship between royal ambitions at the centre and aristocratic power in the localities, matters become more complicated. We certainly cannot see political conflict as the playing out of an inevitable and head-on clash between the central-ising ambitions of kings and the local interests of the aristocracy. Nonetheless, exactly such a view remains so deeply embedded in the historiography as to be almost impossible to budge. Its longevity rests on its historiographical usefulness as a *deus ex machina* which can be invoked to explain long-term change. It is worth remembering, when faced with such a pervasive interpretative scheme, that its validity depends on its evi-dential foundations. In this case, they are weak. The standard tropes about the increasing solidity of aristocratic power in the localities rest on no empirical demonstration of the changing situation on the ground: where changes in local power have been established by argument rather than assertion, the argument has proceeded from narrative accounts of the problems faced by kings, or studies of aristocratic titulature.[99] A proper understanding of the ninth century can clearly only be reached after full weight has been given to the local evidence. Only then should we try to attempt to relate the changing face of local power to the political prob-lems faced by kings.

Before we look at the interrelationship between local and central power, though, we need to address one other historiographical cliché. It is usual to tell the political history of the ninth century as a tragedy, and then to search for the flaw in the Carolingian system which can explain later developments, the 'secret cause' of 'decline and fall'. Political divi-sion is usually seen as the index of political failure. But was it? To write of ninth-century 'division' as if one were carving up something which was, initially, a whole, is misleading: even the 'united Empire' of Charlemagne and Louis the Pious consisted of an agglomeration of regional political units, *regna,* most of which had long pre-Carolingian

[99] Cf. e.g. J. Dhondt, *Etudes sur la naissance des principautés territoriales en France (IXe–Xe siècles)* (Bruges, 1948); K. Brunner, 'Das fränkische Fürstentitel'.

heritages.[100] Under Charlemagne, Louis and their successors, the prolife-
ration of kingships, particularly of sub-kingships granted to royal sons,
was a means of consolidating their family's hold on power, and of supplying effective government to outlying *regna*.[101] Neither Charlemagne
nor Louis, moreover, ever sought to pass on the Empire as a whole to a
single heir: for all the moans of a handful of eloquent but unrepresentative observers, whose views have exercised a disproportionate influence
over later historians, no political realist expected anything other than
division. Division was not a sign of royal weakness, but a means of maintaining royal power within the Carolingian dynasty whilst acknowledging the size of the Empire and the heterogeneity of its constituent units.
To this extent, agreed upon and peaceful division could be seen as an
index of royal strength. Of course, neither Charlemagne nor Louis would
have been entirely happy with the actual shape of the divisions that were
eventually enacted, nor with the process by which they were reached.
But their shared perception, that political division would not alter the fact
that the Empire remained a unit held together by dynastic, aristocratic
and ecclesiastical ties, was surely correct: it was these continuing ties
which made ninth-century politics so messy.[102] What we are watching in
the ninth century is the emergence of a new pattern of segmentation
in an enlarged Empire. It is in the negotiation of this new pattern, not in
the simple fact of its emergence, that the changing balance of political
power can be seen.

We cannot, then, see the mere fact of division as an index of weaker
kingship. Yet the perception that, somehow, in the ninth century kingship did weaken remains difficult to budge. One reason is that we know
a huge amount about ninth-century politics in all its nasty brutishness.
There is an explosion in the quantity of narrative source material
between Louis the Pious' reign and the last decades of the century. We
should pause before we assume that this is an objective reflection of any
increase in the frequency or intensity of political crisis. It was, in fact, a
result of important cultural changes. It is all too easy to be misled by the
narrative sources into thinking that the ninth century, about which they
have so much to say, was a period of disaster, whilst viewing
Charlemagne's reign, for which we have only a handful of court-centred
sources that are guilty of wholesale misrepresentation, through rose-

---

[100] See the seminal work of K.-F. Werner on the *regna* structure of the Empire: *Structures politiques
du monde franc (VIe–XIIe siècles)* (London, 1979).

[101] See now B. Kasten, *Königssöhne und Königsherrschaft. Untersuchungen zur Teilhabe am Reich in der
Merowinger- und Karolingerzeit, Schriften der MGH 44* (Hanover, 1997).

[102] See e.g. S. Airlie, 'After Empire: New Work on the Emergence of Post-Carolingian Kingdoms',
EME, 153–61 at 155–7; Le Jan, 'Structures familiales' pp. 320–5.

tinted spectacles.[103] Early medieval politics was a messy and thoroughly unpleasant business, a fact of which we should not lose sight because we happen to know more about the mess and unpleasantness of the ninth century than of the preceding and succeeding periods. Indeed, the very fact that written polemic was so common in the ninth century must underline the sophistication of the political system.[104]

The time is ripe to look at the politics of the period between Charlemagne and Charles the Fat in its own right, and from a local perspective. The wealth of the charter and letter evidence makes the middle Rhine a region particularly suited to such investigation. The first point is that the foundations of the eighth-century Carolingian settlement held up remarkably well. The half-century centred on 800 saw the emergence of this region as one of the real royal heartlands of the Empire, with the construction of new palaces at Ingelheim and Frankfurt underlining its centrality to the royal itinerary.[105] For a century after the revolt of 785–6, malcontents remained within the *pax Karolina*, respecting the Carolingian monopoly on political legitimacy.[106] Indeed, political conflict was effectively centralised by the end of the eighth century: it was not played out in the localities, but at the royal court. The succession of Louis the Pious in 814, for example, was a traumatic event, and one of the aristocratic groupings central to the conflict it provoked hailed from the middle Rhine, where they were extensive land-

---

[103] For the extreme distortion and misrepresentation of Charlemagne's reign in the sources, see M. Becher, *Eid und Herrschaft*, and R. McKitterick, 'Constructing the Past in the Early Middle Ages: The Case of the Royal Frankish Annals', *Transactions of the Royal Historical Society* 7 (1997), 101–29.

[104] For a preliminary sketch along not dissimilar lines, see M. Innes and R. McKitterick, 'The Writing of History', in R. McKitterick (ed.), *Carolingian Culture: Emulation and Innovation* (Cambridge, 1994), pp. 193–220. See also J. L. Nelson, 'History-writing at the Courts of Louis the Pious and Charles the Bald', in A. Scharer and G. Scheibelreiter (eds.), *Historiographie im frühen Mittelalter*, Veröffentlichungen des Instituts für Österreichisch Geschich 32 (Vienna, 1994), pp. 435–42. This is a subject which I hope to discuss at length elsewhere.

[105] For Ingelheim see P. Classen, 'Die Geschichte der Königspfalz Ingelheim bis zur Verpfändung an Kurpfalz 1375', in J. Autenrieth (ed.), *Ingelheim am Rhein. Forschungen und Studien zur Geschichte Ingelheims* (Ingelheim, 1964), pp. 87–146, and for the archaeology W. Sage, 'Die Ausgrabungen in der Pfalz zu Ingelheim am Rhein, 1960–70', *Francia* 4 (1976), 141–60; for Frankfurt, M. Schalles-Fischer, *Pfalz und Fiskus Frankfurt. Eine Untersuchung zur Verfassungsgeschichte des fränkisch-deutschen Königtums*, VMPIG 20 (Göttingen, 1969). On middle Rhenish palaces in general see W. Schlesinger, 'Die Pfalzen in Rhein-Main-Gebiet', *Geschichte in Wissenschaft und Unterricht* 16 (1965), 487–507, and on the fiscal estates that supported them K. Glöckner, 'Das Reichsgut im Rhein-Maingebiet', *Archiv für Hessische Geschichte und Altertumskunde* 18 (1934), 195–216.

[106] See S. Airlie, '*Semper Fideles*? Loyauté envers les carolingiens comme constituant de l'identité aristocratique', in R. Le Jan (ed.), *La royauté et les élites dans l'Europe carolingienne* (Lille, 1998), pp. 129–44, and on Carolingian efforts to create and maintain aristocratic consensus, J. Hannig, *Consensus Fidelium. Frühfeudale Interpretation des Verhältnisses von Königtum und Adel am Beispiel des Frankenreiches*, Monographien zur Geschichte des Mittelalters 27 (Stuttgart, 1982).

owners descended from the founders of the abbeys of Hornbach and Mettlach. But alliances were forged, programmes were advanced, and consequences were dealt out at Aachen.[107] The revolt of 830 caused ripples in the middle Rhine because one of the key actors, Odo, who had replaced the political fall guy and epicentre of the rebellion, Matfrid, as count of Orléans, was a middle Rhinelander who had served as butler and count at Ingelheim in the 820s.[108] But even in the Orléanais, the bone of their contention, swords were not drawn; conflict was processed at court.

The rebellion of 832 was the first time for half a century that political conflict was not confined to the centre. In our area, this was a result of the efforts of Louis the Pious' son, Louis, king of Bavaria (later known as Louis the German), to carve out a wider eastern Frankish kingdom for himself: conflict took place in the localities, but members of the Carolingian dynasty and their respective claims were the objects of the dispute. Once the rebellion of 832 had broken, Louis led an army to the area of Lorsch. Whilst the Lorsch charters continued to date by the elder Louis' regnal years, his younger namesake evidently could attract enough support in the area to reside safely.[109] Louis the Pious was, however, able to cross the Rhine and menace Louis from the royal palace of Trebur, forcing him to flee to his Bavarian base.[110] Einhard's letters clearly show that the conflict led to divided loyalties and political action in the localities. Late in 832, after Louis the Pious had been reconciled with his eldest son and co-Emperor, Lothar, at Mainz,[111] and left the

---

[107] 'Astronomer', c. 21, ed. Tremp, pp. 348–50.

[108] On Odo, see P. Depreux, *Prosopographie de l'entourage de Louis le Pieux (781–840)* (Sigmaringen, 1997), pp. 190–1, with the important studies of his local support by L. Levillain, 'Les Nibelungen historiques et leurs alliances de famille', II, *Annales du Midi* 50 (1938) 5–72 at 31–46, and K.-F. Werner, 'Untersuchungen zur Frühzeit des französischen Fürstentums', *Die Welt als Geschichte* 19 (1959) 146–93 at 154–5, 163. Levillain argues that the Odo in CL738 was Odo of Orléans, returned to the middle Rhine in 831–2, when the political tide had turned against him. On Matfrid see Depreux, *Prosopographie*, pp. 329–31, and for his kin E. Hlawitschka, *Die Anfänge des Hauses Habsburg-Lothringen. Genealogische Untersuchungen zur Geschichte Lothringens und das Reichs im 9., 10. und 11. Jht.*, Veröffentlichungen der Kommission für saarländische Landesgeschichte und Volkskunst 4 (Saarbrücken, 1969), pp. 154–171.

[109] Thegan, c. 39, ed. Tremp, pp. 224–5; *Ann. Bert.*, s.a. 830, p. 6 gives Lampertheim, 'opposite Worms' as Louis' residence. See Neundörfer, *Studien*, pp. 13–14 pointing out that Lorsch gave Louis the German no 'official' support, at least in that monastic scribes continued to date charters by the regnal year of Louis the Pious. The account of *Ann. Bert.* suggests that the revolt might link to the ripples of aristocratic discontent following imperial actions against Matfrid of Orléans. The 831 division project, *MGH Cap.* II, no. 194, c. 14, acknowledged Louis of Bavaria's influence in the middle Rhine without directly mentioning the region's future fate: Louis got Thuringia and the Rhineland but Charles the Bald the Moselle.

[110] *Ann. Bert.*, s.a. 832, ed. Grat *et al.*, pp. 6–7.

[111] *Ann. Bert.*, s.a. 832, ed. Grat *et al.*, pp. 7–8, stressing the receipt of the annual gifts 'more solito'. Thegan c. 40, ed. Tremp, p. 225 has the Emperor at Frankfurt.

middle Rhine, a series of mandates were sent to key local powerholders ordering them to assemble at Heilbronn on 18 December, where they were to be organised by the *missus* H. and Count Rupert. An unnamed count was told that he would then be instructed 'what to do in our name, along with other faithful counts and vassals, to do it zealously and conduct yourself therein according to the confidence we have in your faithfulness'.[112] An Imperial vassal, H., was 'bid that one of your sons, our vassals, who you know can best do it, be ready, when Count R[upert] and our *missus* H. desire to send us any word by him, to proceed without delay or lack of speed to Tours; there he will find . . . either ourselves or our beloved spouse'.[113] Another vassal was put on similar standby to act as a messenger himself.[114] Louis was using his incumbency of the Imperial throne, and the reserves of legitimacy that he held as Emperor and father, to consolidate his position. These were standard mobilisation procedures – that is, normal techniques of government – which were being adopted as mechanisms for the priming of political support. And mobilising political support in the localities, rather than managing factional conflict at court, was now Louis' central concern.

Political conflict became more dependent still on the ability to mobilise local support as the next act of the drama unfolded. Hearing of brewing rebellion in 833, Louis immediately travelled to Worms (where Count Rupert held sway). Here he spent Lent, Easter and Pentecost.[115] Louis' political problems began when he left this friendly backdrop and travelled to meet his sons in Alsace, and thus moved into the sphere of influence of Hugh, count of Tours and Lothar's father-in-law.[116] Louis, faced with the pope and a united front on the part of his sons, lost power, despite the efforts of the likes of Abbot Adalung of Lorsch.[117] In the aftermath of Louis the Pious' deposition in 833, Louis of Bavaria was able to exert influence on the middle Rhine: from this date onwards the younger Louis styled himself in his charters as 'king in eastern Francia', and through the agency of his archchancellor Grimald, who hailed from the Rhine–Moselle region, he built bridges with the east Frankish

---

[112] Einhard, letter 20.

[113] Letter 21. Note the stress on the role of messengers advocating the emperor's cause.

[114] Letter 22.

[115] *Ann. Bert.*, s.a. 833, ed. Grat *et al.*, pp. 8–9. Note the stress on the festivals, pointing to the use of ritual to buttress Louis' position. *AF*, s.a. 833, p. 26, note that Judith was returned to her husband after her rescue from Italian captivity at Worms.

[116] On Hugh, see Depreux, *Prosopographie*, pp. 262–4; F. Vollmer, 'Die Etichonen. Ein Beitrag zur Frage der Kontinuität früher Adelsfamilien', in G. Tellenbach (ed.), *Studien und Vorarbeiten zur Geschichte des großfränkischen und frühdeutschen Adels*, (Freiburg, 1957), pp. 137–84; C. Wilsdorf, 'Les Etichonides aux temps carolingiens et ottoniens', *Bulletin philologique et historique (jusqu'à 1610) du comité des travaux historiques et scientifiques année 1964* (Paris, 1967), pp. 1–23.

[117] Adalung: Thegan, c. 41, ed. Tremp, p. 228.

aristocracy.[118] On 7 January 834 Louis, residing at Frankfurt, was in sufficient control of the region to grant the *villa* of Langen, which had formed part of the great fiscal complex centred on Trebur and Frankfurt, to Lorsch.[119] In this period Einhard felt compelled to pen an anxious letter to the younger Louis. Einhard, who had somewhat reluctantly placed himself in the service of Lothar, his erstwhile pupil and now Emperor, was concerned about the fate of royal benefices and his estates around Seligenstadt, which now lay in Louis the German's sphere of influence, and pleaded that his personal homage to Lothar was not grounds for Louis to strip him of his eastern benefices. Perhaps Einhard was thinking of the regulations appended to the succession agreements of 806, 817 and 831, when he argued that his personal allegiance to one Carolingian was not incompatible with loyalty and royal favour across the Empire as a whole.[120]

Local conflict finally interlocked with political division at the top with the death of the man who had dominated the area for almost half a century, Count Rupert, probably late in 833.[121] Political leadership on both the regional and the regnal level were now up for grabs. In the resulting vacuum, an intriguing meeting took place at Lorsch on 19 February 834. Rupert's widow gave Lorsch land at Bensheim, for the health of her husband's soul. Her gift was witnessed by her son Rupert, her 'co-inheritor' Guntram (Hraban Maur's brother), and a host of local men of substance.[122] Guntram at least should be numbered amongst the

[118] Fleckenstein, *Die Hofkapelle*, pp. 168–9. On Grimald, Depreux, *Prosopographie*, pp. 221–2, and D. Geuenich, 'Beobachtungen zu Grimald von St.Gallen, Erzkapellan und Oberkanzler Ludwigs des Deutschen', in M. Borgolte and H. Spilling (eds.), *Litterae Medii Aevi. Festschrift J. Autenrieth* (Sigmaringen, 1988), pp. 55–68.   [119] *MGH DLouis the German* 14.

[120] Letter 25, and compare also the appeal Einhard makes for a friend to Louis in letter 34, and the acknowledgement of Louis' *de facto* control in letter 33. The best discussion of Einhard's politics in this period remains M. Bondois, *La translation de Saints Marcellin et Pierre. Etude sur Einhard et sa vie politique de 827 à 834*, Bibliothèque de l'Ecole des Hautes Etudes 160 (Paris, 1907).

[121] Rupert is last definitely seen alive in N14 (ed. Crollius, *Acta Academiae Theodoro-Palatinae* 6 (Mannheim, 1789) p. 252) although see also CL2717, from 829, a joint gift by an untitled Rupert (our count or his son?) and Waltrata, our Rupert's wife; he is dead by February 834 (CL271), the content of this charter (a gift for Rupert's soul by his widow, son and kin) probably placing it in a period of mourning for his death. The key to locating his death within this period is the allusion to the administration of the fisc 'in the time of Count Rupert' in the fiscal register preserved at Lorsch (CL3674a); the context makes it likely that here he was newly deceased, and the *villae* included meant that the register must have been compiled after 7 January 834 (see Gockel, *Königshöfe*, p. 28), thus confirming that Rupert died late in 833. Whether his death was connected with the political conflict of the time or not is unknown.

[122] CL271. Guntram was styled as 'coheres' with Waltrata, Rupert's widow. Other witnesses included Engilhelm (see below, pp. 213–14) and Otakar (below, pp. 214). Note also the presence of a Poppo: a Count Poppo was *de facto* ruler of Thuringia and the area around Fulda, and a loyalist; his eponymous son was a key political figure in the next generation, his father's successor in the Fulda area. For the argument that the Babenbergers (as Poppo's descendants are known to historians) were relations of the Rupertines, see W. Metz, 'Babenberger und Rupertiner in Ostfranken', *Jahrbuch für fränkische Landesforschung* 18 (1958), 295–304, and Friese, *Herrschaftsgeschichte*, esp. pp. 94–107; but compare Gockel, 'Zur Verwandtschaft der Äbtissen Emhilt von Milz', pp. 27–33.

politically active in 834. Louis of Bavaria, anxious about the actions and ambitions of his brother Lothar, eventually rescued his father and aided his restoration to the throne – perhaps playing to residual loyalism as he did so. Louis led 'Bavarians, Austrasians, Saxons, Alemans and Franks from the [western] side of the Ardennes' to Aachen, where Lothar had been holding Louis the Pious prisoner. On 28 February 834 Lothar fled. The younger and the elder Louis publicly celebrated Easter together before turning to deal with Lothar. An army was summoned to Langres to campaign against Lothar in mid-August.[123] Guntram was probably amongst those who freed Louis the Pious and then campaigned against Lothar. In a charter dated 30 August, Guntram gave his family's church at Hofheim to Fulda. The charter is a remarkable document, transmitted in several versions, one of which was evidently modelled on a royal charter and thus underlined the status of Guntram's gift and his political links in 834; in it, Guntram styled himself count.[124] Guntram's charter of August 834 was written by the monk Rudolf of Fulda, the later hagiographer and confessor of Louis of Bavaria, 'on the orders of my lord abbot Hraban', Guntram's brother. Now Rudolf had acted as a charter scribe earlier in his career, but his scribal activities had ended long before 834: his presence writing Guntram's charter in 834 must betoken some special arrangement.[125] It is, therefore, significant that in this period Rudolf was Hraban's political agent.[126] The charter was given no place of enactment. Abbot Hraban of Fulda had been active as a 'loyalist' propagandist, arguing Louis the Pious' case against his sons throughout the rebellions, and had in particular urged Louis of Bavaria to play the dutiful son, a role he eventually took up in February 834.[127] Guntram and Rudolf stood at the head of a contingent of local men, including clients of Fulda,

---

[123] *Ann. Bert.*, s.a. 834, ed. Grat *et al.*, pp. 11–13.

[124] CDF487, and see E. Heydenreich, 'Eine Urkunde für Fulda vom 30 Aug. 834', *Historische Vierteljahrsschrift* 5 (1902), 390–1 and M. Tangl, 'Urkunde für Fulda vom 30 Aug. 834', *Historische Vierteljahrsschrift* 5 (1902), 527.

[125] See Sandmann, 'Wirkungsbereiche Fuldischer Mönche', p. 709.

[126] See the letter chiding Archbishop Otgar of Mainz for disloyalty, *MGH Epp.* V, no. 40, p. 533 and Gerlich, 'Zur Reichspolitik', p. 295, n. 61.

[127] See especially Hraban's long letter on the obedience due by sons to fathers, which implicitly casts the younger Louis as the prodigal son, ed. E. Dümmler, *MGH Epp.* V, pp. 403–15. For comments on Hraban's involvement in politics, see now De Jong, 'The Empire as *Ecclesia*', also B. S. Albert, 'Raban Maur, l'unité de l'empire et ses relations avec les Carolingiens', *Revue d'histoire ecclésiastique* 86 (1991), 5–44, esp. 9–11 on 833–4; Sandmann, 'Hraban als Mönch, Abt und Erzbischof', pp. 148–51, and E. Sears, 'Louis the Pious as *Miles Christi*: The Dedicatory Image in Hrabanus Maurus's *De laudibus sanctae crucis*', in P. Godman and R. Collins, (eds.), *Charlemagne's Heir: New Perspectives on the Reign of Louis the Pious (814–40)* (Oxford, 1990), pp. 605–28 and see also Hraban's letter to the younger Louis, accompanying a commentary on Chronicles, *MGH Epp.* V, p. 423. Note Thegan, c. 53, ed. Tremp, p. 246, on the role of Marcward of Prüm and other *fideles* in sending similar messages on filial duty. Marcward was close to two of Hraban's pupils at least: Hatto, later abbot of Fulda, and Lupus of Ferrières.

following Louis of Bavaria in the name of Louis the Pious. Thanks to his activity in 834, Guntram was able to win an appointment as count, presumably taking over some of the duties of his erstwhile master and kinsman, Rupert. As an influential and experienced local man, he was a safe pair of hands whose appointment did not lead to wider disruption or discontent.[128]

The restoration of Louis the Pious as Emperor led to the restoration of calm on the political surface, both at the centre and in the locality. Even those implicated in the rebellion were, eventually, allowed to demonstrate their renewed loyalty: thus Otgar, archbishop of Mainz and one of Lothar's key advisors in the revolt, was held by Louis until a carefully worded letter 'from the people and clergy of Mainz' facilitated his return to his see.[129] Given the void left by the death of Rupert, and of Odo, who had been killed defending his western *honores*, new names inevitably emerged as leaders of the regional aristocracy. One faction, which had remained loyal to Louis the Pious and was tied to Louis of Bavaria through the person of Grimald, quickly established itself as dominant in the Moselle and middle Rhine. At its centre were Gebhard, count in the Lahn region, his godfather (and the archchancellor Grimald's kinsman) Archbishop Hetti of Trier, Abbot Marcward of Prüm and Count Hatto. Their political outlook was voiced in writing, in the account of Louis' reign written by one of Hetti's suffragan bishops, Thegan.[130] As the loyalties of this grouping indicated, at the base of the new order was a *rapprochement* between the two Louis: open political conflict was again confined to the royal court.

However, calm was always likely to be superficial and temporary; the *rapprochement* was based on an uneasy overlapping of spheres of influence between father and son. The pattern of royal gifts shows this quite graphically. On 10 January 836 Louis the Pious made a gift of land to his *fidelis*, Rupert, the son of the Count Rupert who had dominated the middle Rhine until 833. Louis acknowledged Rupert's 'faithful service' – this youngster had evidently shown his mettle in the crucible of crisis.[131] On

---

[128] On Guntram's earlier political career see above, p. 128; my version differs from previous reconstructions, which make Guntram a count from the 820s onwards on the basis of witnessing and judicial activity, a conclusion which stands at odds with the titulature given Guntram by charter scribes: cf. Schulze, *Grafschaftsverfassung*, pp. 190–1.

[129] *MGH Epp.* V, no. 18, p. 324, and see Gerlich, 'Zur Reichspolitik', pp. 296–7.

[130] On Thegan see E. Tremp, *Studien zu den Gesta Hludovici Imperatoris des Trierer chorbischofs Thegan*, Schriften der MGH 30 (Hanover, 1988).

[131] BM953, edition: *UBMR*64. Some of the land (and Rupert's charter establishing title to that land, which was later copied into the Prüm *Liber Aureus*) ended up being given to Prüm by a Rodulf in 880: *UBMR*118. For Rodulf and his kin and allies, an important aristocratic group who were close to Prüm, see Kuchenbuch, *Bäuerliche Gesellschaft und Klosterherrschaft*, pp. 352–5. The Rupert who was given land in 836 was evidently linked to this group, on the evidence of naming-

26 May 836 Louis of Bavaria made a similar grant to his *fidelis*, Werner, again citing faithful service. It consisted of important estates on the Rhine's east bank, including the *portus* of Zullestein; these strategically important gifts allowed Werner to control access to the Rhine's east bank opposite Worms. Werner, like Rupert, was a member of a family from the middle Rhine.[132] But whereas Werner got lands from his master in the middle Rhine, Rupert got land north of the Moselle. It is significant that, after 834, no diploma of Louis the Pious' concerning property in the region around Mainz, Lorsch and Worms survives. Louis the Pious was able to visit the middle Rhine and draw on the rich fiscal lands there, notably in 836 when he held an assembly at Worms and stayed at Ingelheim and Frankfurt, visiting Einhard at Seligenstadt on the way.[133] Until 838, however, Louis of Bavaria was tacitly allowed to retain control of eastern Francia up to the middle Rhine, where he had gained *de facto* control in 833–4. Hence, although the gift to Werner was made whilst both Louis resided and hunted together at Thionville, the diploma was issued in the name of the younger Louis alone.[134] Louis of Bavaria was, indeed, able to install Ruthard, one of his followers, as a count in the middle Rhine.[135]

The gifts to Rupert and Werner were new in content: previous kings had not been in the habit of making outright gifts of land to their

patterns as well as the fate of the 836 gift – but the family of Rupert had interests down the Moselle, and close links with the aristocracy of the area, which became increasingly important in the course of the ninth century (below, p. 226).

[132] *MGH DLouis the German* 19. On the fiscal estates and rights given to Werner, Gockel, *Königshöfe*, pp. 158–69. The importance of the *portus* at Zullestein is underlined by recent excavations from: W. Jorns, 'Zullestein. Ein Beitrag zur Kontinuität von Bauwerken', in *Deutsche Königspfalzen III* (Göttingen, 1980), pp. 111–35. On Werner's kin, Gockel, *Königshöfe*, p. 304: he was related to Witagowo, who was a follower of Louis', based in Bavaria, so kinship ties may have brought him into Louis' service.   [133] *Ann. Bert.*, s.a. 836, ed. Grat *et al.*, pp. 19–20. *AF*, s.a. 836, p. 27.

[134] *AF*, s.a. 836, p. 27, for the meeting at Thionville. Joint gifts could be made: in the early 820s Lothar and his father issued such documents.

[135] *CL*218 for his witnessing a transaction about land at Pfungstadt in 836, *CL*3770 (dated to 842 following the emended date suggested by Hannig, 'Zentrale Kontrolle', pp. 19–20) for him presiding over an inquest, concerning the extent of a gift made by Louis of Bavaria, *CL*2368 for an exchange between Ruthard and Abbot Samuel of Lorsch in 838x9, *CDF*513 for Ruthard as Louis of Bavaria's count of the palace in 838 (on this document see n. 144). Ruthard's name suggests that he was a kinsman of his master's wife, Emma, and the Empress Judith: on their family see J. Fleckenstein, 'Über die Herkunft der Welfen und ihre Anfänge in Süddeutschland', *Studien und Vorarbeiten*, pp. 71–136. A Ruthard *procurator domus regalis* was active under Arnulf running the middle Rhenish fisc in the last years of the ninth century: see Gockel, *Königshöfe*, pp. 211–13. However the gap of fifty years makes it unlikely that this is the same man who was active from 836–842 (see Gockel, p. 213, n. 730, reinforced if *CL*3770 is redated from 877 to 842). Ruthard is roundly ignored in the standard surveys of local counts: Staab, *Gesellschaft*, p. 420, n. 827, taking account only of *CL*218, tentatively suggests a miscopying of Rupert, but the weight of evidence for Ruthard in the late 830s makes this unlikely. Hannig, 'Zentrale Kontrolle', p. 20, notes Ruthard's importance and suggests links with indigenous middle Rhenish families (on the grounds of name).

aristocratic followers. This change did not go unnoticed: Thegan, who certainly understood what was going on in the localities, commented on it at length.[136] The new kind of gift – of which those to Rupert and Werner were typical – was not an indication that kings were losing control, having to buy up aristocratic support at any price, and alienating invaluable royal resources in the process. For one thing, the gifts were used to reward existing supporters for their past actions (and thereby bind them to the king in the future), not as prizes in some kind of political auction. For another, the property used was carefully chosen, and, in most cases, was not land exploited directly by kings, but land which had previously been granted out as benefices to gain political support. In any case, kings did not lose control of the land so given – there is good evidence for their ability to continue to influence what aristocrats did with land given as outright property, precisely because they had given it and maintained a moral hold over it.[137] The land given to Werner, indeed, ended up being given to the royal abbey of Lorsch, and the monks there remembered it as a species of royal patronage, and gave its original royal owner equal credit with Werner for the gift.[138] But the fundamental point which emerges from the gifts to both Werner and Rupert is that these gifts of royal land were necessary because these young aristocrats needed royal patronage if they were to exercise power on the ground: they show aristocratic insecurity in a world where royal patronage was subject to sudden changes as political tides ebbed and flowed. Perhaps gifts of full property were preferable to benefices because they were harder for rival rulers to revoke if the tide turned.

In spite of Louis the German's evident control of the fisc in the middle Rhine, the charter evidence demonstrates that kings could not ride roughshod over extant patronage networks; the loyalty of men with very local interests needed cultivating and their wishes respecting. The system built up by the elder Rupert continued to be the only viable means of governing the region. Rupert's son, Rupert, and Guntram, one of his erstwhile agents, were able to use their control of this network for their own political ends. In 836 Rupert, a recent beneficiary of royal

---

[136] Thegan, c. 19, ed. Tremp, p. 202, whose perceptions are verified, from the charter evidence, by F. L. Ganshof, 'Note sur la concession d'alleux à des vassaux sous le règne de Louis le Pieux', in *Storiografia e Storia: Studi in onore di E. Dupré Theseider* (Rome, 1974), pp. 589–99; see also D. von Gladiß, 'Die Schenkungen der deutschen Könige zu privaten Eigen (800–1137)', *DA* 1 (1937), 80–136. Ganshof's article is the starting-point on the new pattern of gifts, but in what follows I take issue with his interpretation.

[137] See most recently K. Leyser, 'The Crisis of Medieval Germany', *Proceedings of the British Academy* 69 (1983), 409–43 at 423–41, and the careful discussion of Gladiß, 'Die Schenkungen'.

[138] For more on this phenomenon, Innes, 'Kings, Monks and Patrons', pp. 321–2.

patronage, was playing on his father's former status in his style as he gave Lorsch inherited property at Mettenheim; by 10 April 837 he was styled count and active in the locality. Rupert, indeed, inherited his father's patronage network: he witnessed a gift to Lorsch made by one of his father's clients, Batdagis, alongside other of his father's erstwhile associates, notably his kinsman, Count Guntram, who was Batdagis' present lord.[139] Effective government needed such networks, which were simultaneously comital and familial.

The last two years of Louis the Pious' reign witnessed an astoundingly successful attempt to reassert Imperial power over eastern Francia and Alemannia, as the latent hostilities on a local level broke into the open.[140] The flash point came in 838, when the Emperor decided to move against his son and namesake, citing a 'secret meeting' between Lothar and Louis of Bavaria. Again, official channels were used to mobilise political support.[141] The real cause of conflict was the need to reassert Imperial control over the rich fiscal lands of the middle Rhine; attempts to build a power base for the young Charles the Bald in the west necessarily forced Louis the Pious' itinerary eastwards.[142] The initial actions almost conformed to the older pattern of political conflicts as matters which were played out at court. Certainly, when summoned to meet his father at Nijmegen in the spring of 838, the younger Louis came, and, although 'there was a great argument, quite different from what ought to have happened', the Emperor was still able to have the aristocracy gather at court and make a formal, legal judgement on his son, depriving him of all those areas which he had previously controlled.[143] A Fulda charter suggests some identities for those who travelled to Nijmegen: present, *inter alios*, were the *éminence grise* of the reconstructed regime, Bishop Drogo of Metz, as well as Archbishop Otgar of Mainz and Louis of Bavaria's archchaplain Bishop Baturich of Regensburg, and a long list of counts.[144] Some saw the whole affair as the result of the growing influence at court of Count Adalbert.[145] Adalbert had a formidable range of contacts in the middle Rhine: he and his two brothers, Banzleib, margrave in Saxony,

---

[139] *CL*1826 (donation by 'Rupert, Count Rupert's son'), 219, 222.

[140] See Borgolte, *Geschichte der Grafschaften Alemanniens*, p. 254, and, in general, Nelson, 'The Last Years of Louis the Pious', in *Charlemagne's Heir*, pp. 147–60.

[141] *Ann. Bert.*, s.a. 838, ed. Grat *et al.*, p. 23.   [142] Nelson, 'Last Years', p. 150.

[143] *Ann. Bert.*, ed. Grat *et al.*, pp. 24–5; trans. Nelson. Compare *AF*, s.a. 838, p. 29, stressing that the judgement was written down.

[144] *CDF*513: not the most reliable document but the witness-list shows at the very worst who squared up to whom in the eyes of one informed observer.

[145] *AF*, s.a. 839, p. 29, and see BM932 (accessible edition: M. Bouquet, *Recueil des historiens des Gaules et de la France 6* (Paris, 1749), no. 193), a gift to Adalbert *fidelis* from 834. For Adalbert's earlier career at court, Depreux, *Prosopographie*, pp. 69–72.

and a local count, Hatto, were close to Einhard, Hraban Maur, Archbishop Otgar of Mainz, and another local count, Alberich.[146]

Initially, at least, the Emperor's initiative was remarkably successful, and Louis the Pious was able to winter at Frankfurt. Although Louis of Bavaria rallied his supporters in the localities, even attempting to defend the east bank of the Rhine against his father, the Imperial presence eventually won over the east Franks and the younger Louis fled to Bavaria.[147] Louis the Pious' actions 'to subject [these regions] more firmly to his control' centred around a shake-up in the personnel of government, and reprisals against some of the key backers of the younger Louis. Grimald, the younger Louis' archchancellor, lost the plum abbacy of Wissembourg to Archbishop Otgar of Mainz; the Lorsch monk Samuel, a close contact of Hraban Maur's, got the abbacy of Lorsch in personal union with the bishopric of Worms.[148] Again, Einhard's letters help us follow through the local implications of these actions. In the winter of 839, Louis the Pious was again active in mobilising local support, although this time through a series of messages communicated by Dagulf, an Imperial huntsman, rather than through mobilisation procedures. 'All the counts who are in Austrasia', but in particular 'Hatto and Poppo and Gebhard and their comrades', were ordered 'to come together into one place . . . to consider what is to be done if anything new came up about the region of Bavaria'.[149] The Emperor's long stay at Kreuznach, hunting, and an expedition against the Slavs, doubtless helped regain control and consensus: consensus which was manifested by the swearing of oaths of loyalty to the Emperor.[150] The key figure in the new political configuration of the region, as Einhard's letter suggests, was Count Hatto. Indeed Hatto, with his brothers Adalbert and Banzleib, was the effective political broker for east Francia and Saxony, the points of contact between the regions and the court. Hatto was a survivor of that grouping of easterners who had tried to build bridges between the two Louis, father and son, in the middle 830s; his stature was such that Thegan flattered him with the title *dux ac consul*.[151] Louis of Bavaria's power

---

[146] Friese, 'Einzugsbereich', pp. 1141–2 for the Fulda material on links between these men. Alberich was close to the family of Odo of Orleans (*CDF*395) and lay-abbot of Mosbach (see Einhard, letter 37); his name suggests that he came from a family which dominated the area between the Moselle and Mainz (see below, pp. 218–20).

[147] *Ann. Bert.*, s.a. 838, ed. Grat *et al.*, p. 26. *AF*, s.a. 839, p. 27.

[148] *Ann. Bert.*, s.a. 839, ed. Grat *et al.*, p. 32, following Nelson, *The Annals of St-Bertin*, p. 41; Gerlich, 'Zur Reichspolitik', p. 303; H. Gensicke, 'Samuel, Bischof von Worms 838–856', in *Die Reichsabtei Lorsch*, I, pp. 253–6.

[149] Letter 40, pp. 130–1, and see Airlie, 'Bonds of Power', pp. 192–3, on the role of Dagulf.

[150] *AF*, pp. 30–1, and *Ann. Bert.*, pp. 33–4.

[151] See Tremp, *Studien*, pp. 9–15, on Hatto's family, and *MGH Epp.* V, no. 22, p. 337, for Thegan's flattering letter to Hatto. Note that Gebhard worked with Hatto both in the pages of Thegan and in Einhard's letter 40, from 839: Gebhard's ancestors worked with subsequent local men

in the area might have been fully broken had his father lived. Certainly, when he attempted to regain his influence as far as the Rhine in 840, he was driven beyond the boundaries of Bavaria, even to the Slavs.[152]

But Louis the Pious' death in 840 left the political future of the middle Rhine still unresolved, and this inevitably led to the renewal of conflict, conflict which had to be played out in the localities as there was no longer an agreed political centre. The younger Louis wasted no time in building on his links with the local elite, appointing Einhard's erstwhile notary and successor at Seligenstadt, Ratleig, as his archchancellor in 840.[153] But part and parcel of Louis the Pious' initiatives in the middle Rhine had been an effort to build up support for his eldest son, Lothar, in the region, which he had been granted at an assembly at Worms in 839.[154] Louis the Pious had hoped that Lothar would ally with his youngest son, Charles the Bald, and be content with the eastern half of the Empire, letting Charles rule in western Francia. In an attempt to bind the two kings together, Count Hatto had been made Charles' tutor (*baiolus*).[155] The two leaders of Lothar's party were Archbishop Otgar of Mainz, who had been a key backer as long ago as 833, and Hatto's brother, Count Adalbert. Lothar's trump card was his legitimacy – hence he moved quickly to administer the oath of fidelity across the region.[156] This initiative was, initially, successful: Count Hatto quickly rallied to Lothar and his brother Adalbert.[157] The letters of Abbot Hraban show Lothar soliciting support, and overcoming Hraban's understandable temptation to sit on the fence and wait on events.[158] At Lorsch, Abbot Samuel (also bishop of Worms) was a backer, and Count Rupert a supporter.[159] But Louis of Bavaria

---

named Hatto, too (below, p. 229). Our Hatto was clearly not the Hatto who was a key figure in the last years of Charlemagne's reign: for the evidence for his retirement under Louis the Pious, see Airlie, 'Bonds of Power', p. 194. We should distinguish him, too, from the Hatto who was an Alemannian count, discussed by Tremp: see Einhard, letter 40, for two men named Hatto in 839. But the long historiographical tradition which makes our Hatto count 'near Mainz' actually relies on a nineteenth-century forgery, the Bleidenstadt cartulary. The only discussion which really takes this on board is Gockel, 'Zur Verwandtschaft der Äbtissen Emhilt von Milz', pp. 37–41.

[152] *Ann. Bert.*, ed. Grat *et al.*, p. 36. *AF*, p. 30, talk of many 'east Franks' being won over to the Emperor.

[153] Fleckenstein, *Die Hofkapelle*, p. 171. Einhard died in 840 so Ratlieg's two promotions were virtually simultaneous.   [154] *Ann. Bert.*, s.a. 839, ed. Grat *et al.*, pp. 31–2.

[155] Nelson, *Charles the Bald*, p. 97, following the reinterpretation of *MGH Epp.* VI, no. 2, p. 131, offered by K.-F. Werner, '*Hludovicus Augustus*: Gouverner l'empire chrétien – Idées et réalités', in *Charlemagne's Heir*, pp. 3–123 at p. 77, n. 275.   [156] Nithard II:7, ed. Lauer, pp. 59–60.

[157] Nelson, *Charles the Bald*, p. 99, and see Nithard III:7, p. 114.

[158] See *MGH Epp.* V, no. 38, pp. 475–6, for Lothar's approach, and no. 28, p. 443, for Hraban's response. Hraban later refered to a visit to Lothar at Mainz in August 841, no. 50, p. 500. See De Jong, 'The Empire as *Ecclesia*', pp. 207–10.

[159] On Samuel, Gensicke, 'Samuel'. For Rupert's dalliance with Lothar, see *CL659* from 841, dated by Lothar's regnal year – surprisingly the identity of the donor has been previously ignored, mainly because most authors have accepted Glöckner's reconstruction of Rupert's career.

marched on his brother in 840, besieging the new Emperor and his party in Mainz and forcing an agreement out of them.[160] Lothar then, in his turn, went on the offensive, relying on Adalbert, granted the title '*dux* of the Austrasians' and the position of regional supremo; Louis was forced to flee to Bavaria.[161] But Louis defeated Lothar's forces and slew his enemy Adalbert at a battle near Donauwörth in 841. Following this setback and an alliance between Louis and Charles the Bald, Lothar was driven from the middle Rhine by 842.[162]

The charters from these years vividly show the strains which competition for political loyalty placed on middle Rhenish society, and the insecurity felt by political actors, who could never be wholly sure that they had chosen the right patron. In 841 or 842 Hraban's brother, Guntram, took the extraordinary step of first giving his landed property to his brother's monastery of Fulda, and then receiving it back, with a few extras, as a precarial grant, as we saw earlier. The transaction took place on Guntram's estate at Rohrbach, and was written up by Hraban's trusted agent, the monk Rudolf. It was a pre-emptive move against the confiscation of property should Guntram's chosen patron, Lothar, lose control of the area.[163] On 16 June 842 Count Guntram witnessed a similar transaction, in which one Ratolf made a huge bequest of his landed possessions to a monastery, in this case Hersfeld, and received back the life-interest.[164] The insecurity of such acts at a time of crisis necessitated conspicuous attention to the process of conveyance, witnessing and approval, to leave the whole transaction unchallengeable. Ratolf first had the charter subscribed by a group of witnesses, then recorded the witnesses to a ritual of *vestitura* which was carried out in each of the *villae* concerned, and finally had the whole transaction confirmed by a final group of witnesses, headed by Count Guntram. But, in spite of Guntram's and Ratolf's worries, these documents also show a certain local stability: although Ratolf was a backer of Louis of Bavaria, Guntram

---

[160] *Ann. Bert.*, ed. Grat *et al.*, p. 37; *AF*, pp. 30–1.   [161] Nithard II:7, ed. Lauer, p. 61.

[162] *AF*, s.a. 842, p. 33.

[163] *CDF*534, 535 on 20 May 841 or 842: the incarnation date, followed by Dronke, points to 841 but the charter is dated by Lothar's second year (which might supply a more likely context for Guntram's fears given the revival of Louis the German's cause). Note Guntram's personal bonds with (once again) the monk Rudolf, who writes Guntram's gift, whilst Fulda's 'regular' scribe, Asger, writes the precarial grant.

[164] *UBH*26, and *UBH*27 for the *precaria*. I follow the arguments of K.-U. Jäschke, 'Zu den schriftlichen Zeugnissen für die Anfänge der Reichsabtei Hersfeld', *Blätter für deutsche Landesgeschichte* 107 (1971), 94–135 at 128–32 regarding the date of this document, which the editor had made 815 (the key point is identifying which Louis' second year we are in). The crucial piece of evidence is that the document has a Brunward as abbot of Hersfeld, when royal diplomata make a Bun abbot from 814 to 838: the 815 date is thus difficult to maintain. The document's scribe, Tiethroch, is a Lorsch monk active writing Lorsch charters around 840 (see *CL*265, 1077, 2718 and so on).

still witnessed his transaction, acting as count.[165] Political conflict did not rip the fabric of society apart. Indeed, this civil war was, with the exception of the pitched battles at Fontenoy and Donauwörth, remarkably civil in its conduct. Gerward, a Lorsch monk, sometime librarian of Louis the Pious and a backer of Lothar, could find no greater charge of atrocity to level against Louis of Bavaria and his brother Charles than that the foraging of their followers had brought devastation to the Worms area.[166]

For Guntram and Ratolf these were crucial times, as backing the wrong man would lead to political ruin. They were rooted in the locality, and if the wrong Carolingian ended up ruling it, they were washed up. For younger men from wealthier backgrounds, a more active political strategy was possible: Rupert, for example, soon ended his dalliance with Lothar, and entered the service of Charles the Bald. This possibly took place in 842, when Charles and his brother Louis spent highly visible time together at Worms, where Charles contracted a marriage to Ermentrude, a distant relative of Rupert's.[167] Rupert's loyalty was ensured by the grant of office, and the tenure of land belonging to the vacant see of Rheims.[168] Rupert would have brought with him a gaggle of ambitious youngsters: the most visible was Count Hraban, who had been active in the service of Louis the Pious in Alemannia in 839, and died serving as Charles' standard-bearer in Aquitaine in 844.[169] Once in the west, Rupert was able to draw on the networks which his kinsman, Odo, had put down when count of Orléans: Odo's substantial kin and clients in the west, thanks to the marriages he and his brother had contracted there, became the basis of Rupert's own following, and were consolidated by Rupert's own marriage. Rupert was thus able to find fame in Charles' service in the west, where his descendants eventually replaced the Carolingians on the throne. Through an accident of historiography,

---

[165] Ratolf's support for Louis of Bavaria is suggested by the dating of his charter by Louis' regnal year (and Hersfeld, the abbey Ratolf chose to patronise at this politically sensitive moment, supported Louis).

[166] *Annales Xantenses*, ed. von Simson, s.a. 842, pp. 12–13. On Gerward's authorship, Löwe, 'Studien zu den Annales Xantenses'.

[167] For the impact of Charles' and Louis' joint stay at Worms, see Nithard, III:6, ed. Lauer, pp. 110–12. For this as the point at which Rupert joined Charles, see Nelson, *Charles the Bald*, pp. 130–1, and on Ermentrude's kinship with Rupert, Levillain, 'Les Nibelungen historiques', II, 31–46. Rupert's move west is usually dated to 837: this tradition goes back to Glöckner's classic discussion, 'Lorsch und Lothringen', but is based on no direct evidence, and the charters imply his continued presence in the middle Rhine until 841 at least.

[168] The Rheims land was returned in 845: see *Recueil des actes de Charles II le Chauve*, ed. G. Tessier et al., 3 vols. (Paris, 1943–55), I, no.75.

[169] On Hraban see Borgolte, *Die Grafen Alemanniens*, p. 201. Hraban's name, and origins (son of a Count Ratolf active in the Grabfeld in 838: CDF512) suggest that he was linked to the family of Hraban Maur (already Werner, 'Bedeutende Adelsfamilien', p. 135) – and note that Hraban Maur's brother inherited property jointly with Rupert's morther (CL271).

he is known to posterity through the French transliteration of his name, Robert, and his political success led to the sobriquet 'the Strong'. But middle Rhinelanders did not forget his origins: one Mainz author saw him as a second Maccabeus.[170]

With the defeat of Lothar in 842, the political fate of the middle Rhine was sealed: it was to become a part of the kingdom of Louis, centred initially on his heartland of Bavaria.[171] These geopolitical facts were acknowledged in 843 by the Treaty of Verdun. As well as the area east of the Rhine, Louis was given Mainz, Worms and Speyer, with their hinterlands. The new kingdom was not shaped by political whim, nor was it an artificial unit whose shape was unexpected, the result of the merely 'private' rationale of inheritance within the royal family. The division was concerned to give each Carolingian a rough equality of royal resources, hence the importance of the middle Rhine with its palaces, bishoprics and rich fiscal estates for Louis. But it also had to acknowledge political and social realities. The political geography of the eastern kingdom was determined by the social geology of aristocratic landholding and loyalty: we could see the unrest of the 830s and the political conflict after Louis the Pious' death as a process of brokering between the regional aristocracy as a collective body and their future rulers.[172] Multiple kingship within the Carolingian dynasty had been acknowledged as a necessity for a generation and was a welcome necessity in that it ensured effective government and increased aristocratic access to royal service: it was not an unwelcome departure forced on an unwilling political class by Carolingian dynastic concerns. The negotiation of the ultimate shape which the segments were to take may look messy, and was shocking to contemporaries, but it was done with remarkably little bloodshed. It created a whole new set of problems for Louis the Pious' sons to address.

THE ZENITH OF CAROLINGIAN POLITICS

Did the new political geography alter the pattern of politics? Rebellion and civil war had traumatised the political classes, but they had not

---

[170] *AF*, s.a. 867, p. 66. For Rupert/Robert the Strong, see Glöckner, 'Lorsch und Lothringen'; K.-F. Werner, 'Untersuchungen zur Frühzeit des französischen Fürstentums', *Die Welt als Geschichte* 20, (1960), 87–119.

[171] As already noted by H. Zatschek, 'Die Reichsteilung unter Kaiser Ludwig dem Frommen: Studien zur Entstehung des ostfränkischen Reiches', *MIÖG* 49 (1935), 185–224 esp. 198–201. On royal–aristocratic relations in the division of the Empire, see above all P. Classen, 'Die Verträge von Verdun und von Coulaines 843 als Grundlagen des westfränkischen Reiches', *Historische Zeitschrift* 196 (1963), 1–35.

[172] *Ann. Bert.*, s.a. 843, ed. Grat *et al.*, p. 44, and see F. L. Ganshof, 'On the Genesis and Significance of the Treaty of Verdun (843)', in Granshof, *The Carolingians and the Frankish Monarchy* (London, 1971), pp. 273–88.

unpicked the bonds which held the political system together. Indeed, from a local perspective what emerges again and again is the insecurity of the aristocracy's local power. It was because of this basic insecurity that the kaleidoscope patterns of royal control could shift with bewildering speed.

The charter evidence gives some insight into just what rewards aristocrats were able to extract from kings in the scramble for support. Lothar in particular seems to have attempted to rally his supporters by addressing long-standing family claims, most notably at Mettlach. One of Lothar's key backers, Wido, was a descendant of Mettlach's founders who had found fame and fortune in Italy, where he served as *dux* of Spoleto. Just as Wido's kin had been able to extract confirmation of the privileges of the family's monastery at Hornbach from Lothar in 833, so in 840 they sought to regain control of Mettlach from the bishopric of Trier, under whose control Charlemagne had placed it.[173] In 840 or 841 Lothar rallied Wido's influential and scattered kin group, still potent in the middle Rhine and Moselle but also containing some of the most powerful men in the Loire valley and the Breton march, by ending Mettlach's half-century in Trier's hands and granting it to Wido. In 840 Lothar was prepared to risk dismantling one of the key foundations of the *pax Karolina* in the region – episcopal and thus royal control of the key monastery of Mettlach – to sustain his Imperial dreams. In the summer of 842, when it was clear that Empire was just a dream and regional power in the Moselle would be the key to a successful future, he backtracked and reverted to Charlemagne's policy, returning Mettlach to the bishop of Trier.[174] The controversy over Mettlach fits neatly with an independent account of royal patronage as centring on grants of '*publica* and liberties'. It also demonstrates the extent of aristocratic dependence on royal patronage, and helps us understand why royal threats about the removal of *honores* were such an efficient way of winning over recalcitrants.[175] If politics had been a matter of kings on their knees trying to buy the support of aristocrats who had *de facto* local control, the patterns of patronage and reprisal would have been very different. As it was, Lothar's best gambit, in the autumn of 841 when the stakes were at their highest, was to attempt to rally his followers by dispensing literal, biological, *Königsnähe*,

---

[173] For 833 see *MGH DLothar* 15–17: addressed to the lords of Hornbach, also Lothar's *fideles*, Lambert and Herard, powerful men in the middle Rhine but also, in Lambert's case, one of the key figures in the crucial Loire area.

[174] *MGH DLothar* 67, with useful editorial comments. Tellingly, Trier felt it necessary to have its possession of Mettlach confirmed immediately at the beginning of the next major political crisis, that of 888 (in which Wido's successors were key actors): *MGH DArnulf* 39. Equally tellingly, Wido's family never succeeded in renegotiating the *pax Karolina*: Mettlach remained in Trier's hands.   [175] Nithard, IV:6, ed. Lauer, p. 142.

and marrying off his daughter – just as Charles the Bald married into a key aristocratic family at a crucial juncture, and was accused by one observer of being too liberal in his patronage of his new father-in-law's cronies.[176] Access to royal patronage remained the political trump card.

The winners in this game – men like Rupert – won by anticipating the changing balance of power correctly, and thus gaining effective royal patronage, not by playing off kings and extracting local invulnerability as their price. Insecurity at the centre and insecurity in the localities thus fed off one another. Choosing the wrong Carolingian could ruin a political career. Louis' rule over eastern Francia in the 840s began with a purge of those whose loyalties had lain elsewhere: Count Poppo disappeared from Thuringia, and Hraban's brother, Count Guntram, lost his office. Hraban himself had briefly joined Lothar in the spring of 842, and, when he returned to Fulda, found that the monks, mindful of Louis' control of the region, had elected one of Hraban's pupils, Hatto, as the new abbot. This was a neat way for Hraban and his abbey to get out of a tight political corner: Hraban retired to a nearby monastic cell, the Petersberg, and backed his friend Hatto.[177]

Surprisingly little is known of the local politics of the 840s, after the stabilisation of patterns of royal patronage in 843. This is no accident. In fact, it indicates a largely successful recentralisation of political conflict once the shape of the political map was settled: once again, aristocratic politics came to be played out through royal courts. Until the end of the 840s Louis, although king in the region, avoided the middle Rhine, preferring to wait until entrenched enemies could be replaced with more favourable men; while a few, high-profile individuals could be purged, kings could not cut across the intricate social fabric of local politics too frequently. The key moment came with the death of Archbishop Otgar in 847. Louis made a startling appointment – none other than Hraban. Louis had prepared the ground and built bridges with Hraban, visiting him at Petersberg and holding secret talks in 843 or 845. As Hraban was the guarantor of intellectual orthodoxy, and had an impeccable Mainz pedigree (indeed, he was probably related to his predecessor, Otgar) this was an advantageous appointment for Louis.[178] It was successful. Hraban was able to use his archiepiscopal office to rally the east Frankish church

---

[176] *AF*, s.a. 841, p. 32. For Charles' marriage in 842 and criticism of it, Nithard, IV:6, p. 142. The best account of the various ways in which kings cajoled support from the aristocracy in the civil war is Nelson, 'Public Histories'.

[177] See, in general, Metz, 'Das Kloster Weißenburg', pp. 458–9, and Reuter, *Germany*, p. 75. Poppo and Guntram: Schulze, *Grafschaftsverfassung*, pp. 190–1, and for Guntram after 843, see CDF604, *TAF* c. 42, no. 189, in neither case entitled count. Hraban: De Jong, 'The Empire as *Ecclesia*', pp. 208–9, and see Sandmann, 'Hrabanus', 151–2; Albert, 'Raban Maur', 24–8 is misleading.

[178] *MGH Epp.* V, p. 33, p. 465, and see Sandmann, 'Hrabanus', p. 153.

as a buttress of royal government, beginning a lively synodal tradition. He also won over a circle of contacts, most notably Samuel, a key player as bishop of Worms and abbot of Lorsch.[179]After 847 the middle Rhine, and in particular Frankfurt and Mainz, became central to east Frankish kingship. The *rapprochement* was not wholly untroubled. The military retinue of the archbishop of Mainz were evidently unhappy with Hraban's new line, for in 848 they had to be publicly reconciled with the new archbishop. The charter evidence gives a glimpse of this party which had crystallised around Otgar and distrusted Louis: in 847 Adalbert, 'sometime count', made a gift 'publicly in the city of Mainz' to St Alban's, the archiepiscopal necropolis where Otgar was buried.[180]

The continuing ability of local men to set the political tone is also clear from the charter evidence. Werner, Louis' man in the area since the 830s, was a count by 846 at the latest.[181] Werner had local roots: he had given local land to Lorsch in 825, and his family owned the abbey of Hornbach.[182] These local roots must have helped him build up local support. He was able to win over Engilhelm, a local property-holder who had been close to both Ruperts, and to Guntram.[183] Engilhelm became the *fidelis* of Count Werner, and held, as *precaria* from Lorsch, estates in Weinheim and the *cella* of Birkenau against a payment termed a *pontificium*. Engilhelm and his wife Moda were dead by 846, when Count Werner gave Lorsch land which he had been given by King Louis, and dedicated his gift to the souls of his royal master and his *fideles* Engilhelm and Moda. This intriguing transaction was concluded when Lorsch gave

---

[179] Note that Lorsch's first charter from Louis comes in 847, immediately after the elevation of Hraban., Samuel's friend and erstwhile teacher; thereafter Lorsch enjoyed a close relationship with the east Frankish king (see Wehlt, *Reichsabtei und König*, pp. 32–5). Synods and church: Reuter, *Germany*, pp. 102–11, esp. pp. 109–10.

[180] *AF*, s.a. 848, p. 37, and Adalbert's charter, ed. A. Lamey, *Acta Academiae Theodoro-Palatinae* V (1783), pp. 174–5. On St Alban's, Gierlich, *Die Grabstätten*, pp. 143–84. Note that Adalbert was an ex-count, perhaps another victim of the purge of 842. His name and loyalty point to a link with the family of the Adalbert who had been Lothar's key follower in the area, and was killed in 842. In 841 an Adalbert gave land in the Königssundera, across the Rhine from Mainz, to Fulda: *CDF529*, dated by Lothar's regnal year. Compare also the Count Adalbert in *CL3535/CL2575*. In 827 an Adalbert made an important donation to Hornbach, N13, ed. Lamey, *Acta Academiae Theodoro-Palatinae* I (Mannheim, 1766), pp. 295–6.   [181] *CL27*.

[182] *CL656* for gifts to Lorsch in 825. *MGH DLothar II 24* for Hornbach. The Hornbach evidence confirms Staab, *Gesellschaft*, pp. 410–11, arguing that (*contra* Glöckner, 'Lorsch und Lothringen', p. 308) Werner is no 'new man' owing his position solely to Louis the German's patronage. I cannot, however, agree that his links with Rupert's erstwhile clients make him 'probably the brother of Robert the Strong'. Gockel, *Königshöfe*, p. 304 assembles material suggestive of a relationship to the family of Warin; also Metz, 'Miszellen', p. 5. Werner's lordship of Hornbach is the key to unpicking his kinship ties.

[183] *CL1684*, 271, 219, *UBF76*. Note also his links with the family of Odo of Orleans: *CDF429*. See Staab, *Gesellschaft*, pp. 410–11. Gockel, *Königshöfe*, pp. 269–70, n. 294 claims Engilhelm as a kinsman of Rupert on the grounds of these links.

Count Werner tenure of the *precaria* which had been held by Engilhelm and Moda.[184] The date and content suggests that Werner's gift was part and parcel of the *rapprochement* between Louis 'the German' and his erstwhile opponents in the middle Rhine, which culminated in the appointment of Hraban to Mainz. But the transaction had a local significance, too: Werner had not been able simply to impose his rule on the locality, but had negotiated a complex arrangement with entrenched powerholders, drawing on his local credentials, land and contacts. Engilhelm and Moda's importance is shown graphically in their burial and posthumous commemoration. They were remembered liturgically at Lorsch, and commemorated as *viri spectabiles* who had shown heroic piety – a rare honour for those outside the Carolingian family and the charmed circle of the Imperial aristocracy. Moreover, they were eventually laid to rest alongside their master Count Werner and his masters, the east Frankish kings Louis the German and Louis the Younger, in the *ecclesia varia* constructed in 870s.[185] If this physical manifestation of *Königsnähe* was exceptional, Engilhelm's continued local significance right through the drama of the 830s and 840s was typical. The change of regime and the emergence of new aristocratic rulers did not alter the identity of those who were the real brokers on a local level. One other such man was Otakar who, like Engilhelm, had been close to Count Rupert. Otakar eventually entered the service of Louis the German: in 865 Louis gave the now dead Otakar's erstwhile *beneficium* to Lorsch.[186] Men like Otakar, entrenched in local positions, lay at the basis of Carolingian politics: kings and counts had, in the normal run of things, to come to terms with such men, even if on occasion they could drive them out of office.[187]

If the structures of local power remained unchanged, politics at the level of the court continued to be determined by the wide horizons of the region's aristocracy, whose interests sprawled across the boundaries of the kingdoms created in 843 and periodically renegotiated thereafter. Aristocrats, if they observed the proper etiquette, could expect to hold onto family properties across political boundaries, although high office was normally held in one kingdom alone. Werner, for example, was a count in Louis' kingdom, but had family interests beyond, notably in the middle kingdom, named Lotharingia after its ruler, in which the family monastery of Hornbach was situated. Werner's control of Hornbach –

---

[184] CL27. In CL199, a transaction of Engilhelm's from 822, Count Werner gave permission for the transaction. The date may be mistaken, or alternatively, Werner's permission was added later, after Engilhelm had entered his service: whichever was the case, this confirms the importance of the relationship between Werner and Engilhelm.

[185] Wehlt, *Reichsabtei und König*, pp. 103–5.   [186] CL271; MGH DLouis the German 117.

[187] Cf Airlie, 'The Aristocracy', pp. 449–50.

he was acknowledged as *senior*, lord of the monastery – made him a powerful man in Lotharingia. Werner had access to the Lotharingian court: he was a *fidelis* of the Lotharingian king.[188] Another aristocrat, Nanthar, likewise had interests which straddled the border. He was a count in Lotharingia, but was also active as the advocate of the church of Rheims in the eastern kingdom, and obtained Louis the German's approval for the foundation of an important monastery, Münster-Dreisen, just within the borders of the eastern kingdom.[189] These cross-border links help explain the close ties between Lotharingian and east Frankish polities through the ninth century: hence in 855, on the death of his father Lothar I, Lothar II sought the protection of the east Frankish king, Louis the German, to ensure his succession in Lotharingia; hence in 869, on Lothar II's death, the Lotharingian aristocracy opted into the eastern, rather than the western kingdom, an arrangement confirmed by the Treaty of Meersen in 870; hence in 876, on Louis the German's death, Charles the Bald sought to seize Mainz, Worms and Speyer as the key to wresting Lotharingia from the eastern rulers.[190]

'International' links were vitally important in ninth-century politics; their existence was not just a peculiarity of a region that lay close to a political boundary. The Imperial aristocracy had acquired interests across the Empire as a whole before 843, and these interests survived formal political division.[191] Those at the apex of the aristocracy had access to more than one potential source of royal patronage, and their political activities were not confined to any individual kingdom. This meant that although political conflict was once again centralised, played out at the court and not in the localities, there was now more than one court, and more than one source of legitimacy and patronage, in the system. Look at the career of Adalard, who rose to power at the court of Louis the Pious, and subsequently served Charles the Bald, Lothar I and Lothar II. Adalard's inherited lands centred on the Moselle, but his interests spanned the Frankish world from the Loire to the Rhine. The widow of one of Adalard's clients, Count Nithard of Trier, made testamentary gifts to churches down the Moselle and the Rhine, Lorsch included, in 853. In

---

[188] *MGH DLothar II* 24 (865). Note that the dating and content of this charter fit well with the identity between this Werner and the Werner who fell from Louis the German's favour in 866, suggested below, n. 197.

[189] On Nanthar, see Gockel, *Königshöfe*, pp. 306–7, Metz, 'Das Kloster Weißenburg', p. 459: he probably belongs to a different branch of the same kin-group as Werner. Count and envoy: *Ann. Bert.*, s.a. 863, p. 96. Advocate of Rheims: Flodoard III:26, p. 539. Münster-Dreisen: *MGH DLouis the German* 114 (863–4). Nanthar also owned a *monasteriolum* and a fortified urban residence (*Nanzenburgdor*) in Mainz: see Gockel, *Königshöfe*, p. 306, n. 797.

[190] *AF*, s.a. 855, p. 46; *Ann. Bert.*, s.a. 870, pp. 172–4; *AF*, s.a. 876, pp. 86–7.

[191] Cf Airlie, 'After Empire', pp. 155–7, and Le Jan, 'Structures familiales', pp. 320–5.

855 Adalard himself visited Lorsch, as his current lord, Lothar I, lay dying at Prüm, and a division of Lotharingia between Lothar's three sons, without the intervention of their two jealous uncles, had to be effected. Adalard was clearly not at Lorsch at this juncture to discuss the price of fish! In fact, Adalard's presence at Lorsch can only be explained with reference to discussions over the future of Lothar's realm: on their king's death, 'the *principes* and *optimates* of [Lothar's] kingdom wanted his son Lothar to reign over them, and brought him to Louis, king of the eastern Franks and his uncle, at Frankfurt. With Louis' agreement and support they agreed that he should rule them.'[192]

These international aristocratic links could lead royal policy. In the 850s, when aristocratic discontent with Charles the Bald's regime in the west boiled over into accusations of tyranny, approaches were made to other Carolingians for intervention; revolt, even when expressed, as here, in terms of abstract ideals of just and tyrannous kingship, needed a Carolingian at its head. As leading western aristocrats like Robert the Strong had land and relatives in the east, they approached east Frankish Carolingians for help. In 854 they tempted Louis the Younger into intervention, whilst in 858 Louis the German himself was lured into a western adventure. On this latter occasion, it was only the continued backing of the west Frankish bishops which saved Charles the Bald's bacon, as his aristocracy flocked to Louis.[193] The charters hint at the kind of links which led to Louis the German's dalliance in the west. In the summer of 858, as Louis resided at the west Frankish palace of Attigny, one Tuto approached him and negotiated an exchange of lands in the middle Rhine, recorded in a charter which is dated to Louis' first year as king of western Francia. Tuto had property interests in the middle Rhine, but sought out Louis and demonstrated his *fidelitas* at Attigny at this particularly sensitive juncture, receiving a sizable *beneficium* of lands on the upper Neckar. The easiest explanation is that before 858 his activities had primarily lain in the west, but discontent with Charles the Bald and links with the east led him into Louis' camp in 858.[194] Significantly, one of

---

[192] Adalard: on his political career see Depreux, *Prosopographie*, pp. 80–2; F. Lot, 'Note sur le sénéchal Alard', in Lot, *Recueil des travaux historiques* II (Paris, 1970), pp. 591–607; Nelson, *Charles the Bald*. On his kin and property, Hlawitschka, *Die Anfänge*, is the best discussion. Nithard's widow, Ercanfrida: Wampach, *Urkunden- und Quellenbuch . . . der altluxemburgischen Territorien*, I, no. 87. For 855 see *CL*1922 (18.7.855; Lothar died on 29.9.855 having entered Prüm as a monk in his last months) and *AF*, s.a. 855, p. 46, trans. Reuter, p. 37.

[193] Fried, *König Ludwig der Jüngere in seiner Zeit*, Geschichtsblätter für die Kreis Bergstraße 16 (Lorsche, 1983), pp. 9–11, and see Nelson, *Charles the Bald*, esp. pp. 186–9 for a western perspective.

[194] See *MGH DLouis the German* 94: Tuto is styled *vir fidelisque*. For the subsequent fate of his *beneficium* see *MGH DLouis the Younger* 2: it was subsequently granted to Count Werner and then Lorsch. Although there are influential men named Tuto in the lower Neckar region visible in the Lorsch charters from the late eighth century, there is no evidence for a local Tuto in the 840s, 850s or 860s.

Robert the Strong's kinsmen emerged as a count in the middle Rhine in the immediate aftermath of Louis' 858 campaign in the west. Count Megingoz was a *nepos* of Odo, the son of Robert the Strong, and his property interests and charter activities were in precisely those areas in which the young Robert and his ancestors had held land and been count.[195]

In the 860s it was Louis the German's turn to have an internal political crisis exacerbated by the international dimensions of aristocratic strategy. Gebhard, count in the Lahn area, had been a key backer of Louis the Pious in the 830s, styled 'most noble and faithful *dux*' by Thegan, and his close links to Louis the German allowed him to survive the civil war of 840–3. In 861 Gebhard's sons Odo, Berengar and Waldo were accused of *infidelitas*, having formed a 'reversionary tendency' around Louis' son, Carloman, from whose patronage they hoped to profit. Here, inter-generational conflict within royal and aristocratic families interacted, with Carloman chafing at the bit for real power and allying with these young aristocrats in an attempt to force paternal hands. Although Louis the German did not touch the inherited property *(proprietas)* of the rebels, only removing their *honores*, the sons of Gebhard went a-wandering, in search of Carolingian patronage and thus more *honores*. Through the good offices of their kinsman, Adalard, they moved to greener pastures, one seeking out Charles the Bald in the west, and another Lothar II in the middle kingdom.[196] But they also remembered their lost eastern *honores*. They were thus key actors when renewed conflict between Louis the German and his sons broke out in 865. Following an attempt to settle the succession in which Louis formally partitioned his kingdom, Louis the Younger, who had received Saxony and Franconia, contracted a marriage with Adalard's daughter. This was a powerful assertion of Louis the Younger's power both within his sub-kingdom and on a wider stage. It upset the delicate relations between western, eastern and middle kingdoms; the potential alliance between Louis the Younger and Adalard created a power base for the eastern Carolingian line at the heart of the still independent middle kingdom, on which Charles the Bald in

---

[195] Count Megingoz first appears in 858, witnessing a transaction involving land in the Wingarteiba and Maingau: *Acta Academiae Theodoro-Palatinae* VII (Mannheim, 1789), p. 64. Present at Lorsch in 860, witnessing a donation of property in the Lobdengau: *CL*802. *UBMR*110 shows him as count in the Bingen area in 868; *MGH DLouis the German* 131, again in 870, and finally in *MGH DArnulf* 58. Schulze, *Grafschaftsverfassung*, p. 191 claims he was also active in the Maienfeld, but none of the evidence cited supports this. Fundamental on his relationship to Robert the Strong is Glöckner, 'Lorsch und Lothringen', pp. 342–54, the central pieces of evidence being *CL*1835 (876) concerning land at Mettenheim (where Robert the Strong and his father Rupert had owned land) and making Megingoz *nepos* of Odo, and Regino of Prüm's comments on the kin of Odo, king of West Francia: *Chronicon*, ed. F. Kurze, MGH SRG (Hanover, 1890), s.a. 892, p. 140. For his subsequent career, below pp. 225–7. [196] *AF*, s.a. 861, p. 55.

the west harboured designs. Charles therefore purged Adalard's relatives, including Odo and Berengar, the east Frankish rebels of 861, who quickly sought out Louis the Younger, hoping to win back their eastern *honores*. Another discontented eastern aristocrat, Count Werner (whom Louis the German had stripped of 'public *honores*' earlier in 865) likewise rallied to Louis the Younger's side.[197] In 866 Louis the German travelled to Frankfurt to rally aristocratic opinion against his son. There followed an anxious stand-off, but the whole conflict was brought to a peaceful resolution thanks to the actions of Archbishop Liutbert of Mainz, acting as mediator between father and son; however, the tensions involved in this mediation led to an uprising against Liutbert in Mainz.[198] Even then, the affair was not forgotten: in 871 it was Werner and the sons of Gebhard who rallied again to the side of Carloman and Louis the Younger when tension within the east Frankish Carolingian family boiled over once more.[199] The whole episode underlines the sheer complexity of the ninth-century polity, which comes close to a chaos theory scenario: one set of marriage negotiations set in motion a chain reaction affecting aristocrats and kings right across the Carolingian world.

Politics in the middle of the ninth century was a game of bewildering complexity, played simultaneously on several boards. The articulation of this complexity on a local level is well illustrated by a minor drama involving one aristocratic family and the royal abbey of Prüm, which happened to get caught up in the political crisis surrounding the future of Lotharingia after Lothar II's death in 869. In 868 the *vir illustris* Heriric, about to depart on a pilgrimage to Rome, made a gift of estates at Bingen, Weinsheim and Glan, down the Nahe, to Prüm, for the health of his soul and those of his brothers Hunfrid (bishop of Thérouanne and abbot of St Bertin), Henry and Alberich, and of his father Alberich and his mother Huna.[200] Heriric's family enjoyed land and interests in eastern Francia and Lotharingia, a close relationship with the key Lotharingian

---

[197] *AF*, s.a. 865, p. 63, for Werner. He was accused of stirring up the Moravian ruler, confirming his identity with the Werner active on the Enns: see Mitterauer, *Karolingische Markgrafen*, pp. 125–31, followed by Reuter, *Annals of Fulda*, p. 53, n. 5. But his associates and the sphere of his activities suggests that his interests were not only Bavarian. The middle Rhenish Count Werner was at the Lotharingian court in 865 (*MGH DLothar II* 24) and was rewarded immediately by Louis the Younger on his eventual succession (*MGH DLouis the Younger* 2 to 'our most faithful and venerable Count Werner'): it seems highly likely that he is one and the same man as the rebel of 865.

[198] *AF*, s.a. 866, pp. 64–5, for the 'conspiracy' and its aftermath; *Ann. Bert.*, s.a. 865, pp. 123–4, for the betrothal and western purge; Fried, *König Ludwig der Jüngere*, for analysis.

[199] *AF*, s.a. 871, pp. 72–3.

[200] *UBMR* I 10. On Heriric, his family, and the 868 gift, see Le Jan, 'Structures familiales', 294–301; Kuchenbuch, *Bäuerliche Gesellschaft und Klosterherrschaft*, pp. 348–50; and Staab, *Gesellschaft*, pp. 436–7.

abbey of Prüm (where Hunfrid had been a monk), and high ecclesiastical office in western Francia. The gift was witnessed by fifty-five men, including Bishop Hunfrid, several Prüm monks, the abbey's *vicedominus*, and Count Megingoz, the relative of Robert the Strong who had entered the service of Louis the German in 858. In 870 Louis the German was asked, by the monks of Prüm, to uphold the validity of the Heriric's gift: a relative (*nepos*) of Heriric, none other than the Werner who was a count in the middle Rhine and an important landowner on both sides of the east Frankish–Lotharingian border, was refusing to hand over the estates. Werner lost the case, after the sureties (*fideiussores*) of the original transaction, led by Count Megingoz, attested to the validity of Heriric's gift.[201]

On the surface, the whole dispute looks like a familial conflict of a familiar type. But the status of the family involved meant that the conduct and outcome of the dispute were determined by political pressures. Heriric's father, Alberich, had been a count in the 820s and 830s, when he had been close to Einhard and the brothers Hatto, Adalbert and Banzleib.[202] After 843, Alberich had held onto his inherited lands on the Nahe, but lost his comital office in an area now ruled by Louis the German; his career now lay in the service of Lothar I, and he received a substantial *beneficium* in the Eifel, and was active and influential in the area around Prüm as a royal *vassus*.[203] Heriric, his son, was placed in the service of a different master, none other than Louis the German. Significantly, Heriric received a *beneficium* from Louis in a region close to his inherited lands, on the east Frankish–Lotharingian border.[204] The ecclesiastical career of Heriric's brother, Hunfrid, in west Francia gave the family points of contact with three different Carolingian kings, and enabled them to maintain their interests across the Empire as a whole. Such tactics could pay dividends: in 853 Louis the German approached Lothar, asking that his (Louis') vassal, Heriric, be given a part of a Lotharingian benefice which Count Adalard currently held.[205] The key to understanding the 868 gift is the strategic importance of the lands concerned, on the western border of the east Frankish kingdom. When the gift was made in 868, rival Carolingians were playing for the future of Lotharingia, and

---

[201] *MGH DLouis the German* 131.
[202] See above, p. 206, n. 146, the location of Alberich's interests, and Alberich's future career, making the identity probable: he should probably be identified with the Count Alberich active in the very same area in which Heriric's gift to Prüm lay, and close to the family of Odo of Orleans: CDF395.   [203] *MGH DLothar I* 137; *MGH DLothar II* 31.
[204] Heriric's *beneficium* is known from later charters confirming its gift to the palace chapel at Frankfurt: *MGH DLouis theYounger* 18, *MGH DCharles the Fat* 65.
[205] *MGH DLothar I* 128. I take the 'Adalwardi' of the charter as referring to Adalard: no Adalwards are known to me. Cf. Staab, *Gesellschaft*, p. 436 n. 955.

open conflict between Charles the Bald and Louis the German broke out on Lothar II's death in 869. The fate of Heriric's gift was thus tied up with the outcome of this conflict. Whilst the lands Heriric had given remained in a different kingdom to Prüm, effecting the gift was going to be difficult. But the Treaty of Meersen of 870, in which east Frankish control of the relevant areas of Lotharingia was established, strengthened Prum's hand, and the monks took the case to Louis the German, who upheld their claims, anxious to build a close relationship with this key abbey in a newly-acquired area.[206]

Politics of this ninth-century variety was as difficult for aristocrats as it was for kings: the two were mutually dependent in a polycentric political system in which no one kingdom was a closed entity, aristocratic power seeping through political boundaries yet profoundly dependent on royal favour. The inherent difficulty of politics made for structural instability, in the sense that individual positions were insecure. But, in spite of this, both kings and aristocrats continued to play the game defined by the Carolingian system. It was a game in which aristocratic families sought power through their position within the Carolingian system, and in which royal patronage was central. The multiplicity of potential sources of patronage simply complicated the rules of the game.

Like his brothers, Louis the German was an able ruler who was able to build a powerful kingship within this system. To our eyes, Louis' kingdom might often look different from that of Charles the Bald, largely because the political culture of Louis' court differed from his brother's. However, we should not forget how recently the foundations of an eastern kingship had been laid. Before the middle of the eighth century, beyond the Rhine had lain a 'wild east' of semi-independent polities under varying degrees of influence from the political centre of the Frankish Empire. Although kings had visited the middle Rhine intermittently since *c.* 600, they had never made a habit of residing there for long periods until the advent of the Carolingians. Yet by the 830s Louis was seeking to create a 'kingdom of the eastern Franks', whose western outposts were the palaces and cities of the middle Rhine. After 847, the middle Rhine was developed as a heartland of eastern Frankish kingship. Charlemagne's palace at Frankfurt was redeveloped to the extent that it became an eastern Aachen, 'the principal seat of the kingdom'. Even previously minor royal *villae* like Bürstadt and Trebur were transformed as they become more significant sites for ceremonial

---

[206] The involvement of Werner in the rebellions of Louis the German's sons in 865 and 871 is also clearly important in understanding the context of this judgement.

action and residence.[207] Lorsch was not frequently visited by kings before Louis, but in the second half of the ninth century it was redeveloped as a dedicated royal centre, with the building of a porticoed two-storey hallway (the *Torhalle*) at its entrance, and a new church, the *ecclesia varia*. The roots of redevelopment lie in Louis the German's patronage of the abbey, but it was under his son, Louis the Younger, that the process reached fruition. Lorsch became the mausoleum of the east Frankish dynasty and so a seat of their legitimacy, and St Nazarius was specially honoured in the palace chapel at Frankfurt.[208] These developments were consequent on the region's importance as, economically and politically, the most developed part of Louis' kingdom, and the gateway to the rest of the Empire.[209]

One implication of this changed geopolitical pattern was that local elites saw much more of the king.[210] This may help explain why the promulgation of the Carolingian programme in capitulary form played such a minor role in the political culture of the eastern kingdom: whilst royal decisions could be – and often were – recorded in written form, east Frankish rulers seem in general to have dealt face to face with aristocratic brokers without using the exhortatory medium of the written decree.[211] It is clear that by the end of Louis the Pious' reign, the local power of the aristocracy was both dependent upon, and unambiguously defined in terms of, office. It is no accident that it is in the middle of the

---

[207] Frankfurt: Regino of Prüm, *Chronicon*, s.a. 876, ed. Kurze, p. 111, and see Schalles-Fischer, *Pfalz und Fiskus Frankfurt*, esp. pp. 200–64. Trebur: M. Gockel, 'Die Bedeutung Treburs als Pfalzort', in *Deutsche Königspfalzen* III (Göttingen, 1980), 86–110. Bürstadt: *AF*, s.a. pp. 870, 873, pp. 71, 78. For palaces as *loci regi* see T. Zotz, 'Carolingian Tradition and Ottonian-Salian Innovation: Comparative Observations on Palatine Policy in the Empire', in A. J. Duggan (ed.), *Kings and Kingship in Medieval Europe* (London, 1993), pp. 69–100; in general on palaces and royal resources see T. Zotz, 'Grundlagen und Zentrum der Königsherrschaft', in H. U. Nuber *et al.* (eds.), *Archäologie und Geschichte des ersten Jahrtausends in Südwestdeutschland* (Sigmaringen, 1990), pp. 275–93.

[208] Innes, 'Kings, Monks and Patrons', pp. 319–20, drawing on Wehlt, *Reichsabtei und König*, pp. 32–5, 127–48; Semmler, 'Lorsch', p. 85; Fried, *Ludwig der Jüngere*, p. 13; W. Jacobsen, 'Die Lorscher Torhalle. Zum Probleme ihrer Deutung und Datierung', *Jahrbuch des Zentralinstituts für Kunstgeschichte* 1 (1985), 9–77, and conversations with Matthias Kloft.

[209] On itineraries, Brühl, *Fodrum, Gistum*, pp. 33–9. Royal residences were also developed in Bavaria, Louis' own core area until the 840s, and later in Alemannia.

[210] On the east Frankish kings' management of their aristocracy see T. Zotz, 'Le palais et les élites dans le royaume de Germanie', in R. Le Jan (ed.), *La royauté et les élites dans l'Europe carolingienne* (Lille, 1998), pp. 233–48.

[211] For archives see *AF*, s.a. 863, 876, pp. 58, 89; also *Visio Karoli Magni*, ed. P. Geary, 'Germanic Tradition and Royal Ideology in the Ninth Century: The *Visio Karoli Magni*', in Geary, *Living with the Dead in the Middle Ages* (Ithaca and London, 1994), pp. 49–76 at pp. 74–6. For royal decrees, *AF*, s.a. 852, 882, pp. 43, 99. Cf. also the comments of Hannig, 'Zentralle Kontrolle', pp. 19–23.

ninth century that we first hear of aristocratic discontent and rebellion because of conflict with kings over the control of local offices, above all countships, as in 861 when the sons of Gebhard fled the eastern kingdom because Louis had stripped them of their *honores*.[212] It was not that aristocrats were feeling increasingly possessive about offices which had previously been in the free gift of the king. Local aristocratic power had only been redefined in terms of comital office in the eighth century, and aristocratic families, as we have seen, had always expected to enjoy a loose *de facto* monopoly over local office. This was a workable trade-off for both kings and aristocrats whilst kings remained distant figures. But by the middle of the ninth century, when kings ruled smaller kingdoms and were far closer to the exercise of regional power, the strict definition of office became really useful to kings: dismissal from office acquired a new prominence as a potential threat. Significantly, though, rights of dismissal were not contested directly. Those who nursed grudges about lost *honores* formed an easily-tapped reservoir of support for rebellious sons, like Louis the Younger in 866, and Louis and Carloman in 871. In this new world, the politics of patronage became more crucial than ever, the object of intense aristocratic competition. Rights of dismissal were increasingly necessary to maintain the flow of *honores*, but always dangerous to use. One late Carolingian abbot saw the centrality of their exercise to successful kingship and eulogised Louis the German as a model for his 'discretion, moderation and temperance in the granting and taking away of public office'.[213] It was changing patterns of royal patronage, not an increase in the power of aristocrats against kings, which meant that so much ninth-century politics turned on the politics of royal appointment and dismissal. It was a politics of royal encroachment, not aristocratic self-assertion.

CRISIS, CONFLICT AND CONSOLIDATION

It was only at the very end of the ninth century that the Carolingian system, as reconstituted after the 830s, experienced prolonged structural crisis.[214] Crisis was most clearly visible in a faltering of the Carolingian

---

[212] This is more marked in the west, perhaps because the Annals of St Bertin report this kind of dispute in more depth than the Fulda Annals. But, in the east, see *AF*, s.a. 861, 865, 871, 876 (threat of dismissal), pp. 55, 63, 74–5, 86. Both Regino and Notker make much of aristocratic competition for royal patronage.

[213] Regino, s.a. 876, p. 110. For a catalogue of aristocrats dismissed from *honores*, see A. Krah, *Absetzungsverfahren als Spiegelbild von Königsmacht. Untersuchungen zum Kräftesverhältnis zwischen Königtum und Adel im Karolingerreich und seinen Nachfolgestaaten* (Aalen, 1987).

[214] I make no attempt to give a bibliography of general works on this important period: Hlawitschka, *Lothringen*, is an important analysis of the interplay between kings and the aristocracy of my

dynasty's monopoly on kingship. This was first and foremost a dynastic emergency: it was the lack of adult Carolingians, allied to a pressing need for effective leadership, that led to the crowning of non-Carolingian aristocrats in west Francia and Italy in 888. This was not the result of political division, or the practice of allowing each legitimate Carolingian son a claim to kingship. The immediate backdrop was not political fragmentation but reintegration, a trend which can be detected as early as 869, with the partition of Lotharingia between the eastern and western kingdoms, and reached its culmination in 884 when Charles the Fat was the sole inheritor of the entire Empire of his great-grandfather and namesake, Charlemagne. Reintegration did not lead to the creation of a unitary polity; the constituent parts of the Empire, Lotharingia included, maintained their distinct identities. Indeed, Charles the Fat's problems in the 880s stemmed from the strength of demands for effective and accessible Carolingian kingship, physically present in the regions and offering *Königsnähe* to local elites; demands, that is, for exactly the style of accessible and competing Carolingian kingships which had been the order of the day for the previous half-century. Charles, inevitably, could not fulfil these regional needs. The *regna*, their aristocracies now used to negotiating as collectivities with Carolingian rulers, faced a choice of either brokering a suitable deal with an available Carolingian if they could find one, or creating their own Carolingian-style kingship.

From a local perspective, then, the fundamental political development was the retreat of Carolingian kingship from the localities in the last third of the century. This retreat was tangible and physical. After 869, the crucial Lotharingian regions on the Moselle and Meuse, although places where kings visited, no longer enjoyed sustained royal presence: the regional aristocracy dealt collectively with more distant rulers. After the death of Louis the Younger in 882, the middle Rhine suffered a similar, if not quite identical, fate: it was ruled by kings who frequently stayed at the important palace complexes in the region, and held the most important assemblies there, but who were not intimately involved in local politics. This was not an experience that the aristocracy necessarily enjoyed. Charles the Fat's political problems owed much to the inability of those aristocratic circles centred on Archbishop Liutbert of Mainz to gain access to the king, whose immediate entourage was dominated by Alemannians. In fact, the increased social distance between kings and the

region, whilst Ewig, *Frühes Mittelalter*, and E. Boshof, 'Ottonen- und frühe Salierzeit (919–1056)', in G. Droege and F. Petri (eds.), *Rheinische Geschichte I.3. Hohes Mittelalter* (Dusseldorf, 1983), pp. 1–120, provide useful narratives. The best discussion of this period as a whole is G. Althoff, *Amicitiae und Pacta. Bündnis, Einung, Politik und Gebetsgedenken im beginnenden 10. Jht., Schriften der MGH* 37 (Hanover, 1992), pp. 3–103, to which I am greatly indebted.

regions was politically damaging precisely because aristocratic strategies in the localities relied on a ready and reliable interface with royal patronage. The absence of a trustworthy interface made for chronic insecurity. Local power structures remained simply too complex for powerful aristocrats to establish themselves in total control of closed regional systems, and so when effective royal patronage was not accessible, aristocrats were vulnerable to their local opponents, and stabilising structures of regional alliance and patronage emerged.

The implications of the changed relationship between royal and local power are made clear in the royal charters. The last quarter of the ninth century witnesses a real flurry of such documents in the middle Rhine. This distribution is no accident. Rather than the earlier standard of gifts of land or privileges from kings to the church, charters from the last decades of the ninth century record a greater variety of transactions, and a more complex pattern of endowment. In part, this was an outgrowth of the new patterns of royal patronage which had first emerged in the 830s and continued thereafter, with particularly important *fideles* being granted some land in outright ownership, which they in turn granted to the church. Such gifts remained rare – an important aristocrat might get one such gift in his lifetime – and never replaced the staples of royal endowment with benefices and office. Behind the formulaic facade of the charters lie complex transactions involving kings, their *fideles* and the monks: not only were kings bulking up the local muscle of favoured aristocrats, they were actively regulating and brokering relationships between these aristocratic followers and powerful royal monasteries. The upsurge in this style of endowment in the 880s and 890s reflects the frantic efforts of Charles the Fat and Arnulf to stabilise the position of their local supporters by delegating royal resources to their regional backers. In the short term at least, this was a viable style of kingship.[215] Royal gifts of land have been seen as damaging to kingship in the long term: impoverished kings, so the argument goes, denuded their successors of vital resources. In the middle Rhine at least, such a view is mistaken. Kings granted away much fiscal land, but did not dismantle the complex system which sustained the royal palaces of Ingelheim and Frankfurt. It is quite clear that most of the land given away had never been integral to the palace system and the royal itinerary: the net effect of these gifts was to change the rules of patronage which underscored local politics. Much formerly royal land was 'ecclesiastified' and now accessed via royal abbeys

---

[215] Cf above, pp. 203–4, with references, and my comments in 'Kings, Monks and Patrons', pp. 321–2. Rosenwein, 'The Family Politics of Berengar' is an illuminating study of this aspect of late Carolingian kingship. For the transactions, see *CL*43, 45, 47, 48, 49, 53, 57, 60 and cf. 54, 55, 56, 59; *CDF*602, 603, 629, 647, 650, 653 and cf. *CDF*552, 554, 645.

and bishoprics – which increasingly served as royal 'land banks' – not from kings direct: another index of the increasing social distance between the court and the localities. The few large fiscal complexes which kings did give away were given to powerful local churches who maintained them in the royal service: the classic example of this type of transaction must be Arnulf's grant of the estates supporting the royal post and messenger system at Worms to the bishop, who thereafter maintained the infrastructure on the king's behalf.[216]

Aristocrats were not opting out of the Carolingian system. The locations of royal assemblies, and the patterns of issue of royal charters, conformed to traditional patterns right through the decades around 900. The royal palaces of the middle Rhine and Main continued to act as meeting places and focal points for the east Frankish aristocracy as a collectivity, a fact which reflects a decision to opt into the east Frankish polity.[217] Collective decision and negotiation informed by a political topography defined by royal interests continued as the basic political form. A private charter of 20 May 897 makes the point graphically. In it Adalbero, bishop of Augsburg and abbot of a cluster of key monasteries including Lorsch, regularised his thoroughly irregular status *vis-à-vis* Lorsch. This politically sensitive and controversial action was 'brokered and announced publicly in the city of Worms', in the presence of the great and good of the middle Rhine and Moselle: the archbishops of Mainz and Trier, the bishop of Worms, six counts and a palace official.[218] Here government continued to function on a regional level as the collective action of aristocracy and episcopate.

Not that the continuation of these patterns was a manifestation of organic local consensus – far from it. The 890s and 900s mark a real high point in violent conflict within the aristocracy, and the 897 assembly had met in part to settle one particularly disruptive dispute. The flash point was the murder, in August 892, of Count Megingoz by a Count Alberich

---

[216] For conventional views of impoverishment, see e.g. Dhondt, *Etudes*, esp. pp. 236–53. Cf. J. Martindale, 'The Kingdom of Aquitaine and the Dissolution of the Carolingian Fisc', *Francia* 11 (1985), 131–91, for the careful local study that is needed to contextualise the gifts recorded in royal charters. For Worms and Arnulf, above, pp. 161–2.

[217] E. M. Eibl, 'Zur Stellung Bayern und Rheinfranken im Reiche Arnulfs von Kärnten', *Jahrbuch für Geschichte des Feudalismus* 8 (1984), 73–113; G. Bührier-Thierry, 'Les évêques de Bavière et d'Alémannie dans l'entourage des derniers rois carolingiens en Germanie, 876–911', *Francia* 16 (1989), 31–52, and see now G. Bührier-Thierry, *Evêques et pouvoir dans le royaume de Germanie, 876–973* (Paris, 1997).

[218] *CL53*: 'Consiliatum et ordinatum publice in civitate Wormatia, Hathone et Ratbodone archepiscopis, et Thietelaho episcopo presentibus; insuper Cunrado, Walahone, Gebehardo, Liutfrido, Burkardo, Dragebodo comitibus, Rudhardo domus regalis procuratori, videntibus, et innumerabilibus viris audientibus, cum Liuthero abbate, et cum consensu cunctorum fratrum, Lauresham . . .'

and his *socii* at the monastery of Rethel on the Moselle.[219] Megingoz was a relative of Robert the Strong, and so of the aristocrat who had acquired the west Frankish crown in 888, Odo. He had moved east after entering the service of Louis the German in 858, building on his ancestral claims and kinsmen in the middle Rhine to create a formidable local power base. The charters illuminate the mechanisms through which this was possible. Megingoz was able to build up relationships with local property owners such as Erluin, who had stood at his side at Lorsch in 860. Megingoz's contacts allowed him to deliver patronage to Erluin, in return for local support. Erluin was active defending the rights of Megingoz's contact, the archbishop of Rheims, in the middle Rhine–Vosges area, and was remunerated in gold and silver for his pains, and as a royal agent delimiting the boundaries of royal benefices on the Rhine which were given to Lorsch. Eventually, indeed, Erluin was able to achieve *Königsnähe* himself, thanks to the doors Megingoz had opened for him. His career culminated in the service of Louis the German, running the palace complex at Ingelheim and styled *aulicus praeses*.[220] Megingoz was not only a regional player: his western connections, and particularly his kinship with Odo, made him a player on the Imperial stage as well, and a link between western and eastern courts. This, too, enabled him to cement his local position. Links with the church of Rheims, for example, supported a relative, Rupert, who was a royal vassal and acted on behalf of the archbishop, receiving life-grants of land in the middle Rhine from Rheims in return. In 888 the alliance between the Carolingian ruler of the east, Arnulf, and Odo led to the solidification of Megingoz's regional position still further, with the grant of the key lay-abbacy of St Maximian at Trier, and the immediate granting out of life-interests in the monastery's land to build up local support. Megingoz's domination of Lotharingia from a Trier–Worms axis led to one St Maximian source referring to him as '*dux* of the Lotharingians'.[221]

---

[219] Regino, s.a. 892, p. 140. *Pace* Staab, *Gesellschaft*, pp. 440–1, I seee the Megingoz murdered in 892 as the same man active in the charters since 858: there is no real break in the run of charters. Even if we follow Staab and have two successive local counts named Megingoz, they are father and son, and so my argument is essentially unchanged. Cf. Schulze, *Grafschaftsverfassung*, p. 191. Hlawitschka, *Lothringen*, pp. 110–12, and Ewig, *Frühes Mittelalter*, pp. 242–3. See Althoff, *Amicitiae und Pacta*, pp. 219–23, for the aristocrats around Megingoz.

[220] Herloin and Megingoz at Lorsch in 860: *CL*802. Rheims: Flodoard, c. 26, p. 544. Royal service: *MGH DLouis the German* 117: *missus* here means *ad hoc* royal official. Ingelheim: *MGH DLouis the German* 170. For his local interests, see Staab, *Gesellschaft*, p. 440 with n. 980, and for his career see Hannig, 'Zentralle Kontrolle', 22–3. Note the Herloin, *missus* in northern Neustria in 853, who had sworn to stay loyal to Charles the Bald as Louis invaded the western kingdom in 858: Nelson, *Charles the Bald*, pp. 167, 186 n. 118, with references.

[221] For Megingoz's relationship with Rheims and St Maximian see Staab, *Gesellschaft*, pp. 440–1; Flodoard IV:3, p. 561; Sigehard, *Miracula S. Maximiani*, c. 13, p. 232; *MGH DArnulf* 10.

Thanks to the scope of his contacts, and the increased social distance between the *regnum* and royal courts, Megingoz was able to build up a position in which he mediated royal contact with Lotharingia, and so manipulated royal patronage of the Lotharingian aristocracy. Hence the seething of rival factions, frozen out of the charmed circle of those who enjoyed royal patronage via Megingoz. Megingoz's murderer, Alberich, was a local man whose family were long-standing rivals of Megingoz's; the ancestors of Alberich and Megingoz had been on opposite sides in the 830s.[222] With the murder of 892, Alberich was reacting to his inability to play out this rivalry through local competition for royal patronage, which is how it had been articulated in the previous half-century. Now that Megingoz mediated contact between Lotharingia and the eastern and western courts, Alberich had no alternative but to resort to violence. This was the definitive decentralisation of political conflict.

The murder of Megingoz was a shocking event for contemporaries: even late Carolingian politics was not normally so cold-blooded. The shock waves it sent out continued to reverberate through the region for more than a decade. The initial murder had been a reaction to Megingoz's position as a kind of regional supremo, and the resultant feud became a struggle for his former position. The *scandalum* caused by the murder led to episcopal initiatives at pacification to avoid full-blown feud, and to Arnulf taking on the role of peacemaker, touring Lotharingia and allying himself with the episcopate in 893. Arnulf's actions were not wholly disinterested: he needed a stable regime in this key area. Arnulf attempted to set up his illegitimate son, Zwentibald, in the vacuum left by Megingoz's death. Zwentibald received the key *honor*, the lay-abbacy of St Maximian's, in 893, and Arnulf then attempted to define his son's regional position in the terms appropriate with the lustre of his Carolingian blood, and have him recognised as 'king of the Lotharingians'. The aristocracy, at first suspicious, were eventually persuaded by Arnulf's continued presence and patronage, and recognised Zwentibald at Worms in 895, immediately following the consummation of Arnulf's alliance with the episcopate in a Synod held at nearby Trebur.[223]

The attempt to establish Zwentibald in Lotharingia made eminent political sense, allowing the maintenance of east Frankish control in the region, and embedding Arnulf's line at the very heart of the Empire. Nonetheless, it failed. Since 869, Lotharingia had not had its own,

---

[222] Alberich was a descendent of Heriric and Werner; see pp. 218–20, above for rivalry between them and the family of Robert the Strong and Megingoz.

[223] Regino, s.a. 893, 894, 895, ed. Kurze, pp. 141–4, and for episcopal pacification see Le Jan, *Famille et Pouvoir*, p. 93, with references.

locally-based, king, but had been ruled from distant courts allied with the regional aristocracy. The attempt to set up Zwentibald as 'king of the Lotharingians' thus inevitably involved treading on the toes of regional leaders, who had previously run the *regnum* on behalf of their Carolingian patrons. Within weeks of the acknowledgement of Zwentibald's kingship, some of those who must have been present at Worms were pursuing their political claims with drawn swords. Count Stephan exercised the right of vengeance for Megingoz's murder by striking down Alberich – significantly again on a religious festival. By doing so, Stephen was laying claim to Megingoz's political legacy. His leadership of Megingoz's kin and followers was cemented by the marriage contracted between Megingoz's widow Gisela and Count Burchard, the son of Stephen's brother, Count Walaho. As Walaho's interests lay in the Worms area, where Megingoz had been strong, this group now enjoyed a formidable position in the middle Rhine and the Moselle.[224] The re-eruption of the feud clearly betokened local frustration with the political settlement which Arnulf had brokered: but then Megingoz's kin and followers were the real losers in 895, their honour not satisfied by revenge and the political system Megingoz had built up broken, with the newcomer Zwentibald pulling the levers of patronage.

The latent tension between the new regime and the claims of Stephen and his allies led to Zwentibald's confiscation of their *honores* and *dignitates* in 897 and the division of the confiscated land between Zwentibald's followers. Zwentibald was now directly implicated within the logic of the feud, whilst Stephen and his party were wholly without a stake within the official system and denuded of the ability to deliver patronage to their followers: partisan royal intervention within an aristocratic feud, and the total removal of royal patronage, left them fighting for their political lives. And fight they did. They marched on Trier, Zwentibald's base, and forced the intervention of Arnulf, who staged a reconciliation between his son and the Lotharingian aristocracy. Efforts at pacification were apparently sealed by marriage-alliance, with Zwentibald wedding Oda, daughter of the leading Saxon aristocrat Otto, and an ally of Arnulf's brother-in-law, Count Conrad.[225]

Even the brokering of this complex web of alliance involving the dominant aristocratic groupings in Saxony, Hesse, the middle Rhine and the Moselle, did not save Zwentibald. The aristocracy wanted a stable supra-regional framework and predictable patterns of royal patronage,

---

[224] Regino, s.a. 896, p. 144, and Wolfhard, *Miracula S. Walpurgis*, III:5, ed. Bauch, pp. 268– 70, for the marriage.

[225] Regino, s.a. 897, p. 145, and for the significance of the marriage see Hlawitschka, *Lothringen*, p. 16, n. 34.

not a king who attempted to make or break them, but Zwentibald, desperate to create a Lotharingian power base of his own, continued to remove *honores* and confiscate land with abandon.[226] Significantly, though, the end did not come for Zwentibald until after Arnulf's death in 899, and the succession of an infant but legitimate Carolingian, Louis the Child, to the eastern kingdom in 900. Count Conrad and Archbishop Hatto of Mainz, who had been dominant within Arnulf's regime, were the real powers behind Louis the Child's throne, and allied with key Lotharingian groups to ensure their hegemony over Lotharingia; as Louis' mother was Conrad's sister, they had very good reasons for wishing Zwentibald off the scene. Zwentibald held a public meeting with the various aristocratic factions at St Goar in 899, but in 900 renewed open conflict broke out within the Lotharingian aristocracy, the best part of which finally submitted to Louis the Child. Zwentibald was summarily removed from the equation when his aristocratic opponents killed him at a meeting held on the Meuse on 13 August, thereby opting into the political stability promised by the pliable Carolingian kingship of Louis the Child. On Zwentibald's death his widow, Oda, was immediately married to one of his murderers, an ally of Stephen's called Gerard; Stephen's faction were attempting to consolidate their regional dominance and marry into the east Frankish court elite.[227] Even then, and even following the death of Stephen in an accident in 901, the dispute which had determined the contours of political conflict was not at an end. Violence flared up again in 906, when Count Conrad sent his sons to march on Count Gerard and his brother Count Matfrid to remove them from the *honores* whose devolution had been a matter of dispute since Megingoz's death in 892. After Count Conrad's sons beseiged them in their fortified residence, Gerard and Matfrid submitted to the judgement of an assembly held at Metz which removed the disputed *honores* from their control. It was Conrad's brother, Gebhard, who was to establish himself in Megingoz's counties, and eventually as '*dux* of the Lotharingians'.[228]

---

[226] See Regino, s.a. 898, ed. Kurze, p. 146. Regino's comments on the fall of Zwentibald's regime (s.a. 900, p. 148) are a classic condemnation of the misuse of royal patronage.

[227] Regino, s.a. 899, 900, ed. Kurze, pp. 147–8. Jackman, *Criticism and Critique*, pp. 87–8, suggests that after Gerard's death *c.* 910 Oda went on to remarry again, to Eberhard, brother of Conrad I, which would underline her regional importance.

[228] Regino, s.a. 906, ed. Kurze, pp. 150–1, and see *CL*53, 64, for Gebhard's acquisition of Megingoz's counties and *MGH DLouis the Child* 20 for his 'ducal' title. There is a vast and controversial literature on the family of Conrad: most useful for their involvement in this crucial period is Althoff, *Amicitiae und Pacta*, esp. pp. 240–63. The claims and enmities arising from these events could still break out into feud in the right political circumstances half a century later: Adalbert of Trier, continuation of Regino's *Chronicle*, ed. F. Kurze (Hanover, 1890), s.a. 944, p. 162.

The Lotharingian feud was bloody and long-running because it was a dispute about dispensation of benefices and offices, which were the life-blood of aristocratic power. It was the threat of the removal of royal endowments, on trumped up grounds, that were the flash points of the conflict. It was paralleled by another conflict concerning the disposition of regional power in the area to the east of the middle Rhine, down the Main and beyond. Here a family related to Megingoz's had been domi-nant since at least the 810s, distinguished by the names Poppo and Henry; like Megingoz, these were Imperial aristocrats active on a supra-regional stage, and, indeed, the increased size of political units from the 880s had increased the geographical scope of their activities. The progress of the conflict, and its articulation in terms of feud, followed a near identical pattern to events in Lotharingia: these were not so much spontaneous outbreaks of local tension as the renegotiation of the interaction between regnal and regional political structures. In 892 – even as Zwentibald was being established in Lotharingia – Arnulf removed Count Poppo and made an outsider, Count Conrad, *dux* in Thuringia, a position he instantly gave up to his ally and kinsman Burchard. At a similar date, Conrad's brother, Rudolf, was made bishop of Würzburg. In 897, just as Stephan and his allies sought to reclaim the position held by Megingoz, the sons of Poppo's brother, Henry – Adalbert, Adalard and Henry – resorted to violence to reclaim their family's former dominance. Open conflict between the sons of Henry and of Conrad broke out once again in 902, and in 903 Adalbert, Adalard and Henry were able to drive their opponents 'beyond the Spessart', and seize confiscated lands and offices. Finally, in 906, as Conrad's sons established control in Lotharingia, a lengthy campaign was fought against Adalbert who was finally tried and executed.[229]

The winner in both conflicts was Count Conrad. Conrad's ancestors had dominated Hesse since at least the 830s. Although the struggles for dominance in Lotharingia and Thuringia were articulated as feuds, conflict turned around the royal court, and the ability of rulers to remove *honores*, even to declare recalcitrants outlaws. The occasional outbreaks of 'hot' conflict may catch our eye, as they caught the eye of contemporary writers, but they did not determine the shape or outcome of the conflict:

---

[229] Regino, s.a. 892, 897, 902, 903, 906, ed. Kurze, pp. 121, 145, 149–50, 151–2; see also Widukind of Corvey, *Rerum gestarum Saxonicarum*, ed. P. Hirsch and H.-E. Lohmann, *MGH SRG* (Hanover, 1935) I:22, pp. 32–5. On the descendants of Henry and Poppo see now Althoff, *Amicitiae und Pacta*, pp. 264–9, with references; on the origins of the family see Metz, 'Babenberger und Rupertiner'; and Metz, 'Das Problem der Babenberger in landesgeschichtlicher Sicht', *Blätter für deutsche Landesgeschichte 99* (1963), 59–81. There are hints at opposition to them within Thuringia before 892: *AF*, s.a. 882, 883, pp. 108, 110. For the increased scope of their influence in the 880s see *AF*, s.a. 880, 882, 886, pp. 95, 109, 114.

Conrad won out in both Lotharingia and Thuringia because he controlled the royal court and could use royal patronage – positive and negative – as a political tool, not because he was militarily stronger.[230] The resort to physical violence did not mark the incremental advance of aristocratic power in the localities to the stage where it could be carved out and defended by military campaign. It was rather a reaction to the changes within the political system caused by the increasing reliance of kings on individual figures to monopolise mediation between court and region. These figures were able to skew royal patronage, both positive and negative, to further their own interests. Those groupings which found themselves frozen out of positive patronage, and on the receiving end of negative patronage, turned to violence out of sheer exasperation. Violence, given legal legitimacy by the form of the feud, was the only way for them to force their case into the open. The increasing monopoly of regional power enjoyed by a handful of aristocratic mediators destroyed the balancing mechanisms which in the ninth century had bound all local groups into Carolingian kingship. Political violence was designed to restore, by force, that royal patronage which had previously been enjoyed; it was anything but a universal declaration of independence by powerful aristocrats opting out of the Carolingian system.

The success of Conrad demonstrates the possibilities of these changes in royal patronage for those who controlled it. The processes by which Conrad and his predecessors had built up local power remain shadowy. The acquisition of local power in the middle Rhine and Main regions was, however, not a gradual or organic process taking place over generations, but something which was done suddenly in a quarter of a century: Conrad's ancestors had little land in these areas in the ninth century, and did not hold office in the middle Rhine or Main until the 890s. A Fulda charter, probably to be dated to 894, gives insight into the fragility of their position. It records the property dealings of one Meginfrid, who had received property rights in the Fulda area from a King Louis (presumably Louis the Younger), but who had subsequently come into conflict with Fulda, as he attempted to build up his local position. Eventually Meginfrid's case was heard before Arnulf at the royal palace of Frankfurt. Meginfrid was evidently a client of Conrad's family who had benefited from royal patronage thanks to the *Königsnähe* of his masters: at Frankfurt, Conrad's brother, Gebhard, intervened for him and brokered a compromise. Conrad, Archbishop Hatto and their party dominate the first section of the charter's witness-list. But, in spite of his

---

[230] Royal judgements: *AF*, s.a. 892, p. 121; *MGH DArnulf* 174; Regino, s.a. 896, p. 152. Hot conflict: Regino, s.a. 897, 902, 906, pp. 145, 149, 151–2.

power at court, the essential weakness of Conrad's position in the locality is also made plain. After all, the case turned on the failure of Meginfrid to establish himself in the neighbourhood of Fulda, and the opposition of the abbot of Fulda to Conrad's plans. In fact, Meginfrid had to give the disputed property back to Fulda, in return getting distant land in the Lahn area, the home ground of Gebhard and Conrad.[231]

Even in the 890s, Imperial aristocrats could not simply order people about in the localities. For the decision made in 894 was not enacted behind closed doors. In the charter witness-list behind the bishops and counts who had hammered out the compromise solution stood forty-two property-holders from the Fulda area: public patterns of collective action were not enveloped within aristocratic lordship, but continued to define local politics. To build local support Conrad had to win these men, most of whose forefathers had loyally followed the forefathers of Conrad's opponents, over to his side. Gerd Althoff's magisterial investigation of an entry in the Reichenau confraternity book has shown just how Conrad set about this task: one entry, headed by *dux* Conrad, contains twenty-six further names, almost all of whom can be identified with influential property holders who were active charter witnesses in the neighbourhood of Fulda. There is a particularly close correspondence between those commemorated at Reichenau and those who travelled to Frankfurt in 894, and to another royal palace, Trebur, to witness another controversial transaction concerning Fulda's lands and involving Count Stephen, Zwentibald's opponent, at a crucial juncture in 900; we know that in 900 Stephen's and Conrad's parties were allied in their plans for Lotharingia, an alliance cemented by the remarriage of Zwentibald's widow. Evidently the prayers of the monks of Reichenau in distant Alemannia were an alluring reward for these men, and Conrad and Hatto, by having them included in the Reichenau confraternity book, were sealing a political alliance with spiritual glue. That they had to do so tells us much about the basic continuity of patterns of local power.[232]

The continuing importance of extensive links is underlined by a contemporary account of the miracles wrought at a new and modishly fashionable pilgrimage site, the tomb of St Walpurgis at Monheim near Eichstätt. Both Megingoz's widow, and those involved in the Thuringian feud, made their way to Monheim, a central place in the religious world of the east Frankish aristocracy, at key moments in the 890s.[233] Extensive

---

[231] CDF631, which Dronke dates to 889, but see Althoff, *Amicitiae und Pacta*, pp. 249–50, for the probable date of 894.

[232] See *Das Verbrüderungsbuch der Abtei Reichenau*, eds. Autenrieth *et al.*, f. 71, sectors C3–5, and Althoff, *Amicitiae und Pacta*, pp. 246–51. The charter from 900 is CDF647.

[233] Wolfhard, *Miracula* II:8; III:5; IV:11, ed. Bauch, pp. 234–6, 268–70, 324.

links remained vital not only as a means of winning political support at the political centre, but also – as both the Monheim and Reichenau evidence makes clear – because they allowed the servicing of regional networks of support and allegiance. Nonetheless, changing political structures fundamentally altered the possibilities of geographical mobility within the aristocracy. In the 830s and 840s Robert the Strong had been able to seek his fortune in the west when the tide turned against him in the middle Rhine, and such a strategy, as we have seen, continued to be viable until at least the 860s. By the 880s and 890s, however, the aristocracy was considerably less 'footloose'[234]: Megingoz and those involved in the feud after his death, and his Thuringian counterparts, were engaged in a struggle in which travelling to another region to amass a political base seems not to have been a possibility. They needed extensive links to pursue a political strategy successfully, but their power was far more rooted in a particular region than that of their ancestors. These seismic shifts in the geology of aristocratic society were reactions to, not causes of, changed patterns of royal activity. 'Footloose' strategies had their heyday in the middle decades of the ninth century, when there were rival sources of Carolingian patronage in more or less open competition for aristocratic adherents, but by the end of the century the scarcity of kings made such competitive patronage a thing of the past. The polity was no longer polycentric, and so the parameters of possible politics had altered.

Those aristocrats who established themselves at the head of regional hierarchies came to bear the characteristic title *dux*. We should beware of reading too great an institutional content into the position of the *duces*: it was essentially a form of loose aristocratic dominance based on military leadership, in a long and continuous tradition reaching back beyond the Carolingian period, whose exact content varied from area to area but was never a firm, closed structure.[235] In the middle Rhine, indeed, the development of regional structures was complicated by the continuing interests of kings in a royal heartland. The aristocratic hierarchy which was created in the decades around 900 solidified the power of Conrad and his kin, in the region east from the middle Rhine along the Main and Lotharingia. When, on the death of Louis the Child in 911, Conrad's

---

[234] The term is J. L. Nelson's: *Charles the Bald*, p. 56.

[235] There is a vast bibliography on *duces*. See H.-W. Goetz, ' *"Dux" und "ducatus"'* (Bochum, 1977); K.-F. Werner, 'La génèse des duchés en France et en Allemagne', *Settimane* 27 (1981), 175–207, repr. in his *Vom Frankenreich zur Entfaltung Deutschlands und Frankenreichs* (Sigmaringen, 1984); two regional studies, which help us think about 'ducal' power in practice, are H. Maurer, *Die Herzog von Schwaben* (Sigmaringen, 1978) and T. Zotz, *Der Briesgau und das alemannische Herzogtum*, VF Sonderbard 15 (Sigmaringen, 1974). For Saxony see now M. Becher, *Rex, Dux und Gens. Untersuchungen zur Entstehung des sächsischen Herzogtums im 9. und 10. Jht.* (Husum, 1996).

eponymous son gained the east Frankish crown, these systems of regional dominance fell into the hands of Conrad I's brother, Eberhard. Following the accession of the Saxon leader Henry I to the east Frankish throne on Conrad's death, the ultimate allegiance of the region was up for grabs. The western king, Charles the Simple, was able to follow in the footsteps of Charles the Bald, who made a bid for domination as far as the Rhine's west bank, marching as far as Mainz and Pfeddersheim just outside Worms in 920, whilst there may have been parties in Lotharingia attempting to go it alone under an indigenous aristocrat, Giselbert. In the event, Henry I was able to re-establish his dominance of the crucial area west of the Rhine after a meeting with Charles at Bonn in 921. This dominance was achieved by brokering alliances with the leaders of the region's aristocracy, notably Conrad I's brother Eberhard, '*dux* of the Franks'. The more or less 'horizontal' nature of the bonds of *amicitia* which held the polity together were vividly demonstrated by Henry's initiatives to mobilise support in 930 by visiting Eberhard and the bishops, counts and other nobles of the middle Rhine and Main in person in their churches and homes, where they were honoured to be wined, dined and showered with gifts.[236] Kingship was now essentially concerned with binding together self-standing regional hierarchies; stabilisation of the regnal political framework made regional competition and long-held grudges within the aristocracy less likely to burst into the open in incandescent conflagration.

After the succession of Henry's son, Otto I, these bonds were slowly reworked as the 'vertical' distance between kings and the regional aristocracy once again increased. When fighting broke out between Eberhard's *milites* and those of Otto I's brother, the new king imposed a secular punishment reminiscent of the *harmiscara* imposed by Carolingian kings on aristocratic miscreants. Eberhard was made to hand over war-horses to the biblical value of 100 talents, whilst his followers were made to carry their hunting dogs for a league, into the royal presence at Merseburg. This public humiliation acknowledged in ritual form the prerogatives of royal lordship over regional leaders. Renewed hostilities led to Eberhard's exile, and his alliance with other discontents in Bavaria and Lotharingia: politics at the highest level continued to be played out on a regnal stage. In the revolt and its progress, we see the working out of a series of very local and often long-standing rivalries, some intrafamilial: Eberhard died opposed by two cousins. We also see the ability

---

[236] For these events, see Adalbert of Trier, continuation of Regino's *Chronicle*, ed. F. Kurze, *MGH SRG* (Hanover, 1890), s.a. 923, 924, 925, 931, pp. 157–9. On the changing ties between king and aristocracy from Conrad I to Otto I, I have found Althoff's work particularly valuable.

of the Ottonian dynasty to place itself at the centre of these local rivalries.[237]

After Eberhard's death in 939, Otto's attempts to create a political pyramid with himself at its apex began to bear fruit. Eberhard's title as '*dux* of the Franks' was allowed to atrophy, and Otto concentrated instead on controlling Lotharingia via the middle Rhenish aristocracy in time-honoured east Frankish tradition. In 943 or 944 he appointed Conrad the Red, an aristocrat whose family controlled the abbey of Hornbach and whose inherited interests lay down the west bank of the Rhine, as *dux* of the Lotharingians.[238] Conrad the Red's career demonstrates the continuing significance of royal backing for those wishing to establish a regional hegemony. His constant mention as a petitioner in Otto's royal charters, and his frequent appearance in non-royal charters from Lotharingia, suggests that he established an effective monopoly as the king's regional representative of a type of which his predecessors could only have dreamed.[239] His father, although a well-connected count, was scarcely a figure of the first rank.[240] Conrad the Red's prominence was gained through royal patronage, and his *Königsnähe* was institutionalised by Conrad the Red's marriage to one of Otto I's daughters, Liutgard in 947 or 948: one of a series of actions by which Otto created kinship ties to bind regional leaders to the Ottonian dynasty.[241] The marriage excited considerable controversy, highlighting the intensity of aristocratic competition for royal patronage. One early eleventh-century writer claimed that Conrad the Red had maltreated and dishonoured his wife, and that a duel was fought at Worms in 950, following claims that Liutgard had enjoyed illicit relations with another member of the aristocracy. The

---

[237] On Eberhard's various misadventures from 937 to 939 see Adalbert, s.a. 937–9, ed. Kurze, pp. 160–1; Widukind, II:6, 10, 11, 13, 24–6, ed. Lohmann, pp. 71–2, 73–4, 74–8, 78, 86–9. For the ritual humiliation of carrying one's hound, see B. Schwenk, 'Das Hundetragen. Eine Rechtsbrauch im Mittelalter', *Historisches Jahrbuch* 110 (1990), 289–308; for Carolingian *harmiscara* see De Jong, 'Power and Humility in Carolingian Society: The Public Penance of Louis the Pious', *EME* 1 (1992), 29–52 at 43–7.

[238] See Boshof, 'Ottonen- und Salierzeit', esp. pp. 67–71. On Conrad the Red see most recently W. Glocker, *Die Verwandten der Ottonen und ihre Bedeutung in der Politik* (Vienna and Cologne, 1989), pp. 101–19; R. E. Barth, *Der Herzog in Lotharingien im 10. Jahrhundert* (Sigmaringen, 1990), pp. 105–29.

[239] Barth, *Der Herzog*, pp. 105–29, but esp. pp. 108, 120–1, assembles a vast array of charter evidence which deserves sustained study.

[240] The key evidence for Conrad's father, Count Werner (named in Adalbert, s.a. 943, ed. Kurze, p. 162) comes in a series of entries in the *Liber Memorialis* of Remiremont, esp. f. 54r and f. 5v, 6v: *Liber Memorialis von Remiremont*, eds. E. Hlawitschka, K. Schmid and G. Tellenbach, *MGH Libri Memoriales* I (Dublin and Berlin, 1970), p. 168, interpreted by Althoff, *Amicitiae und Pacta*, pp. 259–60. The key to understanding Conrad's ancestry lies in his lordship over the abbey of Hornbach, which, along with nomenclature, points to descent from the Count Werner who had been the dominant local figure in the mid-ninth century: on him, below, pp. 202–4, 213–15, and on the family see Metz, 'Miszellen'. [241] Adalbert, s.a. 947, ed. Kurze, p. 163.

whole affair smacks of resentment at Conrad's rapid rise and royal favour; it was a descendant of Eberhard, who presumably felt that the upstart Conrad the Red had eclipsed his rightful position, who was alleged to have been involved with Liutgard.[242] Such intense intra- and inter-familial competition for regional power allowed kings to maintain control of a sort. Conrad, although clearly the most powerful individual in the middle Rhine and Lotharingia, was never assured of having his way: in 944, immediately after Conrad's appointment, local opponents accused 'Conrad and his faction' of infidelity to Otto.[243]

Conrad's involvement in the rebellion of 953–4, so vividly described by Widukind, further illuminates Ottonian techniques of human management. Conrad rebelled to save face after reaching a settlement with King Berengar of Italy and being snubbed; he did so not as a regional ruler wanting to cast off the shackles of kingship, but as a member of the east Frankish political community acting alongside one of the king's sons. For all the strength of Conrad's local following, and in particular his alliance of *amicitia* with Archbishop Frederick of Mainz, the most powerful ecclesiastical magnate in his sphere of interest, Otto was able to work with Conrad's local opponents, and Conrad was indeed driven out by the 'Lotharingians' in 953. Just as saving face had escalated conflict at the very beginning, so honour informed Ottonian dealings with Conrad after the collapse of his rebellion: Conrad gave in 'with humility', even refusing to fight the king's army. Otto's regal stature and the 'vertical' nature of his relationship with Conrad were emphasised throughout. Whilst Conrad lost his 'duchy', he was able to lead the Frankish contingent in Otto's army at the battle of the Lech in 955, at which he fell; his cortege made its way back to Worms, where he was buried, with great ceremony.[244]

Although Otto I successfully reshaped the polity into a pyramidal form, and emphasised the special qualities of the king at its apex, Ottonian government remained much more of a 'capstone' affair than its

---

[242] Thietmar of Merseberg, *Chronicon*, II:39, ed. R. Holtzmann, *MGH SRG* (Hanover, 1935), p. 88. This early eleventh-century account must be read next to Adalbert, s.a. 950, p. 164, who says that the duel is about a liaison with a *neptis* of the king. This causes real problems of interpretation (see Jackman, *Criticism and Critique*, and esp. pp. 25–6, 55–7, also 60–1, where he points out royal confiscations which may have taken place at Worms in 950): but even if Thietmar's account is a misunderstanding of exactly what occurred in 950, it is significant for our understanding of reactions to, and the basis of, Conrad the Red's power, and the case in 950 still stands as a striking illustration of aristocratic competition for *Königsnähe* through the marriage bed.

[243] Adalbert, s.a. 944, ed. Kurze, p. 162; Widukind III:17, ed. Lohmann, p. 135.

[244] On the rebellion of 953–4, and Conrad's role therein and thereafter, see Adalbert, s.a. 952–5, ed. Kurze, pp. 165–8; Widukind, III:7–47, ed. Lohmann, pp. 108–126. See also K. Leyser, *Rule and Conflict*; G. Althoff, 'Zur Frage nach der Organisation sächsischer *coniurationes* in der Ottonenzeit', *Frühmittelalterliche Studien* 16 (1982), 129–42.; G. Althoff, 'Königsherrschaft und Konfliktbewältigung im 10. und 11. Jht', *Frühmittelalterliche Studien* 23 (1989), pp. 265–90.

Carolingian predecessor. Its problems and possibilities were the result of this changed profile.[245] Under the Ottonians the theatre of political ritual – well used by the Carolingians – became the central element of a ruling strategy which sought to bind together regional units, not to administer royal wishes in the localities. Ritual humiliation, temporary exile, perhaps the removal of important *honores* such as Conrad the Red suffered in 954, were the punishments meted out to rebels, but by and large the Ottonians did not seek to make or break their aristocracy. The logic was retributive, exacting amends for demonstrable disloyalty; there was no removal of *honores* on account of disfavour or suspicion, nor Carolingian-style disciplinary élan. The type of instrumental literacy used by the Carolingians is hard to trace not because of a deficit in literacy, nor because of political regression, but because it was not relevant to Ottonian needs.[246] The progress of the royal *iter* took on a heightened significance in integrating aristocratic society.[247] The escalation of the rebellion of 953–4 underlines the paramount importance of this ritual progress: Otto had to flee to Saxony rather than lose face on account of his inability to celebrate Easter in the appropriate regal style at Aachen or Mainz.[248]

The Ottonian settlement encouraged a certain level of political stability through the effective abolition of royal caprice. On a local level, this meant the tacit admission of undisturbed family succession to *honores*. The exact mechanisms through which family successions were articulated remain shadowy. There is a widespread assumption that the crisis of the Carolingian Empire resulted in office becoming the outright possession of the aristocracy, inherited as a form of property right.[249] Its evidential basis is embarrassingly scanty. It is quite possible to demonstrate

[245] On Ottonian government see K. J. Leyser, 'Ottonian Government', *English Historical Review* 96 (1981), 721–53; H. Keller, 'Reichsorganisation, Herrschaftsformen und Gesellschaftsstrukturen im Regnum Teutonicum', *Settimane* 38 (1990), 159–95; H. Keller, 'Grundlagen ottonischer Königsherrschaft', in K. Schmid (ed.), *Reich und Kirche vor dem Investiturstreit. Festschrift G. Tellenbach* (Sigmaringen, 1985), pp. 17–34; H. Keller, 'Zum Charakter der "Staatlichkeit"'.

[246] Cf. K. Leyser, 'Ritual, Ceremony and Gesture: Ottonian Germany', in Leyser, *Communications and Power in Medieval Europe* I (London, 1994), pp. 189–213 at pp. 194–6; Keller, 'Reichsorganisation', pp. 169–71.

[247] Brühl, *Fodrum, Gistum, Servitium Regis* is the fundamental study of changing itineraries and their underpinning; for recent advances in the study of Ottonian itinerancy see Bernhardt, *Itinerant Kingship*, summarising much important German scholarship, notably E. Müller-Mertens, *Die Reichsstruktur im Spiegel der Herrschaftspraxis Ottos des Grossen* (Berlin, 1980).

[248] See the famous account in Widukind II:13–14, ed. Lohmann, p. 111.

[249] E.g. Boshof, 'Ottonen-und Salierzeit', pp. 58–9. Cf. also Keller, 'Reichsorganisation', p. 172 (at n. 23 noting the dearth of recent work on this aspect of the shift from Carolingian to Ottonian), and F. Staab, 'Reich und Mittelrhein um 1000', in H. Hinkel (ed.), *1000 Jahre St. Stephan im Mainz*, Quellen und Abhandlungen zur mittelrheinische Kirchengeschichte 63 (Mainz, 1990), pp. 59–100 at pp. 63–4.

that powerful families in fact monopolised countships; indeed, because after the middle of the ninth century royal charters named the count in whose county property or rights were located, we can actually supply a very full list of individual counts for the late Carolingian and Ottonian periods, and it is clear that counts in specific areas tended to come from the same family, and that sons often followed their fathers. We should not let the fuller evidence for the transmission of countships in the late ninth and tenth centuries lead us into concluding that the patterns it reveals were new: as far back as we can go, local office was monopolised by powerful local families, with groups of counties controlled by given individuals.[250] Local families were doubtless less dependent on royal goodwill than they had been under Charlemagne, Louis the Pious and Louis's sons, but this does not necessarily mean that counties had come to be seen as hereditable possessions. The extent to which family control was acknowledged is shown by the early career of Conrad the Red's son, Otto. Otto was acknowledged as his father's successor in a succession of counties well before he reached the age of majority, showing the strength of the expectation that countships were to be transmitted directly from father to son.[251] Where Carolingian kings had room for manoeuvre in the granting of counties, and could intervene in familial succession or manipulate familial patterns, Ottonian rulers kept their hands off.[252]

This does not necessarily mean that counties had become hereditary or proprietorial.[253] There is charter evidence which shows that the position of advocate – far less 'official' than that of count – remained an office whose incumbent was invested by the king at a public assembly in the 920s.[254] Whilst we should not extrapolate too far forward in time from this case, there is actually very little evidence which sheds light on how counts were made counts.[255] The one text habitually cited to demon-

---

[250] J. Prinz, 'Pagus und comitatus in den Urkunden der Karolinger', *Archiv für Urkundenforschung* 17 (1941), 329– 58.

[251] See notably *MGH DOtto I* 178, for 956 when Otto was less than ten. On Otto see Glocker, *Verwandten*, pp. 220–5, and Staab, 'Reich und Mittelrhein', pp. 66–71.

[252] Le Jan, *Famille et Pouvoir*, pp. 249–61, stresses increasing *de facto*, if not *de jure* inheritance, and particularly follows Dhondt, *Etudes*, pp. 21–2, in arguing that straight father–son succession, rather than royal appointments of collateral kin, became the rule.

[253] Nonn, *Pagus und Comitatus*, pp. 239–46, and Zotz, 'Personengeschichte und Grafschafts- verfassung', p. 8

[254] *UBMR*167, for the advocate of St Maximian at Trier receiving his *ministerium* from the king in a *mallus* at Worms in 926. Boshof, 'Ottonen- und Salierzeit', p. 6, points out that the same man was active as advocate already in 923, but the point about the ultimate importance of royal instal- lation stands.

[255] Reuter, *Germany*, pp. 194–5, summarises what little we do know. Late Carolingian texts, in par- ticular the capitulary of Quierzy of 877 (which stated that if any count died whilst Charles the Bald was in Italy his son was to succeed), and various accounts in the annals of individuals whose kin had held countships taking up arms against royal appointees, simply show that familial suc-

strate the inheritance of counties in fact shows the continuation of royal rights of appointment. Adalbert of Trier recorded the death of Count Odo, a nephew of Conrad I, in 949. Odo, we are told, had received royal permission that whatever benefices and offices he held were to be divided, in the manner of inheritance between sons.[256] What this account clearly shows is that the devolution of benefices and offices (*praefecturae*) remained in the ultimate control of the king: hence the need for royal permission. Indeed, the idea of inheritance is introduced as a simile: Odo's benefices and offices are to be treated *as if* (*quasi*) they were transmitted thus. This underlines the fact that neither benefices nor offices were yet seen as being part of the normal mechanisms of inheritance. In some sense counties remained public offices, but ones in which family control was acknowledged as, in the normal run of things, uncontested and incontestable.

It was this reduced room for manoeuvre so far as local office went that made the maintenance of royal control over the church such an important aspect of Ottonian kingship. Rights to make appointments to bishoprics, which as have seen were important to the Carolingians, were assiduously maintained. Indeed, the Ottonians have often been portrayed as pursuing a conscious policy of the imposition of 'court' candidates to key bishoprics to create a network of royal servants in the localities who, allegedly, served as a counterweight to aristocratic localism. In some cases – the classic example is the appointment of Otto I's half-brother, Bruno, as archbishop of Cologne and Conrad the Red's successor as *dux* of Lotharingia – there may be some truth in such a view. But to paint bishops as loyal royal servants lined up against an embedded and restive aristocracy would be mistaken. Loyal bishops were a necessity, but to be effective a bishop also needed to be accepted locally, which usually meant local roots, and the social background of bishops and counts may have normally differed little. Bishops, even where they exercised considerable secular power, were not bulwarks against the aristocracy, but a part of local aristocratic society. The *Life* of Burchard, appointed bishop of Worms in 999, shows the workings of royal policy neatly. Burchard was a member of an aristocratic family from Hesse which specialised in pro-

cession was the norm, as it always had been, not that inheritance was established. We would do well to look at work on post-conquest England which has stressed the complexity of a system in which ancestral rights and notions of family honour led to the pursuit of claims even where no formal law of succession was established: cf. J. C. Holt, 'Property and Politics in Early Medieval England', *P&P* 57 (1972), 3–52.

[256] This is my paraphrase of Adalbert's account: 'Udo comes obiit, qui permissu regis quicquid beneficii aut praefecturarum quasi hereditatem inter filios divisit': s.a. 949, ed. Kurze, p. 164. On the interpretation of this passage, see Jackman, *Criticism and Critique*, esp. pp. 19–21, with bibliography and discussion of other works.

ducing bishops, and was thus educated in the best circles and gained royal
favour; when his predecessor died in 999, Otto III first granted Worms
to Burchard's kinsman Franco, and on Franco's death called for Burchard.
This was not a radically different strategy from that of the Carolingians,
and, again like their Carolingian predecessors, the Ottonians used royal
abbeys to add to episcopal muscle. Bruno of Cologne, for example,
received Lorsch to facilitate his position in the middle Rhine. Bishops
were significant as kings had more initiative in their appointment than
was the case with counts, and so here the Ottonians could attempt to
shape the contours of local politics.[257]

If we want the flavour of the Ottonian system, we need once again to
turn to the local evidence of the charters. One *placitum* concerning
Lorsch's interests gives a vivid glimpse of the exercise of political power
in the localities in the middle of the tenth century. One Gerold and his
wife Idibirga gave property at Wattenheim and Heddesheim in the
Lobdengau 'into the hands' of four named individuals, with complex
instructions regarding its ultimate fate. On Gerold's death the
Wattenheim property was to pass to the brethren of St Peter's at Worms
and that at Heddesheim to Lorsch, in alms for Gerold, Idibirga, their *parentes* and their lord, Count Conrad. Gerold and Idibirga's rather precise
instructions had evidently been given orally: when dispute arose following Gerold's death, it did not turn on documents but on oral testimonies,
and the transmitted record reads as the findings of this first hearing, *c.* 940.
The structure of this hearing is revealing: the advocates of St Peter and
St Nazarius (the former one of Gerold's four 'trustees') contested 'in the
public court (*mallus*) at Ladenburg, in the presence of Count Conrad'.
Seven witnesses swore to the validity of the transaction.[258] The two
parties, in the persons of the bishop of Worms and the abbot of Lorsch,

[257] On the Ottonian *Reichskirche* see T. Reuter, 'The "Imperial church system" of the Ottonian and
Salian rulers: A Reconsideration', *Journal of Ecclesiastical History* 33 (1982), 347–74, with refer-
ences to earlier work, and the response of J. Fleckenstein, 'Problematik und Gestalt der ottonisch-
salischen Reichskirche', in K. Schmid (ed.), *Reich und Kirche vor dem Investiturstreit. Festschrift G.
Tellenbach* (Sigmaringen, 1985), pp. 83–98, and more recently R. Schieffer, 'Der ottonische
Reichsepiskopat zwischen Königtum und Adel', *Frühmittelalterliche Studien* 23 (1989), 291–301.
More is needed on royal exploitation of monasteries and on continuity and changes from
Carolingian church management. For Burchard, see *Vita Burchardi episcopi*, ed. G. Waitz, MGH
SS 4, pp. 829–46, cc. 3–5, pp. 833–5, and W. Metz, 'Zur Herkunft und Verwandtschaft Bischof
Burchards I von Worms', *Hessisches Jahrbuch für Landesgeschichte* 26 (1976), 27–42. For Bruno, see
above all Ruotger, *Vita Brunonis*, ed. I. Ott, MGH SRG (Weimar, 1953): the key text on the
Reichskirche.

[258] It is not clear how these seven are able to swear as they are not the four 'trustees' nor are they
mentioned in the initial account of Gerold and Idibirga's gift as sureties or witnesses. On numbers
of witnesses compare *Lex Ribuaria*, c. 59.1 (sales), 60.1 (gifts), ed. Eckhardt, pp. 60, 62–3 respectively. On numbers of witnesses and law, see H. Fichtenau, 'Forschungen über
Urkundenformeln. Ein Bericht', *MIÖG* 94 (1986), 285–339 esp 329.

were present as were forty-four other witnesses 'who saw and heard in the public court'. Count Burchard headed the list of those watching the contest. *Circa* 960, a new bishop and abbot reopened the case, perhaps in a ceremonial reaffirmation of the previous agreement. Contesting each other's testimony, they saw and heard the record (*traditio*) of the previous judgement. A dozen named men judged on the case this second time.[259] The legal context of this second judgement is more obscure: the *placitum* stresses the presence of bishop and abbot but not count, and names fifteen witnesses. The transmitted document was produced as a record of this second hearing and the case's prehistory. Its final clause was designed to underline the legitimacy of the judgement: 'Enacted in the county of Count Conrad, in the *pagus* of the Lobdengau, in the presence of these *scabini* [20 names follow]'.[260] Ladenburg, as we have already seen, was a 'public city', serving here by the tenth century as the focal point of a 'county'. This case ultimately proceeded according to the Carolingian version of Frankish law. More significantly, it was settled by a series of collective decisions witnessed and affirmed by an assembled community of free property-holders – just as disputes had been settled in the area for centuries. It can be placed alongside a series of other charters which show the continued vitality of local collective action, and the continued importance of the free property-holder as the backbone of society. Thus, when Lorsch was given property rights by Conrad I in 917, their boundaries were established by Count Liutfrid and his *fideles*.[261] Of course, local collective action could be manipulated by the powerful, and Count Conrad, the bishop of Worms and the abbot of Lorsch all clearly attempted to influence the decision made over Gerold's property, with varying degrees of success. This, in itself, was nothing new; the form of the transaction, the forum and processes through which the dispute was handled were traditional. If counts were less dependent on royal favour than previously, there is no sign that the basis of their local power had undergone 'patrimonialisation' or 'privatisation'. Their position remained that of the president of public meetings held according to local tradition.

THE TRANSFORMATION OF THE EARLY MEDIEVAL POLITY

Ending any historical narrative involves distortion: writing a stop implies finding a fixed point of stasis towards which previous developments have

---

[259] Again a significant number in both Roman and Frankish law: *Lex Ribuaria*, c. 60.1, p. 62 demands a dozen witnesses for a 'large' transaction. Was the case reopened so as to get the correct number of witnesses? Or to have a written record made of the judgement?   [260] *CL*532.

[261] *CL*65. Cf. *CDF*675 for comital justice in the area around Fulda dispensed on public meetings, *CDF*692 for justice reached by collective decisions led by a *centurio* who was also Fulda's advocate.

inexorably been leading, but actual societies are not like that. The end of early medieval politics ought, if received views are correct, to be sudden, dramatic and easily identifiable. A long scholarly tradition, perhaps best known through the opening of Marc Bloch's *Feudal Society*, has seen the post-Carolingian period as marked by the rise of a new, intensely local-ised, form of lordship which rent earlier political structures asunder. The precise mechanics of the shift have varied from author to author, and from generation to generation: few now would see change occurring quite so early and dramatically as Bloch, with a social breakdown at the end of the ninth century caused by political division and Viking, Muslim and Magyar raiders, and new, 'feudal', structures growing organically from the ashes.[262] Since Georges Duby's brilliant study of the Mâconnais, and the subsequent series of regional monographs, we have learned to see a bastardised version of the Carolingian system continuing on a local level into the tenth century, before being swept away by a series of changes in the aristocracy at the very end of the tenth century. 'Feudal revolution' marks a fundamental shift in the nature of political and social power: the emergence of a 'private' lordship which was predatory on 'public' governmental structures, whose defining features were violence, vassals and castles, and which led to an increasingly clear social division between warriors and peasants, and a crystallisation of familial structures into lineages focused upon the devolution of the new-style lordship.[263] Although this interpretation was originally developed from France and the Mediterranean, similar forces have since been detected at work in Germany.[264] The causality of 'feudal revolution', even amongst its stu-dents, has been little explored. We have a whole range of different devel-opments – in social stratification, military technology, political power and family structure – tangled into a historiographical knot which is difficult to untie. 'Feudal revolution' has an undoubted intellectual appeal thanks to its sweeping logic, but it can easily become self-referential: each of its individual parts is explained with reference to the others, and difficult to question in isolation because of the complexity of the knots which tie them together.[265]

To query the seductive generality of the 'feudal revolution' is not to deny that politics was fundamentally transformed between the tenth and

---

[262] See M. Bloch, *Feudal Society*, 2 vols. (London, 1962).

[263] Duby, *La société*. For bibliography, including that of regional theses, see Poly and Bournazel, *The Feudal Mutation*.

[264] E.g. Boshof, 'Ottonen- und Salierzeit', esp. pp. 55–72; B. Arnold, *Princes and Territories in Medieval Germany* (Cambridge, 1991); cf. also the comments of T. Reuter, *P&P* 155 (1997), 187–95, with other contributions to the debate on 'The Feudal Revolution' in *P&P* 155 (1997).

[265] The forceful critique by Barthélemy, as voiced in 'La mutation féodale . . .?', is beginning to unravel some of these historiographical knots.

the twelfth centuries, nor to doubt that at the heart of this transformation lay the development of intensive and effectively independent forms of local lordship. As an explanatory device, 'feudal revolution' gets us to the right place, but it is not necessarily the only way there. There is a fundamental problem about where it starts, too: neither Duby, nor any of his successors, investigated the Carolingian system at work, on the ground. They conceptualised change in terms of an antithesis between Carolingian public institutions and feudal private lordship. The antithesis is attractively simple, but fundamentally mistaken: this study has shown that we cannot understand the Carolingian political system as a Heath Robinson prototype for the modern state, with institutions defined by kings and offices resting solely on delegated power. The changing nature of the evidence, indeed, makes drawing a true comparison between the ninth and eleventh centuries, and tracing the progress from one to the other, difficult in the extreme. In the middle Rhine the charters dry up in the tenth century before restarting, in a very different diplomatic tradition, at the end of the eleventh – a very different pattern of distribution to that more familiar to us, from areas like Duby's Mâconnais (where surviving documentation increases dramatically in the post-Carolingian period) – but one which still leaves real problems of tracing change.

Theorists of 'feudal revolution' see Carolingian structures eventually swept aside by raw aristocratic power. The recruitment of large bodies of armed followers and the erection of new, highly fortified residences created a monopoly of force and ushered in a new era of politics as personal lordship. There is even one source from the middle Rhine which, on a superficial reading, could be used to support such a thesis. The anonymous *Life* of Bishop Burchard of Worms, written for one of Burchard's successors after his death in 1025, paints a vivid picture of political struggle following Burchard's appointment in 1000. Worms was dominated by the *dux* Otto, son of Conrad the Red, from a walled fortress, complete with tower, from which Otto's men imposed a reign of terror, using their military muscle to impose themselves on the city, seizing church land and robbing the local population. Burchard, so we are told, was able to remove the threat of Otto, being made sole lord of the city as a condition of his support for the claim of Henry II for the throne, then demolishing Otto's *castellum* and freeing Worms from the 'iniquitous servitude' that Otto had placed on it (the *Life* omits to mention that the 'freedom' which Burchard created was freedom under the lordship of the bishop).[266] But before we proclaim a 'revolution of the year 1000' in Worms, we should pause. This literary account needs handling with care:

---

[266] *Vita Burchardi*, ed. Waitz, cc. 6–9, pp. 835–7.

Heinrich Fichtenau was correct to label it 'excellent . . . but highly misleading'.[267] It used a highly charged inherited rhetoric to attack Otto and
his men as *raptores*, who demolished the city's walls and left the population desolate, prey to wolves and brigands. These ill-doings fit the stereo-
type of the robber baron a little too easily. What was actually a conflict
for political control within Worms between count and bishop is dressed
up in terms of good against evil. Even if we redress this bias, the rhetoric of the text still colours the presentation of the political strategies used:
power becomes a matter of violence. This rhetorical colouring makes it
all too easy for us to simplify the process of political change.[268]

The documentary evidence from Burchard's and Otto's Worms in fact
suggests a very different picture. The city of Worms – a public centre
through which the region was ruled right through the early medieval
period – was vital to Otto's political system. He held royal rights in the
city from the king, in the same manner as his father; these allowed him
one-third of royal income from tolls and justice (the traditional prerogative of the Carolingian count) and control of minting. These rights presumably allowed him to dominate this public stage, which was so
important for the control of the surrounding areas. Although in 979 these
rights were handed over, at the king's command, to the bishop of Worms,
Otto's close relationship with Bishop Hildebold, a political ally at court,
allowed him to continue to dominate the city. The extent of Worms' and
Otto's rights in the woodlands to the south of the city were settled by a
series of exchanges in 992. Even under Burchard, Hildebold's successor,
Otto's relationship was not one of outright hostility: the author of
Burchard's *Vita* was writing with hindsight to paint his hero in the black
and white of hagiography. The royal charter in which Otto handed over
his residence and remaining rights in Worms is paired by a private charter
recording property transactions to supply an endowment for the church
which Burchard erected on the site of Otto's residence: this was a process
of political negotiation, and Otto's stature and pull in Worms and its hinterland clearly continued. What is striking throughout, though, is the
centrality of the city of Worms: controlling Worms was important
because the city remained a forum for local public action.[269]

This examination of the struggle for control of Worms underlines the
danger of invoking violence as a neat catch-all explanation for historical

---

[267] Fichtenau, *Living in the Tenth Century*, p. 429.
[268] Cf. Reuter, 'The "Feudal" Revolution', pp. 177–87.
[269] See Staab, 'Reich und Mittelrhein', esp. pp. 69–70, and for the relationship between Burchard
and Otto, see *MGH DHenry II* 20, *Urkundenbuch der Stadt Worms I*, ed. H. Boos (Worms, 1886),
no. 43 (twelfth-century interpolation of a genuine charter: see Staab, 'Reich und Mittelrhein',
p. 70, n. 42). For Otto's earlier dealings with Worms see *MGH DOtto II* 129 (rights in Worms);
DOtto III 9 and *DOtto III* 85 (woodlands).

change. Armed followings were not new, emerging out of the blue and carrying all before them. We have seen how violence – both 'horizontal', between rivals like Burchard and Otto, and 'vertical', as Otto allegedly used over the inhabitants of Worms – were common social practices long before the year 1000. It is therefore difficult to see how an alleged sudden irruption of political violence could suddenly transform society at the end of the millennium. The development of increasingly complex and costly fortifications, and the eventual emergence of the stone castle in the twelfth and thirteenth centuries, was a very gradual process. We certainly should not imagine that earlier medieval residences were undefended or unadorned. The problem is that before the raising of artificial mounds from the middle eleventh century, and the later adoption of stone for building, such residences are difficult to trace archaeologically. There is good documentary evidence for aristocratic compounds in eighth- and ninth-century Mainz and Worms, some fortified and some even with towers, and the charter evidence shows that the Carolingian aristocracy had dedicated rural residences. We should not assume that such complexes were undefended: in the denouement of the Lotharingian and Thuringian feuds they were capable of withstanding sieges, whilst there is charter evidence for the involvement of the local aristocracy in the building of *castra* as centres of public defence against Magyar raiders in the first half of the tenth century. Defensibility was scarcely a new concern of the post-Carolingian centuries. New styles of aristocratic residence emerge slowly, in a dialectic determined by idioms of status and the demands of military strategy. But, as we have seen, the charter evidence makes it crystal clear that the existence of such centres in the ninth and tenth centuries did not allow aristocrats to rule the localities as an adjunct to their households.

There are similar problems with seeing 'the growth of lordship' as the dynamo driving political and social change. Personal bonds between lords and followers do become increasingly visible in the documentation in the course of the tenth century. This is certainly not an indication of the imposition of lordship where previously there had been none, but it does suggest that personal lordship was becoming increasingly cohesive at law.[270] But the rules of the tenth-century political game were not necessarily dramatically different from those of the contests for local support through informal patronage suggested by the eighth- and ninth-century charters. Even the power of Otto, at the end of the millennium, rested on relatively familiar forms of patronage: control of the monasteries of Hornbach and Wissembourg, and the use of monastic lands, and estates

---

[270] Cf above, pp. 92–3.

granted by the king, to build up local networks of obligation.[271] The use of royal and ecclesiastical land to prime such networks was scarcely new; Otto was simply bidding for local support in a time-honoured fashion. The ultimate forum which processed local affairs remained the public meeting, and there is no indication that Otto's patronage was able to bypass it. The mid-tenth century dispute between the bishop of Worms and the abbot of Lorsch over the bequest of Gerold, which we discussed above, was settled by repeated hearings in the *mallus* at Ladenburg. Although the count who presided, Conrad, had an interest in the case as Gerold's erstwhile lord, this was an avowedly public occasion and the judgement rested on the findings of local *scabini* and on Frankish law. In 1012, Henry II referred simmering disputes, perhaps already evident in the case of Gerold, between Worms and Lorsch over the boundaries of their respective rights in the Odenwald to the judgement of local *scabini* under the leadership of the local count.[272]

In the eleventh century we can begin to detect the reification of power, as property rights came to envelop traditions of local public action. In 1023 Henry acknowledged the problems caused by continuing conflict between Lorsch and Worms, issuing a series of rules for the resolution of quarrels between the two *familie*, whilst shortly afterwards Bishop Burchard of Worms drew up a formal set of rules for the members of his *familia*. In these rules, local counts had a role to play, but the essential logic was one of the two groups making amends with one another: the *familia* was a legally-recognised, coherent unit, under lordly jurisdiction and largely abstracted, in legal terms, from the wider community.[273] In 1065, the members of Lorsch's *familia* – some legally free, others unfree dependants of the abbey who still enjoyed full property rights over inherited land as *ministeriales* – were cohesive enough to defend the abbey's rights by force, in opposition to royal commands.[274] By the twelfth century, lordly jurisdiction was not only personal, but territorial: lords exercised legal rights over the inhabitants of entire areas. The documentary evidence is so sparse that it is difficult to trace the contours of this development, but it marked a fundamental change in the nature of local power.

Carolingian counts ruled roughly territorial units, but their power was exercised through social groups and indigenous habits of collective action, and therefore ultimately defined by local structures of social

---

[271] Staab, 'Reich und Mittelrhein', pp. 66–71, and see *Liber Possessionum Wizenburgensis*, no. 311, a difficult late source discussed by Staab, 'Reich und Mittelrhein', p. 68, n. 33.

[272] CL532; *MGH DHenry II* 247.

[273] *MGH Const.* I, ed. L. Weiland, no. 35, pp. 78–81, no. 438, pp. 639–45.

[274] CLi:393, and see Arnold, *German Knighthood, 1050–1300* (Oxford, 1985), p. 112.

interaction. Local power structures became more formalised in the late Carolingian and Ottonian periods. The tendency of royal charters, from the mid-ninth century, to locate land within an individual's *comitatus* was first and foremost a change in formulae, but it reflected an increasing willingness to talk in jurisdictional terms, culminating in the development of free-standing geographical labels which existed independently of any individual's competence.[275] In the second half of the tenth century and the first half of the eleventh, 'counties' were solid enough to be discussed in the language of property law, as rulers gave the comital rights within particular counties to favoured churches. These gifts transferred the ultimate control of governmental rights, and the attendant revenues. Counts from the same families as their predecessors continued to run things on the ground, their jurisdiction now seen as a benefice held from the church.[276] Interestingly, it is during precisely the period in which such grants were made, in the decades around 1000, that we see Otto of Worms' counties similarly entrusted to loyal followers.[277] The very fact that such arrangements were possible underlines the fact that local power had reified into rights of jurisdiction and revenue, rights which could be treated as property and which were exercised territorially. The process parallels the development of ecclesiastical immunities, which in the tenth century increasingly came to be transformed into territorial jurisdictions, jurisdictions which eventually became likewise defined in terms of property, as a form of tenure.[278] Political power was no longer something embedded in a social context, to do with relationships to local social groups: it was reformulated as a thing in its own right, divorced from its social context.

The royal diplomata of the eleventh century give some idea of the new patterns of power which were emerging. They were not simply formal acknowledgements of shadowy but long-established traditional patterns. In the eleventh century the county of Stockstadt emerged in a large area of the Odenwald on the lower Main, a jurisdiction ultimately owned by the abbey of Fulda. Its basis was the woodland rights which had been appended to the *villa* of Umstadt, which had been given to Fulda in the middle of the eighth century. In the Carolingian period Fulda had property rights over the *villa* of Umstadt in its entirety, and forest rights,

---

[275] E.g. from the 880s documents begin to refer to the 'county of the Lobdengau': *MGH DCharles the Fat* 58, *MGH DArnulf* 30 and subsequently.

[276] H. Hoffmann, 'Grafschaften in Bischofshand', *DA* 46 (1990), 375–480, esp. 464–9.

[277] Staab, 'Reich und Mittelrhein', pp. 66–7.

[278] On immunities in the early middle ages, see W. Davies and P. Fouracre (eds.), *Property and Power in the Early Middle Ages* (Cambridge, 1995), esp. pp. 254–60; for advocacies, Boshof, 'Kirchenvogtei'.

essentially centring on the levying of customary dues, from the surrounding woodland. It was not an area which was home to a count or which could be described as a county. In the eleventh century this was transformed into a territorial unit of rule, a process confirmed by Henry II's gift of 'the county of Stockstadt' to Fulda, after which the abbey owned the royal *bannus* in the territory. The royal gift gave legal form to the territorial jurisdiction, but it may not have been constitutive of the new pattern of power, which rested on the assertion of ultimate political control within an area over which the monks had long held forest rights. Legal rights such as these provided the basis for political power in a new age of armed retinues and territorial power.[279]

Because of the lack of local charters, it is difficult to follow the processes by which such units were created. Although difficult, it is not impossible, thanks to the fact that Lorsch and Worms both resorted to the forgery of false Carolingian privileges to justify claims that they were pursuing in the latter part of the tenth century. Lorsch sought to transform its dominance of its immediate neighbourhood, like Fulda at Stockstadt using customary rights over woodland, allied to its long-standing immunity, as the vehicle to create a territorial jurisdiction. Lorsch's early endowment had centred on Charlemagne's gift of the *villa* of Heppenheim in 773; a *placitum* in 795 had met to confirm the extent of the woodland which pertained to this gift. Later Lorsch scribes rewrote the boundaries, expanding them to take in neighbouring areas where Lorsch's acquisition of landed property made it dominant. The efforts to assert lordship which must have inspired these claims lie behind the long quarrel between Lorsch and Worms, which sought to carve out a similar lordship in an overlapping area. The traces of a systematic effort at colonisation in the area by Lorsch, and reports of Lorsch's armed retainers coming to blows with those of Worms at the beginning of the eleventh century, give a clue as to how these claims were pursued. Like Fulda at Stockstadt, Lorsch eventually received a gift of the royal *bannus* within that part of the Odenwald which pertained to the *villa* of Bürstadt as the confirmation of its lordship.[280] Worms' forgeries were more elaborate

---

[279] See E. Kleberger, *Territorialgeschichte des hinteren Odenwaldes*, Schriften des Hessischen Amts für geschichtliche Landeskunde 26 (Darmstadt, 1958), pp. 12–15; Hoffmann, 'Grafschaften in Bischofshand', 394 and 460–1; *MGH DHenry II* 509. A record of the boundaries of land and woodland at neighbouring Michelstadt, given to Lorsch in 815, survives (*CL*21): here the 'abbot's stream' divides the 'Munitat' from the 'Grapschaft': whether this is, as it purports to be, a Carolingian document or a forgery reflecting a later stage in political development is a moot point.

[280] *CL*6a for the 795 *placitum*, with two versions of the boundary clause, one patently forged to justify claims *c.* 1000, the other not above suspicion but more conservative in its claims. There is a consensus that, leaving aside the boundaries, the record of the actual proceedings of the *placitum* is essentially genuine, although possibly reworked (no forger would have bothered to work out

still, concocted under Bishop Hildebold, who was also head of the royal chancery, and in this position worked up a series of purportedly Carolingian documents granting jurisdictional and other rights in a number of areas to Worms. Worms' primary objective was control of the lower Neckar, and in particular the area around Ladenburg, where Worms had enjoyed important interests since the seventh century. Hildebold's forgeries claimed control over markets, tolls and forest in the Ladenburg area: these rights together defined a territorial unit, which was confirmed in 1012 by Henry II's gift of the 'county of the Lobdengau' and the 'county of the Wingarteiba'.[281] Here the chronology of disputes over territorial boundaries offers a clue to the progress of political change. Grants which had been made under Charlemagne were reworked, and their boundaries became the object of dispute, in the second half of the tenth century, until their extent was finally settled following royal intervention in the first part of the eleventh century. These boundaries were the objects of dispute at this point because the way in which power was being exercised was undergoing important changes, with the emergence of legal rights of territorial control. The extent of these rights, which were effectively new, was what was at issue, and their final establishment in the eleventh century marks the consummation of a new order.

With the emergence of territorial units, power could begin to take on a patrimonial form. In 1012, when Lorsch and Worms had received royal privileges entrenching their territorial control, the precise boundaries of their respective territories had been agreed by a local count and the local *scabini* and *milites*. In spite of this first use of a new label of status, *miles* ('knight'), in the local material, these were traditional structures of local public action.[282] After 1012, however, charters no longer referred to a *pagus* or *comitatus* of the Lobdengau: jurisdiction in the area was now formally under the control of Worms, and cases heard in Worms' court at Ladenburg. Similarly, by 1071 Lorsch was holding three 'principal *malli*'

---

exactly which counts were at which stages in their careers and were close to which locals in 795, nor would a forger have placed the *placitum* in 795 rather than 773, or recited the prehistory of the Heppenheim estate). See H.-P. Lachmann, 'Die frühmittelalterlichen Marken zwischen Rhein und Odenwald unter besonderer Berücksichtigung der Mark Heppenheim', *Berichte zur deutsche Landeskunde* 49 (1975), 31–54 at p. 28. For tenth-century colonisation, H.-J. Nitz, 'The Church as Colonist: The Benedictine Abbey of Lorsch and Planned *Waldhufen* Colonisation in the Odenwald', *Journal of Historical Geography* 9 (1983), 105–26.; for quarrels with Worms, above p. 246 (and note CL532).

[281] For Hildebold's forgeries see Prinz, 'Das Bistum Worms'; Trautz, *Das untere Neckarland* is the best discussion of property holding and settlements in the area; see also Hoffmann, 'Grafschaften in Bischofshand', pp. 449–51. The two gifts are *MGH DHenry II* 226 (county of the Wingarteiba) and 227 (county of the Lobdengau).

[282] *MGH DHenry II* 247, and Büttner, 'Ladenburg am Neckar', 91.

a year for its *familia* at Leutersheim, which were presumably attended by the descendants of those *milites* and *scabini* whose land lay under Lorsch's jurisdiction. These meetings which were known in the vernacular as the *ungeboden ding*, one of the first uses of a phrase which was to have a long historiographical afterlife, were in the nineteenth century interpreted as an ancient, Germanic, tribal moot which survived into the medieval period. In fact, the idea of holding three courts a year comes straight from the Carolingian capitularies, but is here implemented as the locus of collective action within a territorial lordship.[283] The shift in patterns of power involved the acknowledgement of rights of jurisdiction within territorial units, units within which there might still be vigorous traditions of collective action, and which were certainly not wholly at the mercy of lordly whims. It was this change which left political power in the hands of the holders of territorial jurisdiction: holders whose family strategies, always pliable and ready to adjust to the realities of power, became increasingly centred on the transmission of terrritorial jurisdiction.[284]

The shift from informal central places defined by their social significance, to formal jurisdiction, marks the end of rule in its early medieval manifestation. It is a shift from power which remained, in important ways, personal and reciprocal, to power which was based on impersonal rights of command. In the eleventh century, as the *pagus* labels of the early middle ages disappeared, a new terminology emerged to reflect the new reality, as charters began to name the *dominus terrae*, the 'lord of the land'.[285] Political power was no longer embedded in social relationships: it had taken on the form of territorial jurisdiction. This did not come about because post-Carolingian lords were able physically to seize control of all the land in an area, or establish real ownership. It was the creation of formal rights of command, and the resultant definition of territorial jurisdictions within which they were exercised, which marked the end of early medieval politics, leading to important changes in the working of aristocratic family structures, and in notions of status. By the twelfth century, politics was played out through a jigsaw of property rights.

---

[283] *CL*131, and cf R. Schmidt-Weigand, 'Mallus, mallum', in A. Erler (ed.), *Handwörterbuch zur deutsche Rechtsgeschichte* (Berlin, 1971), II, cols. 217–18.

[284] There is a large bibliography on changing family structures, most of it concerned with France. For Germany, see the survey by Arnold, *Princes and Territories*, pp. 135–52, and the case-study by J. Freed, *The Counts of Falkenstein: Noble Self-Consciousness in Twelfth-Century Germany* (Philadelphia, 1984).

[285] The significance of the change is noted by B. Arnold, *German History, 500–1300* (London, 1997), pp. 73–5; see also his *Princes and Territories*, pp. 112–34, with references.

CONCLUSION: STATE AND SOCIETY IN THE EARLY MEDIEVAL WEST

We need to identify the peculiarities of the middle Rhenish experience before attempting comparison and generalisation. The middle Rhine valley was a region whose geopolitical profile underwent a series of dramatic changes between the late Roman period and the high middle ages, changes which affected the relationship of the region to the political centre. In this Roman frontier province political power was transformed by the Imperial infrastructure, which led to the foundation of fortified settlements as the central points of local society, an influx of men and resources in the army, and, in the fourth century, the physical proximity of the Emperor. Eventually, in the fifth century, the middle Rhine found itself cut off from the redistributive system of the Roman army and administration. A new power structure, which expressed itself in the idiom of a 'frontier culture' which had developed through the interaction of barbarian elites and the Roman military, had emerged by the sixth century. The change from Roman to post-Roman, the atrophy of institutionalised forms of power and the emergence of militarised rule which tapped the agrarian surplus directly, was far more abrupt here than elsewhere in Gaul. By 600, rulers began once again to be involved in the region directly; rulers based, as they had been in the fourth century, in northern Gaul, but increasingly interested in exploitation of the 'wild east', the provinces beyond the Rhine, and happy to stay at Worms and Mainz. In the second half of the eighth century, the final consolidation of Frankish royal power in the east placed the Rhine at the heart of Empire, a development consummated by the construction of magnificent palace complexes at Ingelheim and Frankfurt. The symbolic significance of these centres, and the geopolitical centrality of the region, meant that the middle Rhine remained a royal heartland to the end of the early medieval period and beyond.

Power relations in a royal heartland such as the Carolingian and Ottonian middle Rhine will, of course, have differed from those in a peripheral province in which kings were distant figures. But kings were not actors on local stages or in local politics even in regions where they liked to stay, as the rich middle Rhenish evidence makes crystal clear. Although they had favoured residences, kings were itinerant: the political centre was not geographically fixed, but sociologically constructed. Royal power therefore had a stage and audience which were truly regnal. The fact that the middle Rhine was a royal heartland must be borne in mind when offering generalisations based on developments in this region. But it does not invalidate attempts at generalisation: this is Carolingian politics as practised in the dynasty's own backyard, and as such offers an important comparison with the state of affairs in more peripheral regions. Similarly, the evidence for the transformation of political power in the post-Carolingian period is particularly valuable; if this is what happened where kings maintained their power in a more or less continuous Carolingian tradition, it can be usefully placed alongside the numerous studies of structural change in regions where kings ceased to go.

We must begin by admitting huge regional variation across western Europe in the post-Roman experience: the transformation of the Roman world was a series of intensely localised but closely linked processes. Prior to 700 the differing pace and experience of change makes any generalisation difficult: the sixth-century Merovingian Empire encompassed late antique municipalities at one extreme, and societies of free proprietors competing for local pre-eminence at the other. Although it is customary to draw the contrast in terms of differing degrees of Roman survival, we should not forget that even in the middle Rhine the Roman heritage was of fundamental importance. Northern frontier societies had never been that similar to Mediterranean cities even under Rome, and the patterns of local influence which emerged in the post-Roman period on the middle Rhine had clearly visible late Roman foundations. That is, the variation of local structures under Merovingian sway was not the result of differing degrees of disruption of a homogeneous *Romanitas* so much as an outgrowth of long extant patterns of regional diversity, long obscured by the binding force of the late Roman state. By 700, however, it is possible to identify a set of structural characteristics common to societies right across a vast swathe of western Europe, structural characteristics which continued to typify much of western Europe until the eleventh century. The identification of such structural characteristics should not obscure regional differences or negate the dramatic social and political changes which took place between 700 and 1100. But geographical and chronological diversity took place within certain broadly defined parameters which marked them off from both the world of the late Roman state, and the systems of proprietorial jurisdiction over land and people which developed in the eleventh century.

First, early medieval societies were characterised by the centrality of direct control over land. Tenurially, there was very little complexity: possession was normally equated with ownership and property rights over land were manifest. The powerful did not, of course, work their land themselves, and they developed a variety of strategies to control those who laboured for them. Although these strategies most often involved peasant families, some free but most unfree, feeding themselves as well as working the lord's land, labour was effectively tied to the land: these were not negotiable tenures worked for profit. Other than through the exploitation of land they themselves owned, the powerful had few opportunities to tap the agrarian surplus. What 'administration' and 'lordship' that there was impinged relatively lightly on peasant labour and produce, taking the form of customary levies on large areas, in some areas based on late Roman practices fossilised on a local level, in others, like the middle Rhine, more hybrid forms.

Second, as a result of the centrality of land to politics, kings had only a limited impact on local communities. Royal resources were essentially limited to the ownership of land, and were used to feed the royal household, with any 'surplus' holdings being granted out, in a variety of forms, to aristocrats in return for political support. Although kings did maintain control over tolls, there was no central finance system which tapped routinely the agrarian surplus or funded activities beyond the royal household. Where the Roman tax system survived, it did so in local hands, as local dues all but indistinguishable from rent. The absence of routine mechanisms for interaction between the political centre and the localities did not, however, preclude considerable structural power on the part of the centre. This structural power was created by the ability of the centre to intervene in the localities on exceptional but essential occasions. The centre could thus manipulate and canalise essentially local processes to ensure that its strategic goals – the recruitment and supply of armies, the maintenance of roads, bridges and palaces – were met. This is precisely the point that those who argue for a maximalist view of early medieval states miss. Rightly impressed by the organisational capacity of early medieval kings, they assume that it must have been achieved through the types of administration with which we are familiar, when in fact it rested on an entirely different style of consensus-based politics which worked through extant social mechanisms. The Carolingian capitularies need to be read in this light: they were neither mere royal wish-lists nor administrative records pure and simple, but instruments of power which worked through an exhortatory rhetoric, enabling political leaders to meet royal demands in the localities.

This leads us to the third structural characteristic. Power in the localities was exercised through autonomous patterns of collective action, resting on the mobilisation of local groups. Those who ruled in the localities did so by exercising influence through the grain of these patterns, not by command or edict. Cities, bishoprics and monasteries determined the topography of collective action. Control of bishoprics and monasteries was thus central to local power. They were institutions embedded in the localities with which both local and central leaders brokered relationships in the pursuit of political power.

Finally, because of the significance of possession of land, the lack of a centralised political infrastructure, and the self-determination of local communities, political power was diffuse and indirect, based on influence not control. Rule worked through an elite which stood at the apex of local communities, and bound them to the centre. This elite was largely drawn from those communities, and even when it included newcomers despatched from the centre, they had to put down local roots based on land and patronage. That is, although those with local power presented themselves as office-holders, to be effective they needed to build up local purchase. Political power rested on brokerage and patronage, and contained a strong element of reciprocity.

PUBLIC AND PRIVATE, STATE AND SOCIETY

We think of government as a process with its own dedicated space, institutions and rules, reifying a whole complex of discrete power-acts into a single imagined whole.[1] Early medieval politics likewise had a sphere of legitimate ruling action, a political centre which was functionally equivalent to the modern state, but whose location and inner logic were wholly different. Focused on the royal household (the court) and the person of the king, early medieval political action was dominated by the sociability of the ruling elite, in prayer, at table, and on horseback.[2]

---

[1] See P. Abrams, 'Notes on the Difficulty of Studying the State', *Journal of Historical Sociology* 1 (1988), 58–89, for the state as reification; a similar perspective to M. Foucault, 'Governmentality', in G. Burchell, C. Gordon and P. Miller (eds.), *The Foucault Effect: Studies in Governmentality* (Chicago, 1991), pp. 87–104, who usefully problematises the history of government.

[2] Cf. Nelson, 'Public Histories and Private History', 208, stressing that this sphere fulfils the sociological criteria which allow us to analyse it as a 'public domain'; T. Reuter, 'The Making of England and Germany, 850–1050: Patterns of Comparison and Difference', in A. P. Smyth (ed.), *Medieval Europeans* (Basingstoke, 1998), pp. 53–70 at p. 62, for praying, feasting and hunting as the

Historians all too easily assume that the creation of bureaucratic institutions, defined by the king and manned by dedicated, full-time, salaried state servants, is the commonsensical form of political organisation, at which medieval rulers were aiming all along. Early medieval politics, however, was an activity which was defined by inter-personal relationships within the ruling class, rather than one defined in terms of 'governmentality', the management of a bureaucratic machine to meet defined ends. We cannot, that is, take the goals of early medieval politics as the type of institution building we see as a norm, precisely because early medieval political systems were configured differently from those of the modern world.

There are, indeed, severe problems in characterising early medieval political systems as 'states'. This is precisely because statehood is essentially a modern concept coined to describe modern forms of depersonalised political organisation which differ radically from their historical predecessors. Ultimately, whether one puts early medieval political organisations into a box labelled 'states' is an issue for the taxonomist: it depends on what criteria one uses to define statehood. Indeed, such discussions can all too easily fall into the trap of seeing all past politics in modern, bureaucratic and institutional terms, and create a teleology with the modern state as the manifest destiny of historical development. We must not ignore the complex processes by which systems of political power have mutated over time, nor see the 'state' as a timeless concept simply waiting to be invented. Early medieval polities were emphatically not bundles of administrative structures claiming sovereign power. They did, however, define the legitimate exercise of power within given areas, and claim monopolies on strategically important forms of political assertion; they cohered over time and space, too, in spite of the inevitably changing fortunes of individual kingdoms.[3]

The long-established historiographical tendency to see the timeless objective of rulers, always and everywhere, as the creation of a centralised state administered through bureaucratic institutions, has encouraged generations of scholars to view early medieval history in terms of the opposition between 'public' and 'private' power – the former a Good

central practices in early medieval politics. For the anachronism involved in viewing medieval governmentality from the perspective of the modern state, see most recently T. Reuter, 'The Medieval German *Sonderweg*? The Empire and its Rulers in the High Middle Ages', in A. J. Duggan (ed.), *Kings and Kingship in the Middle Ages* (London, 1993), pp. 179–211, and, in the context of a centralised late medieval state, G. L. Harriss, 'Political Society and the Growth of Government in Late Medieval England', *P&P* 138 (1992), 26–57.

[3] S. Reynolds, 'The Historiography of the Medieval State', in M. Bentley (ed.), *Companion to Historiography* (Oxford, 1997), pp. 117–38 reaches a similar conclusion in a useful discussion; see also T. F. X. Noble, *The Republic of St. Peter* (Philadelphia, 1984), pp. 325–36.

Thing identified with kings, the latter a Bad Thing exemplified by the aristocracy. Privileging public vs. private as an interpretative modality creates ahistorical contrasts between order and disorder, harmony and conflict, as the self-image of the modern state as the only guarantor of social peace is read back into the middle ages. Periods of crisis at the political centre have thus normally been seen as necessarily and naturally marked by social disorder – an ingrained assumption which is now challenged both by the empirical evidence and by historiographical worries about the equation of state and social order.[4] The public–private dichotomy also encourages us to separate 'state' and 'society', and to see 'government' as a series of institutions and activities defined by the political centre: this is problematical in a world where the act of ruling cannot be distinguished from the more or less homeostatic processes of social regulation in the localities.[5]

We should avoid assuming that modern understandings of public and private translate unproblematically into the early medieval world. It certainly is anachronistic and highly misleading to postulate a timeless realm of 'private life', the domestic and familial, and to assume that this imagined 'private realm' subsumes the political in societies, like that of the early middle ages, when, most of the time, political relationships were thought about and described in patrimonial terms.[6] There was, however, a rhetoric of public and private status deployed by Carolingian political commentators. It emerged in the first decades of the ninth century, as part of a concerted attempt to understand the Frankish Empire as a Christian *res publica*.[7] The language of the 'public' suffuses this discourse: one ninth-century historian identified the 'iron yoke' with which Charlemagne had forced the aristocracy to respect the public good with the Biblical 'royal road', but tellingly made it a 'royal and public road'.[8]

---

[4] This is implicit in several strands of recent research trying to look at society 'from the bottom up'; it is put very pointedly by J. L. Nelson, 'Kings with Justice, Kings without Justice: An Early Medieval Paradox', *Settimane* 44 (1996), 797–825.

[5] See Bisson, 'The "Feudal" Revolution', with the comments of D. Barthélemy, T. Reuter, S. D. White and C. J. Wickham in the subsequent debate, *P&P*, 152, 155 (1997). See also the trenchant comments of J. L. Nelson in her review of *The Peace of God*, ed. T. Head and R. Landes, *Speculum* 61 (1994), pp. 163–9.

[6] As is argued by G. Duby, 'Private Power, Public Power', in Duby (ed.), *A History of Private Life II: Revelations of the Medieval World*, trans. A. Goldhammer (London, 1988), pp. 3–31 and in the introduction to P. Veyne (ed.), *A History of Private Life I: From Pagan Rome to Byzantium*, trans. A. Goldhammer (London, 1987). J. L. Nelson, 'The Problematic in the Private', *Social History* 15 (1990), 355–65, gives a devastating critique, and, most recently, M. De Jong, 'What was "Public"about Public Penance?' For a regional survey of the use of the word 'public' in early medieval sources see Genicot, '*Publicus*'.

[7] P. Depreux, 'Nithard et la *res publica*: un égard critique sur le règne de Louis le Pieux' *Médiévales* 22–3 (1992), 149–61.

[8] Nithard, *Historiae* IV:7, ed. Lauer, p. 144. See De Jong, 'What was "Public"?', p. 896.

Conclusion: state and society in the early medieval west

The central theme was the need for enlightened concern for the public good. One of Louis the Pious' biographers used a set piece dialogue between the young Louis and Charlemagne to discuss the relationship between the public good and individual self-interest. Charlemagne was horrified at the frugality of Louis' household, and:

> [Louis] told that one who held the name of lord may in fact be left without anything, on account of the private cares of each of the *proceres*, perversely neglectful of the public, until the public was transformed into the private.[9]

The episode was related to the inability of royal resources in Aquitaine to sustain the household of the boy-king Louis, thanks to aristocratic sticky fingers. The author did not see a transformation of public *power* into private *power*. There was no free-standing sphere of private action into which governmental or political power could be withdrawn. Louis' household had become so unroyal that it resembled that of one without public power: he had the name, but not the substance, of king. There are a series of parallel passages. One historian, writing about the deposition of Louis the Pious in 833, could write that:

> Louis was deprived of his rule as Emperor (*a suis imperio privatur*) and given into private custody (*privatus custodiae traditur*).[10]

Note the close connection between deprivation and the private. The latter was not defined in relation to any private sphere. Rather, a private individual was one who did not have the *fides publica* invested in him, who was not involved in public affairs.[11] Another Carolingian historian recounted the deeds of two soldiers who had campaigned with Charlemagne, and drew a contrast between their initial status as 'private men' and their transformation into public figures after receiving endowments (one of land, one of office) from the Emperor.[12] One could be transformed from being a private to a public figure through involvement in public politics, but one could not be a public man with a private life. There was a publicness which attaches itself to the wielders of political power: a point underlined by the vernacular vocabulary, where the linkages between publicness, rule and lordship are manifest. Political power

---

[9] Astronomer, *Vita Hludovici*, c. 6, ed. E. Tremp, *MGH SS* 64 (Hanover, 1995), p. 302: 'dicetque ab illo, quia privatis studens quisque primorum, neglegens autem publicorum, perversa vice, dum publica vertuntur in privata, nomine tenus dominus, factas sit pene omnium indignus'. The best, and only extensive, discussion of Carolingian ideas of public–private is Schlesinger, *Die Entstehung der Landesherrschaft*, pp. 110–27, in which this passage plays an important role.
[10] Regino, *Chronicon*, s.a. 838 [sic], ed. Kurze, p. 74, and see the comments of Goetz, '*Regnum*', p. 165, n. 176.   [11] Le Jan, *Famille et Pouvoir*, p. 122, citing the capitulary evidence.
[12] Notker, *Gesta Karoli Magni*, II:10, ed. Haefele, p. 67. Cf. ibid. pp. 67–8 (on 'private' and royal benefactors). Cf. also Einhard, *Vita Karoli*, c. 26, ed. Holder-Egger, p. 31, on chaplains at Aachen being given 'public' vestments.

was understood as a God-given personal role, a *ministerium*, which one had to fulfil to get to Heaven. This was not an administrative function, but a pastoral vocation which informed one's conduct in its entirety.[13]

Carolingian receptions of the Roman law public:private distinction underline the lack of a clear, free-standing concept of the private: it was used in rhetorical contexts as part of couplets or triplets, stressing scope and breadth ('whether public or private' and so on).[14] Private was not even the most common defining opponent of public: the Carolingian idea of 'public law' was defined in contradistinction to the law of the church, and drew on an opposition between the secular and ecclesiastical, indeed, between the terrestrial and the heavenly.[15] If distinctions between public and private selves only become necessary when one encounters relatively impersonal social structures, distinctions between public and private power are likely to occur where government works through a concrete set of institutions set over and above 'society', which was not the case in the early middle ages. Carolingian usage is comparable to that of early modern England, with private as that which was special, privileged or protected.[16]

Any dichotomy between 'public' and 'private' power is, ultimately, unhelpful. It maps very poorly onto early medieval political structures. Political change, for example, has often been viewed as a struggle between 'private' and 'public' forms of power (read: aristocrats and kings). When the aristocracy find themselves in effective control of local political structures, the modern notion of 'privatisation' is habitually adopted as a metaphor. Yet 'privatisation' is the transfer of tasks carried out by the publicly-funded administrative actions of the modern state to a private sector independent from the state: a fundamental transformation of the location of ruling activity which quite simply could not happen in the early middle ages, when there was no dedicated administrative infrastructure from which governmental activity could be removed. A horse-riding, weapon-carrying aristocracy enjoyed a monopoly on political power at a local level even in the periods of royal strength.

---

[13] H. H. Anton, *Fürstenspiegel und Herrscherethos in der Karolingerzeit*, Bonner Historische Forschungen 32 (Bonn, 1968), esp. pp. 404–14; O. Guillot, 'Une *ordinatio* méconnue: Le Capitulaire de 823/5', in P. Godman and R. Collins (eds.), *Charlemagne's Heir: New Perspectives on the Reign of Louis the Pious (814–40)* (Oxford, 1990), pp. 455–86; J. Fried, 'Der karolingische Herrschaftsverband im 9. Jahrhundert zwischen "Kirche" und "Könighaus"', *Historische Zeitschrift* 235 (1982), 1–43; Goetz, '*Regnum*'; T. Zotz, 'In Amt und Würden. Zur Eigenart "offizieller" Positionen im früheren Mittelalter', *Tel Aviver Jahrbuch für deutsche Geschichte* 22 (1993), 1–23.
[14] On the reception of the Roman law distinction of public and private in ecclesiastical sources see H. Müllejans, *Publicus und privatus im römishcen Recht und im älteren kanonischen Recht* (Munich, 1961).   [15] Köbler, *Das Recht*, pp. 68–70, 93, 141.
[16] Cf. R. Sennett, *The Fall of Public Man* (Cambridge, 1974), p. 16.

We clearly cannot invoke dedicated royal institutions, or agents whose position was wholly defined by the centre, as a norm which we expect to find wherever and whenever we look. The characteristic practices of early medieval kingship – for example, the cultivation of charisma through ceremonial or the political integration of regions through itineracy – cannot be seen as substitutes for 'missing' governmental institutions, precisely because historically they were prior. Rulers did not adopt them because of weakness, or because of their 'archaic' modes of thought, but because they worked. Whilst underlining the qualitative differences between early medieval forms of political organisation and those of later periods, we must also acknowledge the degrees of coherence and effectiveness that early medieval polities could reach. It is all too easy to dismiss the early middle ages as a customary, ritualised, oral and thus stateless Other. Engaging with the early medieval evidence forces us to realise that it was far from self-evident for rulers to have developed these new forms of government, which may in the long term have led to greater concentration of political power, but in the short-term were also contested and disruptive.

INTERPRETING THE EARLY MEDIEVAL WEST

Early medieval politics was defined by the mediating role of the aristocracy as the interface between the political centre and the localities. We therefore cannot see politics as a struggle between king and aristocracy, the former representing centralisation, the latter fragmentation. At the level of local power, royal and aristocratic interests were not distinct, but inter-related in a complex and evolving relationship. If we confine ourselves to the political centre, we may be able to detect changes in the relationship between king and aristocracy, but the system as a whole required symbiosis between king and aristocracy. Political power was not one-dimensional. The metaphor of a balance of power between king and aristocracy, implying that as one side increases its power so the other side must experience an equal and opposite decrease, is misleading precisely because we are not measuring two discrete and separate forms of power in competition with one another, but attempting to assess ultimate control of a kind of power which encompassed both king and aristocracy. In other words, the struggle for political power was not a zero-sum game.

There was a dialectic between royal and aristocratic control within the context of a cumulative, but not steady, accretion of power in the localities. Up to the seventh century, kings meddled with the localities so far as their abilities and resources allowed them, but local power remained a matter of personal influence. The position of the aristocracy as the point of interaction between locality and centre became increasingly solidified in the course of the seventh century. The build-up of supra-regional contacts and holdings necessitated the inclusion of the aristocracy at the political centre, whilst control of bishoprics and the foundation of rural monasteries embedded the aristocracy at the apex of local communities. The centre held, if only because regional power was nowhere so assured that it could be exercised without allying with neighbouring elites. But it only just held, and the decades around 700 were a real high point in unmediated aristocratic power. The coming of the Carolingians initially simply increased the power of many aristocratic groupings, as they extended their interests thanks to Carolingian patronage. But by the second half of the eighth century, and into the first decades of the ninth, the Carolingians rewrote the rulebook, establishing royal lordship over the church and redefining aristocratic local dominance in terms of office. The *pax Karolina* was founded on royal control of the points of contact between centre and locality.

Carolingian reform was not an attempt to centralise, or to build a precursor to the modern state. It was a remarkably successful attempt to restructure power in the localities, which both increased the extent of aristocratic power and placed it within parameters defined by kings. Carolingian problems in the ninth century did not result from partition or royal weakness, but from the inherent complexity of the system. With the necessity of catering for more than one adult male Carolingian in the ninth century, the demands placed on royal goodwill increased dramatically, as did the competition for both royal and aristocratic power. In the last decades of the ninth century, and the first of the tenth, the resulting aristocratic insecurity reached such a level that the mechanisms which had bound all aristocratic factions into the system failed, not least because of the sudden decrease in the sources and availability of royal patronage. Hence the series of sudden incandescent bursts of open conflict over the distribution of power as the relationship between centre and locality was renegotiated. The end result was a tacit recognition of the right of aristocratic families to enjoy the spoils of office as defined by the Carolingian system undisturbed, unless they provoked kings: royal control rested on the church, and on the ability to manipulate the calculus of aristocratic honour. Whereas in some regions – notably southern France and Italy – royal authority gradually withered away whilst the aristocracy continued to exercise Carolingian-style local power, in the middle Rhine a similar aristocratic monopoly on local power was perfectly compatible with the continuation of kingship. Although the political system was now less complex (and correspondingly more stable), from a local perspective what was noticeable was the consolidation of power in the Carolingian style. It was only slowly that new, more intensive systems of local power crystallised. This did not, of course, end the significance of consensus and association as political tactics, or the beginnings of the modern state, but it changed the rules of the game fundamentally: political power was institutionalised in formal rights of command.

If we wish to understand the development of political power, we need to focus on the points of contact between centre and locality.[17] The Roman state had supplied an infrastructure of office which enabled those endowed with it to control a system of surplus expropriation, and thus defined local political power within the framework of the Imperial state. The post-Roman period in the west saw the atrophy of this infrastructure, and correspondingly of the public domain of political discourse which had defined local power in relation to the state: immediately post-Roman states in many areas maintained elements of the Roman taxation system, and of local office, but the new realities of militarised political power defined in ethnic terms made them a thing of the past by the seventh century. Had the infrastructure of the state survived even in the loosest form, the local elite would have inherited a system of local dominance, but also remained dependent on the political centre for that local dominance, which might have been defined in terms of tax law, office, or state control of land. As it was, the state could not define the terms of local power, but without an inherited state infrastructure local elites lacked a regular method of surplus extraction and so had to build up their power through the manipulation of personal relationships and social loyalties; the public domain therefore came to be defined by patterns of elite sociability, rather than the legitimacy of the state. Kings and elites were bound together because both lacked an institutional basis for the exercise of local power, and so both dominated socially rather than administratively, and exercised their domination on an extensive stage that they shared. This is why early medieval polities continued to be extensive: after the fifth- and sixth-century fragmentation of the western Roman

---

[17] I have learnt much from a fascinating debate about the nature of South Asian polities before the impact of the west: see S. Subrahmanyam, 'Aspects of State Formation in South India and Southeast Asia, 1500–1650', *Indian Economic and Social History Review* 23 (1986), 357–77; J. Heitzman, 'State Formation in South India, 850–1280', *Indian Economic and Social History Review* 24 (1987), 35–61; J. Heitzman, 'Ritual Polity and Economy: The Transactional Network of an Imperial Temple in Medieval South India', *Journal of the Economic and Social History of the Orient* 34 (1991), 23–54; J. Mayaram, 'Mughal State-formation: The Mewati Counter-perspective', *Indian Economic and Social History Review* 34 (1997), 169–98. J. H. Kautsky, *The Politics of Aristocratic Empires* (Chapel Hill, 1982), stresses the problems of applying modern notions of centralisation to pre-modern polities run by local elites; cf. Harriss, 'Political Society', for a stimulating discussion of precisely this problem in the highly-governed example of late medieval England.

Empire around barbarian warlords who came to define their dominions as ethnic units, politics on an Imperial scale did re-emerge, albeit an Imperial politics whose geopolitics were different from those of late Rome.[18]

Political power was thus concentrated in the hands of those individuals who mediated between locality and centre. The brokers between the political systems of centre and locality could not, by definition, stand wholly inside either system. They therefore exercised a power which was essentially embodied in their person, encompassing two discrete power networks. Theirs was a power willingly given up by their local clients, who needed solutions to problems that everyday local systems could not resolve, and sought contact with the distant sources of ultimate legitimacy. It frequently became a power which was charismatic in the sense that it became endowed and informed by the sacred. Hence the significance of the church as a hinge between the locality and the centre, and the sacralisation of aristocratic power in the seventh century. Carolingian reform attempted to prevent the development of an exclusively aristocratic charisma, and to replace it with a king-centred descending hierarchy of divinely-ordained *ministerium*. This was an attempt to reintroduce a public discourse about office which would redefine local power in a framework set out by the centre; it was a first step towards reworking the interdependence of central and local power as a matter of public law. It was in redefining this relationship that literacy became significant in Carolingian politics. In the ninth century, the Carolingians succeeded in creating a system in which politics was centred on the endowment and removal of *honores*. But the crisis of the decades around 900 resulted in the aristocracy establishing a *de facto* monopoly on local power as redefined by the Carolingians. Local power was formalised, expressed in terms that were no longer personal but abstract and routine.[19] That this formalisation took place under an aristocratic monopoly resulted in the expression of rights of command in terms of

---

[18] Cf. the comments of C. Wickham, 'The Uniqueness of the East', *Journal of Peasant Studies* 12 (1985), 166–96; H. Berktay, 'Three Empires and the Societies they Governed: Iran, India and the Ottoman Empire', *Journal of Peasant Studies* 18 (1991), 242–63, and J. F. Haldon, *The State and the Tributary Mode of Production* (London, 1993). My perspective on the Frankish state differs from Wickham's discussion of the early medieval west, and from Haldon's discussion of the Franks at pp. 201–15; but like them, I am attempting to explain how the state:elite relationship in the early medieval west differed from that in other pre-industrial empires. For a perspective close to mine see Fouracre, 'Cultural Conformity and Social Conservatism'.

[19] The classic theoretical treatment of this process is M. Weber, *Wirtschaft und Gesellschaft* (4th edition, Tübingen, 1963), II, pp. 662–79; trans. W. G. Runciman, *Weber: Selections* (Cambridge, 1978), pp. 226–50. See also S. N. Eisenstadt, *Max Weber: On Charisma and Institution-building* (London, 1968), with a useful introduction stressing the importance of mediation between different power networks.

property law: the jurisdictional and proprietorial were inextricably inter-twined in the hands of the aristocracy.[20]

Early medieval polities, that is, were above all concerned with the reproduction of a ruling elite. Royal power rested on the ability of kings to manipulate this process so as to shape the ruling elite it wanted, aris-tocratic power on the ability to secure local dominance through plugging securely into the royal court. This mutual interdependence was to have long-term implications of the utmost importance. It left the political centre unable to define the realities of local power. Even the Carolingian discourse of *ministerium* was essentially moral, rather than administrative, in its logic. It aimed at informing the conduct of political leaders, not defining their competence. This meant that when power came to be for-malised, it was discussed in a vocabulary of property law, not administra-tion, fiscality or office. This articulation of political practices as the legal possession of the aristocracy was to cast a long shadow down the centu-ries. The peculiarities of early medieval polities are of fundamental importance in understanding the political development of western Europe.

---

[20] For the long-term significance of this, see T. Ertman, *The Birth of the Leviathan: Building States and Regimes in Medieval and Early Modern Europe* (Cambridge, 1997); S. Clark, *State and Status: The Rise of the State and Aristocratic Power in Western Europe* (Cardiff, 1995); and more generally Mann, *Sources of Social Power*, and J. A. Hall, *Powers and Liberties: The Causes and Consequences of the Rise of the West* (London, 1985).

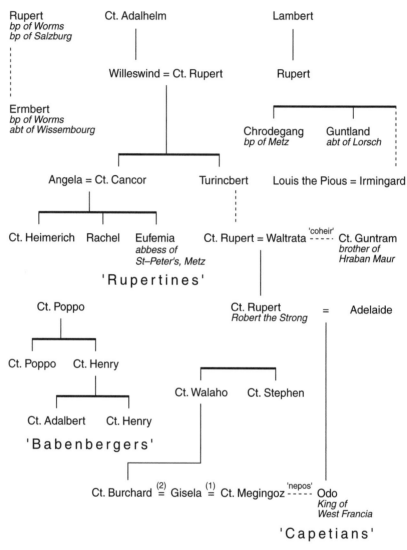

10 Descendants of Lorsch's founders

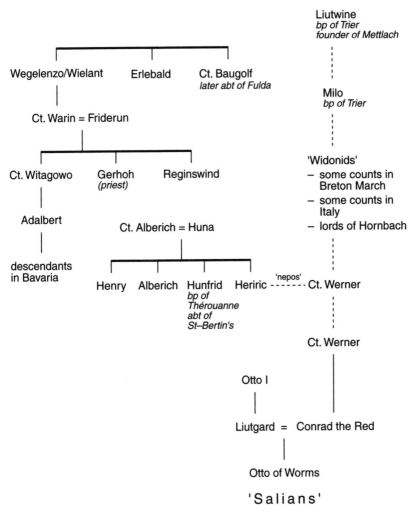

11 Descendants of Hornbach's founders

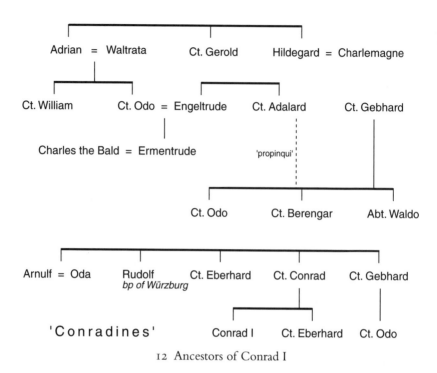

12 Ancestors of Conrad I

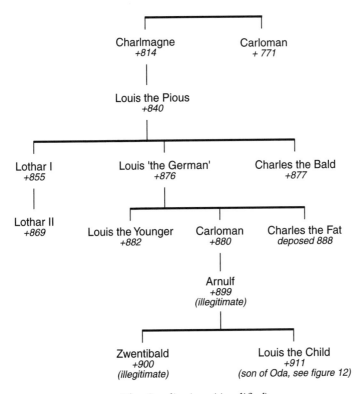

13 The Carolingians (simplified)

LIST OF PRIMARY SOURCES

1 LEGAL SOURCES

1(A) CARTULARIES, COLLECTIONS, POLYPTYCHS (BY INSTITUTION)

Corvey: *Die alten Mönchslisten und die Traditionen von Corvey*, ed. K. Honselmann, Veröffentlichungen der Historischen Kommission für Westfalen 10, Abhandlungen zur Corveyer Geschichtsschreibung 6 (Paderborn, 1982).

Echternach: *Geschichte der Grundherrschaft Echternach im Frühmittelalter*, ed. C. Wampach, I (Luxembourg, 1930).

Flavigny: *The Cartulary of Flavigny*, ed. C. B. Bouchard (Cambridge, MA, 1991).

Freising: *Die Traditionen des Hochstifts Freising*, ed. T. Bitterauf, I, Quellen und Erörterungen zur bayerischen und deutschen Geschichte .; (Munich, 1905).

Fulda: *Urkundenbuch der Kloster Fulda*, ed. E. E. Stengel, Veröffentlichungen der historischen Kommission für Hessen und Waldeck 10, 2 vols. (Marburg, 1913–58).

Codex diplomaticus Fuldensis, ed. E. F. J. Dronke (Kassel, 1850).

Die Klostergemeinschaft von Fulda im früheren Mittelalter, ed. K. Schmid *et al.*, 3 vols. in 5, Münstersche Mittelalter-Schriften 8 (Munich, 1978).

Traditiones et antiquitates Fuldenses, ed. E. F. J. Dronke (Fulda, 1844).

Gorze: *Cartulaire de l'abbaye de Gorze. MS 826 de la Bibliothèque de Metz*, ed. A. d'Herbomez, Mettensia 2 (Paris, 1898).

Hersfeld: *Urkundenbuch der Reichsabtei Hersfeld*, ed. H. Weirich, Veröffentlichungen der historischen Kommission für Hessen und Waldeck 19 (Marburg, 1936).

Hornbach: *Regesta des ehemaligen Benediktinerklosters Hornbach*, ed. A. Neubauer, Mitteilungen des Historischen Vereins der Pfalz 27 (Speyer, 1904). I have also cited full editions of individual charters, where they exist, to supplement Neubauer's summaries.

Lorsch: *Codex Laureshamensis*, ed. K. Glöckner, Arbeiten der historischen Kommission für den Volkstaat Hessen 3, 3 vols. (Darmstadt, 1929–36).

St-Gallen: *Urkundenbuch der Abtei St. Gallen*, ed. H. Wartmann, 2 vols. (Zurich, 1863–6).

St-Trond: *Cartulaire de l'abbaye de St-Trond*, ed. C. Piot, I (Brussels, 1870).

Wissembourg: *Traditiones Wizenburgenses: Die Urkunden des Klosters Weissenburg, 661–864*, ed. K. Glöckner and A. Doll (Darmstadt, 1979).

Liber Possessionum Wizenburgensis, ed. C. Dette, Quellen und Abhandlungen zur mittelrheinische Kirchengeshichte 59 (Mainz, 1987).

List of primary sources

1(B) ROYAL CHARTERS

Regesta Imperii I. Die Regesten des Kaiserreiches unter den Karolingern 751–918, ed. J. F. Böhmer, revised by E. Mühlbacher with J. Lechner, 2nd edn (Innsbruck, 1908).

Die Urkunden Arnulfs, ed. P. Kehr, *MGH Diplomata regum Germaniae ex stirpe Karolinorum/Die Urkunden der deutschen Karolinger* III (Berlin, 1940).

Recueil des actes de Charles II le Chauve, ed. G. Tessier *et al.*, 3 vols. (Paris, 1943–55).

Die Urkunden Heinrichs II und Arduins, ed. H. Bloch and H. Breßlau, *MGH Diplomata regum et imperatorum Germaniae* III (Berlin, 1900–3).

Die Urkunden Karls III, ed. P. Kehr, *MGH Diplomata regum Germaniae ex stirpe Karolinorum/Die Urkunden der deutschen Karolinger* II (Berlin, 1936–7).

Die Urkunden Konrads I, Heinrichs I und Ottos I, ed. T. Sickel, *MGH Diplomata regum et imperatorum Germaniae* I (Berlin, 1879–84).

Die Urkunden Lothars I und Lothars II, ed. T. Schieffer, *MGH Diplomata Karolinorum* III (Berlin, 1966).

Louis the Pious: until the appearance of P. Johanek's *MGH* volume, there is no complete critical edition. Charters have been cited by BM number and then available printed edition. For incomplete editions see M. Bouquet, *Recueil des historiens des Gaules et de la France*, VI (Paris, 1749) and *PL*104.

Die Urkunden Ludwigs des Deutschen, Karlmanns und Ludwigs des Jüngeren, ed. P. Kehr, *MGH Diplomata regum Germaniae ex stirpe Karolinorum/Die Urkunden der deutschen Karolinger* I (Berlin, 1932–4).

Diplomata Merovingorum, ed. K. Pertz, *MGH Diplomata* (Stuttgart, 1872).

Die Urkunden Ottos des II und Ottos des III, ed. T. Sickel, *MGH Diplomata regum et imperatorum Germaniae* II (Berlin, 1888–93).

Die Urkunden Pippins, Karlmanns und Karls des Großen, ed. E. Mühlbacher, *MGH Diplomata Karolinorum* I (Berlin, 1906).

Die Urkunden Zwentibolds und Ludwigs des Kinds, ed. T. Schieffer, *MGH Diplomata regum Germaniae ex stirpe Karolinorum/Die Urkunden der deutschen Karolinger* IV (Berlin, 1960).

1(C) CHARTERS (MISCELLANEOUS)

Acta Academiae Theodoro-Palatinae, vols. 1–7 (Mannheim, 1766–94).

Bündner Urkundenbuch, I, ed. E. Mayer-Marthaler and F. Perret (Chur, 1955).

Chartae Latinae Antiquiores: Facsimile Edition of Latin Charters prior to the Ninth Century, ed. A. Bruckner and R. Marichal (Olten and Lausanne).

Diplomatica Belgica ante annum millenesimum centesimum scripta, ed. M. Gysseling and A. C. F. Koch (Brussels, 1950).

Diplomata, chartae, epistolae, leges aliaque instrumenta ad res gallo-francicas spectantia prius collecta . . ., ed. J. M. Pardessus, 2 vols. (Paris, 1843–9).

'Gerichtsurkunden der fränkischen Zeit. I: Die Gerichtsurkunden aus Deutschland und Frankenreich bis zur Jahre 1000', ed. R. Hübner, *ZSRG GA* 12 (1891): Anhang.

Historia episcopatus Wormatiensis II: *Codex probationum*, ed. J. F. Schannat (Frankfurt, 1724).

Mainzer Urkundenbuch, I, ed. M. Stimming, Arbeiten der historischen Kommission für den Volkstaat Hessen (Darmstadt, 1932).

'Mitteilungen aus Darmstädter Handschriften', ed. A. Schmidt, *Neues Archiv* 13 (1888), 603–22.

Mittelrheinisches Regesten, oder chronologische Zusammenstellung des Quellen-Materials für die

List of primary sources

Geschichte der Territorien der beiden Regierungsbezirke Coblenz und Trier in kurzen Auszügen, I, ed. A. Goerz (Koblenz, 1876).

Monumenta Boica, vols. 28, 31 (Munich, 1829, 1836).

Regesta Alsatiae aevi Merovingici et Karolini (496–918), I (Strasbourg and Zurich, 1949).

Rheinisches Urkundenbuch, ältere Urkunden bis 1100. Erste Lieferung: Aachen-Deutz, ed. E. Wisplinghoff, Publikationen der Gesellschaft für rheinische Geschichtskunde 57 (Bonn, 1972).

'Das Testament des Diakons Adalgisel-Grimo vom Jahre 634', ed. W. Levison, *Aus rheinischer und fränkischer Frühzeit. Ausgewählte Aufsätze* (Düsseldorf, 1948), pp. 118–138.

'Das Testament Fulrads von Saint-Denis', ed. M. Tangl, *Das Mittelalter in Quellenkunde und Diplomatik. Ausgewählte Schriften*, Forschungen zur mittelalterliche Geschichte 12 (Graz, 1966) I, pp. 540–81.

Urkundenbuch zur Geschichte der Bischöfe zu Speyer, I, ed. F. X. Remling (Mainz, 1852).

Urkundenbuch zur Geschichte der, jetzt die Preußischen regierungsbezirke Coblenz und Trier bildenden mittelrheinischen Territorien, I, ed. H. Beyer, L. Eltester and A. Goerz (Koblenz, 1860).

Urkundenbuch der Stadt Strasburg I: Urkunden und Stadtrecht bis zur Jahr 1288, ed. W. Weigand (Strasbourg, 1879).

Urkundenbuch der Stadt Worms, ed. H. Boos, Quellen zur Geschichte der Stadt Worms I (Worms, 1886).

Urkunden- und Quellenbuch zur Geschichte der altluxembourgischen Territorien, I, ed. C. Wampach (Luxembourg, 1935).

I(D) FORMULARIES

Formulae Merowingi et Karolini Aevi, ed. K. Zeumer, *MGH Formulae, Leges sectio* V (Hanover, 1886).

Marculfi Formularum Libri Duo, ed. A. Uddholm (Uppsala, 1962).

I(E) LEGISLATION

Burchard of Worms, *Lex familia Wormatiensis ecclesiae, MGH Const.* I, ed. L. Weigand (Berlin, 1893), no. 438, pp. 639–45.

Capitula Episcoporum, 3 vols., eds. P. Brommer, R. Pokorny and M. Stratmann, R. Pokorny respectively, *MGH Capitula Episcoporum* (Berlin, 1984, 1993, 1995).

Capitularia Regum Francorum, ed. A. Boretius and V. Krause, *MGH Leges sectio* III, 2 vols. (Hanover, 1883–97).

Constitutiones et acta publica imperatorum et regum, I, ed. L. Weigand, *MGH Const.* I (Berlin, 1893).

Hincmar of Rheims, *Collectio de Ecclesiis et Capellis*, ed. M. Stratmann, *MGH Fontes* (Hanover, 1990).

Lex Alamannorum, ed. K. Eckhardt, *Die Gesetze des Karolingerreiches 2. Alemannien und Bayern*, Germanenrechte 2:ii (Weimar, 1934).

Lex Baiuvariorum, ed. K. Eckhardt, *Die Gesetze des Karolingerreiches 2. Alemannien und Bayern*, Germanenrechte 2:ii (Weimar, 1934).

Lex Ribuaria, ed. K. Eckhardt, Germanenrechte 6 (Hanover, 1966).

Notitia de servitio monasteriorum, ed. P. Becker, in K. Hallinger (ed.), *Corpus Consuetudinum Monasticarum* I (Siegburg, 1963), pp. 483–99.

List of primary sources

'Wormser Burgenbauordnung' [Ordinance on the upkeep of Worms' walls, c. 900]: ed. H. Boos, *Monumenta Wormatiensia*, Quellen zur Geschichte der Stadt Worms III (Berlin, 1893), pp. 223–5.

2 COMMEMORATIVE MATERIAL

2(A) 'LIBRI MEMORIALES' AND NECROLOGIES

Fulda: see *Die Klostergemeinschaft von Fulda* (secondary literature) for discussion and registers.

Lorsch: 'Kalendarium necrologium Laureshamense', ed. J. F. Böhmer, *Fontes rerum Germanicarum*, III (Stuttgart, 1853), pp. 144–52.

Reichenau: *Das Verbrüderungsbuch der Abtei Reichenau (Einleitung, Register, Faksimile)*, ed. J. Autenrieth, D. Geuenich, K. Schmid, *MGH Libri Memoriales et Necrologia, n.s.* I (Hanover, 1979).

Remiremont: *Liber Memorialis von Remiremont*, ed. E. Hlawitschka, K. Schmid and G. Tellenbach, *MGH Libri Memoriales* I (Dublin and Berlin, 1970).

2(B) INSCRIPTIONS

Die frühchristliche Inschriften des Mittelrheingebietes, ed. W. Boppert (Mainz, 1971).

3 LETTERS AND LETTER COLLECTIONS

Epistolae Merowingici et Karolini aevi I–IV, *MGH Epp.* 3–6, ed. W. Gundlach and E. Dümmler (Berlin, 1892–1925).

Boniface: ed. M. Tangl, *Die Briefe des heiligen Bonifatius und Lullus*, *MGH Epistolae selectae* I (Berlin, 1955).

Einhard: *Epistolae*, ed. K. Hampe, *MGH Epp.* V (Berlin, 1899), pp. 105–45. Trans. P. Dutton, *Carolingian Civilisation* (Peterborough, Ontario, 1993) or *Charlemagne's Courtier* (Peterborough, Ontario, 1997).

Frothar of Toul: *Epistolae*, ed. K. Hampe, *MGH Epp.* V (Berlin, 1899), pp. 275–98.

Fulda: *Epistolarum Fuldensium fragmenta*, ed. E. Dümmler, *MGH Epp.* V (Berlin, 1899), pp. 517–33.

Supplex Libellus, ed. J. Semmler, in K. Hallinger (ed.), *Corpus Consuetudinum Monasticarum* I (Siegburg, 1963), pp. 319–27.

Hraban Maur: *Epistolae*, ed. E. Dümmler, *MGH Epp.* V (Berlin, 1899), pp. 381–515.

Epistolarum Fuldensium fragmenta, ed. E. Dümmler, *MGH Epp.* V (Berlin, 1899), pp. 517–33.

Lupus of Ferrières: ed. L. Levillain, *Loup de Ferrières: Correspondance*, 2 vols. (Paris, 1930).

Rheims: summaries in Flodoard, *Historiae Remensis Ecclesiae*, ed. G. Waitz and J. Heller, *MGH SS* 13 (Hanover, 1881), pp. 405–599.

4 LITERARY SOURCES

Adalbert of Trier, Continuation of Regino's *Chronicle*, ed. F. Kurze, *MGH SRG* (Hanover, 1890).

List of primary sources

Annales Bertiniani, ed. F. Grat, J. Vielliard, and S. Clémencet (Paris, 1964). Translation and commentary: J. L. Nelson, *The Annals of St-Bertin* (Manchester, 1991).

Annales Fuldenses, ed. F. Kurze, *MGH SRG* (Hanover, 1891). Translation and commentary: T. Reuter, *The Annals of Fulda* (Manchester, 1992).

Annales Iuvavenses, ed. H. Breßlau, *MGH SS* 30:2 (Hanover, 1926), pp. 727–44.

Annales Laureshamenses, ed. G. H. Pertz, *MGH SS* 1 (Hanover, 1829), pp. 22–39.

Annales Mettenses Priores, ed. B. von Simson, *MGH SRG* (Hanover, 1904).

Annales Nazariani, ed. G. H. Pertz, *MGH SS* 1 (Hanover, 1829), pp. 23–45. See also W. Lendi, *Untersuchungen zur frühalemannischen Annalistik. Die Murbacher Annalen* (Freibourg, 1971).

Annales Regni Francorum, ed. F. Kurze, *MGH SRG* (Hanover, 1895).

Annales Xantenses, ed. B. von Simson, *MGH SRG* (Hanover, 1909).

'Astronomer', *Vita Hludovici*, ed. E. Tremp, *MGH SRG* (Hanover, 1995).

Candidus, *Vita Eigil*, ed. G. Waitz, *MGH SS* 15:1 (Hanover, 1887), pp. 221–33.

Candidus, *De Vita Eigil*, ed. E. Dümmler, *MGH PLAC* II (Berlin, 1881), pp. 94–117.

Dhuoda, *Liber Manualis*, ed. P. Riché, Sources Chrétiennes 225 (Paris, 1975).

Eigil, *Vita Sturmi*, ed. O. Holder-Egger, *MGH SS* 2 (Hanover, 1829), pp. 365–77. See also P. Engelbert, *Die Vita Sturmi des Eigil von Fulda*, Veröffentlichungen der Historische Kommission für Hessen und Waldeck 29 (Marburg, 1968).

Einhard, *Vita Karoli*, ed. O. Holder-Egger, *MGH SRG* (Hanover, 1911).

Einhard, *Translatio et miracula sanctorum Marcellini et Petri*, ed. G. Waitz, *MGH SS* 15:1 (Hanover, 1887), pp. 238–64. Trans. P. Dutton, *Carolingian Civilisation: A Reader* (Peterborough, Ontario, 1993) or *Charlemagne's Courtier* (Peterborough, Ontario, 1997).

Ermanic of Ellwangen, *Sermo de Vita Sualonis*, ed. O. Holder-Egger, *MGH SS* 15:1 (Hanover, 1887), pp. 153–63.

Flodoard, *Historiae Remensis Ecclesiae*, eds. G. Waitz and J. Heller, *MGH SS* 13 (Hanover 1881), pp. 405–599.

The Fourth Book of the Chronicle of Fredegar with its Continuations, ed. J. M. Wallace-Hadrill (Oxford, 1960).

Gesta sancti Hrodberti confessoris, ed. W. Levison, *MGH SRM* VI (Hanover, 1913), pp. 140–62.

Gregory of Tours, *Historiae*, ed. B. Krusch and W. Levison, *MGH SRM* I (Hanover, 1951).

Hildebrandslied, trans. J. K. Bostock, *A Handbook on Old High German Literature* (Oxford, 1976), 2nd edn, rev. K. C. King and D. R. McLintock, pp. 76–7.

Hincmar of Rheims, *Vita Remigii*, ed. B. Krusch, *MGH SRM* III (Hanover, 1896), pp. 239–341.

Hraban Maur, *Carmina*, ed. E. Dümmler, *MGH PLAC* II (Hanover, 1881), pp. 154–258.

Hraban Maur, adaptation of Vegetius' *De Re Militarii*, ed. E. Dümmler, 'De procinctu Romanae militia', *Zeitschrift für deutsches Altertum* III (1872), 443–52.

Huneberc of Heidenheim, *Vita Willibaldi episcopi Eichstetensis*, ed. O. Holder-Egger, *MGH SS* 15:1 (Hanover, 1887), pp. 86–106.

Huneberc of Heidenheim, *Vita Wynebaldi abbatis Heidenheimensis*, ed. O. Holder-Egger, *MGH SS* 15:1 (Hanover, 1887), pp. 106–17.

Jonas of Bobbio, *Vita Columbani*, ed. H. Haupt, *Quellen zur Geschichte des 7. und 8. Jahrhunderts*, ed. A. Kusterning and H. Wolfram (Darmstadt, 1982). Also ed. B. Krusch, *MGH SRG* (Hanover and Leipzig, 1905).

List of primary sources

Nithard, *Historiae*, ed. P. Lauer, *Histoire des fils de Louis le Pieux* (Paris, 1926).

Notker of St-Gallen, *Gesta Karoli Magni*, ed. H. F. Haefele, *MGH SRG* (Hanover, 1959). Trans. L. Thorpe, *Two Lives of Charlemagne* (London, 1971).

Regino of Prüm, *Chronicon*, ed. F. Kurze, *MGH SRG* (Hanover, 1890).

Rudolf of Fulda, *Vita Leobae abbatissae Biscofesheimensis*, ed. G. Waitz, *MGH SS* 15:1 (Hanover, 1887), pp. 118–31.

Rudolf of Fulda, *Miracula sanctorum in Fuldensium ecclesias translatorum*, *MGH SS* 15:1 (Hanover, 1887), pp. 328–41.

Ruotgar, *Vita Brunonis*, ed. I. Ott, *MGH SRG* (Weimar, 1951).

Sigehard of St-Maximian, *Miracula S. Maximini*, ed. G. H. Pertz, *MGH SS* 4 (Hanover, 1841), pp. 230–4.

Thegan, *Gesta Hludovici Imperatoris*, ed. E. Tremp, *MGH SRG* (Hanover, 1995).

Thietmar of Merseberg, *Chronicon*, ed. R. Holtzmann, *MGH SRG* (Berlin, 1935).

Venantius Fortunatus, *Carmina*, ed. F. Leo, *MGH AA* IV:i (Berlin, 1881).

Visio Karoli Magni, ed. P. Geary, as an appendix to 'Germanic Tradition and Royal Ideology in the Ninth Century: The *Visio Karoli Magni*', in Geary, *Living with the Dead in the Middle Ages* (Ithaca, 1994), pp. 74–6.

Vita Burchardi episcopi Wormatiensis, ed. G. Waitz, *MGH SS* 4 (Hanover, 1841), pp. 829–46.

Vita Eucherii episcopi Aurelianensis, ed. W. Levison, *MGH SRM* VII (Hanover, 1920), pp. 46–53.

Wandalbert of Prüm, *Miracula S. Goaris*, ed. O. Holder-Egger, *MGH SS* 15:1 (Hanover, 1887), pp. 361–73. Also edited by H. Steine, *Lateinische Sprache und Literatur des Mittelalters* 11 (Frankfurt, 1981).

Widukind of Corvey, *Rerum gestarum Saxonicarum*, ed. P. Hirsch and H.-E. Lohmann, *MGH SRG* (Hanover, 1935).

Willibald, *Vita Bonifatii*, ed. W. Levison, *MGH SRG* (Hanover, 1905).

Wolfhard of Herrieden, *Miracula S. Waldburgis Monheimensis*, ed. A. Bauch, *Ein bayerisches Mirakelbuch aus der Karolingerzeit. Die Monheimer Walpurgis-Wunder des Priesters Wolfhard* (Regensburg, 1979). Also ed. O. Holder-Egger, *MGH SS* 15:1 (Hanover, 1887), pp. 535–55.

BIBLIOGRAPHY OF SECONDARY WORKS

Abels, R., *Lordship and Military Obligation in Anglo-Saxon England* (London, 1988)

Abrams, P., 'Notes on the Difficulty of Studying the State', *Journal of Historical Sociology* 1 (1988), 58–89

Airlie, S., 'The Political Behaviour of the Secular Magnates in Francia, 829–879' (unpublished D.Phil. thesis, Oxford, 1986)

'Bonds of Power and Bonds of Association in the Court Circle of Louis the Pious', in P. Godman and R. Collins (eds.), *Charlemagne's Heir: New Perspectives on the Reign of Louis the Pious (814–40)* (Oxford, 1990), pp. 191–204

'After Empire: New Work on the Emergence of Post-Carolingian Kingdoms', *EME* 2 (1993), 153–61

'The Aristocracy', in *NCMH*, pp. 431–50

'*Semper Fideles*? Loyauté envers les Carolingiens comme constituant de l'identité aristocratique', in R. Le Jan (ed.), *La royauté et les élites dans l'Europe carolingienne* (Lille, 1998), pp. 129–44

Albert, B. S., 'Raban Maur, l'unité de l'empire et ses relations avec les Carolingiens', *Revue d'histoire ecclésiastique* 86 (1991), 5–44

Althoff, G., 'Zur Frage nach der Organisation sächsischer *coniurationes* in der Ottonenzeit', *Frühmittelalterliche Studien* 16 (1982), 129–42

'Königsherrschaft und Konfliktbewältigung im 10. und 11. Jht.', *Frühmittelalterliche Studien* 23 (1989), 265–90

Verwandte, Freunde und Getreue. Zum politischen Stellenwert der Gruppenbindungen im früheren Mittelalter (Darmstadt, 1990)

Amicitiae und Pacta. Bündnis, Einung, Politik und Gebetsgedenken im beginnenden 10 Jht., Schriften der MGH 37 (Hanover, 1992)

Otto III (Darmstadt, 1996)

Spielregeln der Politik im Mittelalter. Kommunikation im Frieden und Fehden (Darmstadt, 1997)

'*Ira Regis*: Prolegomena to a History of Royal Anger', in B. H. Rosenwein (ed.), *Anger's Past: The Social Uses of an Emotion in the Middle Ages* (Ithaca and London, 1998), pp. 59–74

Ament, H., *Fränkische Adelsgräber aus Flonheim in Rheinhessen*, Germanische Denkmälern der Völkerwanderungszeit B 5 (Berlin, 1970)

'Die Franken in der Römerstädten der Rheinzone', in K. van Welck (ed.), *Die Franken. Wegbereiter Europas*, 2 vols. (Mainz, 1997), I, pp. 129–38

274

Bibliography of secondary works

Anderson, P., *Passages from Antiquity to Feudalism* (London, 1974)

Angenendt, A., 'Pirmin und Bonifatius. Ihr Verhältnis zu Mönchtum, Bischofsamt und Adel', in A. Borst (ed.), *Mönchtum, Episkopat und Adel zur Gründungszeit der Abtei Reichenau*, VF 20 (Sigmaringen, 1974), pp. 251–303

'Theologie und Liturgie der frühmittelalterliche Toten-Memoria', in K. Schmid and J. Wollasch (eds.), *Memoria. Die geschichtliche Zeugniswert des liturgischen Gedenkens im Mittelalter*, Münstersche Mittelalter Schriften 48 (Munich, 1984), pp. 79–199

Anton, H. H., *Fürstenspiegel und Herrscherethos in der Karolingerzeit*, Bonner Historische Forschungen 32 (Bonn, 1968)

Arnold, B., *German Knighthood, 1050–1300* (Oxford, 1984)

Princes and Territories in Medieval Germany (Cambridge, 1991)

German History, 500–1300 (London, 1997)

Bachrach, B. S., *Merovingian Military Organisation 481–751* (Minneapolis, 1972)

'Animals and Warfare in Early Medieval Europe', *Settimane* 31 (1985), 707–51

Balzaretti, R., 'The Monastery of Sant' Ambrogio and Dispute Settlement in Early Medieval Milan', *EME* 3 (1994), 1–18

'Cities and Markets in Early Medieval Europe', in G. Ausenda (ed.), *After Empire: Towards an Ethnology of Europe's Barbarians* (San Marino, 1995), pp. 113–34

'Cities, Emporia and Monasteries: Local Economies in the Po Valley, c.700–875', in N. Christie and S. T. Loseby (eds.), *Towns in Transition* (Woodbridge, 1997), pp. 213–34

Barnwell, P. S., *Emperor, Prefects and Kings: The Roman West, 395–565* (London, 1992)

Barth, R. E., *Der Herzog in Lotharingien im 10. Jahrhundert* (Sigmaringen, 1990)

Barthélemy, D., 'La mutation féodale a-t-elle eu lieu?', *Annales: ESC* 47 (1992), 767–77

La societé dans le comté de Vendôme de l'an mil au XIVe siècle (Paris, 1993)

'Debate: The "Feudal" Revolution', *P&P* 152 (1996), 196–205

Bartlett, R., *Trial by Fire and Water: The Medieval Judicial Ordeal* (Oxford, 1986)

Beaujard, B., 'Dons et pieté à l'égard des saints dans la Gaule des Ve et VIe siècles', in M. Sot (ed.), *Haut Moyen Age. Festschrift P. Riché* (Paris, 1993), pp. 59–68

Becher, M., *Eid und Herrschaft. Untersuchungen zum Herrscherethos Karls des Großen*, VF Sonderband 39 (Sigmaringen, 1993)

Rex, Dux und Gens. Untersuchungen zur Entstehung des sächsischen Herzogtums im 9. und 10. Jht. (Husum, 1996)

Behn, F., 'Ein vorfränkisches Gräberfeld bei Lampertheim im Rheinhessen', *Mainzer Zeitschrift* 30 (1935), 56–65

'Ausgrabungen in Lorsch', in *Laurissa Jubilans. Festschrift zur 1200-Jahrfeier von Lorsch* (Lorsch, 1964), pp. 115–20

Bergengruen, A., *Adel und Grundherrschaft im Frankenreich*, Vierteljahrsschrift für Sozial- und Wirtschaftsgeschichte Beihefte 41 (Berlin, 1958)

Berktay, H., 'Three Empires and the Societies they Governed: Iran, India and the Ottoman Empire', *Journal of Peasant Studies* 18 (1991), 242–63

Bernhard, H., 'Die frühmittelalterliche Siedlung Speyer "Vogelgesang"', *Offa* 39 (1982), 217–33

Bernhardt, J. W., *Itinerant Kingship and Royal Monasteries in Germany, 919–1056* (Cambridge, 1994)

Beumann, H., 'Zur Textgeschichte der Vita Ruperti', in *Festschrift für Hermann Heimpel*, 3 vols., VMPIG 36 (Göttingen, 1972), III, pp. 166–96

Beyerle, F., 'Zur Wehrverfassung des Hochmittelalters', in *Festschrift Ernst Mayer (Würzburg)* (Weimar, 1932), pp. 31–91

Bibliography of secondary works

Bischoff, B., *Lorsch im Spiegel seiner Handschriften*, Münchener Beiträge zur Mediävistik und Renaissance-Forschung (Munich, 1974)

Bisson, T. N., 'The "Feudal" Revolution', *P&P* 142 (1994), 6–42

Bleiber, W., 'Grundherrschaft und Markt zwischen Loire und Rhein während des 9. Jahrhunderts: Untersuchungen zu ihrem wechselseitigen Verhältnis', *Jahrbuch für Wirtschaftsgeschichte* 3 (1982), 105–35

Bloch, M., *Feudal Society*, trans. L. Manyon, 2 vols. (London, 1962)

Blok, D. P., 'Le notariat franc: a-t-il existé?', *Revue du Nord* 42 (1960), 320–1

Böhme, H.-W., *Germanische Grabfunde des 4. und 5. Jahrhunderts zwischen Elbe und Loire*, 2 vols. (Munich, 1974)

'Adelsgräber im Frankenreich. Archäologische Zeugnisse zur Herausbildung einer Herrenschicht unter den merowingischer Königen', *Jahrbuch des Römisch-Germanischen Zentralmuseums Mainz* 40 (1995), 397–534

'Adel und Kirche bei den Alemannen der Merowingerzeit', *Germania* 74 (1996), 477–507

Böhne, W. (ed.), *Hrabanus Maurus und seine Schule. Festschrift der Rabanus-Maurus-Schule* (Fulda, 1980)

Böhner, K., 'Urban and Rural Settlement in the Frankish Kingdom', in M. W. Barley (ed.), *European Towns: Their Archaeology and Early History* (London, 1977), pp. 185–207

Bois, G., *The Transformation of the Year 1000: The Village of Lournand from Antiquity to Feudalism*, trans. J. Birrell (Cambridge, 1992)

Bondois, M., *La translation de Saints Marcellin et Pierre. Etude sur Einhard et sa vie politique de 827 à 834*, Bibliothèque de l'Ecole des Hautes Etudes 160 (Paris, 1907)

Bonnassie, P., *La Catalogne du milieu du Xe à la fin du XIe siècle* (Toulouse, 1975)

'On the Survival and Extinction of the Slave Regime in Early Medieval Europe', in Bonnassie, *From Slavery to Feudalism in South-western Europe*, trans. J. Birrell (Cambridge, 1991), pp. 1–59

Borgolte, M., 'Die Geschichte der Grafengewalt im Elsaß von Dagobert I bis Otto dem Großen', *ZGO* 131 (1983), 3–54

Review of K. Heinemeyer, 'Das Erzbistum Mainz', *ZGO* 131 (1983), 467–8

'Gedenkstiftungen im St Galler Urkunden', in K. Schmid and J. Wollasch (eds.), *Memoria. Die geschichtliche Zeugniswert des liturgischen Gedenkens im Mittelalter*, Münstersche Mittelalter Schriften 48 (Munich, 1984), pp. 578–602

Geschichte der Grafschaften Alemanniens in fränkischer Zeit, VF Sonderband 31 (Sigmaringen, 1984)

Die Grafen Alemanniens im merowingischer und karolingischer Zeit. Eine Prosopographie (Sigmaringen, 1986)

'Die Alaholfingerurkunden. Zeugnisse vom Selbstverständnis einer adligen Verwandtengemeinschaft des frühen Mittelalters', in Borgolte and D. Geuenich (eds.), *Subsidia Sangallensia I. Materialen und Untersuchungen zu den Verbrüderungsbüchern und zu den älteren Urkunden des Stiftsarchivs St. Gallen* (St Gallen, 1986), pp. 297–354

Borst, A., 'The Invention and Fissure of the Public Persona', in Borst, *Medieval Worlds: Barbarians, Heretics and Artists in the Middle Ages* (Cambridge, 1991), pp. 37–60

Boshof, E. 'Untersuchungen zur Kirchenvogtei in Lothringen im 10. und 11. Jht.', *ZSRG KA* 65 (1979), 55–119

'Ottonen- und frühe Salierzeit (919–1056)', in F. Petri and G. Droege (eds.), *Rheinische Geschichte*, I:iii, *Hohes Mittelalter* (Düsseldorf, 1983), pp. 1–120

Bibliography of secondary works

Bosl, K., 'Pfalz und Försten', in *Deutsche Königspfalzen. Beiträge zu ihrer historischen und archäologischen Erforschung*, I, VMPIG 11 (Göttingen, 1963), pp. 1–29

'*Potens* und *pauper*. Begriffsgeschichtliche Studien zur gesellschaftlichen Differenzierung im frühen Mittelalter und zur "Pauperismus" des Hochmittelalters', in Bosl, *Frühformen der Gesellschaft in mittelalterlichen Europa. Ausgewählte Beiträge zu einer Strukturanalyse der mittelalterlichen Welt* (Munich and Vienna, 1964), pp. 106–34

'Der Adelsheilige. Idealtypus und Wirklichkeit, Gesellschaft und Kultur in merowingerzeitlichen Bayern des 7. und 8. Jhts', in C. Bauer *et al.* (eds.), *Speculum Historiale. Festschrift J. Spörl* (Munich, 1965), pp. 167–87

Franken um 800. Strukturanalyse einer fränkischen Königsprovinz (2nd edn, Munich, 1969)

Bouchard, C. B., *Sword, Miter and Cloister: Nobility and the Church in Burgundy, 980–1198* (Ithaca and London, 1987)

Bourdieu, P., *Outline of a Theory of Practice*, trans. R. Nice (Cambridge, 1977)

Breßlau, H., 'Urkundenbeweis und Urkundenschreiber im älteren deutschen Recht', *Forschungen zur deutsche Geschichte* 26 (1886), 1–66

Handbuch der Urkundenlehre für Deutschland und Italien, 2 vols. (Leipzig, 1912–17)

Brooks, N. P., 'The Development of Military Obligations in Eighth and Ninth Century England', in P. Clemoes and K. Hughes (eds.), *England Before the Conquest* (Cambridge, 1974), pp. 69–84

'Arms, Status and Warfare in late Saxon England', in D. Hill (ed.), *Ethelred the Unready*, British Archaeological Reports British Series 59 (Oxford, 1978), pp. 81–103

'Church, Crown and Community: Public Work and Seigneurial Responsibility at Rochester Bridge', in T. Reuter (ed.), *Warriors and Churchmen in the High Middle Ages: Essays presented to Karl Leyser* (London, 1992), pp. 1–20

'Medieval Bridges: A Window onto Changing Concepts of State Power', *Haskins Society Journal* 7 (1997), 11–29

Brown, P. R. L., 'The Rise and Function of the Holy Man in Late Antiquity', *Journal of Roman Studies* 61 (1971), 80–111

'Society and the Supernatural: A Medieval Change', *Daedalus* 104 (1975), 133–51

The Cult of the Saints: Its Rise and Function in Latin Christianity (Chicago, 1981)

'Vers la naissance de purgatoire', *Annales: ESC* 52 (1997), 1247–62

Brühl, C.-R., 'Königspfalz und Bischofstadt in fränkischer Zeit', *Rheinische Vierteljahrsblätter* 23 (1958), 161–274

Fodrum, Gistum, Servitium Regis. Studien zu den wirtschaftlichen Grundlagen des Königtums im Frankenreich und in den fränkischen Nachfolgestaaten Deutschland, Frankreich und Italien vom 6 bis zur Mitte 14. Jahrhunderts, Kölner Historische Abhandlungen 14, 2 vols. (Cologne and Graz, 1968)

Brunner, K., 'Das fränkische Fürstentitel im neunten und zehnten Jahrhundert', in H. Wolfram (ed.), *Intitulatio II: Lateinische Herrscher- und Fürstentitel im neunten und zehnten Jahrhundert*, MIÖG Ergänzungsband 23 (Vienna, 1973), pp. 179–340

Oppositionelle Gruppen im Karolingerreich, Veröffentlichungen des Instituts für österreichische Geschichtsforschung 25 (Vienna, 1979)

'Auf den Spuren verlorener Traditionen', *Peritia* 2 (1983), 1–22

Brunner, O., *Land and Lordship: Structures of Governance in Medieval Austria*, trans. H. Kaminsky and J. Melton (Philadelphia, 1992)

Bührier-Thierry, G., 'Les évêques de Bavière et d'Alémannie dans l'entourage des derniers rois carolingiens en Germanie, 876–911', *Francia* 16 (1989), 31–52

Evêques et pouvoir dans le royaume de Germanie, 876–973 (Paris, 1997)

Bibliography of secondary works

'"Just Anger" or "Vengeful Anger"? The Punishment of Blinding in the Early Medieval West', in B. H. Rosenwein (ed.), *Anger's Past: The Social Uses of an Emotion in the Middle Ages* (Ithaca and London, 1998), pp. 75–91

Büttner, H., 'Frühes fränkisches Christentum am Mittelrhein', *Archiv für mittelrheinische Kirchengeschichte* 3 (1951), 9–55

'Das mittlere Mainland und die fränkische Politik des 7. und früher 8. Jahrhunderts', in *Herbipolis Jubilans. 1200 Jahre Bistum Würzburg*, Würzburger Diözesangeschichtsblätter 14/15 (Würzburg, 1952), pp. 83–90

'Zur Stadtentwicklung von Worms im Früh- und Hochmittelalter', in *Aus Geschichte und Landeskunde. Festschrift F. Steinbach* (Bonn, 1960), pp. 389–407

'Ladenburg am Neckar und das Bistum Worms bis zum Ende des 12. Jahrhunderts', *Archiv für Hessische Geschichte und Altertumskunde* 28 (1963), 83–98

'Mission und Kirchenorganisation des Frankenreiches bis zum Tode Karls des Großen', in H. Beumann (ed.), *Karl der Große: Lebenswerk und Nachleben. I: Persönlichkeit und Geschichte* (Düsseldorf, 1965), pp. 454–86

'Die politische Kräfte zwischen Rhein und Odenwald bis zum 11. Jahrhundert', in Büttner, *Zur frühmittelalterlichen Reichsgeschichte am Rhein, Main und Neckar*, ed. A. Gerlich (Darmstadt, 1975), pp. 253–66

'Mainz im Mittelalter. Gestalten und Probleme', in Büttner, *Mittelrhein und Hessen. Nachgelassene Studien*, ed. A. Gerlich, Geschichtliche Landeskunde 33 (Stuttgart, 1989), pp. 1–50

Büttner, H., and Duft, J., *Lorsch und St-Gallen*, VF Sonderband 1 (Sigmaringen, 1963)

Bullough, D., '*Europae Pater*: Charlemagne and his Achievement in the Light of Recent Scholarship', *English Historical Review* 85 (1970), 59–105

'Burial, Community and Belief in the Early Medieval West', in P. Wormald *et al.* (eds.), *Ideal and Reality in Frankish and Anglo-Saxon Society* (Oxford, 1983), pp. 177–201

'*Alboinus deliciosus Karoli regis*: Alcuin of York and the Shaping of the Early Carolingian Court', in L. Fenske *et al.* (eds.), *Institutionen, Kultur und Gesellschaft in Mittelalter. Festschrift J. Fleckenstein* (Sigmaringen, 1984), pp. 73–92

'*Aula Renovata*: The Carolingian Court before the Aachen Palace', in Bullough, *Carolingian Renewal: Sources and Heritage* (Manchester, 1991), pp. 123–60

Friends, Neighbours and Fellow-Drinkers: Aspects of Community and Conflict in the Early Medieval West, H. M. Chadwick Memorial Lecture (Cambridge, 1991)

Busch, J. W., 'Vom Attentat zur Haft. Die Behandlung von Konkurrenten und Opponenten der frühen Karolinger', *Historische Zeitschrift* 263 (1996), 561–88

Butzen, R., *Die Merowinger östlich des mittleren Rheins. Studien zur militärischen, politischen, rechtlichen, religiösen, kirchlichen, kulturellen Erfassung durch Königtum und Adel im 6. sowie 7. Jahrhundert* (Würzburg, 1987)

Caciola, N., 'Wraiths, Revenants and Ritual in Medieval Culture', *P&P* 152 (1996), 3–45

Campbell, J., 'The Sale of Land and the Economics of Power in Early England: Problems and Possibilities', *Haskins Society Journal* 1 (1989), 23–37

'England in 991', in J. P. Cooper (ed.), *The Battle of Maldon: Fact and Fiction* (London, 1993), pp. 1–17

'The Late Anglo-Saxon State: A Maximum View', *Proceedings of the British Academy* 87 (1994), 39–65

Cardot, F., *L'espace et le pouvoir. Etude sur l'Austrasie mérovingienne* (Paris, 1987)

Carpenter, C., 'Gentry and Community in Medieval England', *Journal of British Studies* 33 (1994), 340–80

Bibliography of secondary works

Charles-Edwards, T., 'The Distinction between Land and Moveable Wealth in Anglo-Saxon England', in P. H. Sawyer (ed.), *Medieval Settlement* (London, 1979), pp. 97–104

Cheyette, F. L., '"Suum cuique tribuere"', *French Historical Studies* 6 (1970), 287–99
'The Invention of the State', in B. K. Lackner and K. R. Phillip (eds.), *Essays in Medieval Civilization: The Walter Prescott Webb Memorial Lectures* (Austin, 1979), pp. 143–76

Claessen, H. J. M., and Skalník, P. (eds.), *The Early State* (The Hague, 1977)

Clanchy, M. T., 'Remembering the Past and the Good Old Law', *History* 55 (1970), 165–79

Clark, S., *State and Status: The Rise of the State and Aristocratic Power in Western Europe* (Cardiff, 1995)

Classen, P., 'Bemerkungen zur Pfalzenforschung am Mittelrhein', in *Deutsche Königspfalzen: Beiträge zu ihrer historischen und archäologischen Erforschung*, I, VMPIG 11 (Göttingen, 1963), pp. 75–96
'Die Verträge von Verdun und von Coulaines 843 als Grundlagen des westfränkischen Reiches', *Historische Zeitschrift* 196 (1963), 1–35
'Die Geschichte der Königspfalz Ingelheim bis zur Verpfändung an Kurpfalz 1375', in J. Autenrieth (ed.), *Ingelheim am Rhein. Forschungen und Studien zur Geschichte Ingelheims* (Ingelheim, 1964), pp. 87–146
'Fortleben und Wandel spätrömischen Urkundenwesens im frühen Mittelalter', in P. Classen (ed.), *Recht und Schrift im Mittelalter*, VF 23 (Sigmaringen, 1977), pp. 13–54

Claude, D., 'Untersuchungen zum frühfränkischen Comitat', *ZSRG GA* 42 (1964), 1–79
'Zu Fragen frühfränkischer Verfassungsgeschichte', *ZSRG GA* 83 (1966), 273–80

Colman, R., 'Reason and Unreason in Early Medieval Law', *Journal of Interdisciplinary History* 4 (1974), 571–91

Constable, G., '*Nona et Decima*: An Aspect of the Carolingian Economy', *Speculum* 35 (1960), 224–50
Monastic Tithes from their Origins to the Twelfth Century (Cambridge, 1964)

Coss, P. R., *Lordship, Knighthood and Locality: A Study of English Society, c.1180–c.1280* (Cambridge, 1991)

Costambeys, M. J., 'An Aristocratic Community on the North Frankish Frontier, 690–726', *EME* 3 (1994), 39–62

Coulson, C., 'Fortresses and Social Responsibility in late Carolingian France', *Zeitschrift für die Archäologie des Mittelalters* 4 (1976), 29–37

Dannenbauer, H., *Grundlagen der mittelalterlichen Welt. Skizzen und Studien* (Stuttgart, 1958)
'Die Freien im karolingischen Heer', in Dannenbauer, *Grundlagen der mittelalterlichen Welt. Skizzen und Studien* (Stuttgart, 1958), pp. 240–56
'Fränkische und schwäbische Dörfer am Ende des 8. Jahrhunderts', in Dannenbauer, *Grundlagen der mittelalterlichen Welt. Skizzen und Studien* (Stuttgart, 1958), pp. 271–83
'Paraveredus-Pferde', in Dannenbauer, *Grundlagen der mittelalterlichen Welt. Skizzen und Studien* (Stuttgart, 1958), pp. 257–70

Davies, W., 'Priests and Rural Communities in East Brittany in the Ninth Century', *Etudes Celtiques* 20 (1983), 177–97
'Disputes, their Conduct and their Settlement in the Village Communities of Eastern Brittany in the Ninth Century', *History and Anthropology* 1 (1985), 289–312

Bibliography of secondary works

'People and Places in Dispute in Ninth-Century Brittany', in Davies and P. Fouracre (eds.), *The Settlement of Disputes in Early Medieval Europe* (Cambridge, 1986), pp. 65–84

Small Worlds: The Village Community in Early Medieval Brittany (London, 1988)

'On Servile Status in the Early Middle Ages', in M. L. Bush (ed.), *Serfdom and Slavery: Studies in Legal Bondage* (London, 1996), pp. 225–46

Davies, W., and Fouracre, P. (eds.), *The Settlement of Disputes in Early Medieval Europe* (Cambridge, 1986)

Property and Power in the Early Middle Ages (Cambridge, 1995)

Davis, J., *Land and Family in Pisticci* (London, 1973)

De Jong, M., 'Power and Humility in Carolingian Society: The Public Penance of Louis the Pious', *EME* 1 (1992), 29–52

'Carolingian Monasticism: The Power of Prayer', in *NCMH*, pp. 622–53

In Samuel's Image: Child Oblation in the Early Medieval West (Leiden, New York and Cologne, 1996)

'What was "Public" about Public Penance? *Paenitentia Publica* and Justice in the Carolingian World', *Settimane* 44 (1996), 863–902

'The Empire as *Ecclesia*: Hrabanus Maurus and Biblical *Historia* for Kings', in Y. Hen and M. Innes (eds.), *Using the Past in the Early Middle Ages* (Cambridge, 2000), pp. 191–226.

Depreux, P., 'Nithard et la *res publica*: un égard critique sur le règne de Louis le Pieux', *Médiévales* 22–3 (1992), 149–61

Prosopographie de l'entourage de Louis le Pieux (781–840) (Sigmaringen, 1997)

Dette, C., 'Einige Bemerkungen zum ältesten Weißenburger Urbar', in A. Verhulst (ed.), *La grande domaine aux époques merovingienne et carolingienne* (Ghent, 1985), pp. 112–24

'Die Grundherrschaft Weißenburg im 9. und 10. Jahrhundert im Spiegel ihrer Herrenhöfe', in W. Rösener (ed.), *Strukturen der Grundherrschaft im frühen Mittelalter*, VMPIG 92 (Göttingen, 1989), pp. 181–96

'Kinder und Jugendliche in der Adelsgesellschaft des frühen Mittelalters', *Archiv für Kulturgeschichte* 76 (1994), 1–34

Devroey, J.-P., 'Polyptyques et fiscalité à l'époque carolingienne: une nouvelle approche', *Revue belge de philologie et d'histoire* 63 (1985), 783–93

'Problèmes de critique autour du polyptyque de l'abbaye de Saint-Germain-des-Prés', in H. Atsma (ed.), *La Neustrie. Les Pays au Nord de la Loire de 650 à 850*, I, Beihefte der Francia 16 (Sigmaringen, 1989), pp. 441–65

'*Ad utilitatem monasterii*. Mobiles et préoccupations de gestion dans l'économie monastique du monde franc', *Revue bénédictine* 103 (1993), 224–40

Etudes sur le grand domaine carolingien (Aldershot, 1993)

Dhondt, J., *Etudes sur la naissance des principautés territoriales en France (IXe–Xe siècles)* (Bruges, 1948)

[Dienemann-]Dietrich, I., 'Die Traditionsnotiz des *CL* Nr.3139 und ihr vermeintliches Datum von 772/73', *Hessisches Jahrbuch für Landesgeschichte* 3 (1953), 283–91

Diepenbach, W., 'Die Münzpragungen am Mittelrhein im Zeitalter der Merowinger', *Mainzer Zeitschrift* 44–5 (1949–50), 141–52

Doll, A., 'Das Pirminskloster Hornbach. Gründung und Verfassungsentwicklung bis Anfang des 12 Jahrhunderts', *Archiv für mittelrheinische Kirchengeschichte* 5 (1953), 108–42

Dronke, P., *Women Writers of the Middle Ages* (Cambridge, 1984)

Dubled, H., '"Allodium" dans les textes latins du moyen âge', *Le Moyen Age* 57 (1951), 241–6

'La notion de propriété en Alsace du VIIIe au Xe siècle', *Le Moyen Age* 14 (1959), 429–52

Duby, G., *La société au XIe et XIIe siècles dans la région mâconnaise* (Paris, 1953)

The Early Growth of the European Economy: Warriors and Peasants from the Seventh to the Twelfth Century, trans. H. B. Clarke (Ithaca, 1974)

'Private Power, Public Power', in Duby (ed.), *A History of Private Life II: Revelations of the Medieval World*, trans. A. Goldhammer (London, 1988), pp. 3–31

Durliat, J., 'Le polyptyque d'Irminon et l'impôt pour l'armée', *Bibliothèque de l'Ecole des Chartes* 141 (1983), 183–208

'Qu'est-ce qu'un polyptyque? A propos des documents de Tours (ChLA 659)', in *Media in Francia . . . Recueil des Mélanges offerts à Karl-Ferdinand Werner* (Paris, 1989), pp. 129–38

Les finances publiques de Dioclétian aux Carolingiens (284–888), Beihefte der Francia 21 (Sigmaringen, 1990)

Effros, B., 'Symbolic Expressions of Sanctity: Gertrude of Nivelles in the Context of Merovingian Mortuary Custom', *Viator* 27 (1996), 1–10

Eibl, E.-M., 'Zur Stellung Bayern und Rheinfranken im Reiche Arnulfs von Kärnten', *Jahrbuch für Geschichte des Feudalismus* 8 (1984), 73–112

Eisenstadt, S. N., 'The Study of the Process of Institutionalisation', in Eisenstadt, *Essays on Comparative Institutions* (New York, Sydney and London), pp. 1–68

Elton, H., *Frontiers of the Roman Empire* (London, 1996)

Erkens, F.-R., '*Divisio legitima* und *unitas imperii*. Teilungspraxis und Einheitsstreben bei der Thronfolge im Frankenreich', *DA* 52 (1996), 423–85

Ertman, T., *Birth of the Leviathan: Building States and Regimes in Medieval and Early Modern Europe* (Cambridge, 1997)

Esch, A., 'Überlieferungs-Chance und Überlieferungs-Zufall als methodisches Problem des Historikers', *Historische Zeitschrift* 240 (1985), 529–70

Estey, F. N., 'The *Scabini* and the Local Courts', *Speculum* 26 (1951), 119–29

Ewig, E., 'Volkstum und Volksbewußtsein im Frankenreich des 7. Jhts.', in Ewig, *Spätantikes und fränkisches Gallien. Gesammelte Schriften (1952–73)*, I, ed. H. Atsma, Beihefte der Francia 3 (Munich, 1976), pp. 231–73

'Der Mittelrhein im Merowingerreich. Eine historische Skizze', in Ewig, *Spätantikes und fränkisches Gallien. Gesammelte Schriften (1952–73)*, I, ed. H. Atsma, Beihefte der Francia 3 (Munich, 1976), pp. 435–49

'Die Stellung Ribuariens in der Verfassungsgeschichte des Merowingerreiches', in Ewig, *Spätantikes und fränkisches Gallien. Gesammelte Schriften (1952–73)*, I, ed. H. Atsma, Beihefte der Francia 3 (Munich, 1976), pp. 450–71

'Die Civitas Ubiorum, die Francia Rinensis und das Land Ribuarien', in Ewig, *Spätantikes und fränkisches Gallien. Gesammelte Schriften (1952–73)*, I, ed. H. Atsma, Beihefte der Francia 3 (Munich, 1976), pp. 472–503

'Civitas, Gau und Territorium in den Trierischen Mosellanden', in Ewig, *Spätantikes und fränkisches Gallien. Gesammelte Schriften (1952–73)*, I, ed. H. Atsma, Beihefte der Francia 3 (Munich, 1976), pp. 504–22

'Milo et eiusmodi similes', in Ewig, *Spätantikes und fränkisches Gallien. Gesammelte Schriften (1952–73)*, II, ed. H. Atsma, Beihefte der Francia 3 (Munich, 1979), pp. 189–219

Bibliography of secondary works

'Beobachtungen zur Entwicklung der fränkischer Reichskirche unter Chrodegang von Metz', in Ewig, *Spätantikes und fränkisches Gallien. Gesammelte Schriften (1952–73)*, II, ed. H. Atsma, Beihefte der Francia 3 (Munich, 1979), pp. 220–31

'Saint Chrodegang et la réforme de l'église franque', in Ewig, *Spätantikes und fränkisches Gallien. Gesammelte Schriften (1952–73)*, II, ed. H. Atsma, Beihefte der Francia 3 (Munich, 1979), pp. 232–59

'Probleme der fränkischen Frühgeschichte in den Rheinlanden', in H. Beumann (ed.), *Historische Forschungen W. Schlesinger* (Cologne and Vienna, 1974), pp. 47–74

'Die Franken am Rhein', in H. Beumann and W. Schröder (eds.), *Aspekte der Nationenbildung im Mittelalter* (Sigmaringen, 1978), pp. 109–26

'Zu Wimpfen und Worms, St-Dié und Trier im 7. Jahrhundert', *Jahrbuch für westdeutsche Landesgeschichte* 1 (1975), 1–9

'Zur Bilihildisurkunde für das Mainzer Kloster Altmünster', in K.-U. Jäschke and R. Wenskus (eds.), *Festschrift für H. Beumann* (Sigmaringen, 1977), pp. 137–48

'Der Raum zwischen Selz und Andernach von 5 bis zur 7 Jahrhundert', in Ewig and J. Werner (eds.), *Von der Spätantike zum frühen Mittelalter. Aktuelle Probleme in historischer und archäologischer Sicht*, VF 25 (Sigmaringen, 1979), pp. 271–96

Frühes Mittelalter: Die Rheinlande in fränkischer Zeit (Düsseldorf, 1980) (vol. I:ii of F. Petri and G. Droege (eds.), *Rheinische Geschichte*)

Falck, L., *Mainz im frühen und hohen Mittelalter (Mitte 5. Jht. bis 1244)* (Düsseldorf, 1972) (vol. II of A. P. Brück and L. Falck (eds.), *Geschichte der Stadt Mainz*)

Fehring, G. P., and Stein, F., 'Frühmittelalterliche Kirchenbauten unter St. Dionysius zu Esslingen am Neckar', *Germania* 44 (1966), 354–85

Felten, F. J., *Äbte und Laienäbte im Frankenreich. Studien zum Verhältnis von Staat und Kirche im früheren Mittelalter*, Monographien zur Geschichte des Mittelalters 20 (Stuttgart, 1980)

'Herrschaft des Äbtes', in F. Prinz (ed.), *Herrschaft und Kirche. Beiträge zur Entstehung und Wirkungsweise episkopaler und monastischer Organisationsformen*, Monographien zur Geschichte des Mittelalters 33 (Stuttgart, 1988), pp. 147–296

Fichtenau, H., *Arenga. Spätantike und Mittelalter im Spiegel der Urkundenformeln*, MIÖG Ergänzungsband 18 (Graz, 1957)

Das Urkundenwesen in Österreich vom 8. bis zum frühen 13. Jahrhundert, MIÖG Ergänzungsband 23 (Vienna, 1971)

'Forschungen über Urkundenformeln. Ein Bericht', *MIÖG* 94 (1986), 285–339

Living in the Tenth Century: Mentalities and Social Order, trans. P. Geary (Philadelphia, 1991)

Fleckenstein, J., 'Fulrad von St-Denis und der fränkische Ausgriff in dem süddeutschen Raum', in G. Tellenbach (ed.), *Studien und Vorarbeiten zur Geschichte des großfränkischen und frühdeutschen Adels*, Forschungen zur oberrheinische Landesgeshichte 4 (Freiburg, 1957), pp. 9–39

'Über die Herkunft der Welfen und ihre Anfänge in Süddeutschland', in G. Tellenbach (ed.), *Studien und Vorarbeiten zur Geschichte des großfränkischen und frühdeutschen Adels*, Forschungen zur oberrheinische Landesgeshichte 4 (Freiburg, 1957), pp. 71–136

Die Hofkapelle der deutschen Könige I. Grundlegung: Die karolingische Hofkapelle, Schriften der MGH 16:i (Stuttgart, 1959)

'Einhard, seine Gründung und sein Vermächtnis im Seligenstadt', in K. Hauck (ed.), *Das Einhardskreuz. Vorträge und Studien der Münsteraner Diskussion zur arcus Einhardi*,

Bibliography of secondary works

Abhandlungen der Gesellschaft der Wissenschaften in Göttingen, philologische-historische Klasse 87 (Göttingen, 1974), pp. 96–121

'Adel und Kriegertum und ihre Wandlung in Karolingerreich', *Settimane* 27 (1981), 67–94

'Problematik und Gestalt der ottonisch-salischen Reichskirche', in K. Schmid (ed.), *Reich und Kirche vor dem Investiturstreit. Festschrift G. Tellenbach* (Sigmaringen, 1985), pp. 83–98

Fleming, R., 'Rural Elites and Urban Life in Late-Saxon England', *P&P* 141 (1993), 3–37

Fossier, R., 'Les tendances de l'économie: stagnation ou croissance?', *Settimane* 27 (1981), 261–74

Foucault, M., 'Governmentality', in G. Burchell, C. Gordon and P. Miller (eds.), *The Foucault Effect: Studies in Governmentality* (Chicago, 1991), pp. 87–104

Fouracre, P., '"Placita" and the Settlement of Disputes in later Merovingian Francia', in W. Davies and P. Fouracre (eds.), *The Settlement of Disputes in Early Medieval Europe* (Cambridge, 1986), pp. 23–44

'Merovingian History and Merovingian Hagiography', *P&P* 127 (1990), 3–38

'Cultural Conformity and Social Conservatism in Early Medieval Europe', *History Workshop Journal* 33 (1992), 152–60

'Carolingian Justice: The Rhetoric of Improvement and the Contexts of Abuse', *Settimane* 42 (1995), 771–803

'Frankish Gaul to 814', in *NCMH*, pp. 85–109

'Eternal Light and Earthly Needs: Practical Aspects of the Development of Frankish Immunities', in W. Davies and P. Fouracre (eds.), *Property and Power in the Early Middle Ages* (Cambridge, 1995), pp. 53–81

Fouracre, P. and Gerberding, R., *Late Merovingian France: History and Hagiography, 640–720* (Manchester, 1996)

Freed, J., *The Counts of Falkenstein: Noble Self-Consciousness in Twelfth-Century Germany* (Philadelphia, 1984)

Freedman, P., *The Origins of Peasant Servitude in Medieval Catalonia* (Cambridge, 1991)

Fried, J., 'Der karolingische Herrschaftsverband im 9. Jahrhundert zwischen "Kirche" und "Königshaus"', *Historische Zeitschrift* 235 (1982), 1–43

König Ludwig der Jüngere in seiner Zeit, Geschichtsblätter für die Kreis Bergstraße 16 (Lorsch, 1983)

Friese, A., *Studien zur Herrschaftsgeschichte des fränkischen Adels. Der mainlandische-thuringische Raum von 7. bus 11. Jahrhunderts* (Stuttgart, 1979)

Friese, E., 'Studien zur Einzugsbereich der Kloster von Fulda', in *Klostergemeinschaft* II:iii, pp. 1003–1269

'Zum Geburtsjahr des Hrabanus Maurus', in R. Kottje and H. Zimmermann (eds.), *Hrabanus Maurus. Lehrer, Abt und Bischof* (Wiesbaden, 1982), pp. 18–74

Ganshof, F. L., 'Benefice and Vassalage in the Age of Charlemagne', *Cambridge Historical Journal* 6 (1939), 147–75

Feudalism, trans. P. Grierson (London, 1953)

'La preuve dans le droit franc', in *La Preuve*, 2 vols., Recueil de la Société Jean Bodin 17 (Paris, 1965), II, pp. 71–98

Frankish Institutions under Charlemagne (Providence, 1968)

'Charlemagne's Use of the Oath', in Ganshof, *The Carolingians and the Frankish Monarchy* (London, 1971), pp. 111–124

Bibliography of secondary works

'On the Genesis and Significance of the Treaty of Verdun (843)', in Ganshof, *The Carolingians and the Frankish Monarchy* (London, 1971), pp. 273–88

'Note sur la concession d'alleux à des vassaux sous le règne de Louis le Pieux', in *Storiografia e Storia: Studi in onore di E.Dupré Theseider* (Rome, 1974), pp. 589–99

Geary, P. J., *Aristocracy in Provence: The Rhône Basin at the Dawn of the Carolingian Age* (Stuttgart and Philadelphia, 1985)

Furta Sacra: Thefts of Relics in the Central Middle Ages (2nd edn, Princeton, 1990)

'The Uses of Archaeological Sources for Religious and Cultural History', in Geary, *Living with the Dead in the Middle Ages* (Ithaca and London, 1994), pp. 30–48

'Exchange and Interaction between the Living and Dead in Early Medieval Society', in Geary, *Living with the Dead in the Middle Ages* (Ithaca and London, 1994), pp. 77–94

'Living with Conflicts in Stateless France: A Typology of Conflict Management Mechanisms, 1050–1200', in Geary, *Living with the Dead in the Middle Ages* (Ithaca and London, 1994), pp. 125–62

Phantoms of Remembrance: Memory and Oblivion at the End of the First Millennium (Princeton, 1994)

'Extra-Judicial Means of Conflict Resolution', *Settimane* 42 (1995), 569–605

Genicot, L., '*Publicus*. Sur la survivance de la notion de l'état', in L. Fenske *et al.* (eds.), *Institutionen, Gesellschaft und Kultur im Mittelalter. Festschrift J. Fleckenstein* (Sigmaringen, 1984), pp. 147–64

Gensicke, H., 'Samuel, Bischof von Worms 838–856', in F. Knöpp (ed.), *Die Reichsabtei Lorsch. Festschrift zum Gedenken an ihre Stiftung 764*, 2 vols. (Darmstadt, 1974–77), I, pp. 253–6

Gerlich, A., '"Fidelis noster Otakarus". Aus den Anfängen der Bonifatiusverehrung am Mittelrhein', *Mainzer Zeitschrift* 48/49 (1953–4), 1–3

'Zur Reichspolitik des Erzbischofes Otgar von Mainz', *Rheinische Vierteljahrsblätter* 19 (1954), 286–316

Geuenich, D., 'Beobachtungen zu Grimald von St Gallen, Erzkapellan und Oberkanzler Ludwigs des Deutschen', in M. Borgolte and H. Spilling (eds.), *Litterae Medii Aevi. Festschrift J. Autenrieth* (Sigmaringen, 1988), pp. 55–68

Gierlich, E., *Die Grabstätten der Rheinische Bischöfe vor 1200*, Quellen und Abhandlungen zur mittelrheinische Kirchengeschichte 65 (Mainz, 1990)

Gladiß, D., 'Die Schenkungen der deutschen Könige zu privaten Eigen (800–1137)', *DA* 1 (1937), 80–136

Glocker, W., *Die Verwandten der Ottonen und ihre Bedeutung in der Politik* (Vienna and Cologne, 1989)

Glöckner, K., 'Ein Urbar des rheinfränkischen Reichsgutes aus Lorsch', *MIÖG* 38 (1920), 381–98

'Das Reichsgut im Rhein-Maingebiet', *Archiv für Hessische Geschichte und Altertumskunde* 18 (1934), 195–216

'Lorsch und Lothringen, Robertiner und Capetinger', *ZGO* 50 (1936), 301–54

Gockel, M., *Karolingische Königshöfe am Mittelrhein*, VMPIG 31 (Göttingen, 1970)

'Zur Verwandtschaft der Äbtissin Emhilt von Milz', in H. Beumann (ed.), *Festschrift für Walter Schlesinger*, 2 vols., Mitteldeutsche Forschungen 74 (Marburg, 1974), II, pp. 1–70

Review of F. Staab, 'Untersuchungen zur Gesellschaft der Karolingerzeit am Mittelrhein', *Naßauische Annalen* 87 (1976), 309–15

'Die Träger von Rodung und Siedlung in Hünfelder Raum in der Karolingerzeit', *Hessisches Jahrbuch für Landesgeschichte* 26 (1976), 1–26
'Die Bedeutung Treburs als Pfalzort', in *Deutsche Königspfalzen: Beiträge zu ihrer historischen und archäologischen Erforschung*, III, VMPIG 11 (Göttingen, 1979), pp. 86–110
Godelier, M., and Strathern, M. (eds.), *Big Men and Great Men* (Cambridge, 1991)
Godman, P., and Collins, R. (eds.), *Charlemagne's Heir: New Perspectives on the Reign of Louis the Pious (814–840)* (Oxford, 1990)
Goetz, H.-W., *'Dux' und 'ducatus'* (Bochum, 1977)
'*Nobilis*: Der Adel im Selbstverständnis der Karolingerzeit', *Vierteljahrsschrift für Sozial und Wirtschaftsgeschichte* 70 (1983), 153–91
'Herrschaft und Recht in der frühmittelalterlicher Grundherrschaft', *Historisches Jahrbuch* 104 (1984), 392–410
'*Regnum*. Zum politische denken der Karolingerzeit', *ZSRG GA* 104 (1987), 110–90
'Serfdom and the Beginnings of a "Seigneurial System" in the Carolingian Period: A Survey of the Evidence', *EME* 2 (1993), 29–51
Goffart, W., 'From Roman Taxation to Medieval Seigneurie: Three Notes', in Goffart, *Rome's Fall and After* (London, 1989), pp. 167–211
'Old and New in Merovingian Taxation', in Goffart, *Rome's Fall and After* (London, 1989), pp. 213–31
'Merovingian Polyptyques: Reflections on Two Recent Publications', in Goffart, *Rome's Fall and After* (London, 1989), pp. 255–73
Goody, J., 'Inheritance, Property and Women: Some Comparative Considerations', in Goody, J. Thirsk and E. P. Thompson (eds.), *Family and Inheritance: Rural Society in Western Europe, 1200–1800* (Cambridge, 1976), pp. 10–36
The Development of the Family and Marriage in Europe (Cambridge, 1983)
Grünewald, M., 'Worms zwischen Burgunden und Saliern', in K. van Welck (ed.), *Die Franken. Wegbereiter Europas*, 2 vols. (Mainz, 1996), I, pp. 160–2
Guillot, O., 'Une *ordinatio* méconnue: Le Capitulaire de 823/5', in P. Godman and R. Collins (eds.), *Charlemagne's Heir: New Perspectives on the Reign of Louis the Pious (814–40)* (Oxford, 1990), pp. 455–86
Gurevich, A., 'Représentations et attitudes à l'égard de la propriété pendant le haut moyen âge', *Annales: ESC* 27 (1972), 523–47
Habermas, J., *The Structural Transformation of the Public Sphere: An Inquiry into a Category of Bourgeois Society*, trans. T. Berger (London, 1989)
Hägermann, D., 'Die Abt als Grundherr: Kloster und Wirtschaft im frühen Mittelalter', in F. Prinz (ed.), *Herrschaft und Kirche. Beiträge zur Entstehung und Wirkungsweise episkopaler und monastischer Organisationsformen*, Monographien zur Geschichte des Mittelalters 33 (Stuttgart, 1988), pp. 345–85
Hahn, H., 'Eihloha – Sturm und das Kloster Fulda', *Fuldaer Geschichtsblätter* 56 (1980), 50–82
Haldon, J. F., *The State and the Tributary Mode of Production* (London, 1993)
'Military Service, Military Lands and the Status of Soldiers: Current Problems and Interpretations', *Dumbarton Oaks Papers* 47 (1993), 1–67
Hall, J. A., *Powers and Liberties: The Causes and Consequences of the Rise of the West* (London, 1985)
Hall, S. et al., *Policing the Crisis* (London, 1973)

Halsall, G., 'The Origins of the *Reihengräberzivilisation* – Forty Years On', in J. F. Drinkwater and H. Elton (eds.), *Fifth-Century Gaul:A Crisis of Identity?* (Cambridge, 1992), pp. 196–207

'Social Change around 600: An Austrasian Perspective', in M. Carver (ed.), *The Age of Sutton Hoo* (Woodbridge, 1992), pp. 265–78

Settlement and Social Organisation:The Merovingian Region of Metz (Cambridge, 1995)

'Female Status and Power in Early Medieval Central Austrasia: The Burial Evidence', *EME* 5 (1996), 1–24

'Towns, Societies and Ideas: The Not-so-strange Case of late Roman and early Merovingian Mez', in N. Christie and S. T. Loseby (eds.), *Towns in Transition* (Woodbridge, 1997), pp. 235–61

'Burial Ritual and Merovingian Society', in J. Hill and M. Swan (eds.), *The Community, the Family and the Saint* (Turnhout, 1998), pp. 325–38

'Social Identities and Social Relationships in early Merovingian Gaul', in I. N. Wood (ed.), *Franks and Alamanni in the Merovingian Period: An Ethnographic Perspective* (Woodbridge, 1998), pp. 141–65

'Archaeology and the late Roman Frontier in northern Gaul: The so-called *Federatengräber* Reconsidered', in W. Pohl and H. Reimitz (eds.), *Grenze und Differenz im früheren Mittelalter* (Vienna, forthcoming)

Halsall, G. (ed.), *Violence and Society in the Early Medieval West* (London, 1997)

Hamerow, H., 'The Archaeology of Rural Settlement in Early Medieval Europe', *EME* 3 (1994), 167–79

'Shaping Settlements: Early Medieval Communities in Northwest Europe', in J. Bintliff and H. Hamerow (eds.), *Europe between Late Antiquity and the Middle Ages*, British Archaeological Reports International Series 617 (Oxford, 1995), pp. 8–37

Hammer, C. I., 'Family and *familia* in Early Medieval Bavaria', in R. Wall *et al.* (eds.), *Family Forms in Historic Europe* (Cambridge, 1983), pp. 217–48

'*Lex scripta* in Early Medieval Bavaria: Use and Abuse of *Lex Baiuvariorum*', in E. B. King and S. Ridyard (eds.), *Law in Medieval Life and Thought* (Sewanee, 1990), pp. 185–95

'Servile Names and Seigneurial Organisation in Early Medieval Bavaria', *Studi Medievali* 36 (1995), 917–28

'Land Sales in Eighth- and Ninth-century Bavaria: Legal, Economic and Social Aspects', *EME* 6 (1997), 47–76

Hampel, A., *Der Kaiserdom zu Frankfurt am Main, Ausgrabungen 1991–3* (Nußloch, 1994)

Hannig, J., *Consensus Fidelium. Frühfeudale Interpretation des Verhältnisses von Königtum und Adel am Beispiel des Frankenreiches*, Monographien zur Geschichte des Mittelalters 27 (Stuttgart, 1982)

'*Pauperiores vassi de infra palatio?* Zur Entstehung der karolingischen Königsbotenorganisation', *MIÖG* 91 (1983), 309–74

'Zentralle Kontrolle und regionale Machtbalance. Beobachtungen zum System der karolingischen Königsboten am Beispiel des Mittelrheingebietes', *Archiv für Kulturgeschichte* 66 (1984), 1–46

'Zur Funktion der karolingischen "missi dominici" im Bayern und in den südostlichen Grenzgebieten', *ZSRG GA* 101 (1984), 256–300

'*Ars donandi*: Zur Ökonomie des Schenkungs im früheren Mittelalter', *Geschichte in Wissenschaft und Unterricht* 3 (1986), 149–62

Bibliography of secondary works

Hardt-Friederichs, F., 'Markt, Münze und Zoll im ostfränkischen Reich bis zum Ende der Ottonen', *Blätter für deutsche Landesgeschichte* 116 (1980), 1–32

Härke, H., 'Warrior Graves? The Background of the Anglo-Saxon Weapon Burial Rite', *P&P* 126 (1990), 22–43

Harrison, R., *The Early State and Cities in Lombard Italy* (Lund, 1993)

Harriss, G., 'Political Society and the Growth of Government in Late Medieval England', *P&P* 138 (1993), 28–57

Hartung, W., 'Adel, Erbrecht, Schenkung. Die strukturellen Ursachen der frühmittelalterlichen Besitzübertragungen an die Kirche', in F. Seibt (ed.), *Gesellschaftsgeschichte: Festschrift für K. Bosl zum 80. Geburtstag*, 2 vols. (Munich, 1988), II, pp. 417–38

Hauck, K., 'Tiergärten im Pfalzbereich', in *Deutsche Königspfalzen: Beiträge zu ihrer historischen und archäologischen Erforschung*, I, VMPIG 11 (Göttingen, 1963), pp. 30–74

Hay, D. et al., *Albion's Fatal Tree: Crime and Society in Eighteenth-century England* (London, 1974)

Head, T., *Hagiography and the Cult of the Saints: The Diocese of Orléans 800–1200* (Cambridge, 1990)

Heidrich, I., 'Titulatur und Urkunden der arnulfingischen Hausmeier', *Archiv für Diplomatik* 11/12 (1965–6), 71–279

Heinemeyer, K., *Das Erzbistum Mainz in römischer und fränkischer Zeit I. Die Anfänge der Diözese Mainz*, Veröffentlichungen der Historischen Kommission für Hessen und Waldeck 39 (Marburg, 1979)

'Die Gründung des Klosters Fulda im Rahmen der bonifatianischen Kirchenorganisation', *Fuldaer Geschichtsblätter* 56 (1980), 83–132

Heinzelmann, M., 'L'aristocratie et les évêchés entre Loire et Rhin jusqu'à la fin du VIIe siècle', *Revue d'Histoire de l'Eglise de France* 62 (1976), 75–90

Translationsberichte und andere Quellen des Reliquienkultes, Typologie des sources du Moyen Age occidental 33 (Turnhout, 1979)

'Bischof und Herrschaft vom spätantiken Gallien bis zur den karolingischen Hausmeiern: Die institutionellen Grundlagen', in F. Prinz (ed.), *Herrschaft und Kirche. Beiträge zur Entstehung und Wirkungsweise episkopaler und monastischer Organisationsformen*, Monographien zur Geschichte des Mittelalters 33 (Stuttgart, 1988), pp. 23–82

'"Villa" d'après les œuvres de Grégoire de Tours', in E. Magnou-Nortier (ed.), *Aux sources de la gestion publique* (Lille, 1993), pp. 45–70

Heitzmann, J., 'State Formation in South India, 850–1280', *Indian Economic and Social History Review* 24 (1987), 35–61

'Ritual Polity and Economy: The Transactional Network of an Imperial Temple in Medieval Southern India', *Journal of the Economic and Social History of the Orient* 34 (1991), 25–54

Hen, Y., *Culture and Religion in Merovingian Gaul* (New York, Leiden and Cologne, 1995)

Herlihy, D., 'Church Property on the European Continent, 701–1200', *Speculum* 36 (1961), 81–102

Heß, W., 'Geldwirtschaft am Mittelrhein in karolingischer Zeit', *Blätter für deutsche Landesgeschichte* 98 (1962), 26–63

Heydenreich, E., 'Eine Urkunde für Fulda vom 30 Aug. 834', *Historische Vierteljahrschrift* 5 (1902), 390–1

Hlawitschka, E., *Lothringen und das Reich an der Schwelle der deutschen Geschichte*, Schriften der MGH 21 (Stuttgart, 1968)

Bibliography of secondary works

Die Anfänge des Hauses Habsburg-Lothringen. Genealogische Untersuchungen zur Geschichte Lothringens und das Reichs im 9., 10. und 11. Jht., Veröffentlichungen der Kommission für saarländische Landesgeschichte und Volkskunst 4 (Saarbrücken, 1969)

'Waren die Kaiser Wido und Lambert Nachkommen Karls des Großen?', *Quellen und Forschungen aus italienischen Archiven und Bibliotheken* 49 (1969), 366–86

'Zu den Grundlagen des Aufstiegs der Karolinger. Beschäftigung mit zwei Büchern von Matthias Werner', *Rheinische Vierteljahrsblätter* 49 (1985), 1–61

Hodges, R., *Dark Age Economics: The Origins of Towns and Trade AD 600–1000* (London, 1982)

Hoffmann, H., 'Kirche und Sklaverei im frühen Mittelalter', *DA* 42 (1988), 1–47

'Grafschaften in Bischofshand', *DA* 46 (1990), 375–480

Holt, J. C., 'Property and Politics in Early Medieval England', *P&P* 57 (1972), 3–52

Hülsen, F., *Die Besitzungen des Klosters Lorsch in der Karolingerzeit. Ein Beitrag zur Topographie Deutschlands im Mittelalter*, Historische Studien 104 (Berlin, 1913)

Humphreys, S., 'Social Relations on Stage: Witnesses in Classical Athens', *History and Anthropology* 1 (1985), 313–69

Hussong, U., 'Studien zur Geschichte der Reichsabtei Fulda bis zur Jahrtausendswende', Parts I–II, *Archiv für Diplomatik* 31 (1985), 1–255; 32 (1986) 129–304

Innes, M., 'Charlemagne's Will: Politics, Inheritance and Ideology in the Early Ninth Century', *English Historical Review* 112 (1997), 833–55

'Memory, Orality and Literacy in an Early Medieval Society', *P&P* 158 (1998), 3–36

'Kings, Monks and Patrons: Political Identity at the Abbey of Lorsch', in R. Le Jan (ed.), *La royauté et les élites dans l'Europe carolingienne* (Lille, 1998), pp. 301–24

'*A Place of Discipline*: Aristocratic Youth and Carolingian Courts', in C. Cubitt (ed.), *Court Culture in the Early Middle Ages* (forthcoming)

'Keeping it in the Family: Women and Aristocratic Memory, 700–1200', in E. van Houts (ed.), *Medieval Memories: Men, Women and the Past, 700–1300* (London, 2001)

'Space, Place and Power in Carolingian Society', in M. De Jong and F. Theuws (eds.), *Topographies of Power in the Early Middle Ages* (Leiden, forthcoming)

Innes, M., and McKitterick, R., 'The Writing of History', in R. McKitterick (ed.), *Carolingian Culture: Emulation and Innovation* (Cambridge, 1994), pp. 193–220

Jackman, D. C., *Criticism and Critique: Sidelights on the Konradiner* (Oxford, 1997)

Jacobi, F., 'Die weltlichen und geistlichen Magnaten im Fuldaer Totenannalen', in *Klostergemeinschaft* II:ii, pp. 792–887

Jacobsen, W., 'Die Lorscher Torhalle. Zum Probleme ihrer Deutung und Datierung', *Jahrbuch des Zentralinstituts für Kunstgeschichte* 1 (1985), 9–77

Jahn, J., '*Tradere ad sanctum*. Politische und gesellschaftliche Aspekte der Traditionspraxis im agilolfingischen Bayern', in F. Seibt (ed.), *Gesellschaftsgeschichte. Festschrift für K. Bosl zum 80. Geburtstag*, 2 vols. (Munich, 1988), II, pp. 400–16

James, E., 'Cemeteries and the Problem of Frankish Settlement in Gaul', in P. H. Sawyer (ed.), *Names, Words and Graves: Early Medieval Settlement* (Leeds, 1979), pp. 55–89

The Franks (Oxford, 1988)

'Burial and Status in the Early Medieval West', *Transactions of the Royal Historical Society* 39 (1989), 23–40

Janssen, W., 'Dorf und Dorfformen des 7. bis 12. Jhts. im Lichte neuer Ausgrabungen in Mittel- und Nordeuropa', in H. Jankuhn *et al.* (eds.), *Das Dorf der Eisenzeit und des frühen Mittelalters*, Abhandlungen der Akademie der Wissenschaften in Göttingen, philologische-historische Klasse 101 (Göttingen, 1977), pp. 285–356

Bibliography of secondary works

Jarnut, J., 'Die frühmittelalterliche Jagd unter rechts- und sozialgeschichtlichen Aspekten', *Settimane* 31 (1985), 765–808

'Ein Bruderkampf und seine Folgen. Die Krise des Frankenreiches (768–71)', in G. Jenal (ed.), *Herrschaft, Kirche, Kultur. Festschrift F. Prinz*, Monographien zur Geschichte des Mittelalters 32 (Sigmaringen, 1992), pp. 165–77

Jarnut, J., Nonn, U., and Richter, M. (eds.), *Karl Martell in seiner Zeit*, Beihefte der Francia 37 (Sigmaringen, 1994)

Jäschke, K.-U., 'Zu den schriftlichen Zeugnissen für die Anfänge der Reichsabtei Hersfeld', *Blätter für deutsche Landesgeschichte* 107 (1971), 94–135

Burgenbau und Landesverteidigung um 900, VF Sonderband 16 (Sigmaringen, 1975)

Jobert, P., *La notion de donation: Convergances 630–750*, Publications de l'Université de Dijon (Paris, 1977)

Johanek, P., 'Zur rechtlichen Funktion von Traditionsnotiz, Traditionsbuch und früher Siegelkunde', in P. Classen (ed.), *Recht und Schrift im Mittelalter*, VF 23 (Sigmaringen, 1977), pp. 131–62

John, E., *Land Tenure in Early England: A Discussion of Some Problems* (Leicester, 1960)

John, W., 'Formale Beziehungen der privaten Schenkungsurkunden Italiens und des Frankenreiches und die Wirksamkeit der Formulare', *Archiv für Urkundenforschung* 14 (1936), 1–104

Jorns, W., 'Zullestein. Ein Beitrag zur Kontinuität von Bauwerken', in *Deutsche Königspfalzen: Beiträge zu ihrer historischen und archäologischen Erforschung*, III, VMPIG 11 (Göttingen, 1979), pp. 111–35

Kaiser, R., 'Steuer und Zoll in der Merowingerzeit', *Francia* 7 (1979), 1–17

Kasten, B., 'Erbrechtliche Verfügungen des 8. und 9. Jhts. Zugleich ein Beitrag zur Organisation und zur Schriftlichkeit bei der Verwaltung adeliger Grundherrschaft am Beispiel des Grafen Heccard aus Burgund', *ZSRG GA* 107 (1990), 236–338

Königssöhne und Königsherrschaft. Untersuchungen zur Teilhabe am Reich in der Merowinger- und Karolingerzeit, Schriften der MGH 44 (Hanover, 1997)

Kautsky, J. H., *The Politics of Aristocratic Empires* (Chapel Hill, 1982)

Keller, H., 'Grundlagen ottonischer Königsherrschaft', in K. Schmid (ed.), *Reich und Kirche vor dem Investiturstreit. Festschrift G. Tellenbach* (Sigmaringen, 1985), pp. 17–34

'Zum Charakter der "Staatlichkeit" zwischen karolingischer Reichsreform und hochmittelalterliche Herrschaftsausbau', *Frühmittelalterliche Studien* 32 (1989), 248–64

'Reichsorganisation, Herrschaftsformen und Gesellschaftsstrukturen im Regnum Teutonicum', *Settimane* 38 (1990), 159–95

Keller, H. *et al.*, 'Mittelalterliche Städte auf römischer Grundlage im einstigen Dekumatenland', *ZGO* 96 (1987), 1–64

Kessler, P. T., 'Merowingisches Fürstengrab von Planig in Rheinhessen', *Mainzer Zeitschrift* 35 (1940), 1–12

Kessler, P. T., and Schnellenkamp, W., 'Ein frühmerowingisches Grab bei Rommersheim (Eichloch) in Rheinhessen', *Mainzer Zeitschrift* 28 (1933), 118–25

Kienast, W., *Die fränkische Vasallität von den Hausmeiern bis zu Ludwig dem Kind und Karl dem Einfältigen* (Frankfurt, 1990)

Kleberger, E., *Territorialgeschichte des hinteren Odenwalds*, Schriften des Hessischen Amts für geschichtliche Landeskunde 26 (Darmstadt, 1958)

Kletschke, H., *Die Sprache der Mainzer Kanzlei nach den Namen der Fuldaer Urkunden*, Hermaea 29 (Halle, 1933)

289

Bibliography of secondary works

Knöpp, F. (ed.), *Die Reichsabtei Lorsch. Festschrift zum Gedenken an ihre Stiftung 764*, 2 vols. (Darmstadt, 1974–7)

Köbler, G., *Das Recht im frühen Mittelalter. Untersuchungen zu Herkunft und Inhalt frühmittelalterlicher Rechtsbegriffe im deutschen Sprachgebiet*, Forschungen zur deutschen Rechtsgeschichte 7 (Cologne and Vienna, 1971)

'Eigen und Eigentum', *ZSRG GA* 95 (1978), 1–33

Kottje, R., 'Schriftlichkeit im Dienst der Klosterverwaltung und des klösterlichen Lebens unter Hrabanus Maurus', in G. Schrimpf (ed.), *Kloster Fulda in der Welt der Karolinger und Ottonen*, Fuldaer Studien 7 (Frankfurt, 1996), pp. 177–92

Kottje, R., and Zimmermann, H. (eds.), *Hrabanus Maurus. Lehrer, Abt und Bischof*, Mainzer Akademie der Wissenschaften und der Literatur, Abhandlungen der Geistes- und Sozialwissenschaften 4 (Wiesbaden, 1982)

Kraft, R., *Das Reichsgut im Wormsgau*, Quellen und Forschungen zur Hessischen Geschichte 16 (Darmstadt, 1934)

Krah, A., *Absetzungsverfahren als Spiegelbild von Königsmacht. Untersuchungen zum Kräftesverhältnis zwischen Königtum und Adel im Karolingerreich und seinen Nachfolgestaaten* (Aalen, 1987)

Kuchenbuch, L., *Bauerliche Gesellschaft und Klosterherrschaft im 9. Jht. Studien zur Sozialstruktur der Familia der Abtei Prüm*, Vierteljahrsschrift für Sozial- und Wirtschaftsgeschichte Beihefte 66 (Wiesbaden, 1978)

'Die Klostergrundherrschaft im Frühmittelalter: Eine Zwischenbilanz', in F. Prinz (ed.), *Herrschaft und Kirche. Beiträge zur Entstehung und Wirkungsweise episkopaler und monastischer Organisationsformen*, Monographien zur Geschichte des Mittelalters 33 (Stuttgart, 1988), pp. 297–343

Kuhn, T. S., *The Structure of Scientific Revolutions* (Chicago, 1962)

Kutsch, K., 'Frühfränkisches Grab aus Biebrich', *Germania* 5 (1921), 27–35

Lachmann, H.-P., 'Die frühmittelalterlichen Marken zwischen Rhein und Odenwald unter besondere Berücksichtigung der Mark Heppenheim', *Berichte zur deutsche Landeskunde* 49 (1975), 27–37

La Rocca, C., 'Segni di distinzione. Dai corredi funerari alle donazioni "post obitum" nel regno langobardo', in L. Paroli (ed.), *L'Italia centro-settentrionale in età langobarda* (Florence, 1997), pp. 31–54

Lauranson-Rosaz, C., *L'Auvergne et ses marges (Velay, Gévaudan) du VIIIe au XIe siècle: la fin du monde antique?* (Le Puy-en-Velay, 1987)

Le Jan, R., '"Pauperes" et "Paupertas" dans l'occident carolingien aux IXe et Xe siècle', *Revue du Nord* 50 (1968), 169–87

'Structures familiales et politiques au IXe siècle: un group familiale de l'aristocratie franque', *Revue Historique* 265 (1981), 289–333

'Aux origines du douaire médiéval (VIe–Xe siècles)', in M. Parisse (ed.), *Veuves et Veuvage dans le Haut Moyen Age* (Paris, 1993), pp. 107–21

'Domnus, illuster, nobilissimus: les mutations de pouvoir au Xe siècle', in M. Sot (ed.), *Haut Moyen Age. Festschrift P. Riché* (Paris, 1993), pp. 439–48

Famille et Pouvoir dans le Monde Franc, VIIIe–Xe siècles, Publications de la Sorbonne (Paris, 1995)

'Justice royale et pratiques sociales dans le royaume franc au IXe siècle', *Settimane* 44 (1997), 47–86

Le Jan, R. (ed.)., *La royauté et les élites dans l'Europe carolingienne* (Lille, 1998)

Lechner, J., 'Die älteren Königsurkunden für das Bistum Worms und die Begründung der bischöflichen Fürstenmacht', *MIÖG* 22 (1901), 361–409, 529–74

Lemarignier, J.-F., 'La dislocation du "pagus" et le problème des "consuetudines" (Xe–XIe siècles)', in *Mélanges d'histoire du moyen âge dédiés à la mémoire de Louis Halphen* (Paris, 1951), pp. 401–10

Lesne, E., 'Les diverses acceptions du terme "beneficium" du VIIIe au IXe siècle', *Revue historique du droit français et étranger* 3 (1924), 5–56

Levillain, L., 'Les Nibelungen historiques et leurs alliances de famille', Parts I–II, *Annales du Midi* 49 (1937) 337–407; 50 (1938) 5–72

Levison, W., *England and the Continent in the Eighth Century* (Oxford, 1946)

Levy, E., *West Roman Vulgar Law: The Law of Property* (Philadelphia, 1951)

Leyser, K., *Rule and Conflict in an Early Medieval Society* (Oxford, 1979)

'Ottonian Government', *English Historical Review* 96 (1981), 721–53

'The Crisis of Medieval Germany', *Proceedings of the British Academy* 69 (1983), 409–43

'Early Medieval Canon Law and the Beginnings of Knighthood', in L. Fenske *et al.* (eds.), *Institutionen, Kultur und Gesellschaft im Mittelalter. Festschrift J. Fleckenstein* (Sigmaringen, 1984), pp. 549–66

'Ritual, Ceremony and Gesture: Ottonian Germany', in Leyser, *Communications and Power in Medieval Europe I: The Carolingian and Ottonian Centuries*, ed. T. Reuter (London, 1994), pp. 189–213

Liebeschuetz, J. H. W. G., *Barbarians and Bishops: Army, Church and State in the Age of Arcadius and Chrysostom* (Oxford, 1991)

Little, L. K., *Benedictine Maledictions: Liturgical Cursing in Romanesque France* (Ithaca and London, 1993)

Lot, F., *L'impôt foncier et la capitation personnelle sous le bas-Empire et à l'époque francque*, Bibliotheque de l'Ecole des Hautes Etudes 253 (Paris, 1928)

'Note sur le sénéchal Alard', in Lot, *Recueil des travaux historiques* (Paris, 1970), II, pp. 591–607

Löwe, H., 'Studien zu den Annales Xantenses', *DA* 8 (1950), 59–99

Lund, N., 'The Armies of Swein Forkbeard and Cnut: *Leding* or *Liđ*?', *Anglo-Saxon England* 15 (1984), 105–18

MacCormack, S., 'Sin, Citizenship and the Salvation of Souls: The Impact of Christian Practices on late Roman and post-Roman Society', *Comparative Studies in Society and History* 39 (1997), 644–73

McKitterick, R., *The Frankish Church and the Carolingian Reforms, 789–895* (London, 1977)

The Frankish Kingdoms under the Carolingians, 751–987 (London, 1983)

The Carolingians and the Written Word (Cambridge, 1989)

'Frauen und Schriftlichkeit im Frühmittelalter', in H.-W. Goetz (ed.), *Weibliche Lebensgestaltung im frühen Mittelalter* (Cologne, Weimar and Vienna, 1991), pp. 65–118; English trans., 'Women and Literacy in the Early Middle Ages', in McKitterick, *Books, Scribes and Learning in the Frankish Kingdoms, 6th to 9th Centuries* (Aldershot, 1994), no. XIII

'Perceptions of Justice in Europe in the Ninth and Tenth Centuries', *Settimane* 44 (1997), 1075–1102

'Constructing the Past in the Early Middle Ages: The Case of the Royal Frankish Annals', *Transactions of the Royal Historical Society* 7 (1997), 101–29

Bibliography of secondary works

McKitterick, R. (ed.), *Carolingian Culture: Emulation and Innovation* (Cambridge, 1994)

New Cambridge Medieval History II: 700–900 (Cambridge, 1995)

McLaughlin, M., *Consorting with Saints: The Ideology of Prayer for the Dead in Early Medieval France* (Ithaca, 1993)

Maddern, P., *Violence and Social Order: East Anglia, 1422–42* (Oxford, 1992)

Magnou-Nortier, E., 'La gestion publique en Neustrie: les moyens et les hommes (VIIe–IXe siècles)', in H. Atsma (ed.), *La Neustrie. Les Pays au Nord de la Loire de 650 à 850*, I, Beihefte der Francia 16 (Sigmaringen, 1989), pp. 271–320

'La chute de Rome a-t-elle eu lieu?', *Bibliothèque de l'Ecole des Chartes* 152 (1994), 521–41

Mann, M., *The Sources of Social Power I: A History of Power from the Beginning to A.D.1760* (Cambridge, 1986)

Martindale, J., 'The French Aristocracy in the Early Middle Ages: A Reappraisal', *P&P* 75 (1977), 5–45

'The Kingdom of Aquitaine and the Dissolution of the Carolingian Fisc', *Francia* 11 (1985), 131–91

'The Nun Immena and the Foundation of the Abbey of Beaulieu: A Woman's Prospects in the Carolingian Church', *Studies in Church History* 27 (1990), 27–42

'"His Special Friend"? The Settlement of Disputes and Political Power in the Kingdom of the French, Tenth to Twelfth Centuries', *Transactions of the Royal Historical Society* 5 (1995), 22–42

Matthews, J. F., *Western Aristocracies and the Imperial Court, AD 364–425* (Oxford, 1975)

Maurer, H., *Der Herzog der Schwaben* (Sigmaringen, 1978)

Mauss, M., *The Gift: Forms and Functions of Exchange in Archaic Societies*, trans. I. Cunnison (New York, 1967)

Mayaram, J., 'Mughal State-formation: The Mewati Counter-perspective', *Indian Economic and Social History Review* 34 (1992), 169–97

Mayer, T., 'Die Ausbildung der Grundlagen des modernen deutsches Staat im hohen Mittelalter', *Historische Zeitschrift* 159 (1938–9), 457–87

Metz, W., 'Babenberger und Rupertiner in Ostfranken', *Jahrbuch für fränkische Landesforschung* 18 (1958), 295–304

Das karolingische Reichsgut. Eine verfassungs- und verwaltungsgeschichtliche Untersuchung (Berlin, 1960)

'Das Problem der Babenberger in landesgeschichtlicher Sicht', *Blätter für deutsche Landesgeschichte* 99 (1963), 59–81

'Miszellen zur Geschichte der Widonen und der Salier, vornehmlich in Deutschland', *Historisches Jahrbuch* 85 (1965), 1–27

'Das Kloster Weißenburg und der Vertrag von Verdun', in C. Bauer *et al.* (eds.), *Speculum Historiale. [Festschrift J. Spörl]* (Munich, 1965), pp. 458–68

'Austrasische Adelsherrschaft des 8 Jahrhunderts. Mittelrheinische Grundherren in Ostfranken, Thüringen und Hessen', *Historisches Jahrbuch* 87 (1967), 257–304

'Forschungen zur Reichsgut im Rhein-Main-Gebiet', in J. Bärman *et al.* (eds.), *Geschichtliche Landeskunde* 7 (Wiesbaden, 1972), pp. 209–17

'Zur Herkunft und Verwandtschaft Bischof Burchards I von Worms', *Hessisches Jahrbuch für Landesgeschichte* 26 (1976), 27–42

'Zu Wesen und Strukturen der geistlichen Grundherrschaft', *Settimane* 27 (1981), 147–69

'Zum Lorscher Reichsurbar', *Historisches Jahrbuch* 106 (1986), 407–17

Miller, D. H., 'Frontier Societies and the Transition between Late Antiquity and the Early Middle Ages', in H. Elton and H. Sivan (eds.), *Shifting Frontiers in Late Antiquity* (Aldershot, 1996), pp. 158–71

Miller, W. I., *Bloodtaking and Peacemaking: Feud, Law and Society in Saga Iceland* (Chicago, 1990)

Mitterauer, M., *Karolingische Markgrafen im Südosten. Fränkische Reichsaristokratie und bayerischer Stammesadel im österreichischen Raum*, Archiv für österreichische Geschichte 123 (Vienna, Graz and Cologne, 1963)

'Herrenburg und Burgstadt', in Mitterauer, *Markt und Stadt im Mittelalter. Beiträge zur historischen Zentralitätsforschung*, Monographien zur Geschichte des Mittelalters 21 (Stuttgart, 1980), pp. 192–234

Morimoto, Y., 'Autour du grand domaine carolingien', in Morimoto and A. Verhulst (eds.), *Economie rurale et économie urbaine au moyen âge* (Kyushu, 1993), pp. 25–79

Müllejans, H., *Publicus und privatus im römischen Recht und im älteren kanonischen Recht*, Münchener theologische Studien 14 (Münich, 1961)

Müller-Mertens, E., *Karl der Große, Ludwig der Fromme und die Freien. Wer waren die liberi homines der karolingischen Kapitularien (742/3–832)? Ein Beitrag zur Sozialgeschichte und Sozialpolitik des Frankenreiches*, Forschungen zur mittelalterlichen Geschichte 10 (Berlin, 1963)

Die Reichstruktur im Spiegel der Herrschaftspraxis Ottos des Großen (Berlin, 1980)

Murray, A. C., *Germanic Kinship Structure: Studies in Law and Society in Antiquity and the Early Middle Ages* (Toronto, 1983)

'The Position of the *Grafio* in the Constitutional History of Merovingian Gaul', *Speculum* 64 (1986), 787–805

'From Roman to Frankish Gaul: *Centenarii* and *Centenae* in the Administration of the Merovingian Kingdom', *Traditio* 44 (1988), 59–100

Neale, W. C., 'Land is to Rule', in R. E. Frykenberg (ed.), *Land Tenure and Social Structure in Indian History* (Madison, Milkwaukee and London, 1965), pp. 3–16

Nehlsen-von Stryck, K., *Die boni homines des frühen Mittelalters unter besondere Berücksichtigung der fränkischen Quellen*, Freiburger Rechtsgeschichtlichen Abhandlungen 2 (Berlin, 1981)

Nelson, J. L., 'Public Histories and Private History in the Work of Nithard', *Speculum* 60 (1985), 251–93; reprinted in Nelson, *Politics and Ritual in Early Medieval Europe* (Woodbridge, 1986), pp. 195–238

'Dispute Settlement in Carolingian West Francia', in W. Davies and P. Fouracre (eds.), *The Settlement of Disputes in Early Medieval Europe* (Cambridge, 1986), pp. 45–64

Politics and Ritual in Early Medieval Europe (Woodbridge, 1986)

'The Lord's Anointed and the People's Choice: Carolingian Royal Ritual', in D. Cannadine and S. Price (eds.), *Rituals of Royalty: Power and Ceremonial in Traditional Societies* (Cambridge, 1987), pp. 137–80

'Making Ends Meet: Poverty and Wealth in the Carolingian Church', *Studies in Church History* 24 (1987), 25–35

'Ninth-Century Knighthood: The Evidence of Nithard', in C. Harper-Bill *et al.* (eds.), *Studies in Medieval History presented to R. Allen Brown* (Woodbridge, 1989), pp. 255–66

'The Last Years of Louis the Pious', in P. Godman and R. Collins (eds.), *Charlemagne's Heir: New Perspectives on the Reign of Louis the Pious (814–40)* (Oxford, 1990), pp. 147–60

'Literacy in Carolingian Government', in R. McKitterick (ed.), *The Uses of Literacy in Early Medieval Europe* (Cambridge, 1990), pp. 258–96

'The Problematic in the Private', *Social History* 15 (1990), 355–65

Charles the Bald (London, 1992)

'Kingship and Empire in the Carolingian World', in R. McKitterick (ed.), *Carolingian Culture: Emulation and Innovation* (Cambridge, 1994), pp. 52–87

Review of T. Head and R. Landes (eds.), 'The Peace of God', *Speculum* 61 (1994), 163–9

'Parents, Children and the Church in the Early Middle Ages', *Studies in Church History* 31 (1994), 81–114

'History-writing at the Courts of Louis the Pious and Charles the Bald', in A. Scharer and G. Scheibelreiter (eds.), *Historiographie im frühen Mittelalter*, Veröffentlichungen der Institut für Österreichische Geschichte 32 (Vienna, 1994), pp. 435–42

The Frankish World, 750–900 (Woodbridge, 1994)

'Kingship and Royal Government', in *NCMH*, pp. 383–430

'The Wary Widow', in W. Davies and P. Fouracre (eds.), *Property and Power in the Early Middle Ages* (Cambridge, 1995), pp. 82–113

'Kings without Justice, Justice without Kings: An Early Medieval Paradox', *Settimane* 44 (1996), 797–825

'Violence in the Carolingian World and the Ritualisation of Ninth-century Warfare', in G. Halsall (ed.), *Violence and Society in the Early Medieval West* (London, 1997), pp. 90–107

Neundörfer, D., *Studien zur ältesten Geschichte des Kloster Lorsch*, Arbeiten zur deutschen Rechts- und Verfassungsgeschichte 3 (Berlin, 1920)

Niemeyer, W., *Der Pagus des frühen Mittelalters in Hessen*, Schriften des Hessischen Landesamtes für geschichtliche Landeskunde 30 (Marburg, 1968)

Nitz, H.-J., 'The Church as Colonist: The Benedictine Abbey of Lorsch and Planned *Waldhufen* Colonisation in the Odenwald', *Journal of Historical Geography* 9 (1983), 105–26

Noble, T. F. X., *The Republic of St.Peter:The Birth of the Papal State, 680–825* (Philadelphia, 1984)

Nonn, U., *Pagus und comitatus in Niederlothringen. Untersuchungen zur politischen Raumgliederung im früheren Mittelalter*, Bonner Historische Forschungen 49 (Bonn, 1983)

'Probleme der frühmittelalterlichen Grafschaftsverfassung am Beispiel des Rhein-Mosel Raum', *Jahrbuch für westdeutsche Landesgeschichte* 17 (1991), 29–50

Odegaard, C. E., *Vassi and Fideles in the Carolingian Empire* (Cambridge, MA, 1945)

Oexle, O. G., 'Gilden als soziale Gruppen in der Karolingerzeit', in H. Jankuhn et al. (eds.), *Das Handwerk in vor- und frühgeschichtlicher Zeit I*, Abhandlungen der Akademie der Wissenschaften in Göttingen, philologisch-historische Klasse 122 (Göttingen, 1981), pp. 284–354

'Die Gegenwart der Toten', in W. Verbeke and D. Verhelst (eds.), *Death in the Middle Ages* (Louvain, 1983), pp. 15–77

'Mahl und Spende im mittelalterlichen Totenkult', *Frühmittelalterliche Studien* 18 (1984), 401–14

'Conjuratio und Gilde im frühen Mittelalter. Ein Beitrag zum Problem der sozialgeschichtlichen Kontinuität zwischen Antike und Mittelalter', in B. Schwineköper (ed.), *Gilden und Zünfte. Kaufmännische und gewerbliche*

Bibliography of secondary works

Genossenschaften im frühen und hohen Mittelalter, VF 28 (Sigmaringen, 1985), pp. 151–214

Ogris, W., 'Festuca', in A. Erler *et al.* (eds.), *Handwörterbuch zur deutsche Rechtsgeschichte*, I (Berlin, 1971), cols. 1111–14

Oldenstein, J., 'Die letzten Jahrzehnte des römischen Limes zwischen Andernach und Selz unter besonderer Berücksichtigung des Kastells Alzey und der Notitia Dignitatum', in F. Staab (ed.), *Zur Kontinuität zwischen Antike und Mittelalter am Oberrhein*, Oberrheinische Studien 11 (Sigmaringen, 1994), pp. 69–112

Oswald, F., and Störmer, W. (eds.), *Die Abtei Amorbach im Odenwald* (Sigmaringen, 1984)

Parisse, M. (ed.), *Veuves et Veuvage dans le Haut Moyen Age* (Paris, 1993)

Patze, H. (ed.)., *Die Burgen im deutsche Sprachraum: ihre rechts- und verfassungsgeschichtliche Bedeutung*, 2 vols., VF 19 (Sigmaringen, 1976)

Paxton, F. S., *Christianising Death: The Creation of a Ritual Process in Early Medieval Europe* (Ithaca and London, 1990)

Percival, J., 'Seigneurial Aspects of late Roman Estate Management', *English Historical Review* 82 (1969), 449–73

Pohl-Resl, B., 'Vorsorge, Memoria und soziales Ereignis: Frauen als Schenkerinen in den bayerischen und alemannischen Urkunden des 8. und 9. Jahrhunderts', *MIÖG* 103 (1995), 265–87

Poly, J.-P., and Bournazel, E., *The Feudal Mutation* (London, 1990)

Prinz, F., 'Herzog und Adel im agilulfingischen Bayern: Herzogsgut und Konsensschenkungen vor 788', *Zeitschrift für bayerische Landesgeschichte* 25 (1962), 225–63

    Frühes Mönchtum im Frankenreich. Kultur und Gesellschaft in Gallien, den Rheinländen und Bayern am Beispiel der monastischen Entwicklung (4 bis 8 Jahrhundert) (Munich and Vienna, 1965)

    'Stadtrömisch-Italienische Märtyrreliquien und fränkischer Reichsadel im Maas-Moselraum', *Historisches Jahrbuch* 87 (1967), 1–25

    'Heiligenkult und Adelsherrschaft im Spiegel merowingischer Hagiographie', *Historische Zeitschrift* 204 (1969), 529–44

    Klerus und Krieg im früheren Mittelalter. Untersuchungen zur Rolle der Kirche beim Aufbau der Königsherrschaft, Monographien zur Geschichte des Mittelalters 2 (Stuttgart, 1971)

Prinz, J., 'Pagus und comitatus in den Urkunden der Karolinger', *Archiv für Urkundenforschung* 17 (1941), 329–58

Quarthal, F. (ed.), *Alemannien und Ostfranken im Frühmittelalter*, Veröffentlichung des Alemannisches Instituts Freiburg-im-Br. 48 (Bühl and Baden, 1984)

Raach, T., *Kloster Mettlach/Saar und sein Grundbesitz. Untersuchungen zur Frühgeschichte und zur Grundherrschaft der ehemaligen Benediktiner Abtei im Mittelalter*, Quellen und Abhandlungen zur mittelrheinische Kirchengeschichte 19 (Mainz, 1974)

Radding, C., *The Origins of Medieval Jurisprudence: Pavia and Bologna 850–1150* (London and New Haven, 1988)

Reuter, T., 'Saint Boniface and Europe', in Reuter (ed.), *The Greatest Englishman: Essays on St Boniface and the Church at Crediton* (Exeter, 1980), pp. 69–93

    'The "Imperial Church System" of the Ottonian and Salian Rulers: A Reconsideration', *Journal of Ecclesiastical History* 33 (1982), 347–74

    'Plunder and Tribute in the Carolingian Empire', *Transactions of the Royal Historical Society* 35 (1985), 75–94

    'The End of Carolingian Military Expansion', in P. Godman and R. Collins (eds.),

Bibliography of secondary works

Charlemagne's Heir: New Perspectives on the Reign of Louis the Pious (814–40) (Oxford, 1990), pp. 391–405

Germany in the Early Middle Ages, 800–1056 (London, 1991)

'The Medieval German *Sonderweg*? The Empire and its Rulers in the High Middle Ages', in A. J. Duggan (ed.), *Kings and Kingship in the Middle Ages* (London, 1993), pp. 179–211

'"Kirchenreform" und "Kirchenpolitik" in Zeitalter Karl Martells: Begriffe und Wirklichkeit', in J. Jarnut et al. (eds.), *Karl Martell in seiner Zeit*, Beihefte der Francia 37 (Sigmaringen, 1994), pp. 35–59

'Debate: The "Feudal" Revolution', *P&P* 155 (1997), 177–95

'The Making of England and Germany, 850–1050: Patterns of Comparison and Difference', in A. P. Smyth (ed.), *Medieval Europeans* (Basingstoke, 1998), pp. 53–70

Reynolds, P. L., *Marriage in the Western Church: The Christianization of Marriage during the Patristic and Early Medieval Periods* (Leiden, New York and Cologne, 1994)

Reynolds, S., *Kingdoms and Communities in Western Europe 900–1300* (Oxford, 1984)

Fiefs and Vassals: The Medieval Evidence Reconsidered (Oxford, 1994)

'The Historiography of the Medieval State', in M. Bentley (ed.), *Companion to Historiography* (London, 1997), pp. 117–38

Richter, M., '. . . *Quisquis scit scribere, nullam potat abere labore*. Zur Laienschriftlichkeit im 8. Jahrhundert', in J. Jarnut et al. (eds.), *Karl Martell in seiner Zeit*, Beihefte der Francia 37 (Sigmaringen, 1994), pp. 393–404

Roberts, S., *Order and Dispute: An Introduction to Legal Anthropology* (London, 1977)

'The Study of Disputes: Anthropological Perspectives', in J. Bossy (ed.), *Disputes and Settlements: Law and Human Relations in the West* (Cambridge, 1983), pp. 1–24

Rösener, W., 'Strukturformen der adeligen Grundherrschaft in der Karolingerzeit', in Rösener (ed.), *Strukturen der Grundherrschaft im frühen Mittelalter*, VMPIG 92 (Göttingen, 1989), pp. 126–80

Grundherrschaft im Wandel, VMPIG 102 (Göttingen, 1991)

'Die Grundherrschaft des Kloster Fulda in karolingische und ottonische Zeit', in G. Schrimpf (ed.), *Kloster Fulda in der Welt der Karolinger und Ottonen*, Fuldaer Studien 7 (Frankfurt, 1996), pp. 202–24

Rösener, W. (ed.), *Strukturen der Grundherrschaft im frühen Mittelalter*, VMPIG 92 (Göttingen, 1989)

Rosenwein, B. H., *To Be the Neighbor of Saint Peter: The Social Meaning of Cluny's Property, 909–1049* (Ithaca and London, 1989)

'The Family Politics of Berengar I, King of Italy (888–924)', *Speculum* 71 (1996), 247–81

Rosenwein, B. H. (ed.), *Anger's Past: The Social Uses of an Emotion in the Middle Ages* (Ithaca and London, 1998)

Rosenwein, B. H., Head, T., and Farmer, S., 'Monks and their Enemies: A Comparative Approach', *Speculum* 66 (1991), 764–96

Rouche, M., 'L'héritage de la voierie antique dans la Gaule du haut Moyen Age (Ve–XIe siècles)', in *L'homme et la route en Europe occidentale*, Flaran 3 (Auch, 1982), pp. 13–32

Rubin, M., 'Small Groups: Identity and Solidarity in the Late Middle Ages', in J. Kermode (ed.), *Enterprise and Individuals in Fifteenth-Century England* (Stroud, 1991), pp. 132–50

Rubner, H., 'Vom römischen Saltus zum fränkischen Forst', *Historisches Jahrbuch* 83 (1964), 271–7

Bibliography of secondary works

Runciman, W. G., *A Treatise on Social Theory II: Substantive Social Theory* (Cambridge, 1989)

Sage, W., 'Die Ausgrabungen in der Pfalz zu Ingelheim am Rhein, 1960–70', *Francia* 4 (1976), 141–60

Sahlins, M., 'Poor Man, Rich Man, Big-Man, Chief', *Comparative Studies in Society and History* 5 (1962–3), 285–303

Saint Chrodegang (Metz, 1967)

Samson, R., 'The Merovingian Nobleman's Home: Castle or Villa?', *Journal of Medieval History* 13 (1987), 287–315

'Social Structures in the *Reihengräber*: Mirror or a Mirage?', *Scottish Archaeological Review* 4 (1987), 116–26

Sandmann, M., 'Die Folge der Äbte', in *Klostergemeinschaft* I, pp. 178–204

'Wirkungsbereiche Fuldischer Mönche', in *Klostergemeinschaft* II:ii, pp. 692–791

'Hraban als Mönch, Abt und Erzbischof', *Fuldaer Geschichtsblätter* 56 (1980), 133–80

Sato, S., 'L'*agrarium*: la charge paysanne avant le régime domanial, VIe–VIIIe siècles', *Journal of Medieval History* 24 (1998), 103–25

Schaab, M., 'Die Zent im Franken von der Karolingerzeit bis ins 19. Jahrhundert. Kontinuität und Wandel einer aus dem Frühmittelalter stammenden Organisationsform', in W. Paravicini and K.-F. Werner (eds.), *Histoire comparée de l'adminstration (IVe–XVIIIe siècles)*, Beihefte der Francia 9 (Munich, 1980), pp. 345–62

Schäfer, A., 'Mauerbaupflicht fränkischer Königsleute zu Ladenburg und an der karolingerzeitliche Ringwallanlage "Heidenlöcher" bei Deidesheim. Eine Quelle der Karolingerzeit aus dem Nonnenmünster bei Worms', *ZGO* 113 (1965), 429–35

'Die Abtei Weissenburg und das karolingische Königtum', *ZGO* 114 (1966), 1–53

Schaller, D., 'Der Junge "Rabe" am Hof Karls des Grossen', in J. Autenrieth and F. Brunhölzl (eds.), *Festschrift B. Bischoff* (Stuttgart, 1971), pp. 123–41

Schalles-Fischer, M., *Pfalz und Fiskus Frankfurt. Eine Untersuchung zur Verfassungsgeschichte des fränkisch-deutschen Königtums*, VMPIG 20 (Göttingen, 1969)

Schallmeyer, E., 'Die Lande rechts des Rheins zwischen 260 und 500 nach Christ', in F. Staab (ed.), *Zur Kontinuität zwischen Antike und Mittelalter am Oberrhein*, Oberrheinische Studien 11 (Sigmaringen, 1994), pp. 53–68

Schefers, H., 'Einhards römische Reliquien. Zur Bedeutung der Reliquientranslation Einhards von 827/828', *Archiv für Hessische Geschichte und Altertumskunde* 48 (1990), 272–92

Einhard – ein Lebensbild aus karolingischer Zeit, Geschichtsblätter für die Kreis Bergstraße 26 (Heppenheim, 1993)

Schieffer, R., 'Der ottonische Reichsepiskopat zwischen Königtum und Adel', *Frühmittelalterliche Studien* 23 (1989), 291–301

Schieffer, R. (ed.), *Schriftkultur und Reichsverwaltung unter den Karolingern*, Abhandlungen der Nordrhein-Westfalische Akademie der Wissenschaften 97 (Opladen, 1996)

Schieffer, T., *Winfrid-Bonifatius und die christliche Grundlegung Europas* (Freiburg, 1954)

Schlesinger, W., *Die Entstehung der Landesherrschaft. Vorwiegend nach mitteldeutschen Quellen* (2nd edn, Darmstadt, 1964)

'Die Pfalzen in Rhein-Main-Gebiet', *Geschichte in Wissenschaft und Unterricht* 16 (1965), 487–507

'Zur politische Geschichte der fränkischen Ostbewegung vor Karl dem Großen', in Schlesinger (ed.), *Althessen im Frankenreich*, Nationes 2 (Sigmaringen, 1975), pp. 9–62

Bibliography of secondary works

Schlesinger, W (ed.), *Althessen im Frankenreich*, Nationes 2 (Sigmaringen 1975)

Schmid, K. *Gebetsgedenken und adliges Selbstverständnis im Mittelalter. Ausgewählte Beiträge* (Sigmaringen, 1983)

Schmid, K. et al., *Die Klostergemeinschaft von Fulda im früheren Mittelalter*, 3 vols. in 5, Münstersche Mittelalter-Schriften 8 (Münich, 1978)

Schmid, K., and Wollasch, J. (eds.), *Memoria. Die geschichtliche Zeugniswert des liturgischen Gedenkens im Mittelalter*, Münstersche Mittelalter Schriften 48 (Munich, 1984)

Schmidt-Weigand, R., 'Mallus, mallum', in A. Erler *et al.* (eds.), *Handwörterbuch zur deutsche Rechtsgeschichte*, II (Berlin, 1971), cols. 217–18

'Das Dorf nach den Stammesrechten des Kontinents', in H. Jankuhn *et al.* (eds.), *Das Dorf der Eisenzeit und des frühen Mittelalters*, Abhandlungen der Akademie der Wissenschaften in Göttingen, philologisch-historische Klasse 101 (Göttingen, 1977), pp. 408–443

'Stammesrecht und Volkssprache in karolingischer Zeit', in H. Beumann and W. Schröder (eds.), *Aspekte der Nationenbildung im Mittelalter*, Nationes 3 (Sigmaringen, 1978), pp. 171–204

Schmitt, J., *Untersuchungen zu den Liberi Homines der Karolingerzeit* (Frankfurt, 1977)

Schneider, G., 'Reims und das Remigiusland in frühen Mittelalter (6 bis 9 Jahrhundert)', *ZGO* 119 (1971), 47–80

Schnellenkamp, W., 'Ein Grabhügel bei Wallterstädten in Hessen-Starkenburg mit Bestattungen der Hallstatt-, Latène- und Merowingerzeit', *Mainzer Zeitschrift* 27 (1932), 59–74

Schreibmuller, H., 'Die Ahnen Kaiser Konrads II und Bischof Brunos von Würzburg', in *Herbipolis Jubilans. 1200 Jahre Bistum Würzburg*, Würzburger Diözesangeschichts-blätter 14/15 (Würzburg, 1952), pp. 173–233

Schrimpf, G. (ed.), *Kloster Fulda in der Welt der Karolinger und Ottonen*, Fuldaer Studien 7 (Frankfurt, 1996)

Schulze, H. K., *Die Grafschaftsverfassung der Karolingerzeit in den Gebieten östlich des Rheins*, Schriften zur Verfassungsgeschichte 19 (Berlin, 1973)

'Rodungsfreiheit und Königsfreiheit. Zu Genesis und Kritik neuer verfassungs-geschichtlicher Theorien', *Historische Zeitschrift* 219 (1974), 529–50

'Reichsaristokratie, Stammesadel und fränkischer Freiheit', *Historische Zeitschrift* 227 (1978), 353–73

'Ostfranken und Alemannien in der Politik des fränkischen Reiches', in F. Quarthal (ed.), *Alemannien und Ostfranken im Frühmittelalter*, Veröffentlichung des Alemannisches Instituts Freiburg-im-Br. 48 (Bühl and Baden, 1984), pp. 13–37

'Grundprobleme der Grafschaftsverfassung', *Zeitschrift für Württembergische Landesgeschichte* 44 (1985), 265–82

'Die Grafschaftsorganisation als Element der frühmittelalterlichen Staatlichkeit', *Jahrbuch für Geschichte des Feudalismus* 14 (1990), 29–46

Schulze, M., 'Die Wüstung Wülflingen in Nordwürttemberg', *Offa* 39 (1982), 235–43

Schütte, S., 'Continuity Problems and Authority Structures in Cologne', in G. Ausenda (ed.), *After Empire:Towards an Ethnology of Europe's Barbarians* (San Marino, 1995), pp. 163–76

Schütz, J., 'Die Deutung alte fränkische Bezeichnungen: Ortsname "Vougastisburch"-"ostarstuopha"-"Trusnasteti"', *Jahrbuch für fränkische Landesforschung* 56 (1996), 111–22

Schwenk, B., 'Das Hundetragen. Eine Rechtsbrauch im Mittelalter', *Historisches Jahrbuch* 110 (1990), 289–308

Schwind, F., 'Die Franken in Althessen', in W. Schlesinger (ed.), *Althessen im Frankenreich*, Nationes 2 (Sigmaringen, 1975), pp. 211–80

'Beobachtungen zur inneren Struktur des Dorfes in karolingischer Zeit', in H. Jankuhn *et al.* (eds.), *Das Dorf der Eisenzeit und des frühen Mittelalters*, Abhandlungen der Akademie der Wissenschaften in Göttingen, philologisch-historisch Klasse 101 (Göttingen, 1977), pp. 444–93

'Zu karolingerzeitlichen Klöstern als Wirtschaftsorganismen und Stätten handwerklicher Tätigkeit', in L. Fenske *et al.* (eds.), *Institutionen, Gesellschaft und Kultur im Mittelalter. Festschrift J. Fleckenstein* (Sigmaringen, 1984), pp. 101–23

Sears, E., 'Louis the Pious as *Miles Christi*: The Dedicatory Image in Hrabanus Maurus's *De laudibus sanctae crucis*', in P. Godman and R. Collins (eds.), *Charlemagne's Heir: New Perspectives on the Reign of Louis the Pious (814–40)* (Oxford, 1990), pp. 605–28

Semmler, J., 'Studien zum Supplex Libellus und zur anianischen Reform in Fulda', *Zeitschrift für Kirchengeschichte* 69 (1958), 268–98

'Episcopi potestas und karolingische Klosterpolitik', in A. Borst (ed.), *Mönchtum, Episkopat und Adel zur Gründungszeit des Klosters Reichenau*, VF 20 (Sigmaringen, 1974), pp. 305–95

'Die Geschichte der Abtei Lorsch von der Gründung bis zum Ende der Salierzeit, 764 bis 1125', in F. Knöpp (ed.), *Die Reichsabtei Lorsch. Festschrift zum Gedenken an ihre Stiftung 764*, I (Darmstadt, 1974), pp. 75–173

'Chrodegang, Bischof von Metz, 747–766', in F. Knöpp (ed.), *Die Reichsabtei Lorsch. Festschrift zum Gedenken an ihre Stiftung 764*, I (Darmstadt, 1974), pp. 229–45

'Pippin III und die fränkische Klöster', *Francia* 3 (1975), 88–146

'Mission und Pfarrorganisation in den rheinischen, mosel- und maasländischen Bistümern 5–10 Jahrhundert', *Settimane* 28 (1982), 813–88

'Zehntgebot und Pfarrtermination in karolingischer Zeit', in H. Mordek (ed.), *Aus Reich und Kirche. Festschrift F. Kempf* (Sigmaringen, 1983), pp. 33–44

Sennett, R., *The Fall of Public Man* (Cambridge, 1974)

Siems, H., *Handel und Wücher im Spiegel frühmittelalterlicher Rechtsquellen*, Schriften der MGH 35 (Hanover, 1992)

Smith, J. M. H., *Province and Empire: Brittany and the Carolingians* (Cambridge, 1992)

'The Problem of Female Sanctity in Carolingian Europe', *P&P* 146 (1995), 3–37

'Religion and Lay Society', in *NCMH*, pp. 654–78

Southall, A., 'A Critique of the Typology of States and Political Systems', in M. Banton (ed.), *Political Systems and the Distribution of Power* (London, 1965), pp. 113–40

Sprandel, R., *Der merovingische Adel und die Gebiete östlich des Rheins*, Forschungen zur oberrheinische Landesgeschichte 5 (Freiburg, 1957)

'Dux und comes in der Merovingerzeit', *ZSRG GA* 70 (1957), 41–84

Das Kloster St. Gallen in der Verfassung des karolingischen Reiches, Forschungen zur oberrheinischen Landesgeschichte 7 (Freiburg, 1958)

'Struktur und Geschichte des merowingische Adels', *Historische Zeitschrift* 193 (1961), 33–71

'Grundherrlicher Adel, rechtsständige Freiheit und Königszins. Untersuchungen über die alemannischen Verhältnis in der Karolingerzeit', *DA* 19 (1963), 1–29

Bibliography of secondary works

'Bemerkungen zum frühfränkischen Comitat', *ZSRG GA* 82 (1965), 288–91

'Gerichtsorganisation und Sozialstruktur Mainfrankens im früheren Mittelalter', *Jahrbuch für fränkische Landesforschung* 38 (1978), 7–38

'Die frühmittelalterliche Grundbesitzverteilung und Gerichtsordnung im fränkischen und alemannischen Raum', in F. Quarthal (ed.), *Alemannien und Ostfranken im Frühmittelalter*, Veröffentlichung des Alemannisches Instituts Freiburg-im-Br. 48 (Bühl and Baden, 1984), pp. 47–59

Staab, F., *Untersuchungen zur Gesellschaft am Mittelrhein in der Karolingerzeit*, Geschichtliche Landeskunde 11 (Wiesbaden, 1975)

'A Reconsideration of the Ancestry of Modern Political Liberty: The Problem of the so-called "King's Freedmen" (*Königsfreie*)', *Viator* 11 (1980), 52–69

'Zur Organisation des früh- und hochmittelalterlichen Reichsgutes an der unteren Nahe', in A. Gerlich (ed.), *Beiträge zur Geschichtliche Landeskunde*, Geschichtliche Landeskunde 21 (Wiesbaden, 1980), pp. 1–29

'Der Grundbesitz der Abtei Fulda bis zur Mitte des 9. Jahrhunderts und seine Stifter', in W. Böhne (ed.), *Hrabanus Maurus und seine Schule: Festschrift der Rabanus-Maurus-Schule* (Fulda, 1980), pp. 48–63

'Wann wurde Hrabanus Maurus Mönch in Fulda? Beobachtungen zur Anteilnahme seiner Familie an den Anfängen seiner Laufbahn', in R. Kottje and H. Zimmermann (eds.), *Hrabanus Maurus. Lehrer, Abt und Bischof*, Mainzer Akademie der Wissenschaften und der Literatur, Abhandlungen der Geistes- und Sozialwissenschaften 4 (Wiesbaden, 1982), pp. 75–101

'Speyer im Frankenreich', in W. Eger (ed.), *Geschichte der Stadt Speyer* I (Stuttgart, Cologne and Mainz, 1982), pp. 163–247

'Aspekte der Grundherrschaftsentwicklung von Lorsch vornehmlich auf Grund der Urbare des Codex Laureshamensis', in W. Rösener (ed.), *Strukturen der Grundherrschaft im frühen Mittelalter*, VMPIG 92 (Göttingen, 1989), pp. 285–333

'Reich und Mittelrhein um 1000', in H. Hinkel (ed.), *1000 Jahre St. Stephan im Mainz*, Quellen und Abhandlungen zur mittelrheinische Kirchengeshichte 63 (Mainz, 1990), pp. 59–100

'Kirchliche Raumerschließung in den Diözesen Trier, Mainz, Worms, Speyer, Straßburg und Konstanz im 7. Jht. durch die Abtei Weissenburg', *Archiv für mittelrheinische Kirchengeschichte* 42 (1990), 13–56

'Agrarwissenschaft und Grundherrschaft. Zum Weinbau der Klöster im Frühmittelalter', in A. Gerlich (ed.), *Weinbau, Weinhandel und Weinkultur*, Geschichtliche Landeskunde 40 (Stuttgart, 1993), pp. 1–48

'*Rudi populo rudis adhuc presul*. Zu den wehrhaften Bischöfe der Zeit Karl Martells', in J. Jarnut et al. (eds.), *Karl Martell in seiner Zeit*, Beihefte der Francia 37 (Sigmaringen, 1994), pp. 249–75

'Heidentum und Christentum in der Germania Prima zwischen Antike und Mittelalter', in Staab (ed.), *Zur Kontinuität zwischen Antike und Mittelalter am Oberrhein*, Oberrheinische Studien 11 (Sigmaringen, 1994), pp. 117–52

'Die Königin Fastrada', in R. Berndt (ed.), *Das Frankfurter Konzil von 794: Kristallisationspunkt karolingische Kultur*, Quellen und Abhandlungen zur mittelrheinische Kirchengeschichte 80 (Mainz, 1997), pp. 183–217

Staab, F. (ed.), *Zur Kontinuität zwischen Antike und Mittelalter am Oberrhein*, Oberrheinische Studien 11 (Sigmaringen, 1994)

Bibliography of secondary works

Stafford, P., 'La mutation familiale: A Suitable Case for Caution', in J. Hill and M. Swan (eds.), *The Community, the Family and the Saint* (Turnhout, 1998), pp. 103–25

Stein, B., *Peasant, State and Society in Medieval South India* (Delhi, 1980)

Stein, G., 'Kontinuität im spätrömischen Kastell Altrip (Alta ripa) bei Ludwigshafen am Rhein', in F. Staab (ed.), *Zur Kontinuität zwischen Antike und Mittelalter am Oberrhein*, Oberrheinische Studien 11 (Sigmaringen, 1994), pp. 113–17

Stengel, E. E., *Abhandlungen und Untersuchungen zur Hessischen Geschichte*, Veröffentlichungen der Historischen Kommission für Hessen und Waldeck 26 (Marburg, 1960)

Steuer, H., 'Standortverscheibunger früher Siedlungen – von der vorrömischen Eisenzeit bis zum frühen Mittelalter', in G. Althoff *et al.* (eds.), *Person und Gemeinschaft im Mittelalter. Festschrift K. Schmid* (Sigmaringen, 1988), pp. 25–59

'Archaeology and History: Proposals on the Social Structure of the Merovingian Empire', in K. Randsborg (ed.), *The Birth of Europe: Archaeology and Social Relations in the First Millennium AD* (Rome, 1989), pp. 100–22

'Zur Berechnung von Bevölkerungsgröße und Bevölkerungsentwicklung in einer Siedlungslandschaft der Merowingerzeit', *Saeculum* 39 (1988), 119–28

Stoclet, A., *Autour de Fulrad de Saint-Denis (v.710–784)* (Geneva, 1993)

Störmer, W., *Früher Adel. Studien zur politischen Führungsschicht im fränkisch-deutschen Reich von 8. bis 11. Jahrhundert*, 2 vols., Monographien zur Geschichte des Mittelalters 6 (Stuttgart, 1973)

'Die Reichskirche im Spessart-Odenwald-Gebiet von der Karolinger bis zur Salierzeit', *Jahrbuch für fränkische Landesforschung* 48 (1988), 1–16

'Zu Herkunft und Wirkungkreis der merowingerzeitlichen "mainfränkischen" Herzöge', in K. R. Schnith and R. Pauler (eds.), *Festschrift für E. Hlawitschka* (Munich, 1993), pp. 11–21

Strayer, J. R., *On the Medieval Origins of the Modern State* (Princeton, 1970)

Sullivan, R. E., 'The Carolingian Age: Reflections on its Place in the History of the Middle Ages', *Speculum* 64 (1989), 267–306

Szàbo, T., 'Antikes Erbe und karolingisch-ottonische Verkehrspolitik', in L. Fenske *et al.* (eds.), *Institutionen, Gesellschaft und Kultur im Mittelalter. Festschrift J. Fleckenstein* (Sigmaringen, 1984), pp. 125–45

Tangl, M. ,'Urkunde für Fulda vom 30 Aug. 834', *Historische Vierteljahrsschrift* 5 (1902), 527

Tellenbach, G., 'Zur ältesten Geschichte der Welfen in Süddeutschland', in Tellenbach (ed.), *Studien und Vorarbeiten zur Geschichte des großfränkischen und frühdeutschen Adels*, Forschungen zur oberrheinische Landesgeschichte 4 (Freiburg, 1957), pp. 335–40

Tellenbach, G. (ed.), *Studien und Vorarbeiten zur Geschichte des großfränkischen und frühdeutschen Adels*, Forschungen zur oberrheinische Landesgeshichte 4 (Freiburg, 1957)

Theuws, F., 'Landed Property and Manorial Organisation in Northern Austrasia: Some Considerations and a Case Study', in N. Roymans and F. Theuws (eds.), *Images of the Past: Studies on Ancient Societies in Northwestern Europe* (Amsterdam, 1991), pp. 299–407

Thompson, E. P., 'The Grid of Inheritance: A Comment', in J. Goody, J. Thirsk and E. P. Thompson (eds.), *Family and Inheritance: Rural Society in Western Europe, 1200–1800* (Cambridge, 1976), pp. 328–60

Customs in Common (London, 1991)

Tits-Dieuaide, M. J., 'Grands domaines, grandes et petites exploitations en Gaule mérovingienne. Remarques et suggestions', in A. Verhulst (ed.), *Le grand domaine aux époques mérovingienne et carolingienne* (Ghent, 1985), pp. 23–50

Toubert, P., *Les structures du Latium médiéval* (Paris, 1973)

Trautz, F., *Das untere Neckarland im Mittelalter*, Heidelberger Veröffentlichungen zur Landesgeschichte und Landeskunde 1 (Heidelberg, 1953)

Tremp, E., *Studien zu den Gesta Hludovici Imperatoris des Trierer chorbischofs Thegan, Schriften der MGH* 30 (Hanover, 1988)

Ullmann, W., 'Public Welfare and Social Legislation in the Early Medieval Councils', *Studies in Church History* 7 (1971), 1–39

Van Dam, R., *Leadership and Community in Late Antique Gaul* (Berkeley and London, 1985)

Van Es, W., 'Dorestad Centred', in J. C. Besteman *et al.* (eds.), *Medieval Archaeology in the Netherlands* (Assen, 1990), pp. 151–82

Verbruggen, J. F., 'L'armée et la stratégie de Charlemagne', in H. Beumann (ed.), *Karl der Große: Lebenswerk und Nachleben. I: Persönlichkeit und Geschichte* (Düsseldorf, 1965), pp. 420–36

Verhulst, A., 'La génèse du régime domanial classique en France au haut moyen âge', *Settimane* 13 (1966), 135–60

'La diversité du régime domanial entre Loire et Rhin à l'époque carolingienne', in W. Janssen and D. Lohrmann (eds.), *Villa-curtis-grangia. Landwirtschaft zwischen Loire et Rhein von der Römerzeit zum Hochmittelalter*, Beihefte der Francia 11 (Munich and Zurich, 1983), pp. 133–48

'Die Grundherrschaftsentwicklung im ostfränkischen Raum vom 8. bis 10. Jahrhundert. Grundzüge und Fragen aus westfränkischer Sicht', in W. Rösener (ed.), *Strukturen der Grundherrschaft im frühen Mittelalter*, VMPIG 92 (Göttingen, 1989), pp. 29–46

'Etude comparative du régime domanial classique à l'est et à l'ouest du Rhin à l'époque carolingienne', in *La croissance agricole du Haut Moyen Age*, Flaran 10 (Auch, 1990), pp. 87–101

Rural and Urban Aspects of Early Medieval Northwest Europe (Aldershot, 1992)

Verhulst, A. (ed.), *Le grand domaine aux époques mérovingienne et carolingienne* (Ghent, 1985)

Vollmer, F., 'Die Etichonen. Ein Beitrag zur Frage der Kontinuität früher Adelsfamilien', in G. Tellenbach (ed.), *Studien und Vorarbeiten zur Geschichte des großfränkischen und frühdeutschen Adels*, Forschungen zur oberrheinische Landesgeshichte 4 (Freiburg, 1957), pp. 137–84

Vollrath, H., 'Herrschaft und Genossenschaft im Kontext frühmittelalterlicher Rechtsbeziehungen', *Historisches Jahrbuch* 102 (1982), 33–71

Wagner, G., 'Comitate zwischen Rhein, Main und Neckar', *ZGO* 64 (1955), 1–34

Waitz, G., *Deutsche Verfassungsgeschichte*, 8 vols. (Berlin, 1876–96)

Wallace-Hadrill, J. M., 'The Bloodfeud of the Franks', in Wallace-Hadrill, *The Longhaired Kings* (London, 1962), pp. 121–147

'A Background to St Boniface's Mission', in P. Clemoes and K. Hughes (eds.), *England Before the Conquest* (Cambridge, 1971), pp. 35–48

Wamers, E., 'Frühmittelalterliche Funde aus Mainz. Zur karolingische-ottonischen Metalschmuck und seinen Verhältnissen zum angel-sächsischen Kunsthandwerk', in

Wamers *et al.* (eds.), *Frankfurter Beiträge zur Mittelalter-Archäologie* I (Bonn, 1986), pp. 1–55

Die frühmittelalterlichen Lesefunde aus der Löhrstraße (Baustelle Hilton II) in Mainz (Mainz, 1994)

Weber, M., *Wirtschaft und Gesellschaft* (4th edn, Tübingen, 1963)

On Charisma and Institution Building, ed. and trans. S. N. Eisenstadt (London, 1968)

Weber: Selections, ed. W. G. Runciman, trans. E. Matthews (Cambridge, 1978)

Wehlt, H.-P., *Reichsabtei und König. Dargestellt am Beispiel der Abtei Lorsch mit Ausblicken auf Hersfeld, Stablo und Fulda*, VMPIG 28 (Göttingen, 1968)

Weidemann, K., 'Die Topographie von Mainz in der Römerzeit und dem frühen Mittelalter', *Jahrbuch des Römisch-Germanisches Zentralmuseums Mainz* 15 (1968), 146–99

Weidemann, M., 'Urkunden und Viten der Heiligen Bilihildis aus Mainz', *Francia* 21/1 (1994), 17–84

Weidinger, U., 'Untersuchungen zur Grundherrschaft des Klosters Fulda in der Karolingerzeit', in W. Rösener (ed.), *Strukturen der Grundherrschaft im frühen Mittelalter*, VMPIG 92 (Göttingen, 1989), pp. 247–65

Weiner, A., *Inalienable Possessions: The Paradox of Keeping-while-Giving* (Berkeley, Los Angeles and New York, 1992)

Weise, G., 'Staatliche Baufronden in fränkischer Zeit', *Vierteljahrsschrift für Sozial- und Wirtschaftsgeschichte* 15 (1921), 341–80

Weitzel, J., *Dinggenossenschaft und Recht. Untersuchungen zum Rechtsverständnis im fränkisch-deutschen Mittelalter*, 2 vols., Quellen und Forschungen zur Höchsten Gerichtsbarkeit im Alten Recht 15 (Cologne and Vienna, 1985)

Werner, K.-F., 'Untersuchungen zur Frühzeit des französischen Fürstentums (9.–10. Jahrhundert)', Parts I–V, *Die Welt als Geschichte* 18 (1958), 256–89; 19 (1959), 146–93; 20 (1960), 87–119

'Bedeutende Adelsfamilien im Reich Karls des Großen', in H. Beumann (ed.), *Karl der Große: Lebenswerk und Nachleben. I: Persönlichkeit und Geschichte* (Düsseldorf, 1965), pp. 83–142; trans. T. Reuter, 'Important Noble Families in the Kingdom of Charlemagne', in Reuter, *The Medieval Nobility: Studies on the Ruling Classes of France and Germany from the Sixth to the Twelfth Centuries* (Amsterdam, 1979), pp. 137–202

'Heeresorganisation und Kreigführung im deutschen Königreich des 10. und 11. Jahrhunderts', *Settimane* 15 (1968), 791–845

'Le rôle de l'aristocratie dans la christianisation du nord-est de la Gaule', *Revue de l'Histoire de l'Eglise de France* 62 (1976), 45–73

Structures politiques du monde franc (VIe–XIIe siècles) (London, 1979)

'Missus-marchio-comes. Entre l'administration centrale et l'administration locale de l'empire carolingien', in W. Paravicini and K.-F. Werner (eds.), *Histoire comparée de l'administration IVe–XVIIIe siècles*, Beihefte der Francia 9 (Munich, 1980), pp. 191–239

'La genèse des duchés en France et en Allemagne', *Settimane* 27 (1981), 175–207

Vom Frankenreich zur Entfaltung Deutschlands und Frankenreichs (Sigmaringen, 1984)

'*Hludovicus Augustus*: Gouverner l'empire chrétien – Idées et réalités', in P. Godman and R. Collins (eds.), *Charlemagne's Heir: New Perspectives on the Reign of Louis the Pious (814–40)* (Oxford, 1990), pp. 3–123

Werner, M., *Der Lütticher Raum in frühkarolingischen Zeit. Untersuchungen zur Geschichte einer karolingischen Stammeslandschaft*, VMPIG 62 (Göttingen, 1980)

Adelsfamilien im Umkreis der frühen Karolinger. Die Verwandtschaft Irminas von Oeren und Adelas von Pfalzel, VF Sonderband 28 (Sigmaringen, 1982)

White, S. D., 'Pactum . . . legem vincit et amor judicium: The Settlement of Disputes by Compromise in Eleventh-century Western France', *American Journal of Legal History* 22 (1978), 281–308

'Feuding and Peacemaking in the Touraine around the Year 1100', *Traditio* 42 (1986), 195–263

'Inheritances and Legal Arguments in Western France, 1050–1150', *Traditio* 43 (1987), 55–103

Custom, Kinship and Gifts to Saints: The Laudatio Parentum in Western France, 1050–1150 (Chapel Hill, 1988)

'Debate: The "Feudal" Revolution', *P&P* 152 (1996), 205–23

Whittaker, C. R., 'Rural Labour in Three Roman Provinces', in P. Garnsey (ed.), *Non-slave Labour in the Greco-Roman World* (Cambridge, 1980), pp. 73–99

'Circe's Pigs: From Slavery to Serfdom in the Roman World', *Slavery and Abolition* 8 (1987), 88–122

'Landlords and Warlords in the later Roman Empire', in J. Rich and G. Shipley (eds.), *War and Society in the Roman World* (London, 1993), pp. 277–302

Frontiers of the Roman Empire (Baltimore and London, 1994)

Wickham, C. J., *Early Medieval Italy: Central Authority and Local Society, 400–1000* (London, 1981)

'The Other Transition: From the Ancient World to Feudalism', *P&P* 103 (1984), 3–36

'The Uniqueness of the East', *Journal of Peasant Studies* 12 (1985), 166–96

'Land Disputes and their Social Framework in Lombard–Carolingian Italy, 700–900', in W. Davies and P. Fouracre (eds.), *The Settlement of Disputes in Early Medieval Europe* (Cambridge, 1986), pp. 105–24

The Mountains and the City: The Tuscan Apennines in the Early Middle Ages (Oxford, 1989)

'European Forests in the Early Middle Ages: Landscape and Land Clearance', *Settimane* 37 (1989), 479–548; reprinted in Wickham, *Land and Power: Studies in Italian and European Social History, 400–1200* (London, 1994), pp. 155–200

'Problems of Comparing Rural Societies in Early Medieval Western Europe', *Transactions of the Royal Historical Society* 6 (1992), 221–46

'La chute de Rome n'aura pas lieu. A propos d'un livre récent', *Le Moyen Age* 49 (1993) 107–26

Land and Power: Studies in Italian and European Social History, 400–1200 (London, 1994)

'Italy and the Early Middle Ages', in Wickham, *Land and Power: Studies in Italian and European Social History, 400–1200* (London, 1994), pp. 99–118

'Rural Society in Carolingian Europe', in *NCMH*, pp. 510–37

'Debate: The "Feudal" Revolution', *P&P* 155 (1997), 196–207

Wieczorek, A., 'Die Ausbreitung der fränkischen Herrschaft in das Rheinland vor und seit Chlodwig I', in K. van Welck (ed.), *Die Franken. Wegbereiter Europas*, 2 vols. (Mainz, 1996), I, pp. 241–80

Wightman, E., 'Peasants and Potentates: An Investigation of Social Structure and Land Tenure in Roman Gaul', *American Journal of Ancient History* 3 (1978), 97–128

Gallia Belgica (London, 1985)

Bibliography of secondary works

Wilsdorf, C., 'Les Etichonides aux temps carolingiens et ottoniens', in *Bulletin philologique et historique (jusqu'à 1610) du comité des travaux historiques et scientifiques année 1964* (Paris, 1967), pp. 1–23

Wolfram, H., 'Der heilige Rupert und die antikarolingische Adelsopposition', *MIÖG* 80 (1972), 4–34

'Vier Fragen zur Geschichte des heiligen Rupert. Eine Nachlese', *Studien und Mitteilungen zur Geschichte des Benediktiner-Ordens und seiner Zweige* 93 (1982), 2–25

Die Geburt Mitteleuropas: Geschichte Österreiches vor seiner Entstehung (Vienna, 1987)

'Karl Martell und das fränkische Lehenswesen. Aufnahme eines Nichtbestandes', in J. Jarnut *et al.* (eds.), *Karl Martell in seiner Zeit*, Beihefte der Francia 37 (Sigmaringen, 1994), pp. 61–77

Wollasch, J., 'Gemeinschaftsbewußtsein und soziale Leistung im Mittelalter', *Frühmittelalterliche Studien* 9 (1975), 268–86

Wood, I. N., *The Merovingian North Sea* (Alsingas, 1983)

'Disputes in Fifth- and Sixth-century Gaul', in W. Davies and P. Fouracre (eds.), *The Settlement of Disputes in Early Medieval Europe* (Cambridge, 1986), pp. 7–22

The Merovingian Kingdoms, 480–751 (London, 1993)

'Teutsind, Witlaic and the History of Merovingian *precaria*', in W. Davies and P. Fouracre (eds.), *Property and Power in the Early Middle Ages* (Cambridge, 1995), pp. 31–52

'The Frontiers of Western Europe: Developments East of the Rhine in the Sixth Century', in W. Bowman and R. Hodges (eds.), *The Sixth Century: Production and Demand* (Leiden, Boston and Cologne, 1998), pp. 231–57

Wormald, J., 'The Bloodfeud in Early Modern Scotland', in J. Bossy (ed.), *Disputes and Settlements: Law and Human Relations in the West* (Cambridge, 1983), pp. 101–44

Wormald, P., *Bede and the Conversion of England: The Charter Evidence*, Jarrow Lecture 1984 (Jarrow, 1985)

Young, B., 'Paganisme, christianisme et rites funéraires', *Archéologie Médiévale* 7 (1977), 5–81

'Exemple aristocratique et mode funéraire dans la Gaule mérovingienne', *Annales: ESC* 41 (1986), 379–407

Zatschek, H., 'Die Benutzung der Formulae Marculfi und anderer Formelsammlungen in den Privaturkunden des 8. bis 10. Jahrhunderts', *MIÖG* 42 (1927), 165–267

'Die Reichsteilung unter Kasier Ludwig dem Frommen: Studien zur Entstehung des ostfränkischen Reiches', *MIÖG* 49 (1935), 185–224

Zöllner, E., 'Woher stammte der heilige Rupert?', *MIÖG* 57 (1949), 1–22

Zotz, T., *Der Breisgau und das alemannische Herzogtum*, VF Sonderband 19 (Sigmaringen, 1974)

'Adel, Oberschicht, Freie', *ZGO* 125 (1977), 3–20

'Grafschaftsverfassung und Personengeschichte. Zu einen neuen Werk über das karolingerzeitliche Alemannien', *ZGO* 97 (1988), 1–14

'Beobachtungen zur königlichen Grundherrschaft entlang und östlich des Rheins vornehmlich im 9. Jahrhundert', in W. Rösener (ed.), *Strukturen der Grundherrschaft im frühen Mittelalter*, VMPIG 92 (Göttingen, 1989), pp. 74–124

'Grundlagen und Zentrum der Königsherrschaft', in H. U. Nuber *et al.* (eds.), *Archäologie und Geschichte des ersten Jahrtausends in Südwestdeutschland* (Sigmaringen, 1990), pp. 275–93

'Carolingian Tradition and Ottonian–Salian Innovation: Comparative Observations on Palatine Policy in the Empire', in A. J. Duggan (ed.), *Kings and Kingship in the Middle Ages* (London, 1993), pp. 69–100

'In Amt und Würden. Zur Eigenart "offizieller" Positionen im früheren Mittelalter', *Tel Aviver Jahrbuch für deutsche Geschichte* 22 (1993), 1–23

'Le palais et les élites dans le royaume de Germanie', in R. Le Jan (ed.), *La royauté et les élites dans l'Europe carolingienne* (Lille, 1998), pp. 233–48

INDEX

Aachen 160, 198, 200, 220, 237
Adalard, Count 40, 215–19, fig. 12
Adalbero, bishop of Augsburg and abbot of
  Lorsch 225
Adalbert, bishop of Trier and chronicler 239
Adalbert, brother of Otakar 60–3, fig. 6
Adalbert, son of Witagowo 191, fig. 11
Adalbert, count of Trier 205–8
Adalbert, Count 213
Adalgisel-Grimo, deacon at Verdun 112,
  177
Adalhelm, Count, father of Willeswind 55,
  figs. 5, 10
Adalung, abbot of Lorsch 199
administration 4–12, 251–63; mechanics of
  141–64; Roman 166–70; *see also* capitularies,
  counts, government, state
advocate 44–5, 47, 238, 240–1; of Fulda 44–5;
  of Rheims 215; of Seligenstadt 44–5, 124
Aetius, master of the soldiers 167–8
Agantheo, client of Einhard's 92
Aggiold, local landowner 114
agri decumates 166
Alahfrid, client of Einhard's 194
Alans 167
Alapsi, scribe 116
Alberich, Count in 830s 206, 218–19, fig. 11
Alberich, Count in 890s, descendant of Count
  Alberich 225–9
Alberich, son of Count Alberich (830s) 218,
  fig. 11
Alemans, Alemannia 8–9, 27–9, 55, 127, 151,
  170, 180, 185, 205, 209, 223, 232
allod (*allodium*) 73
alms 32–3, 37–40, 69–72, 161
Alsace 28, 99, 117, 155, 180, 199
Altheim 23
Althoff, Gerd, historian 232
Altrip 168, 190
Altstadt 146

Alzey 23, 76, 168–9
Amorbach, monastery 28
Andernach 116
Angela, wife of Cancor 51–9, fig. 5, 10
Angers 145
Annales Nazariani 186
Annales school of historians 7
Annals of Fulda 1, 3
Aquitaine 209, 257
archaeology: importance of, 6; used as source,
  27 (church foundation), 33–6 (grave-goods),
  109–10 (rural settlements), 168–70
  (transition from Roman to Merovingian),
  172–4 (Merovingian society); *see also* burial,
  grave-goods
aristocracy, definition of 82–5
arms, *see* weapons
army, Frankish 143–53; mobilisation orders and
  politics 194, 199, 206
army, Roman 166–9; *see also* horses, military
  service, soldiers, violence, weapons
Arnulf, Emperor 76, 157–8, 161–2, 224–32,
  fig. 13
Askmundesheim 154
associations, sworn 37–8, 69–70; *see also*
  oaths
Attigny 216
Auerbach 80
Austrasia 175, 177–8, 187; *see also* Liège,
  Lotharingia, Meuse, Moselle

Bad Kreuznach, *see* Kreuznach
bannus 5, 143, 247–9
banquets, *see* feasts, feasting
Banzleib, Margrave of Saxony 205–6, 219
Batdagis, local landowner 92, 205
Baturich, bishop of Regensburg 205
Baugolf, Count, then abbot of Fulda 66, 87,
  186, 188, 189, fig. 11
Baumerlenbach, nunnery 25–6

Index

Index

Index

estates: in Carolingian period 51–68, 77–82; in Merovingian period 73–7; and military obligations 143–53; and royal service 143–64; *see also* land

ethnicity, ethnic identity: and archaeology 169–70; of Austrasians and Neustrians 177–8; of Franks 152–53, 169–72; and Roman frontier 166; of Thuringians 185–6

Eucherius, bishop of Orleans 179

Eufemia, daughter of Count Cancor 51–9, fig. 5, 10

evidence, 2–3; reliance of historians upon 3, 6–7, 13, 15–16, 25x; survival of 2–3, 13–18, 112

excavation, *see* archaeology

exchanges of land 45–6, 72, 103–4, 105

exemptions, from royal service and tax 141–3, 146–7, 155, 157, 211; *see also* immunities

faithful men, *see fideles*

family, *see* kinship

Fastrada, wife of Charlemagne 185–6, 187, 192

feasts, feasting: and burial 37–8; and commemoration 39–40; political and social function 175, 234, 254

festivals, religious as occasions for political events 199, 200, 201, 226, 228, 237; *see also* monasteries, lay visits to

feud 129–33, 136, 187, 225–31, 245

feudalism, feudal revolution, feudal society: meanings of 8, 11; and military service 151–3; 'feudal revolution', emergence of 'feudal society' 6, 242–50; *see also* benefice, lordship, vassals

Fichtenau, Heinrich, historian 244

fideles, fidelity: definition of 90–1, 181, 187; military service of 151–3; specific examples of 202–3, 213, 215, 216, 224, 241; *see also* infidelity

Fischbach, monastery 23

Flonheim 33–4, 124, 150–1, 169–70

Florstadt 157

foederati 167–9

Folcnand, tribune 44–5

Fontenoy, battle (841) 209

forests 133, 142–3, 160, 247–9; *see also* hunting

forfeiture of offices and royal lands 186, 217, 218, 221–2, 228, 229, 230, 237–8

forgery 158, 164, 248–9

fortifications 162–4, 169, 243–5

Franco, brother of Burchard of Worms 240

Frankfurt 35–6, 187, 197, 200, 206, 213, 216, 218, 220, 221, 225, 231–2, 251

Frederick, archbishop of Mainz 236

Friese, Eckhard, historian 23

Freising 191

freedom: definition of 82–5, 90, 108–9, 111; and military service 143–53; and royal service 156–64; and taxation and tribute 153–6; and tenurial structures 48–9, 73–82, 83, 85; threats to 48–9, 87; *see also* peasants

friendship (*amicitia*), as form of alliance 130, 131, 234, 236

Frisians, 21, 97–8; at Worms 162–4

frontier: east Frankish–Lotharingian, 210, 214–15; Frankish–Aleman (*c.*500) 170, fig. 9; Frankish–Thuringian 176, 251; Roman 166–9; Rhine as 2, 166–9, 176, 210

Frumold, royal vassal 86–7

Fulco, bishop of Worms 193

Fulda, monastery 2, 14–15, 21–3, 28–30, 33, 46, 59, 60–8, 69–71, 74, 102–4, 110, 121–2, 125, 126, 186, 187–9. 201–2, 205–6, 208, 231–2, 247–8

Fulrad, abbot of Saint-Denis 27–9, 57, 179, 180

Ganshof, F.-L., historian 5

Gaul 75, 95, 112, 167, 169, 172, 173–4, 187; *see also* Loire, western Francia

Gebhard, Count 202, 206, 217, 222, fig. 12

Gebhard, Count, son of Count Gebhard 222, 229, 231–2, fig. 12

Geilrat, daughter of Otakar 61–3, fig. 6

Geismar 121–3

Gengenbach, monastery 28

gentry, definition 84–5

Gerard, Count 229

Gernsheim 164

Geroin, scribe 115–16

Gerold, Count 150–1, fig. 12

Gerold, local landowner 92, 240–1, 246

Gerward, Lorsch monk 209

Gewilib, bishop of Mainz 175

Ghent 90

gifts, gift-giving: to church 13–50; and honour 130; and inheritance 34–40; and law 130–1; and lordship 91–2, 149; to kings 158–9; from kings 202–4, 224–5, 234; *see also* benefices, precarial grants, reciprocity

'gilds', *see* associations, sworn

Gisela, wife of Count Megingoz 228, fig. 10

Giselbert, Count 234

Giselhelm, local landowner 108, 147–52

Glan, river 218

Göllheim 125

Gonsenheim 63

Gorze, monastery 18, 19, 26, 27, 28, 51–3, 102, 181

Index

Index

Index

315

Index

316

Cambridge Studies in Medieval Life and Thought
Fourth series

Titles in series

★ *Also published as a paperback*